Dear readers

Purpose of book:

I really do not want that people a
hours due to making a nice graphs or chart for their reports, assignments, presentation, meeting materials. Let's do not work overtime because of this!

Simply, let's get rid of any stress from making nice Excel charts!

I hope that this book saves your precious time for creating Excel charts and provides good results with you.

"This Book!"

- **Definitely, you are able to create your own unique Excel charts after mastering the chart techniques in this book**.
- You make yourself like a superstar with beautiful & amazing charts in your presentations or reports.
- You can walk away from the same Excel charts which everybody creates.
- Without knowing these techniques, it is quite difficult to create these charts.

How to use "This Book!"

- **Are you crazy? No need to read whole book.** Just jump into the chart you like to make.
- **I am so busy! Just use the example charts** in Excel file with some adjustments.

　　1. *Creating techniques = How to catch fish*
　　2. *Example charts in Excel file = fish which already caught*

- No need to buy the newest Microsoft office package.

- **Excel 2013, Excel 2016, 2019, Excel 365** are suitable for this book.
- **However, <u>Excel 2010 or older versions does NOT fit for this book.</u>** This is because combined charts are used a lot in this book.

- Is it possible to combine these chart techniques one another?

  Yes, of course, you can!

  - This book contains all different methods to create unique Excel charts.
  - The description for chart creations in the book is straightforward.

- I do not know about Excel functions. Is it okay?

  Definitely, no problem.

  The usage of Excel functions is quite limited on the chart creation in this book. Don't worry about fancy Excel functions.

Who needs this book:

- who wants to show beautiful charts in her/his meeting materials, presentation, reports, etc.
- who wants to create unique charts for her/his dash board
- who does not overwork due to making nice charts for quarterly or annual reports

Contents:

E-book (444 pages in A4 with Font size 12) & 26 Uniqiue Infographic Charts' techniques (incl. practice worksheets).

- Each worksheet contains one Excel chart technique or reference data. All charts are dynamically changed by input values' movements.

Applied Excel version:

Professional Plus 2016 is used in this book. The applied Excel version does not include 'ICON functionality & its usage'.

However, the ICON functionality is not really necessary for this book.

About Author

Brilliant Brilliant has worked for one of well-known global financial firms as a senior analyst over 19 years. He has various working experience with financial modelling, reporting, presentations and multiple projects over a decade.
In addition, he is running an Excel YouTube Channel and the name of channel is "Excel Tutorial" (see below link).

https://www.youtube.com/@excel-tutorial

Infographics in Excel Charts

Copyright © 2024 by Brilliant Brilliant

All rights reserved. Copyright and permission should be obtained from the publisher prior to any prohibited reproduction, storage in a retrieval system, or transmission in any form or by any means, electronic, mechanical, photocopying, reordering, or likewise.

Contents

OVERVIEW OF MAIN CHARTS IN THE BOOK 7

BASIC KNOWLEDGE: 20

HOW TO MAKE A CHART (FOR BEGINNER) 26

1. VERTICAL GENDER ICON CHART 32

2. HORIZONTAL MALE FEMALE ICON CHART 51

3. MIXED GENDER ICON CHART 65

4. PEOPLE GRAPH 74

5. 3D METAL BAR CHART 80

6. 3D METAL GLASS BAR CHART 97

7. VERTICAL TRANSPARENT BAR CHART WITH CIRCLE ICON............112

8. 3D DONUT CHART 126

9. WIND CHART WITH AVERAGE LINE 138

10. CIRCLE BUBBLE CHART 156

11. ERROR BAR CHART 167

12. WAFFLE CHART 185

13. MAKING A CHART WITHOUT CHART FUNCTIONALITY 195

14. VERTICAL BAR CHART WITH ARROW PERCENTAGE 204

15. HALF-CIRCLE DONUT CHART 227

16. DYNAMIC COLOUR-CHANGED BAR CHART 245

17. TWO-SIDES HORIZONTAL BAR CHART 259

18. UNIQUE 2D & 3D DONUT CHART 279

19. HIGHLIGHTING BAR CHART 295

20. 2D & 3D INDEX-MEASURE BAR CHART 309

21. INFOGRAPHIC CHART WITHOUT CHART FUNCTIONALITY.........327

22. BAR OF BAR CHART 347

23. WORLD MAP CHART 365

24. SPECIAL RANGE BAR CHART 388

25. STYLISH DONUT CHART 410

26. STYLISH BAR CHART WITH ERROR BARS 430

Overview of Main Charts in the book

- **Note1: Allow to jump.** You can jump to the chart you like to make. No need to read one section after another.
- **Note2: Be creative!** The following charts are just examples of chart-creating techniques in this book. You can create your unique charts.

1. Vertical gender icon chart, Text chart & People graph

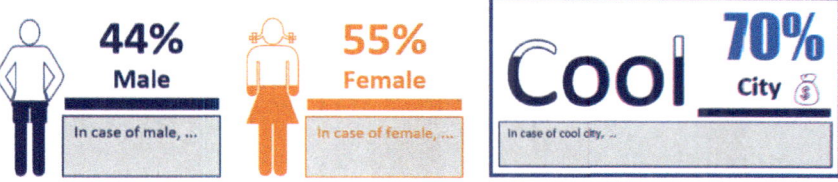

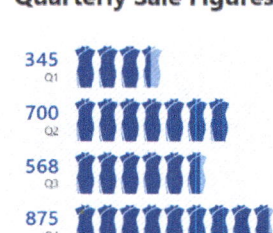

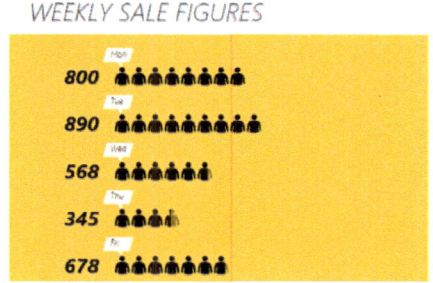

2. Horizontal gender icon chart & Mixed gender icon chart

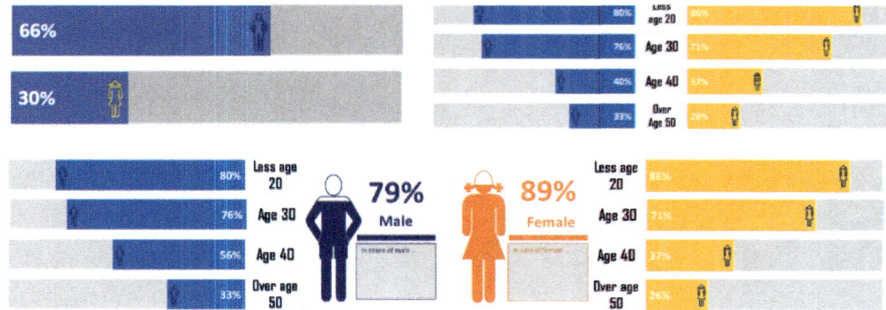

3. 3D metal bar chart

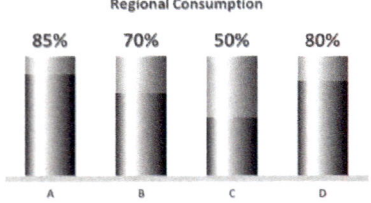
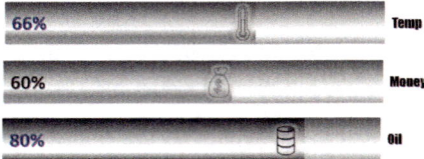

4. 3D metal glass bar chart

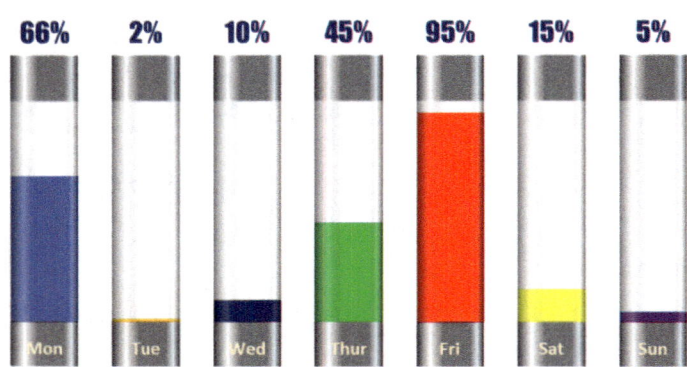

5. Vertical transparent bar chart with circle icon

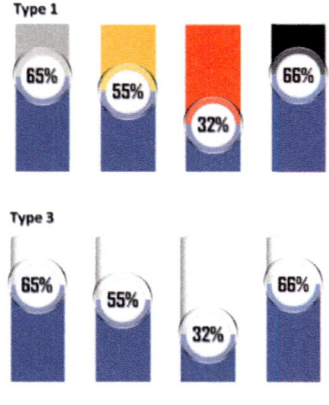
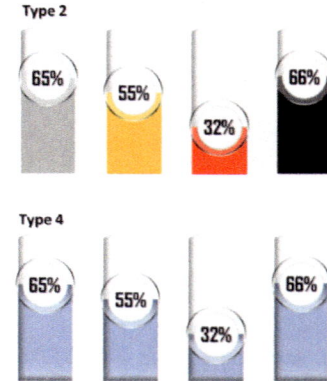

6. 3D donut chart

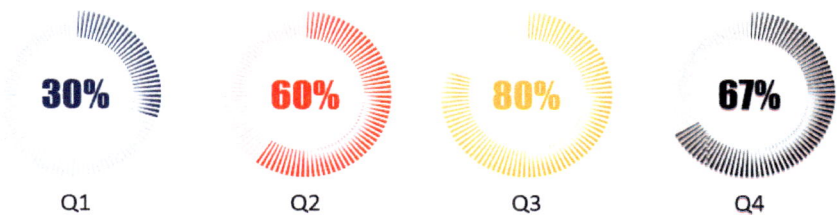

7. Wind chart with average line

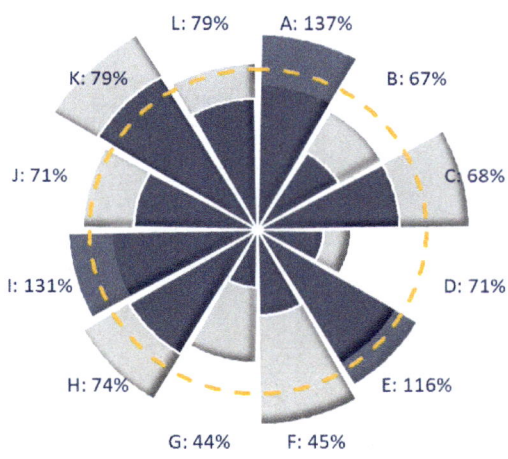

8. Circle Bubble Chart

9. Error Bar chart

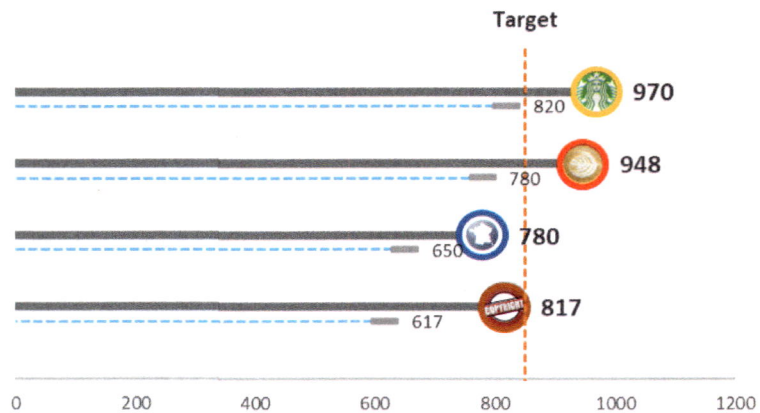

10. Waffle Chart

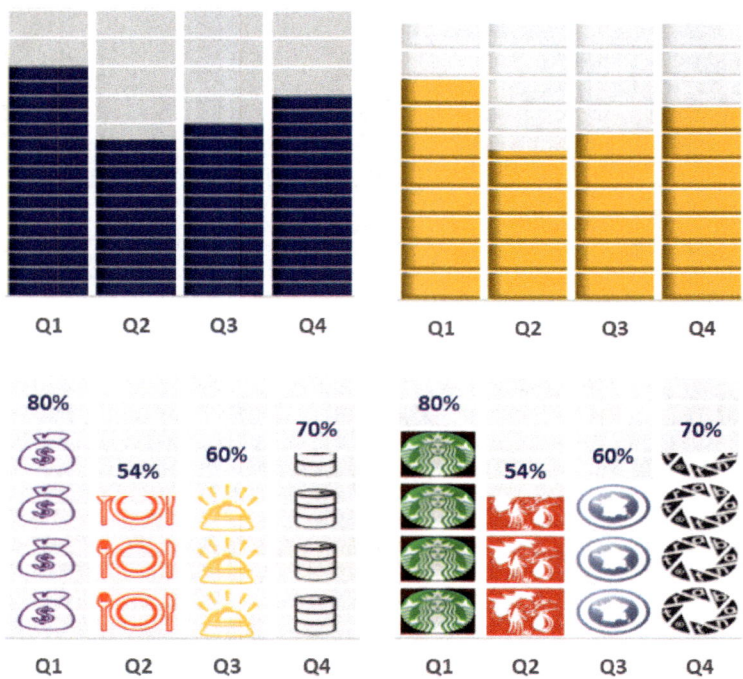

11. Making a chart with chart functionality

12. Vertical bar chart with arrow percentage

13. Half-circle donut charts (3 different types)

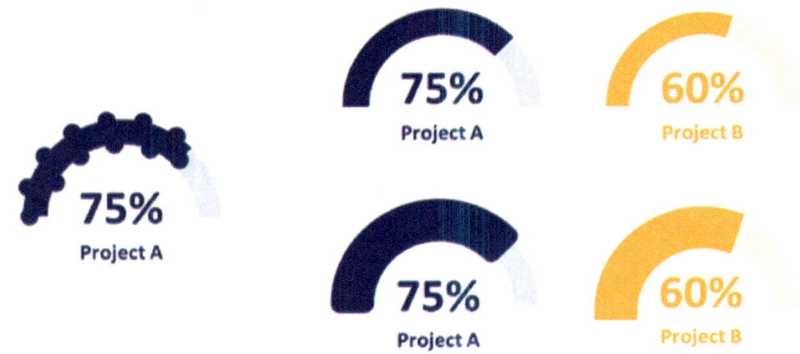

14. Dynamic Color-changed Bar Chart (depends on input)

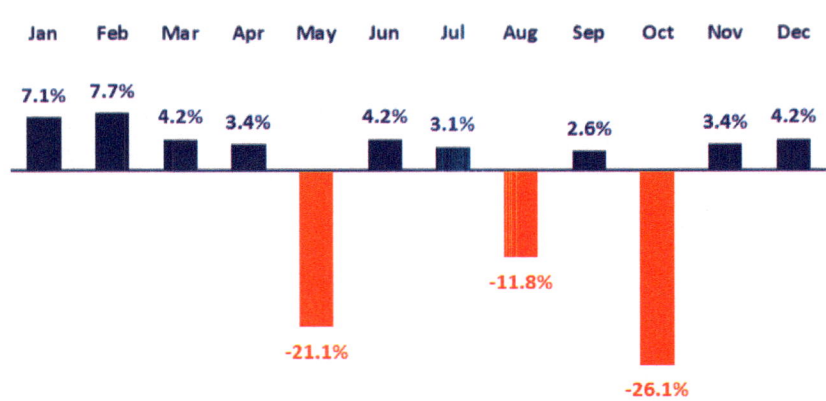

15. 2-sided Horizontal Bar Chart

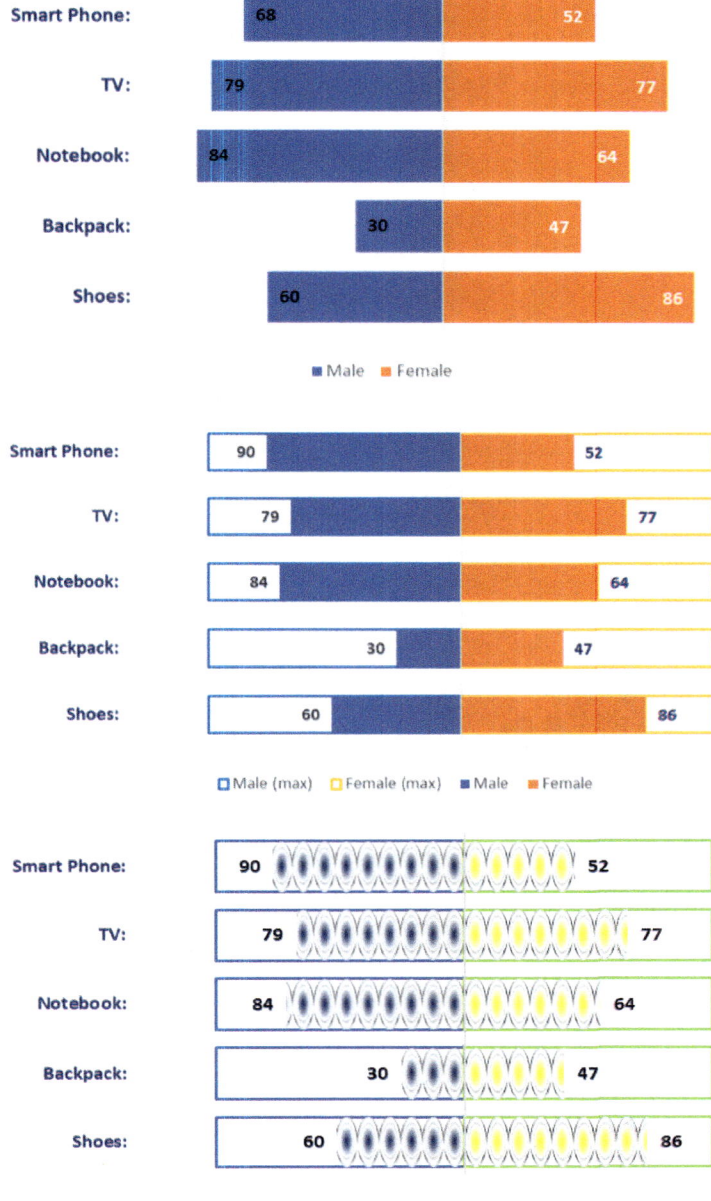

16. Unique 2D & 3D donut chart

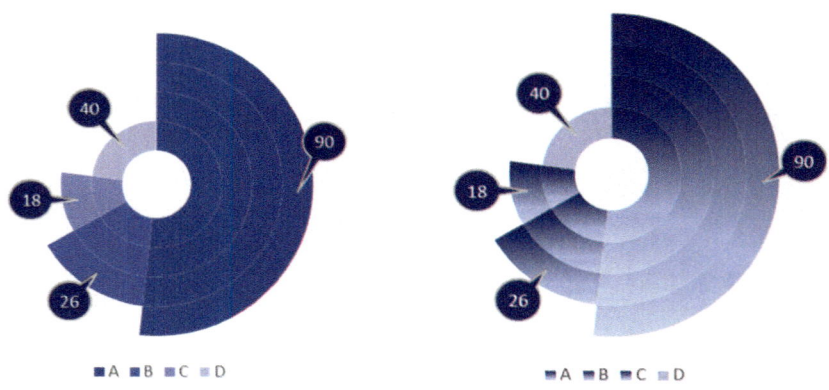

17. <u>Automatic highlighted</u> bar chart (depends on selection)

18. 3D index measure bar chart (2 different types)

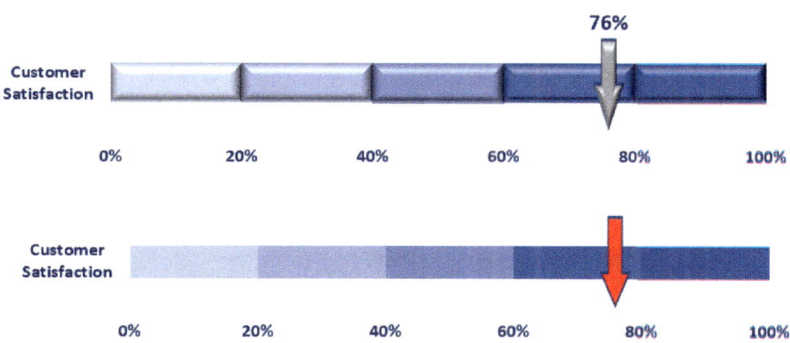

19. Infographic Chart (<u>color-changed</u> by input values)

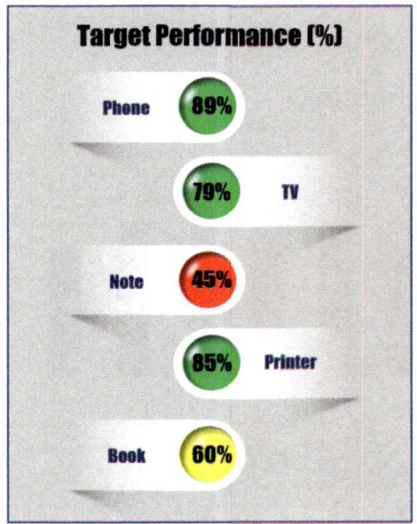

20. Bar of Bar Chart (complication makes it simple)

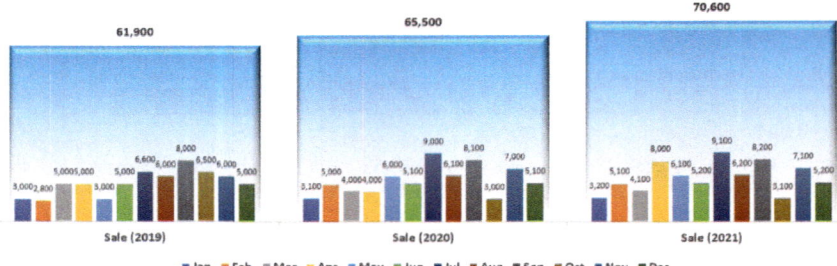

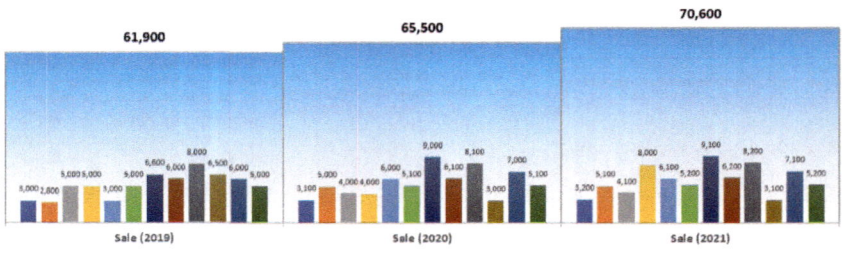

21. World Map Chart (2D & 3D icon & Excel version free)

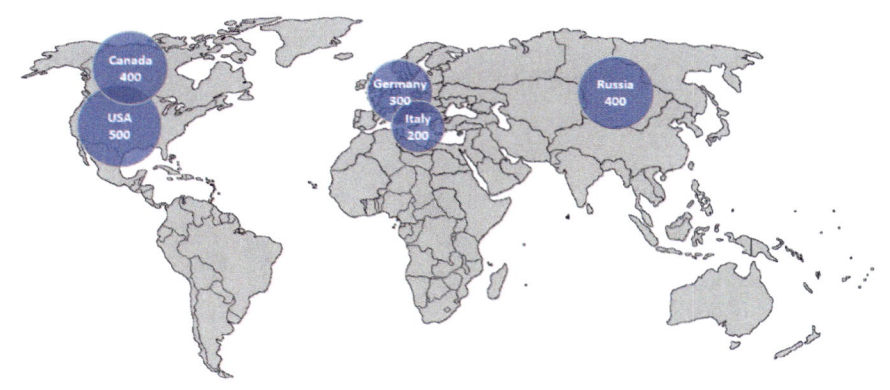

22. **Special Ranged** Bar Chart (you can define the range)

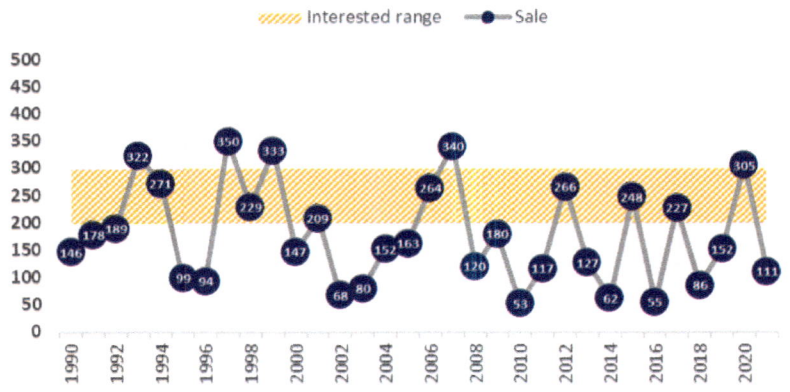

23. Stylish Donut Charts

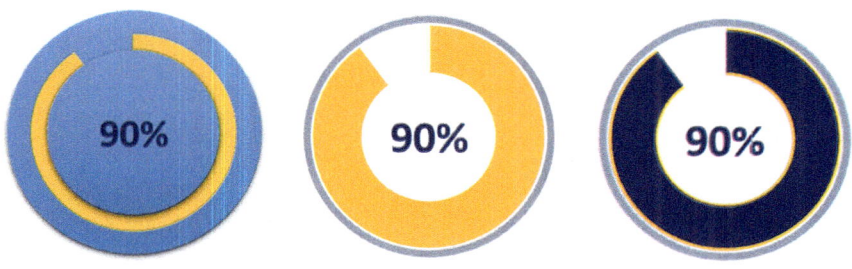

24. Stylish Bar Chart with Error Bars

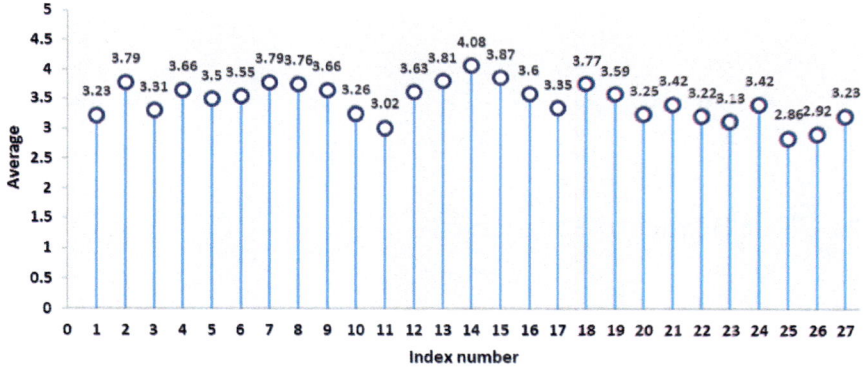

- **Note3:** *This book does not include the techniques for the following charts. However, you can see the free tutorial from my YouTube channel & also download the complete version of infographics Excel charts in the YouTube video.*

25. Background-Band Line Chart

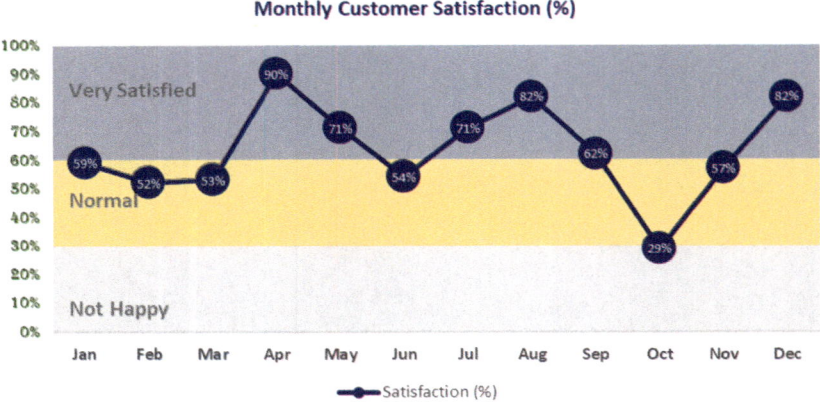

26. Chart Beautiful Line Chart

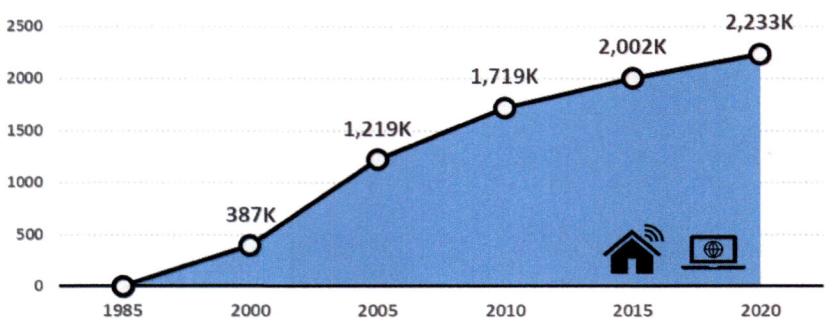

27. Bullet Chart

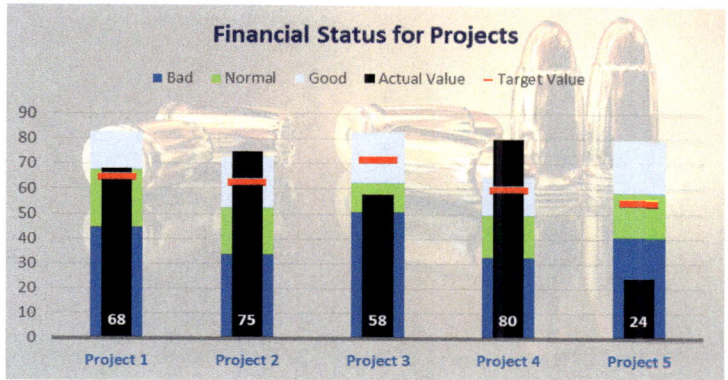

28. Difference Bar Chart

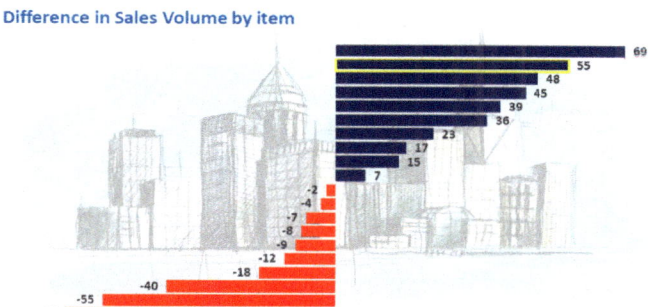

29. Expected Trend Line Chart

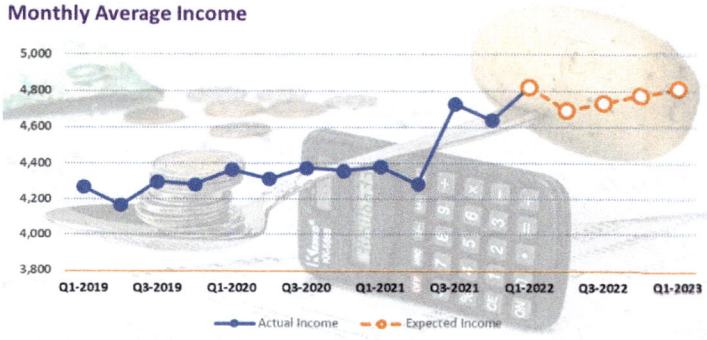

30. Horizontal Timeline Chart

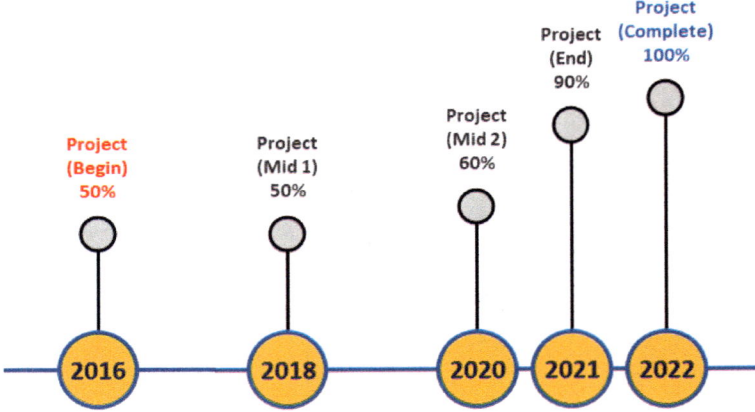

31. Infographic Doughnut Chart

32. Max & Min Line Chart

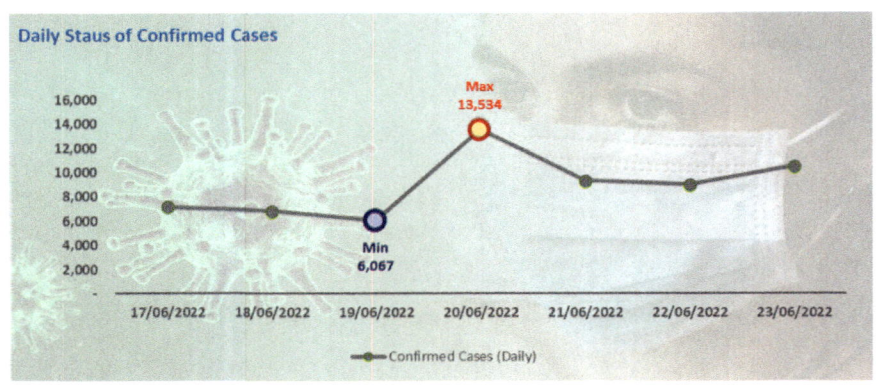

33. Multi-Bubble Chart

34. Vertical Icon Chart

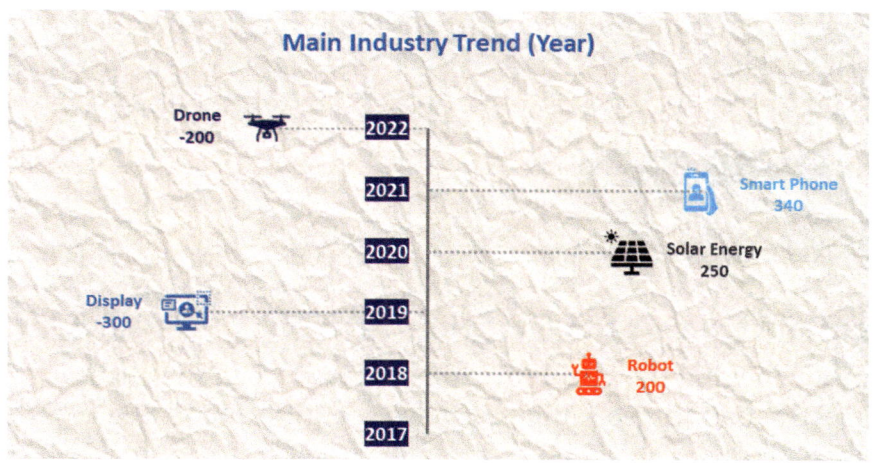

Basic knowledge:

If you already know how to make a chart in Excel, just skip entire this section!

The basic, general and common steps of creating a chart are explained here. This is a section for a person who is not familiar with Excel before. *This section is optional.*
In addition, there is one more section for beginner: '**How to make a chart (for beginner)**' in appendix.

How to select input data:

Put the cursor at the starting cell (i.e. 44% below example) which you want to select, you can select input values by dragging a left button of mouse until the end of cell which you want to select.

	Input	
	Male	Female
	44%	55%
help	56%	45%

How to select the chart (=graph):

Simply clicking the graph by mouse. If you click the chart correctly, you can see small 8 circles around a chart. See below.

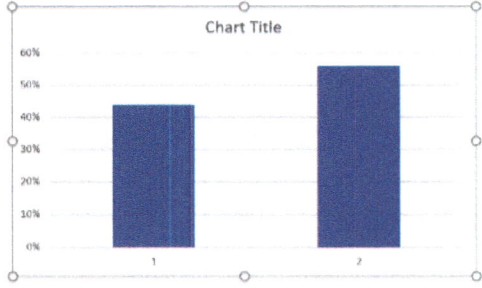

Ribbon or Tab?

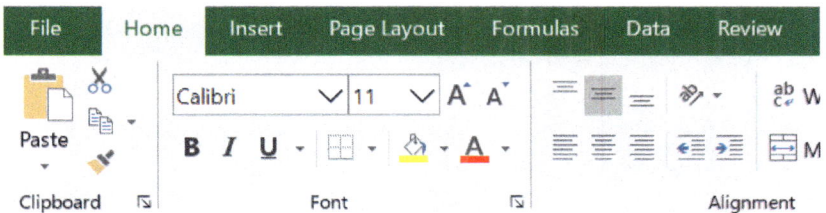

Ribbon (the green line in the above picture) is the official name, but we call them just **tabs** in this book (i.e. Home tab, Insert tab). This is because it just sounds better.

Graph or Chart?

We will simply use both a graph or a chart as the same meaning or same thing in this book.

'>>>' means a next step. (i.e.: click **Insert tab** >>> **Chart** >>> **2-D Stacked column** chart)

How to go to 'Format Axis':

Click one of axis in the chart. press **CTRL+1**. We can see **Format Axis** on the right-hand side.

How to go to chart elements:

After clicking a chart, we can see the plus (+) sign on right hand side. This is the location where we can control the chart elements.
  - Go to chart elements = click (+) sign in gray in the chart
- **Remove the chart elements** = Unclick the chart elements which you want to remove

How to remove 'Shape Fill' and 'Shape Outline':

You will also see the following steps a lot in the later sections. Click a chart >>> Go to **Format** tab. We will change the default settings of **Shape Fill** and **Shape Outline** of the chart.

- **Shape Fill** = No Fill
- **Shape Outline** = No Outline

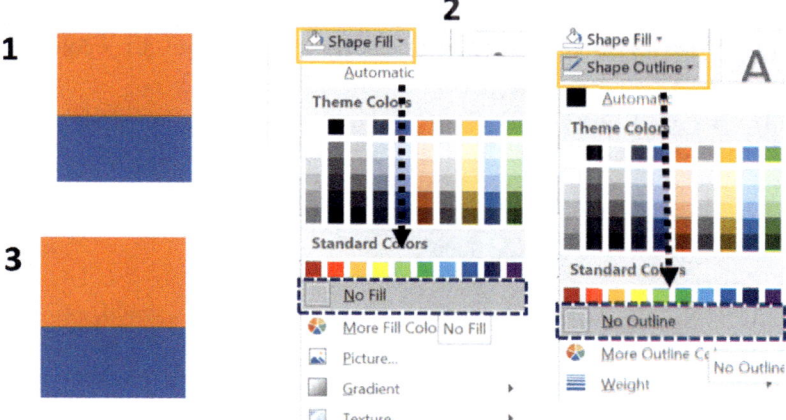

How to remove Gridlines:

- Go to **View** tab and unclick **Gridlines**.

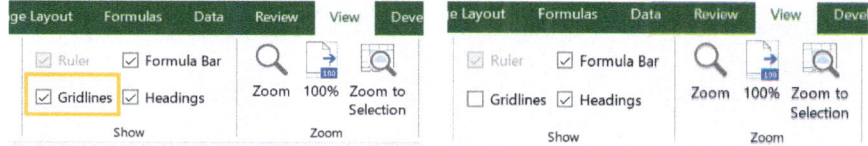

How to group objects (or items):

Select more than 2 objects, then click right-hand button on the mouse, you can see '**Group**'. Select Group. More than 2 objects become one object. You can also ungroup it or regroup them.

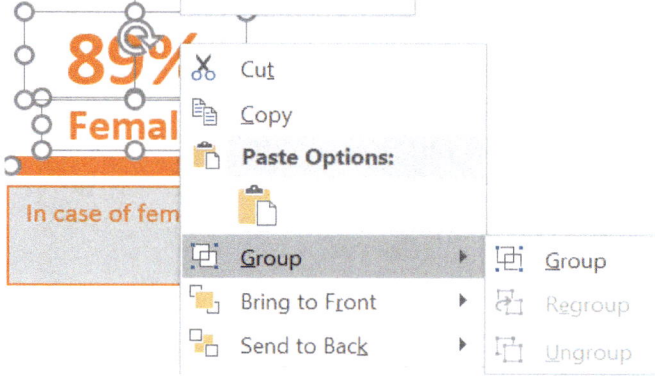

How to make a text box which shows input values:

- Make a text box: **Insert** tab >>> **Shapes** >>>select **Text box**.
- Put a cursor inside of text box & click function box (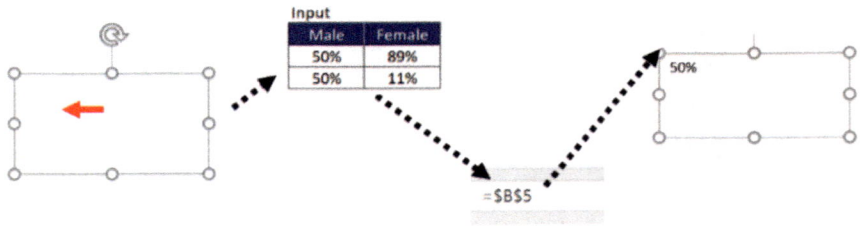)
- Write '**= cell location** (i.e. =B5)' and then hit 'Enter' button.

How to make the text box looking good:

Clicking a text box, removing Shape Fill & Shape Outline.
- **Shape Fill** = No Fill
- **Shape Outline** = No Outline

The rest elements (font size, font color, font type, etc.) can be changed by Font tab (see below)

How to update 'Chart Title':

- Click a 'Chart Title' box in the chart by a mouse.
- Go to function bar (= fx) and put '='.
- Next to '=', Click the cell which you want to use it for the chart title (in the function bar).
i.e. ='3D Metal Bar'!$A$1
- Hit an 'Enter' button.

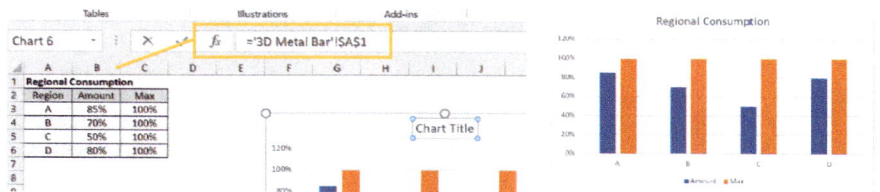

From now on, the chart title will change whenever you can the cell text for the chart title.

How to add Labels in the chart:

- Click the bar which you want to add labels
- Click a right-hand side mouse button >>> Click **'Add Data Labels'**
- Go to **Format Data Labels** >>> Select **"Value from Cells"**
- Select **the actual values** from the input table.

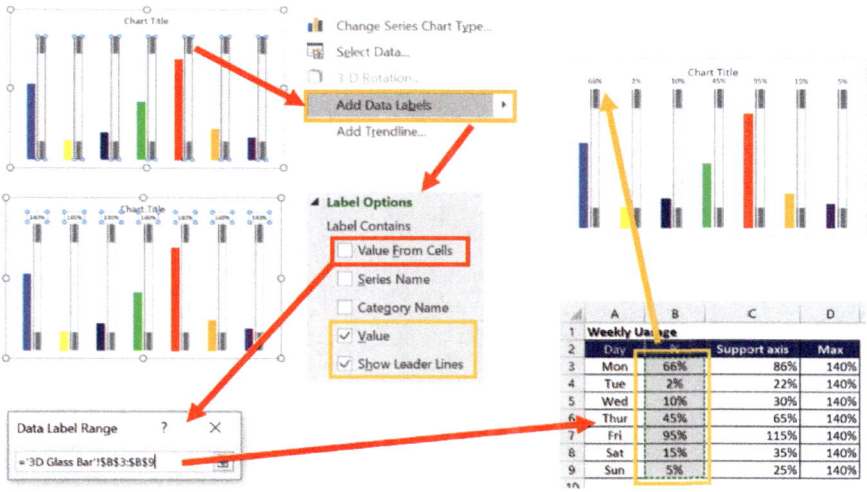

(Note) This functionality is available from Excel version 2013. In case of older versions, it needs to click each data label and link to the actual values in the table one by one.

How to make a chart (for Beginner)

This is a section for someone who has very limited experience on Excel. We will create a basic simple chart. If you already know how to create a chart, kindly please skip this section.

How to insert input values into worksheet:

Once you open the excel, the default tab is Home. It is possible to enter a value in a cell.
After putting values, press Enter button. The cursor is moving the below cell.

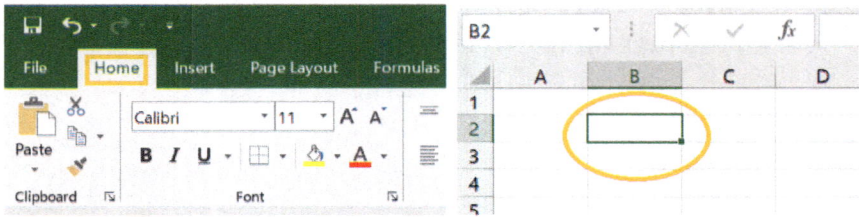

It is possible to make an input table like below.

	A	B	C
1			
2		100	
3			
4			

	A	B	C
1		Input1	Input2
2		100	123
3		145	167
4		125	122

How to read input location:

For example, Cell C3 means column C (vertical) and row 3 (horizontal). C3 = 167.

	A	B	C
1		Input1	Input2
2		100	123
3		145	167
4		125	122

How to select input values:

- Put the cursor into the starting point of input values
- Press a left-hand mouse button, holding & dragging it until the end of the range.

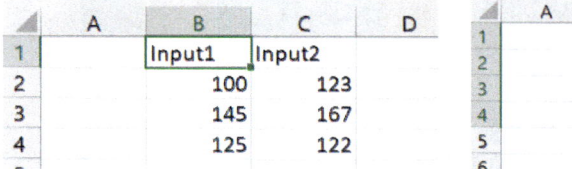 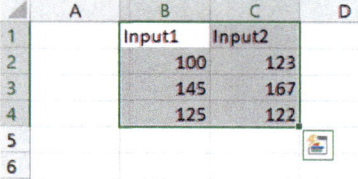

How to make a chart:

After selecting input values, go to Insert tab. Select a chart from the available selections.

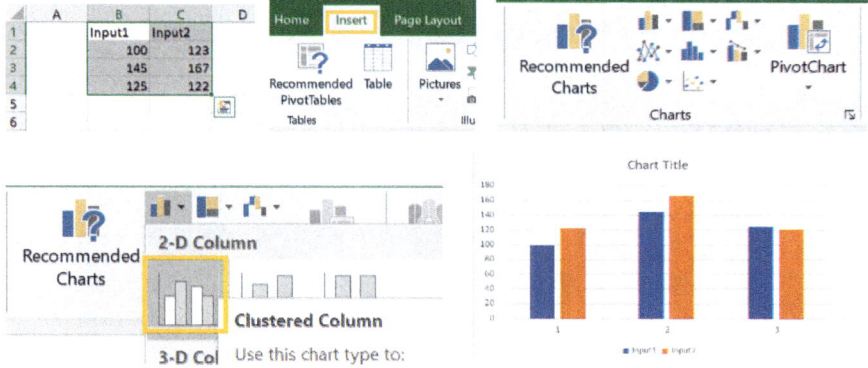

Design tab in Chart:

Go to the end of tabs, it is possible to see Design tab. Click the tab. Choose the design which you like.

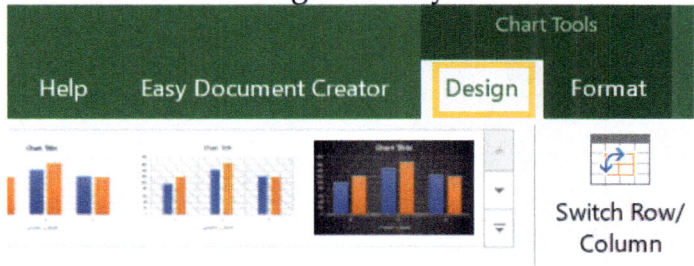

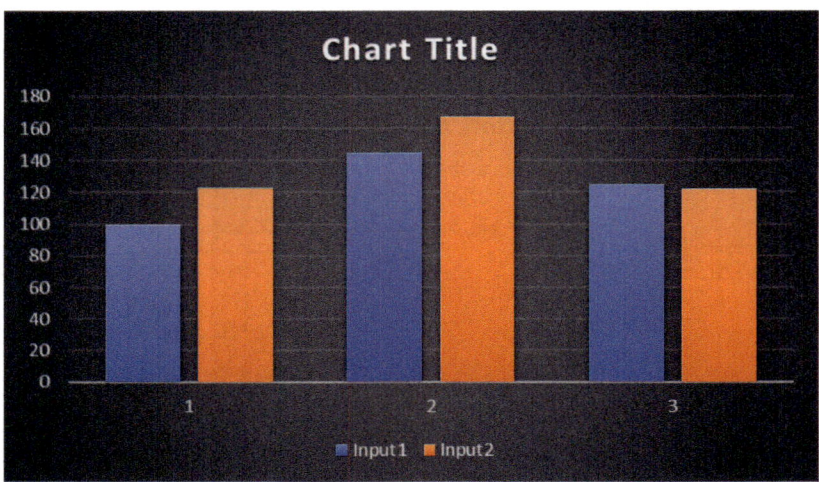

How to insert Title:

As a simple approach, click the chart title. Change the title of chart.

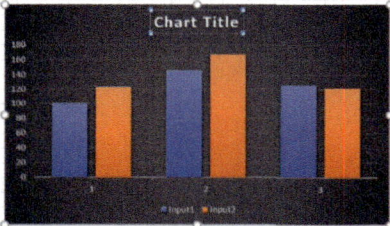 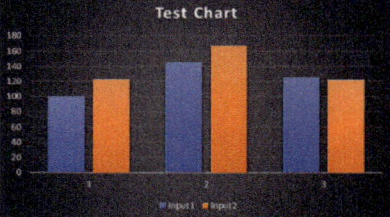

Complete a chart.

Example chart excel file:

Unfortunately, Amazon KDP does NOT support downloading any attached files directly from KDP directly. Therefore, kindly please visit the link below & download the example of infographic Excel chart file:

https://drive.google.com/drive/folders/1SG8dBkvEEAlR39q5G6KcTcQcFSQj8Tlv?usp=sharing

As a bonus, you can also download the complete version of infographics in Excel charts from my YouTube video.

https://www.youtube.com/@excel-tutorial

Typo & Errors in the book:

Kindly please contact to me by the following e-mail address:
life96336@gmail.com

Dynamic Icon charts:

Let's start! The first target chart looks like below. Actually, this chart is a combined chart.

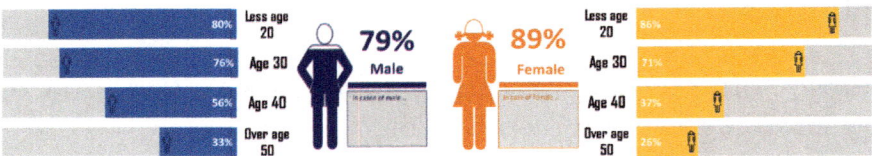

It can split into 3 different charts like below:

- Vertical gender icon chart

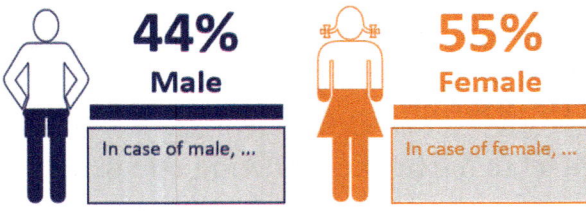

- Horizontal male female icon chart

- Mixed gender icon chart (combining them & the below are 2 examples of mixed charts)

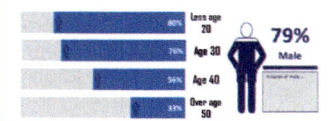

Note that we will tackle how to create the above 3 charts in the following 3 sections. Each section will introduce new techniques of creating charts.

1. Vertical gender icon chart

We are going to make a vertical man & woman icon chart which the inside of chart will be changed by input values. Using icon technique is quite useful and handy to create various infographic charts.

Target picture:
What we are going to make is the following chart: The arrow is pointing at the actual input values.

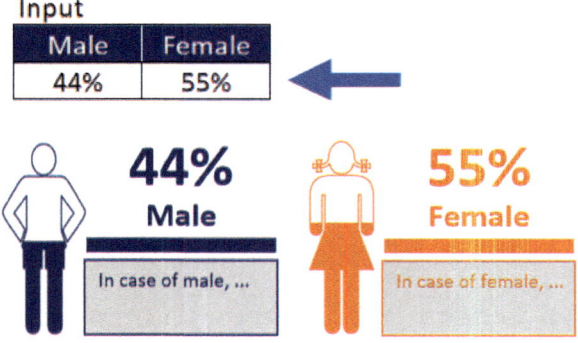

First, create **input cells** and **helping cells** in an empty worksheet.
The input values are presented by percentage (%). This is because, normally, reports are used % a lot and % is easy to communicate.
The help cells have a simple formula which is '**1-input value**'.

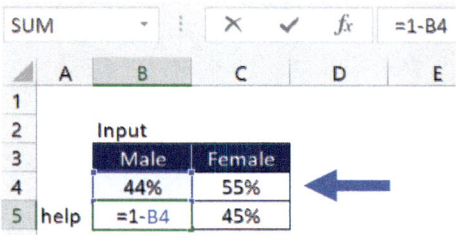

Next, make a **2D stacked column chart**. As an example, we are going to create a male case in this book.

After selecting the range of input values, go to an **Insert** tab. (See below)

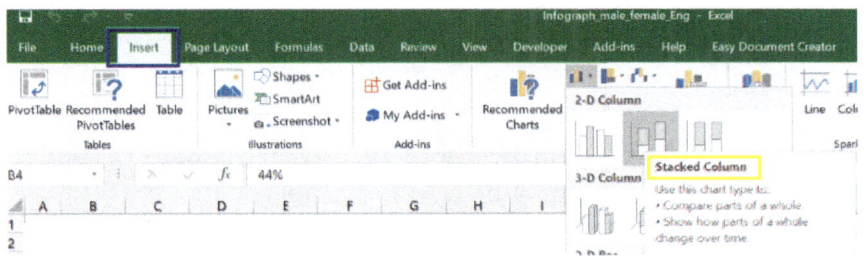

Go to **Chart** tab, select **2-D Stacked column** (see below).

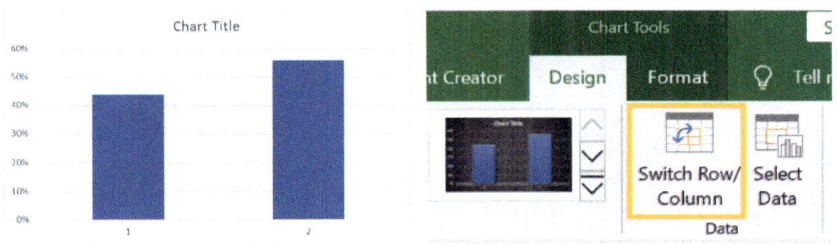

Go to **Design** >>> **Switch Row/Column**.

We can get the below chart as an outcome.

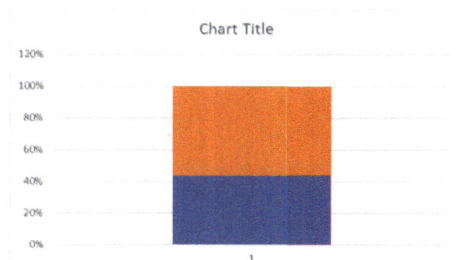

Go to '**Format Axis**' (= click an axis in the chart & **CTRL +1**). We can see Format Axis (see right hand part in the below picture)

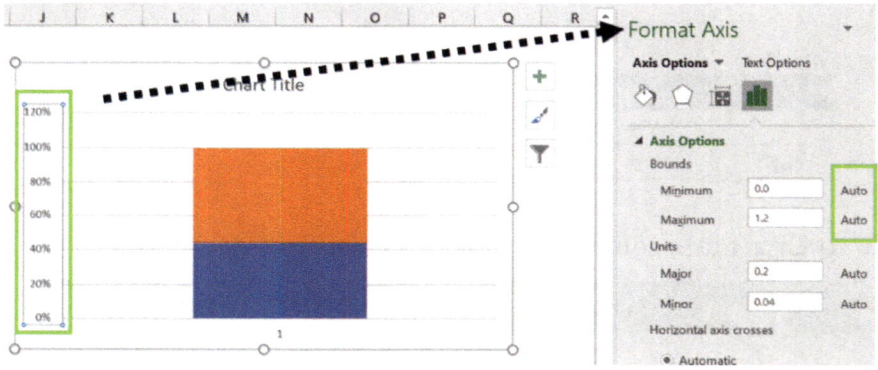

Switching **Min** & **Max** values by **re-typing '0'** instead of **'0.0'** for a **Min** value & putting **1** as a **Max** value.
Then, the bounds setting is changed from **Auto** to **Reset**. It means that the axis bounds are not automatically changed anymore. The default setting is always **Auto**.
You can see the max is 100% in the vertical axis.

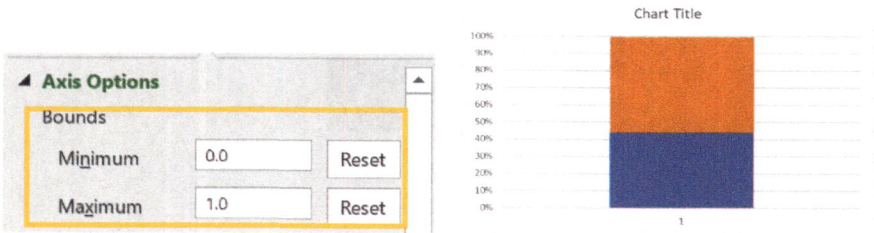

How to clean up the chart elements:

After clicking a chart, we can see the plus sign. This is the location where we can clean up the chart elements.

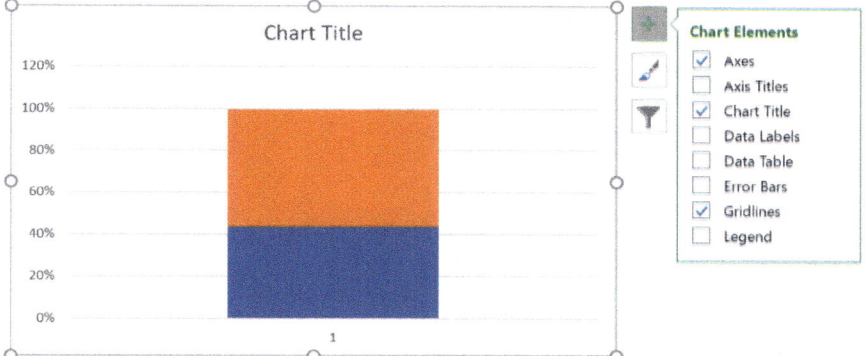

We can clean up all chart elements by unclicking these elements. (Axes, Chart Title, Gridlines, etc.)
The meaning of **clean up** chart elements = **Unclicking** the default setting elements.

Next, change **Gap Width** from 150% to **100%** after selecting only the actual input value.

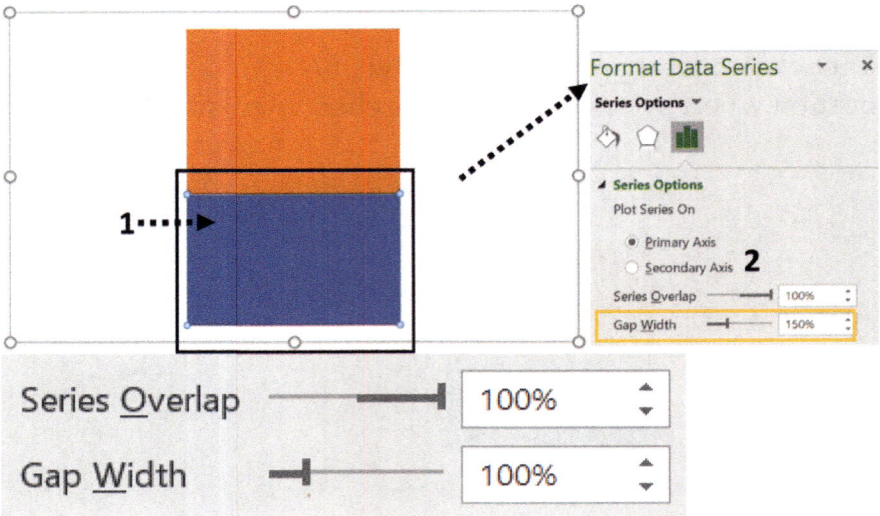

How to remove Shape Fill and Shape Outline:

We will change the default setting of **Shape Fill** and **Shape Outline** of the chart.

In **Insert** tab, go to **Shape Fill** and **Shape Outline** and then select **No Fill** and **No Outline**.

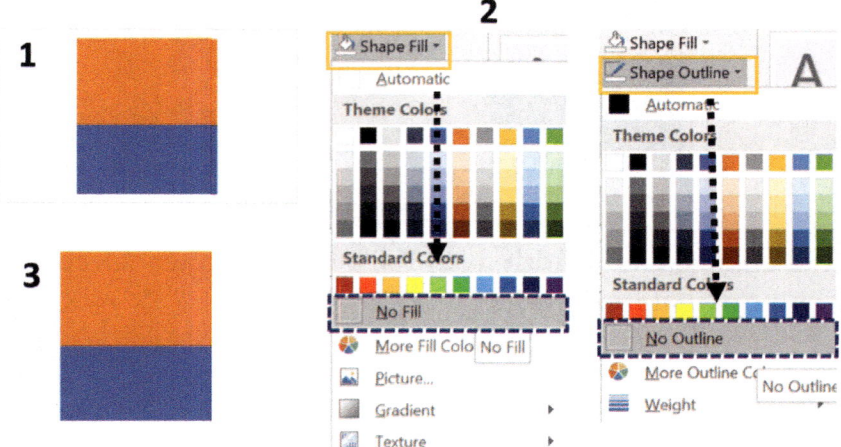

You can see the outline is gone in the above no.3 picture.

How to remove Gridlines:

- Go to **View** tab and unclick **Gridlines**.

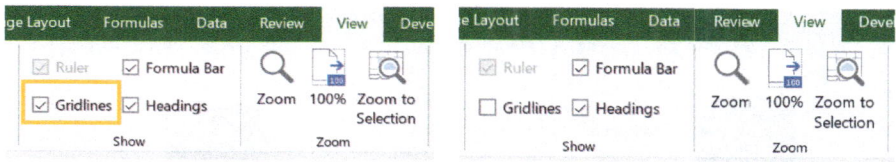

After finishing this step, it might look like the below:

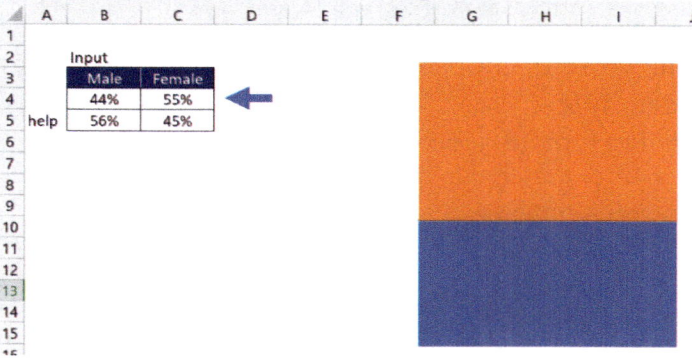

Next, we are going to change the color of bars:
- Helping bar = **No color**
- Actual input bar = you can choose the color you like

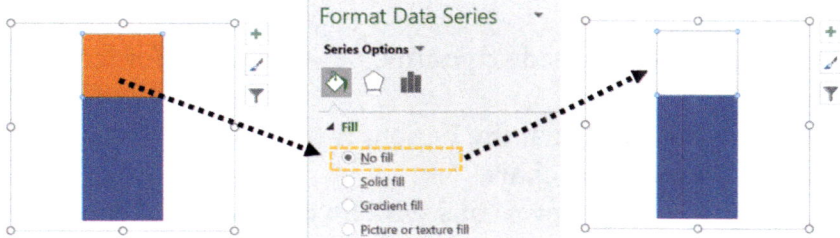

go to '**Format Data Series**' = click the upper axis in the chart & CTRL + 1 >>>
- **Helping bar** = Click **No fill**

- **Actual input bar = Solid fill** >>> Choose the color which you like (i.e. dark blue)

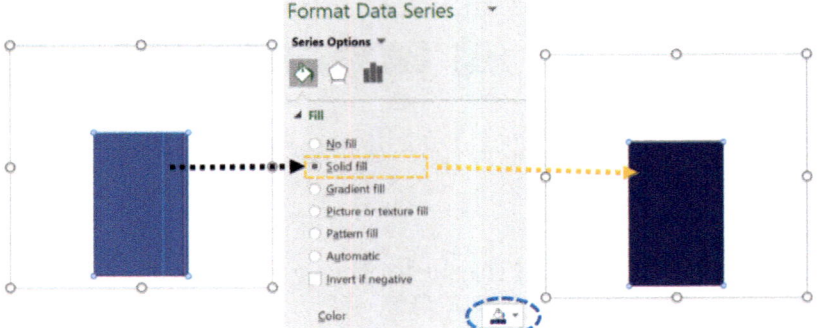

In case of female, you can choose the color which you like. (i.e. Orange in this example)

In case of inputs for female, we need to select female inputs.

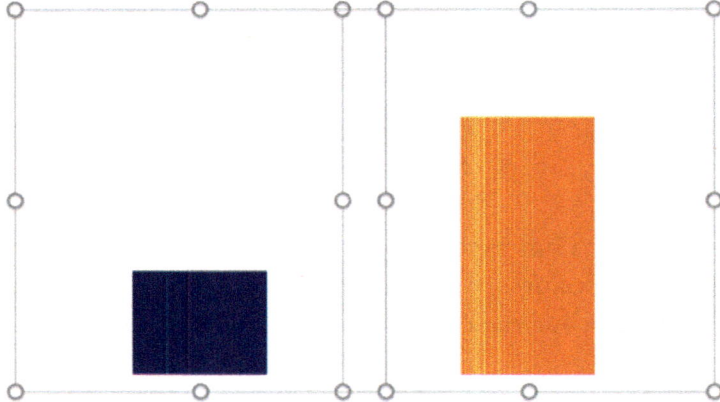

We just finished the inside dynamic bar chart part for icon charts.

In order to save time, just the bar chart (up to now) from Example files for your chart.

Just change or create new icons which you want to create.

How to make an Icon:

Note: In case of **Microsoft 365** or **later versions**, there is a new function called '**Icon**'. It looks like a bird in the insert tab which helps to create various icons easily.

However, it assumes that not everybody has the most recent Microsoft package. In fact, there is *no need to buy a newer Microsoft package because of a few new functionalities.*

Let's assume that we do not have the icon function in this book. (Using Excel 2016)
Therefore, alternatively, we will use **Symbol** as an icon with combining PowerPoint. More correctly speaking, we only need **Merge Shapes function** in **PowerPoint** to convert Symbol to Icon.
Before the usage of Merge Shapes function, it does not matter to use the function either in Excel or PowerPoint for the below steps. In this example, we will use PowerPoint only for **Merge Shapes function**.

Now, we are going to create an icon. The following steps are feasible for both in Excel or PowerPoint.
(In case of PowerPoint, open a new empty slide in PowerPoint. In Excel, just create the below.)

Go to **Insert** tab, create **1 rectangle** and **1 text box**.

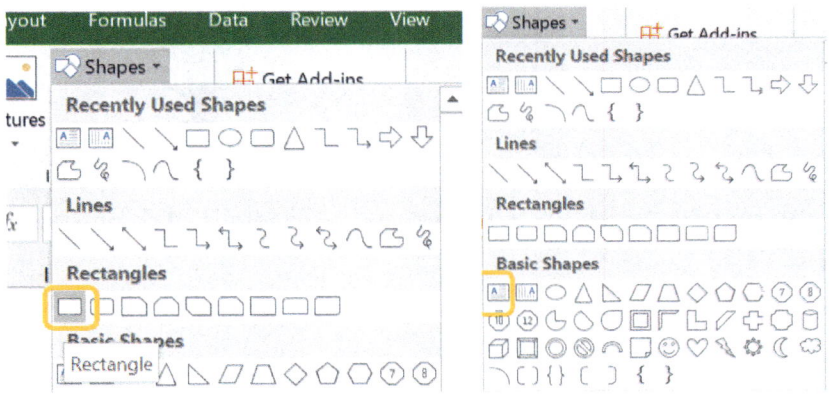

After creating text box, go to **insert** tab >>> **Symbol** >>> **Webdings** >>> choose an Icon.

Possible options: **Webdings, Wingdings or Wingdings 2**

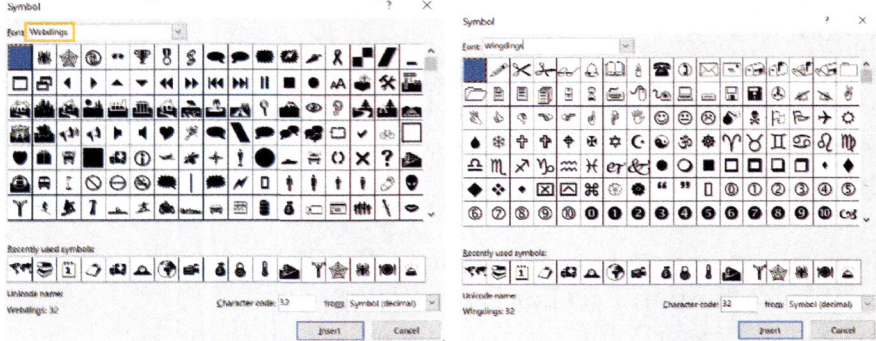

As a default setting, the font size is 11. Therefore, it would be nice to make it bigger like **72** or even bigger. Just used a dummy icon below.

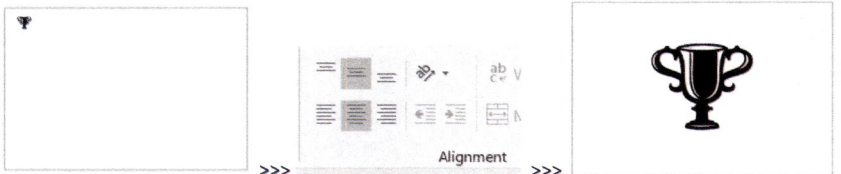

Click the text box with an icon, removing Shape Fill & Shape Outline.
- **Shape Fill** = No Fill
- **Shape Outline** = No Outline

Now, overlapping with the rectangle and the text box.
Copy & Paste them into a new slide in PowerPoint.

Please note that "Merge Shapes" functionality is only available in PowerPont.

Go back to our actual male icon.

Select both of the files >>> **Format** tab >>> **Merge Shapes** >>> **Combine**

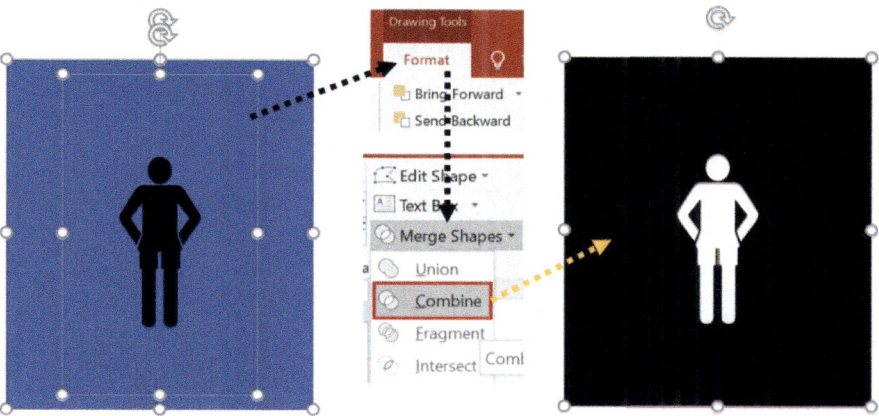

(in PowerPoint) The next is:
- **Shape Fill** = White
- **Shape Outline =** Dark blue (The color which you like)

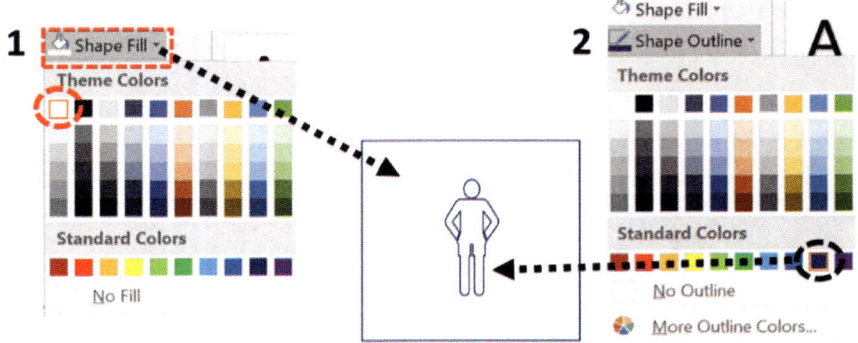

The part for PowerPoint is over!
Copy and **Paste** into Excel as a **Picture**.

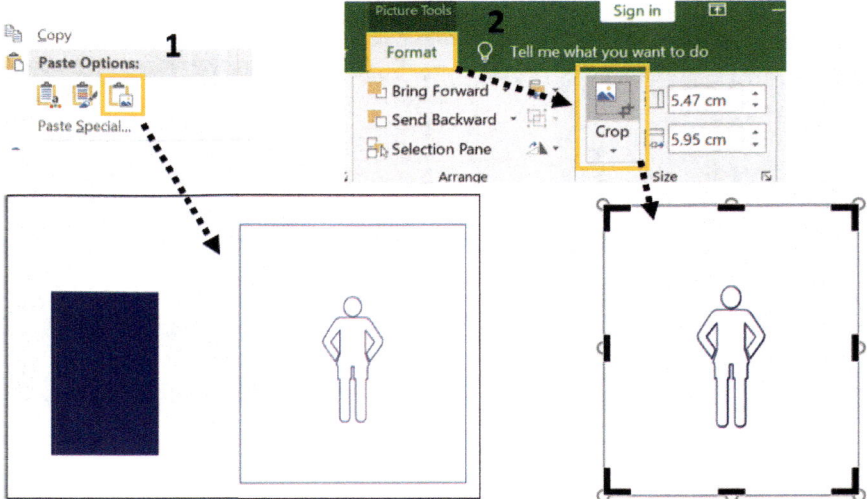

What we are going to is **to crop** its picture to remove any unwanted part.
What we need is the only icon part.

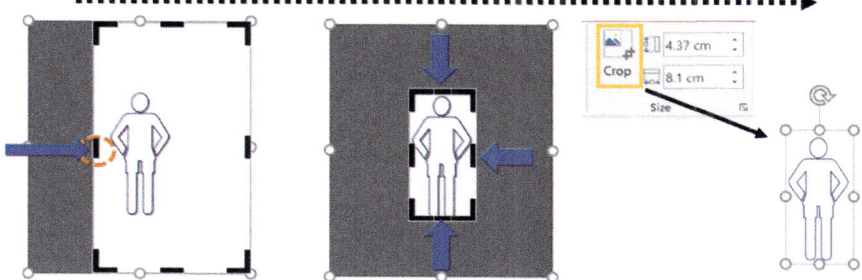

By using mouse, dragging & push a black T shape towards the icon (See the first picture above). After finishing the shape, click Crop button again.
For female icon (or any other icons), the method to create is exactly the same (except Shape Outline).

- **Shape Outline** = Dark blue (Male)
- **Shape Outline** = Orange (Female)

The icon part is also over. If you obtain icons like them, you did awesome job.
The reason why I choose male & female is that a gender comparison is frequently & commonly used.

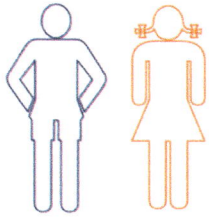

Please make sure the icon color and bar color are identical.

The next step is combining between the vertical bar chart and icons.
- Put an icon in front of the bar chart.

- Set the input as 100%. Drag the icon to cover the entire bar chart.
Please make sure the icon can cover the entire bar chart. Also check with lower input values like 3%.

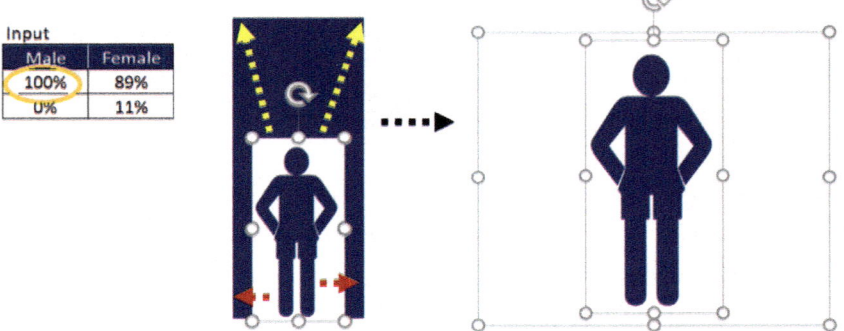

How to group objects (or items):

This is also used a lot in the later sections. Select more than 2 objects, then click right button on the mouse, you can see '**Group**'. Select Group. More than 2 objects become one object. You can ungroup it or regroup them.

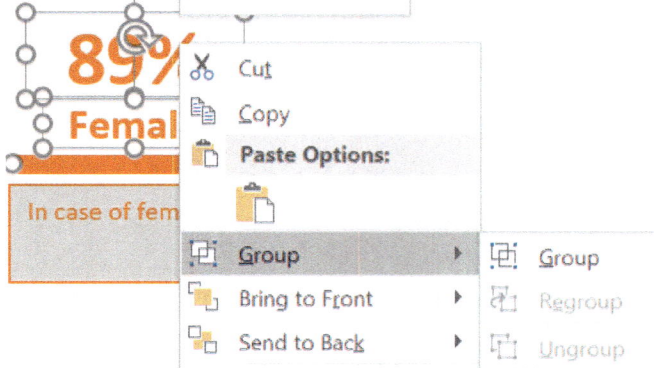

Next, grouping the icon & the bar chart. The main part of creating chart is done.
You can see that each icon has the corresponding chart and input value.

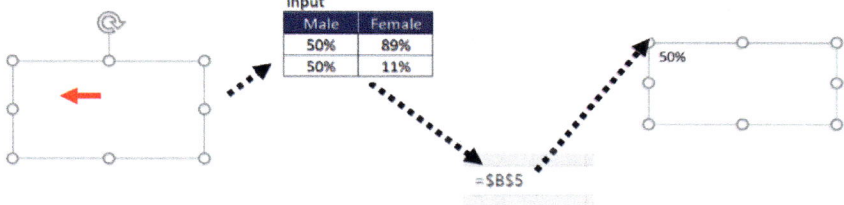

The next steps are to decorate the icon chart.

How to make a text box which shows input values:

- First, make a text box. **Insert** tab >>> **Shapes** >>> **Text box**.
- Put cursor inside and click function box ( )
- Write '= cell location (i.e. B5)' and then hit Enter button

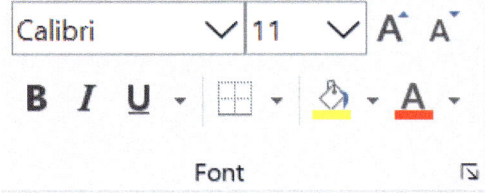

How to make the text box looking good:

Clicking a text box, removing Shape Fill & Shape Outline.
- **Shape Fill** = No Fill
- **Shape Outline** = No Outline

The rest elements (font size, font color, font type, etc.) can be changed by Font tab elements (see below)

For the horizontal line, **Insert** tab >>> **Shapes** >>> **Rectangle box**. Fill with the color which you like.

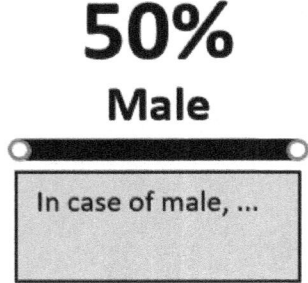

Next, grouping them into one object.

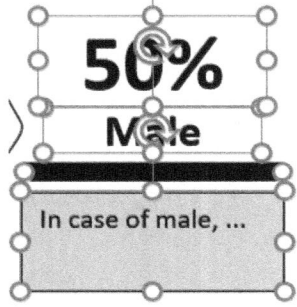

The above parts (color, size, location, etc.) are fully depends on your preference.
The helping cells is relocated to one of corners of sheet.

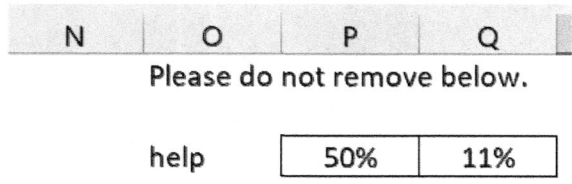

Finally, we complete the vertical icon chart. Looks good.

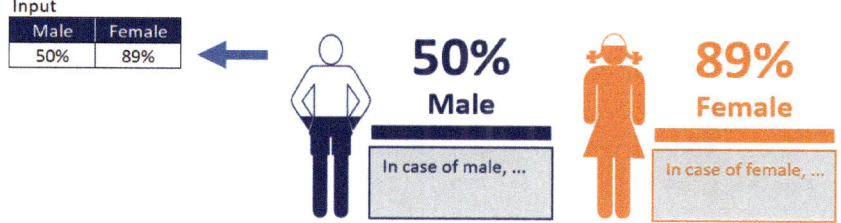

The method of icon chart is quite handy for infographic and also reports.
This is because each icon is a separate chart. Therefore, you can easily locate the icon chart.

Also, by google search for '**Unicode in Excel**', you can find various possibilities to obtain icons.
I will share one simple approach to more icons. "**Win button + .**" in this book.

Before using the icons from internet website, please check the copyrights of icons.

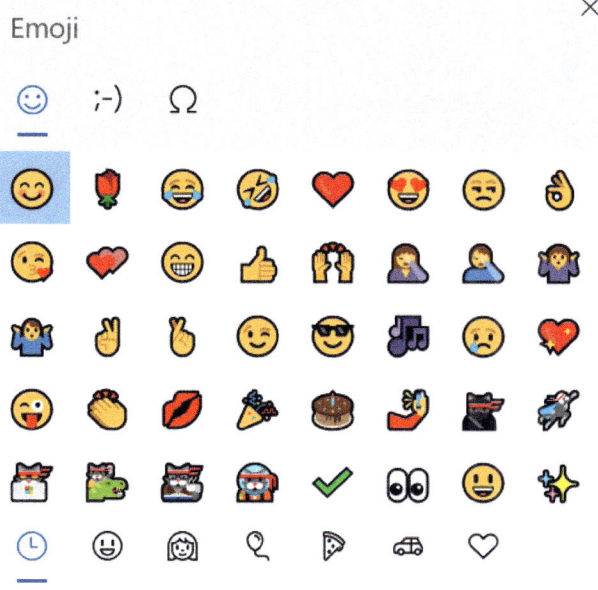

All icons from 'Microsoft Icon functionality' for Free:

Youtuber '**PowerPoint University**' collected all icons from 'Microsoft Icon functionality' and share it for Free in the following link: (The below link is also available in Example chart excel file)

https://drive.google.com/file/d/10virioA2V1Km4ao94ssX8CO YryXftO6A/view

Please note that <u>the above link is nothing to do with the author</u>, but I would like to share the link. It allows you to use all icons in Microsoft Icon functionality.

How to make letter icon chart:

Now, we will challenge one more example with the icon chart method. In this example, we will use letters as an icon. Please see the below picture.

Note: When you use letter as an icon, please be careful with the form of letters.
For the symbol icon chart, we changed the size of icon itself to fit the bar chart. For letter icon, the bar chart has to be changed to fit the letter icon.

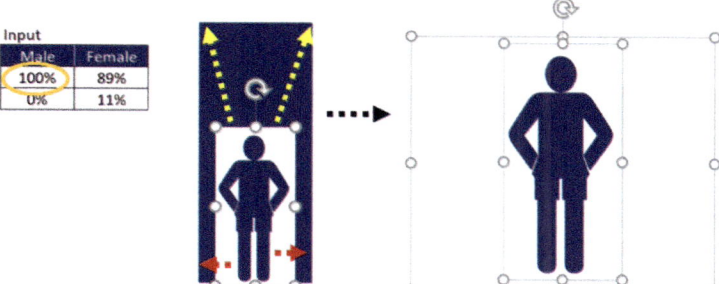

Please control the size of the bar chart to fit the letter icon.

Based on this example, we learn that any letters can be used in an icon chart.

In conclusion, the method of icon chart is quite handy to create unique charts for infographic & various reports.

Trouble shooting (Tip):

How to avoid destroy original chart shape after adding new col or rows

After adding completing your chart task, it was realized that you need to add one more column.

After adding the column, your completed chart is destroyed due to adding or adjusting a new column.

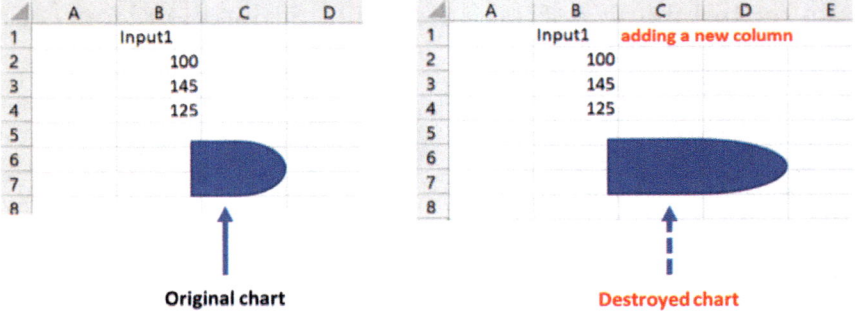

Q: What should I do with it?

The solution is to go to '**Size and Properties**' and click '**Move but don't size with cells**.

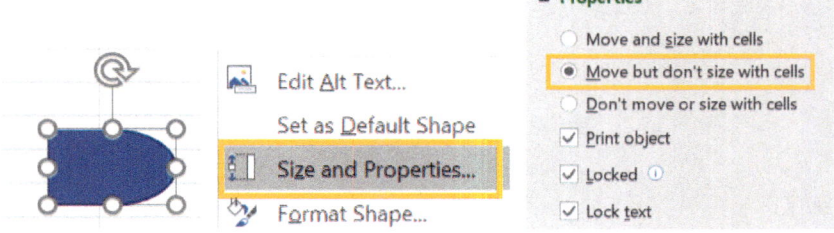

2. Horizontal male female icon chart

In this section, we are going to create a horizontal male female icon chart.
This chart is also using the icon technique, but the icon is sitting inside of chart and the icon is moving horizontally.
This technique is also quite useful and handy to create various infographic charts.

For this chart, we will use a combo chart with both scatter plot and a bar chart with icons.
Once again, it is not possible to create a combo chart with Excel 2010 version or older ones.

Target picture:

What we are going to make is the following graph:

First, we will create a new input table which includes input values and the helping values.

In the same manner, the input values are presented by percentage (%) because of common usage in reports. It is normally easy to communicate.

	Male	Female
Input	66%	80%
Max value	100%	100%

In this example, we will create an icon first. The way how to create icon is very similar to a vertical icon chart.
The most different part would be the shape fill color.
After combining symbol & rectangle box (**Format** tab >>> **Merge Shapes** >>> **Combine**):
- **Shape Fill = White** for Vertical chart
- **Shape Fill = Transparent** for Horizontal chart

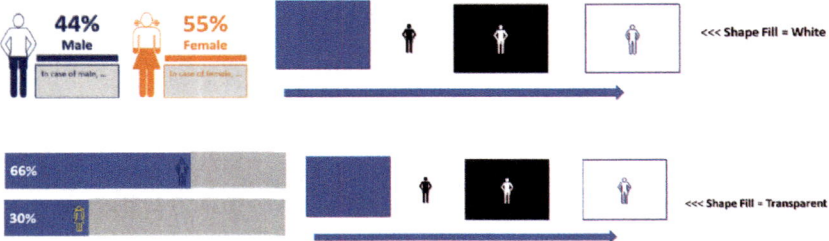

How to make an Icon:
Making an icon is very similar to the vertical chart. Therefore, the explanation is simplified here.

In Excel, go to **Insert** tab, create **1 rectangle** and **1 text box**. (See below)

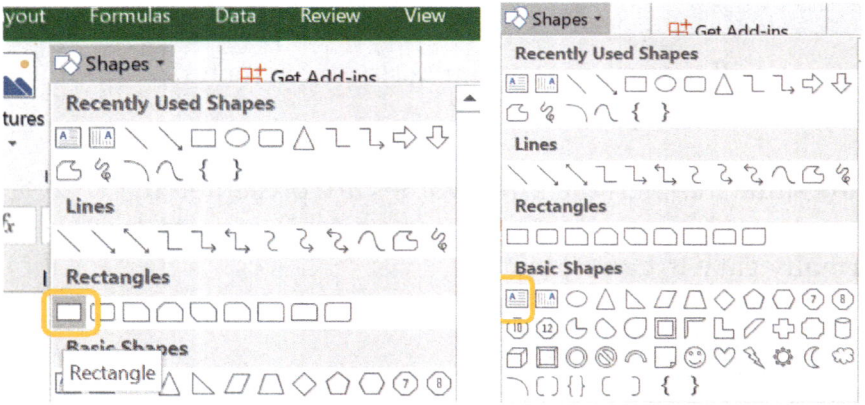

After creating text box, go to **Insert** tab >>> **Symbol** >>> **Webdings** >>> choose an Icon.

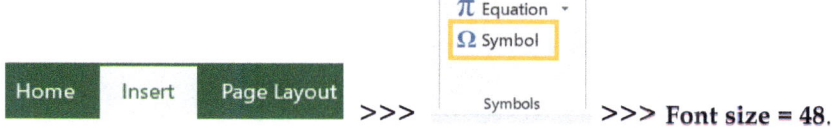 >>> Font size = **48**.

Click the text box with an icon, removing **Shape Fill & Shape Outline** (in Excel).
- **Shape Fill** = No Fill
- **Shape Outline** = No Outline

Now, overlapping with the rectangle and the text box (the text box is in front of the rectangle).

Copy & Paste them into a new slide in PowerPoint.
Select both files >>> **Format** tab >>> **Merge Shapes** >>> **Combine**

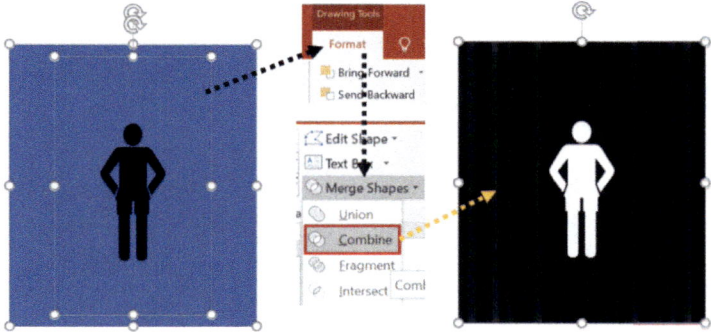

The next is:
- **Shape Fill** = **Transparent**
- **Shape Outline** = Dark blue (The color which you like)

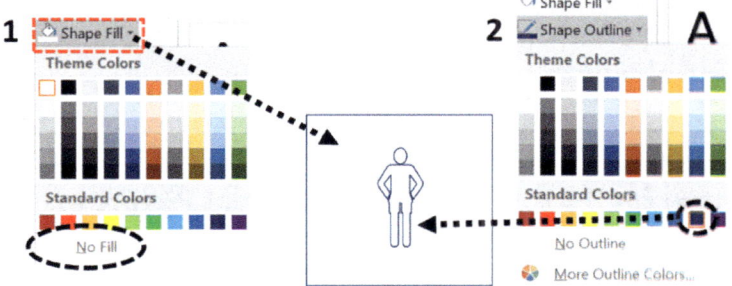

The part for PowerPoint is over.
- **Copy** & **Paste** back into Excel as a **Picture**.
- Conduct **Crop**.

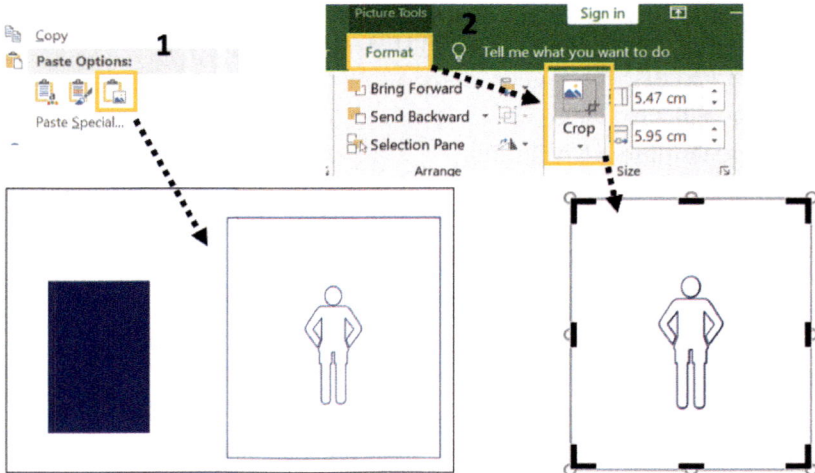

Size of icon:

The size of icons is a lot smaller than the vertical ones because horizontal icons will be located inside of bar. For the female, the creating step are identical except the outline color and icon itself.

How to control height & width of the icon:

It is easier to control the size of multiple icons by using '**Format Picture**':
- Click an icon & **CTRL +1** >>> can see **Format Picture** on the right-hand side
- Unclick '**Lock aspect ratio**'

- Control **Height** & **Width** of the icon (as you wished)

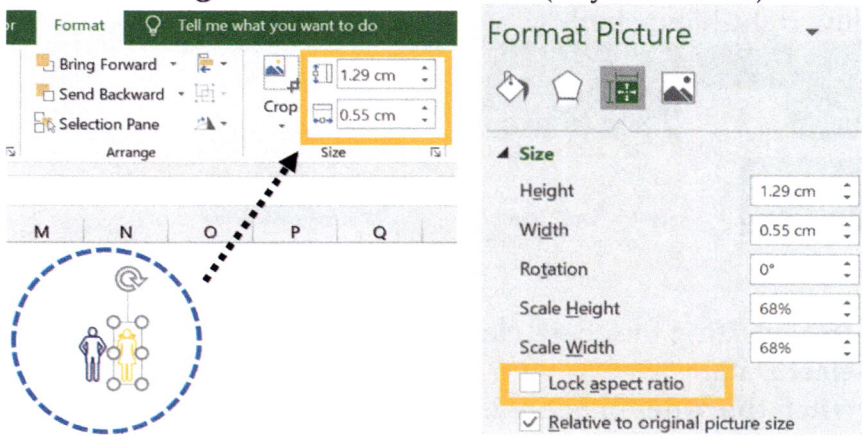

How to create 2-D Clustered horizontal bar chart:

First, remove Gridlines (**View** tab >>> unclick **Gridlines**).
After selecting inputs (i.e. input value & max value for male),
go to Insert tab. Select **2-D bar** >>> **Clustered Bar**.
The Max value (100%) represents the maximum range of bar chart.

	Male	Female
Input	66%	80%
Max value	100%	100%

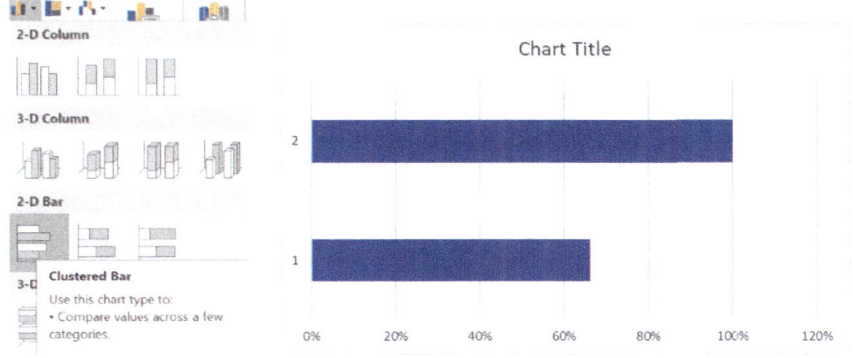

Go to **Design >>> Switch Row/Column**. We can see the below right-hand chart.

- After selecting the chart, click a right-hand button and go to **Select Data**.
- **Switch the order** of Series2. Put it above Series1 by clicking a triangle button.
- Click the bar in the chart and change **Series Ovelap: 100%** and **Gap Width: 0%**.

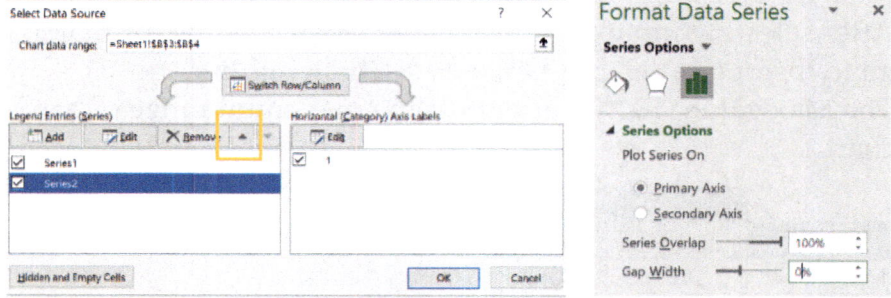

How to change the range of Axis:

- Click an Axis and then **CTRL +1**
- Go to **Format Axis** and change **Min: 0 & Max values: 1**
- Also, changed from **Auto** to **Reset** (fixed the axis range of chart)

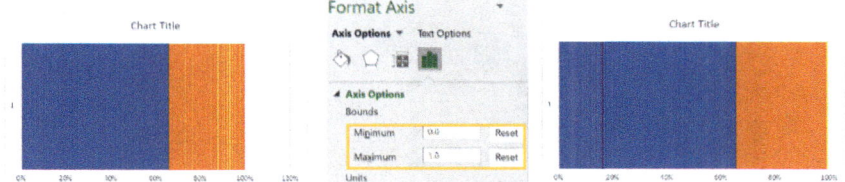

You can see the axis range is changed from **120%** to **100%** in the above picture.

After removing chart elements:
- Go to chart elements = click (+) sign in the chart
- **Remove the chart elements** = Unclick the chart elements which you want to remove

After removing 'Shape Fill' and 'Shape Outline':
- **Shape Fill** = No Fill
- **Shape Outline** = No Outline

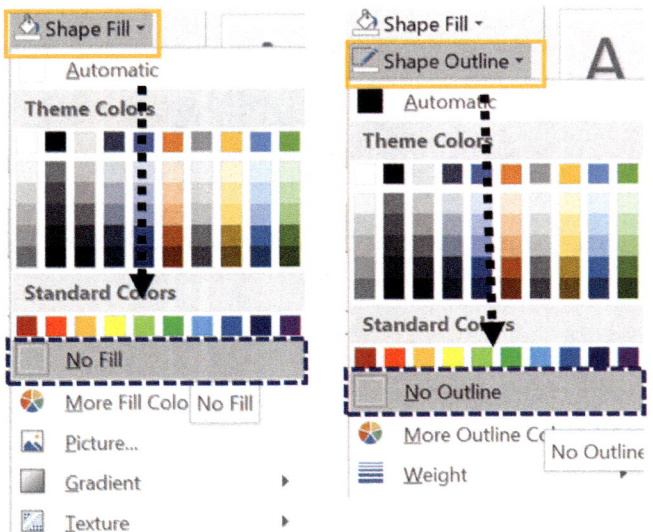

Next, adjusting the shape of chart by dragging the chart
- **Change the color of bar** to your wished color. **Note: Please select only bar at a time.**
- For the max bar, the white color is not recommendable because it is difficult to see the max bar.

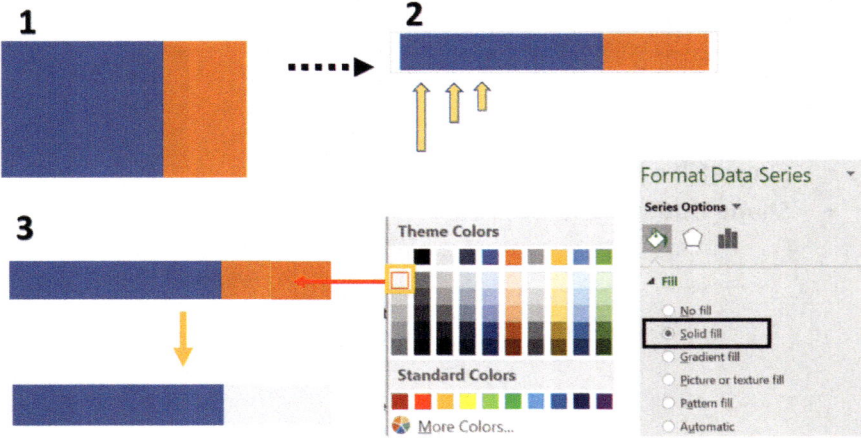

How to combine icon & bar chart (by using scatter plot):

We are going to combine the icons which we made with the bar chart.

We will use a female icon for creating the combining part of the chart.
The icon is going to move whenever the input value is changed. Therefore, we need a new series for the action.

Creating a new series: Click the chart and click a right-hand mouse button.
- Click **Select Data** >>> **Add** >>>
- Entering **Series name** = Icon & **Series values** = **0.5**

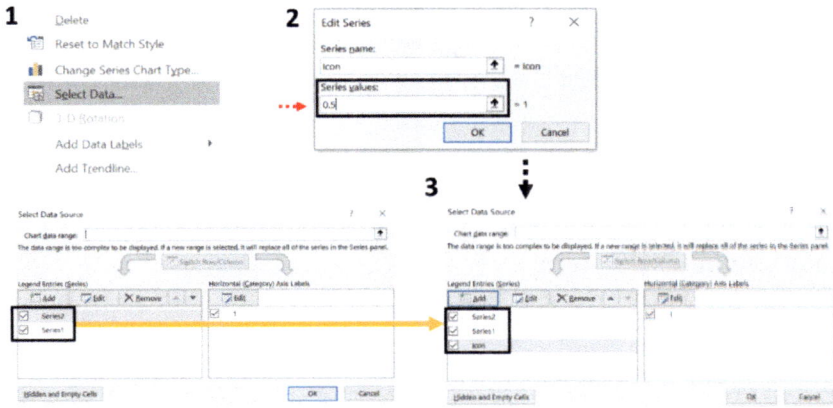

We can see the additional bar in the chart. There are 3 series in the chart.

How to switch to combo chart:

In order to change the bar chart to combo chart, select the chart and click a right-hand mouse button.
- Go to **Change Series Chart Type** (see below) and
- Change chart type **for icon series** from '**Clustered bar**' to '**Scatter**'

You can find a small dot at the end of bar. (In fact, the dot is not so recognizable!)
We are going to switch the dot to the female icon later on. The location of icon will depend on this dot input value.

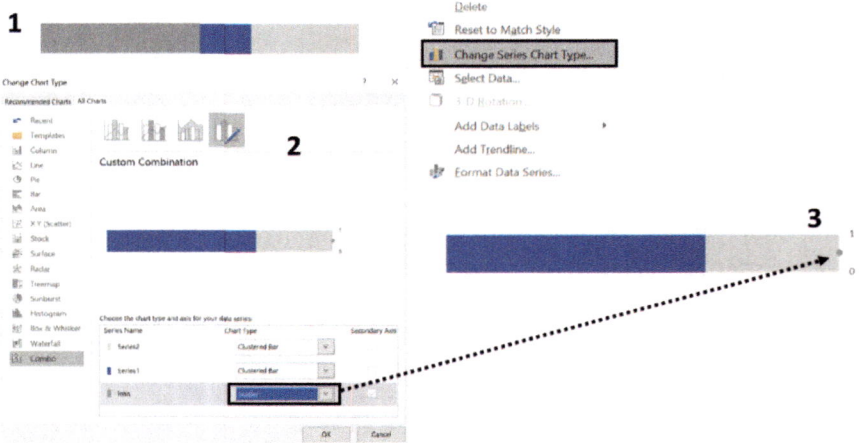

As you can see, the dot appears at the end of bar. We need to change the setting of scatter plot range.
Please see below 5 steps.

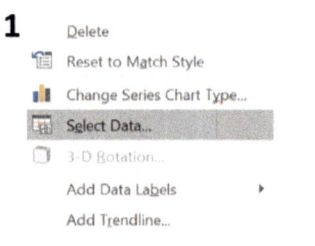
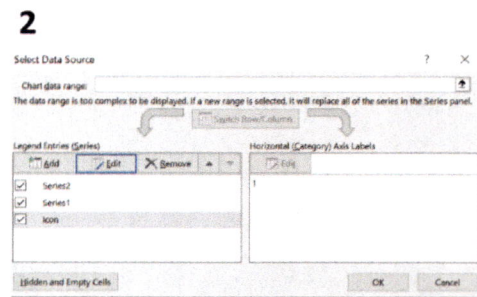

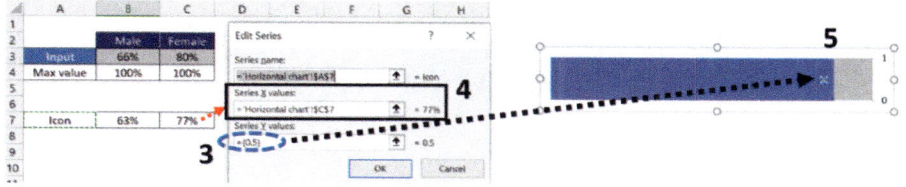

- Go to **Select Data** >>> Select 'Icon' series >>> **Edit**
- **X value = select Icon cell location** (picture No. 3) >>>
Explain this part later

At the moment, just use a dummy fixed value. (the explanation at the end of this section)
- **Y value = 0.5** (this is a fixed value)
The dot location is changed by icon cell value. From now on, we create a bar chart with a female icon.

How to combine an icon picture and the dot in the chart:

(Note) This technique is quite useful and handy. We will use it a lot in the later section.
First, click the axis (at the end of right-hand side) for scatter plot and remove it.

Please follow these steps.
- Click the female icon >>> **Ctrl + C**
- Click the scatter plot dot >>> **Ctrl + V**

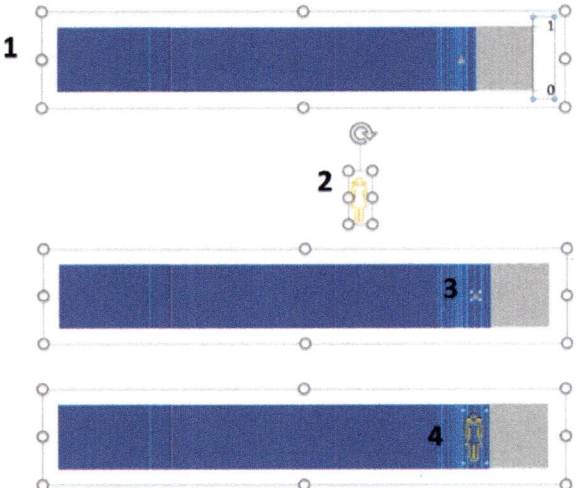

(Note) It is required to adjust the size of icon after pasting to the bar chart. For example, the size of icon is too big for the chart, make the icon smaller and paste it again or vice versa.

How to add Data Labels & control the location of labels:

As a next step, we will add data label for the actual input value and locate it near the left-hand side of the bar chart.

- Click the **inner bar** & click right-hand side mouse button
- Select **Format Data Labels** & Click
- Click the label >>> **CTRL+1** >>> Go to **Label position** >>> Click **Inside Base**

After these steps, you can see the last picture below.

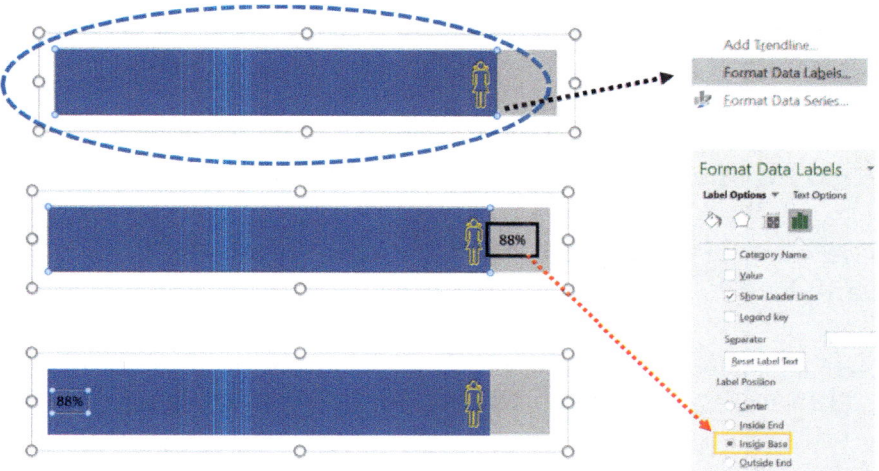

How to change the format of labels:

This is pretty easy. Click the label and go to **Home** tab. Change the size of label (i.e. 18), color (white), etc.

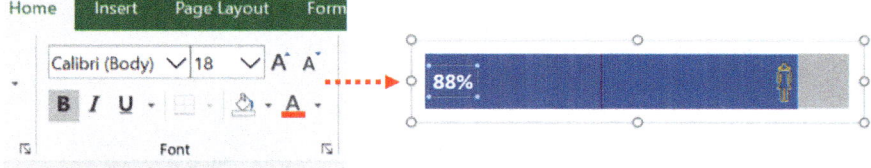

Let's go back to the location cell for icon ('**X value = select Icon cell location of scatter plot**').
In this part, we need to apply a formula in order to position the icon properly on the chart.

Problem is:

When we use a small input value like 3% or lower, the problem of overlapping label and the icon is occurred. In order to make a smooth dynamic movement of icon, the following formula is introduced.

Formula for icon location =IF($C$3<=10%, $C$3*0.5+3%, $C$3-3%)

==IF(actual input value <=10%, actual input value *0.5+3%, actual input value -3%)==

Where actual input value = 80% (i.e. cell C3) in the below example.

- Actual input value is lower or equal to 10%, input value times 0.5 and add 3% more.

- Actual input value is bigger than 10%, input value minus 3%.

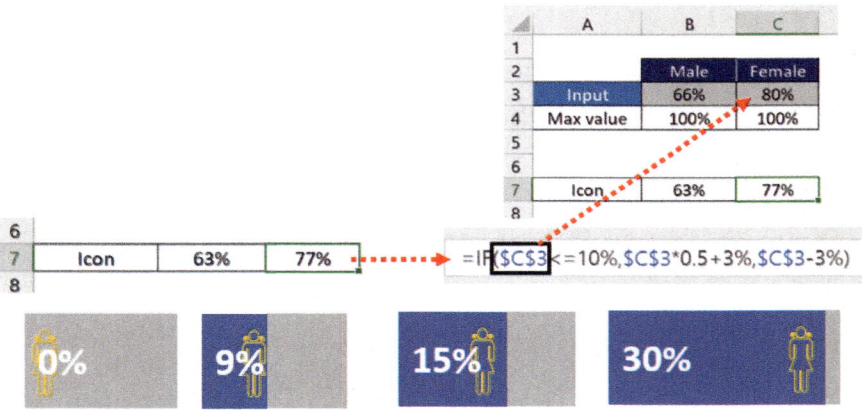

If you use the above formula, the icon will move like the above pictures when we are using a small input value. If you don't like the above location, it is possible to adjust +3% or -3% or **times 0.5** part as well.

Finally, we manage to create the horizontal male female icon chart. We just changed vertical to horizontal, but the method of creating the chart is quite different.

Type 1:

Type 2:

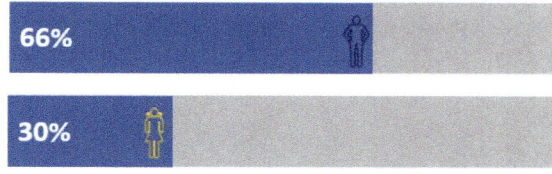

3. Mixed gender icon chart

In this section, we are going to touch 2 topics. The first one is to make a reverse horizontal gender icon chart. The 0% starts & moves from a right-hand side to a left-hand side in this chart.

The target picture is as follows:

The second part is to make a combined chart by using both a reverse and non-reverse horizontal male & female icon chart. As an applied example, we will compare the gender differences by different age groups.

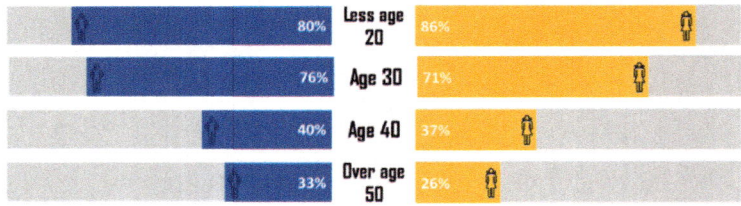

First, we are going to create the reverse chart. How to create an icon part will be skipped because the creating method is identical as the previous icon charts.

In case of input values, we create new input-helping values which is the original values times -1.

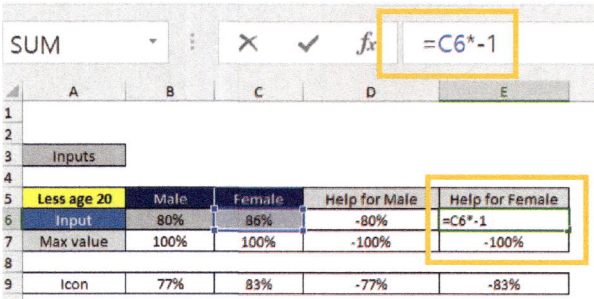

The new input-helping values are directly used as new input values for the charts to move an icon reversely. The original inputs are not using to create a reverse chart except a label.

2-D clustered horizontal bar chart

The creating method is quite similar to the horizontal bar chart except taking new inputs. Therefore, the detail explanation of how to create a bar chart will be skipped. Please refer to the horizontal gender bar chart.

One main difference would be the negative range of Axis:
- Click an Axis and then **CTRL +1**
- Go to **Format Axis** and change **Min: -1** & **Max values: 0**
- Also, changed from **Auto** to **Reset** (fixed the axis range of chart)

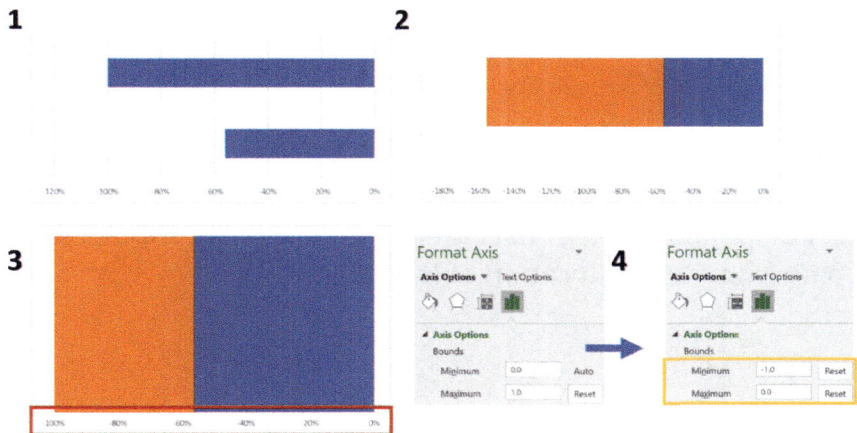

Once again, all the below steps are also very similar to the horizontal icon chart. Therefore, the detail explanation of below steps will be also skipped. Please refer to the previous section.

After adding data, the high-level main steps of creating charts are as follow:
1. Creating a reverse bar chart
2. Adding a scatter plot

3. Adjusting a location of scatter plot
4. Copy & paste icon into scatter plot
5. Adjusting colors of bars
6. Adding labels into bar chart
7. Adjusting the size of labels

(Note) please put inside for the location label.

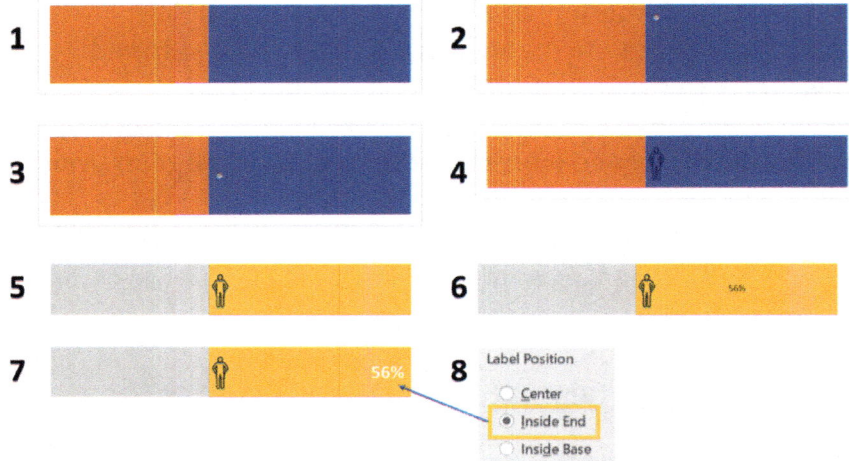

The reverse horizontal icon chart is completed.
The key points for this chart are to have negative inputs, range of axis from -1 to 0, location of labels.

Applied version of icon chart1:

Next step would be to make a combined chart by using both a reverse and non-reverse horizontal gender icon chart. The way how to make is very easy.

Put a reverse horizontal chart, a text box in the middle and horizontal chart in a line on the sheet. Grouping them. Please see the below picture.

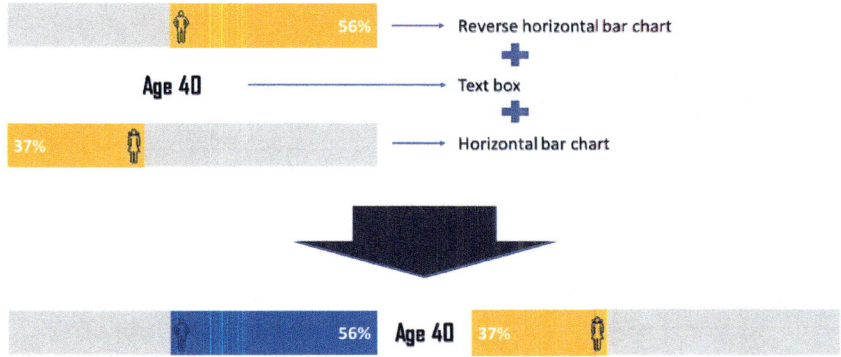

Next, based on this example, we are going to make 3 more new inputs.

Copy & paste the combining chart 3 times more.
The total input sets consist of 4 sets of input values. In each set, it consists of inputs for horizontal chart and for the reverse chart. Please see below.

Inputs				
Less age 20	Male	Female	Help for Male	Help for Female
Input	80%	86%	-80%	-86%
Max value	100%	100%	-100%	-100%
Icon	77%	83%	-77%	-83%
Age 30	Male	Female	Help for Male	Help for Female
Input	76%	71%	-76%	-71%
Max value	100%	100%	-100%	-100%
Icon	73%	68%	-73%	-68%
Age 40	Male	Female	Help for Male	Help for Female
Input	40%	37%	-40%	-37%
Max value	100%	100%	-100%	-100%
Icon	37%	34%	-37%	-34%
Over age 50	Male	Female	Help for Male	Help for Female
Input	33%	26%	-33%	-26%
Max value	100%	100%	-100%	-100%
Icon	30%	23%	-30%	-23%

The most careful point would be to link the input values and the charts correctly.

Based on this example, input values and the corresponding 8 charts (4 horizontal and 4 reverse horizontal charts) are needed to link properly.
It can be irritating. Also, it requires to distinguish the positive and negative inputs when you link the input values to the charts.

Useful Tip:

When you are dealing with multiple charts, text boxes, please use the alignment functionality. It allows you to allocate these charts & text boxes very easily.

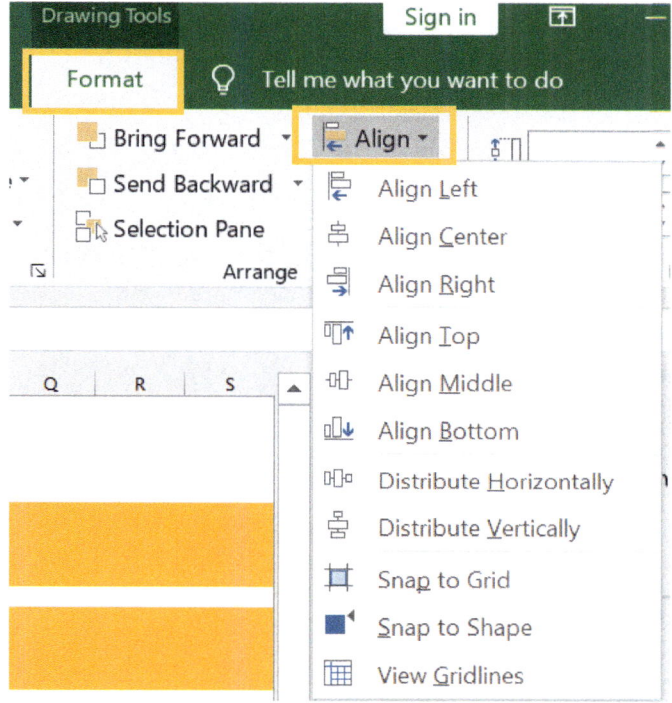

After using Align functionality, we can complete the mixed gender icon chart.

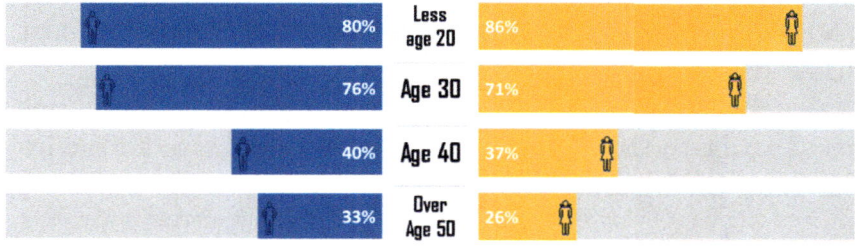

Applied version of icon chart2:

We are moving to the applied versions. Let's call it. 'When vertical charts meet horizontal charts,'.
We will combine the vertical icon chart and the mixed horizontal and reverse horizontal charts together.

The way how to make it is very simply. Just allocate these charts as you like. For this example, the following way is applied. I believe that it is a good infographic chart. This infographic shows the total gender differences on your pursued analysis.

In the below part of the chart, it also shows the age differences in each gender.

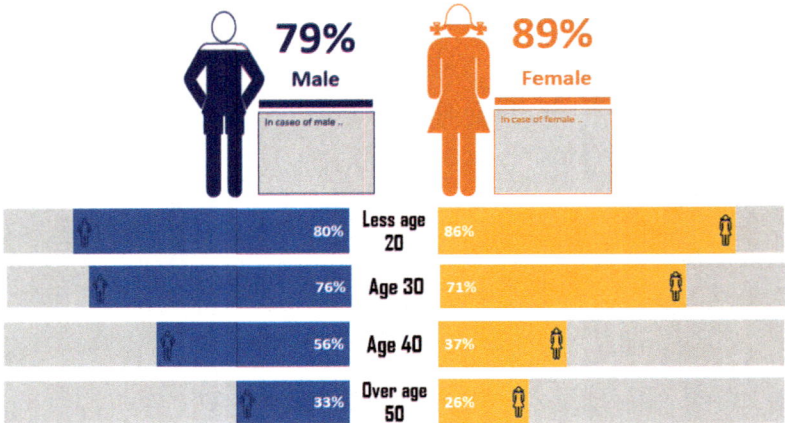

Applied version of icon chart3:

In term of effort, it is not much. Just separate the above chart and re-allocate them by each gender.
However, this applied version of chart might be useful when you describe the behavior of one specific gender at a time in your report, blog and paper.

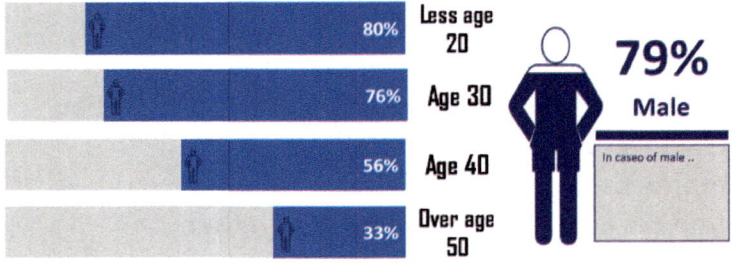

Sample: usage of chart in the report

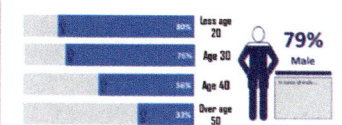

In case of male, when they are more interested in electronic product A than product B. In terms of age differences, ...

In case of female, please find the following:

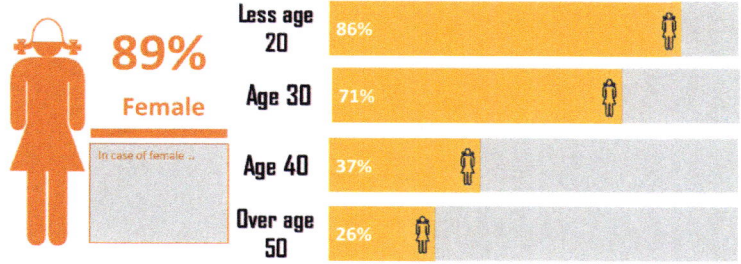

Sample: usage of chart in the report

In case of female, when they are more interested in electronic product A than product B. In terms of age differences, ...

The last applied one would be combining all charts horizontally. Please see below:

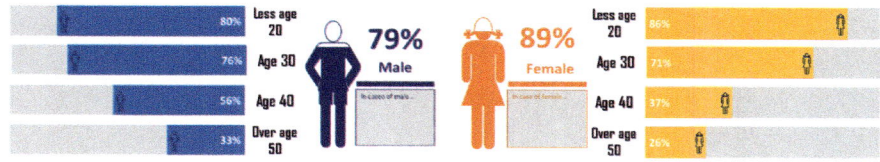

Finally, it looks quite nice. When we are creating one small icon chart, it was good. However, once we combine them all together, it looks quite neat and ready to use for your reports, presentations or books. In addition, each chart is an independent element. It means that you can allocate these charts as you wish.

Furthermore:
Although we only focus on the gender differences in this section, it is also possible to apply for products, travelling preference, company comparisons, etc.
The technique of vertical icon chart, horizontal and reverse horizontal icon chart are quite useful to create your own charts in various different manner.

4. People graph

In this section, we are going to create a graph which does not require a lot of effort. However, the graph looks quite nice and easy to create it.

The main idea of this section is **how to use 'Add-ins in Excel'**. There are various Add-in functionalities in Excel. Some of them are provided by Microsoft directly or by external providers. Also, some of them are free and some of them are required some cash payments to obtain the Add-ins in your Excel.

As you can expect, we are going to deal with an **Add-in function** provided **by Microsoft & for free**.
Sounds good, isn't it?

Let's start it. The name of Add-in graph (which we will use in this section) is called '**People graph**'.
As examples, our target graphs are as follows:

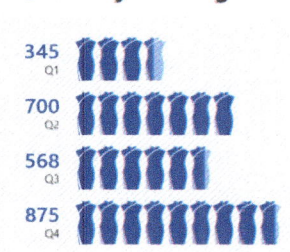

The method to create this graph is quite simple. First, Go to **Insert** tab and click '**Get Add-ins**'.

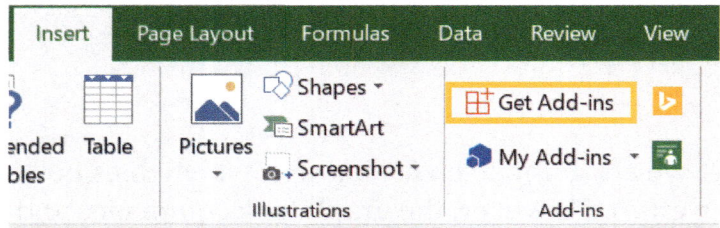

In Add-ins, type '**People graph**' in the search box on the upper left-hand side. You can see the following picture. Click '**Add**' button of People graph from the search window.

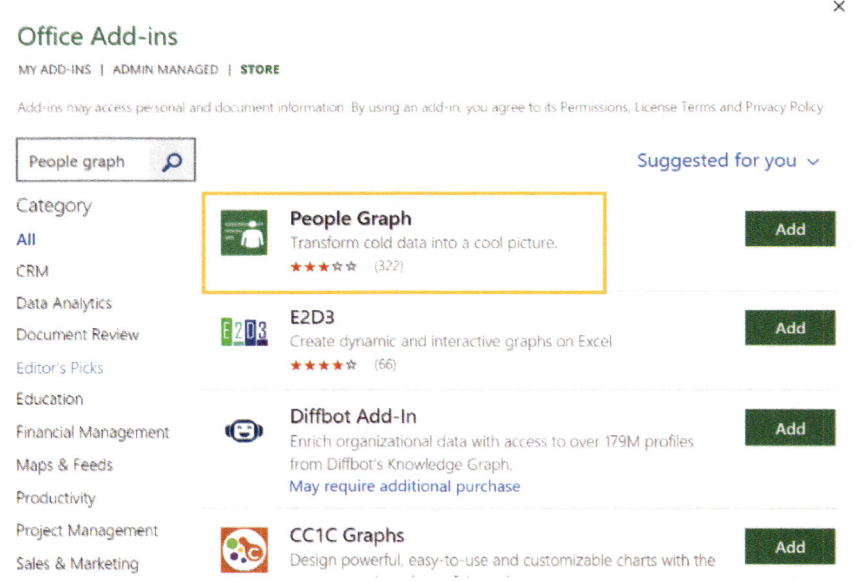

Next, you can see the following picture. The input values are prepared as well (See below on the right-hand side).

If you click the upper right-hand side of the graph (see below), you can see the '**Data**' button and '**Setting**' button.
First, click '**Data**' button.

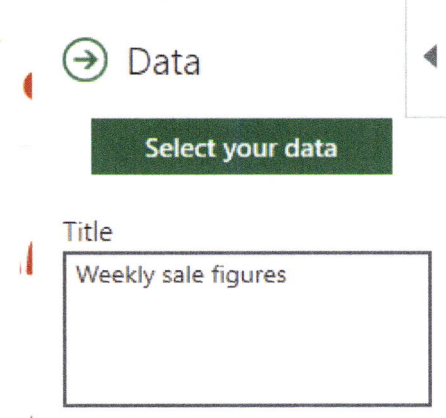

Now, we can copy & paste the title of chart into the '**Title**' box. Click '**Select your data**' button.

After click the '**Select your data**' button, you can see the following picture.

As you can see, the '**Create**' button is not activated yet in the below pop-up window.
Next, select the input values.

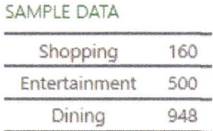

It is possible to click the '**Create**' button after selecting the input values. Click '**Create**' button.

(Note) **This graph allows only 2 columns of input form to create the people graph.**

Actually, we are almost done.

In order to obtain our target graph, we need to go to '**Setting**'. Click '**type**' and click '**Type 2**'.

We can create our target graph.

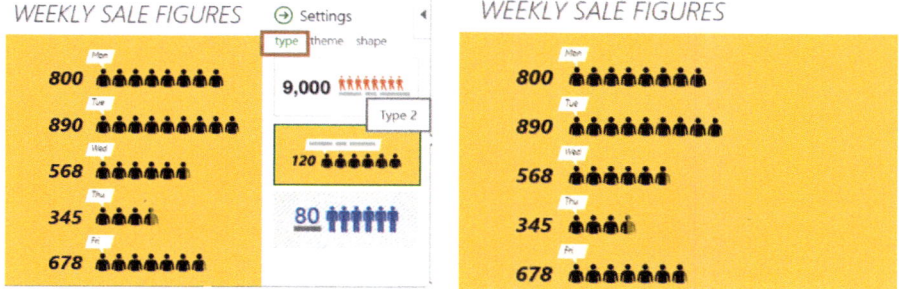

Under '**Setting**', there are 3 possible options (type, theme, shape). If you click each option, you can see the following pictures.

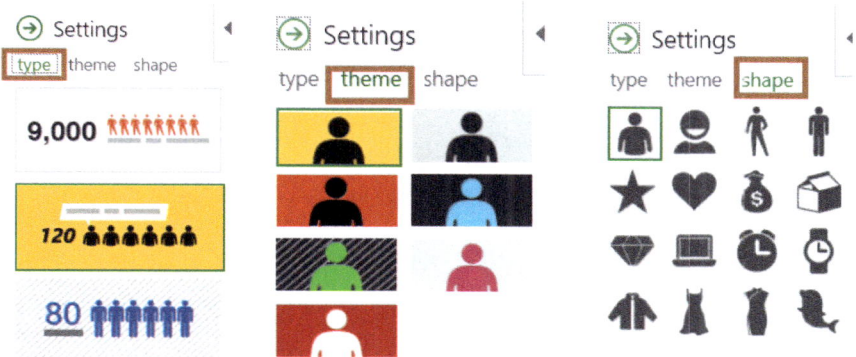

The '**People graph**' is provided by Microsoft. Therefore, this Add-in functionality would be more trustful compared to external Add-ins. Please find the benefits and drawbacks of this graph.

- Benefit: very easy to use.
- Drawback: difficulty to adjust this graph. Therefore, the modification is very limited.

In addition, please note that the graph has the minimum size of contents. As a result, if you try to reduce the graph size more than the minimum size. It is possible to display all of the contents in the graph.

Please see the below comparisons. We can see that the Friday figure is missing on the right-hand side graph.

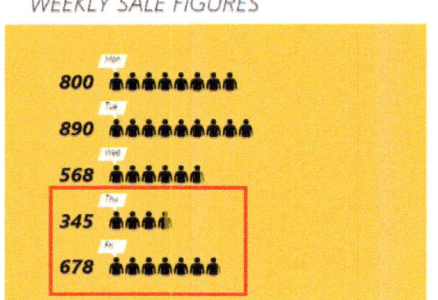 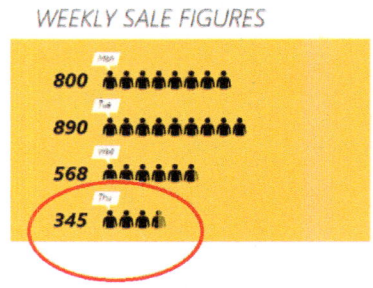

If you want to use this function again, click '**My Add-ins**'. It is possible to find the 'People Graph' without searching it.

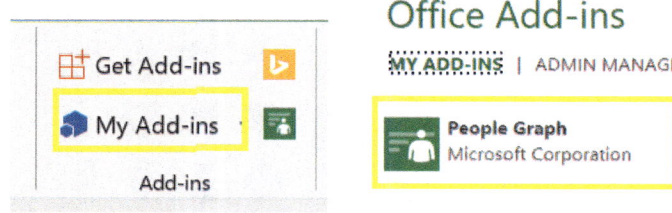

Note: the explanation of the second people graph is skipped because the graph creation method is very similar to the first example.

5. 3D metal bar chart

In this section, we are going to create a 3D vertical metal bar chart. In general, there are several ways to create 3D graphics. In this book, as expected, we will create 3D charts by using Excel built-in function.
Our target chart looks like the below:

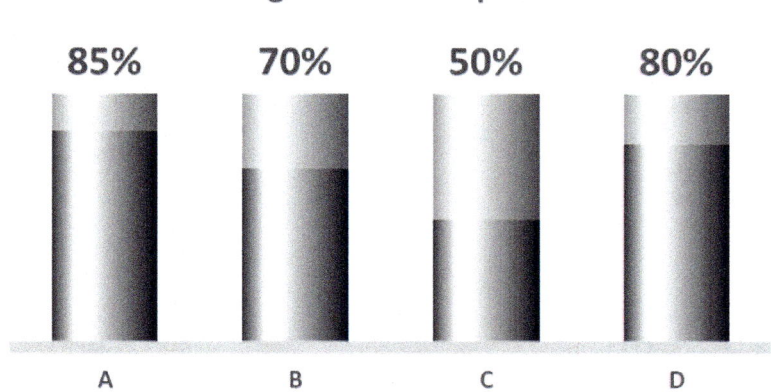

Main idea of this section is to learn how to make a 3D chart in Excel.
The chart improvement would be like the following:

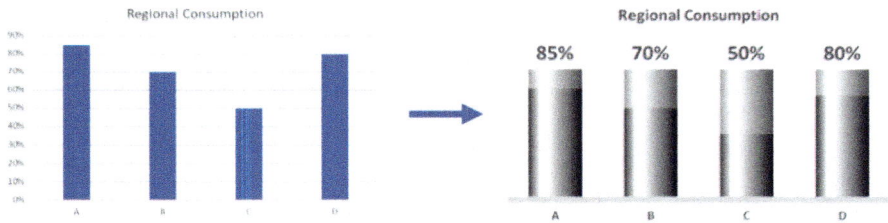

Let's start it. First, we are going to create helping cells which represent the max range of the chart.

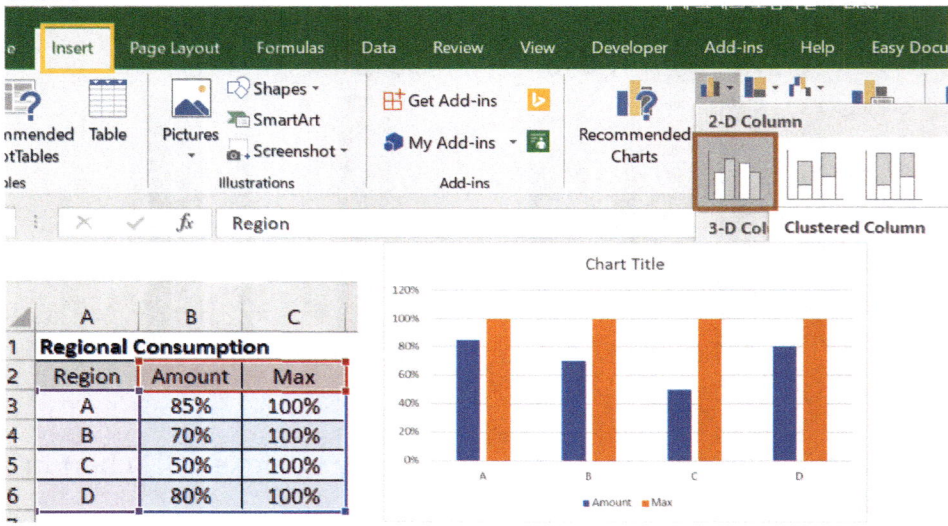

How to make 2D clustered column chart:
Select inputs >>> **Insert** tab >>> choose **2D clustered column chart**

Next is how to clean up chart elements.
- Go to chart elements = click (+) sign in the chart
- **Remove the chart elements** = Unclick the chart elements which you want to remove

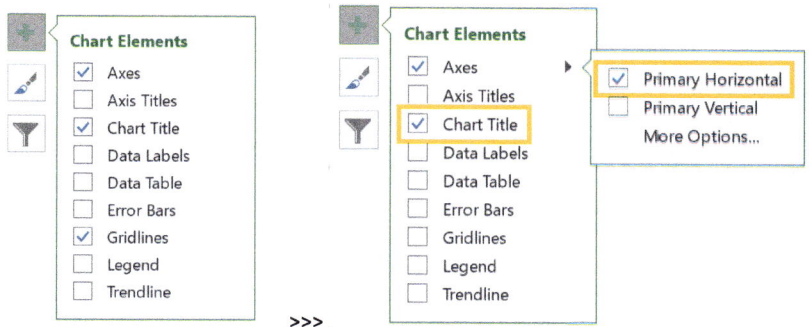

Find an error of Excel:

If you click and unclick '**Axes**' in the chart elements, the end of horizontal axis is changed into an unexpected shape. (See below circle part in the chart)

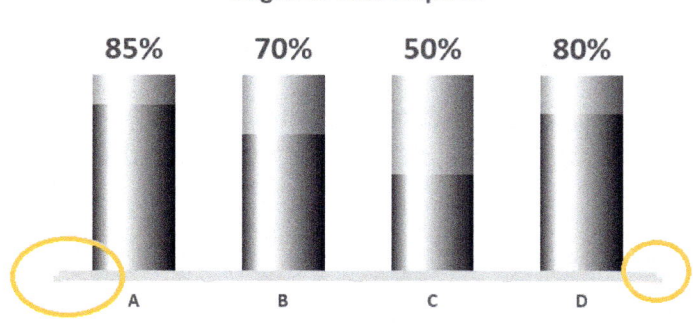

As a remedy, once you clean up the chart element, please do not click & unclick 'Axes' in the chart elements to avoid this error.

How to update 'Chart Title':

- Click a '**Chart Title**' box in the chart
- Go to function bar (= fx) and put '='.
- Next to '=', Click the cell which you want to use it for the chart title (in the function bar).
  i.e. ='3D Metal Bar'!$A$1
- Hit an '**Enter**' button.

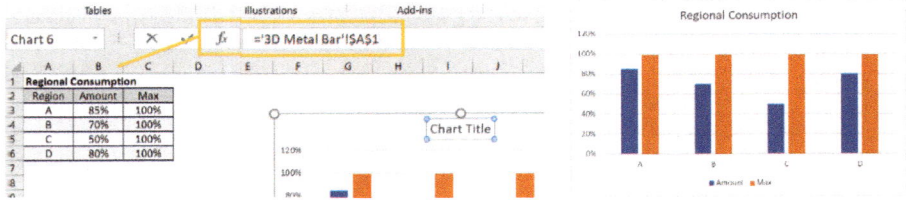

From now on, the chart title will change whenever you can the cell text for the chart title.

For a vertical axis, click a **vertical axis** >>> **CTRL +1** >>> **Format Axis**.
Switching Min & Max values by **re-typing '0'** instead of 0.0
- **min** value = 0
- **max** value = 1 in **Axis Options** in **Format Axis**.

Then, the bounds setting is changed from **Auto** to **Reset**. It means that the axis bounds are not automatically changed anymore.

(Note) The default setting is normally **Auto**.
You can see that the max value is 100% in the vertical axis.

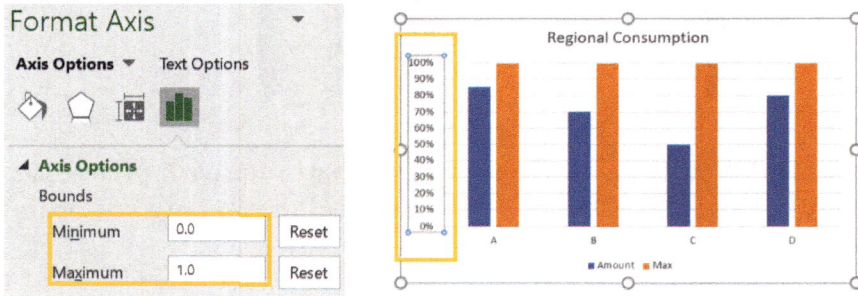

Now, we are moving to add 3D effect into the chart.

How to make a 3D metal box:
- Go to **Insert** tab and select a **rectangle box**, create it on the worksheet
- Click a chart >>> Go to **Format** tab. Shape Outline = No Outline
- Go to **View** tab and unclick **Gridlines**.

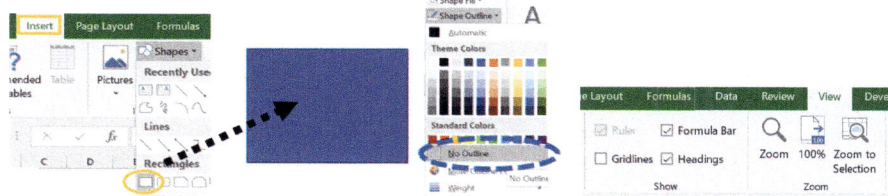

Next, we are going to give an **3D effect** by using **gradient fill**.

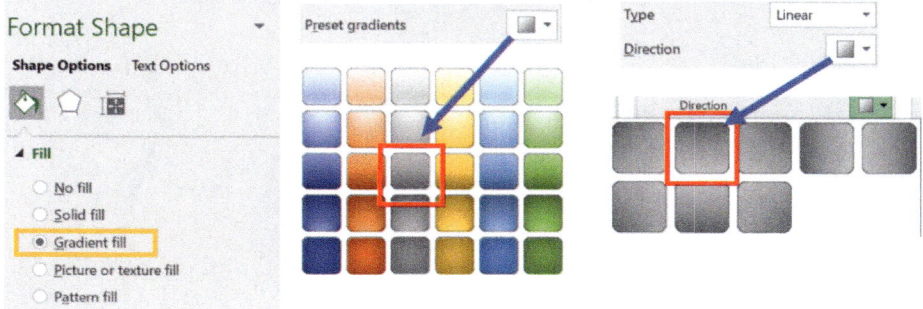

Next is **Gradient stops**.

If you click somewhere in the middle of Gradient stops bar, it is possible to add stop points.
How to remove the stop point: click and select and delete button.

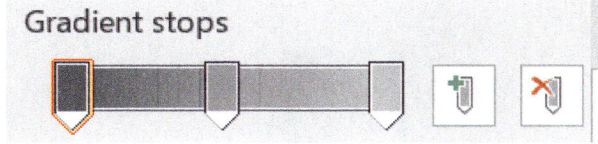

Key idea:
By changing location & color the stop points, it is possible to create a 3D effect.

Please find the following settings for the stop points.

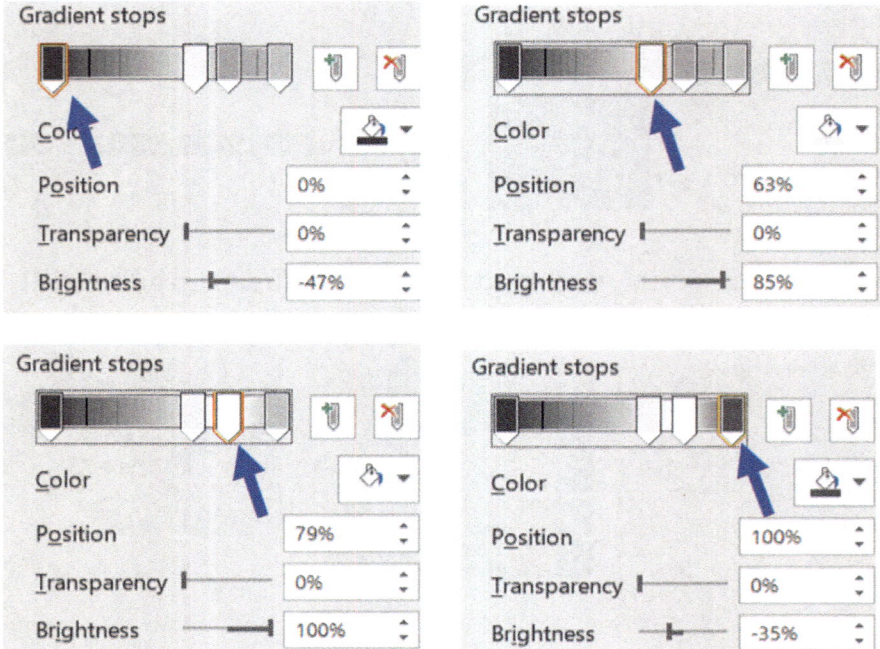

Now, the box is transposed by 90 degrees to the clockwise direction. Drag it like a bar.
We already make a metal bar. This bar will be used for the max value.

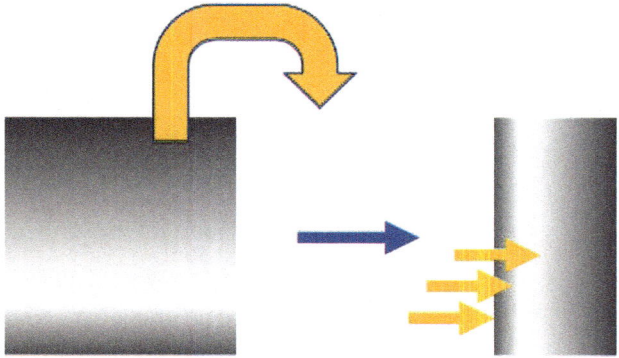

By using copying and pasting the metal bar, we can create the second bar which shows the actual input value.

Please find the following settings for the stop points.

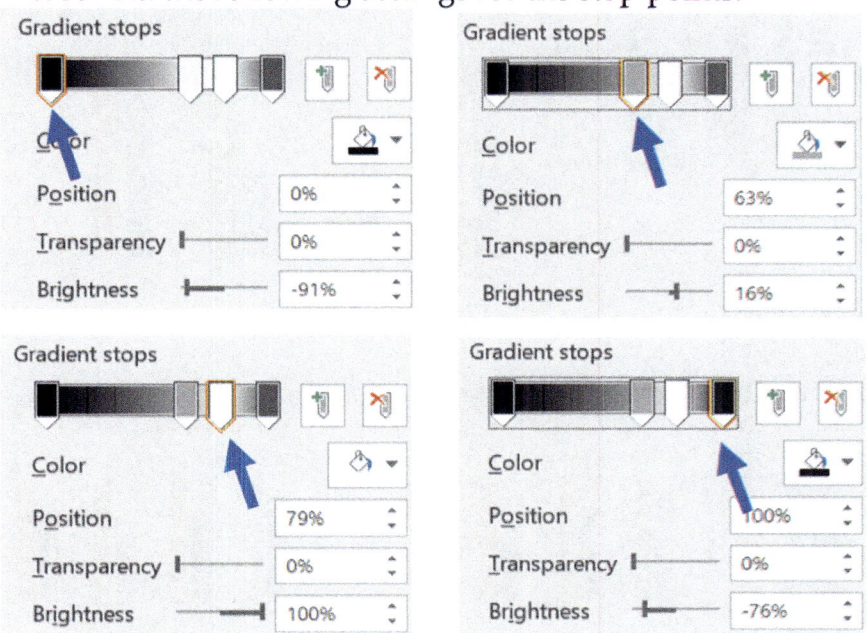

Finally, we managed to create two 3D metal bars.

How to combine the clustered bar chart with the metal bar shapes:

- Click the actual bar shape (darker color) >>> **Ctrl + C**
- Click the actual bar (smaller bars) chart >>> **Ctrl + V**

Do the same thing for the max bar shape (lighter color).

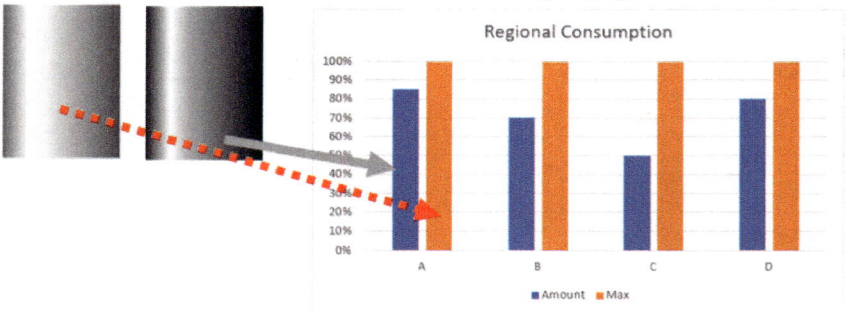

For the actual bar shape (darker color):

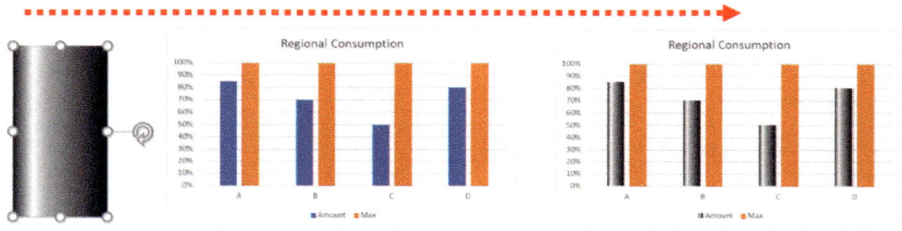

After applying the max bar shape:

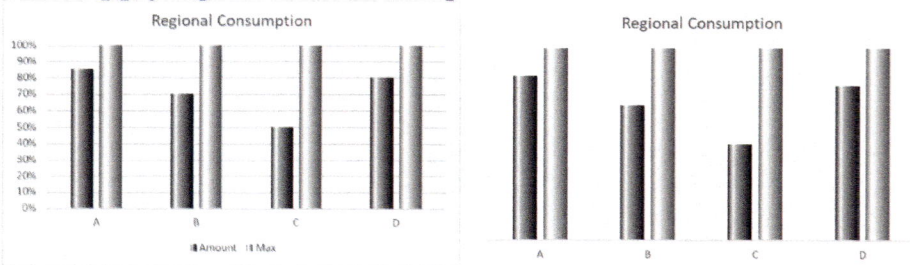

The difference between right-hand side and left-hand side is with chart elements or not in above two pictures. The reason why the chart elements are appeared above is in order to explain to you easily.

If you are here, you are almost done.

How to combine 2 vertical bars in the chart:
- Click one of the bars in the chart >>> **CTRL + 1**
- **Series Overlap**: 100%
- **Gap Width**: 80%

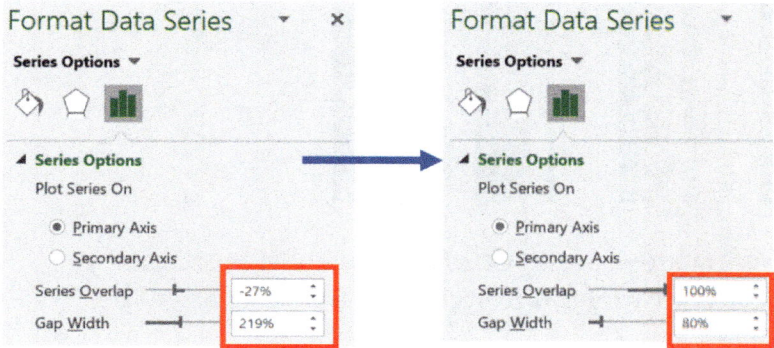

What's happening!

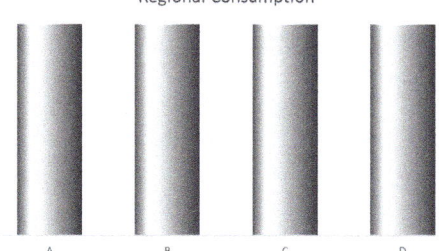

After selecting the chart, click the left-hand button in the mouse.

Go to **Select Data** >>> **Move up 'Max' series** to the top of list.

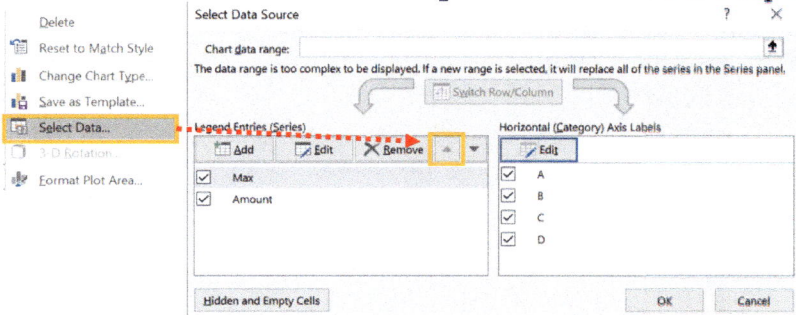

We can create the following graph.

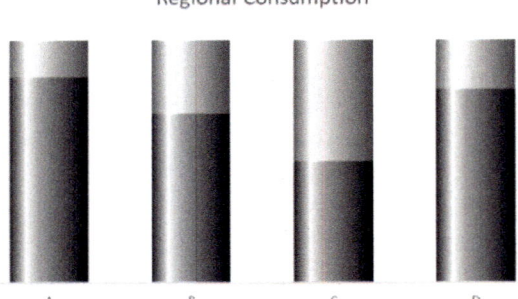

The following steps are to decorate the chart more nicely. If you wish your preferable style, feel free to change the settings.

The following set-ups are based on the example file.
In **Home** tab, it is possible to change the general format of the chart (the chart title size, color and font type, etc.).

- Font size: **16** & **Bold**
- Font color: see below

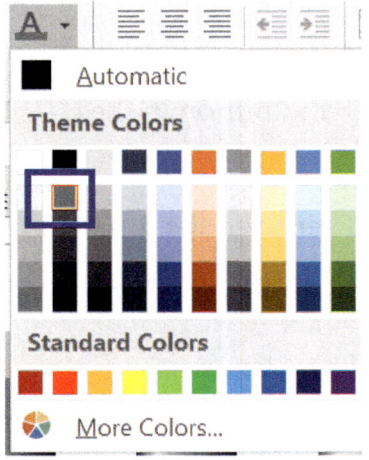

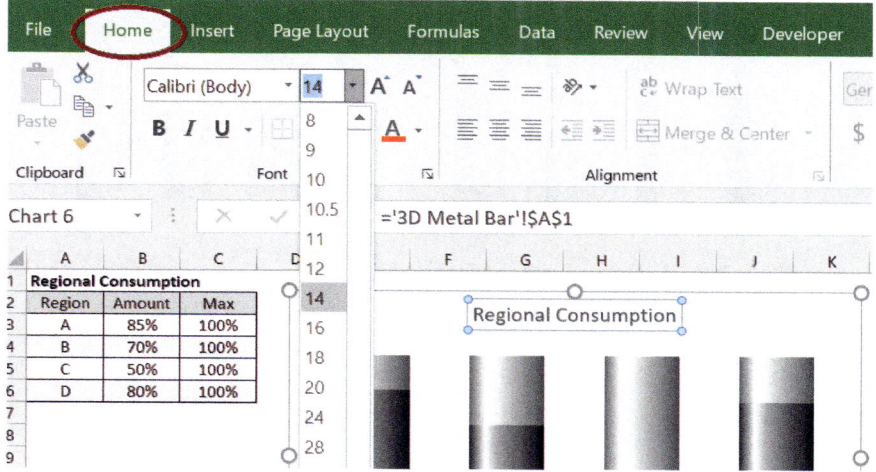

How to add data labels in the chart:

As a next step, we will add the actual input values and locate it on top of each bar.

- Click the **inner bar** & click a right-hand side mouse button.
- Select **Add Data Labels** >>> Click

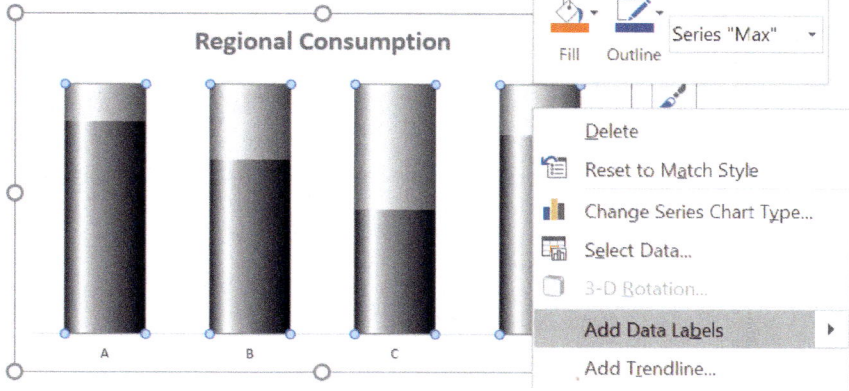

First, the data label shows the max bar value which is 100%. Click the max values by the mouse.

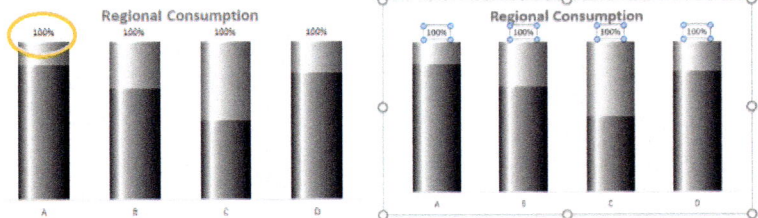

- Click **Ctrl +1**, Go to **Format Data Labels**
- Select "**Value from Cells**" and select **the actual values** from the input table.

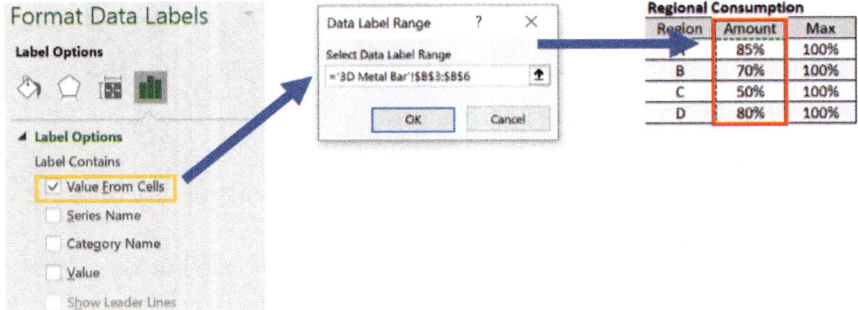

(Note) This functionality is available from Excel version 2013. In case of older versions, it needs to click each data label and link to the actual values in the table one by one.

It is possible to see the actual value on top of each bar in the chart.

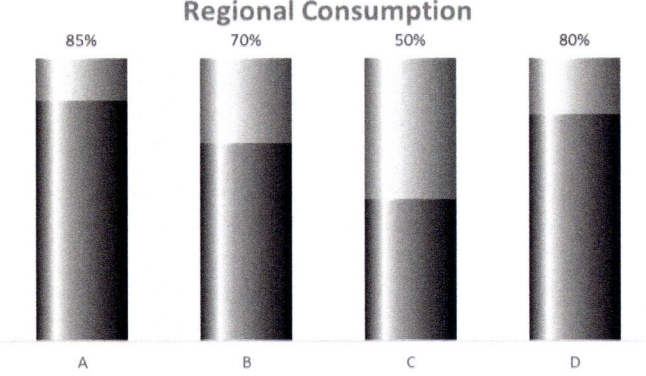

- In **Home** tab, change Font size: **20** & **Bold**.
- Select the "**Plot Area**" in the chart.
- Drag it down to avoid the overlapping labels.

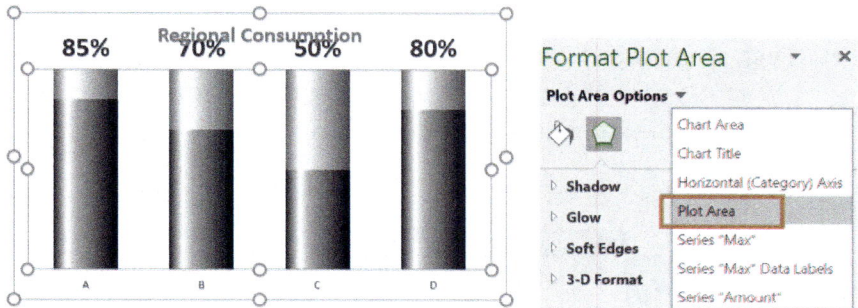

Select the horizontal axis and change the format of the font.
- In **Home** tab, change **Font size: 12** & **Bold**.
- In **Format Axis**, change the **width** to **5**.

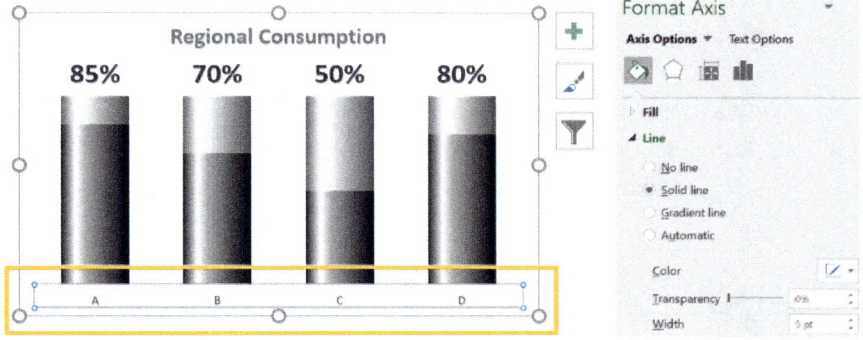

Finally, we can create the following chart.

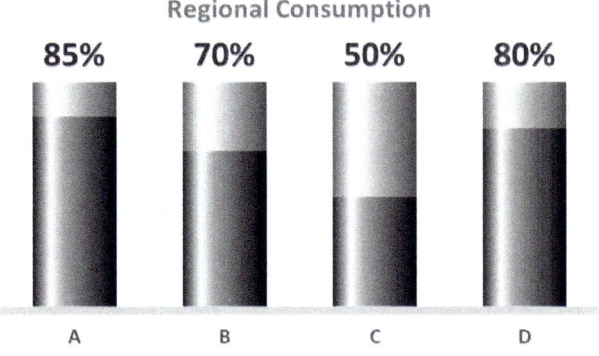

Applied example:

In this example, we will apply the 3D technique to the horizontal icon chart.

- First, sheet-copy & paste the gender icon chart in the new sheet.
    - In case of 2 icons, just use the gender chart.
    - More icons cases, it requires to modify the input tables.

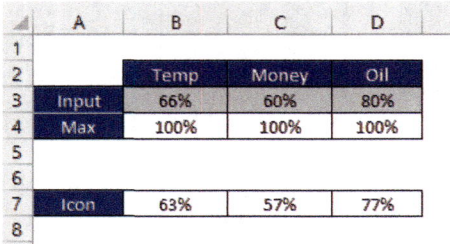

- Copy & paste the 3D metal bars in the new sheet
- By using how to create the icon, create 3 new icons (Money, Temp, Oil)

- Copy & paste the 3D metal bar into the icon chart.
- Exchange the male & female icon into 3 new icons.
    - For having more options, a new 3D bar has been created.

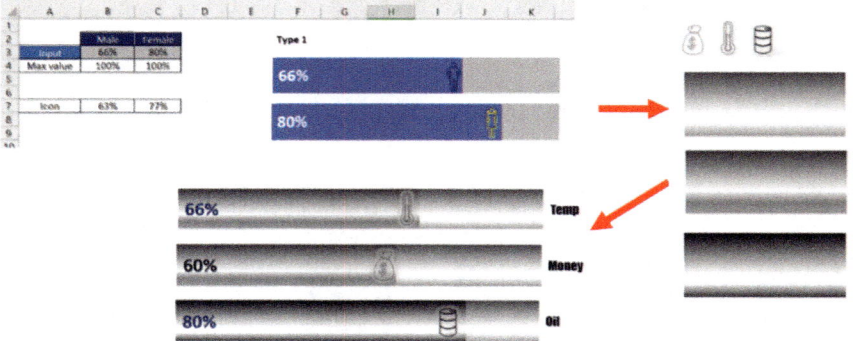

How to add Label into the chart:

Simply speaking, how to add the letter "Temp", "Money", "Oil" in the chart.

The method is identical by using **Format Data Labels**.

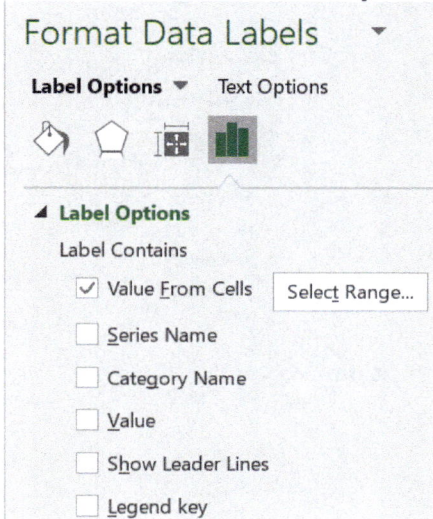

In case of the inner bar, it is already used for showing actual percentage % value. Therefore, we need to use the bar used for max value.

Click the max bar and go to **Format Data Labels**. **Add label** and 100% will be appeared like below.

As you can see, the location of label is a bit awkward. Therefore, it is necessary to adjust the size of max bar. Select the Plot Area and adjust the size of the plot area in the chart.

Issue: Difficult to select the 'Plot Area' by mouse?

- Click any series in the chart & Click **CTRL + 1**
- go to **Format Data Series**.
- Click a reversed triangle next to **Series Options**.
- Select **Plot Area**. After selecting, adjust the size of plot area.

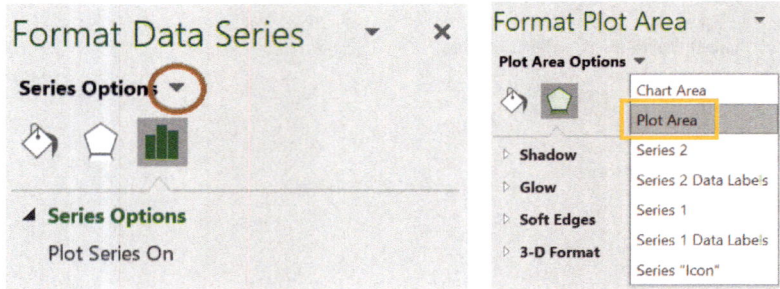

- Select **Outside End** for **Label Position**

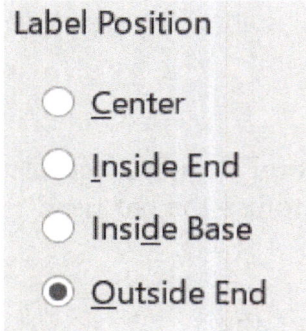

The following chart will be appeared.

Glow Effect:

As a new learning, the Glow effect will be used to visualize the icon more clearly.

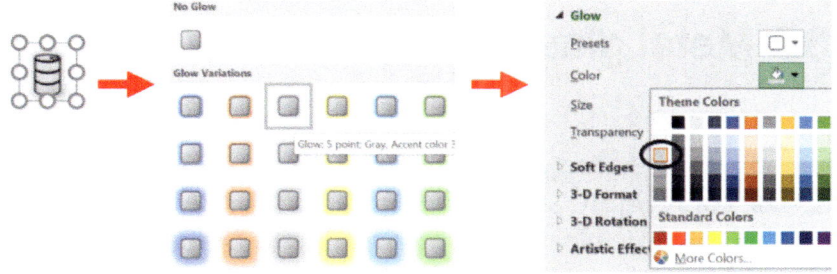

Finally, we complete the horizontal 3D metal icon bar chart.

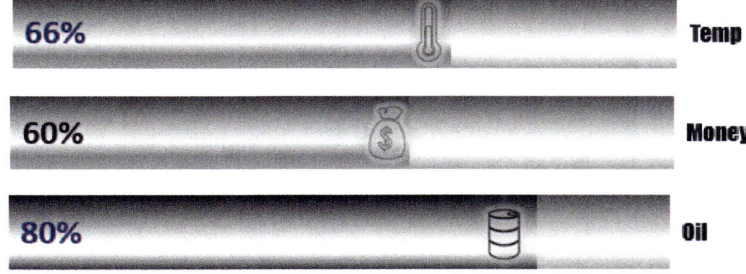

In this section, we learnt about:
- creating 3D effect metal bar,
- adding 2 labels in the horizontal chart and
- using Glow effect.

6. 3D Metal glass bar chart

In this section, we are going to create a 3D metal glass bar chart. The color liquid shows the actual amount of each bar in the chart. It is quite clear that you are able to create a completely new type of chart after learning this section.

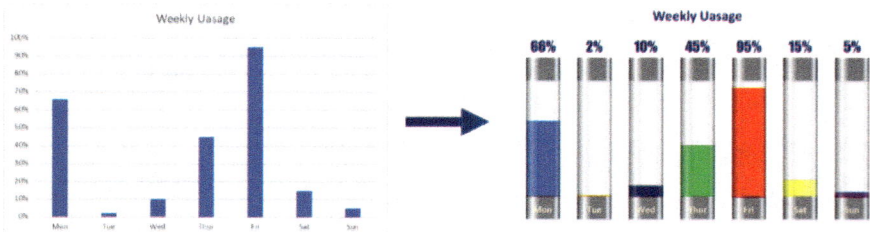

(Note) **The most difficult part is how to assign the length of glass bar and the actual input values.**

If the length allocations are not correct, the color liquid does not show the actual value correctly.

As a starting point, we are creating a new input table and also supporting axis and max values.
In addition, **'Lengths Proportion of Bar'** table is created. See below.

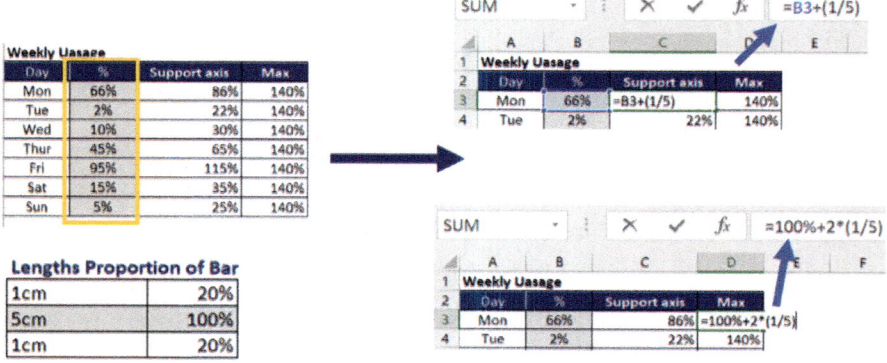

Formula for Support axis & Max (=Allocation settings) are following:
- **Supporting axis = Actual values (%) + (1/5)**
- **Max = 100% + 2*(1/5)**

The above formulas are allocated because the height of metal parts and glass part (1cm, 5cm, 1cm).

How to make 3D metal and glass bar:

In Insert tab, select a rectangle and remove outline.

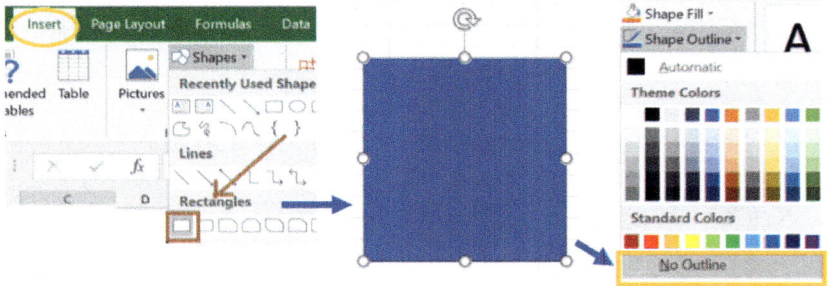

How to remove Gridlines:

- Go to **View** tab.
- **Gridlines** = Unclick Gridlines

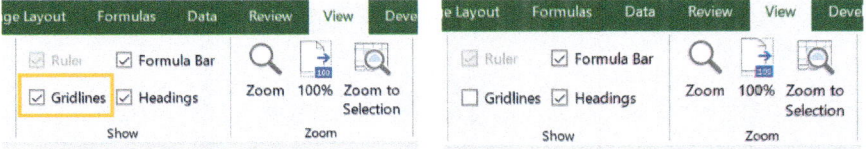

Next, we are going to give an 3D effect by using gradient fill.

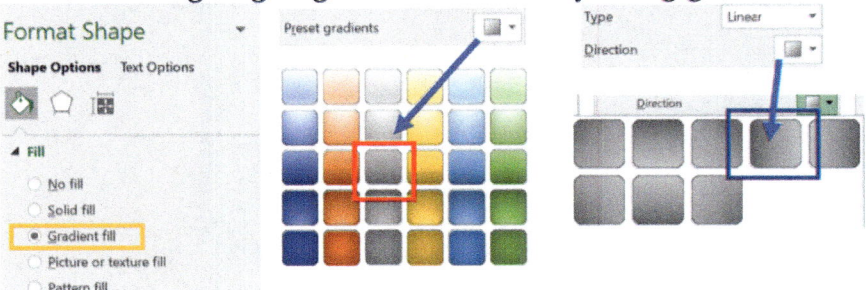

Next is **Gradient stops**.

If you click somewhere in the middle of Gradient stops bar, it is possible to add stop points.
How to remove the stop point: click and select and delete button.

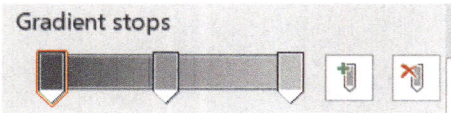

Key idea:
By changing locations & color the stop points, it is possible to create a 3D effect.

Please find the following settings for the stop points.

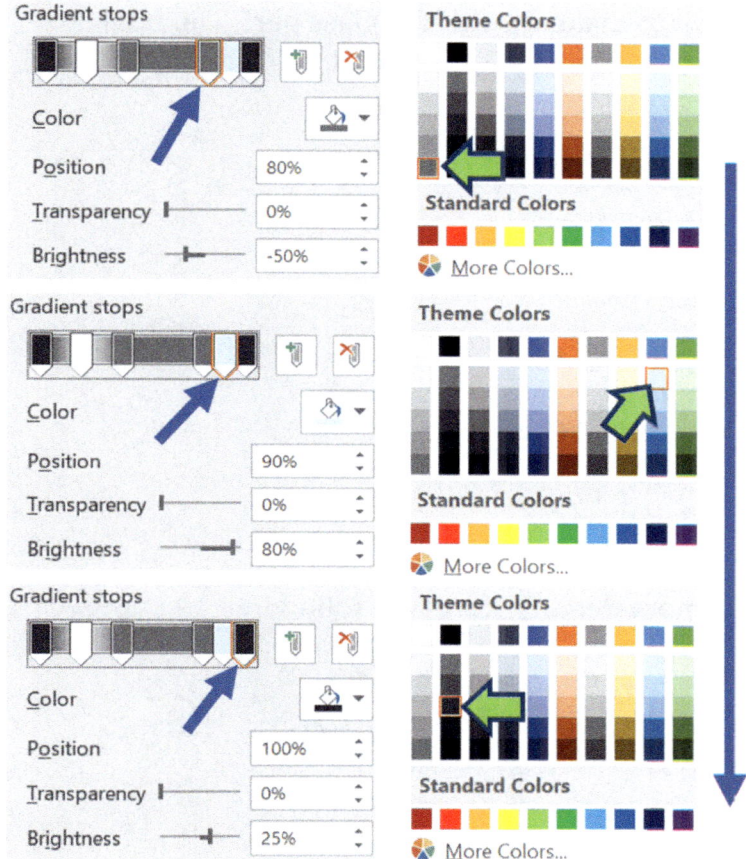

After **selecting the rectangle**, go to **Format**. Choose **1cm** for height.

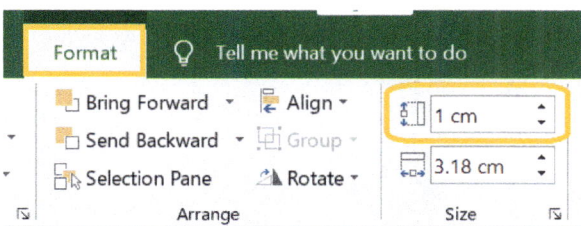

It is possible to create the below shape.

Copy & paste it to make the middle glass part. The total process are as follows (Step 1 to 4):

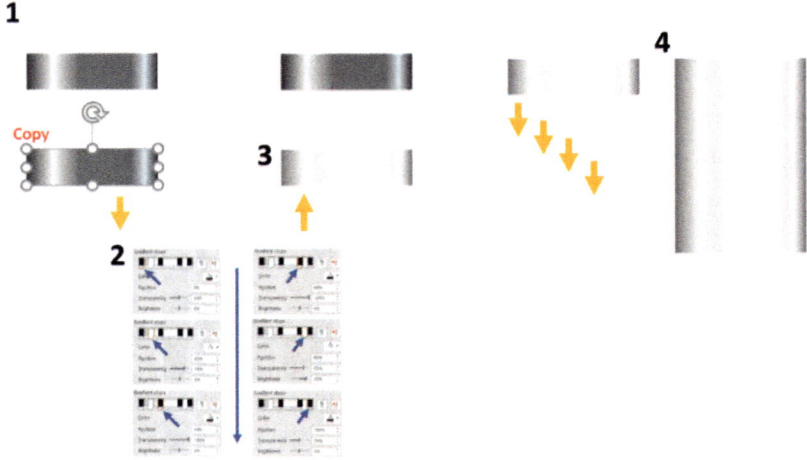

In step 2, the more detail settings are following.

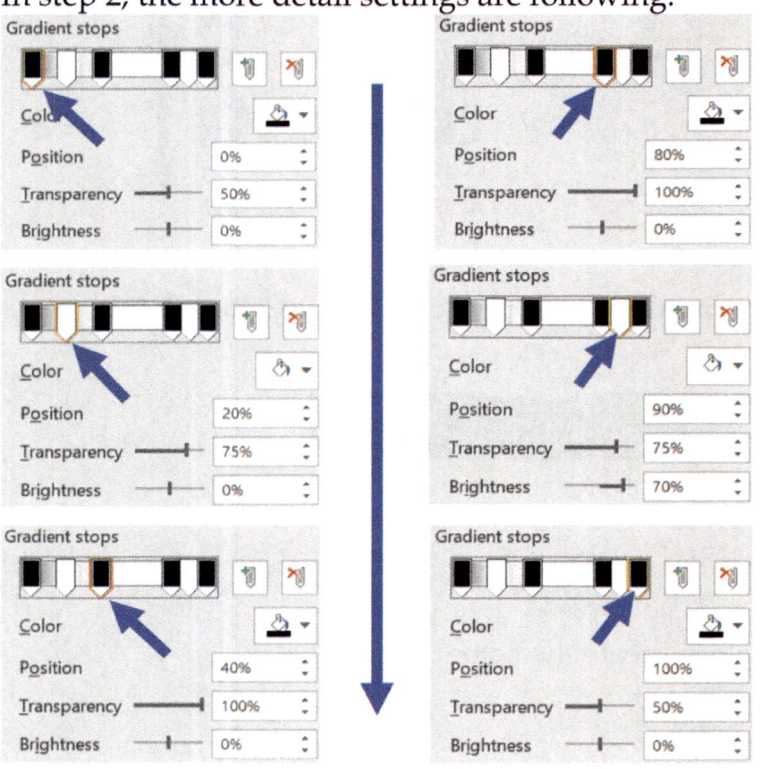

In case of colors, only **black** and **white** color are used for this step in the above settings. It is easy to recognize it by the color of Gradient stops.

Copy & paste the metal part again after completing the glass part.

After selecting each metal parts and glass part, go to **Format**. Choose **1cm** for metal height & **5cm** for glass height. For width, **3.18cm** is selected in this example.

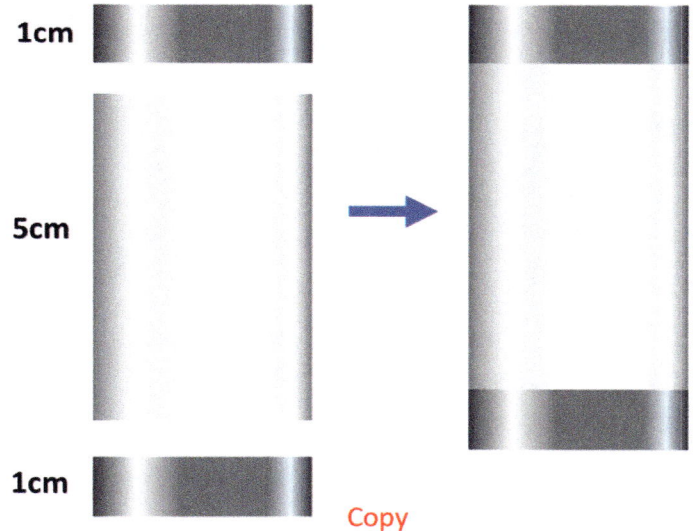

Copy

Setting of height & widths.

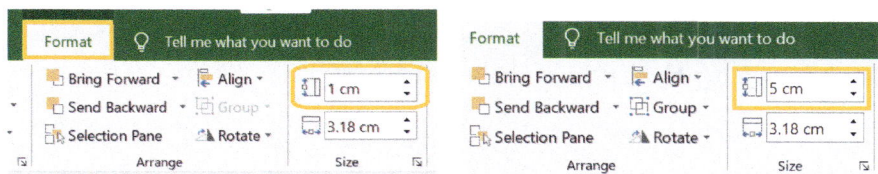

The last step would be a grouping of 3 parts into one part. We can create a metal glass bar icon.

How to create the inside chart:

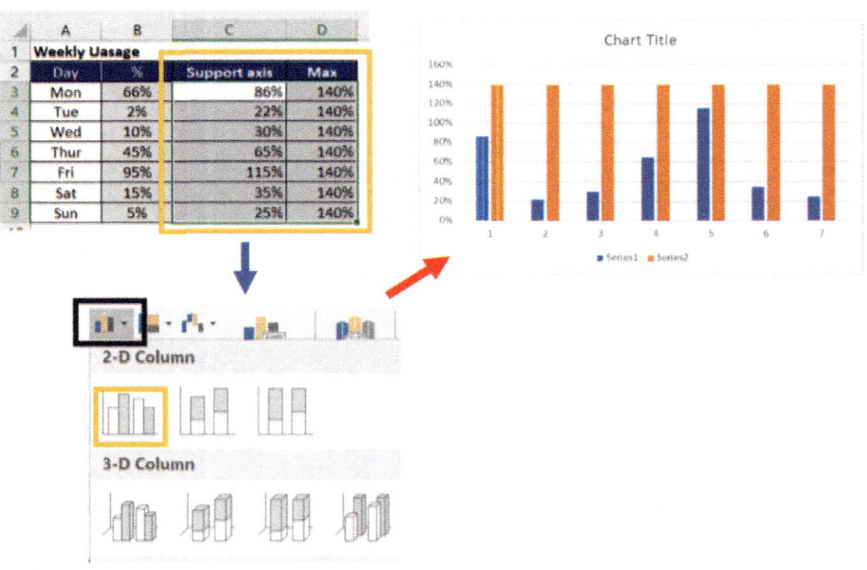

How to set up the format axis (Vertical):

(Important) The max values for vertical axis is 1.4. This is because the max value is linked to display of actual values in the glass chart. If you change the proportion of metal & glass ratio, the max value of axis bound has to be adjust accordingly as well.

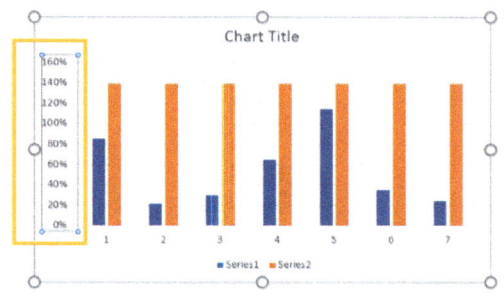 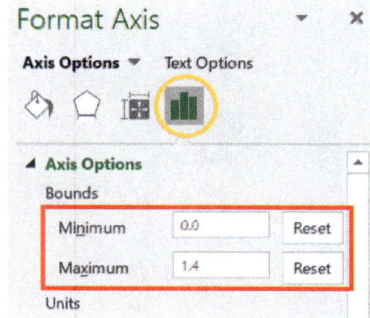

Clean up the chart elements:

After completing axis bounds, click a chart. You can see the plus sign. This is the location where we can clean up the chart elements.

Chart Elements
- ☐ Axes
- ☐ Axis Titles
- ☑ Chart Title
- ☐ Data Labels
- ☐ Data Table
- ☐ Error Bars
- ☐ Gridlines
- ☐ Legend
- ☐ Trendline

How to combine 3D bar & bar chart:

- Click 3D glass bar & **CTRL + C**
- Click a max series in the chart & **CTRL + V**

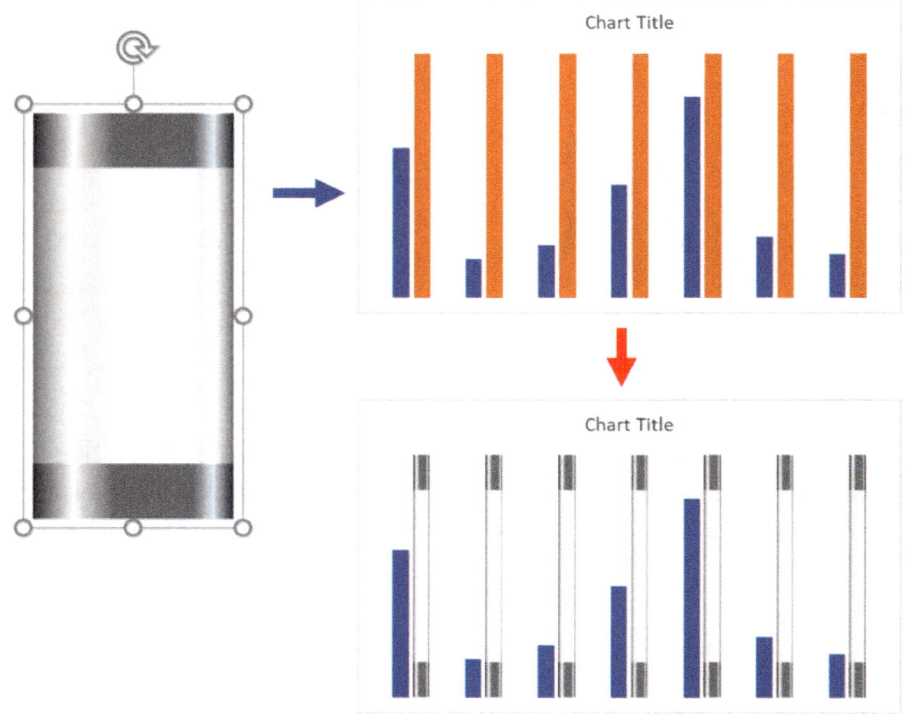

For the inner color, you can simply choose what you like.
- **CTRL + 1**, Go to '**Format Data Point**'.
- Select **Fill** and **Solid Fill**.
- Choose the color you like for the chart.

(Note) click only one bar in chart.
- The first click = selecting all bars in the chart
- The second click = selecting one bar in the chart

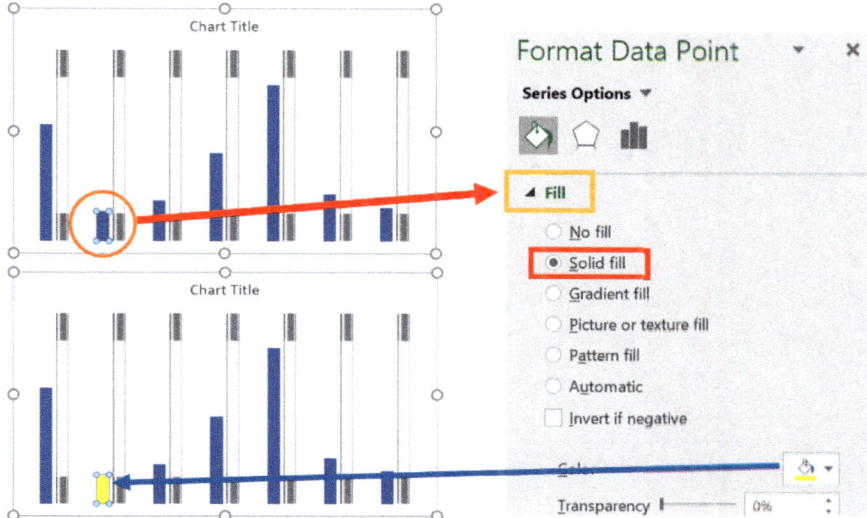

In this example, the following colors are chosen.

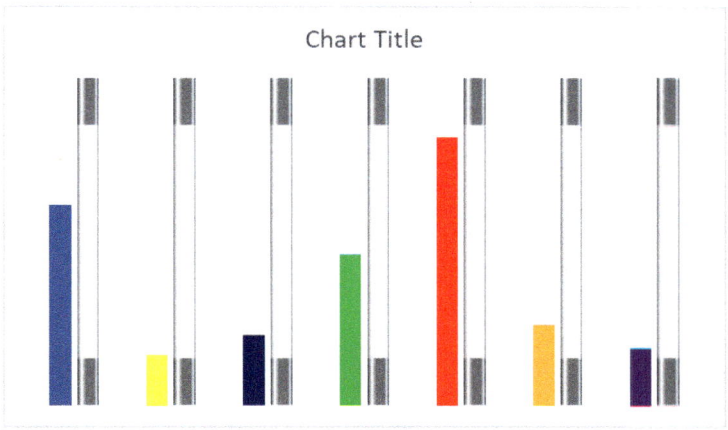

How to add Labels in the chart:

Click the bar which you want to add labels & Click **CTRL +1** >>> Click **'Add Data Labels'**.

Go to **Format Data Labels** >>> Select **"Value from Cells"** and **select the actual values** from the input table.

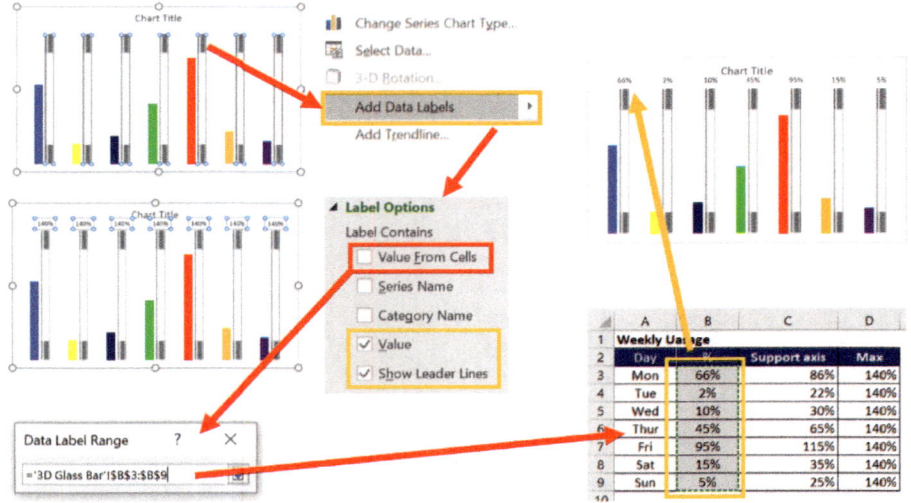

(Note) This functionality is available from Excel version 2013. In case of older versions, it needs to click each data label and link to the actual values in the table one by one.

In the same manner, it is possible to add 'Day' into the actual value bars. See below.

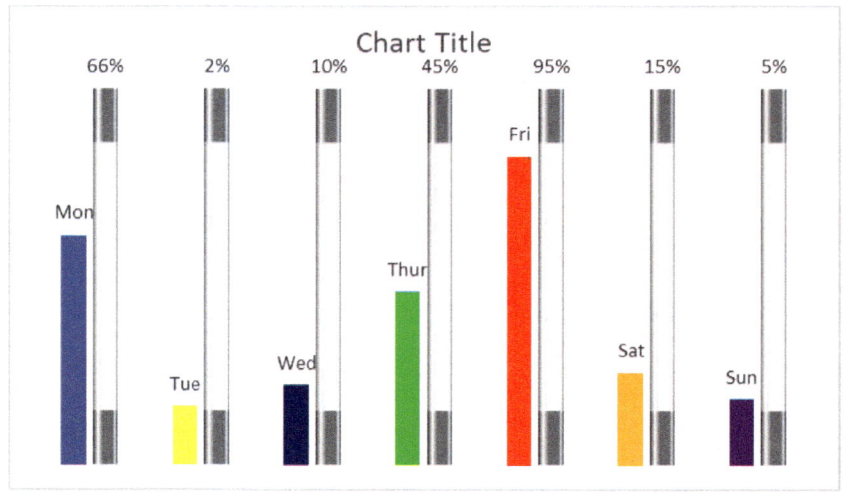

In '**Format Data Labels**', select '**Inside Base**' in **Label Position**.

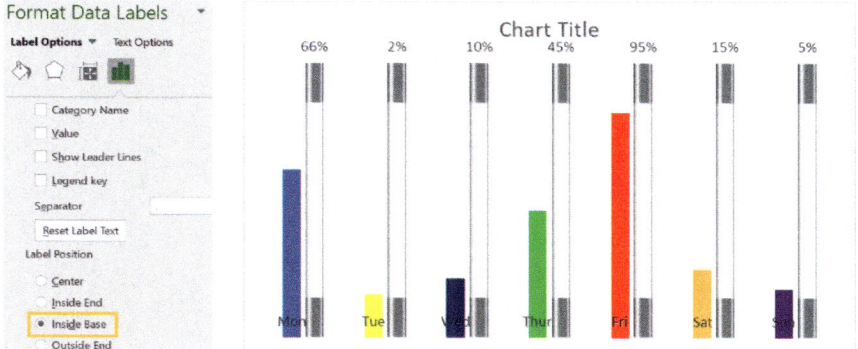

We combined the inner bars and the glass bars by adjusting **Series overlap = 100% & Gap Width = 50%**.

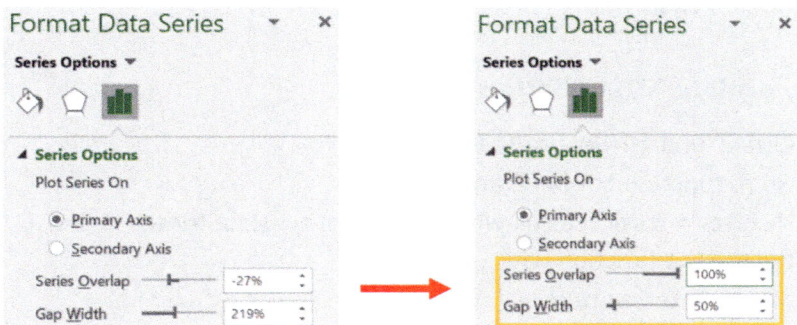

Change of the color of 'day' labels in the chart with the below color.

After these adjustments, it is possible to create the below chart.

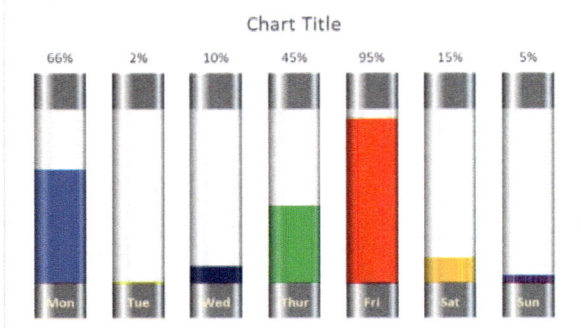

In addition,
- **Shape Outline** = No Outline
- Adjust the size & color of actual input values
- Update chart title

How to update 'Chart Title':

- Click a **'Chart Title'** box in the chart
- Go to function bar (= fx) and put '='.
- Next to '=', click the cell which you want to use it for the chart title (in the function bar).
- Hit an **'Enter'** button.

Finally, we can complete to create 3D metal glass chart.

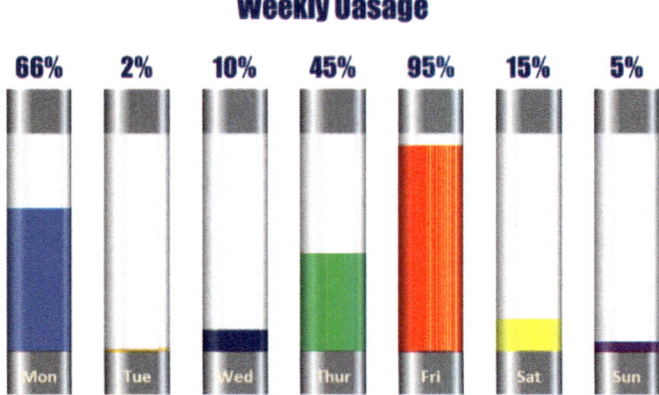

Applied example:

Just change into the identical color for each chart and copy & create 3 more charts.
It is easy to create a regional comparison chart.

(Note) The below charts are used the same input. Therefore, all the chart figures are identical.

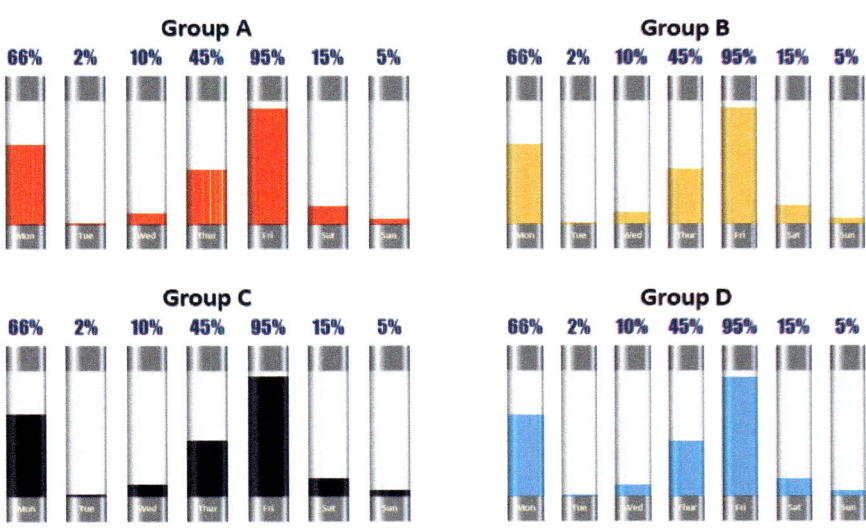

How to change the inner bar color after completing the chart:

Just select any series and **CTRL+1**
Switch 'Series overlap' = 100% >>> 50%

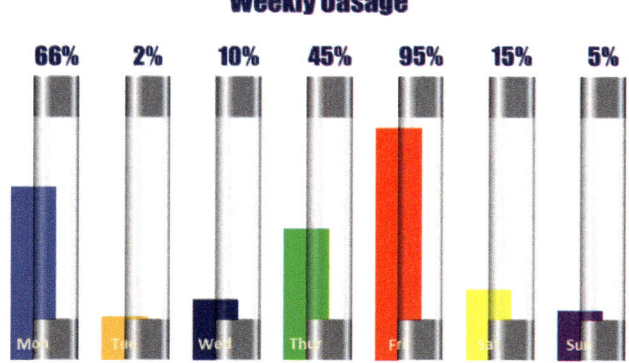

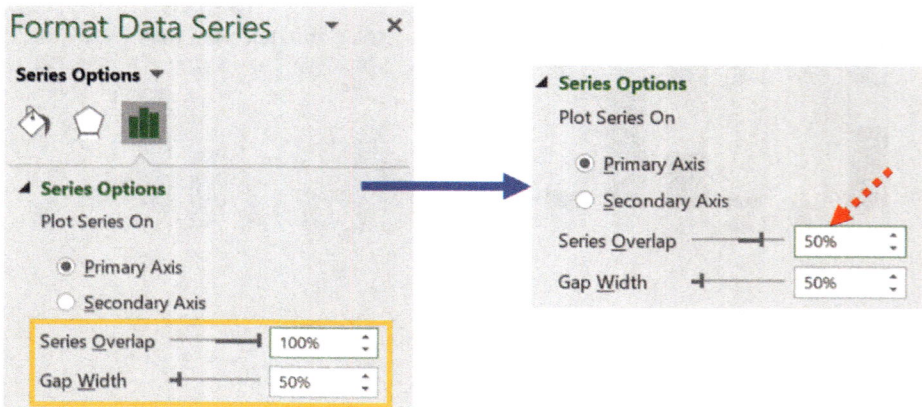

Change the color of inner bar color
Switch 'Series overlap' = 50% >>> **100%**

7. Vertical transparent bar chart with circle icon

The circle in the chart will change depends on the input values.
One of the characteristics of this chart is to use an icon which you made it, not pre-defined ones. It means that you can create your personalized chart after mastering this technique.

Our target chart looks like the below:

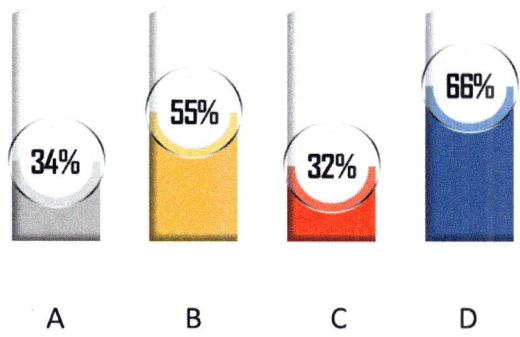

First of all, create input values (%), Max value (=100%).

	A	B	C	D	E	F
1						
2				A	B	C	D
3			Input	65%	55%	32%	66%
4			Max	100%			

How to remove Gridlines:
- Go to **View** tab
- unclick **Gridlines**.

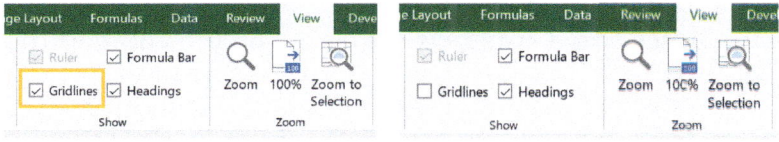

It mainly consists of 4 parts.

- Creating transparent bar (for max value) & colored bar (for actual value)
- Creating inner & outer circle
- Creating vertical bar chart
- Combining them all together

First, we will create the personalized transparent bar icon.
- In **Insert** tab, go to **Shapes** and click the **rectangle** with top edge-cute.
- Click **CTRL + 1** and go to **Shadow**. Select the shadow like below one.
- Select color **white**, Shape Outline = **No Outline**

Below step 1 to 4, the transparent bar is completed.

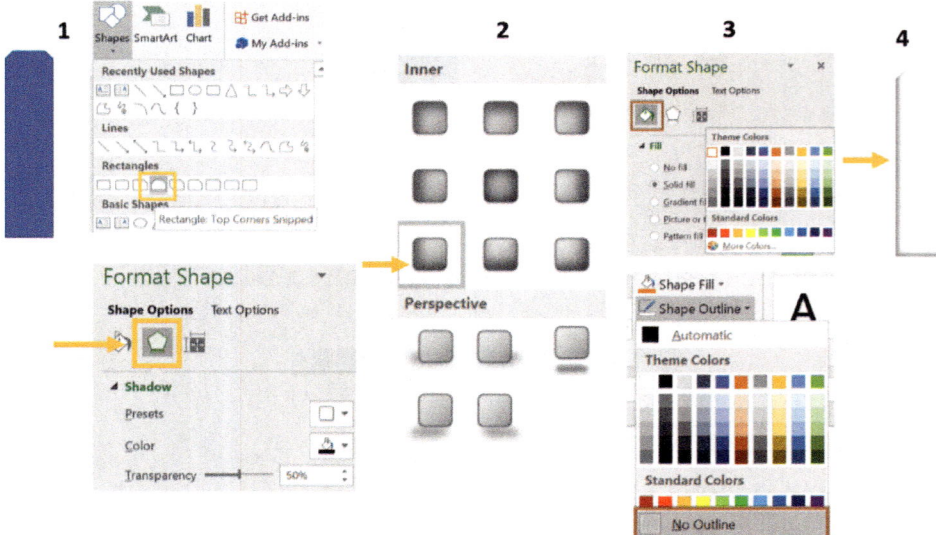

Next, we are going to make a personalized circle which will be used as an icon.

First, the outer circle, inner circle, last will be combined them.

For the **outer circle**:

- In **Insert** tab, go to **Shapes** and click the circle.
- Click **CTRL + 1** and go to Format Shape.
- Select Transparency **60%**, color = **White**

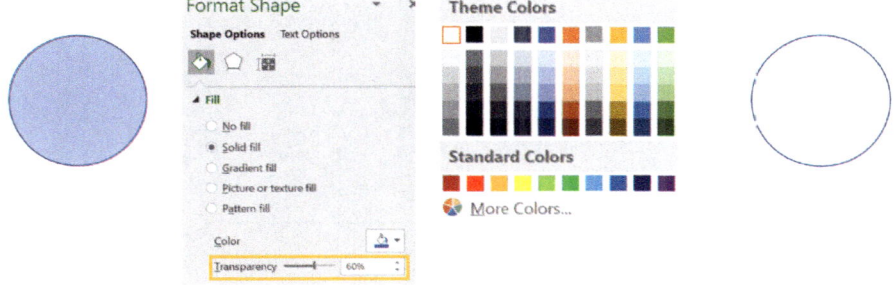

For **line**, select **Gradient fill**.

The detail gradient settings for the outer circle are as follows: Color is **White & Black**, positions of gradient stops are 0%, 30%, 60%, 83%, 100%.

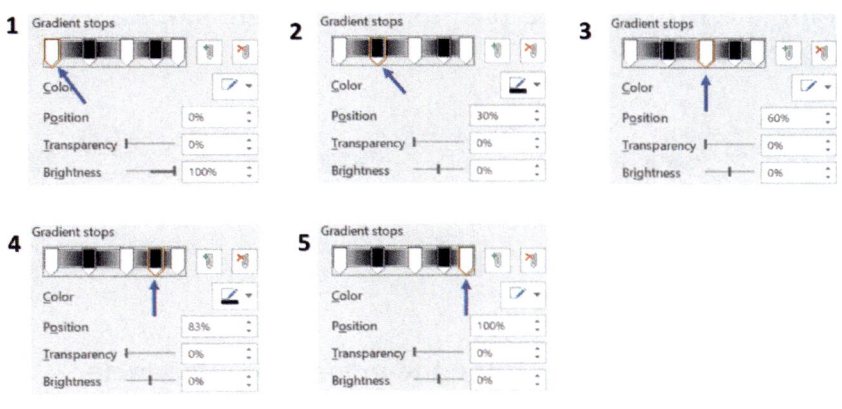

The outer circle is completed.

Next, we are going to create the **inner circle**.
- Copy & paste the outer circle for making an inner circle. Just make it smaller to put it into the outer circle.
- For line, put line = **No line**
- For fill, select **Gradient Fill**.
- Type = **Radial**
- Direction = **from center**

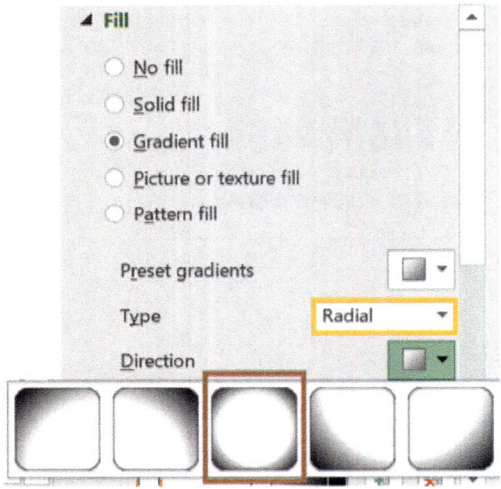

The detail gradient settings for the inner circle are as follows: Color is **White & Black**, positions of gradient stops are 0%, 60%, 100%.

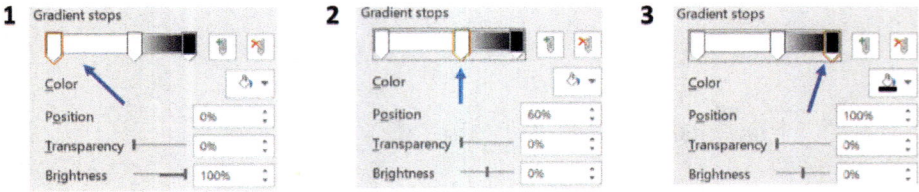

Last step would be grouping the inner and outer circle.

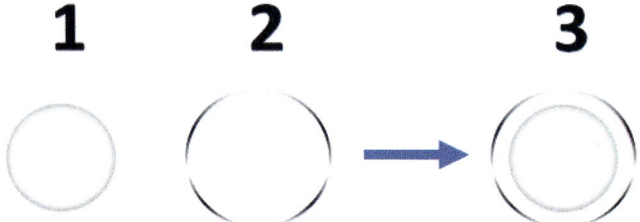

How to create 2-D Clustered bar chart:

The method to create this chart is similar to a horizontal bar chart, but switched to a vertical direction.

After selecting inputs (i.e. input value & max value), go to **Insert** tab. Select **2-D bar >>> Clustered Bar**.

The Max value (100%) represents the maximum range of bar chart.

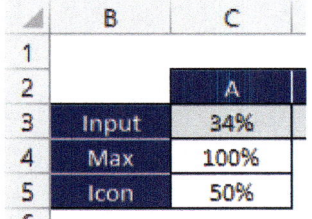 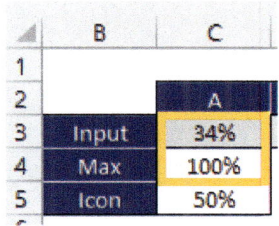

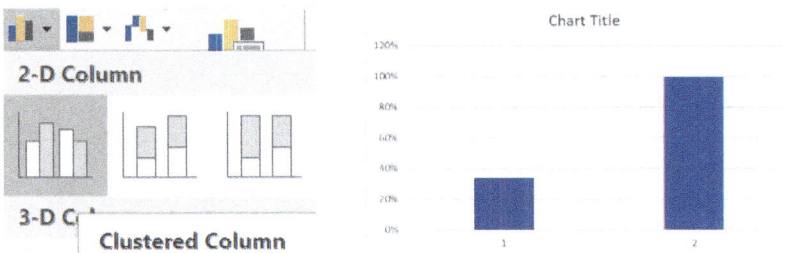

Go to **Design >>> Switch Row/Column**.
We can see the below right-hand chart.

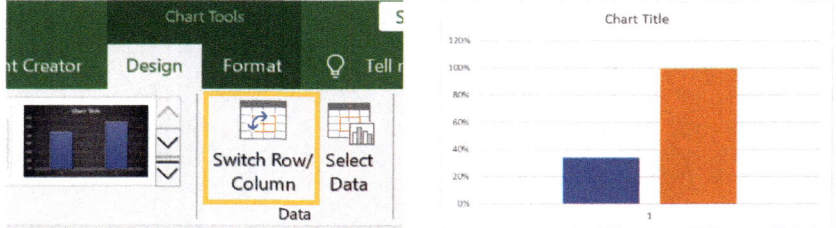

- After selecting the chart, click a right-hand button and go to **Select Data**.
- **Switch the order** of Series2. Put it above Series1 by clicking a up triangle button.
- Click the bar in the chart and change **Series Ovelap: 100%** and **Gap Width: 0%**.

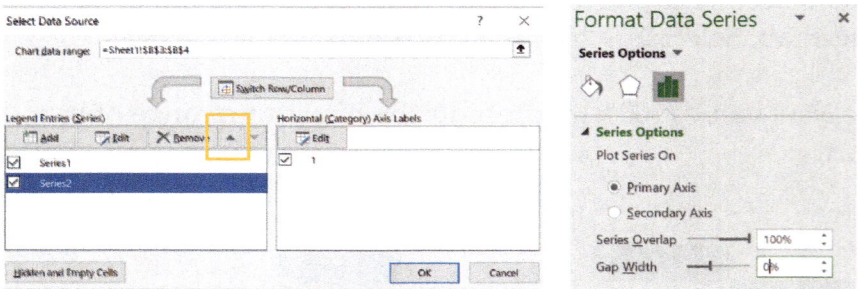

How to change the range of Axis:

- Click an Axis and then **CTRL + 1**
- Go to Format Axis and change **Min: -0.2** & **Max values: 1.2**

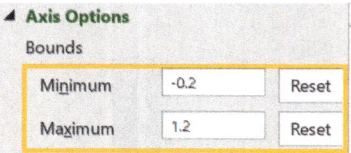

- Also, changed from **Auto** to **Reset** (fixed the axis range of chart)

You can see the axis range is from **-20%** to **120% in the below** picture.

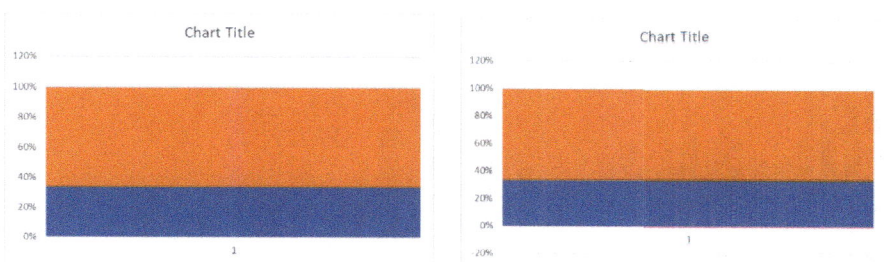

After removing chart elements:
- Go to chart elements = click (+) sign in the chart
- **Remove the chart elements** = Unclick the chart elements which you want to remove

After removing 'Shape Fill' and 'Shape Outline' (in '**Format**' tab in '**Chart Tools**'):
- **Shape Fill** = No Fill (for chart, but each series has filled color)
- **Shape Outline** = No Outline

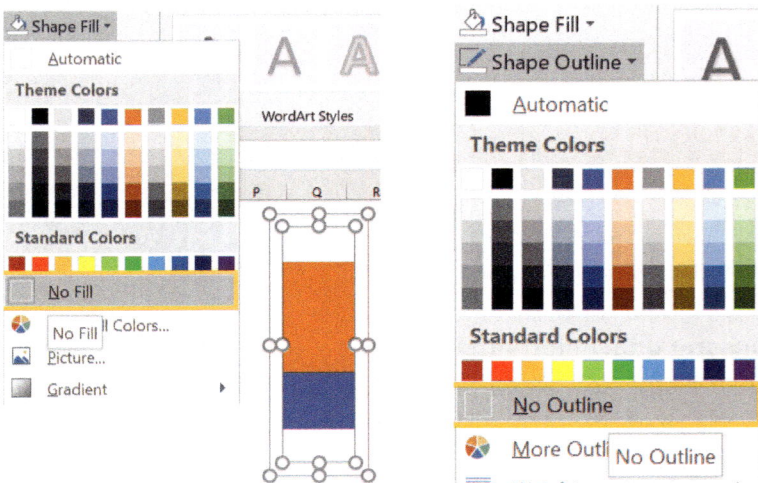

- Next, adjusting the shape of chart by dragging the chart
- **Change the color of bar** to your wished color. **Note: Please select only bar at a time.**
- For the max bar, the white color is not recommendable because it is difficult to see the max bar.
- Adjust the width to make a rectangle bar chart by using mouse dragging.

We can complete up to the following bar.

How to combine icon & bar chart (by using scatter plot):

We are going to combine the circle icon with the vertical bar chart.

The icon is going to move whenever the input value is changed.
Therefore, we **need a new series** for the action. For creating a new series:
- Click the vertical bar chart and click a right-hand mouse button.
- Click **Select Data** >>> **Add** >>>
- Entering **Series name** = "Icon" & **Series values** = 0.5

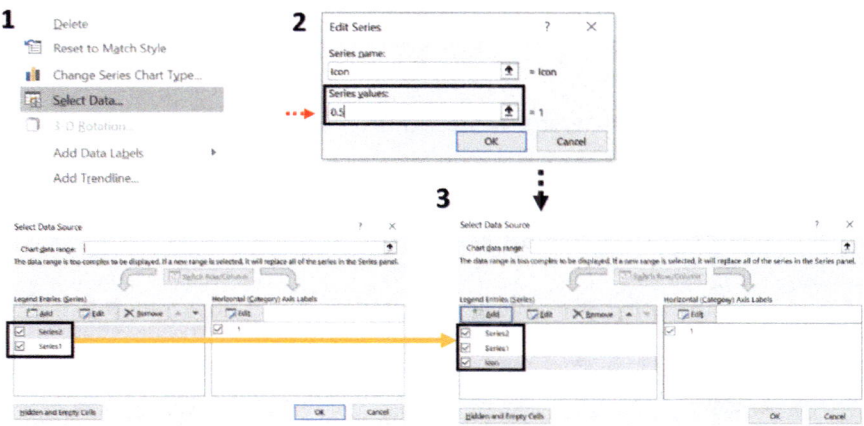

How to switch from 2-D Clustered bar chart to Combo chart:

In order to do so, select the chart and click a right-hand mouse button.
- Go to **Change Series Chart Type** (see below) and
- Change chart type **for icon series** from '**Clustered bar**' to '**Scatter**'

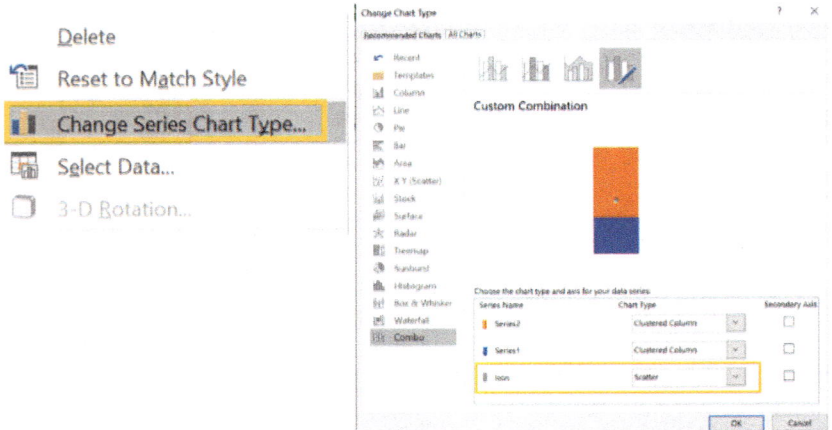

After this step, you can find a small dot on the bar chart. (In fact, the dot is not so recognizable!)

In case of scatter plot, we need to add 2 new X & Y vlaues for the plot in '**Select Data Source**'.
- X values = **1**
- Y values = **Actual input value**

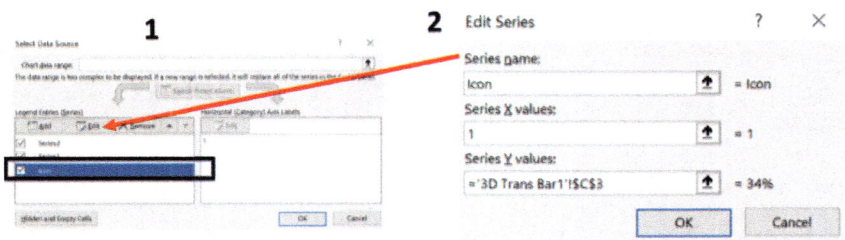

In summary,
- Add a new series for icon movements
- **Switch** bar chart to **combo chart** (in scatter plot, it needs one more input value than bar chart)
- Change X (=1) & Y vlaues (= acutal input) for the scatter plot.

How to combine an icon picture and the dot in the chart:

- Click the circle icon >>> **Ctrl + C**
- Click the scatter plot dot in the chart >>> **Ctrl + V**

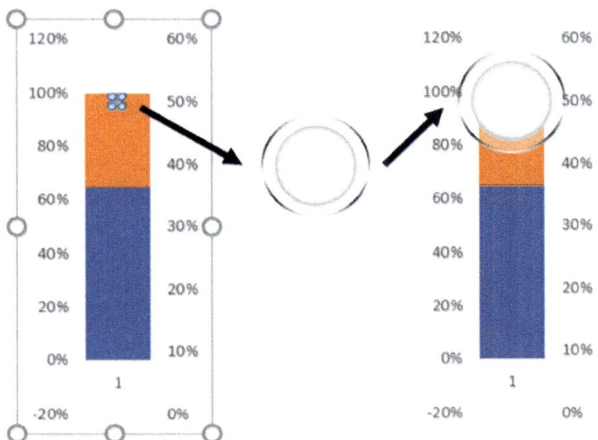

For the transparent bar, the method is very similar.
- Click the **transparent bar icon** >>> **Ctrl + C**
- Click the **max bar** in the chart >>> **Ctrl + V**

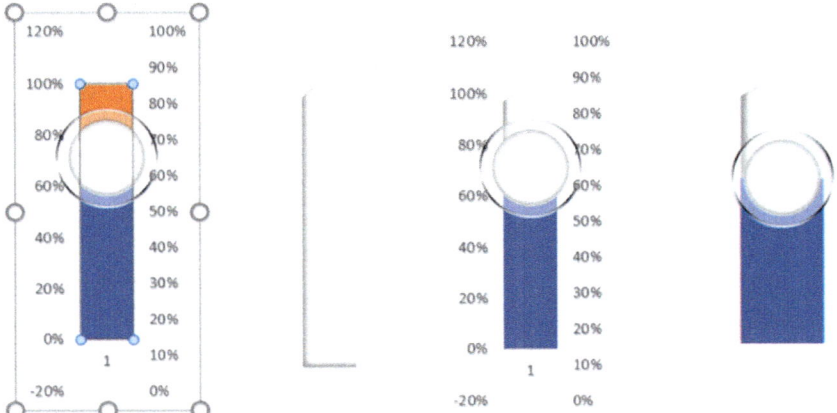

For explanation, the axis ranges are added in the above picture.

How to add Labels in the chart:

- Click the icon circle which you want to add labels
- Click right-hand side mouse button >>> Click **'Add Data Labels'**.
- Go to **Format Data Labels** >>> Select "**Value from Cells**" in Label Options
- Select **the actual values** from the input table.
- Put **Label Position = Center**

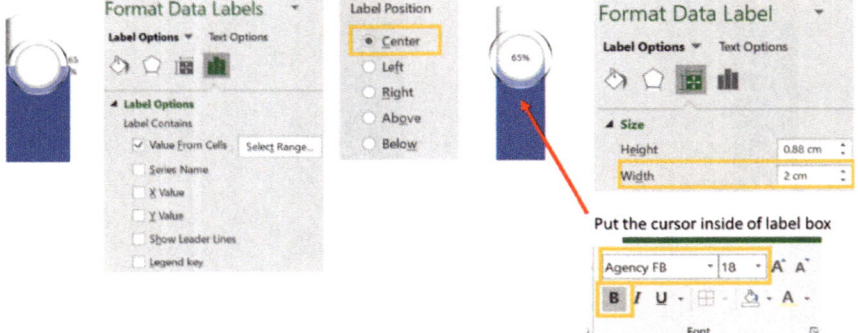

In order to adjust the size of font, the cursor must be in side of the label box.
- Width = **2cm**
- Font style= **Agency FB, 18, Bold**

How to change inner colored bar:

- Copy & paste the transparent bar and change the color which you like.

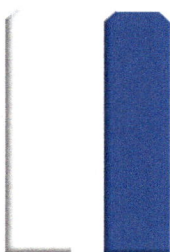

- Click the **colored bar icon** >>> **Ctrl + C**
- Click the **max bar** in the chart >>> **Ctrl + V**

Finally, we can create the following vertical transparent bar chart with circle icon.

To add the text box below the chart is omitted because it is quite straightforward.
Depends on your input values, you can create more bar charts and combine them by grouping.

Finally, we complete the vertical transparent bar chart with circle icon.

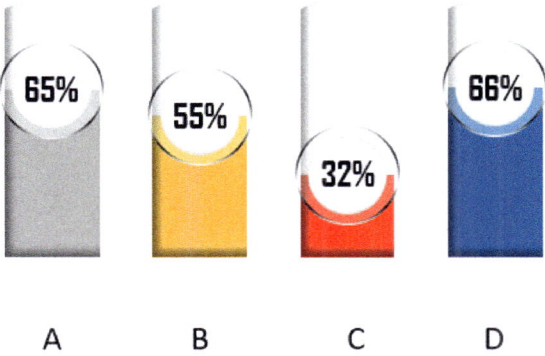

Applied examples:

In addition, it is easy to create a different style of bar chart as well.

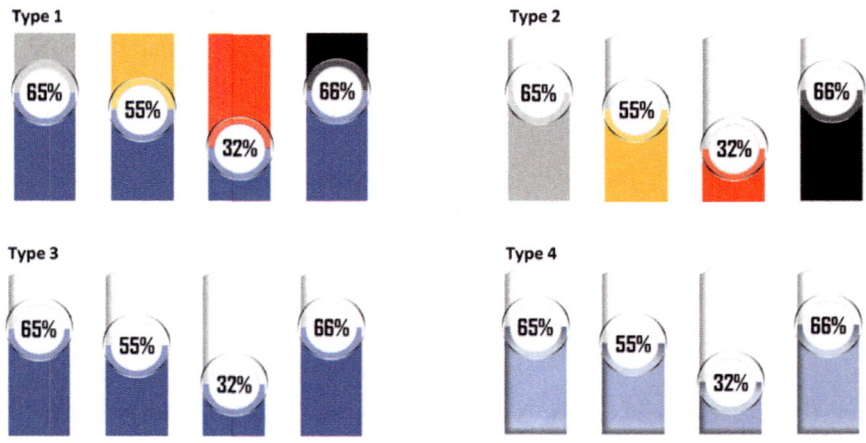

8. 3D donut chart

In general, we can create the following donut chart by using a built-in function easily.

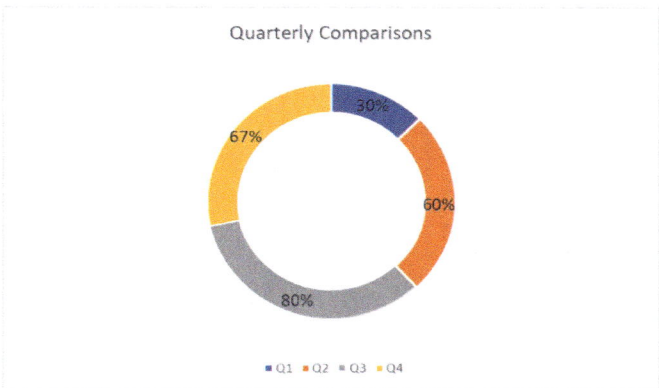

However, as you can see below, the below donut charts are more intuitive and clearer than the above one. The below chart is our target chart in this section:

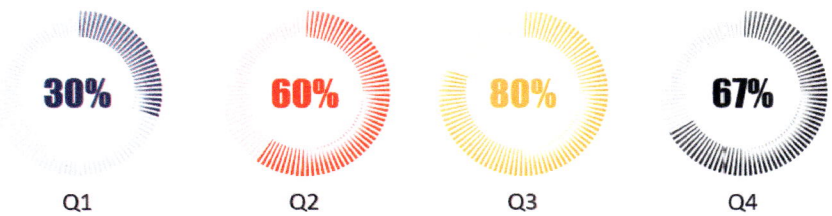

(Note) it is not possible to make this chart with Excel 2010 version or older version. This is because these versions are not supporting combo chart.

How to remove Gridlines:

- Go to **View** tab
- unclick **Gridlines**.

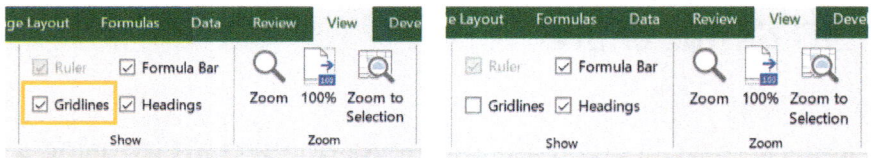

First of all, create input values (%), Supporting value **(=100% - Actual input value)**.

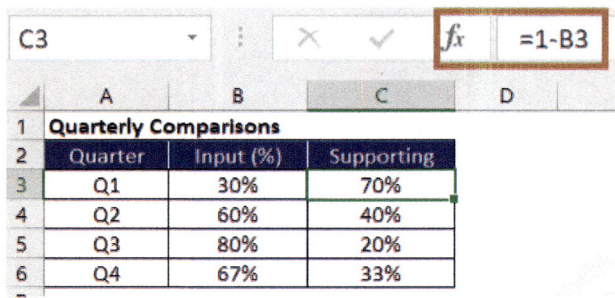

Quarter	Input (%)	Supporting
Q1	30%	70%
Q2	60%	40%
Q3	80%	20%
Q4	67%	33%

How to create a sliced donut form:

First, create an empty donut chart.

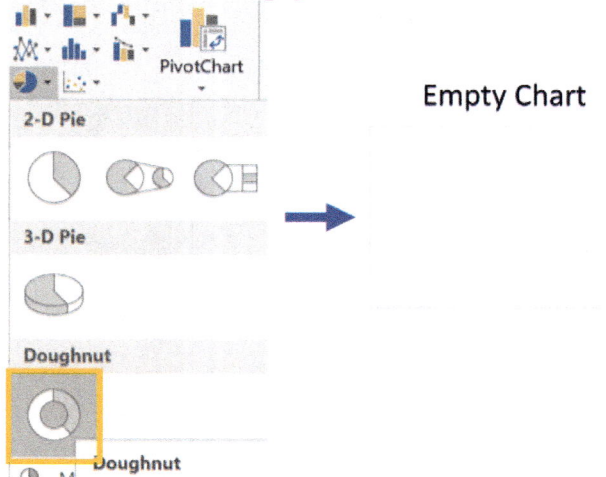

Empty Chart

(Note) our original donut chart has 100 sliced donut charts. However, we will use 10 sliced one for better explanation of creating the chart.

Second, prepare the slice inputs for the chart.
- In an empty cell, insert '1,1,1,1,1,1,1,1,1,1'
- Copy '1,1,1,1,1,1,1,1,1,1' part.
- Select the empty donut chart
- Select **'Select Data'** after right-click of mouse button & click **'Add'**
- Paste '1,1,1,1,1,1,1,1,1,1' in **Series values** and click **OK**.

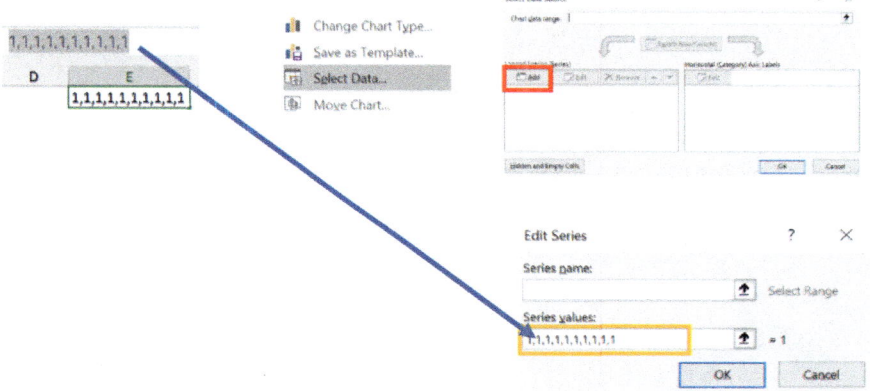

We can see the empty chart changes to sliced donut chart.

How to adjust the sliced donut chart:

- Click the series in the chart & Click a right-hand side mouse button
- Click **Format Data Series**
- Set **65%** for **Doughnut Hole Size**

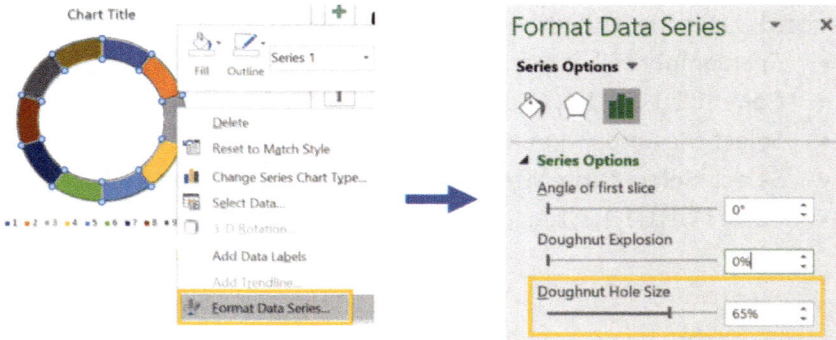

(For the case of example)
- Go to Format tab and Shape Fill = **Dark blue**
- Shape Outline color = **White**
- Shape Outline weight = **1.5**

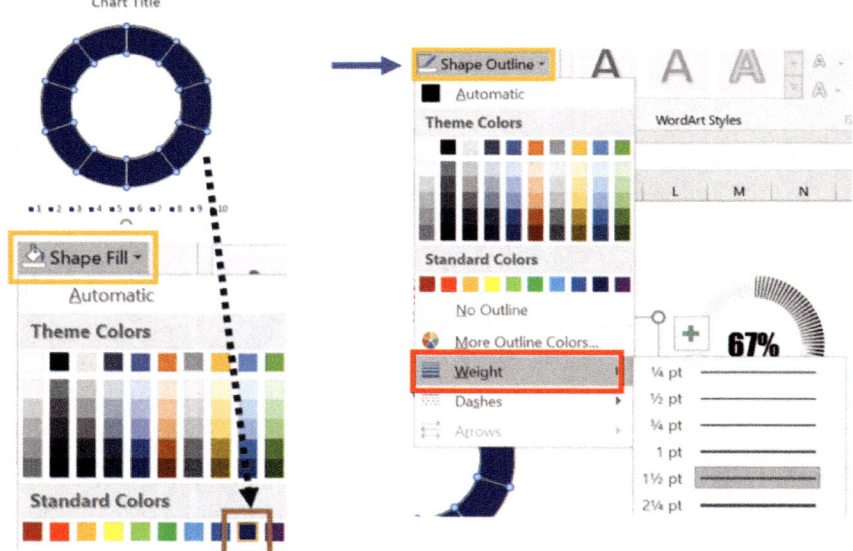

We complete the slice form for the donut chart.

Question: Why do we create & use the 1s in the chart?

The number of 1 represents the number of slices. In the below example, you can fine the case of 10, 20, 100. In terms of percentage, 10 = 10%, 20 = 5%, 100 = 1% for each slice in the donut chart.

(You can find the below in the reference sheet in the example Excel file.)

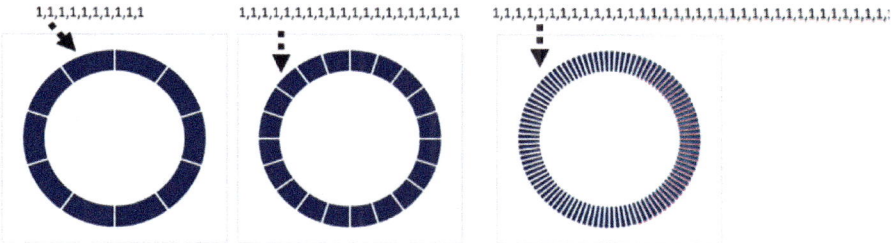

In addition, 4 different color of donut charts are already ready in the example file.

How to add 3D effect into 2D sliced donut chart form:

Select **Gradient fill**.
The detail gradient settings for the outer circle are as follows:

Color is **White & Dark Blue**, positions of gradient stops are 0%, 40%, 80%, 100%.

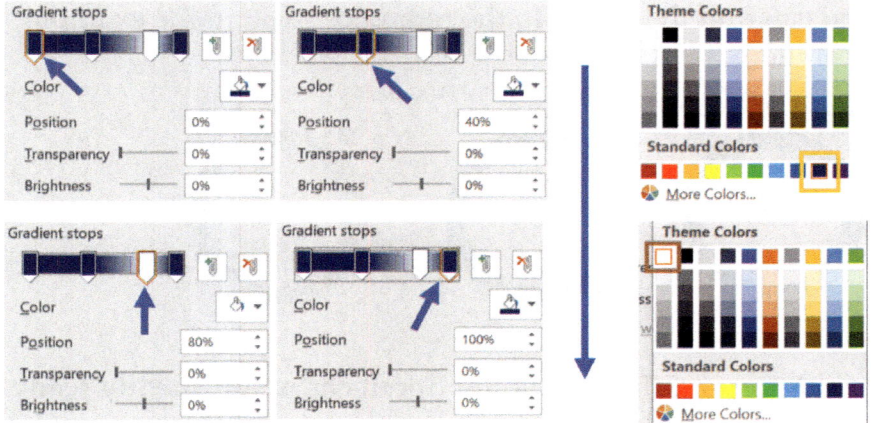

In addition, 4 different 3D color of donut charts are already ready in the example file.

How to add a NEW series in the donut chart:

Next, the new series will create & use for the actual input value. For creating a new series:
- Click the chart and click a right-hand mouse button.
- Click **Select Data** >>> **Add** >>>
- Select **Series name** = input value name & **Series values** = range of **actual input values**

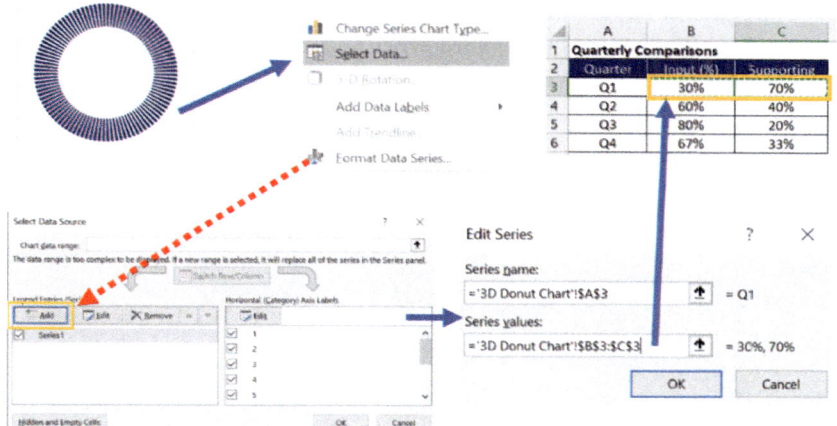

We can create the following one.

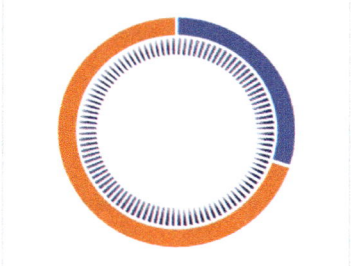

How to create the actual input values in donut chart:

(Note) the following processes are required correct orders & correct selections of chart parts in each step.

- **Click the purple part** in the donut chart & click right mouse button.
- Click '**Change Series Chart Type**'

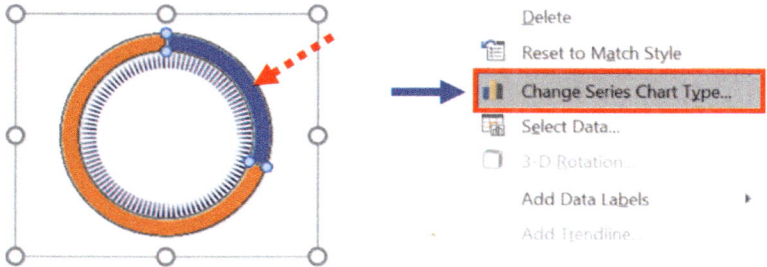

- Change chart type from **Doughnut** to **Pie** for the actual input value (= Q1 series in this example)
- Click OK.

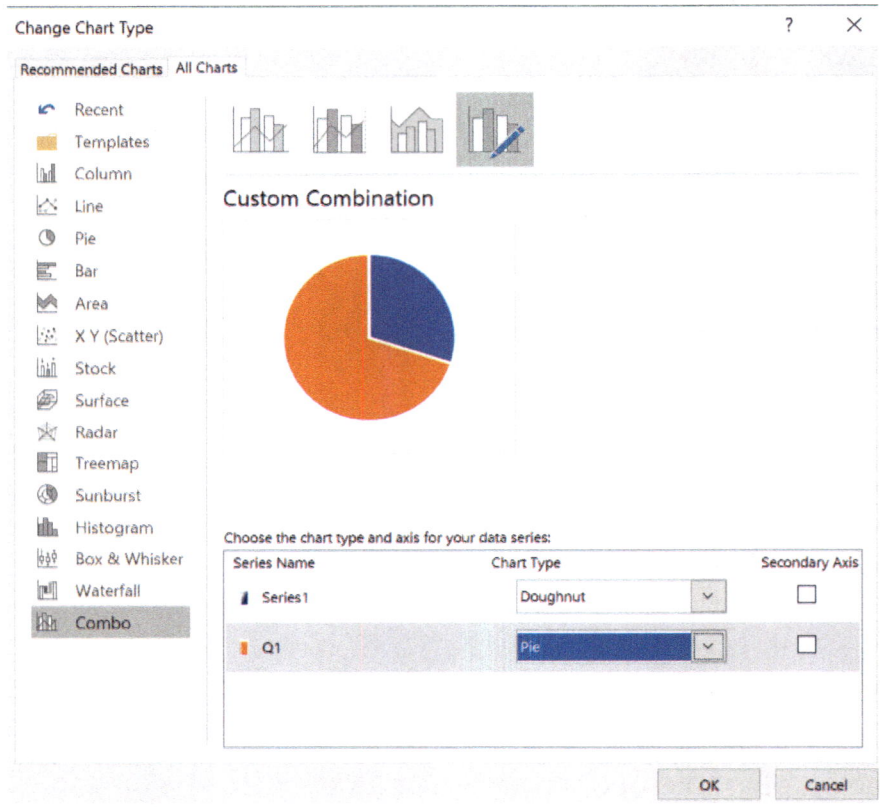

We can see only pie chart instead of our donut chart. We are going to disappear the supporting series from the donut chart.

- Double clicks of the **supporting pie part**
- Click **CTRL+1** and go to '**Format Data Point**'.
- Select **solid fill**
- Color = **White** & Transparency = **15%**

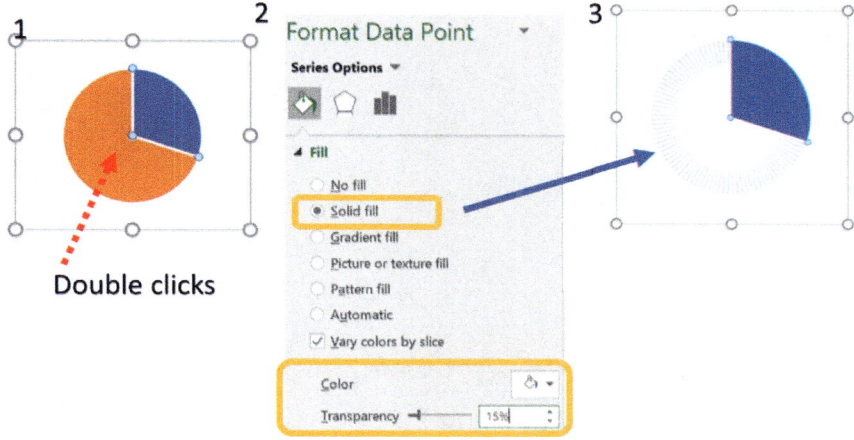

Now, we move on the actual value part in the chart.
- **Double clicks** of the actual value part
- Click **CTRL+1** and go to '**Format Data Point**'
- Select **No fill**

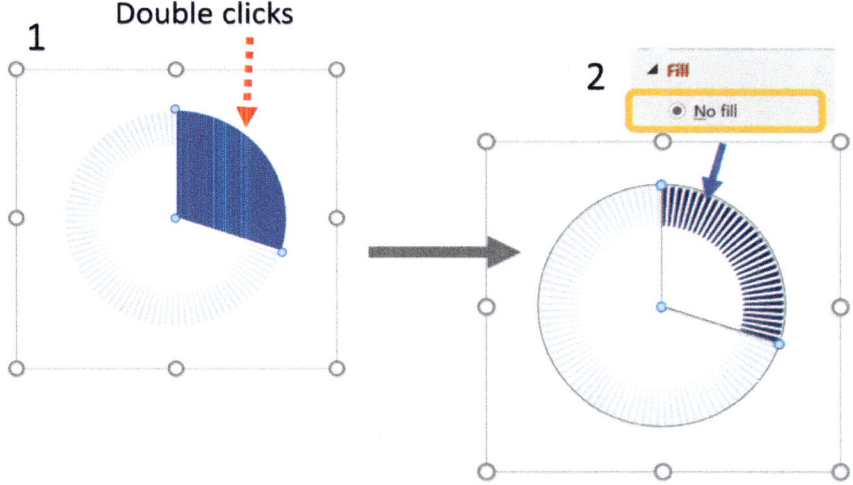

Finally, we can have the following 3D donut chart which can change by input value.

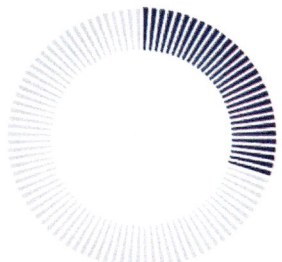

How to set up chart area in pie chart:

- Click the chart itself by mouse
- Click 'Shape Fill' and click white color

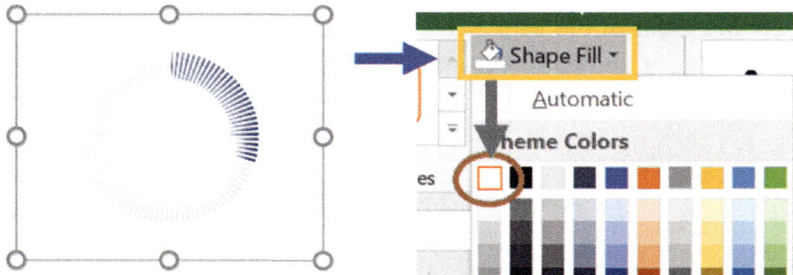

- Click **'Shape Outline'** and click **'No Outline'**

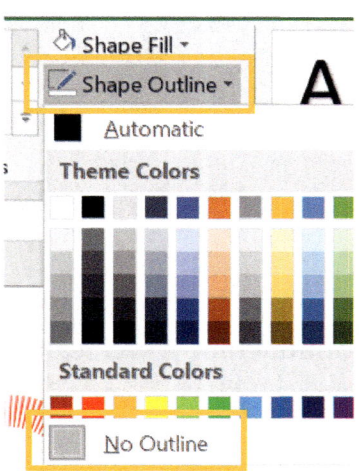

How to add Labels in the chart:

- Click **Text Box** in **Shapes** in **Insert** tab
- Create a text box in a sheet by dragging a mouse

- Go to function bar (= fx) and put '='.
- Next to '=', click the cell which you want to use it for the label (in the function bar).
- Hit an 'Enter' button.

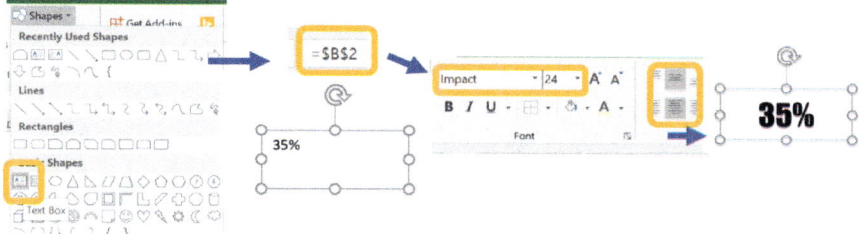

In order to adjust the size of font, click the text box.

In the **Home** tab:
- **No fill** & **No line** for the text box
- Font style = **Impact, 24, Bold**

How to assign multiple objects (i.e. chart & labels) nicely:

Click both donut chart & text box at the same time, go to **Format** tab and go to **Align**.

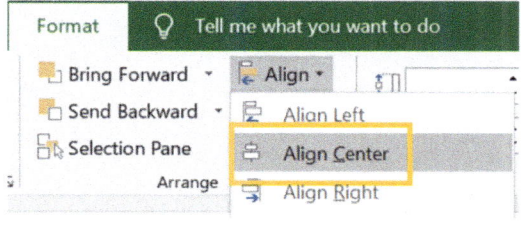
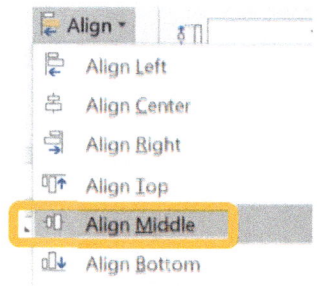

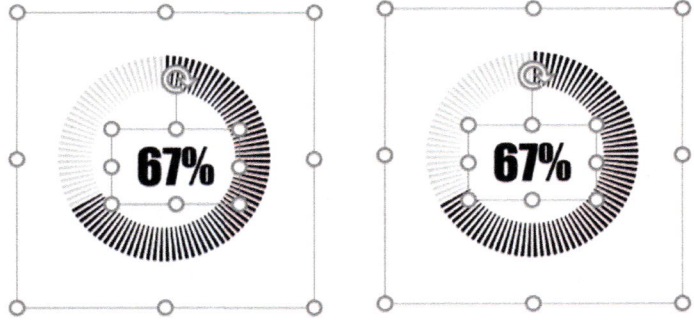

Finally, we complete the 3D donut chart.

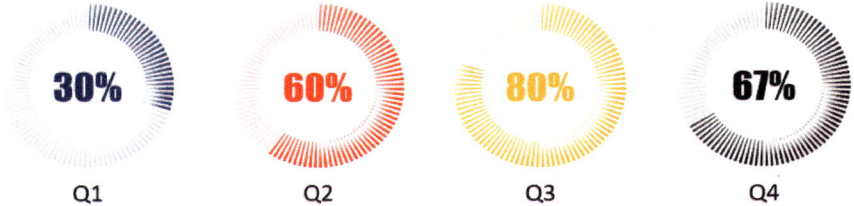

9. Wind chart with Average line

In this section, we are going to create a wind chart. The target chart looks like below:

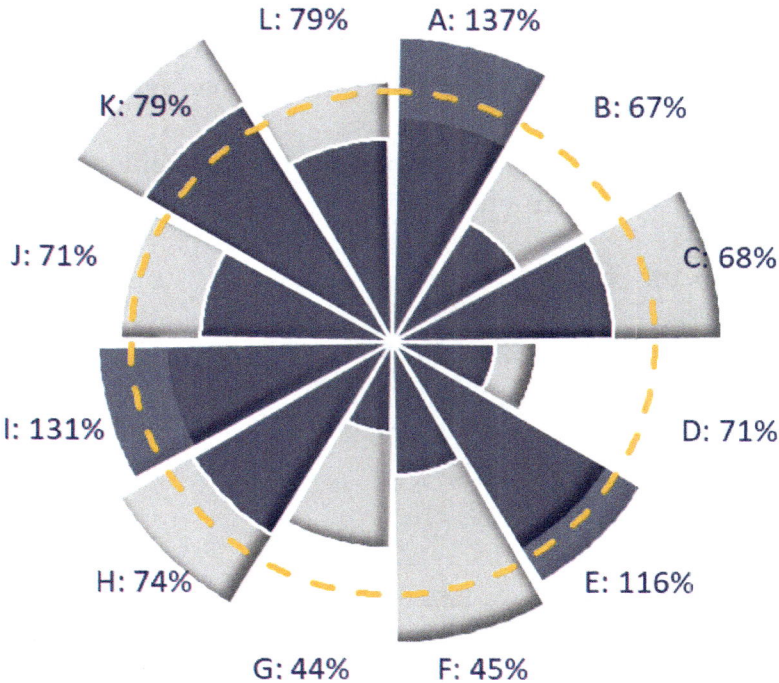

How to interpret the chart:

In this example, there are 12 companies (Company A to L) in the industry. The chart compares the expected sale values, actual values and average expected values in one chart. (Note) There is no need to be 12 companies. The reason why 12 is used for monthly comparisons as a possible applied example.
- Gray color: Expected value for each company
- Dark blue (transparency 40%): Actual value for each company
- Orange line: Average expected value

According to the chart, Company A, E, I exceed their expected values (over 100%), and also their sale figure is higher than the average expected value. However, the remain companies are not able to reach their expected value.

If the company's value is below the orange line, the company value is lower than the expected average value.
In case of company K, it does not exceed the target value, the company's actual value is higher than the average value.

As you can see, the benefit of this chart is to be able to include a lot of information in one chart.

Inputs for the chart:

A	B	C	D
		input	input
	Company	Actual value	Expected value
	A	78	57
	B	36	54
	C	54	80
	D	25	35
	E	71	61
	F	34	76
	G	23	52
	H	57	77
	I	72	55
	J	47	66
	K	71	90
	L	52	66

Unlike other charts, it requires some input preparation processes. For label,

SUM × ✓ fx =B3&": "&ROUND(C3/D3,2)*100&"%"

A	B	C	D	E	F
		input	input		
	Company	Actual value	Expected value	Label	
	A	78	57	)*100&"%"	
	B	36	54	B: 67%	
	C	54	80	C: 68%	
	D	25	35	D: 71%	
	E	71	61	E: 116%	
	F	34	76	F: 45%	
	G	23	52	G: 44%	
	H	57	77	H: 74%	
	I	72	55	I: 131%	
	J	47	66	J: 71%	
	K	71	90	K: 79%	
	L	52	66	L: 79%	

How to create a label function (for inputs):

The interpretation of function of label is as follows (i.e. Company A).
- A: 137% =B3&": "&ROUND(C3/D3,2)*100&"%"
- A: 137% = Company name A & Actual value (78) / expected value (57) = 1.37 times 100 & %
- Round is a function for removing digit numbers in this case.
- Output: "A: 137%"

How to calculate 'Width of each piece':

There are 12 companies, the degree of circle is 360. Therefore, the formula is:

Width of each piece = 360/12 = 30

Total companies	12
Width of each pieace	30
Average expected value	64

As another example, there are 10 companies. The width of each piece is:

Width of each piece = 360/10 = 36

For the donut chart, we need 30s for 12 times in a row. The idea is similar to 1s in 3D donut chart.

30,30,30,30,30,30,30,30,30,30,30,30

This is a bit tricky part. We need to create a below chart. The table contains 360 rows. The detail of column is as follow.

index1	index2	help1	help2	Avg
1	1	0	0	64
2	1	78	57	64
3	1	78	57	64
4	1	78	57	64
5	1	78	57	64
6	1	78	57	64
⋮				
28	1	78	57	64
29	1	78	57	64
30	1	78	57	64
31	2	0	0	64
32	2	36	54	64
33	2	36	54	64
⋮				
354	12	52	66	64
355	12	52	66	64
356	12	52	66	64
357	12	52	66	64
358	12	52	66	64
359	12	52	66	64
360	12	52	66	64

- **index1**: the number is increase from 1 to 360. (360 rows)
- **index2**: 1s for 30 times, 2s for 30 times, …, 12s for 30 times

- **help1**: in the same manner as index2, listing the **actual values** of each company from A to L.
  However, **the starting value is 0** (please see above)
  In other words, 0, and then 78 (=Company A actual value) for 29 times, 0, and then 36 (=Company B actual value) for 29 times, …, until 52 for 29 times for Company L.

- **help2**: in the same manner as help1, listing the **expected values** of each company from A to L.

- **Avg**: listing the average values (=64) for entire rows

For help1 & help2, the following function is used. (i.e. help1)

	f_x	=IF(MOD($O3,30)=1,0,OFFSET($C$3,$P3-1,0))				
N	O	P	Q	R	S	

	index1	index2	help1	help2	Avg
	1	1	P3-1,0))	0	64
	2	1	78	57	64

How to create help function: (i.e. help1)

=IF(MOD($O3,30)=1,0,OFFSET($C$3,$P3-1,0))
=IF(MOD($O3,30)=1,0 means:

- If index1 reaches 30 times numbers (30, 60, 90, …), the index1 calls 0.
- If not, actual values are calling by using offset function for 29 times.

Please refers to the detail in the Excel file.
In addition, 'Explanation for help1 (Step by step)' has been added in the Excel file. The input preparation for wind chart is done now.

V	W	X	Y
Explanation for help1 (Step by step)			combine
step1	step2	step3	step4
1	0	78	0
2	1	78	78
3	1	78	78
4	1	78	78
5	1	78	78
6	1	78	78
7	1	78	78
8	1	78	78

How to create Wind chart:

Select entire column help1,2 & Avg. Put the cursor at cell Q3 (=starting input value).

Hold both **CTRL** & **Shift** key. With holding these two buttons, press right-hand direction arrow and then press down arrow. You can select the entire columns.

O	P	Q	R	S
Supporting inputs for chart ($C$18=30)				
index1	index2	help1	help2	Avg
1	1	0	0	64
2	1	78	57	64
3	1	78	57	64
4	1	78	57	64
5	1	78	57	64
6	1	78	57	64
7	1	78	57	64
8	1	78	57	64
9	1	78	57	64
10	1	78	57	64

- After selecting all columns, go to **Insert** tab.
- Click **Recommended Charts** >>> **All Charts**.
- Select **Radar**. **OK**.

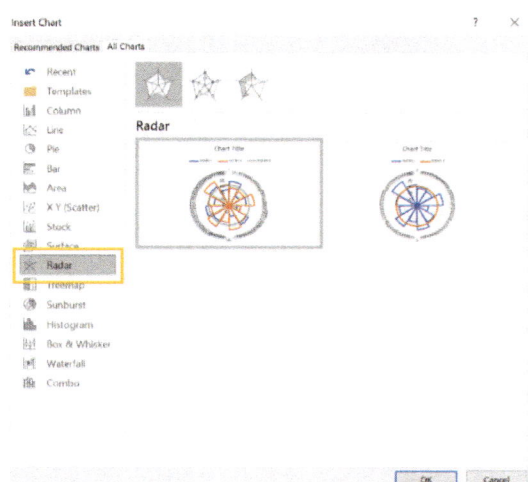

Click the chart and click a right-hand mouse button.
Select '**Change Chart Type**'.

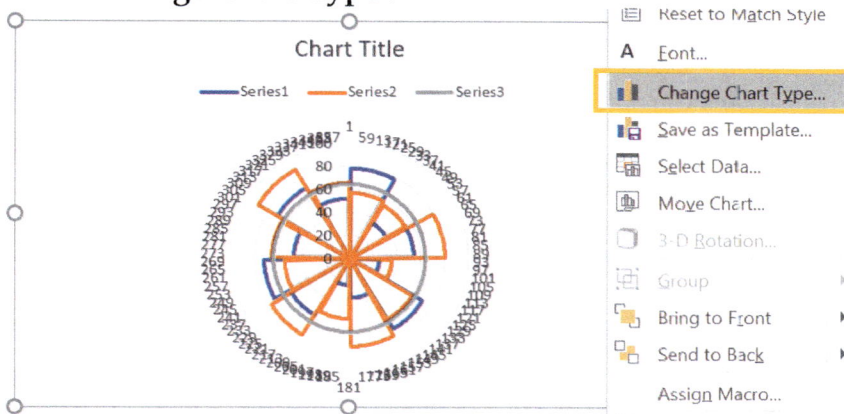

Go to '**Combo**' chart
- Series1(=help1): **Filled Radar**
- Series2 (=help2): **Filled Radar**
- Series3 (=Avg): **Radar with Markers**

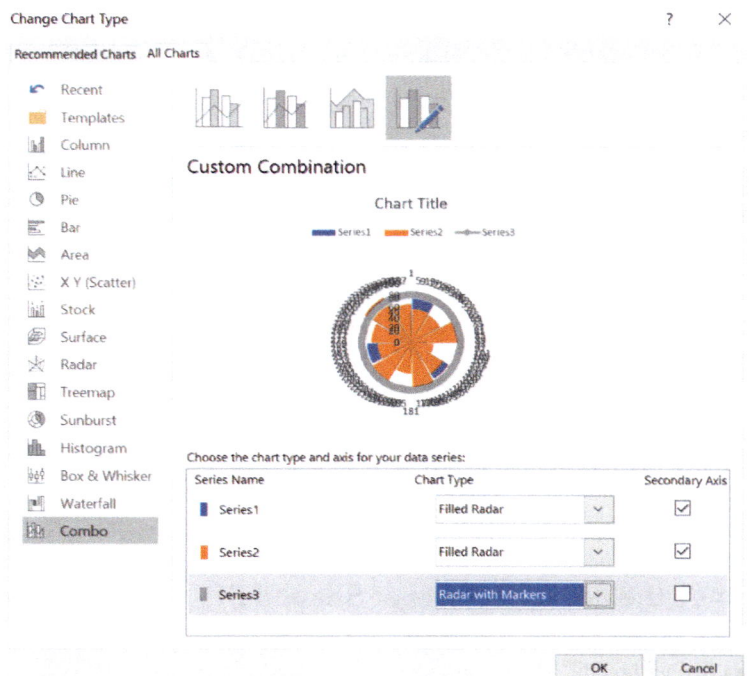

Already, the average line is completed.

How to remove chart elements:

After clicking a chart, we can see the plus (+) sign on right hand side. This is the location where we can control the chart elements.

- Go to chart elements = click (+) sign in the chart
- **Remove the chart elements** = Unclick the chart elements which you want to remove

Somehow, some numbers are appearing. Click the various numbers, press delete button.

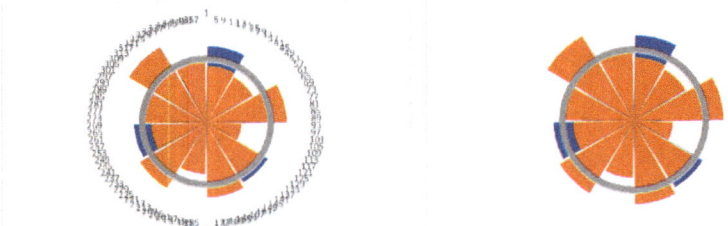

How to remove 'Shape Fill' and 'Shape Outline':

You will also see the following steps a lot in the later sections. Click a chart >>> Go to **Format** tab.

We will change the default setting of **Shape Fill** and **Shape Outline** of the chart.

- **Shape Fill** = No Fill
- **Shape Outline** = No Outline

How to remove Gridlines:

- Go to **View** tab and unclick **Gridlines**.

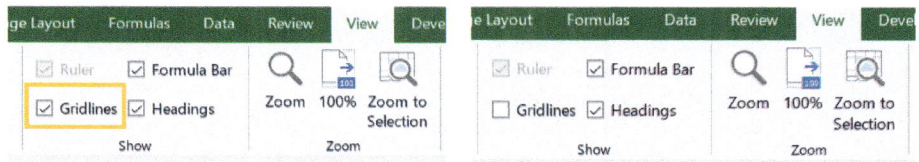

It is possible to create up to the below chart.

How to add a new series (for label) in the chart:

(Note) The new series will be used for label in the chart.
- In an empty cell, insert '30,30,30,30,30,30,30,30,30,30,30,30' (similar as donut chart)
- Copy '30,30,30,30,30,30,30,30,30,30,30,30' part.

- Select the chart
- Select **'Select Data'** after right-click of mouse button & click **'Add'**
- Paste '30,30,30,30,30,30,30,30,30,30,30,30' in **Series values** and click **OK**.
- Ignore '={1}' in **Series values**

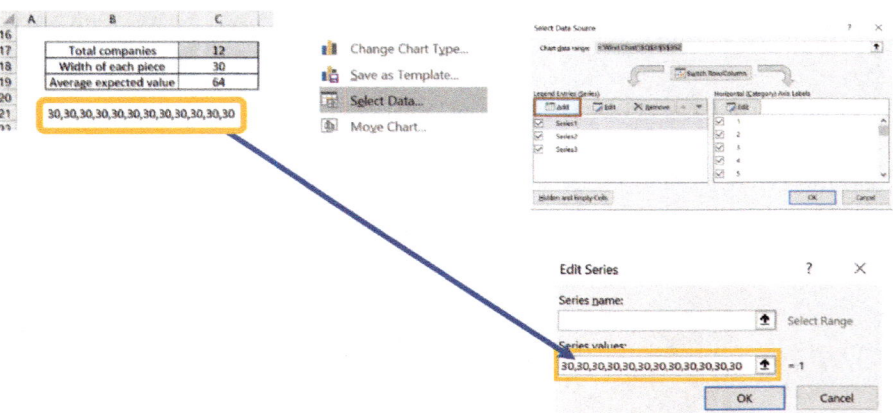

Click the chart and click a right-hand mouse button. Select **'Change Chart Type'**.

Go to **'Combo'** chart >>> **Series4 (=30, 30,30, 30, …):** **Doughnut**

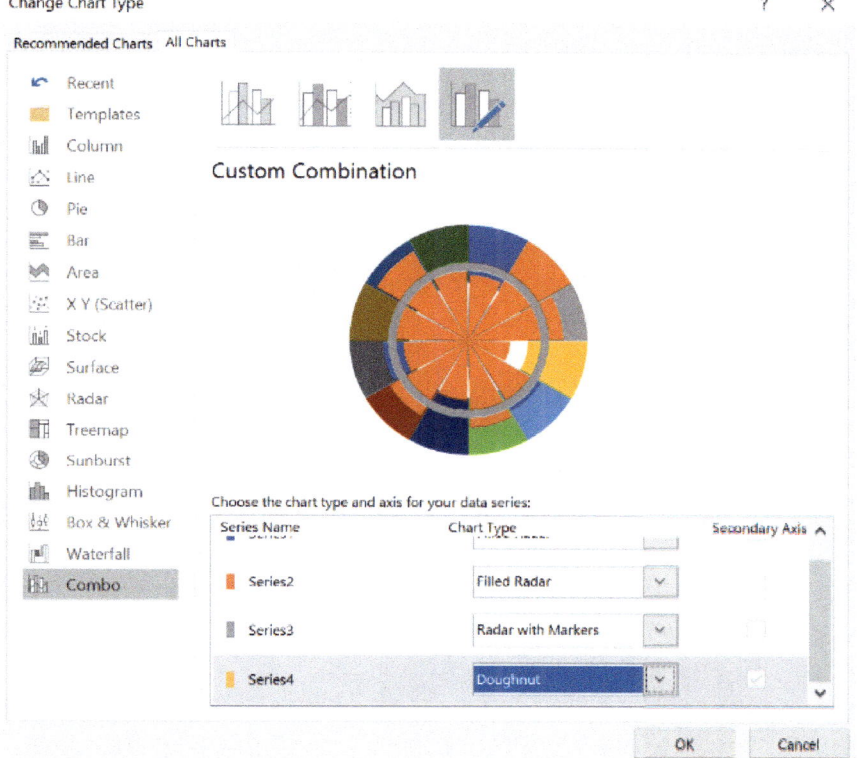

After selecting the doughnut chart, click **CTRL + 1** and
- Select '**No fill**'.
- Select **Doughnut Hole Size** = **90%**

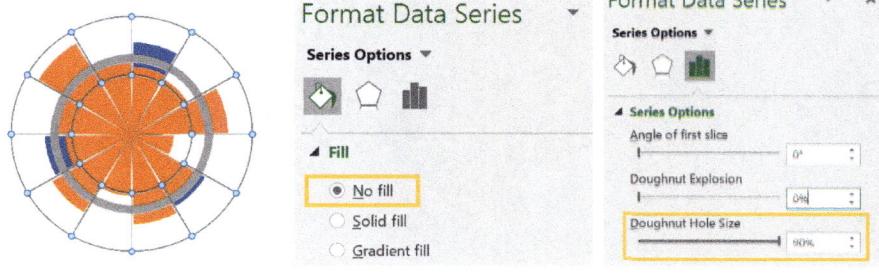

How to select the donut chart in the wind chart?

As mentioned before, the donut chart will be used for adding labels. However, it is quite difficult to select the donut chart. After selecting the doughnut chart, click **CTRL + 1** and go to **'Format Data Series'**.

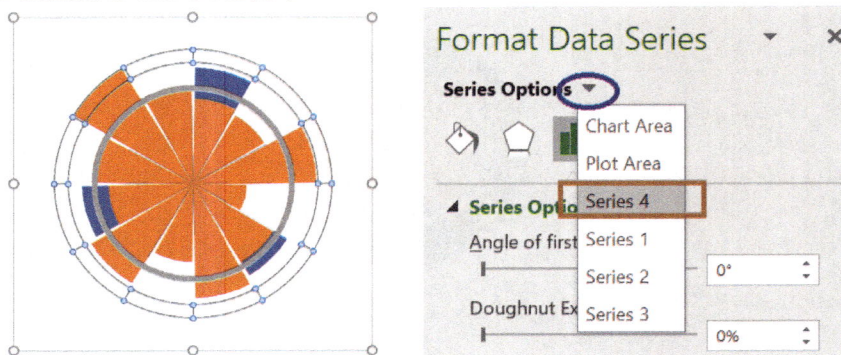

After selecting the Series 4 (Labels), click a right-hand mouse button and select **'Add Data Labels'**.

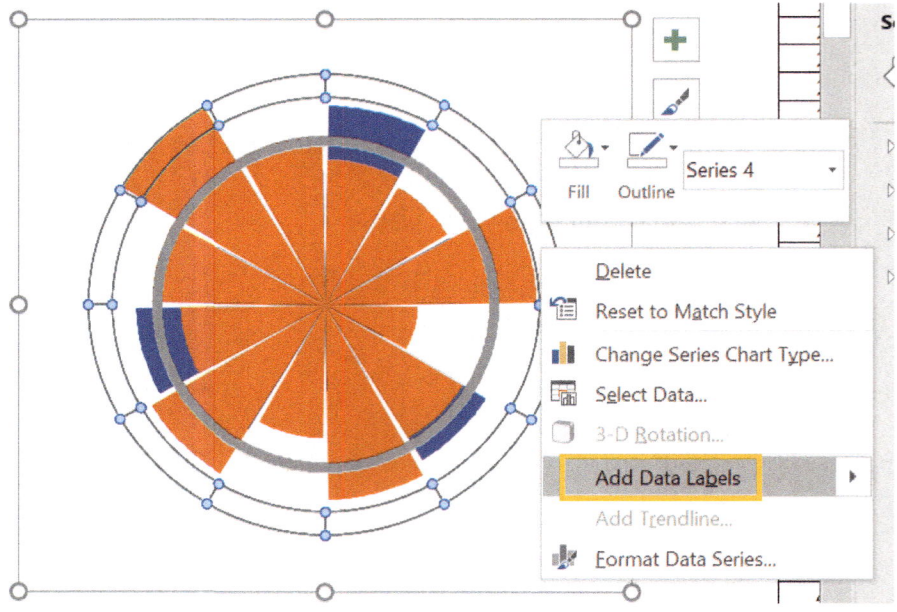

The following chart will appear.

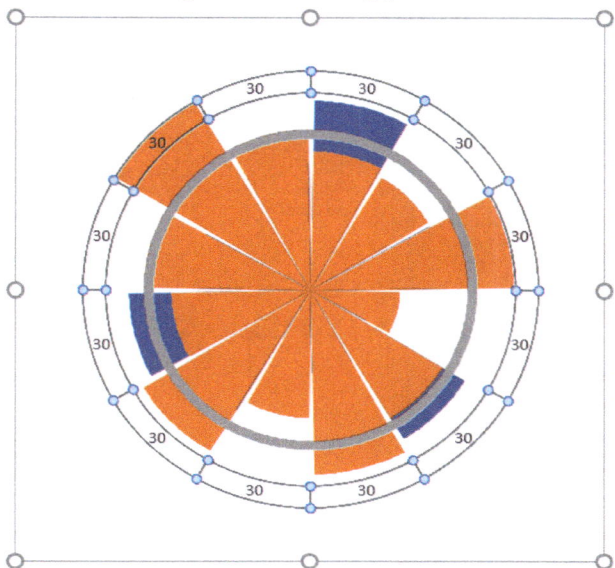

How to read label from the input table:

- Select labels (=30) in the chart and you can see like the below.

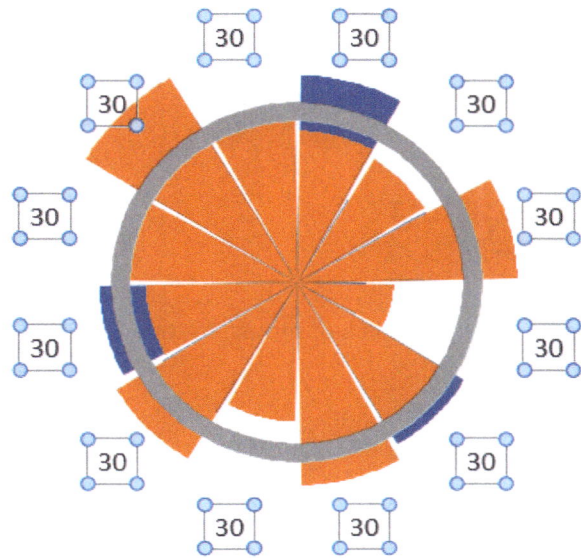

- Select **'Value From Cells'** in **'Format Data Labels'**.
- Select the label ranges from the input table (see below)

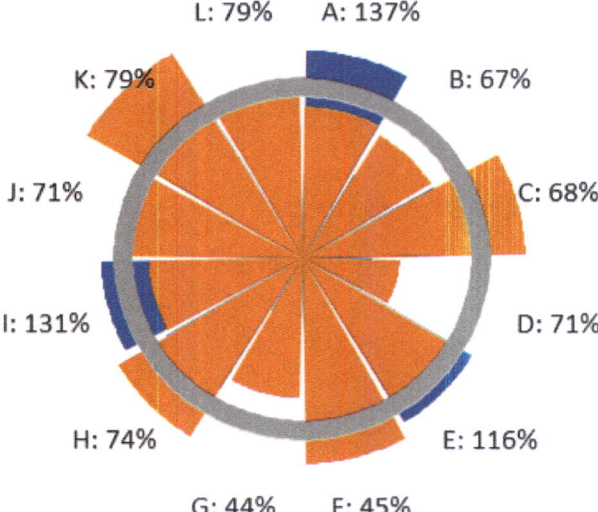

Re-adjusting series order.
- Select the chart
- Select **'Select Data'** after right-click of mouse button & click 'Series2 (=help2)'
- Put it on the top of series.

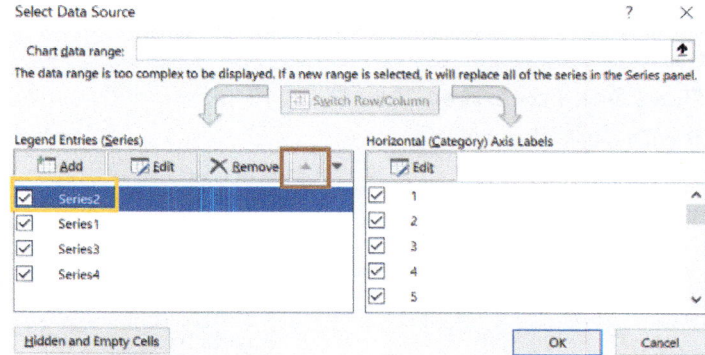

After changing the order, the actual values come front & the expected values set back in the wind chart. (please compare the above chart.)

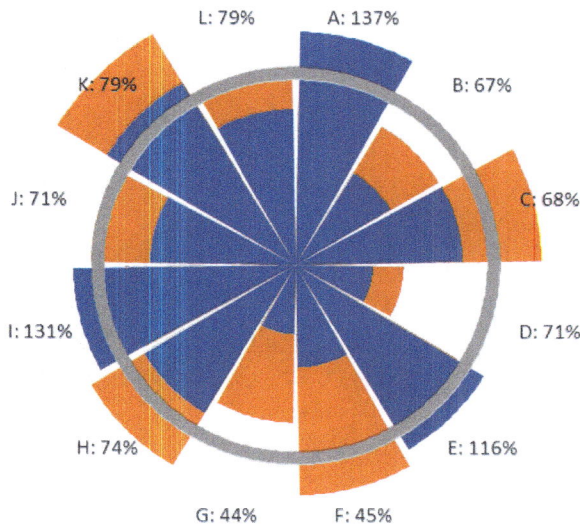

How to change the color in wind chart:

(Note) the following settings are based on the given example. It can be changeable by your personal preferences.

Settings for actual value:
- Select the **Actual value** pieces in the chart
- Click **CTRL+1** & Select **Marker**
- **Solid fill** with **Dark blue** color
- Transparency = **40%**

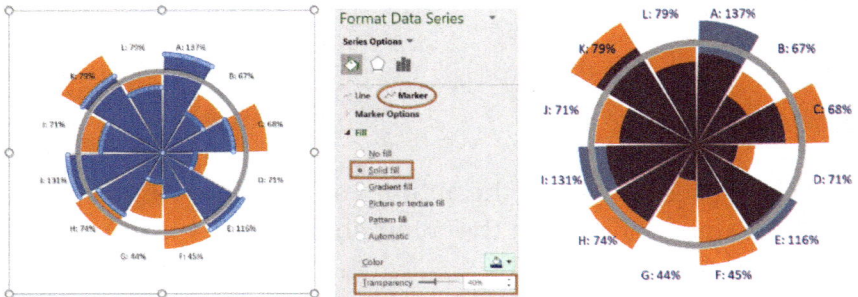

Settings for expected value:
- Select the **Expected value** pieces in the chart
- Click **CTRL+1** & Select **Marker**
- **Solid fill** with **Gray** color
- Transparency = **0%**

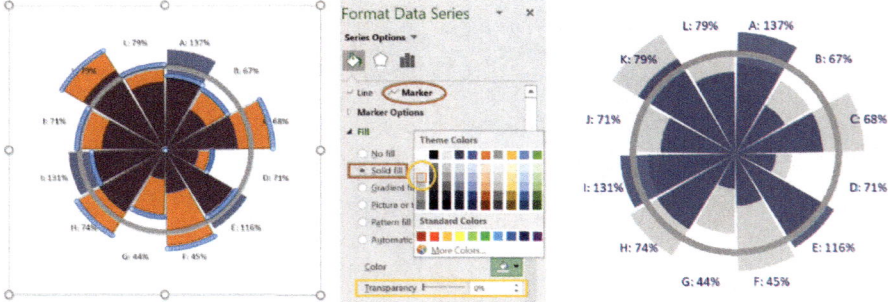

Settings for actual value:
In order to make the inside color more clearly, we need to add additional settings.
- Select the **Actual value** pieces in the chart
- Click **CTRL+1** & Select **Effect**
- **Presets** with the below inner effect (see below)
- Transparency = **50%**

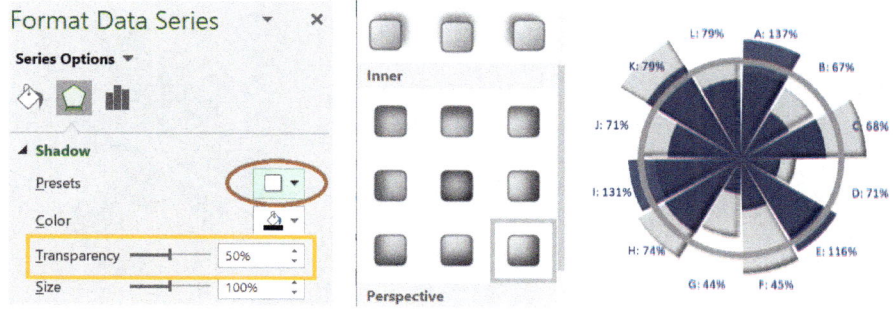

Settings for orange line (average expected value):
- Select the **Average value line** in the chart
- Click **CTRL+1** & Select **Marker Option = None**
- Select **Line** & **Solid line** with **Orange** color
- Dash type = **Square Dot**

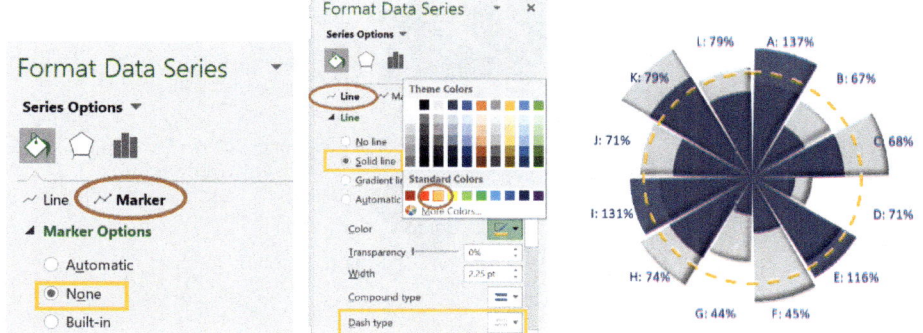

Settings for the lines for each piece:
- Select the **Actual value** pieces in the chart
- Click **CTRL+1** & Select **Line** & **Solid line** with **White** color
- Width = **1.5**

You can see the difference between before and after setting changes (see below).
It is possible to control the space of each piece with width.

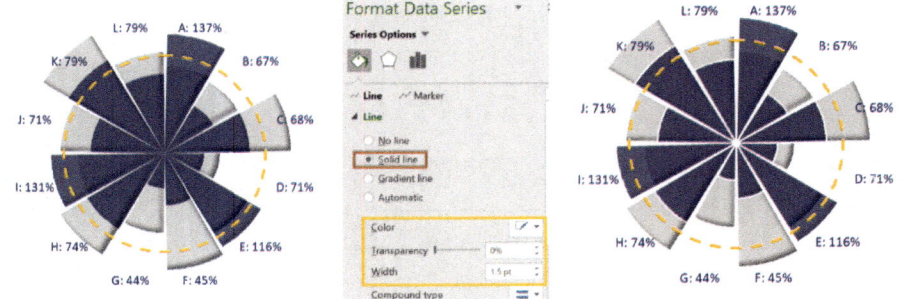

Finally, we can complete the wind chart.

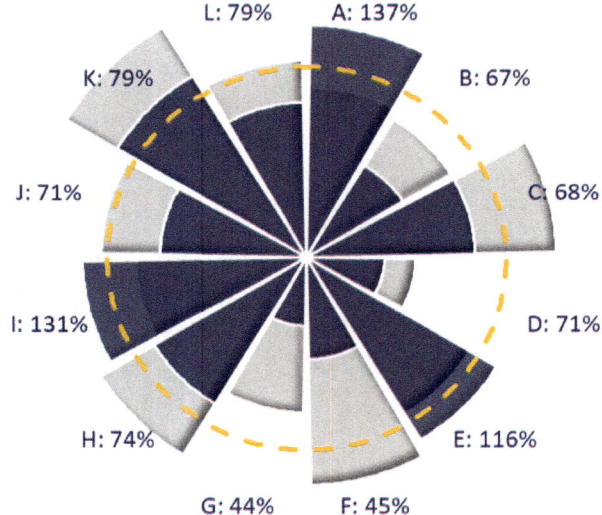

10. CIRCLE BUBBLE CHART

This chart consists of 2 parts.
- First part: how to use a circle chart
- Second part: to combine the circle chart & a bubble chart together with icon techniques.

On a circle chart:
In general, it is easy to create a linear or a bar chart by changing X & Y values. However, it is not easy to create a curve shape chart with X & Y value changes. In order to solve this problem, this chart has been introduced.
The circle chart looks like below:

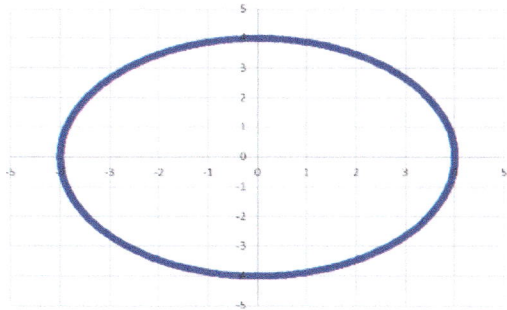

As a starting point, you do not need to worry about the Sin & Cos function in the circle chart at all. What we need to know is how to use this chart for creating a new chart.

More precisely, **the X & Y values from the circle chart will use as input values for a new curved-shape chart.** Therefore, there is no need to create this chart & the chart is already created.

How to use the circle chart:
- X axis: Horizontal move of the circle chart
- Y axis: Vertical move of the circle chart
- Radius: control the size of circle

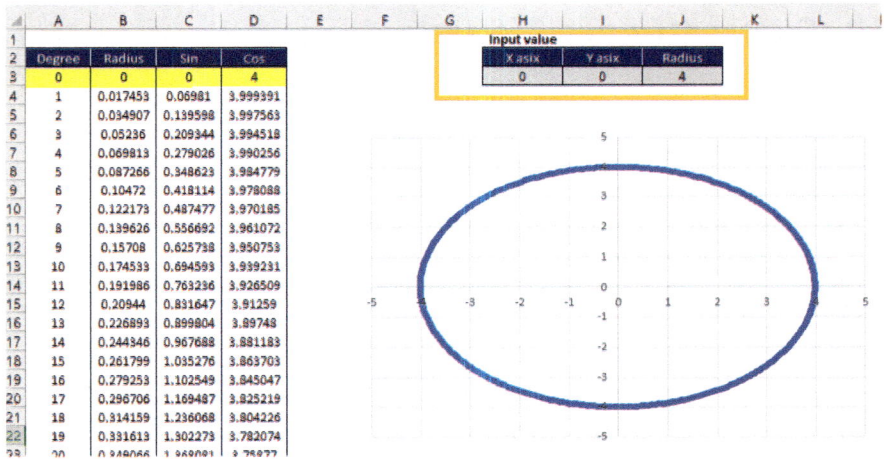

How to define a name:

We are going to create an input data table, so-called "**circle**" in this example.

- Select the entire range from row 2 to row 368.
- Go to the cell-location-showing box (see below)
- Hit "Enter" button
- You can find "circle" in this box.
- If you select it, the pre-defined range is selected.

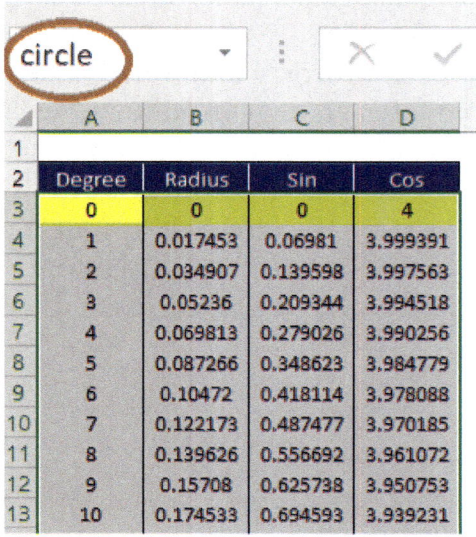

How to build input-reading tool:

`fx  =VLOOKUP($B8,circle,2,FALSE)`

The above formula is 0.3839724 Radius cell. B8 is 22.

Function Arguments		? ×
VLOOKUP		
Lookup_value	$B8	= 22
Table_array	circle	= {0,0,0,4;1,0.0174532925199433,0.06980962...
Col_index_num	2	= 2
Range_lookup	FALSE	= FALSE
		= 0.383972435

Looks for a value in the leftmost column of a table, and then returns a value in the same row from a column you specify. By default, the table must be sorted in an ascending order.

Lookup_value is the value to be found in the first column of the table, and can be a value, a reference, or a text string.

Extend the formula until Y values.

By using the below table, we are able to call any X, Y & Radius values from the "circle" table depends on the degree inputs (yellow part)

Input Degree	Radius	X asix Sin	Y asix Cos	Bubble Size
0	0	0	4	0
22	0.3839724	1.498426374	3.7087354	400
55	0.9599311	3.276608177	2.2943057	200

How to create a half circle by using a scatter plot:

By using this tool, plug in 0,22, ..., 180 in degree. We can obtain corresponding input values.

Input Degree	Radius	X asix Sin	Y asix Cos	Bubble Size
0	0	0	4	0
22	OOKUP($B8,c	1.498426374	3.7087354	400
55	0.9599311	3.276608177	2.2943057	200
90	1.5707963	4	2.45E-16	800
125	2.1816616	3.276608177	-2.294306	300
158	2.7576202	1.498426374	-3.708735	500
180	3.1415927	4.90059E-16	-4	0

Next, select a **scatter plot** from chart type (after selecting input ranges).

Input		X asix	Y asix	Bubble
Degree	Radius	Sin	Cos	Size
0	0	0	4	0
22	0.3839724	1.498426374	3.7087354	400
55	0.9599311	3.276608177	2.2943057	200
90	1.5707963	4	2.45E-16	800
125	2.1816616	3.276608177	-2.294306	300
158	2.7576202	1.498426374	-3.708735	500
180	3.1415927	4.90059E-16	-4	0

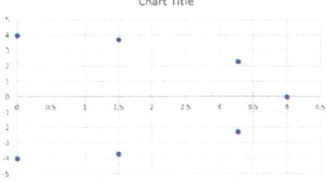

Clean chart elements in scatter plot
- **Shape Fill** = No Fill
- **Shape Outline** = No Outline

The half-circle chart is completed.
(Note) If you want to make more dots, simply extend the table.

Select the last row (like below), drag the small square by mouse.

158	2.75702	1.498420571	-3.70875342	100
180	3.141593	4.9006E-16	-4	0

Applied example: Combine the half circle with circle Icon

You might remember the transparent circle icon which we made in the previous section.
- Click the circle icon >>> **Ctrl + C**
- Click the scatter plot dot in the chart >>> **Ctrl + V**

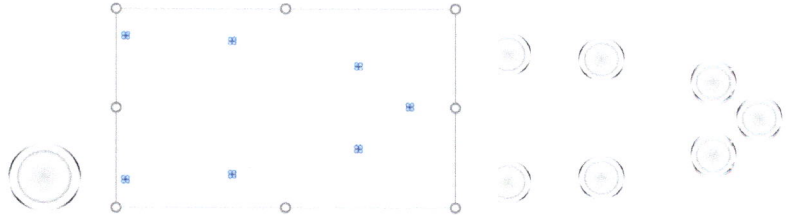

From the above last picture, the shape of chart is a bit awkward. Therefore, the size of chart is adjusted by a mouse.

In this example, we actually need only 5 dots. Therefore, we reduced the input values from 7 to 5 values.

Input		X asix	Y asix	Bubble
Degree	Radius	Sin	Cos	Size
0	0	0	10	0
22	0.3839724	3.746065934	9.2718385	400
55	0.9599311	8.191520443	5.7357644	200
90	1.5707963	10	6.126E-16	800
125	2.1816616	8.191520443	-5.735764	300
158	2.7576202	3.746065934	-9.271839	500
180	3.1415927	1.22515E-15	-10	0

Combining 'half circle' with 'circle icon' part is completed.

Applied Example1:

The target chart looks like below:
- The donut figure represents total percentage (%) of a gender or a region
- Each small bubble & horizontal bar means the percentage for each generation or group.

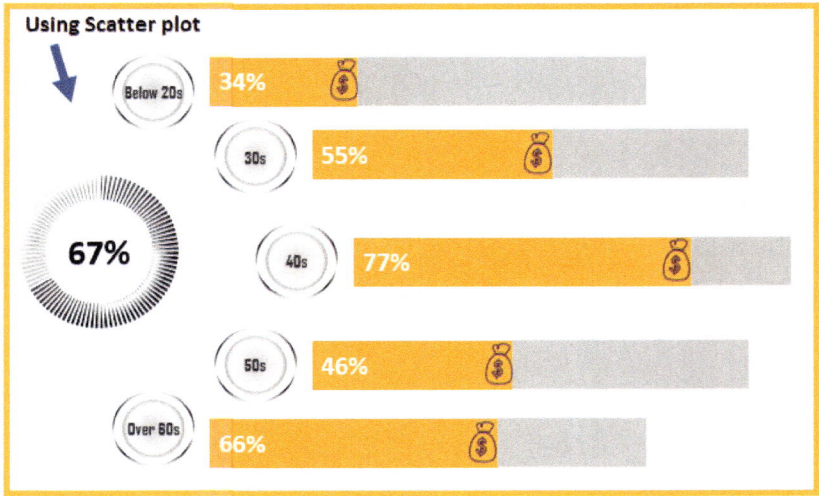

In terms of structure: it consists of
- 3D Donut chart
- Circle bubble chart (we learnt this section)
- Icon horizontal bar chart

In fact, it looks quite nice. If we use this chart in the report, it might give a good impression of the data analysis.

How to make this chart:

The way to make this chart is quite simple and straightforward.
- Copy and paste the 3 charts (incl. input values) into one sheet and grouping it.
- The most time-consuming part would be re-linking input values and the corresponding charts.

The detail explanation of how to change linkage between input values and charts will omit because this is just changing input values correctly. Please refer to the Excel file for further details.

In addition, it is possible to create more than a half circle shape as well. Altough we do not create the actual chart, it is a useful method to create a non-liner shape chart eaisily. Please find the 2 examples.

Applied Example2: Applying Bubble chart:

If you want to contain more information into the chart, we can use a bubble chart instead of scatter plot. Compared to the scatter plot, it is possible to add more series (or information). See below table.

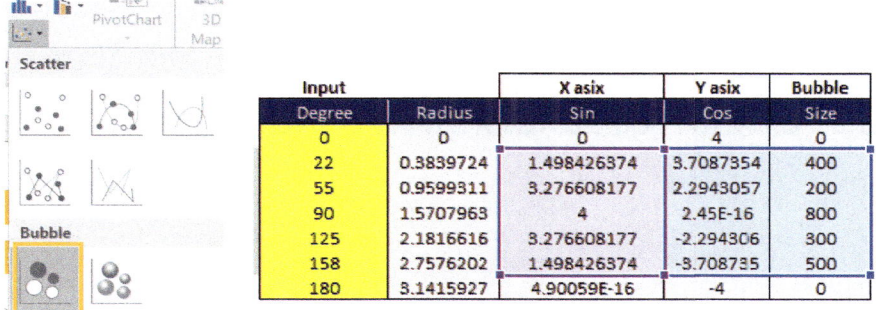

By using the input "**Size**", the size of bubble can be changeable.

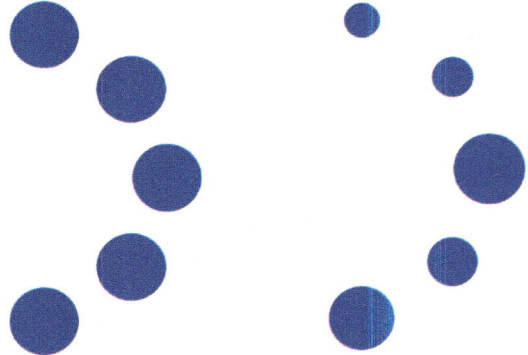

(Note) if the size of bubble is changing, the combined chart shape is also changing.
In order to avoid this situation, click one of the axes in the chart.
- Click **CTRL+1** & Go to **Format Axis**
- Fixed Min = **-5** & Max bound = **5**
- Set **Radius** (=4) **value** is **Bound +1**

In the below picture, the axis range intentionally shows for the explanation.

After fixing the bound, remove the axis in chart element.

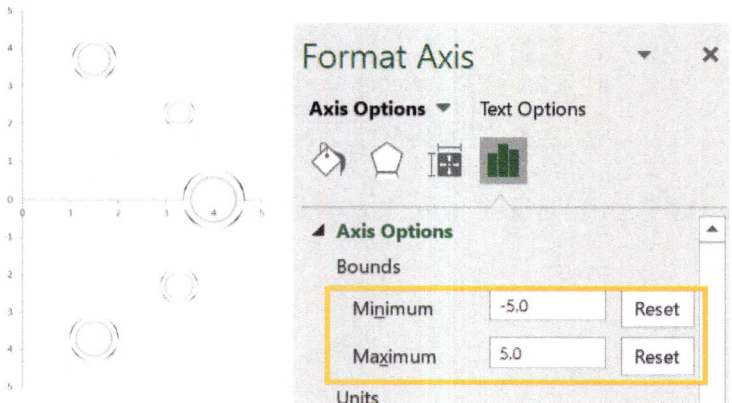

The rest of processes are identical as the previous section.

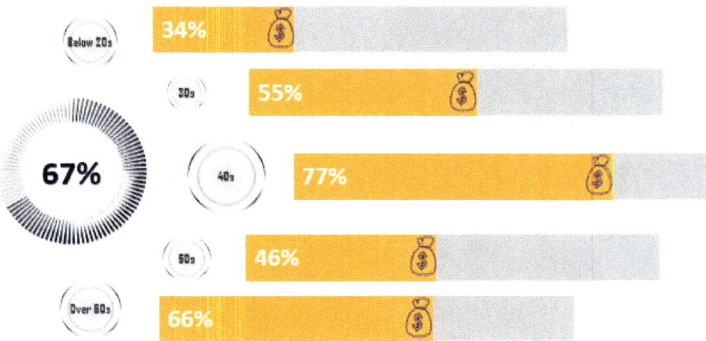

Applied Example3: How to use photo into the chart:

In this section, we will put the photos into the bubbles in a scatter plot. For example, if you want to use your company logo, it is possible to apply by using this technique.
- Select the bubble (=scatter plots) by clicking a mouse
    - one click = select all plots
    - double click = select one plot

- Select the circle icon & **CRTL+1** >>> Go to **Format Data Series**
- Select **Picture or texture fill**
- Click **Insert** >>> click **"From a file"** >>> Choose your own picture.

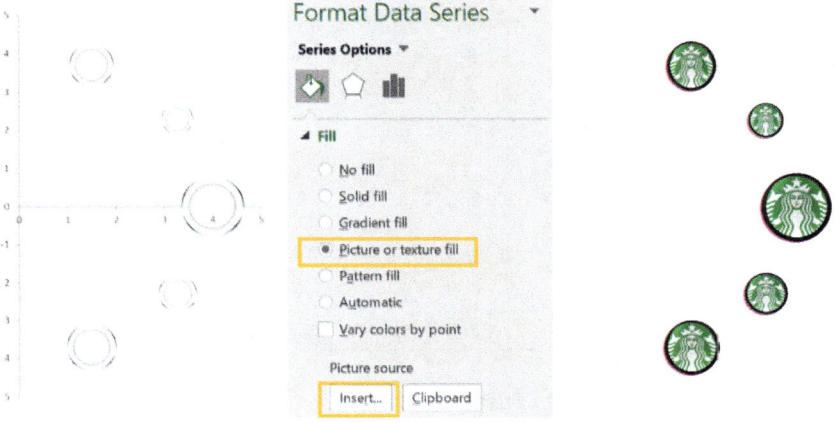

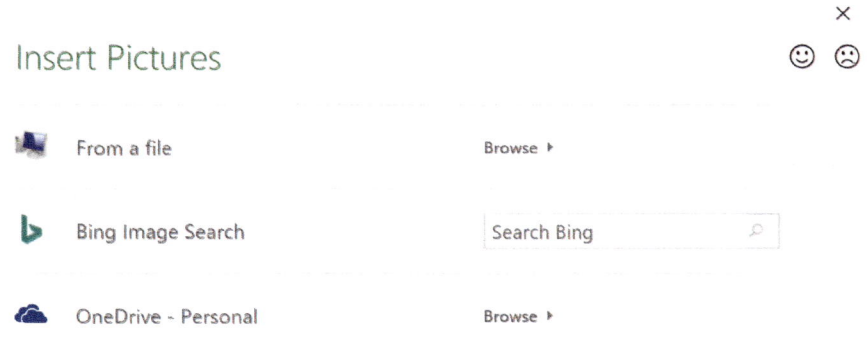

If we apply this method, it is not possible to put label in inside of the icon circle.

In order to solve this problem, we need to switch the location label.

- Click the icon circle which you want to add labels
- Click right-hand side mouse button >>> Click **'Add Data Labels'**.
- Go to **Format Data Labels** >>> Select "**Value from Cells**" in Label Options
- Select **the actual values** from the input table.
- Put **Label Position** = **Right**

It is completed for the chart.

Copyright issue with photo:

Lastly, the copyright is a big issue these days. However, there are some possibilities to walk away this issue. You can use the photo from the below sites without copyright issue for commercial use.

Just in case, kindly please re-check the guideline of copyright again. This is because they can change their policy.

https://www.cleanpng.com/

11. Error Bar chart

3 Error Bar chart will be tackled in this section. The first target chart looks like below:

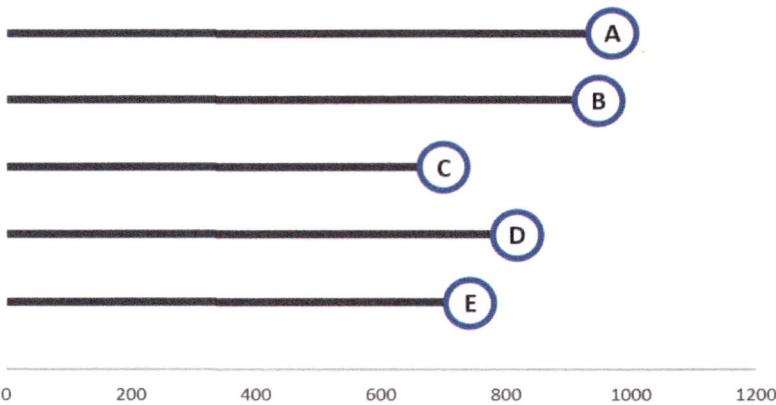

Where we can use:

The chart will be useful to compare the performance or sale figures among multiple groups.
The chart comparatively looks more nicer than a normal bar chart. (See below)

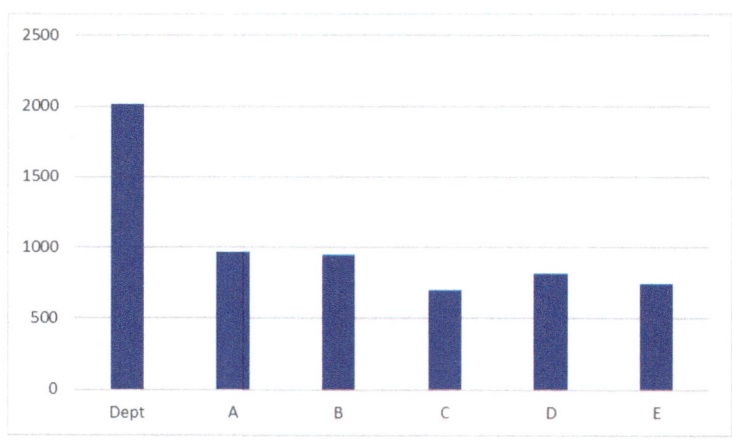

How to remove Gridlines:

Go to **View** tab and unclick **Gridlines**.

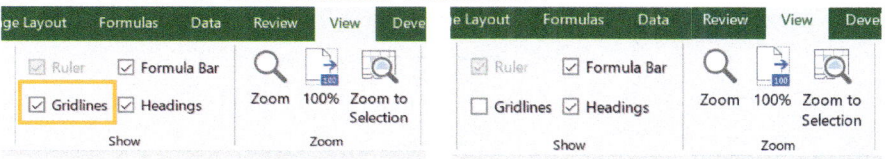

How to create input values in Error Bar chart:

First, we will create a new input table which includes input values and the Y axis (=helping values).
The input values are presented by percentage (%) because of common usage in reports. It is normally easy to communicate.

For the supporting values,
- The last value (= E dept) set **0.5**.
- **Add 0.5** more for other value. (E = 0.5, D = 1, C= 1.5, until A = 2.5) reversely
- Y axis values will be used for y values in a scatter plat later.

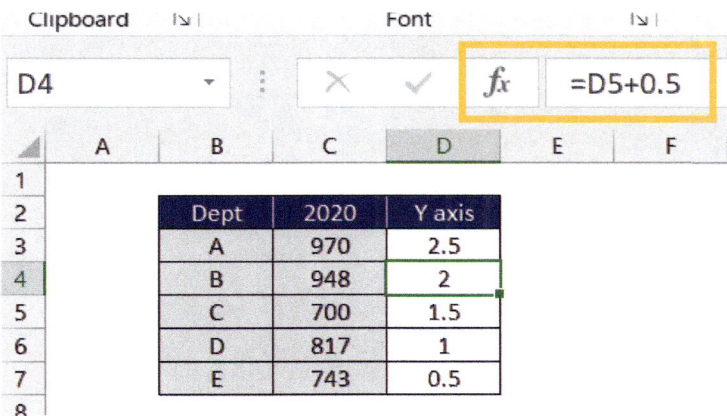

How to create a scatter plot:

Select input range and '**Scatter plot**' in **Insert** tab. Remove all chart elements except horizontal axis.

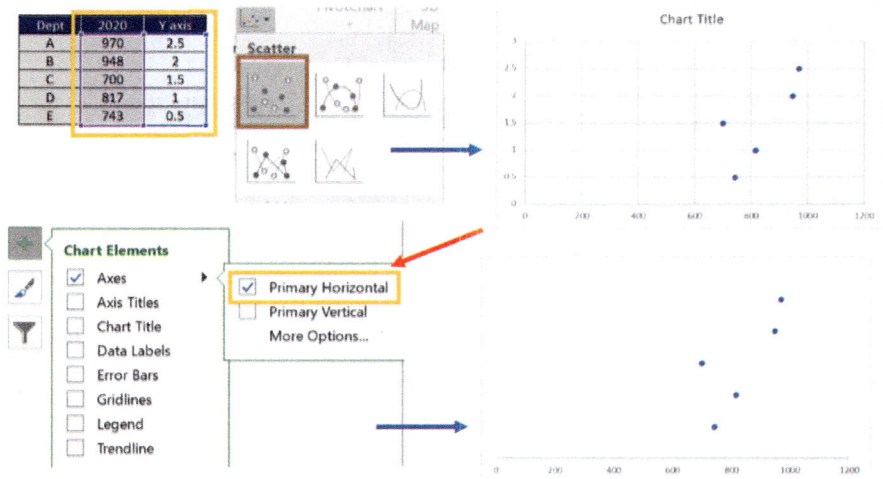

How to make a bubble in scatter plot:

- Click plots (select all points) & **CTRL+1**
- Click **Marker** & Built-in, circle and Size = **21**
- Click **Fill** & Solid fill & Color = **white**
- Click **Border** & Solid fill & Color = **purple**, Width = **2.75**

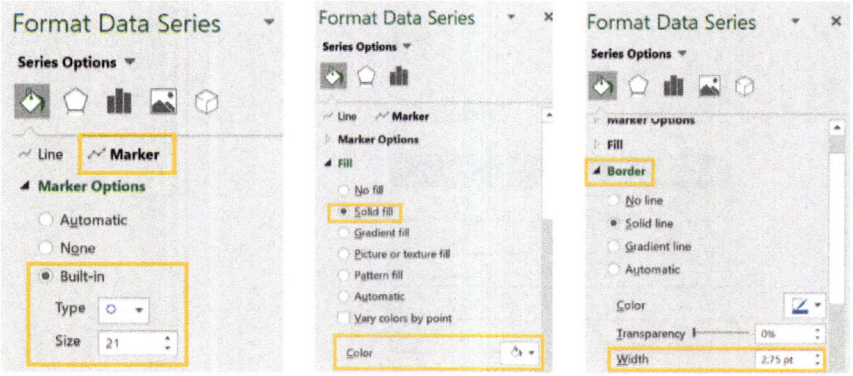

Simply, we can have the following chart.

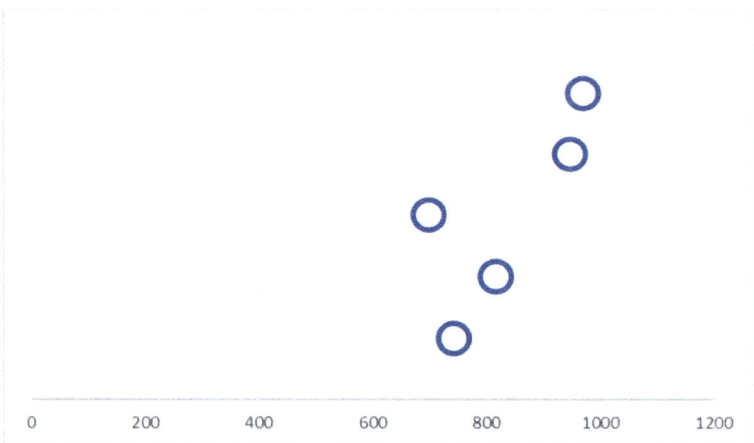

How to use Error Bar functionality:

- Click chart element (plus sign) in the chart.
- Select '**Error Bars**' & '**More Options…**'
- Select a small triangle & Select '**X Error Bars**'
- Select **Minus** & **No Cap**

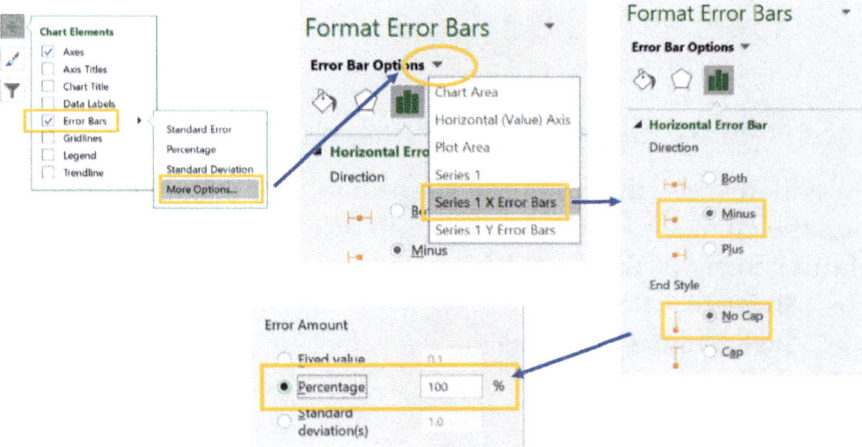

We can have a left-hand side chart below. Click a vertical Error Bars and remove them.

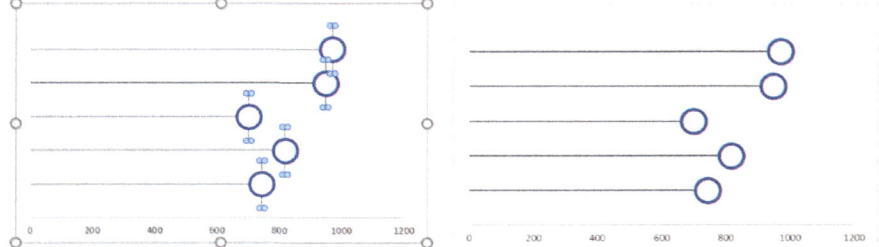

Select the **Error Bars (=lines attached the scatter plot)** in chart. Adjust the format of the lines.

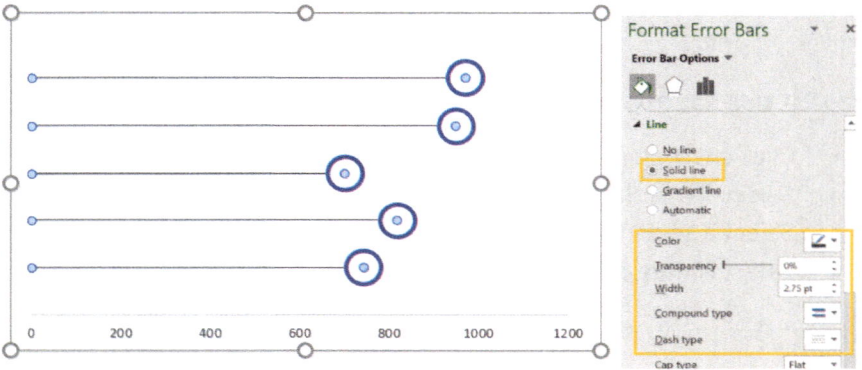

How to remove 'Shape Fill' and 'Shape Outline':

You will also see the following steps a lot in the later sections. Click the chart >>> Go to **Format** tab. We will change the default setting of Shape Fill and Shape Outline of the chart.
- **Shape Fill** = No Fill
- **Shape Outline** = No Outline

How to add Label in Error Bars:

- Click the scatter plot which you want to add labels
- Click **CTRL +1** >>> Click **'Add Data Labels'**.
- Go to **Format Data Labels** >>> Select **"Value from Cells"**
- Select **the actual values** from the input table. Click **OK**.

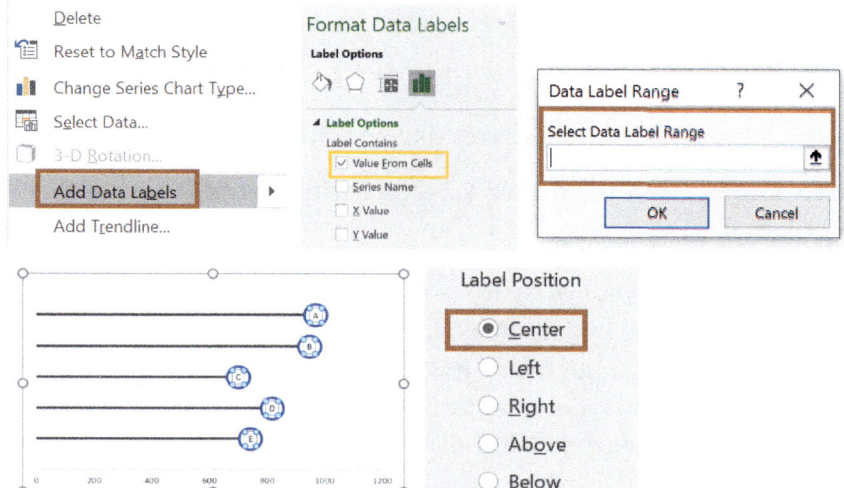

We can complete the base error bar chart.

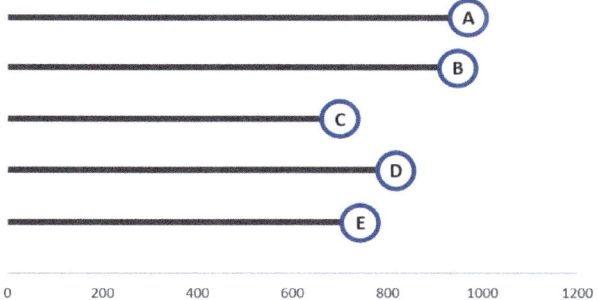

Applied example1:

The target chart looks like below. 4 companies have the same sale target.

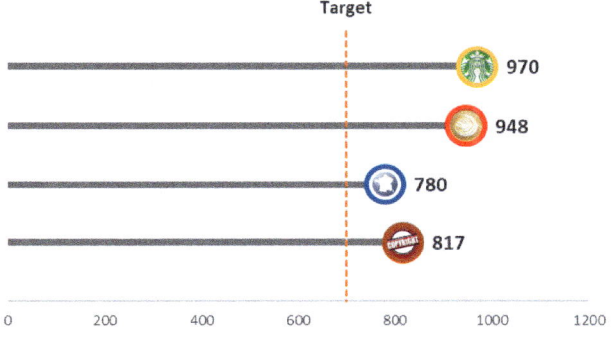

In order to create this chart, we need to add a new series for adding the target line.

Adding new inputs into Error Bar chart:

Create a new Target input & Y2 axis input in the input table (see below).

- For a new target (=700), it is a fixed common value which represents the target value for all companies.
- For Y2 axis (in input table), it will be used for Y values for Target value as a new series in a scatter plot.
    - Starting with **2.3** and increased by **0.5**.

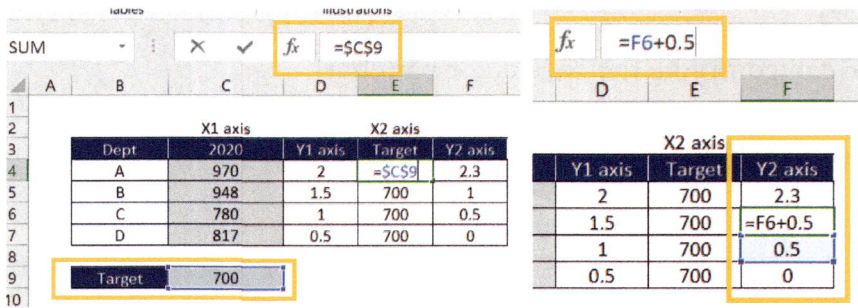

How to add the new series into the chart:

Click the chart & right-hand mouse button and select '**Select Data**'.

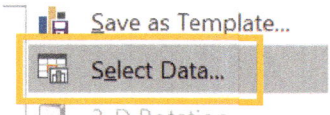

Add a new series and define this series like below.
- X values = **Target values** (E column)
- Y values = **Y2 axis values** (F column)

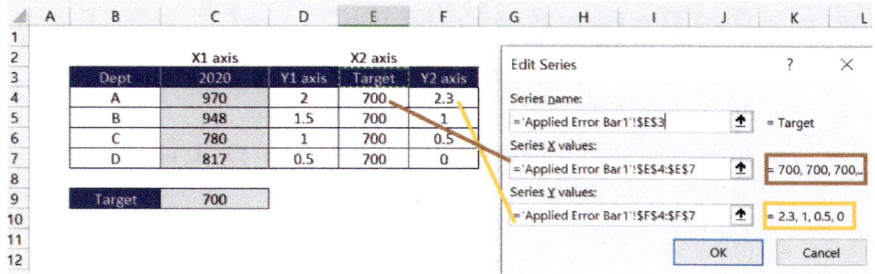

How to switch from scatter plot to Combo chart:

In order to do so, select the chart and click a right-hand mouse button.
- Go to **Change Series Chart Type** (see below) and
- Change chart type **Target series** from '**Scatter**' to '**Scatter with smooth Line**'

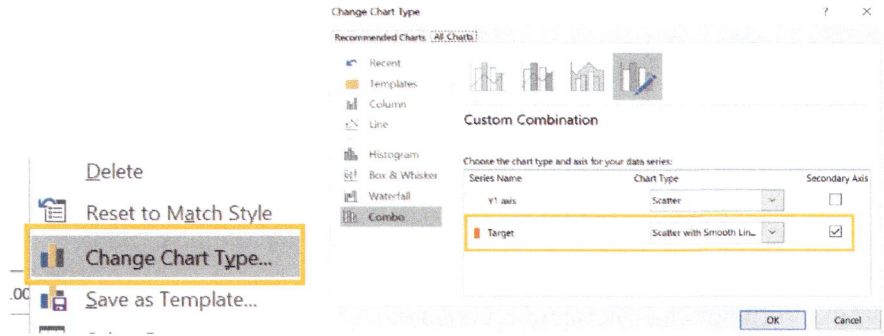

After click OK, we can see the new vertical line in the chart.

How to control the position of the vertical line (= Target line):

You can control the height of Target line by the starting value of Y2 axis input.
In this example, **2.3** is used for the control of Target line's height.

How to adjust the format of target line:

- Click the line in the line and **CTRL+1**
- Go to **Format Data Series** and select **Solid line**.
- For the detail settings, please see below. (you can change these formats by your preferences)

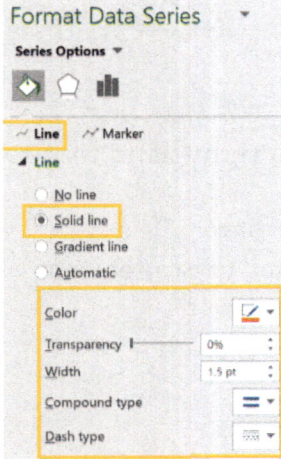

How to add the letter "Target" in the target line:

- Click **only the top dot** from the target line **by double clicking** of the top dot.
- With holding the top dot, click a right-hand mouse button.
- Go to '**Format Data Label**' and select '**Value From Cells**'.
- Click '**Select Range**' and select **one cell** which contains the letter 'Target'.
- Go to **Label Position** and select '**Above**'. OK.

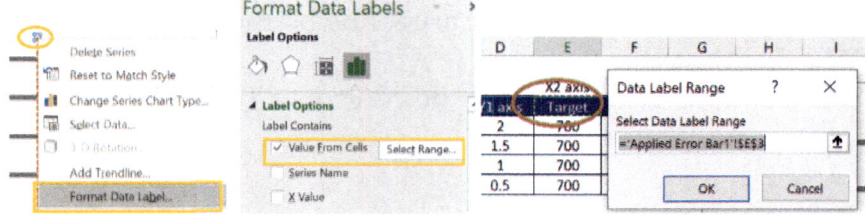

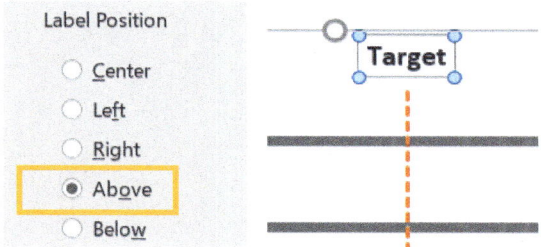

How to use photo into the chart:

Now, we will put the photos into the bubbles in a scatter plot. For example, if you want to use your company logo, it is possible to apply by using this technique.
- Select the bubble (=scatter plots) by clicking a mouse
    - one click = select all plots
    - double clicks = select one plot

- **CRTL+1** & Go to **Format Data Series**
- Select **Picture or texture fill**
- Click **Insert** >>> click "**From a file**" >>> Choose your own picture.

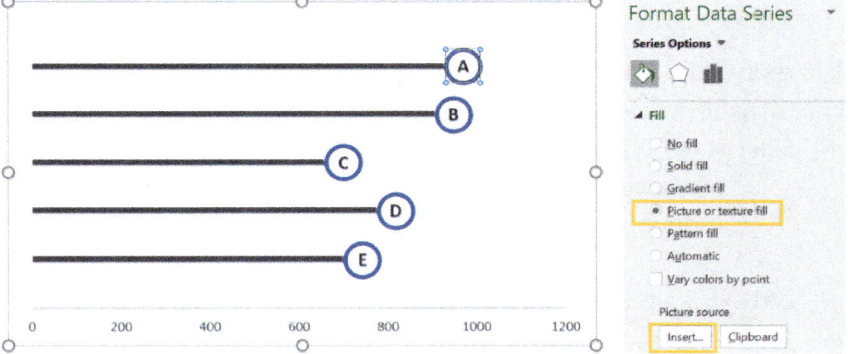

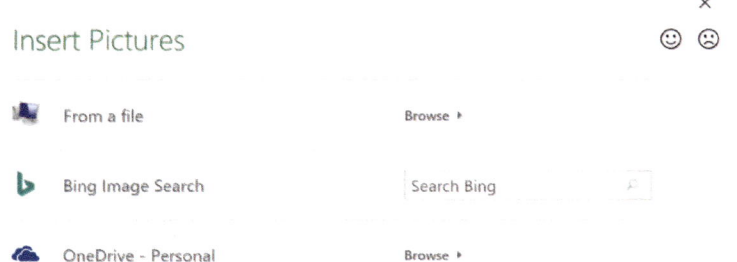

After applying this method, it is not possible to put labels (A, B, C, D, E) in inside of the icon circle.
In order to solve this problem, we need to switch the location label.

- Click the icon circle which you want to add labels
- Click right-hand side mouse button >>> Click **'Add Data Labels'**.
- Go to **Format Data Labels** >>> Select "**Value from Cells**" in Label Options
- Select **the actual values** from the input table.
- Put **Label Position** = **Right**

In this example, a new border line of marker (=color of scatter plot) is applied due to each logo color.
- Select the bubble (=scatter plots) by clicking a mouse
    - one click = select all plots
    - double clicks = select one plot

- **CRTL+1** & Go to **Format Data Point**
- Select **Marker** & **Solid line**
- Choose the color which you like

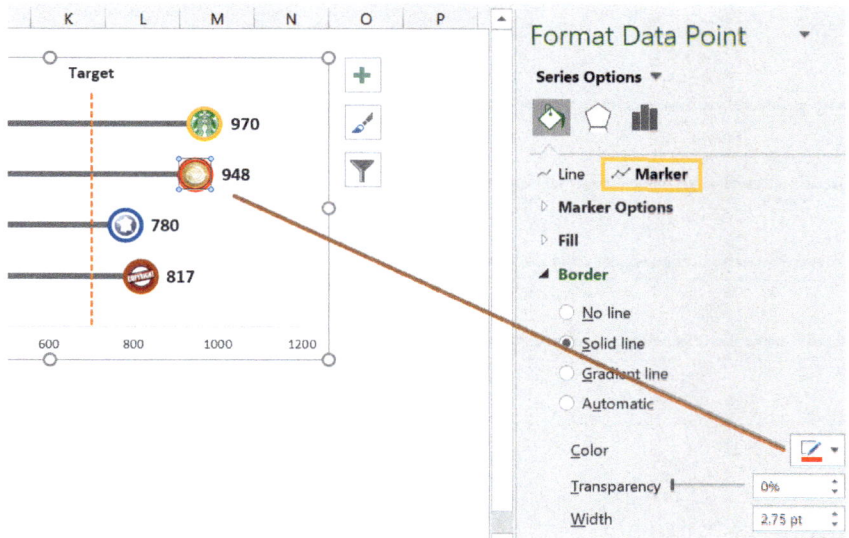

Finally, we can create a chart with a target line & each company logo in the chart.

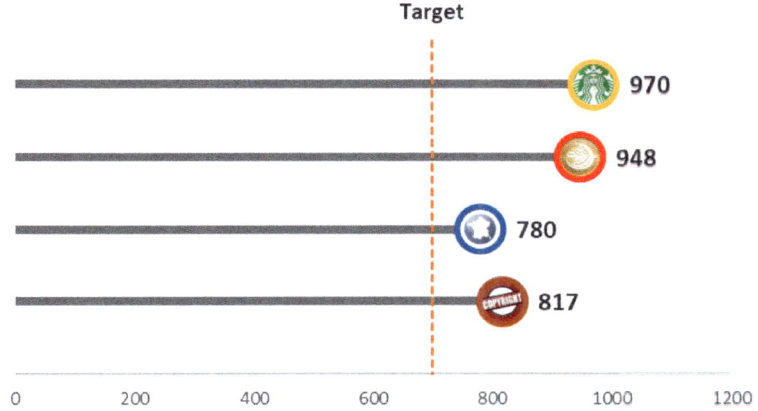

Applied examples 2:

In this example, we assume that each company has **a different target value**.
The dash line (below the bold line) represents each company's target line.

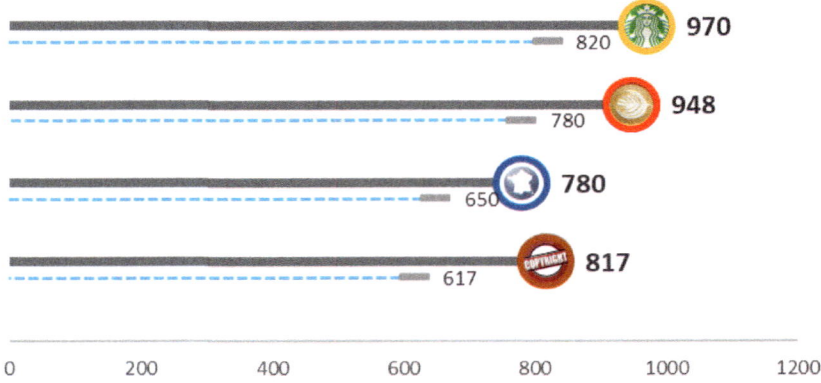

Applied examples 3:

In this example, we assume that each company has **a different target value** and also has **a common target line or an average line** (=vertical dashed line).

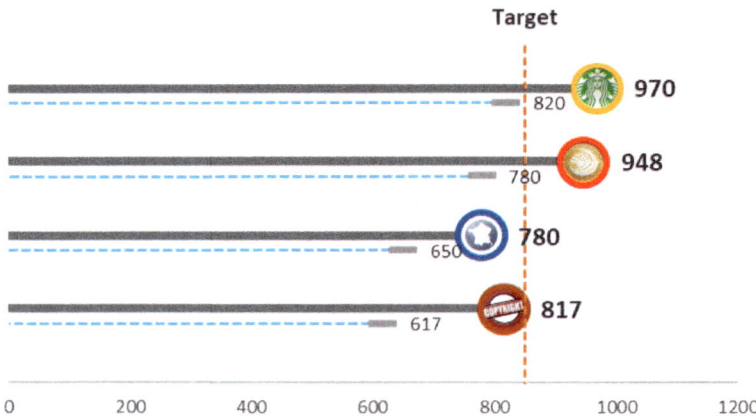

(Note) The main difference between example 2 & 3 is to have a common target line or not.

In case of the common target line, how to make it is already explained earlier. Therefore, we will only tackle how to make an individual target line in the chart.

A good starting is an applied example1. You can easily create example 2 & 3 from 1.

For example2, remove target line. For example3, keep the target line.

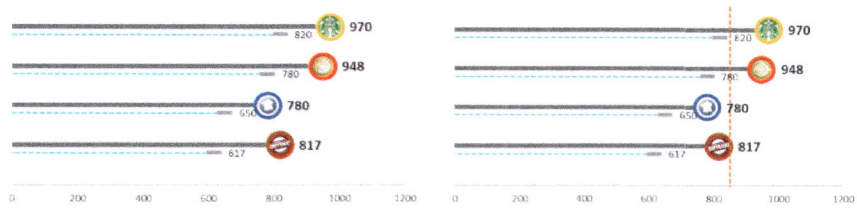

How to make an individual target line:

First, insert the expected input values into input table. Please note that we will use Y1 axis as a main vertical value for the chart.

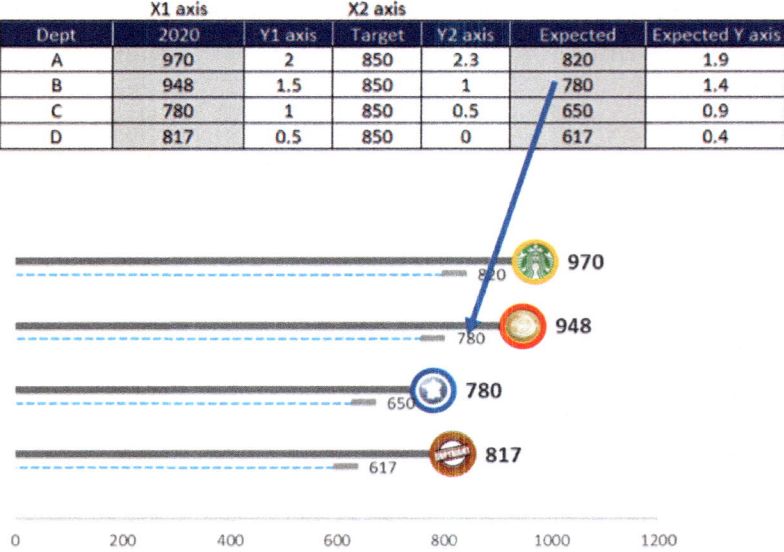

Adding the 2nd Y axis value into Error Bar chart:

The 2nd Y axis will be located below the existing Y axis. Therefore, the input for the 2nd Y axis is Y1 axis input -0.1 (**=Y1 input - 0.1**). If you want put the above, please use +0.1.

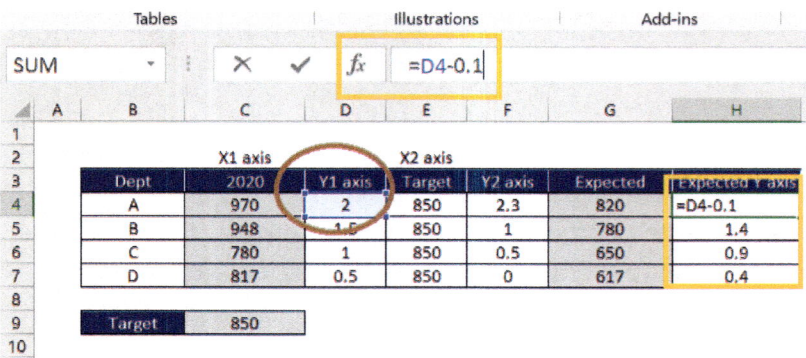

How to add the new series into the chart:

Click the chart & right-hand mouse button and select '**Select Data**'.

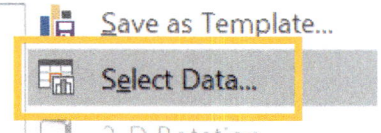

Add a new series and define this series like below.
- X values = **Expected values** (G column)
- Y values = **Expected Y axis values** (H column)

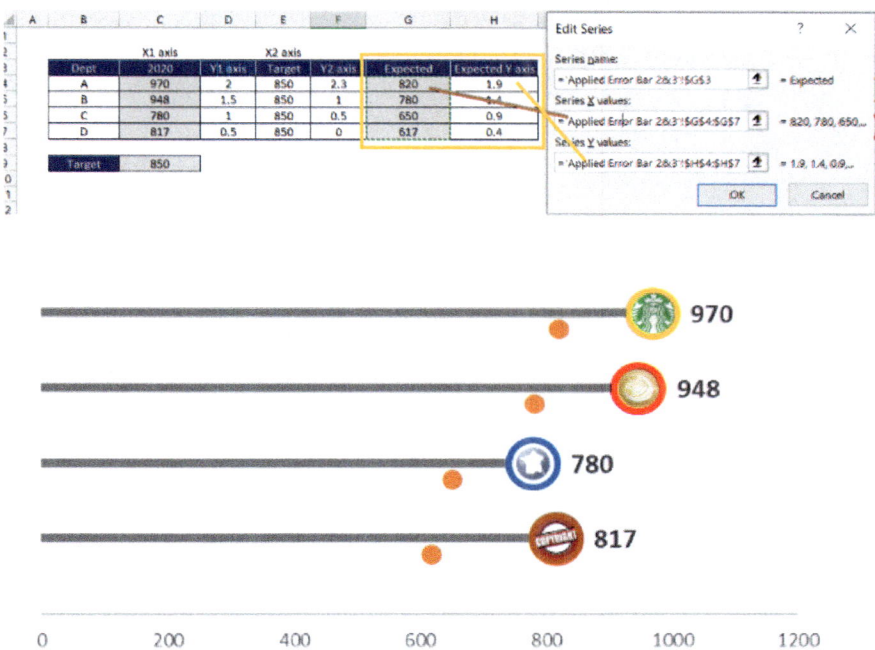

We can see a new series of dots in the chart. (See above)
- Click & select the new expected values (select all points) & **CTRL+1**
- Click **Marker** & Built-in, circle and Size = **12**
- Choose the type which you like.

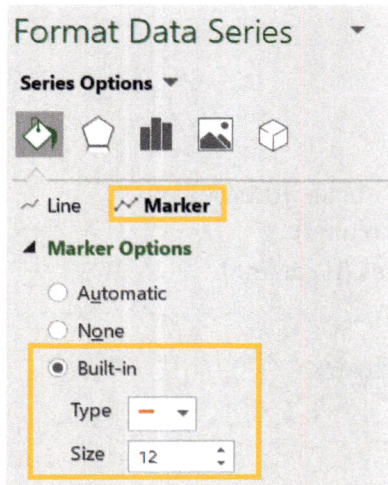

How to use Error Bar functionality:

The way how to create the Error Bar lines is very similar as what we made it before.

- Click & select the expected values.
- Click chart element (plus sign) in the chart.
- Select '**Error Bars**' & '**More Options...**'
- Select a small triangle & Select '**Expected**' (new series)
- Select **Minus** & **No Cap**

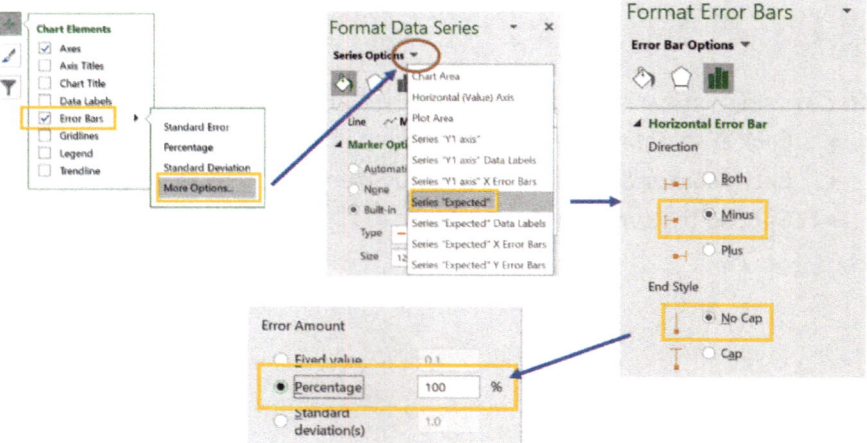

- Click a vertical Error Bars in the chart and **remove vertical Error Bars**.
- Select the error bars and adjust the format of error bars in '**Format Error Bars**'.

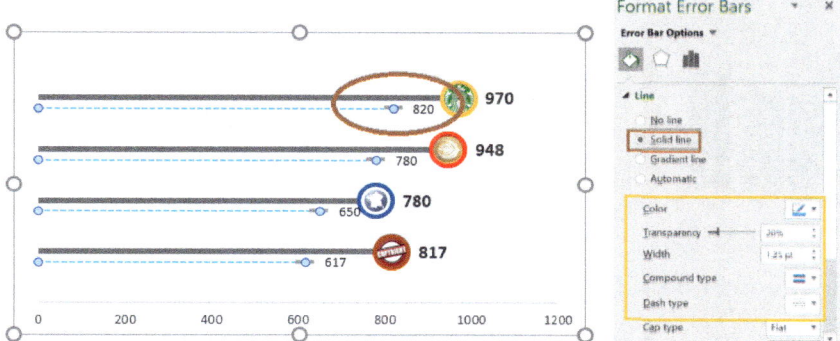

We complete the applied error bar chart.

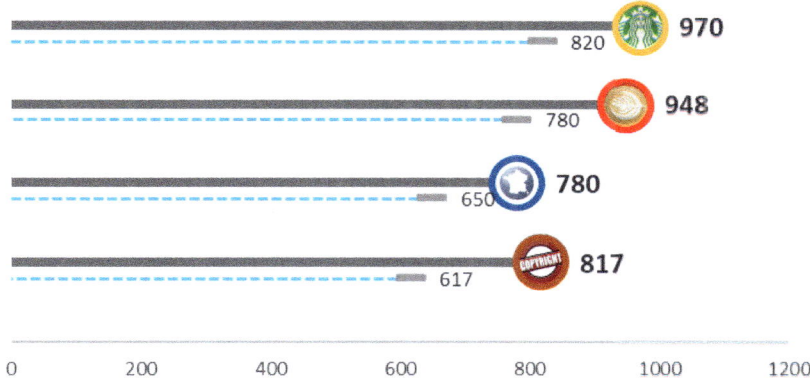

12. WAFFLE CHART

In this section, the target chart looks like below. Compared to the bulit-in bar char, the waffle looks more fancy.

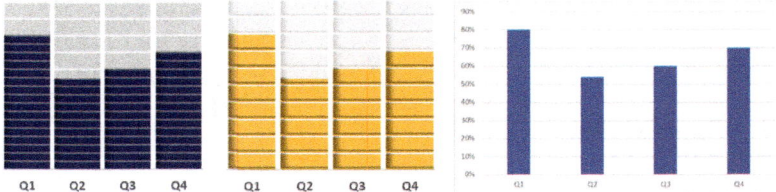

One of main benefits of this chart is:

Once you made a right-square shape of any image, you can directly apply these right-square images to charts.

How to create 2-D Clustered bar chart:

After selecting inputs (i.e. input value & max value), go to **Insert** tab.
Select **2-D bar >>> Clustered Bar**. The Max value (100%) represents the maximum range of bar chart.

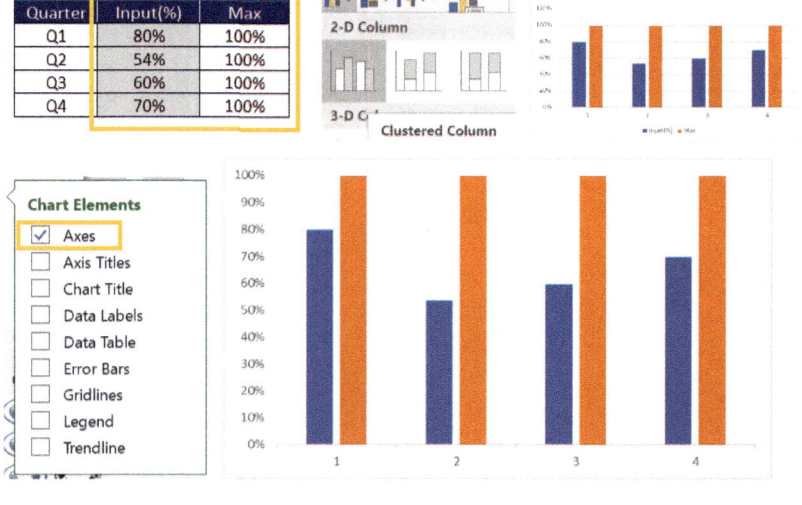

How to change the range of Axis:

- Click an Axis in the chart and then **CTRL + 1**
- Go to **Bounds** in **Axis Options** in **Format Axis** and change **Min: 0** & **Max values: 1.0**

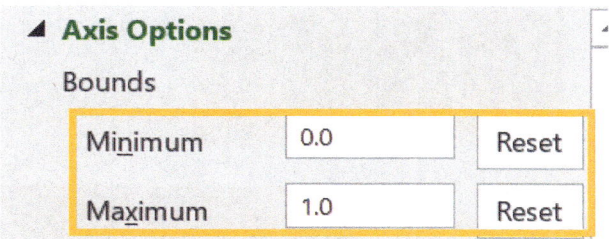

- Also, changed from **Auto** to **Reset** (fixed the axis range of chart). You can see the axis range is from **0%** to **100%** in the above picture.
- Click Axes in the chart elements

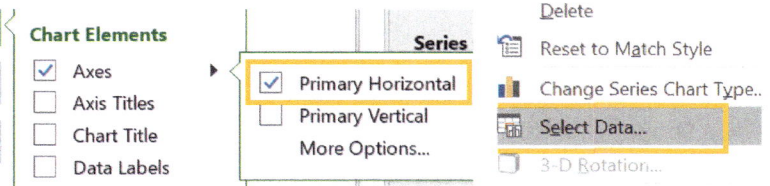

- Click a Series in the chart and then **CTRL + 1** (see below)
- Click right mouse button & Go to **Select Data** >>> **'Edit'**.
- Choose a range for "Q1, Q2, Q3, Q4" into Axis label range.

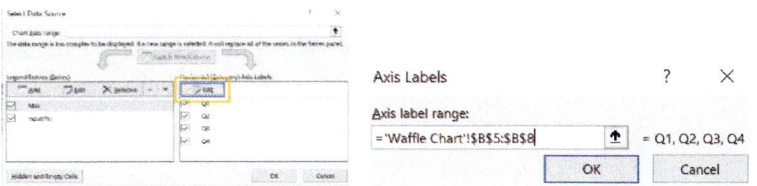

- Click a Series in the chart and then **CTRL + 1** (see below)
- Go to **Format Data Series** &
    - Series Overlap: 100%
    - Gap Width: 0%

- Click right mouse button & Go to **Select Data** >>> Move up **'Max' series** to the top of list.

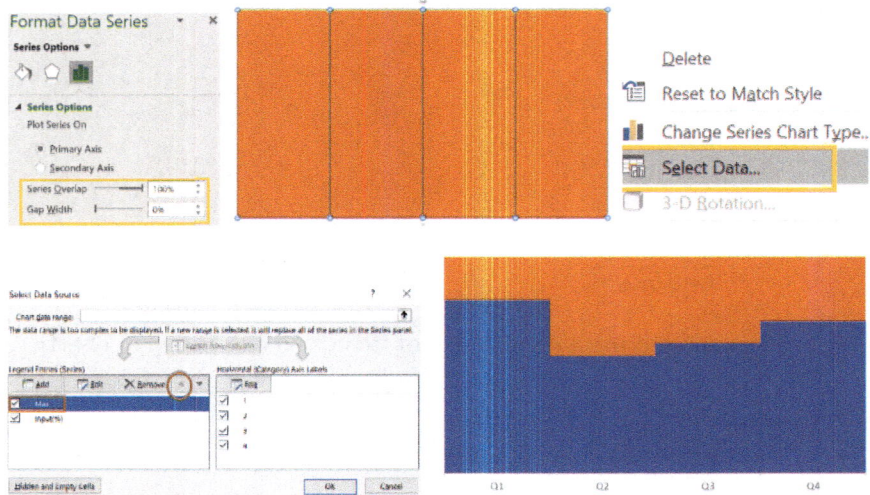

Click a chart >>> Go to **Format** tab.
- **Shape Fill** = No Fill
- **Shape Outline** = No Outline

How to make a right square box:

- Go to **Insert** tab, select **rectangle** and create it on worksheet.
- For Fill, select color = choose the color you like
- For Line, select color = **White**
- For Size, make sure that **Height & Width are same**. Unclick **Lock aspect ratio**.

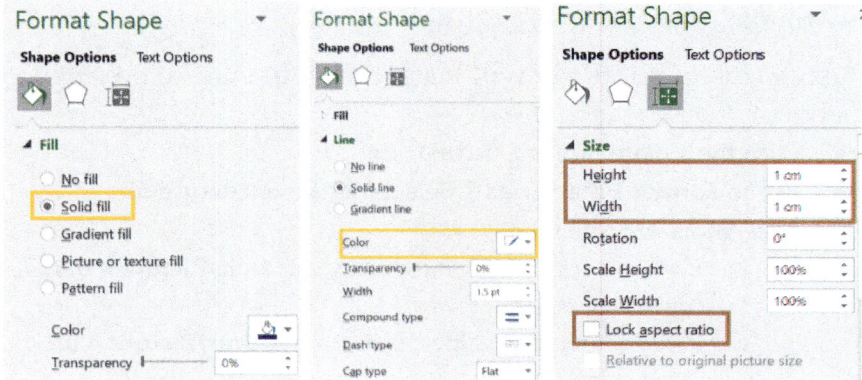

In the same manner, we can create another right square box. We can make the following.

How to combine the right square box with bar chart:

- Click the square box >>> **Ctrl + C**
- Click the bar series in the chart >>> **Ctrl + V**

In this example, the gray color is applied to max & the dark blue is for the actual values.

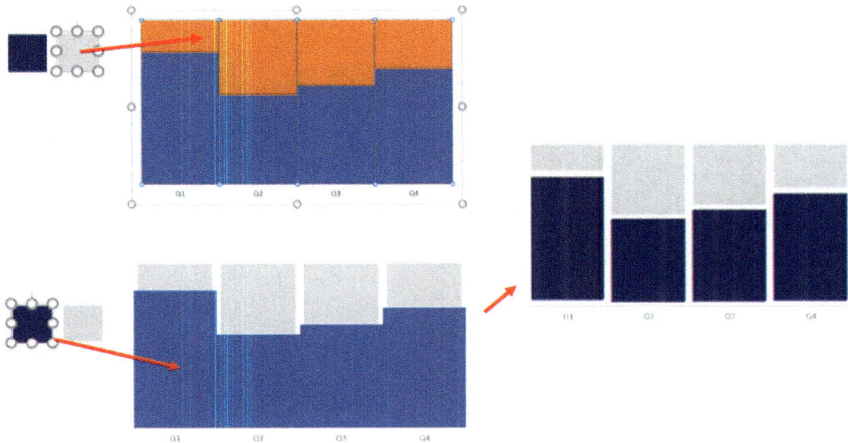

How to use 'Stack & Scale with' in chart:

By using this method, we will stack the right square boxes in the chart.
- Click the square box >>> **Ctrl + 1**
- Go to **Format Data Series** & Select **Picture or texture fill**
- Click **'Stack & Scale with'** >>>
    - If you select actual value series, put **Unit/Picture = 0.05** (dark blue color)
    - If you select max value series, or put **Unit/Picture = 0.1** (gray color).

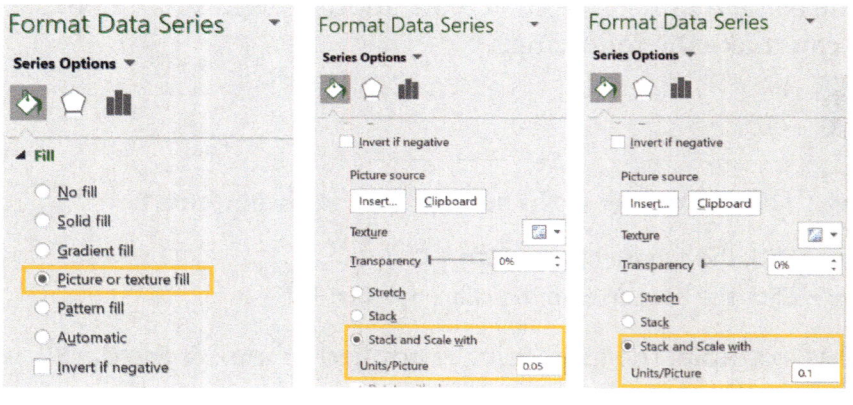

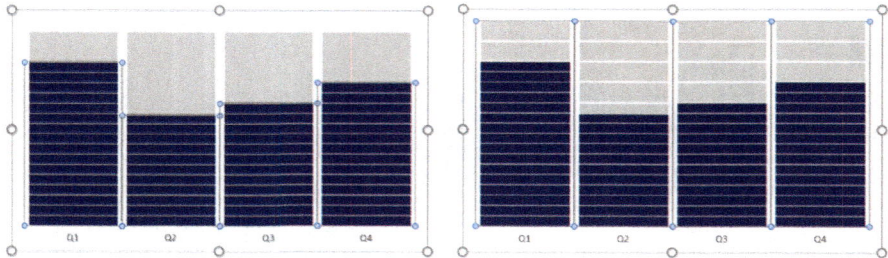

In this example, select the dark blue series first, and then select the gray color series later.
- The **max** (=background) series is divided by **0.1** (=10%)
- The **actual value series** is divided by **0.5** (=5%)

How to change the size of chart:

In order to make it like the below (right side),

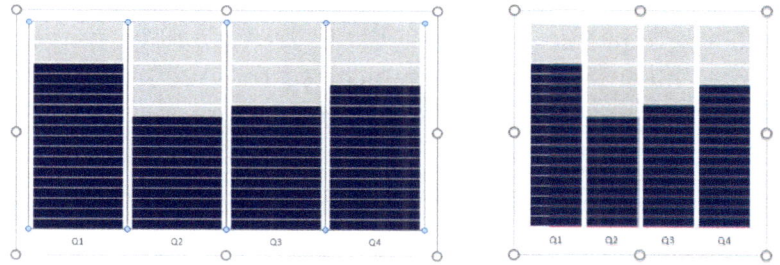

- Click the chart >>> **Ctrl + 1** >>> Go to **Format Data Series**
- Select **Chart Area** by using reverse triangle.
- Go to Size in Format Chart Area. Set Height & Width = **7cm**

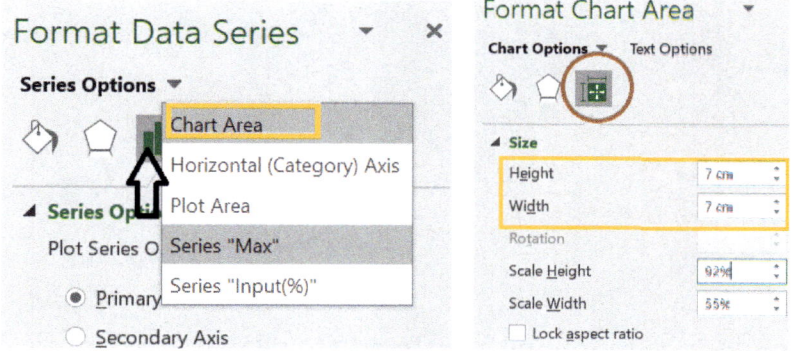

How to make Mini Chart:

The meaning of min chart would be putting a chart in one cell.
- Decrease the chart which you want to put it into a call.
- Press Alt, drag and put it into a call.

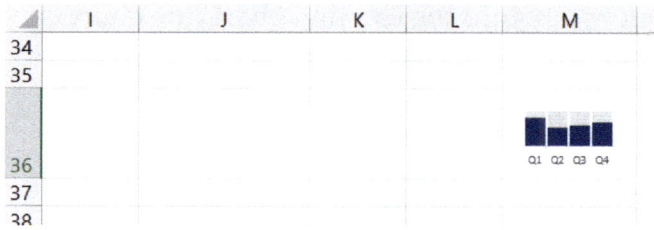

When you make a dashboard, this method will be useful.

Applied example 1 (with waffle chart):

By using 3D effect, it is possible to create a new image of waffle chart. As you already noticed that we try to use the methods which we learnt before into applied examples.

- Copy & paste the existing square box (make a new one)
- Click the square box >>> **Ctrl + 1**
- Go to **Format Data Series** & Select **Solid fill** & choose the color you like.
- Go to **Effect** & choose one pre-set in **Presets**
  - If you select actual value series, transparency = **50%**
  - If you select max value series, transparency = **85%**

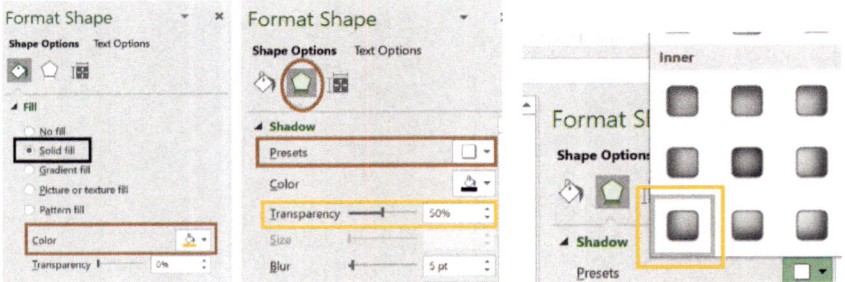

As examples, the following are already available in example excel file.

After applying a new box into the existing chart, the chart is changed liked below.

(Note) Apply **Unit/Picture = 0.1** (for actual value)

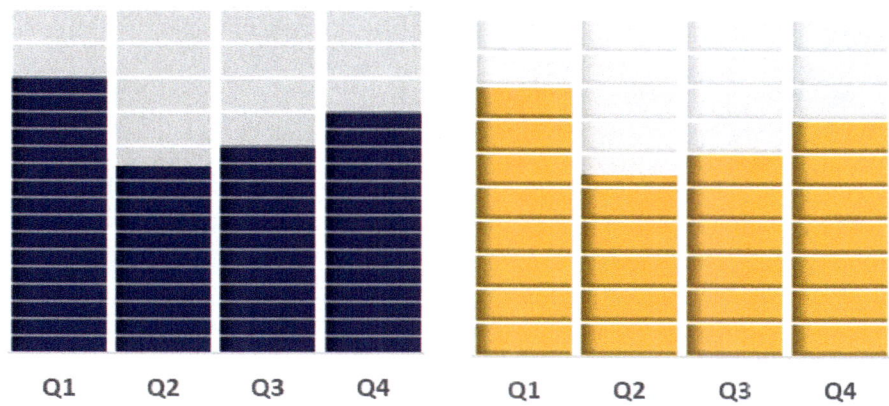

Applied example 2 (with waffle chart):

Based on the transparent 3D circle in the earlier section, it is possible to create the following circle with different colors. **One important thing:** make sure your icon, box or circle is that **height is the same as width.**

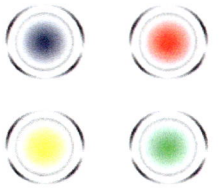

How to combine the right square box with bar chart:

- Click the circle >>> **Ctrl + C**
- Click the actual value bar in the chart >>> **Ctrl + V**

In this example, the gray color is applied to max.

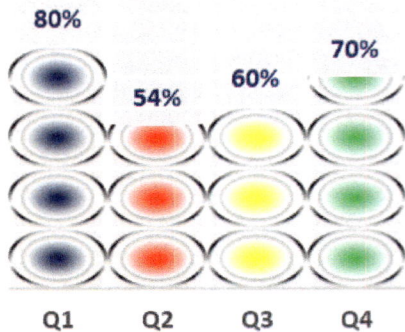

By using the built-in icons: it is also possible to apply the same approach as above.

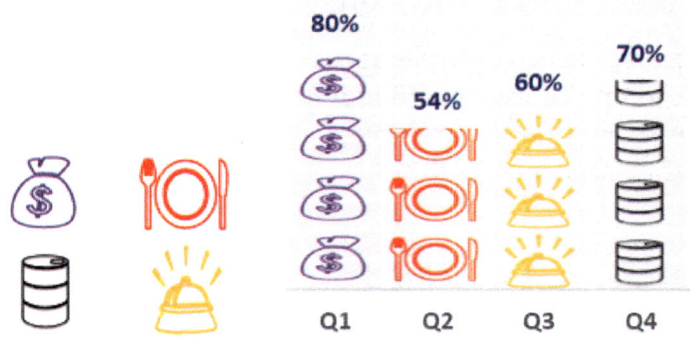

In addition, the photos can apply for the waffle chart as well like above.

Copy & paste your photos on the worksheet. By line width, you can control the distance between photos.

(Note) set the **line color** around photo = **White & Width = 1.5**cm

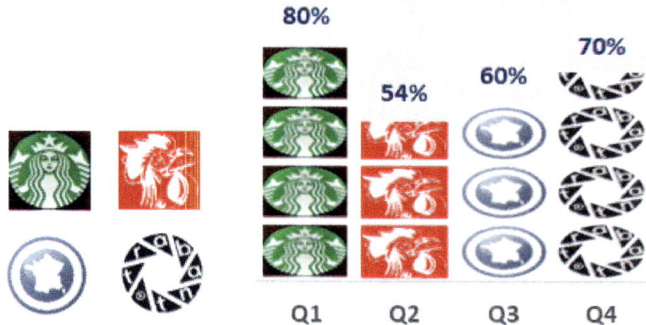

The main benefit of Waffle chart is that you can directly apply any type of items if the item is a right- square form.

Combining Mini chart with Waffle chart:

As a next applied case, the above 5 different waffle charts become mini charts. It is possible to put them into a cell by using holding Alt + Mouse dragging. (See below)

(Note) the same inputs are used for the 5 waffles chart in the example. Therefore, the 5 charts show the same values.

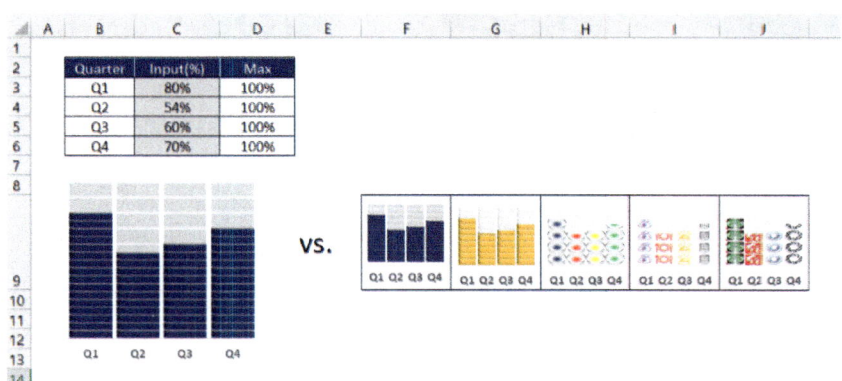

13. Making a chart without chart functionality

In this section, we are going to create a chart with using a built-in chart function (Chart in 'Insert' tab).
Basically, we will make a chart from the scratch.

This chart looks a bit simpler compared to other charts. In order to avoid too-simple chart, 3D effect is added in this chart.

The target chart looks like below.

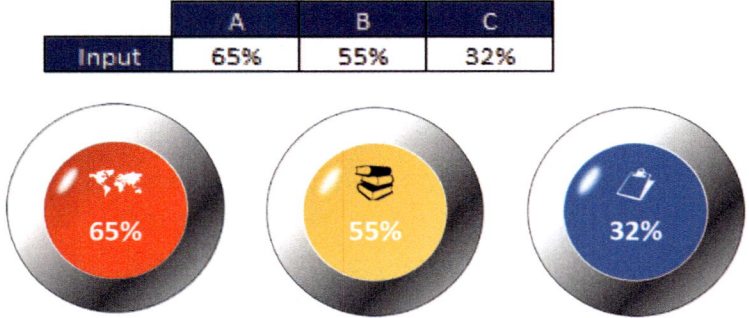

The main benefit of this chart is that there is no limitation. The following description is fully based on the given example.

How to make an outer circle:

Please note that all the following settings are based on the given example above.

Insert a circle. The size of outer circle = **6cm**. Line color = **Black** & Width = **0.5**pt.

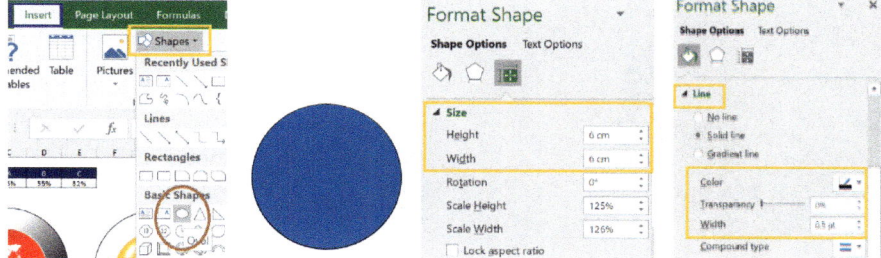

Select **Gradient fill** & Select degree for **225** degree (see below).

The feeling we want to create is the light is coming from 225 degree to downside.

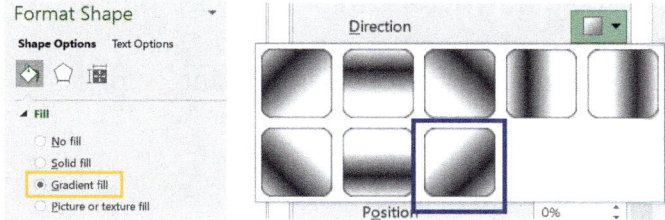

Settings for Gradient stops:
- Color is white except the second stop (Black)
- Positions are 0%, 30%, 66% and 100%.

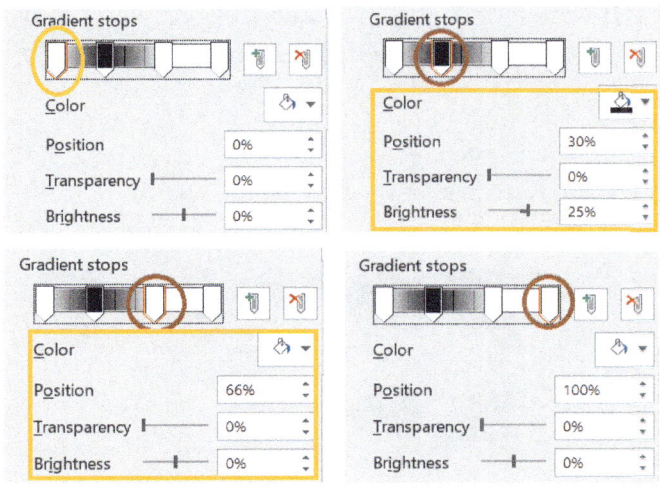

The outer circle is completed.

How to make an inner circle:

The method is pretty much same as the outer circle.
Please note that all the following settings are based on the given example above.
Insert a **circle**. The size of outer circle = **4cm**. Line color = **Black** & Width = **1**.

Select **Gradient fill** & Select degree for **225** degree (see below). The feeling we want to create is the light is coming from 225 degree to downside.

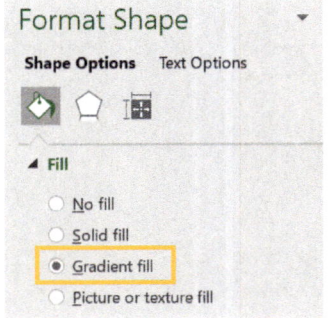
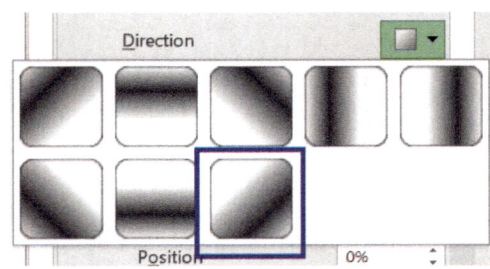

Settings for Gradient stops:

- Color is all **Red** & specify the red color (click '**More Colors ...**' >>> select the color you like)
  Why '**More Colors ...**'? in order to show you more possibility to choose colors.

- Positions are 0%, 56% and 100%.

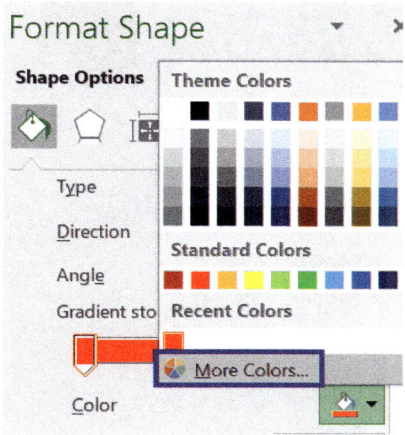

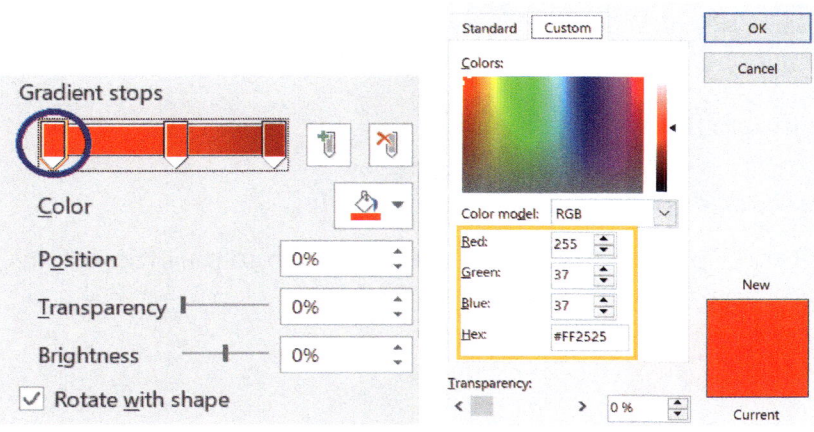

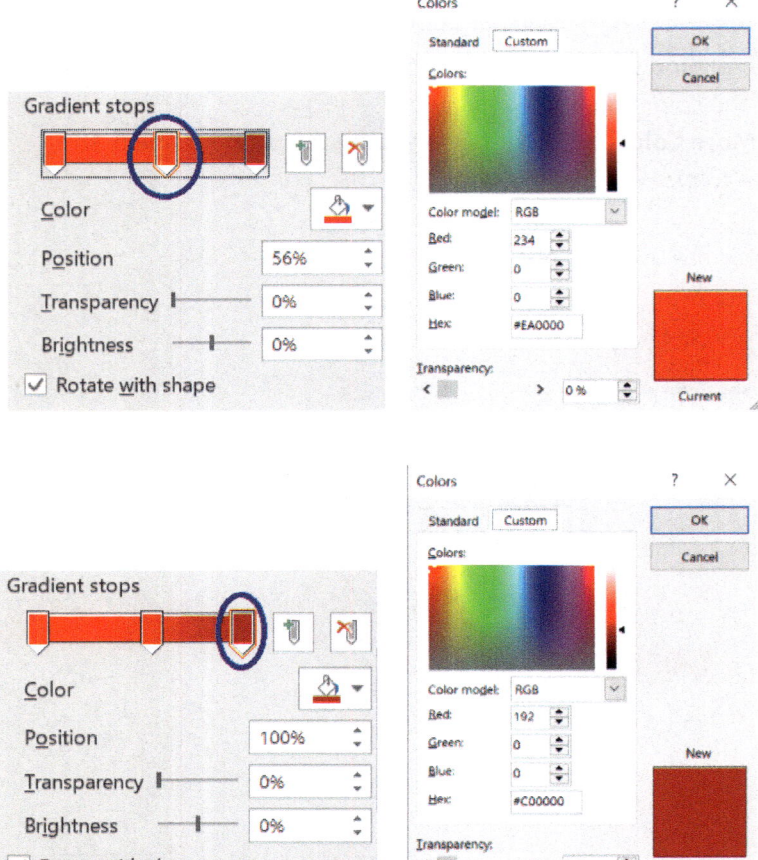

The inner circle is completed.

How to add the reflection on the circle:

The target picture looks like the inside white part (See below):

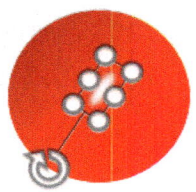

- Select a **circle** in **Insert** tab
- Squeeze the circle like overall shape.
- Select **solid fill** with **white** color
- Go to **Effect** & Select **Soft Edges**. Choose the **third one**.

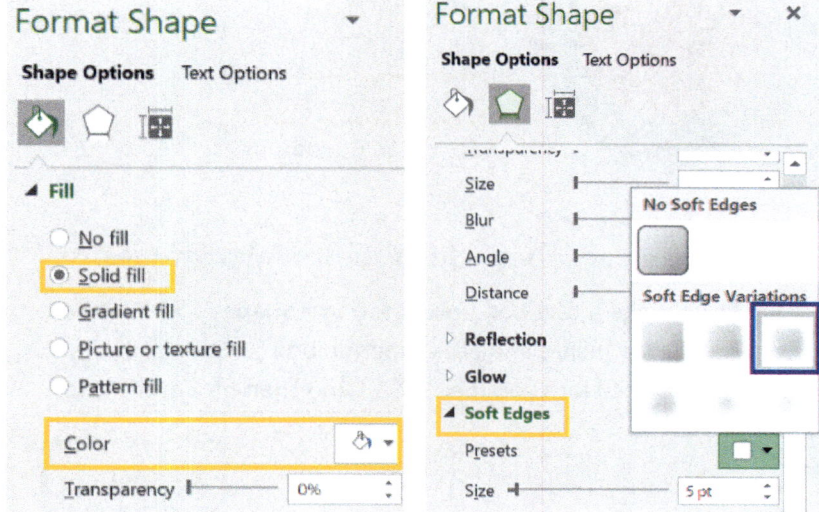

- Put this into the inner circle somewhere at 225 degrees area. Group them.

How to align 2 circles:

Put the inner circle somewhere inside of outer circle.
Go to **Format** & select **Align Center** & **Align Middle**.

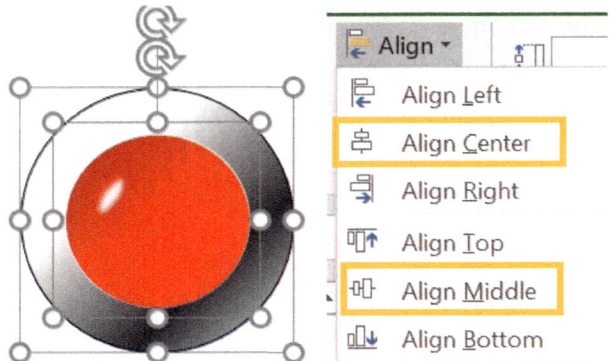

How to make a text box which shows input values:

- First, make a text box. **Insert** tab >>> **Shapes** >>> **Text box**.
- Put cursor inside and click function box ( )
- Write '= cell location (i.e. $C$3)' and then hit Enter button

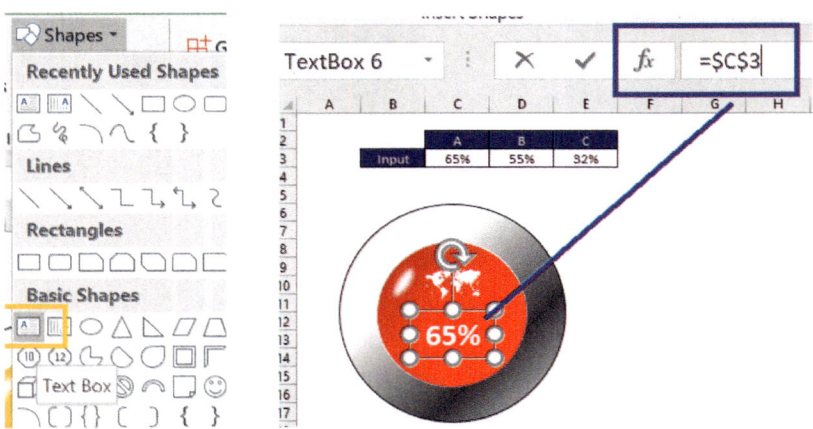

The format of text is as follows: (Color is white)

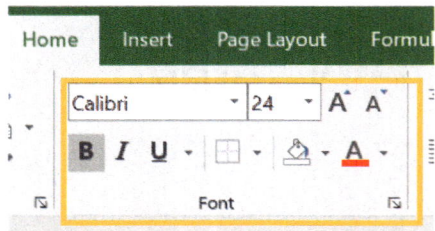

How to make an icon:

- First, make a text box. **Insert** tab >>> **Shapes** >>> **Text box**.
- Put cursor inside & go to **insert** tab >>> **Symbol** >>> **Webdings** >>> choose an Icon.
  - Possible options: Webdings, Wingdings or Wingdings 2 in Symbol in Excel

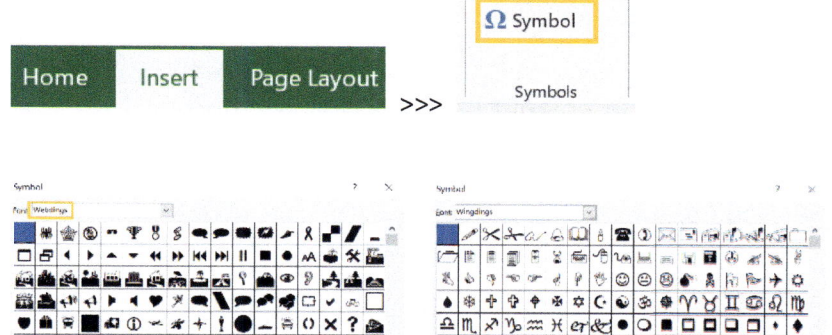

Click the text box, removing **Shape Fill & Shape Outline**.
- **Shape Fill** = No Fill
- **Shape Outline =** No Outline

We can create an icon for the chart.

How to align multiple objects:

Put the icon on top of text box inside of inner circle.
Select all objects & Go to **Format** & select **Align Center**. Group them (optional).

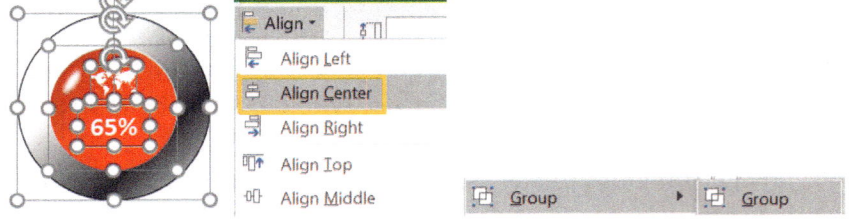

For 2nd and 3rd circle, copy & paste it into worksheet. Click the inner circle and change the color from Red to other color.

By using the align in Format tab, it is easy to allocate the 3 circle charts nicely.

Finally, the target chart is completed.

14. VERTICAL BAR CHART WITH ARROW PERCENTAGE

The target chart looks like below:

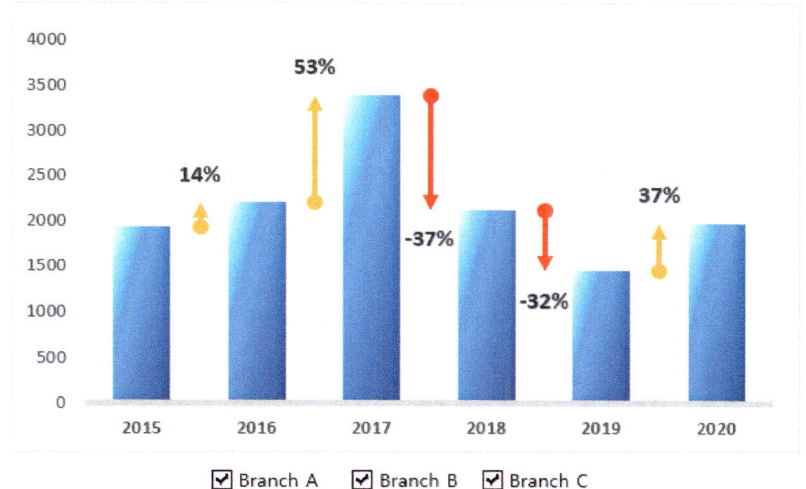

The main benefit of this chart is to see the movements between years easily. In addition, it is allowable to see the result of all or selected branches by selecting check box in the bottom of chart.

Please note that this chart is required to prepare input adjusting processes before creating a chart.

Input:

The following input table has been made for this chart creation.

Input		
Branch	Year	Sale
A	2015	550
A	2016	1000
A	2017	700
A	2018	720
A	2019	390
A	2020	690
B	2015	500
B	2016	740
B	2017	1910
B	2018	690
B	2019	500
B	2020	450
C	2015	890
C	2016	470
C	2017	780
C	2018	720
C	2019	560
C	2020	850

Let's tackle the hardest part for this chart creation.
We need to use a function called '**SUMIF**' for the input adjusting processes

SUMIF function is to sum the values in a specific range that meet criteria that you specify.

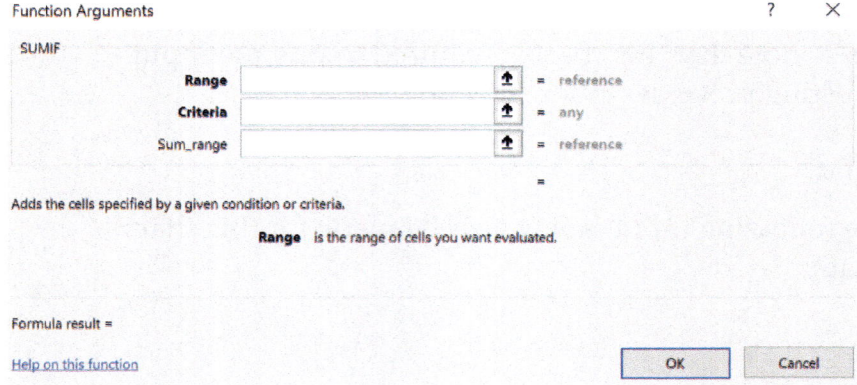

As an example, **Range** would be from column L (from 2015 to 2020) and **Criteria** = 2015.

Sum_range would be column M (from 550 to 690).
As a result, we can see that the criteria = 2015 is true in column M is only **550**.

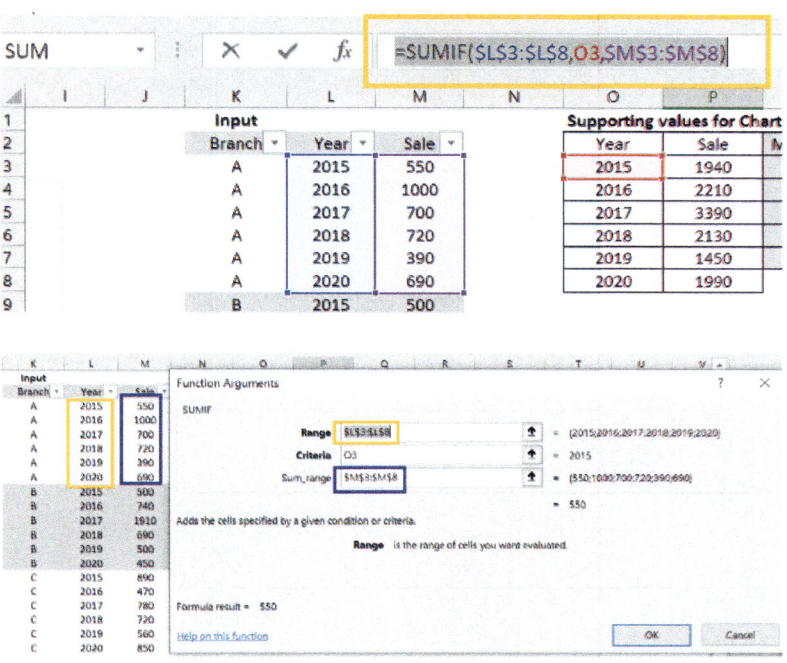

For the preparation of chart, we can create 3 SUMIF functions for 3 branches. (See below)

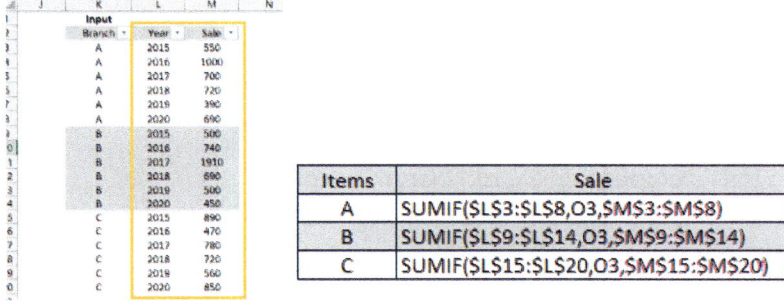

Items	Sale
A	SUMIF($L$3:$L$8,O3,$M$3:$M$8)
B	SUMIF($L$9:$L$14,O3,$M$9:$M$14)
C	SUMIF($L$15:$L$20,O3,$M$15:$M$20)

i.e. Branch A: = SUMIF($L$3:$L$8,O3,$M$3:$M$8)
=SUMIF(total sale years, specific year, Branch A)
=SUMIF(from 2015 to 2020, 2015, Sale for A in 2015)

How to see 'Developer' tab:

In a default setting, it is not possible to see Developer tab.

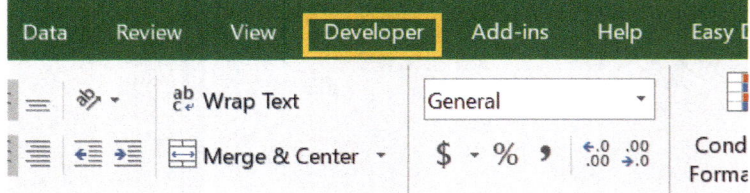

In order to see this tab, please follow the below steps.
File >>> Options >>> Customize Ribbon >>> Main Tabs (right-hand side) **>>> Developer >>> OK**

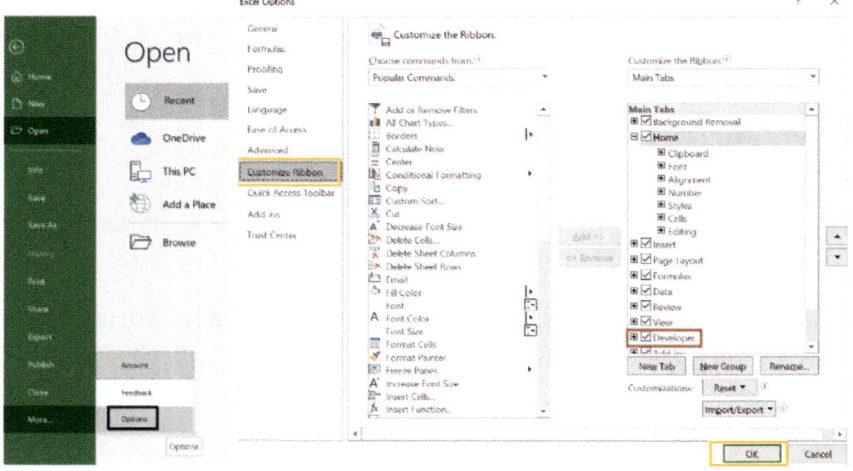

How to make check box:

- Go to **Developer** tab & Click '**Insert**' button
- Select '**Check Box (Form Control)**' & Click any location in Worksheet
- Drag the check box until the size you would like to have.
- Put the cursor inside of check box & change the name

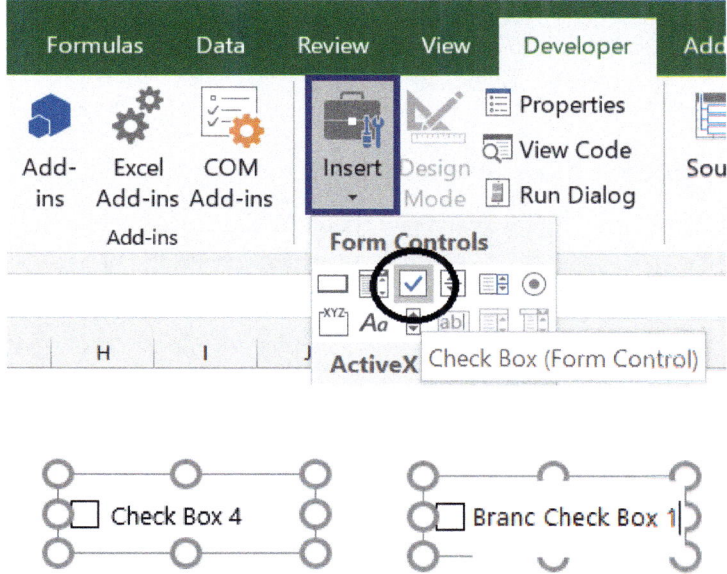

- After selecting the box, click a right-hand mouse button & go to **Format Control** (see below)
- Go to **Control** & Put the cursor inside of '**Cell link:**'
- **Select a cell** for the 'Cell link' which you will control the check box either tick or untick.

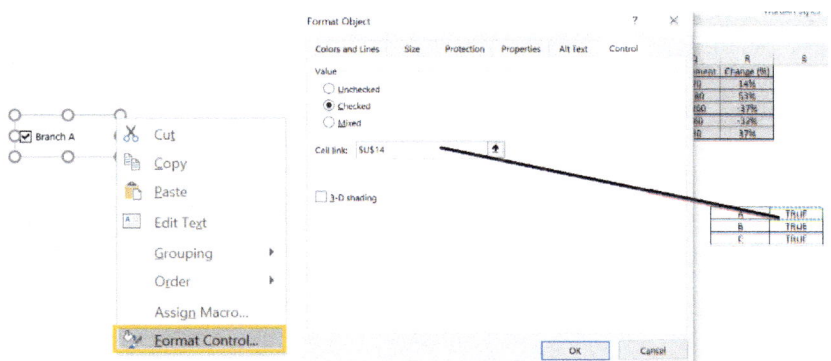

In the same manner, it is possible to create 3 check boxes and also the Cell link related cells.

☑ Branch A   ☑ Branch B   ☑ Branch C

A	TRUE
B	TRUE
C	TRUE

For checking, Branch B & C are unticked.

☑ Branch A   ☐ Branch B   ☐ Branch C

A	TRUE
B	FALSE
C	FALSE

How to align multiple objects:

Select all objects & Go to **Format** & select **Align Center**. **Group** them (optional).

How to combine 'SUMIF functions' & 'Check Boxes':

By using if statement, it is possible to combine SUMIF function with Check Boxes.

- Step1: **IF (Check Box linked cell value = either (TRUE or FALSE), SUMIF Function, 0)** for each branch.
- Step2: Sum these '3 if statements' up like the following way.
  =IF($U$14,SUMIF($L$3:$L$8,O3,$M$3:$M$8),0)+IF($U$15,SUMIF($L$9:$L$14,O3,$M$9:$M$14),0)+IF($U$16,SUMIF($L$15:$L$20,O3,$M$15:$M$20),0)

Note that unticked check-box brings 0 as a result.

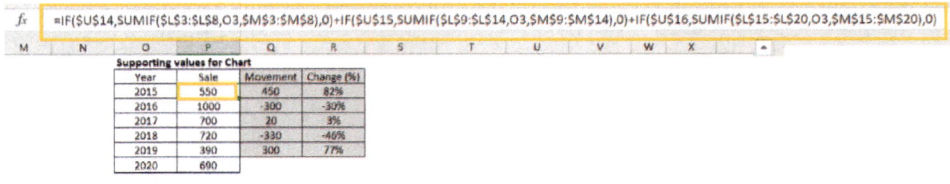

- Step3: Copy & paste the formula until the 2020 (starting from 2015).

How to add movement inputs:

Create an absolute difference & relative differences based on the SUMIF sale figure above.

O	P	Q	R
Supporting values for Chart			
Year	Sale	Movement	Change (%)
2015	550	=P4-P3	82%
2016	1000	-300	-30%
2017	700	20	3%
2018	720	-330	-46%
2019	390	300	77%
2020	690		

O	P	Q	R
Supporting values for Chart			
Year	Sale	Movement	Change (%)
2015	550	450	=P4/P3-1
2016	1000	-300	-30%
2017	700	20	3%
2018	720	-330	-46%
2019	390	300	77%
2020	690		

- Absolute Difference: Sale 2016 – Sale 2015)
- Relative Difference: Sale 2016 / Sale 2015 - 1)

Copy & paste these formulas until the 2020 (starting from 2015).

We can complete the first chart-supporting-value table.

Supporting values for Chart

Year	Sale	Movement	Change (%)
2015	550	450	82%
2016	1000	-300	-30%
2017	700	20	3%
2018	720	-330	-46%
2019	390	300	77%
2020	690		

(Note) It seemes like that there are a lot steps for creating the chart-supporting-value table.
In fact, the steps are not so complicated. The long explaination is coming from the detail explaination for each step.

How to create the second chart-supporting-value table:

Next, we are going to create the second chart-supporting-value table below.

2nd Axis	Increase	Decrease
1.5	1000	#N/A
2.5	#N/A	700
3.5	720	#N/A
4.5	#N/A	390
5.5	690	#N/A

For 'Increase':
Increase = IF(Absolut Difference >=0, 2016 sale figure, NA())

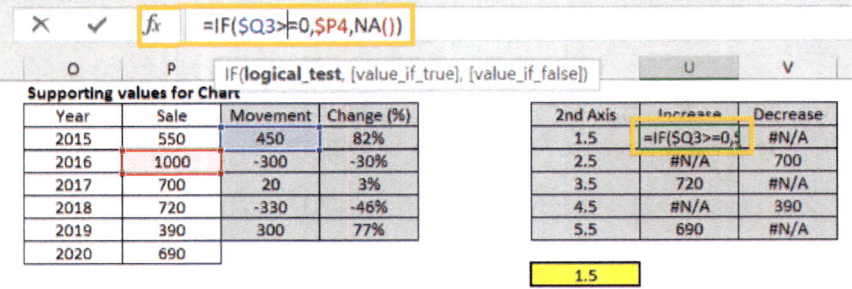

NA() = nothing will be returned.

For 'Decrease':
Decrease = IF(Absolut Difference <0, 2016 sale figure, NA())

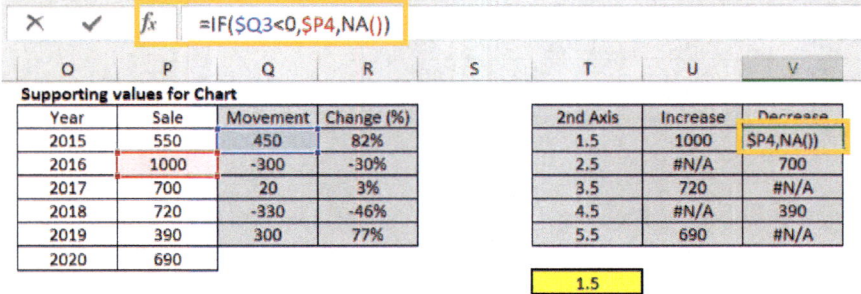

Copy & paste the formula until the 2020 (starting from 2015).
For '2nd Axis':

Create a new axis for the chart. The starting value is control by the yellow cell (=1.5)
The axis value is increased by 1.

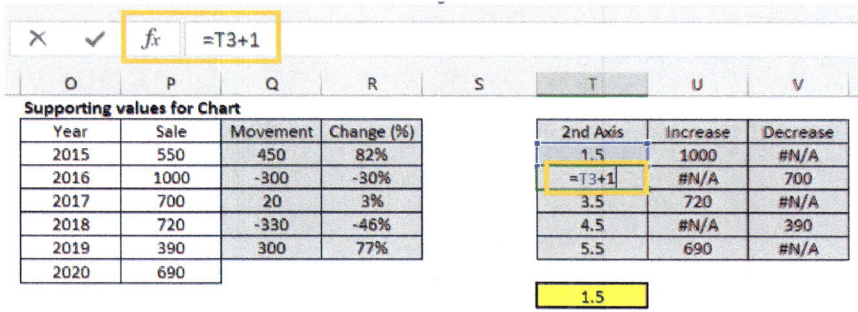

In summary,
- Create & combine SUMIF functions with Check Boxes
- Create an absolute difference & relative differences based on the SUMIF sale figure.
- Create the second chart-supporting-value table (Increase, Decrease & 2nd Axis)

Now, complete the preparation for chart input values.

How to create 2-D Clustered bar chart:

After selecting inputs, go to **Insert** tab.
Select **2-D bar >>> Clustered Column Bar**.

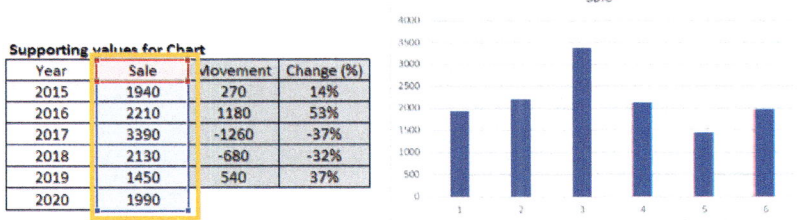

By using **Select Data**, (after clicking Edit,) add year for the x axis. OK

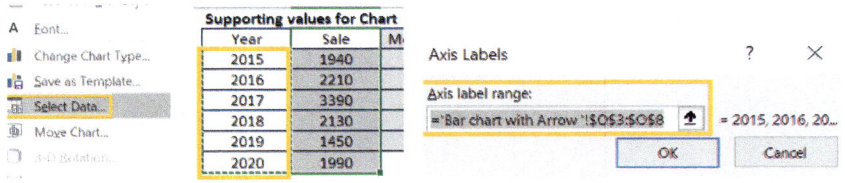

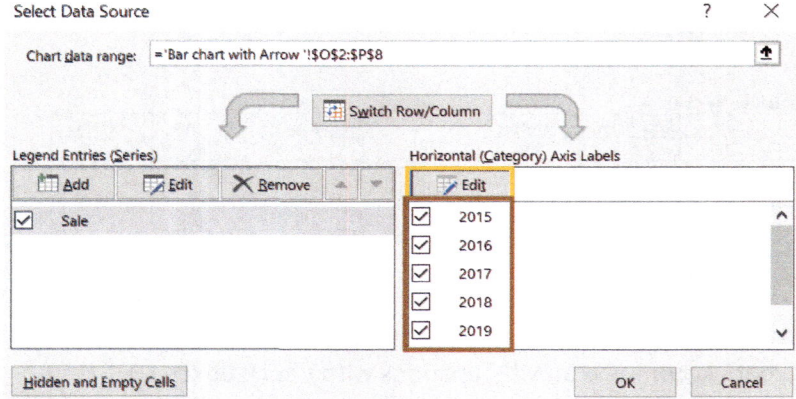

By using '**Select Data**', (after clicking Add,) add 2 series (Increase & Decrease) for the chart from the second chart-supporting-value table (Increase, Decrease & 2nd Axis).

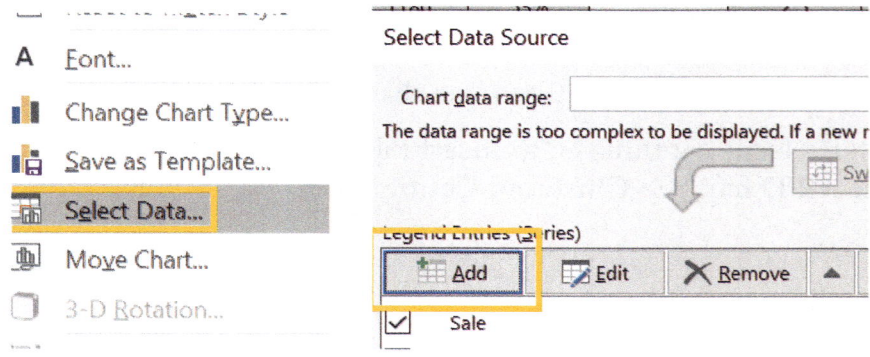

For 'Increse' series:

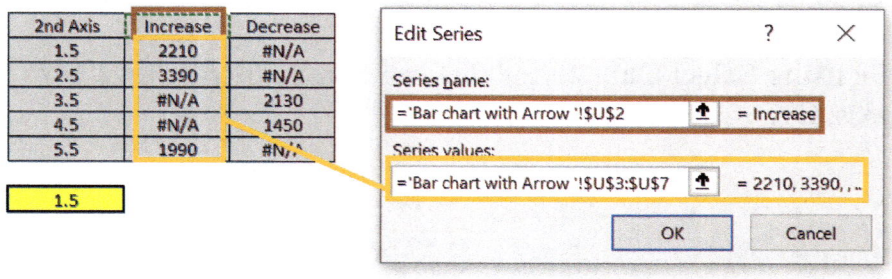

For 'Decrease' series:

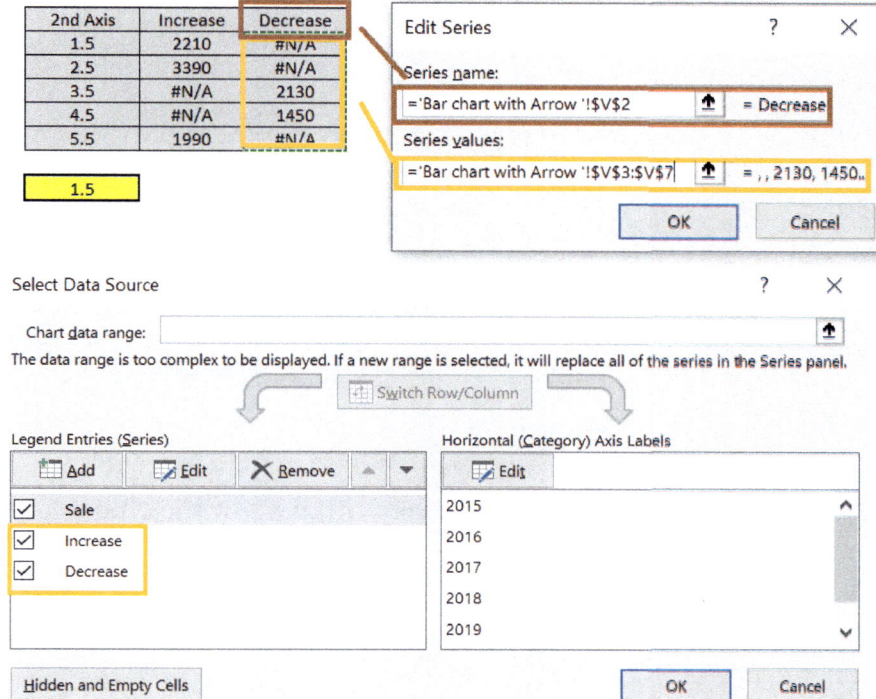

It is possible to create the below chart. Note that #N/A values in the table is not appearing in the chart.

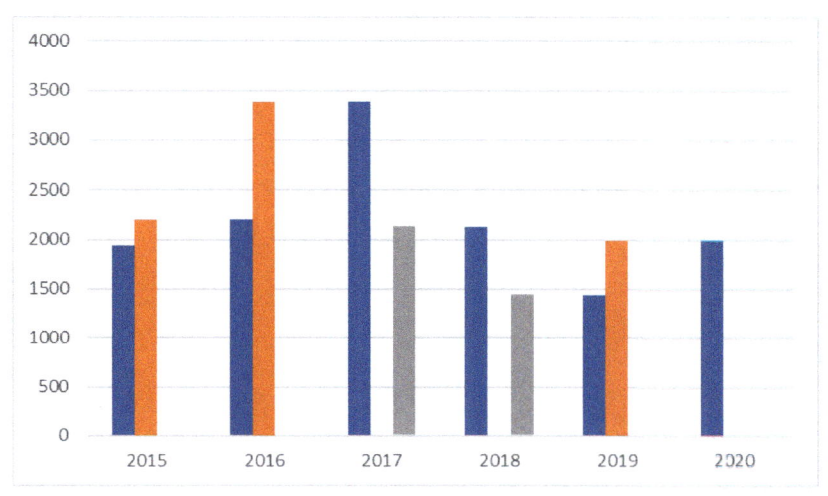

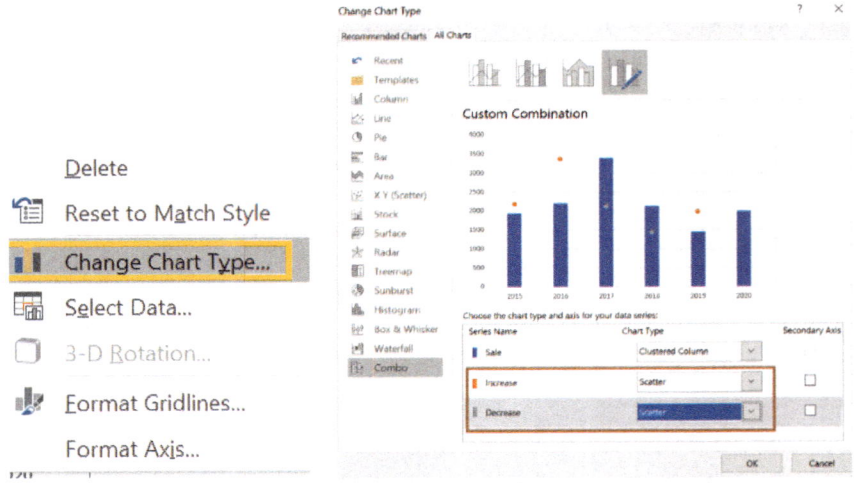

You can see that the dots are in line with bars in the chart.

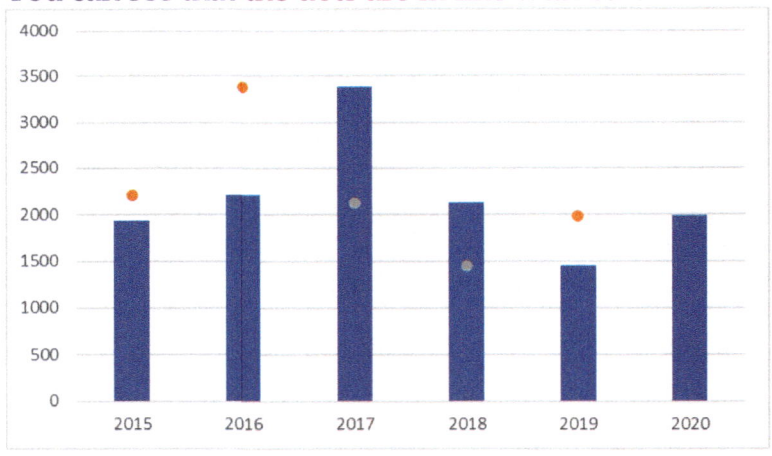

By adjusting of series X values, it is possible to change locations of dots in between bars.
For Increase:

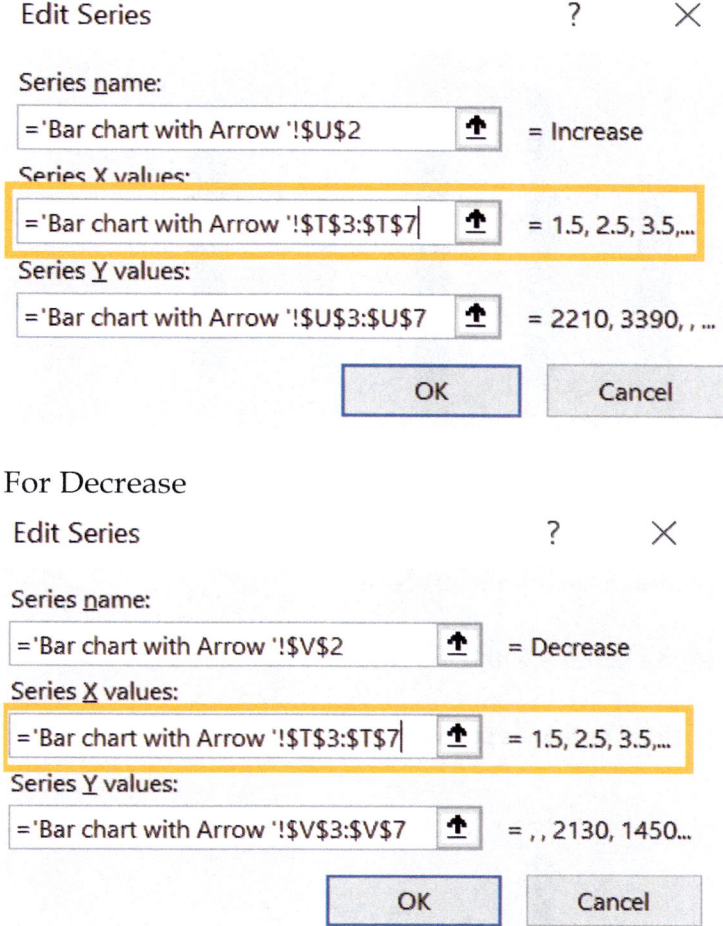

For Decrease

You can see that the locations of dots are changed. The dots are located in the middle of vertical bars.

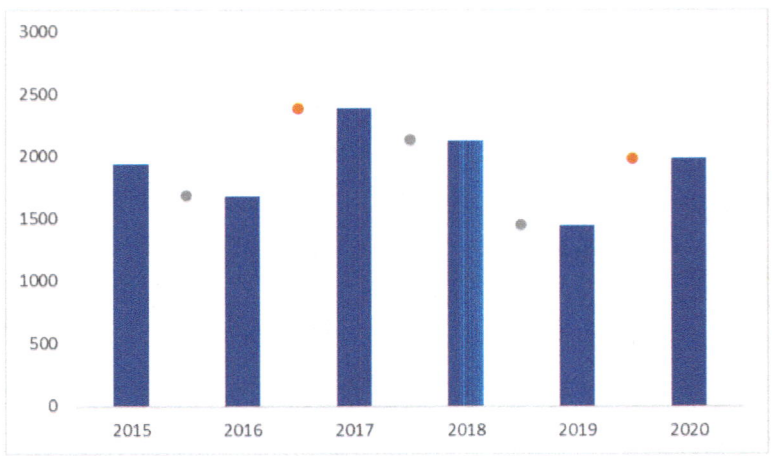

How to add Error bars into scattor plot dots:

Note that the following steps have to conduct for increase sereies and decrease series **seperately**.

- Click & select a series (i.e. the Increase values) in the chart by mouse.
- Click chart element (= plus sign) in the chart on the right-hand side.

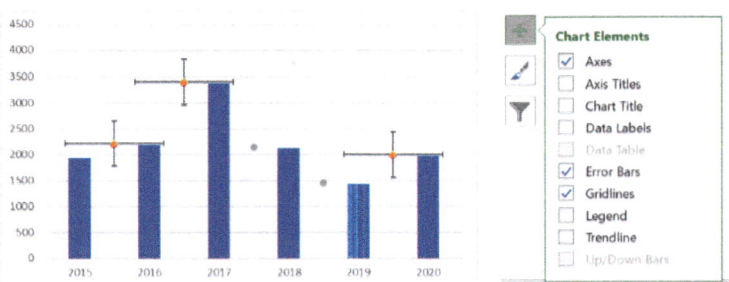

- Select '**Error Bars**' in the chart element (see above) & go back to worksheet.
  You can see the plus shape error bars for the increase series.

- Click only horizontal Error Bars in the chart (see below) and **remove horizontal Error Bars**.
  by a delete button after selecting them.

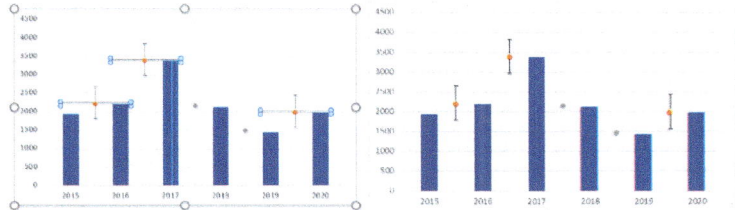

- Go back & click '**Error Bars**' & continuously click '**More Options…**'
- Select **Minus** & **No Cap**

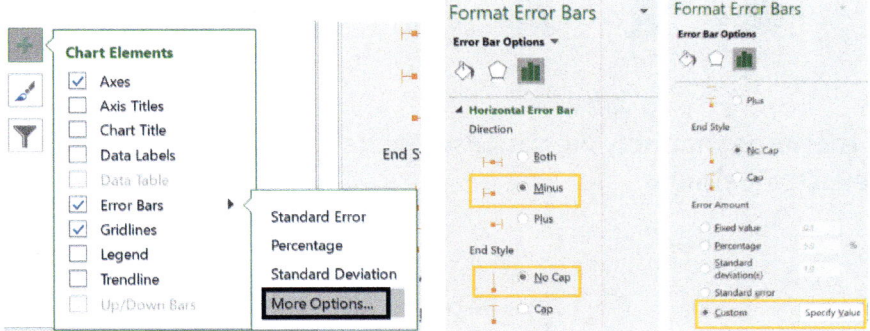

- Select '**Custom**' in **Error amount** & click '**Specify Value**'.
- Select the movements (column Q & see below table) for '**Specify Value**' range.

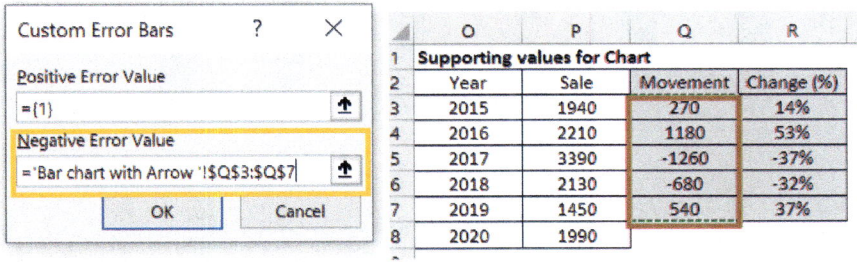

Now, it is possible to see the increase movements in error bars. (see below)

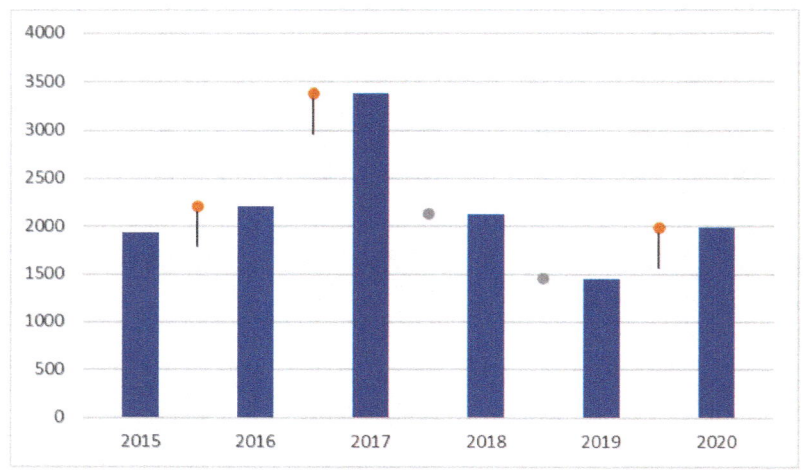

In the same manner, we can also create the decrease series as well. (see below)

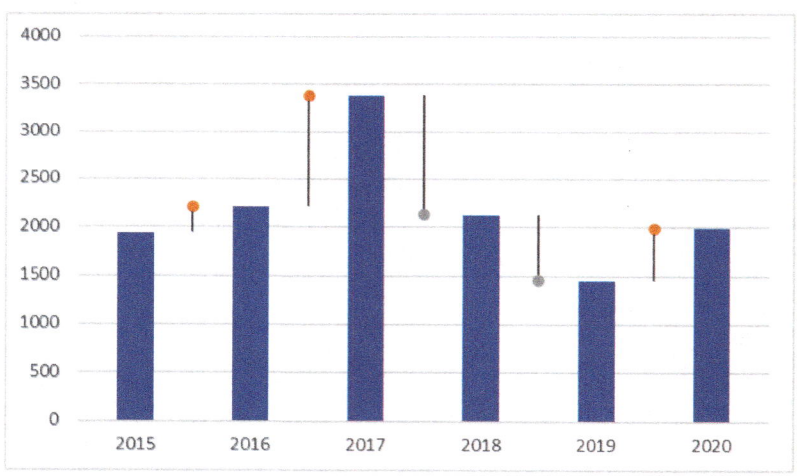

How to remove marker in the chart:

- Click a sereis which you want to remove (i.e. the increase series dots) by mouse & **CRTL + 1**
- Go to **Format Data Series** & Click **Marker** >>> Select **None** for the **Marker Options**.

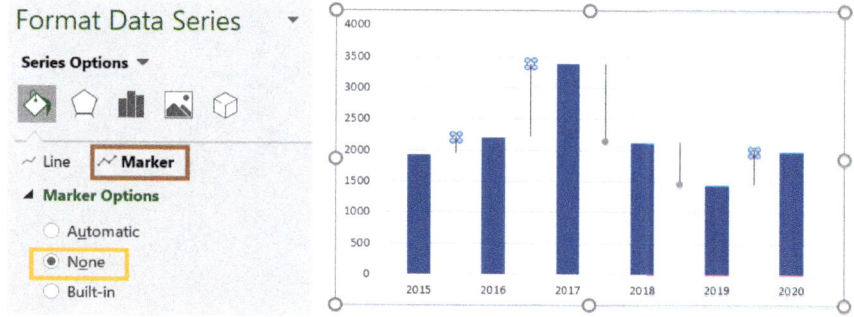

How to add arrow & adjust format of the movement lines:

For movement line format (i.e. Increase series):
- Select the error bar (movement lines) by mouse & **CRTL+1**
- Go to **Line** & change the **color & width** (color = orange & width = 2.5)

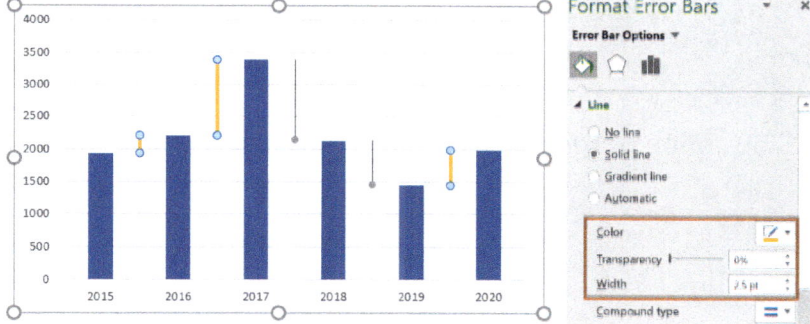

- Go down to **Begin Arrow type** >>> **select the arrow** which you like
- Go to **End Arrow type** >>> **select the circle**

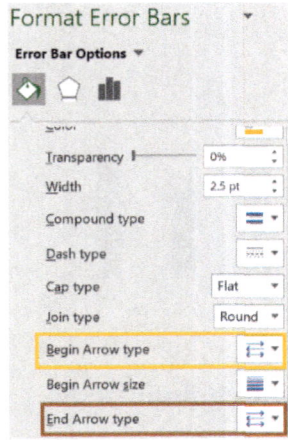

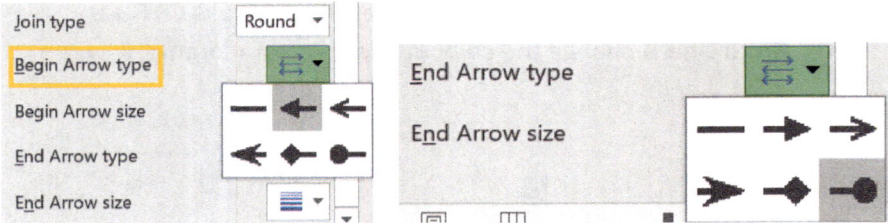

The shape of the movement line is changed like below.

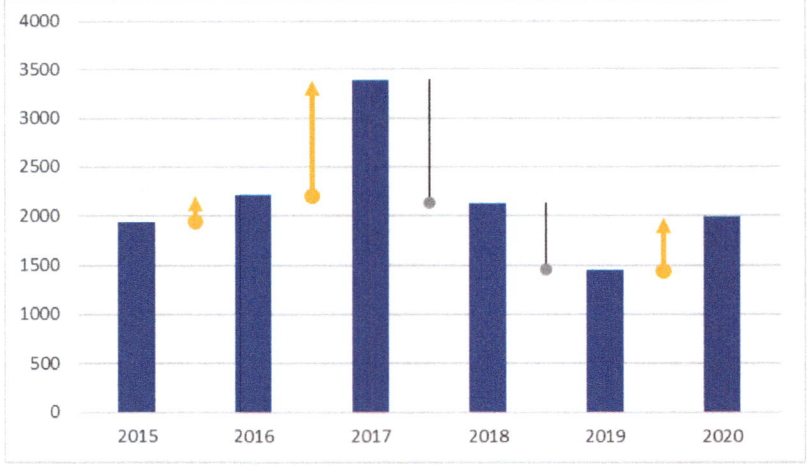

In the same manner, we can also create the decrease series as well. The red color is applied for the decrease series. (see below)

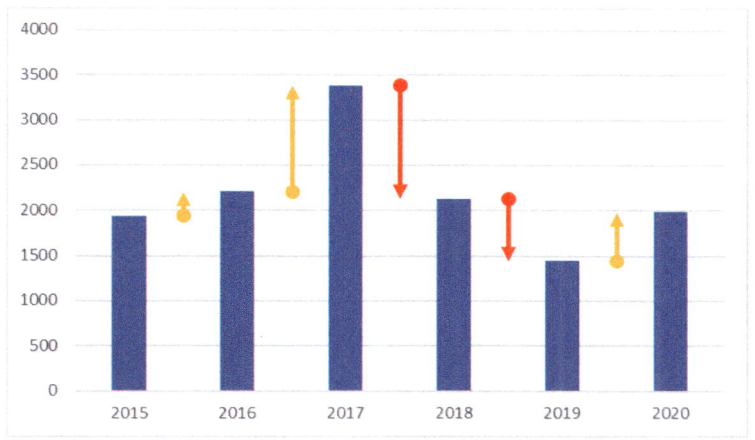

Drawback: if the movements are too small, the circle & arrow are overlapping.

If you select **empty** for **End Arrow size**, you can avoid the drawback.

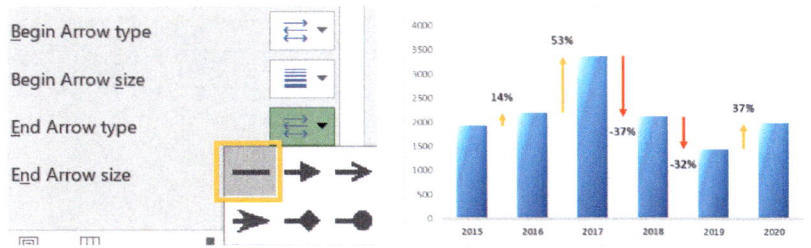

How to add Labels in the chart:

After clean up chart element (removing Grid line), please follow the following steps:
- Click hidden scatter plots (i.e. increase series) by mouse
- Click a right-hand mouse button >>> Click **'Add Data Labels'**.
- Go to **Format Data Labels** >>> Select "**Value from Cells**"
- Select **'Change (%)'** series from the supporting input table.
- **Label position**
   o   Increase series = **Above**
   o   Decrease series = **Below**

Add Data Labels:

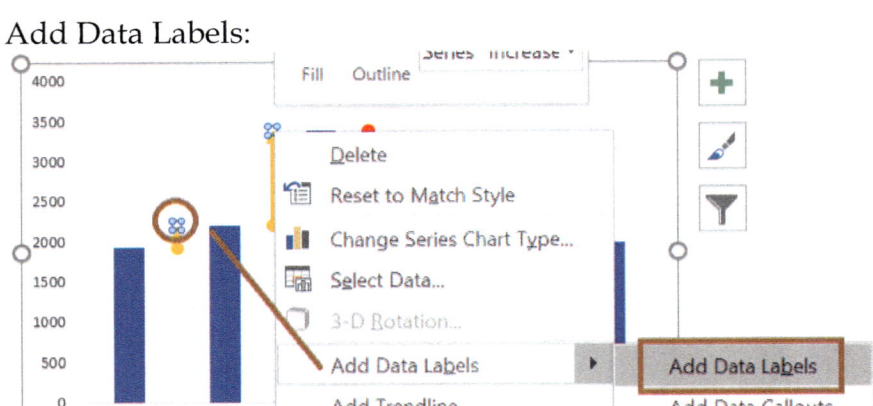

Data Label Range:

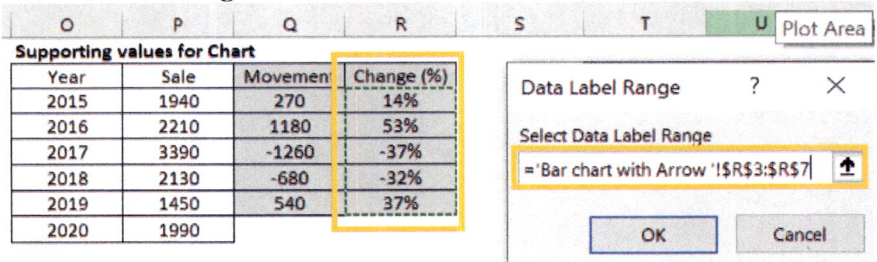

Label Position:

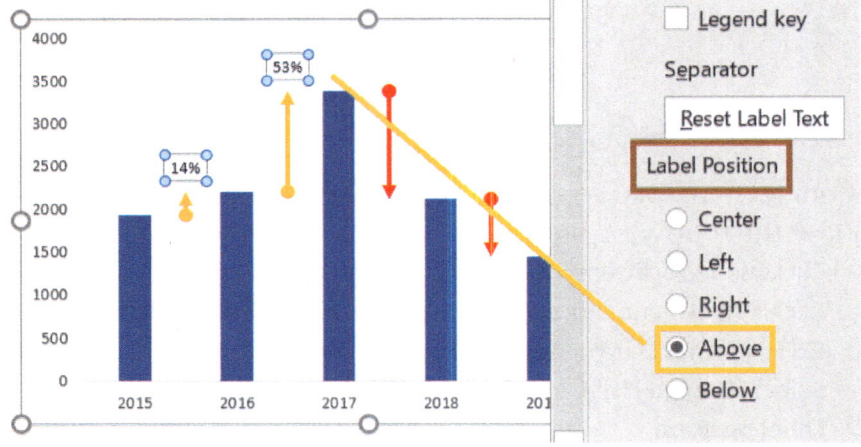

Label font format change is **font size =12 & bold**.

How to change the format of x axis: (Optional)

- Click the x axis & **CTRL+1**
- **Width = 3.25**

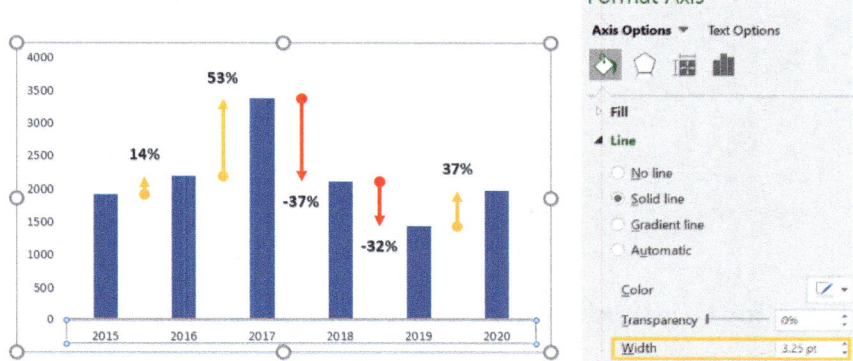

Combine with check box & the chart:
Put the check box into below chart & group them.

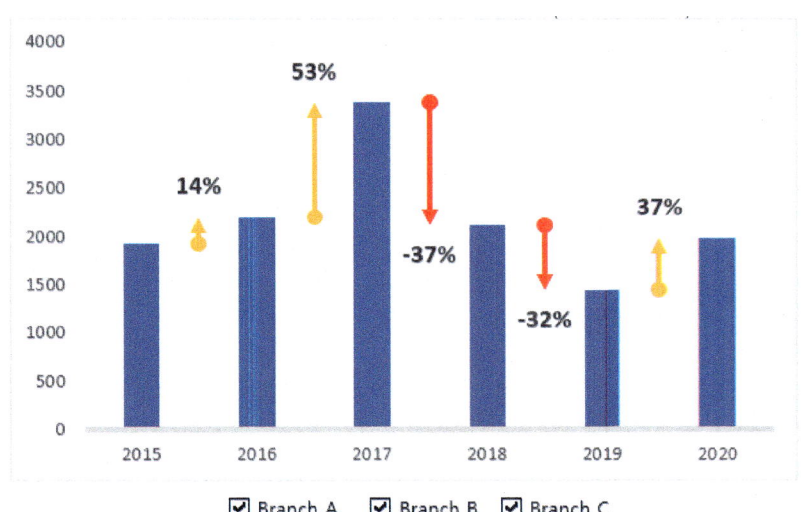

Optional: adding 3D effect into bars

- Select the vertical bars by mouse & CTRL + 1.
- Select **Gradient fill** & Select degree for **15** degree (see below).

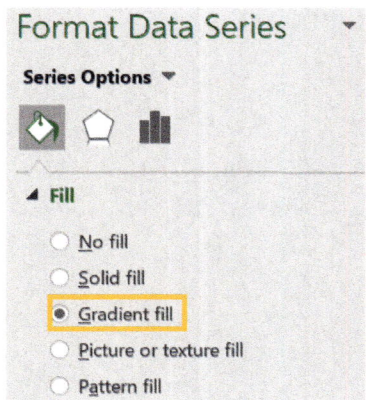 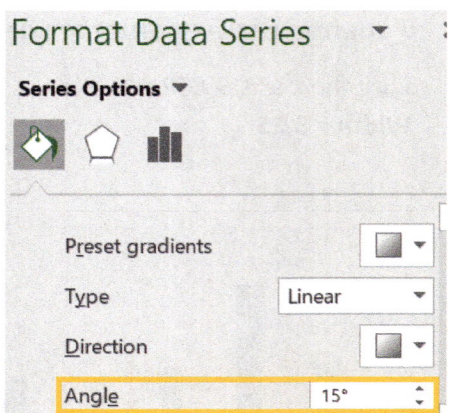

Settings for Gradient stops:

- Color is **white** (first one), **light blue** (middle 2 stops) & **blue** (last one)
- Positions are **0%, 29%, 41%, 100%**.

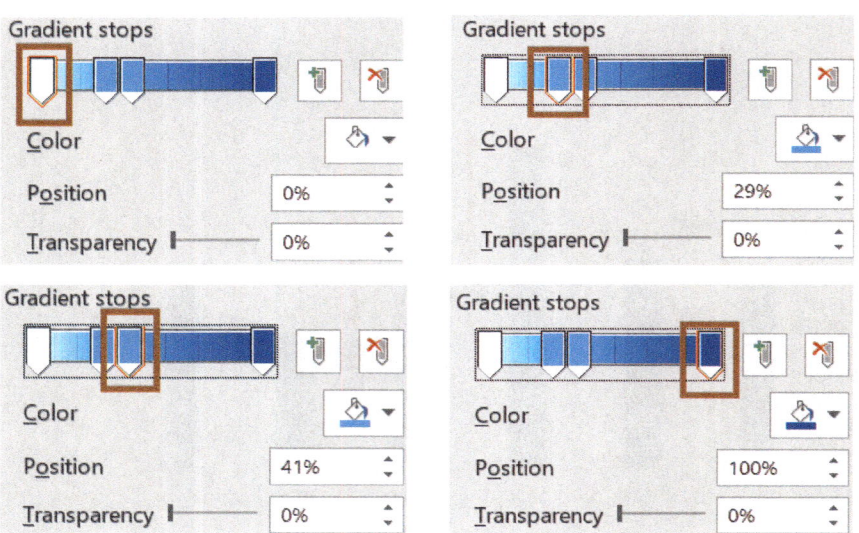

Go to **Shadow** & set **Transparency = 85%** & select **Presets** like below.

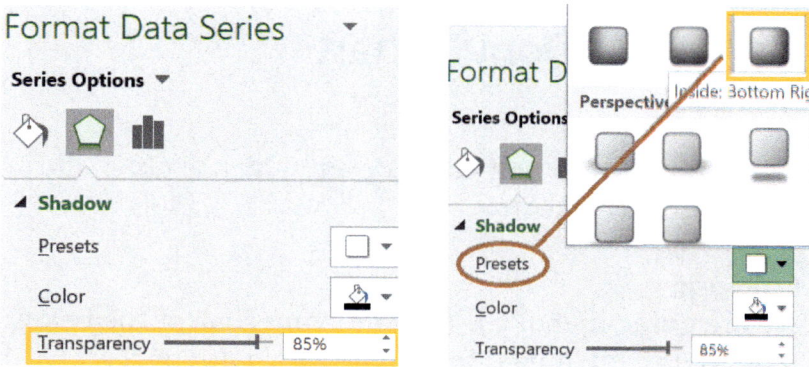

Finally, we can complete the chart.

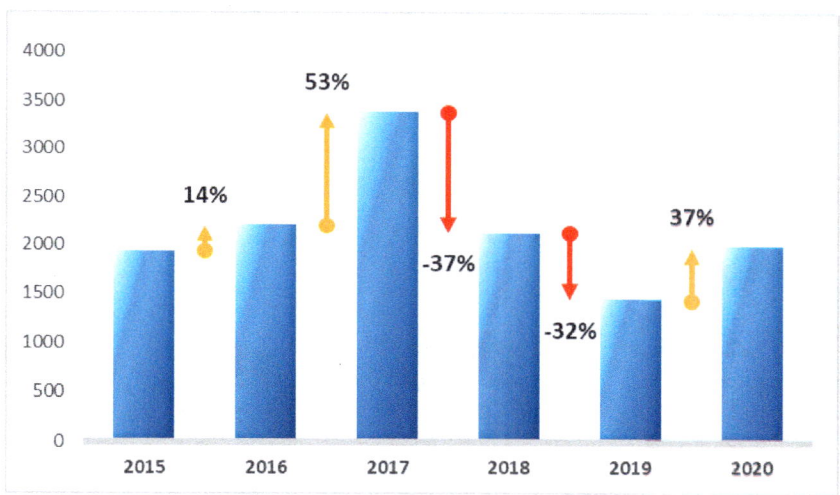

15. Half-circle Donut Chart

We are going to make a half-circle donut which is not really straightforward to make it.

Target picture:
What we are going to make is the following charts: The below input table is directly linked to the half-circle donut charts.

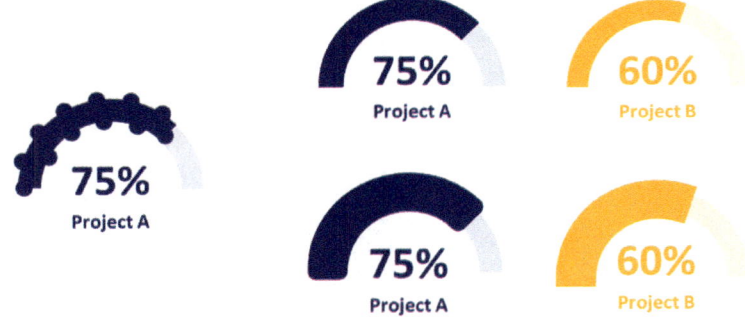

How to set up input values:

First, create **input cells** and **helping cells** in an empty worksheet.
The input values are presented by percentage (%). This is because, normally, reports are used % a lot and % is easy to communicate.

The help cells have a simple formula which is '**1-input value**'.

	P	Q	R	S
	Actual inputs for the graphs			
	Project	Status	Helping cells	Total
	A	75%	=1-Q3	100%
	B	60%	40%	100%

In order to hide both helping cells and total cells, we can create another separate 2 input values. Cell B2 and B3 are actual values and Q2 and Q3 are linked values.

total value = actual value + helping value

	P	Q	R	S
	Actual inputs for the graphs			
	Project	Status	Helping cells	Total
	A	75%	25%	=Q3+R3
	B	60%	40%	100%

How to create donut chart:
As a starting point, you can simply think that 1 raw of input (above table) means one donut chart.

Select input range by dragging mouse with holding right-hand side button from the starting cell to the end of input data cell.

	P	Q	R	S	T
	Actual inputs for the graphs				
	Project	Status	Helping cells	Total	
	A	75%	25%	100%	
	B	60%	40%	100%	

Next, make a **Donut chart**.
- Go to **Insert** tap >>> select **Doughnut**

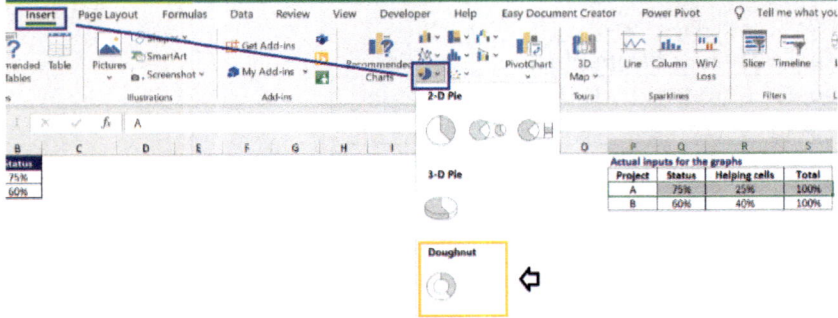

We can see the below chart.

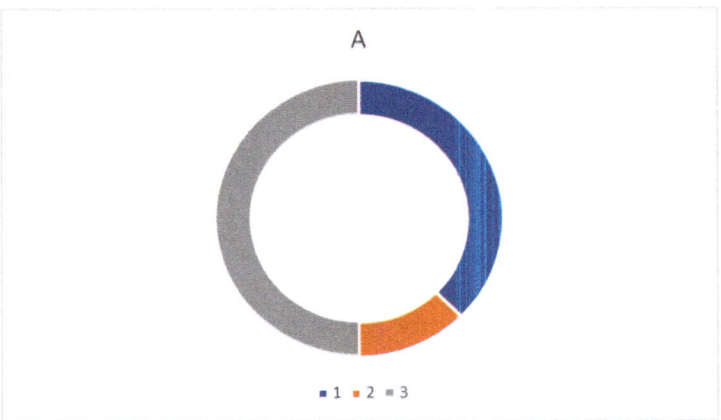

How to remove chart elements:

After clicking a chart, we can see the plus (+) sign on right hand side. This is the location where we can control the chart elements.

- Go to chart elements = click **(+)** sign in gray in the chart
- **Remove the chart elements** = Unclick the chart elements which you want to remove

In this case, we unclicked both chart title and legend from chart elements.

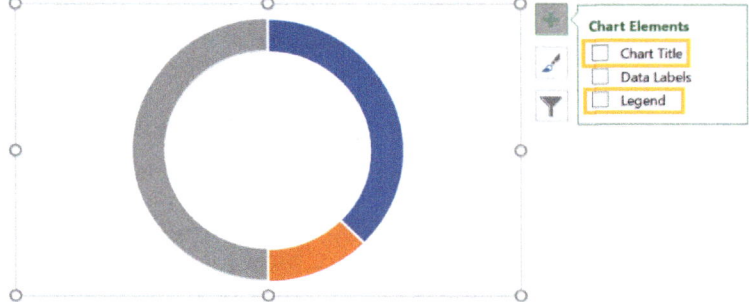

Difference between 'Chart area' and 'Plot area':

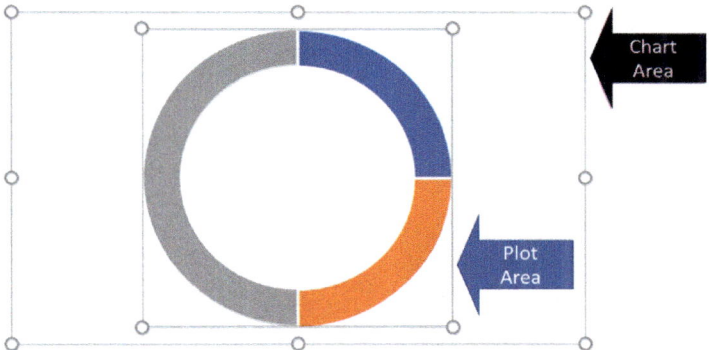

How to select Chart Area:
In general, you can click the area by using mouse.

Alternatively, you can use the following way:
- Click the graph >>> **Ctrl + 1** (Format Chart Area) >>> click reverse **small triangle** next to '**Chart Options**' >>> select **Chart Area**

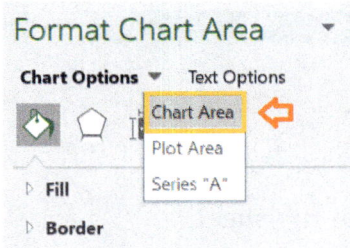

After selecting chart area, making it as a right square shape. In order to do:

- Click chart >>> **Format** tab >>> change size by adjusting values.

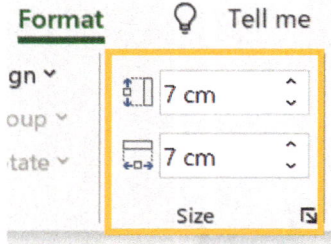

We can see like below.

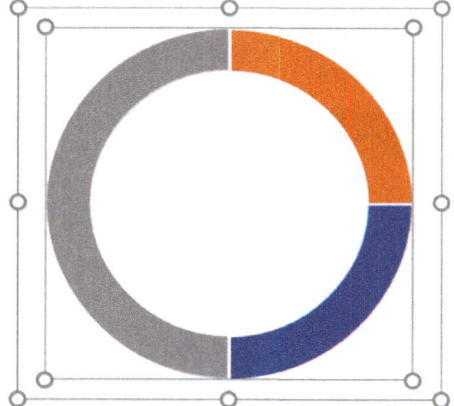

How to remove Gridlines:

- Go to **View** tab and unclick **Gridlines**.

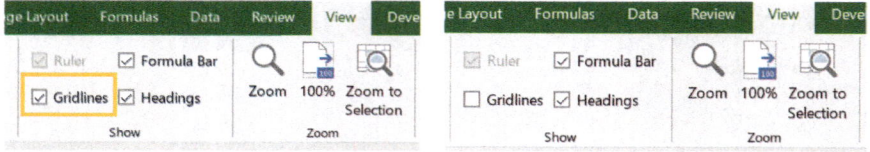

All the grid lines are disappeared in the sheet.

How to remove 'Shape Fill' and 'Shape Outline':

Click a chart >>> Go to **Format** tab. We will change the default settings of **Shape Fill** and **Shape Outline** of the chart.

- **Shape Fill** = No Fill
- **Shape Outline** = No Outline

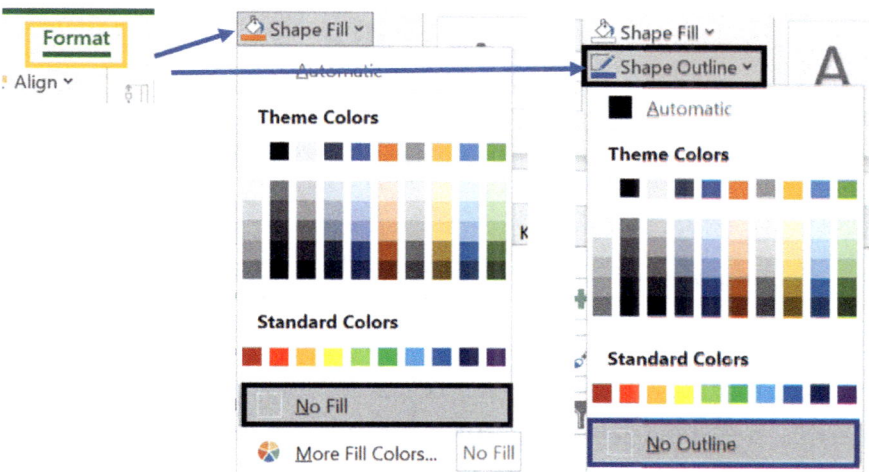

As a result, we can see the following chart.

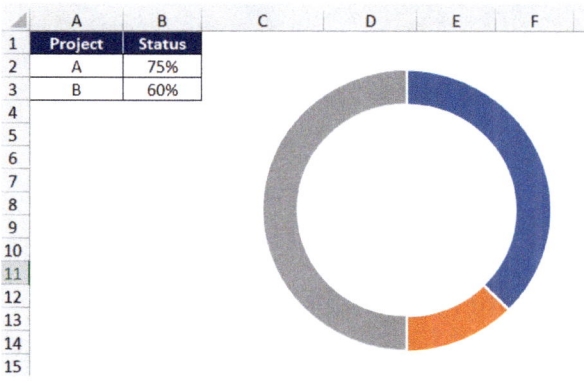

How to make a half donut chart:

As a result, we can see the following chart.

Click one of series in the chart (**select one of pieces**) >>>
Ctrl + 1 >>> **Format Data Series** >>>
Set **270** degree in **Angle of first slice**

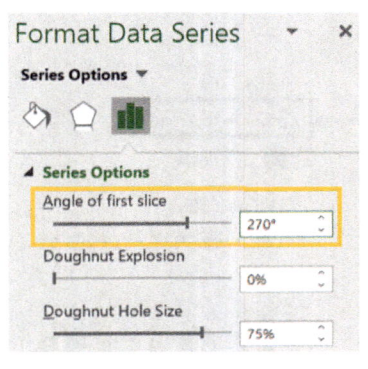 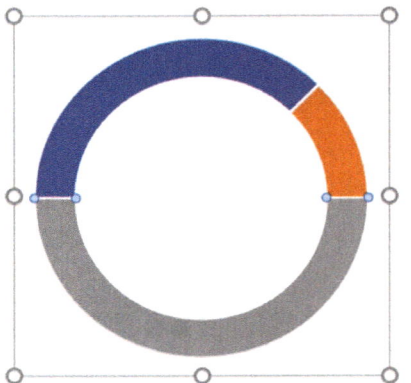

In order to hide the below half of circle, select only the below half of the circle (using a mouse) by **double clicks** in the chart.

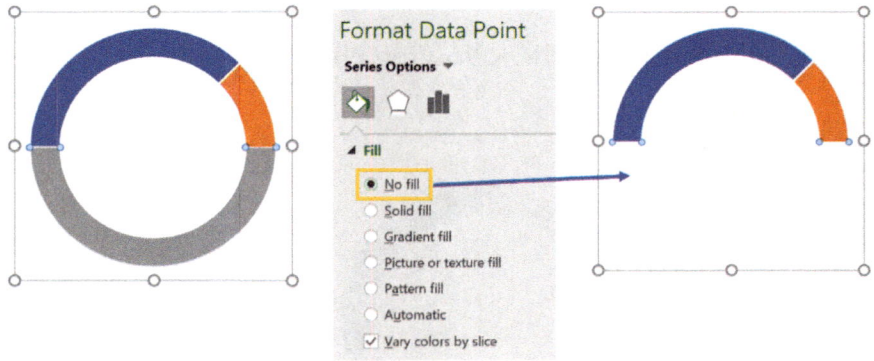

Up to now, we create a donut chart and make it a half donut chart by disappearing color of the below half part in the chart.

How to change colors in the chart:

Please note that we need to **change the color <u>one by one</u>**. We can start the main donut part and supporting part.

For the main donut part:
- Click one of series in the chart (**select one of pieces**) >>>
- **Ctrl + 1** >>> **Format Data Series** >>> **Fill** >>>
- Select **Solid fill** >>> Select a color (i.e., dark blue) which you wish to choose.

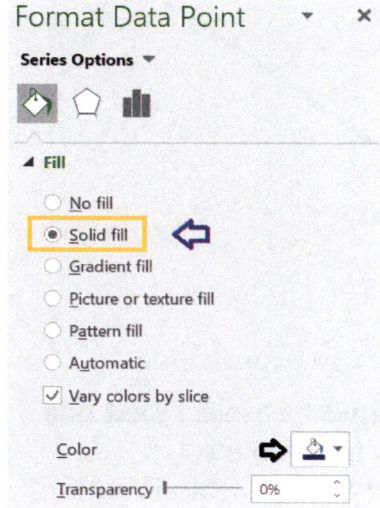

For the supporting donut part, see below.

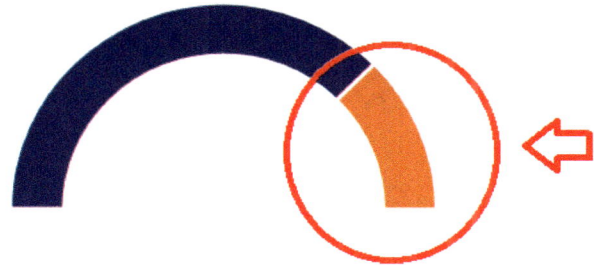

Select the same color as the main donut part.

All settings are identical both main donut and support donut part **except transparency**.

- **Transparency = 90%**

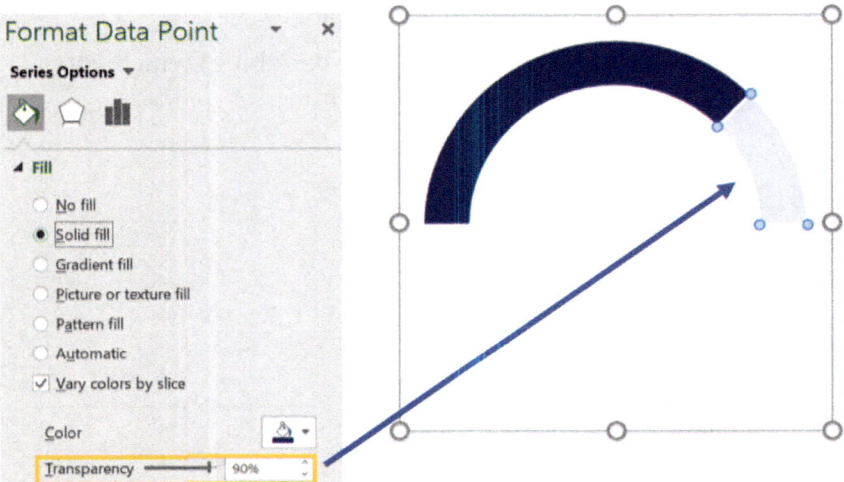

How to make a text box which shows an input value:

- Make a text box: **Insert** tab >>> **Shapes** >>>select **Text box**.
- Put a cursor inside of text box & click function box ( )
- Write '**= cell location** (i.e., =B5)' and then hit '**Enter**' button.

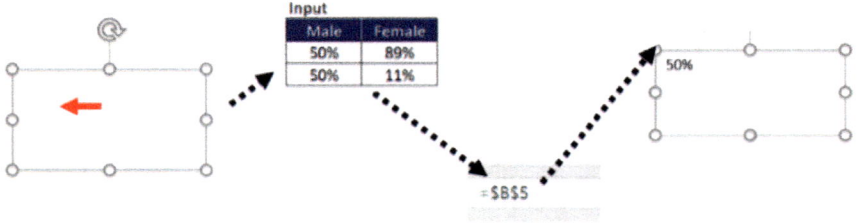

In this example, we need to add =$B$2
Please see below.

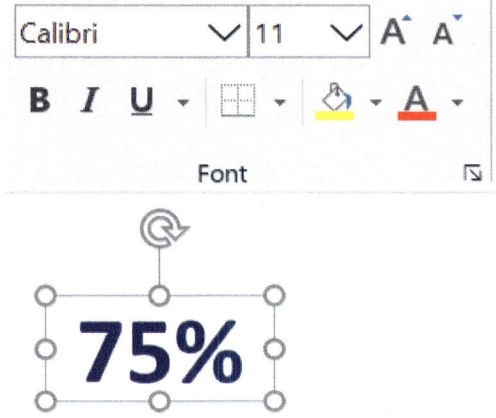

How to make the text box looking good:

Clicking a text box, removing Shape Fill & Shape Outline.
- **Shape Fill** = No Fill
- **Shape Outline** = No Outline

In the **Home** tap, the rest elements (font size, font color, font type, etc.) can be changed by Font tab elements (see below)

In the same manner, we can make another text box for the Project name.

How to align multiple text boxes or charts:

Now, we have 3 pieces of components (half donut chart, 2 text boxes). In order to make them align nicely, please use the following steps which is much easier than by using mouse.

- **Holding Ctrl** button >>> select chart and text boxes by clicking a left-hand mouse button.

It is possible to select multiple items in the sheet.

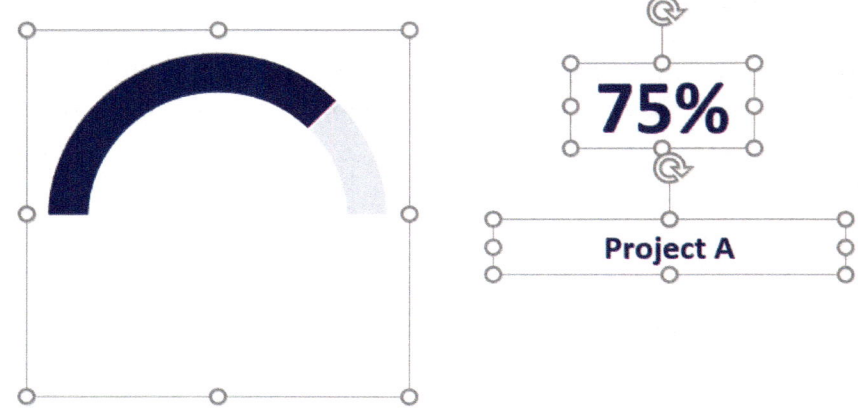

Go to **Shape Format** >>> **Align** >>> **Align Center**

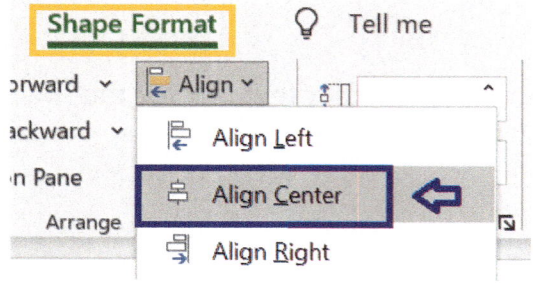

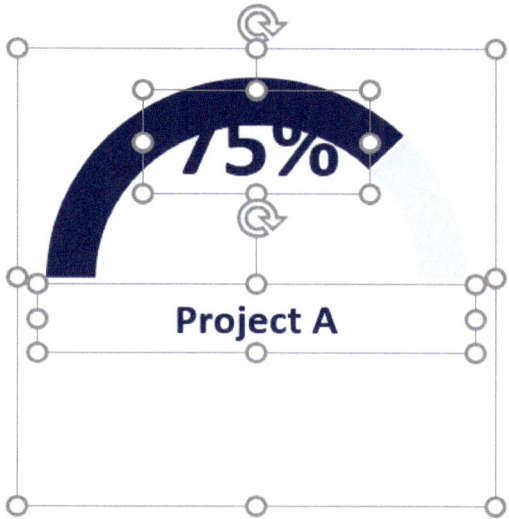

Deselect all items and select only 75% text box.
Adjust height to the adequate location by using a direction key.

In this example, hitting downward direction key will be the right one.

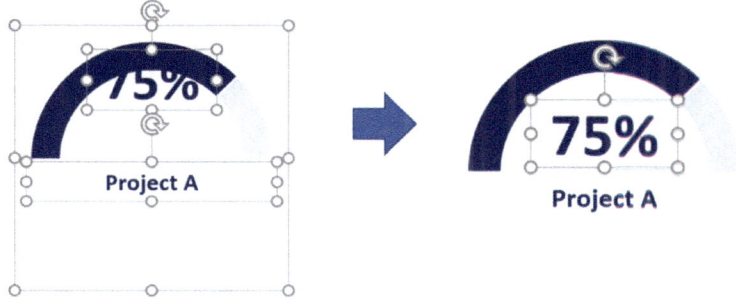

Depends on the location of items, the align elements are changeable.

All of align elements are very handy to allocate various charts or text boxes at once.

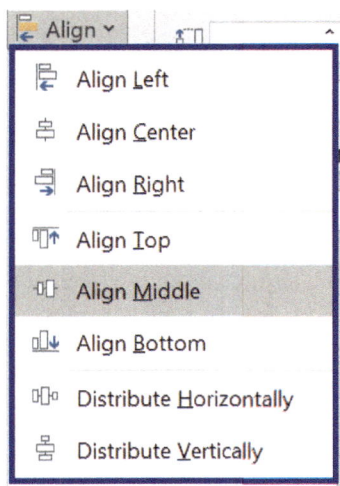

Optional: How to group objects (or items):

Select more than 2 objects, then click a right-hand button on the mouse, you can see '**Group**' in **Shape Format**. Select Group.

More than 2 objects become one object which is handy.
If you don't like it, you can also ungroup it or regroup them.

Select multiple items >>> Go to **Shape Format** >>> **Group**

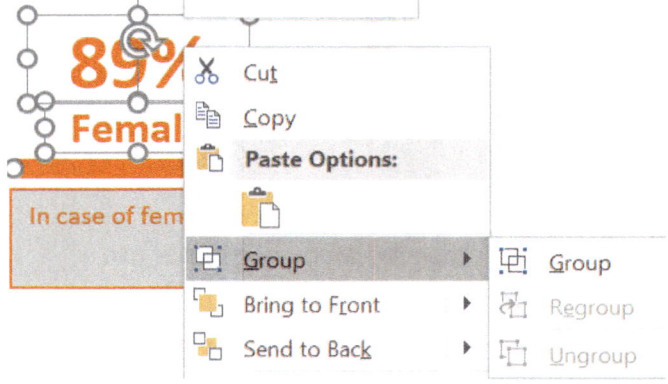

Believe it or not, we already complete a half-circle donut chart. This chart is ready to use for your report, blog (as picture), teaching materials.

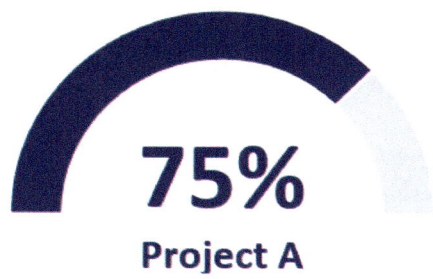

Now, we can challenge ourselves to generate more applied version from the basic half-circle donut chart.

Applied version 1:

In term of effort, it is not much. Copy & paste the base half-circle donut chart.

Select the main donut part which shows the actual input value (=i.e., 75%).

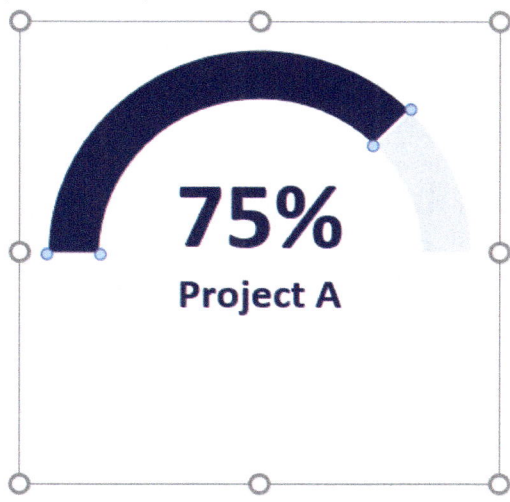

Please note that we need to **change the line color one by one**.

- Click main donut chart part >>>
- **Ctrl + 1 >>> Format Data Series >>> Border** >>>
- Select **Solid line** >>> Select a small color (i.e., dark blue) as filled color.
- Width = **15pt**

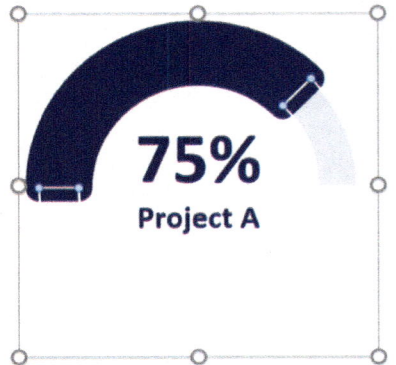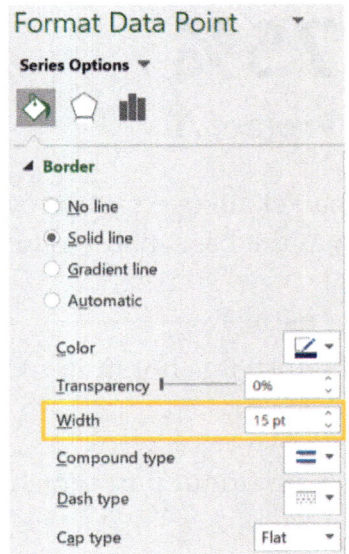

- Select **supporting donut** >>> Select **No line** in Border

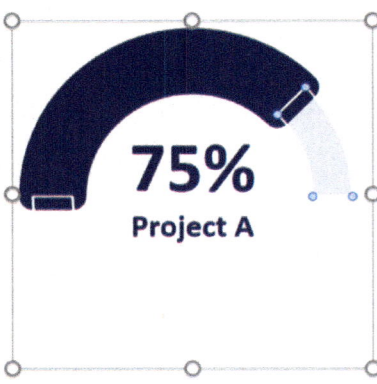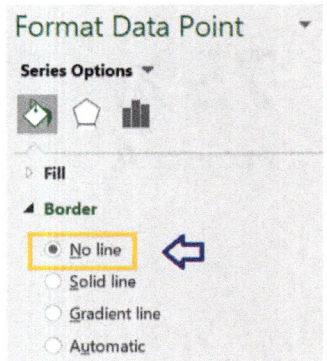

For the below disappeared donut part:
We can set up in the same manner for as well. (**No line** in **Border** in **Format Data Series**)

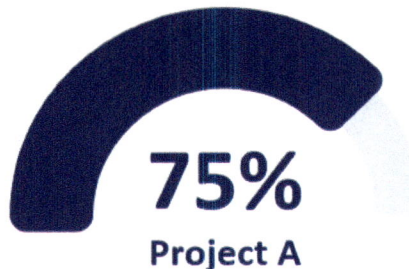

After applying no line, the white lines are disappeared.

Applied version 2:

In term of effort, it is also not much. Copy & paste the applied version 1 chart.

- Click main donut chart part >>>
- **Ctrl + 1** >>> **Format Data Series** >>> **Border** >>>
- Select **Solid line** >>> Go to a dash type
- Select Round Dot

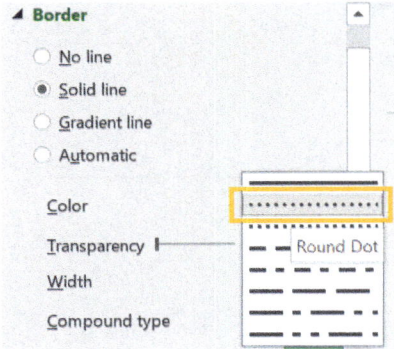

We can already complete the new type of half-circle donut chart.

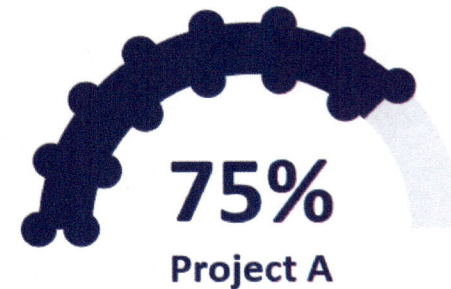

In case of change of color of donut chart, we did not discuss because this is rather straightforward to do it.

Finally, we can create the below types of charts.

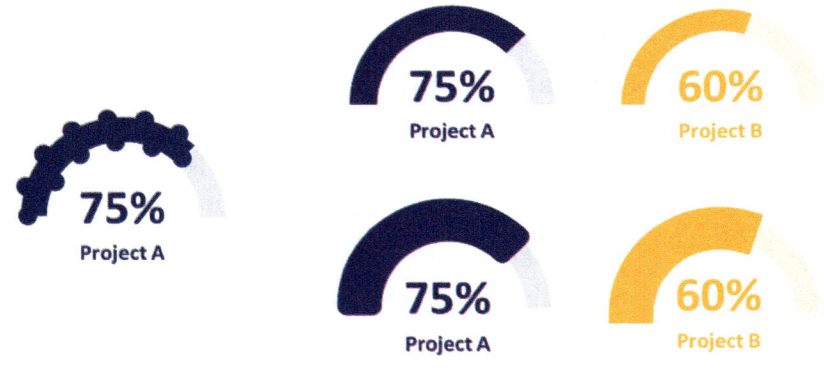

Trouble shooting (Tip):

How to avoid destroy original chart shape after adding new col or rows

After adding completing your chart task, it was realized that you need to add one more column.
After adding the column, your completed chart is destroyed due to adding or adjusting a new column.

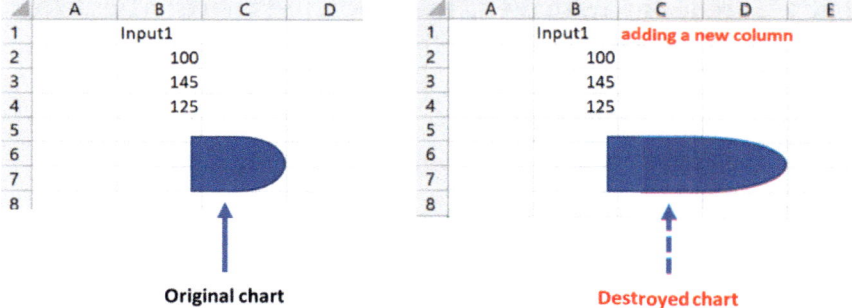

Original chart   Destroyed chart

Q: What should I do with it?

The solution is to go to '**Size and Properties**' and click '**Move but don't size with cells**.

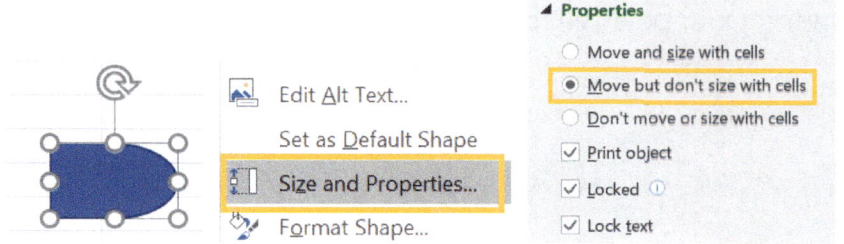

16. Dynamic Colour-changed Bar Chart

We are going to make a dynamic color-changed bar chart **(depends on input values)** which is not really straightforward to make it without knowing the trick.

Target picture:
What we are going to make is the following charts: The below input table is directly linked to the color-changed bar chart.

Example:
- If the input value is negative, the bar color is red.
- If the input value is positive, the bar color is dark blue.

In terms of graphical perspective, the chart looks like a normal bar chart.

However, the dynamic color-changed chart is very practical and handy for your daily work. The beauty of the char is that you do not need to change the color when input values are changing from positive to negative or vice versa.

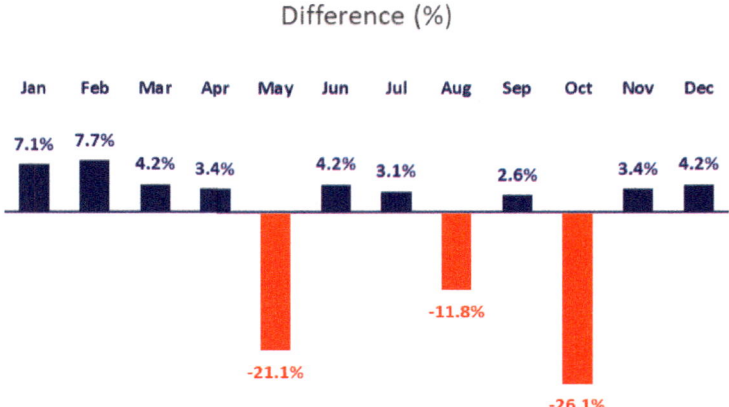

How to set up input values:

First, create actual **input columns, Difference column** in an empty worksheet (as an example).

The input values are presented by absolute value and the difference is in percentage (%).

For this section, we are going to use the following table as an example. The difference column is a mixture with positive values and negative values.

Month	Sale (2020)	Sale (2019)	Difference (%)
Jan	3,000	2,800	7.1%
Feb	2,800	2,600	7.7%
Mar	5,000	4,800	4.2%
Apr	6,000	5,800	3.4%
May	3,000	3,800	-21.1%
Jun	5,000	4,800	4.2%
Jul	6,600	6,400	3.1%
Aug	6,000	6,800	-11.8%
Sep	8,000	7,800	2.6%
Oct	6,500	8,800	-26.1%
Nov	6,000	5,800	3.4%
Dec	5,000	4,800	4.2%

- Difference (%) = Sale (2020) / Sale (2019) – 1

How to create 2-D Clustered bar chart:

- After selecting inputs values (Difference column by using mouse dragging), go to **Insert** tab.
- Select **2-D bar** >>> **Clustered Bar**.

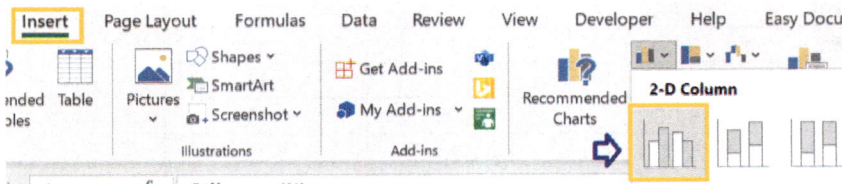

	A	B	C	D
1	Month	Sale (2020)	Sale (2019)	Difference (%)
2	Jan	3,000	2,800	7.1%
3	Feb	2,800	2,600	7.7%
4	Mar	5,000	4,800	4.2%
5	Apr	6,000	5,800	3.4%
6	May	3,000	3,800	-21.1%
7	Jun	5,000	4,800	4.2%
8	Jul	6,600	6,400	3.1%
9	Aug	6,000	6,800	-11.8%
10	Sep	8,000	7,800	2.6%
11	Oct	6,500	8,800	-26.1%
12	Nov	6,000	5,800	3.4%
13	Dec	5,000	4,800	4.2%

We can create the following chart.

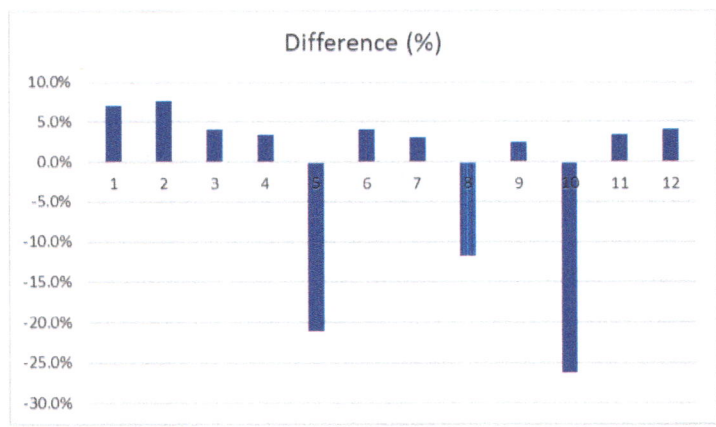

- After **selecting the chart**, click a right-hand mouse button and go to **Select Data**.

- Click **Edit** in **Horizontal Axis Labels**

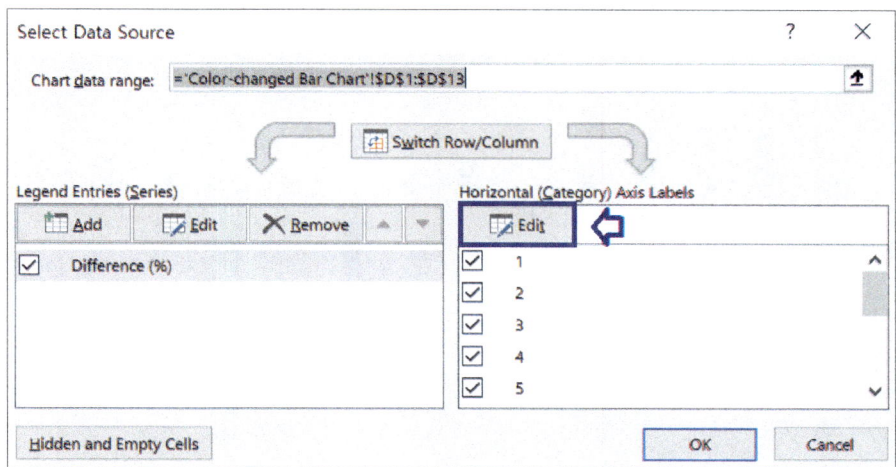

- Select **Month cloumn** (Column A) and click **OK.**

- click **OK** again.

We can create the following bar chart.

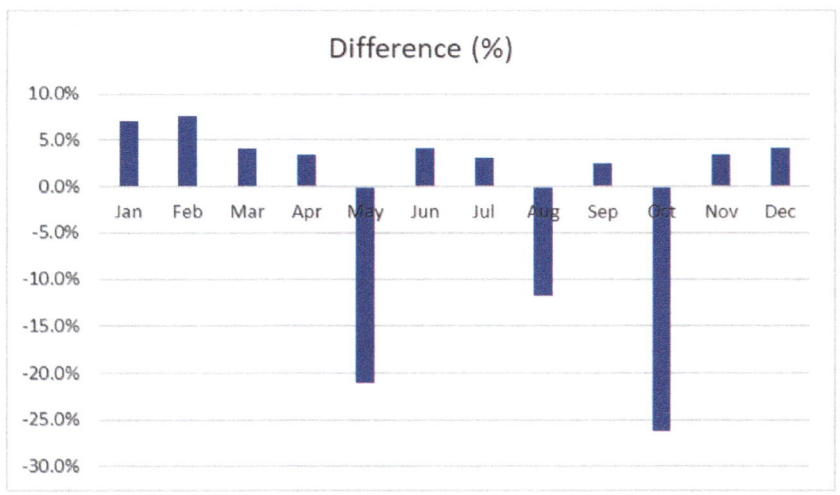

How to remove Gridlines:

- Go to **View** tab and unclick **Gridlines**.

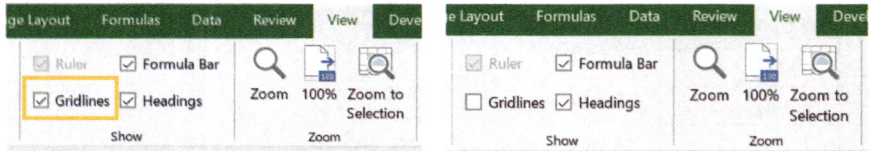

All the grid lines are disappeared in the sheet.

How to remove 'Shape Fill' and 'Shape Outline':

Click a chart >>> Go to **Format** tab. We will change the default settings of **Shape Fill** and **Shape Outline** of the chart.

- **Shape Fill** = No Fill
- **Shape Outline** = No Outline

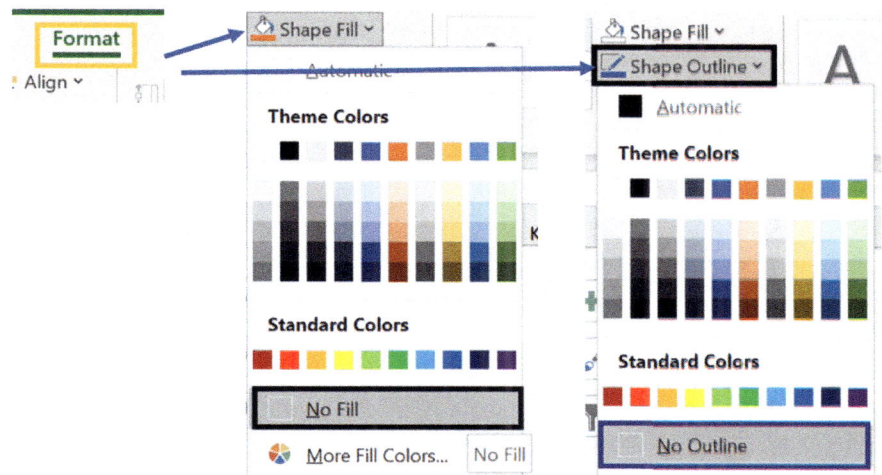

How to move Label in the chart:

- Select **horizontal axis** (Jan, Feb, …) >>> **Ctrl +1**
- Go to **Label** in **Format Axis** >>> **Label Position**
- Select **High** in **Label Position**

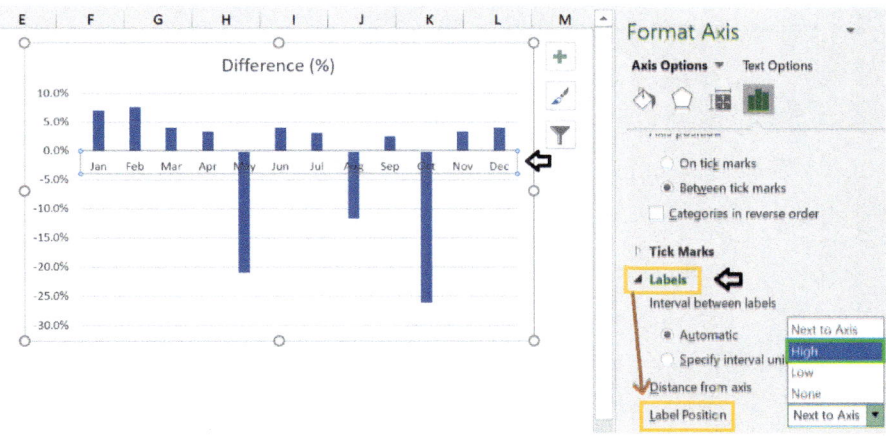

As a result, we can see the following chart.

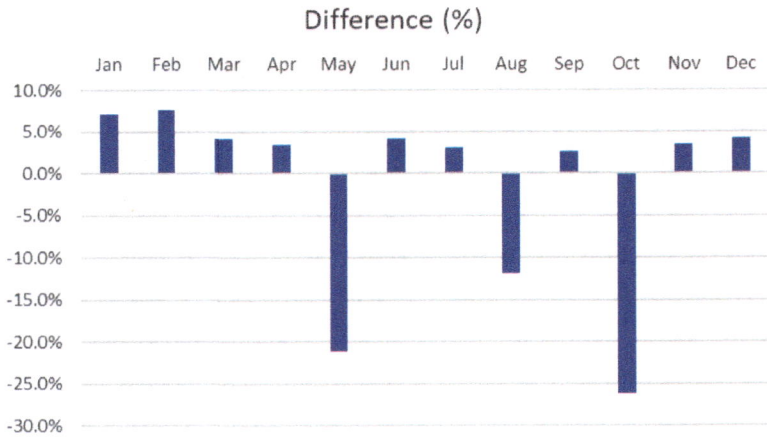

Setup for how to change the color of bar depends on input value:

- Select one of bars in the chart (by mouse clicking) >>> **Ctrl +1**
- Go to **Fill** in **Format Data Series**
- Select **Invert if negative** in Fill

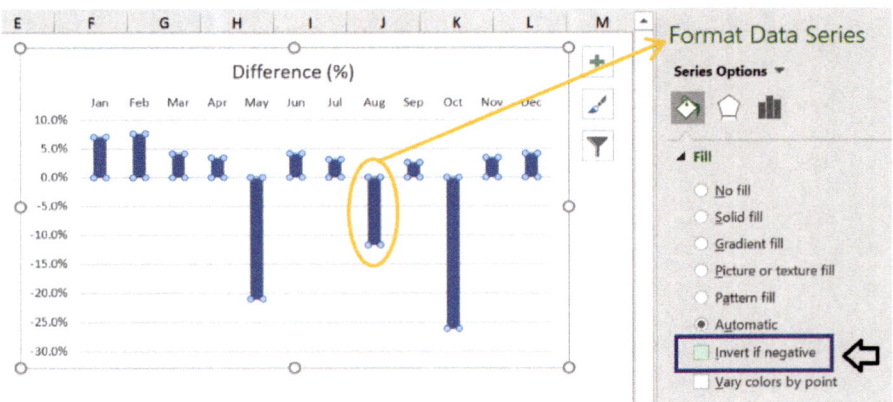

- Select **Solid fill** in **Fill**
- You can see 2 colors are popping up after selecting Solid fill.
- The **first color is positive value** and the **second one is negative value**.

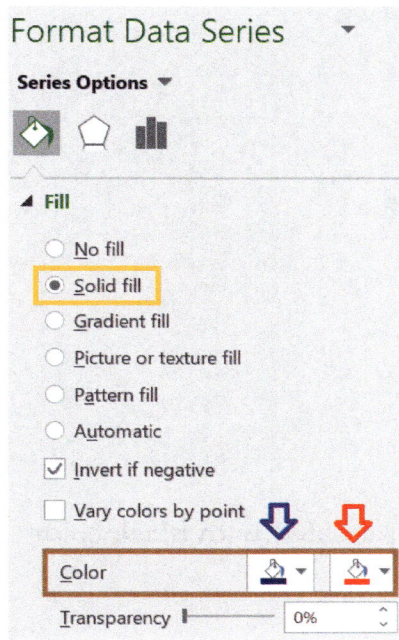

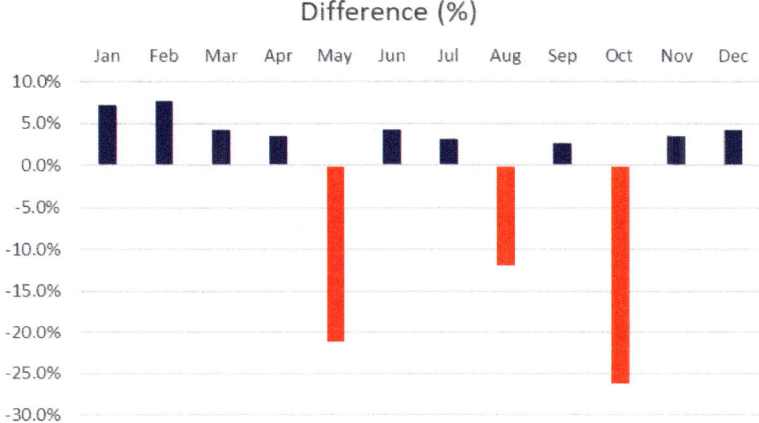

How to adjust the middle line in the graph:

- Select horizontal axis (Jan, Feb, …) >>> **Ctrl +1**
- Go to **Line** in **Format Axis**
- Select **Solid line** in Line
- Change color of line, width (as you wish)

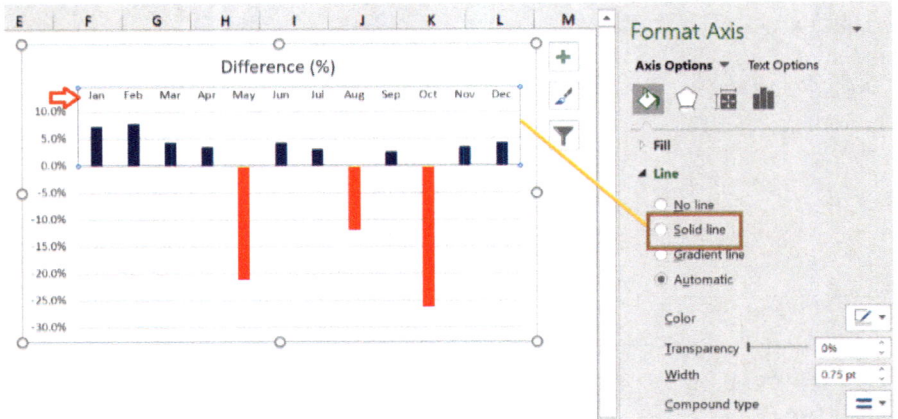

As an example, the following one is created with **black** color and **width 1.25pt**.

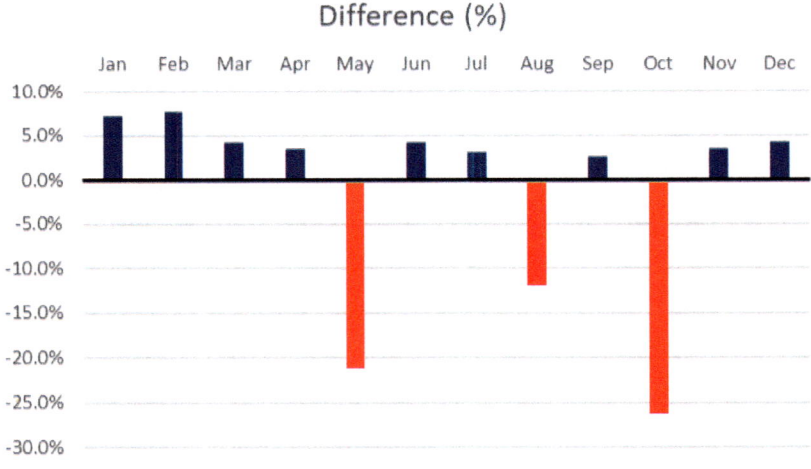

How to add labels on the bars:

- Select **horizontal bars** (Jan, Feb, ...)
- Click a **right-hand mouse button** >>> click **Add Data Labels**

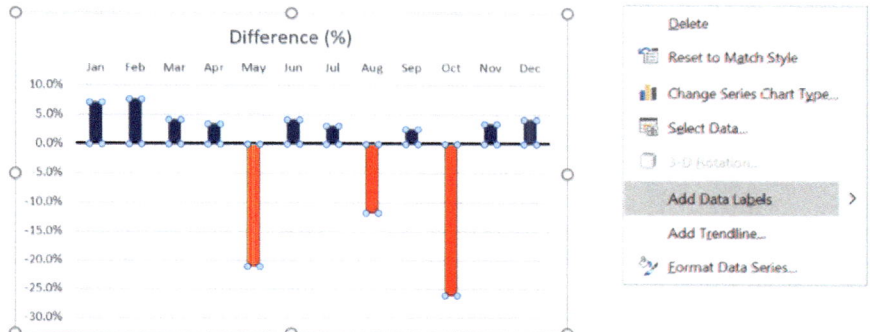

- Select the **labels on bar** by using mouse
- Adjust color of letter, size (as you wish)

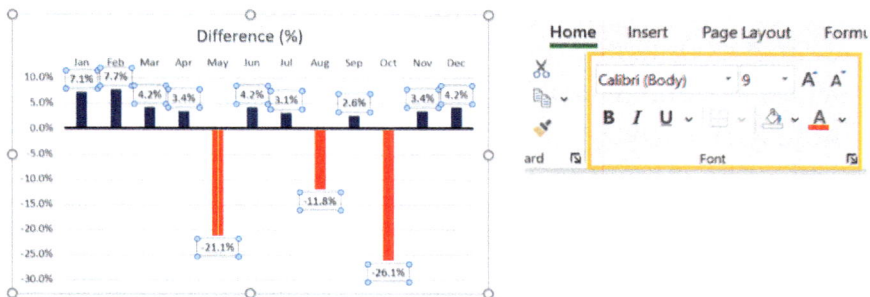

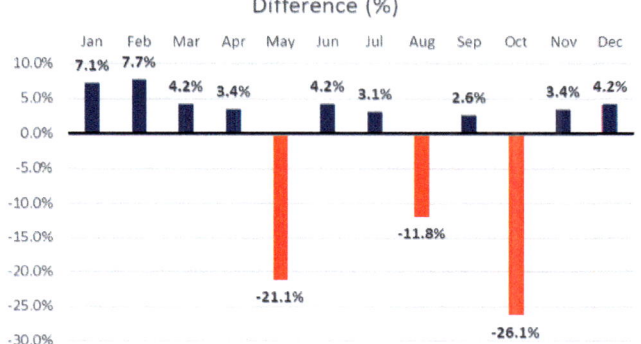

How to adjust labels on the bars in the chart:

As you can see below, labels and axis are too close.
In order to solve this situation, we need to adjust Format Axis.

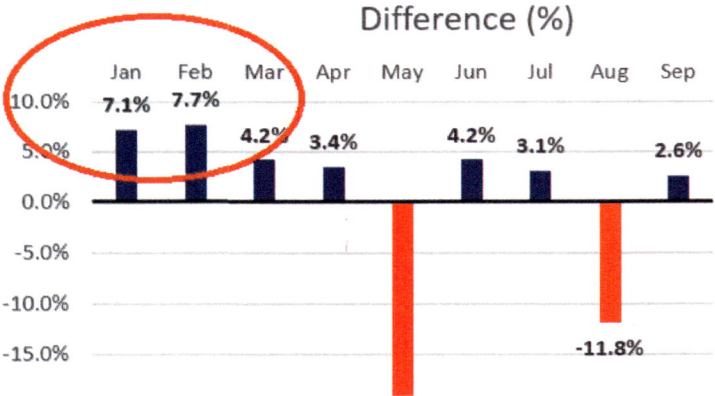

- Click a **vertical axis** in the chart >>> **Ctrl + 1**
- Go to **Axis Option**
- Adjust **Maximum** number
- **Auto** is changed to **Reset**.

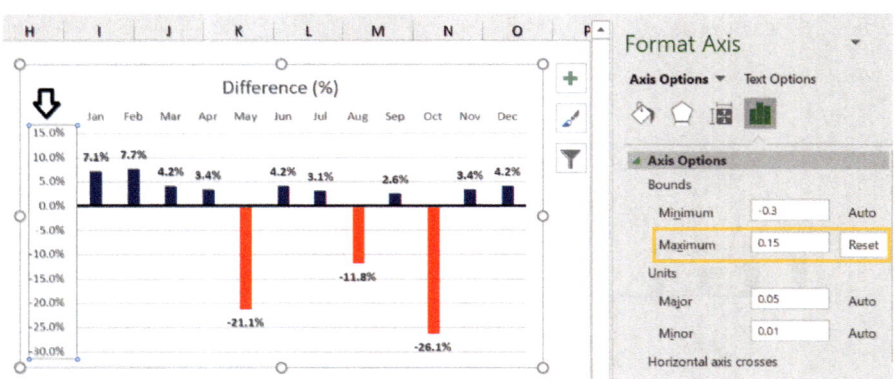

Please note that you need to adjust the maximum axis number manually.

How to remove chart elements:

After clicking a chart, we can see the plus **(+) sign** on right hand side. This is the location where we can control the chart elements.

- Go to **Chart Elements** = click **(+)** sign in gray in the chart
- **Remove the chart elements** = **Unclick** the chart elements which you want to remove

In this case, we unclicked both **Gridlines** and **Primary Vertical Axis** from chart elements.

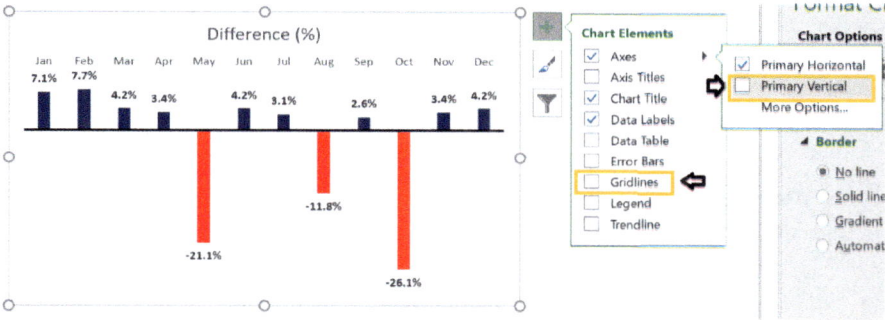

How to select 'Plot Area':

In general, it is possible to select the area by using mouse.

Alternatively, you can use the following way:
- Click the graph >>> **Ctrl + 1** (**Format Chart Area**) >>> click a **small inverse triangle** next to 'Chart Options' >>> select **Plot Area**

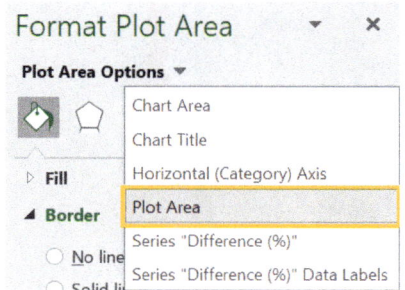

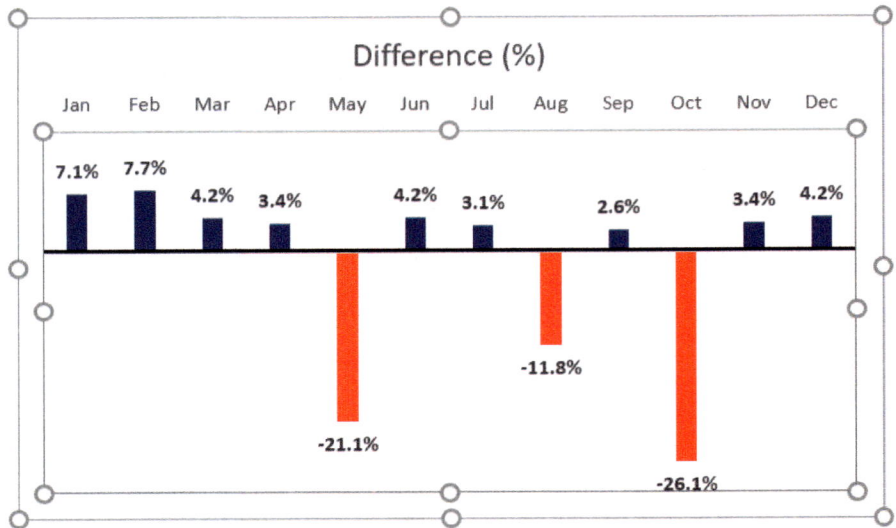

By a **mouse dragging**, you can adjust the distance between the horizontal axis and Chart title.

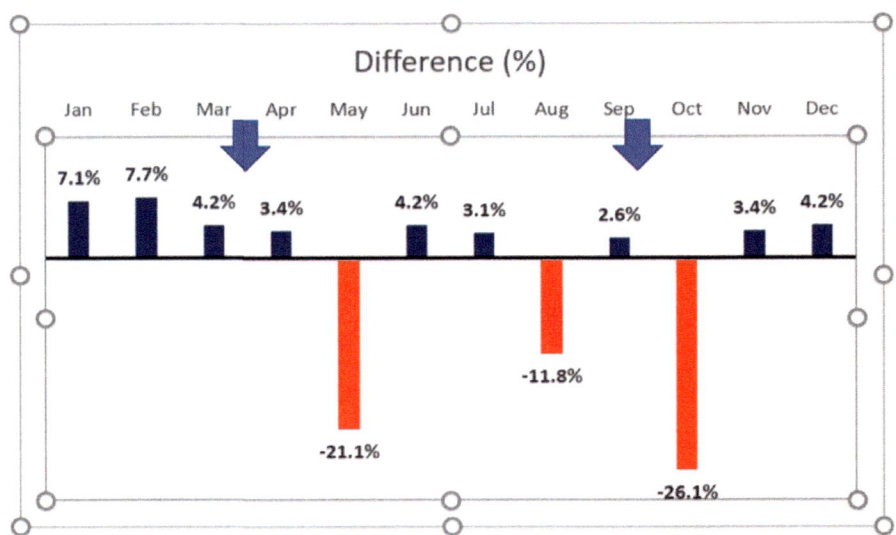

Finally, we can complete to create this chart.

For the shake of completeness, the horizontal values (Jan, Feb, …) are adjusted (Bold, Dark blue in **Home** tab)

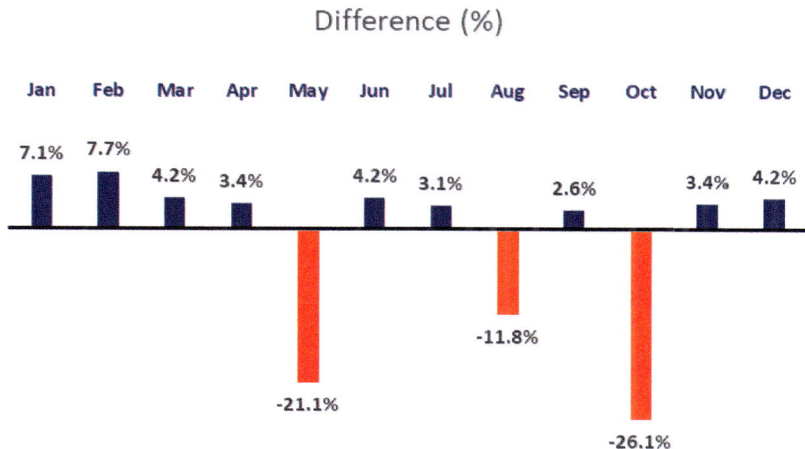

As a test, actual input values are changed. Correspondingly, the color-changed bar charted is also updated. (See Jan)

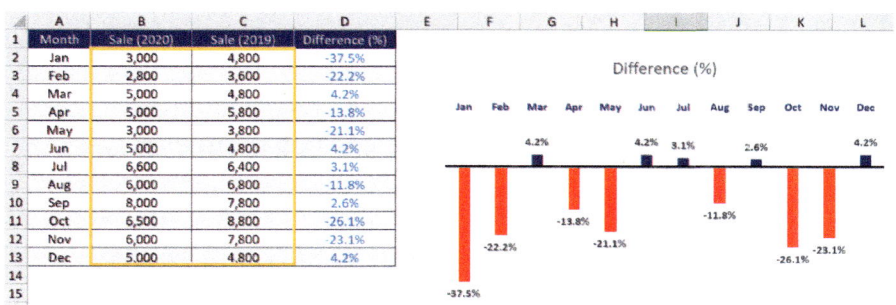

Please be aware again that you need to adjust the maximum axis number manually depends on the movements of Difference (%) column. This is because we change the setting to a manual mode.

17. Two-sides Horizontal Bar Chart

We are going to make a 2 sides horizontal bar chart. It looks like an easy chart to create it. However, it is not really straightforward to make it without knowing the trick.

Target picture:
What we are going to make is the following charts:

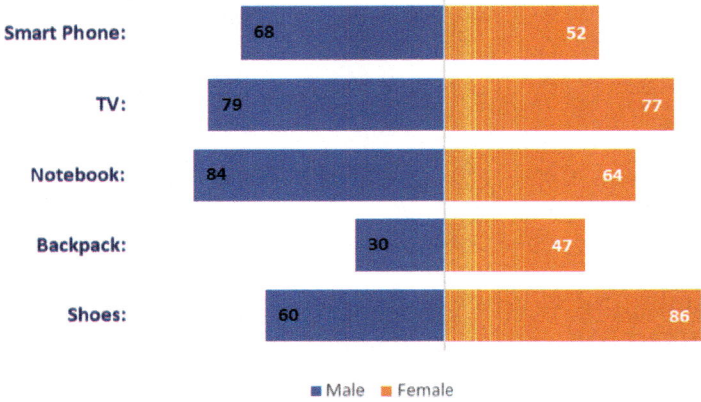

How to set up input values:

First, create actual input value table **2 times** in an empty worksheet.

For the second table, one of the input values columns is required to have a formula. (i.e., male)

- Male = Male (from another table) * – 1

Only one of input columns is needed to have an above formula. This step is to make a negative values' column.

	A	B	C	D
	SUM		✗ ✓ fx	=B3*-1
1	Input Value			
2	Product	Male	Female	
3	Smart Phone:	68	52	
4	TV:	79	77	
5	Notebook:	84	64	
6	Backpack:	30	47	
7	Shoes:	60	86	
8				
9	Graph			
10	Product	Male	Female	
11	Smart Phone:	=B3*-1	52	
12	TV:	-79	77	
13	Notebook:	-84	64	
14	Backpack:	-30	47	
15	Shoes:	-60	86	

Later on, **as a clean-up process**, we can **relocate the second graph** somewhere in the hidden place.

How to create 2-D Stacked bar chart:

- After selecting inputs values (see below range selection & by using mouse dragging), go to **Insert** tab.
- Select **2-D bar** >>> **Stacked Bar**.

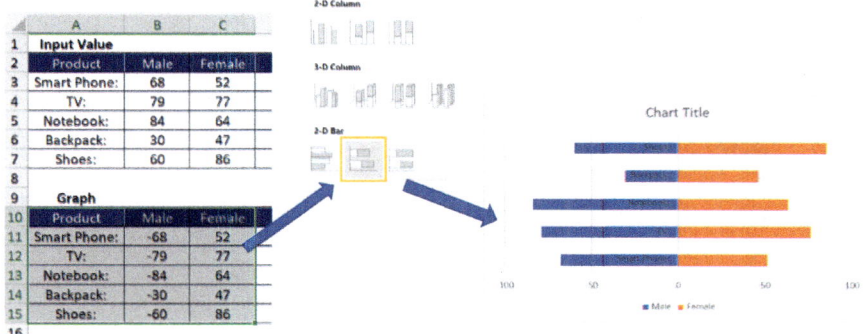

How to adjust order of bars in the chart:

After creating the horizontal bar chart, we can find a problem that the order of bars is reversed compared to the original input table.

(Note) In order to visualize vertical axis values, the color is changed to white in below chart. (**This is definitely no need to make this chart.**)

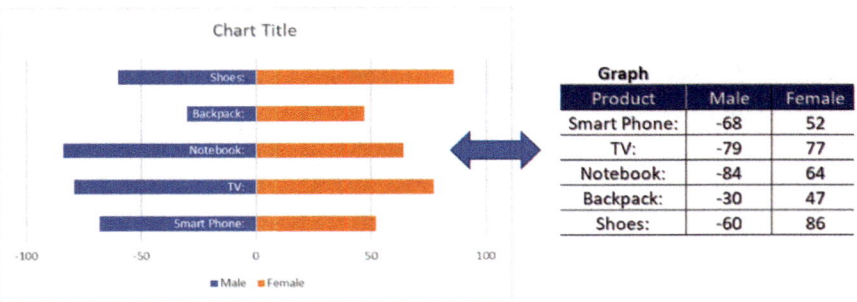

- Click **vertical axis** using mouse >>> **Ctrl + 1**
- Go to **Axis position** >>> click **'Categories in reverse order'**

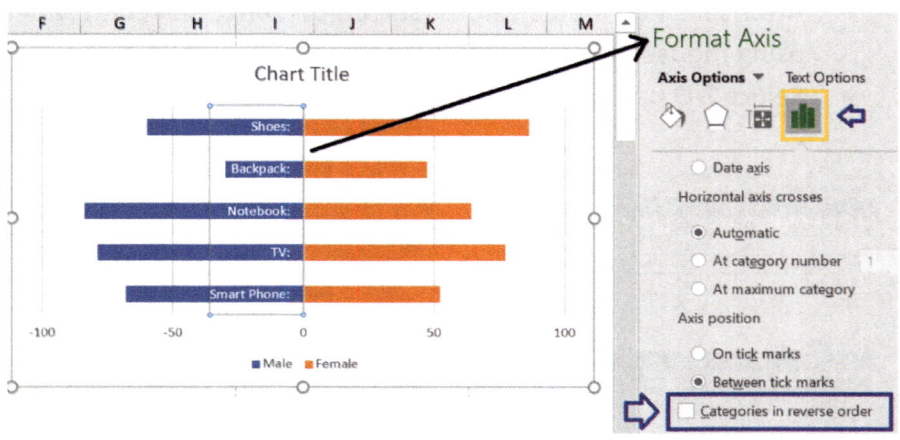

How to change location values in the vertical axis:

- Click **vertical axis** using mouse >>> **Ctrl + 1**
- Go to **Labels** >>> select **'Low'** in **Label Position**

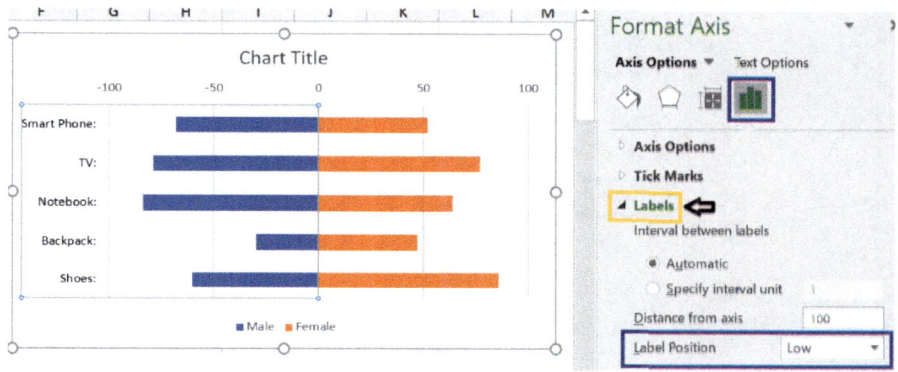

How to remove Gridlines:

- Go to **View** tab and unclick **Gridlines**.

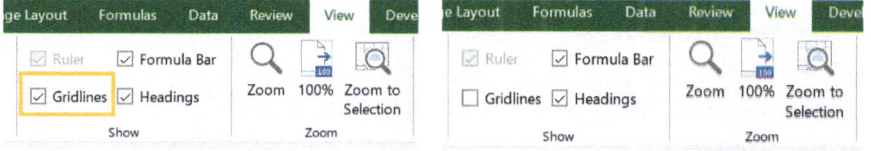

All the grid lines are disappeared in the sheet.

How to remove 'Shape Fill' and 'Shape Outline':

Click a chart >>> Go to **Format** tab. We will change the default settings of **Shape Fill** and **Shape Outline** of the chart.

- **Shape Fill** = No Fill
- **Shape Outline** = No Outline

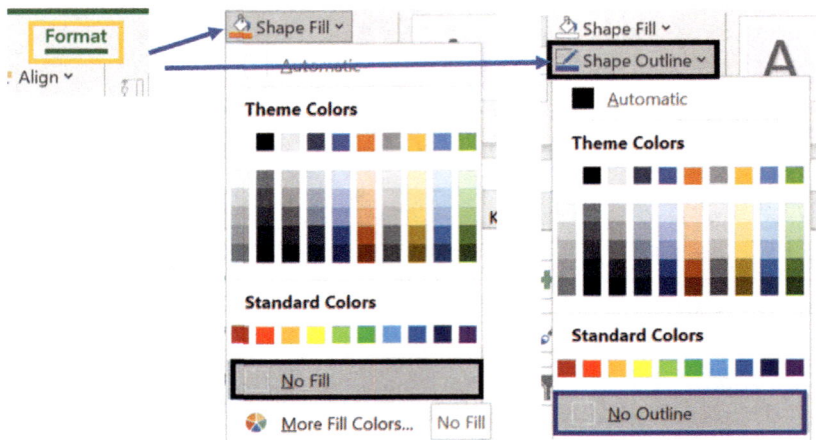

How to remove chart elements:

After clicking a chart, we can see the plus **(+) sign** on right hand side. This is the location where we can control the chart elements.

- Go to chart elements = click **(+)** sign in gray in the chart
- **Remove the chart elements** = Unclick the chart elements which you want to remove

In this case, we unclicked both **Chart Title** and **Gridlines** from chart elements.

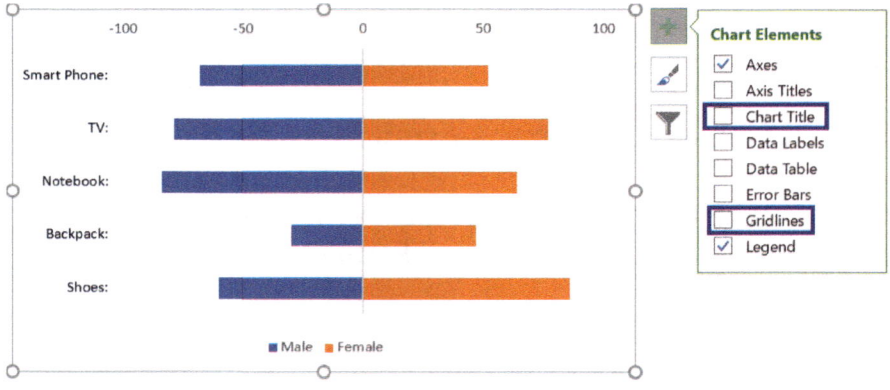

How to adjust gab among horizontal bars in the chart:

- Click **horizontal bars** using mouse >>> **Ctrl + 1**
- Go to Series Options in **Format Data Series** >>> select **'35%'** in **Gap Width** (you can choose what you wish)

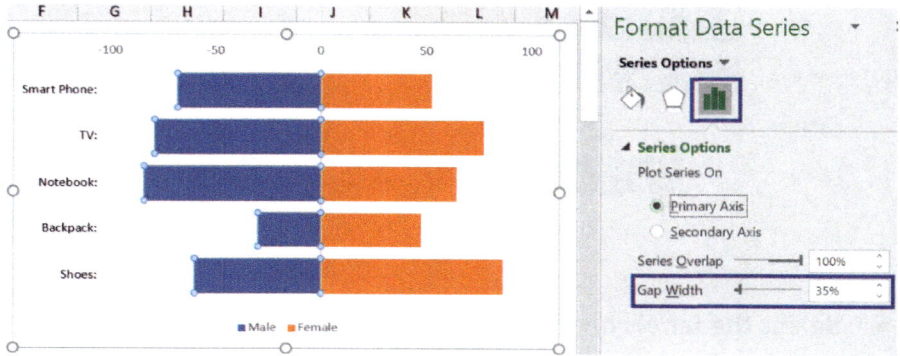

How to add labels on the bars:

- Select horizontal bar
- Click a **right-hand mouse button** >>> click **Add Data Labels**

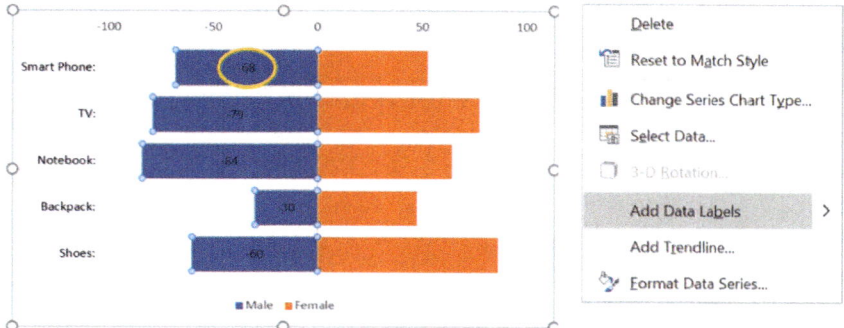

It is required to do it **twice for both directions** (left and right side). In this book, we are going to show only the left side. In the same manner, we can add labels on the right side.

How to adjust label's locations:

- **Select labels** by using mouse >>> **Ctrl + 1 (Format Data Labels)**
- Go to **Label Position** >>> click **Inside End**

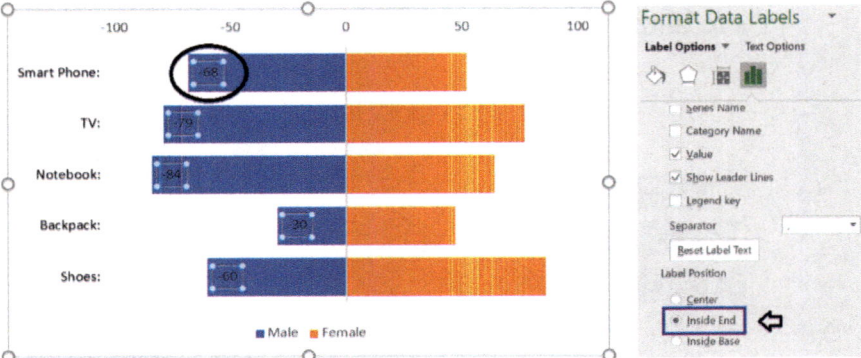

- **Select the labels** on the bars by using a mouse
- Adjust color of letter, size (as you wish) in **Home** tab

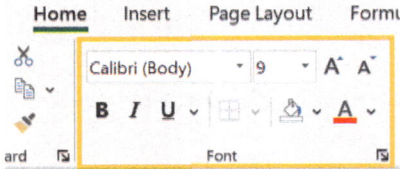

It is also required to do it **twice** for both directions (left and right side).

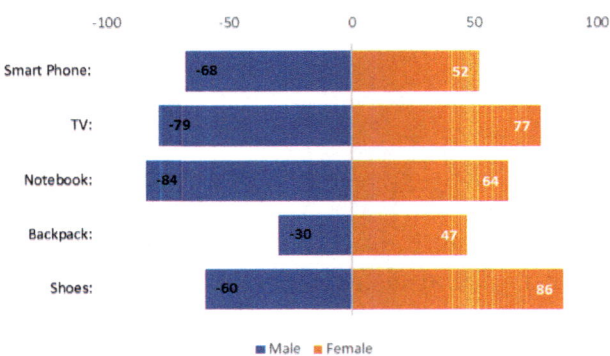

In the above case, the following setting is applied.
- Left side: **black** color (for label) with **bold**
- Right side: **white** color (for label) with **bold**

Problem!!!!

How to deal with 'negative value' in left side bars:
- **Select left-side labels** by using mouse >>> **Ctrl + 1 (Format Data Labels)**
- Go to **Number** >>> **Format Code** >>> **0;0** >>> **Add**

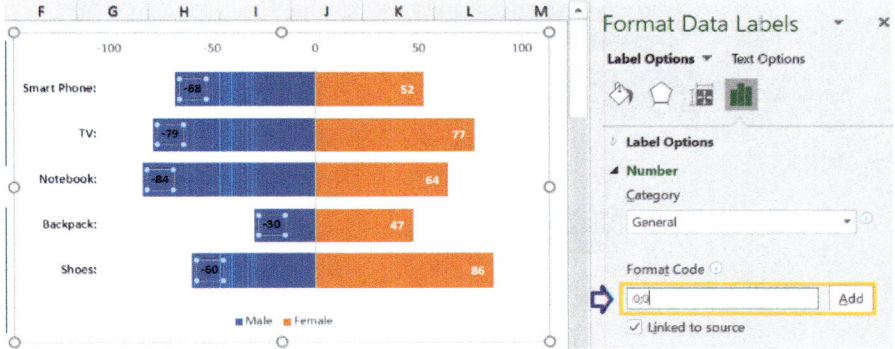

You can see that the negative values are changed to positive ones.

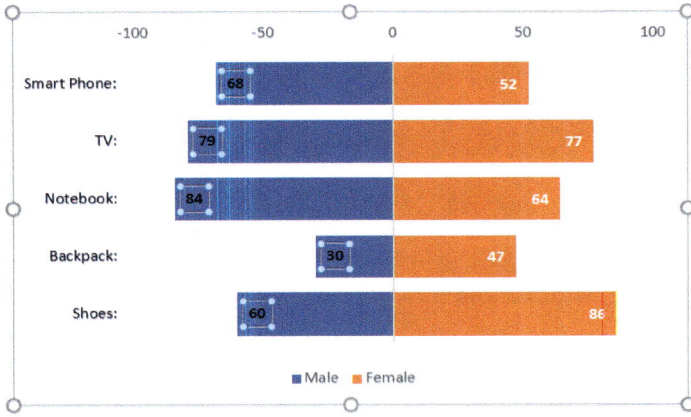

Please be aware that the negative values are actually still negative numbers.

What we did it that these values look like positive ones by using **Format Code**.

How to remove the vertical axis:

Click the **vertical axis** >>> press **delete** button

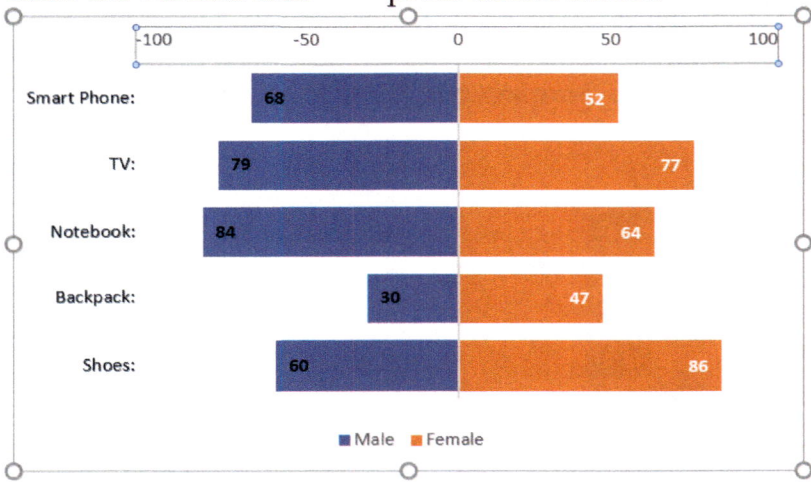

Finally, we can complete this graph.

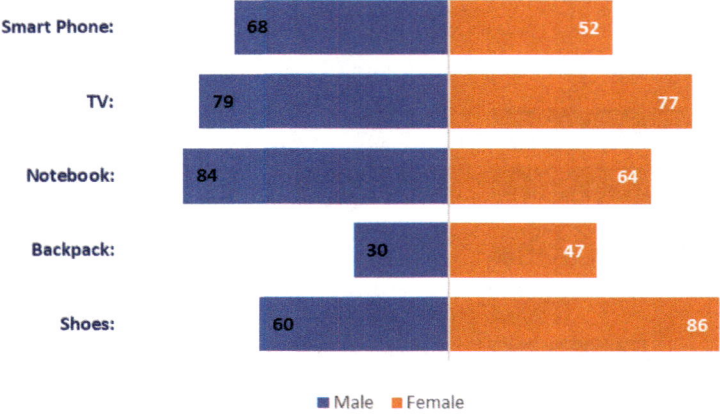

Applied Version 1:

Target picture:

What we are going to make is the following charts:

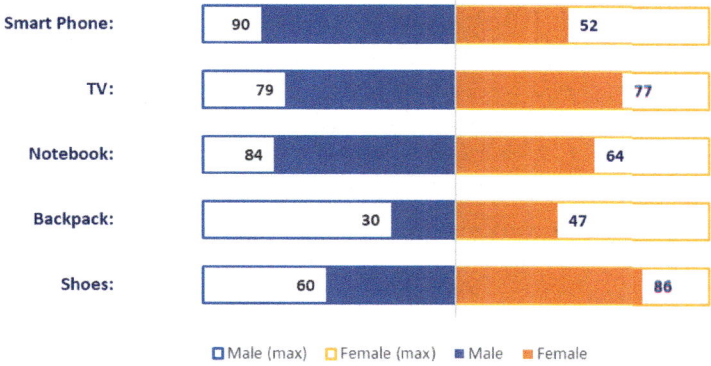

How to set up input values:

First, we need to create new 2 additional columns (=max values) for both input value tables.

In case of Input Value table:

- Male (max) = **MAX($B$3:$C$7)*1.3**

	A	B	C	D	E
1	Input Value				
2	Product	Male	Female	Male (max)	Female (max)
3	Smart Phone:	90	52	=MAX($B$3:$C$7)	117
4	TV:	79	77	117	117
5	Notebook:	84	64	117	117
6	Backpack:	30	47	117	117
7	Shoes:	60	86	117	117
8					
9	Graph				
10	Product	Male	Female	Male (max)	Female (max)
11	Smart Phone:	-90	52	-117	117
12	TV:	-79	77	-117	117
13	Notebook:	-84	64	-117	117
14	Backpack:	-30	47	-117	117
15	Shoes:	-60	86	-117	117

The applied formula is same for both max columns.
In order to make the **$ sign** in the range, press **F4 button** after selecting the range in the formula.

For the second table ('Graph'), one of the input values columns is required to have a formula. (i.e., male)

- Male (max) = Male (from another table) * – 1

Only one of input columns is needed to have an above formula. This step is to make negative values' columns.

	A	B	C	D	E
1	**Input Value**				
2	Product	Male	Female	Male (max)	Female (max)
3	Smart Phone:	90	52	117	117
4	TV:	79	77	117	117
5	Notebook:	84	64	117	117
6	Backpack:	30	47	117	117
7	Shoes:	60	86	117	117
8					
9	**Graph**				
10	Product	Male	Female	Male (max)	Female (max)
11	Smart Phone:	-90	52	-117	117
12	TV:	-79	77	-117	117
13	Notebook:	-84	64	-117	117
14	Backpack:	-30	47	-117	117
15	Shoes:	-60	86	-117	117
16					

How to add the new input values (2 max series):

- **Copy and paste the chart** (which we created) into a worksheet somewhere.
- **Select the new chart** by using mouse
- Click a **right-hand button** in the mouse
- Select **'Select Data'**

We can see a new pop-up window.

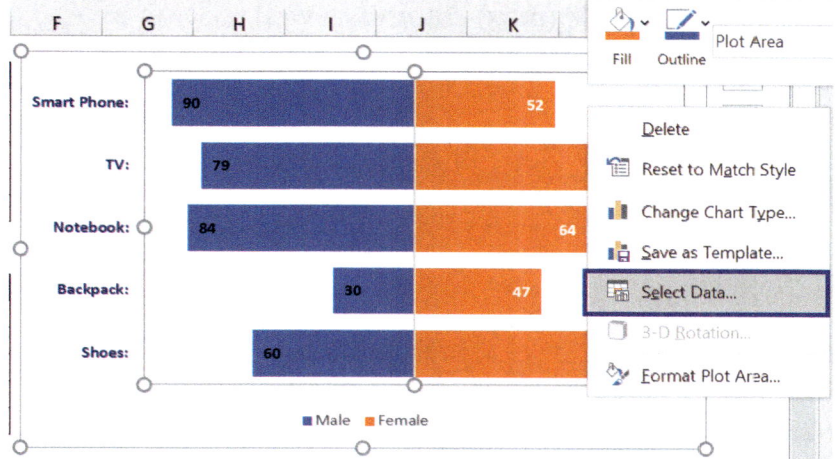

- Click **Add** button in the **'Select Data Source'**.

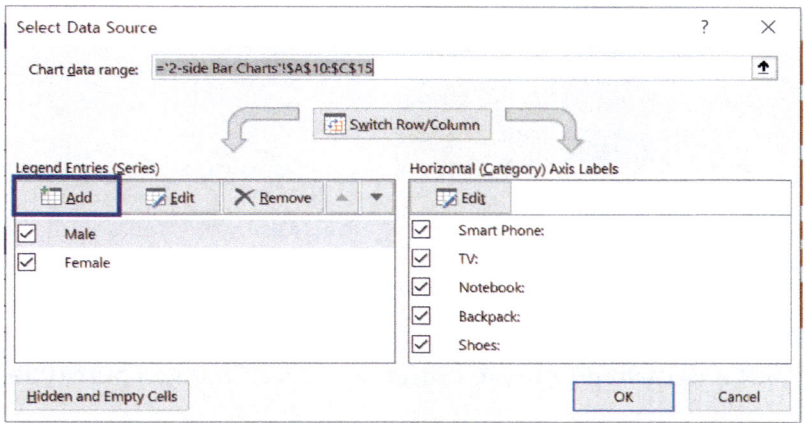

- Select **Series name** (D10 for Male (max)) & **Series value**.

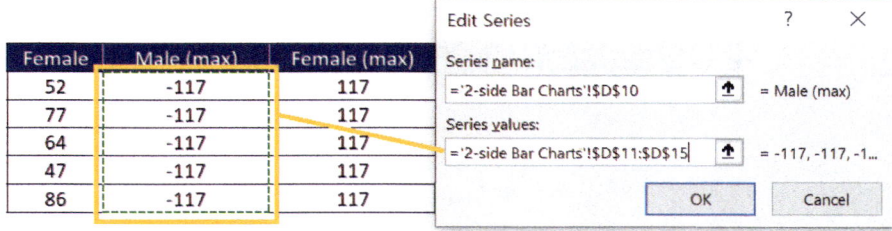

We need to add Female (max) column as well.

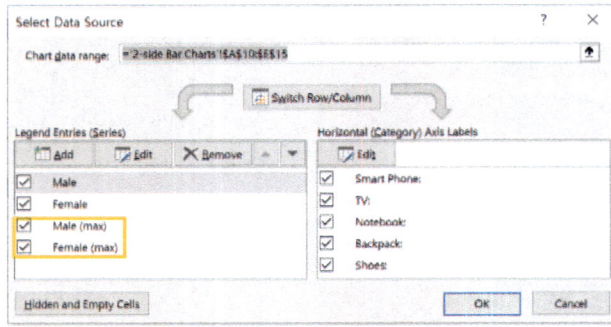

After adding 2 columns, it looks like below.

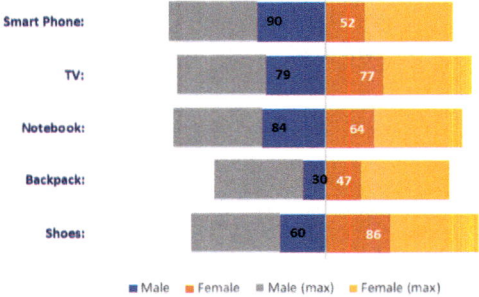

How to change chart type:

We need to change the chart from **Stack bar** to **Clustered bar**.
- Click a **right-hand mouse** button >>> click **Change chart type**.

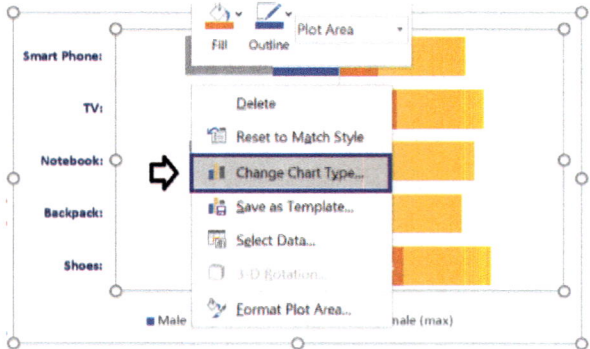

In a new pop-up, select **Clustered Bar**.

- Click **horizontal bars** using mouse >>> **Ctrl + 1**
- Go to **Series Options** in **Format Data Series** >>> select '**100%**' in **Series Overlap**

We have the following graph which looks strange.

In order to solve this situation, we need to switch the order of series in the chart. Both 2 new series are needed to be higher than the original series.

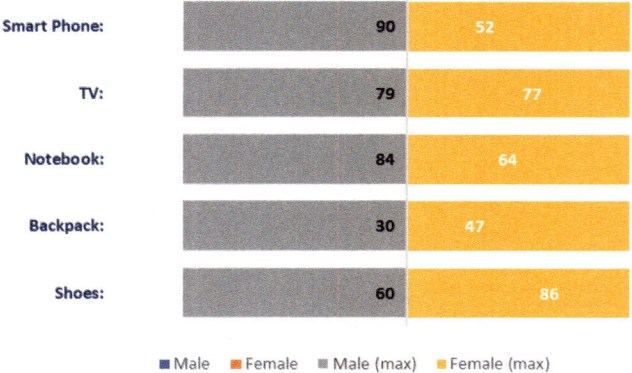

How to change the order of series in the chart:

- **Select the chart** by using mouse
- Click a **right-hand button** in the mouse
- Select '**Select Data**'

We can see a new pop-up window.

- Move up both Male (max) and Female (max) in the '**Select Data Source**' by using **triangle**.
- Select series >>> press the **triangle button** to be the top.
- Both Male (max) and Female (max) need to be **higher** than Male and Female series.

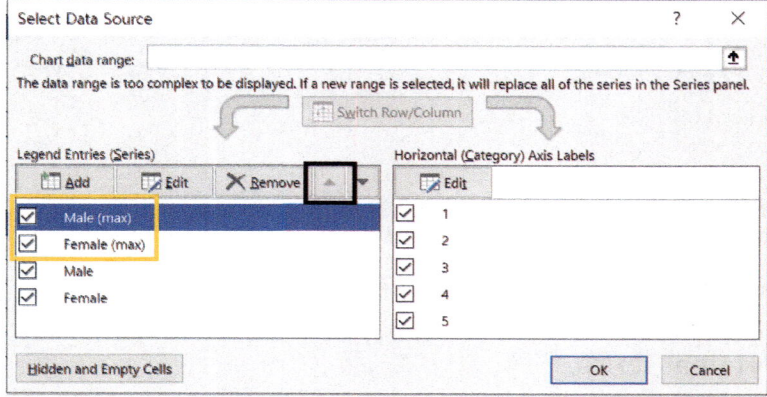

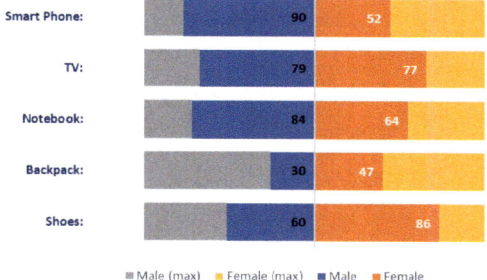

How to adjust the max bars in the chart:

- **Select one of max series** by using mouse >>> **Ctrl + 1**
- **No fill** in Fill & **Solid line** with selecting **same color** as bars
- **Line width = 1.5pt** (in the same manner, the female part)

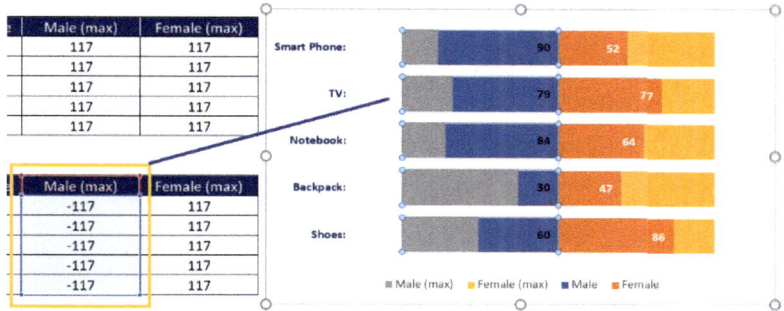

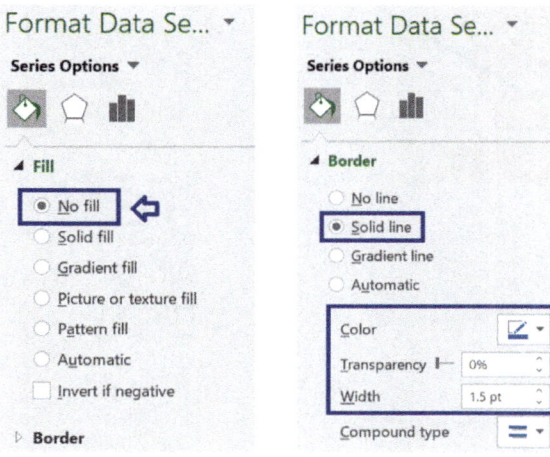

How to adjust the legend in the chart:

- **Select the legend** by using mouse (all selection)
- **Click one more time with one legend** which you want to remove (you see select like below)
- Press **delete** button

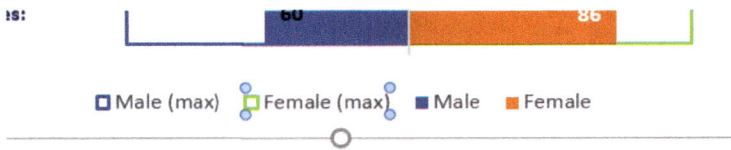

In this way, we can remove both max series.

Option: How to change label location:

- Select **one of labels** >>> **Ctrl +1**
- Go to **Label Position**
- Select **Outside End** in **Label Position**

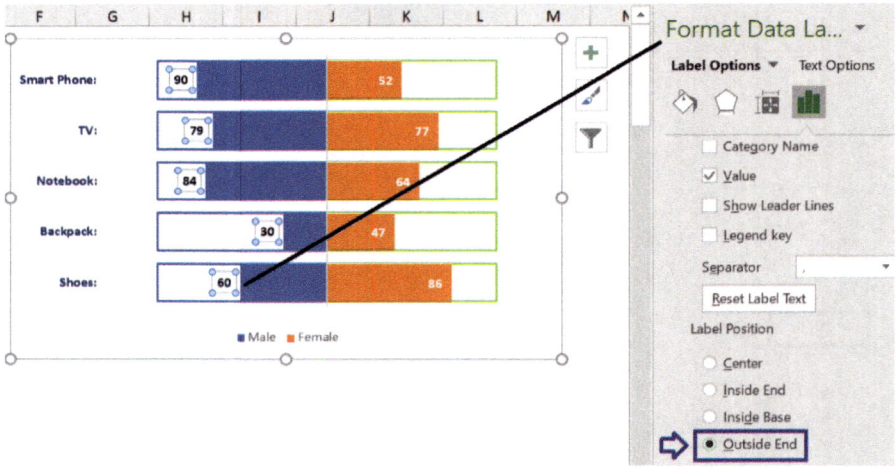

Applied Version 2:

Target picture:
What we are going to make is the following charts:

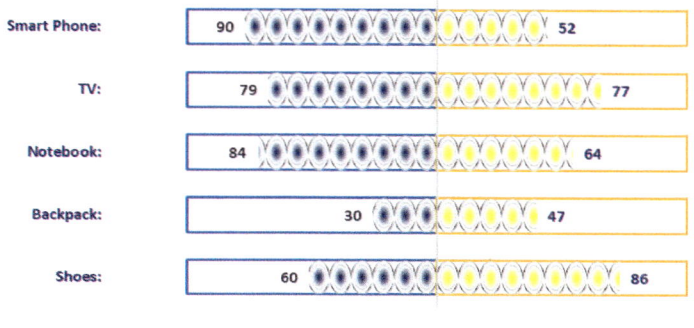

Let's assume that the following icons are available. Actually, you can find these icons in the example file.

How to combine an icon picture and the dot in the chart:

- Click the icon >>> **Ctrl + C** from **applied version 1 bar chart**
- Click the horizontal bar in the chart >>> **Ctrl + V**

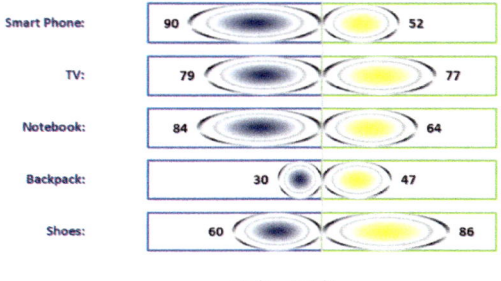

How to use 'Stack & Scale with' in chart:

By using this method, we will stack the right square boxes in the chart.

- Click the **icon-combined bar** >>> **Ctrl + 1**
- Go to **Format Data Series** & Select **Picture or texture fill**
  o Click **'Stack & Scale with'** >>> **Unit/Picture = 10**

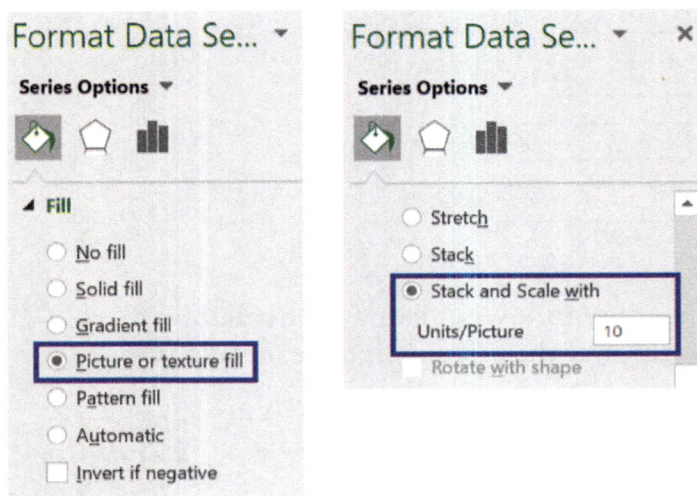

We can complete this applied bar chart.

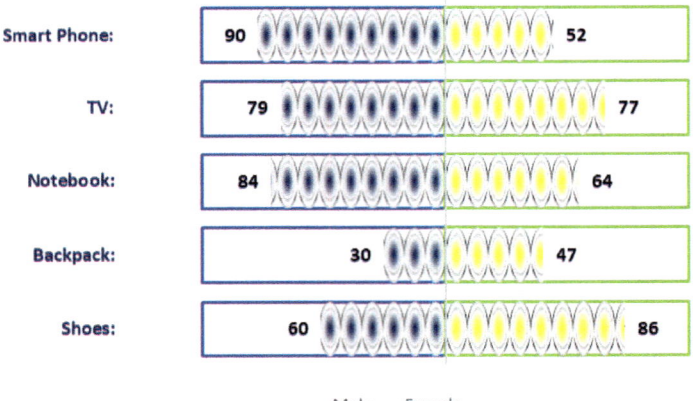

Applied Version 3 & 4:

Target picture:
What we are going to make is the following charts:

How to combine an icon picture and the dot in the chart:

- Click the icon >>> **Ctrl + C** into the **base bar chart**
- Click the horizontal bar in the chart >>> **Ctrl + V**

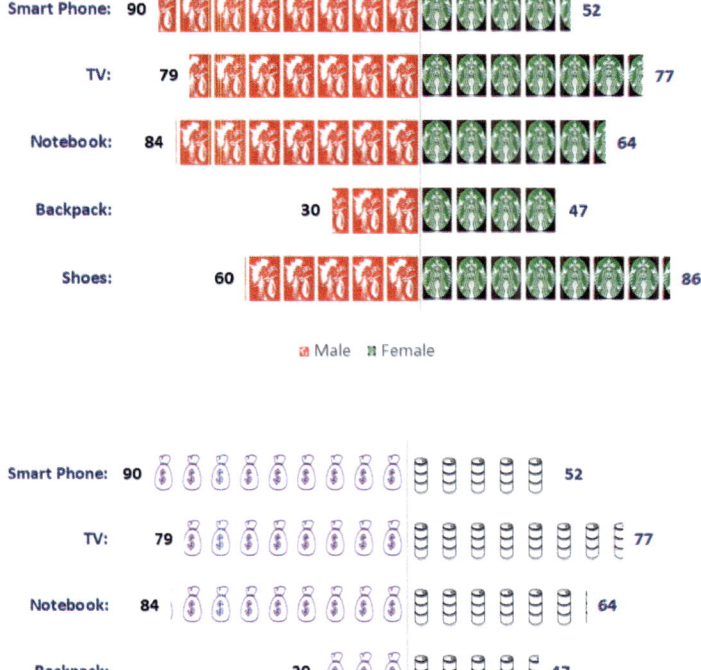

Please use already prepared icons in excel file for the above charts.

18. Unique 2D & 3D Donut Chart

We are going to make a 2 sides horizontal bar chart which is not really straightforward to make it without knowing the trick.

Target picture:
What we are going to make is the following charts:

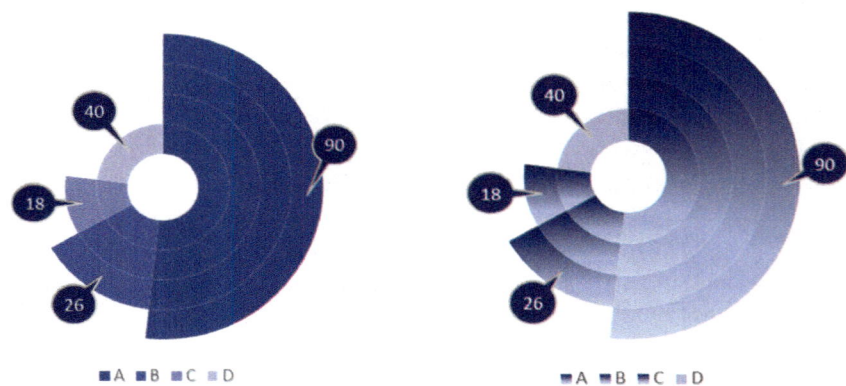

How to set up input values:

First, create **input cells** and **4 supporting cells** in an empty worksheet. The 4 supporting cells have **simply the same** values as the actual input values.

	A	B	C	D	E
1					
2		Input	supporting1	supporting2	supporting3
3	A	38	38	38	38
4	B	26	26	26	26
5	C	18	18	18	18
6	D	40	40	40	40

How to create donut chart:

Select input range by dragging mouse with holding right-hand side button from the starting cell to the end of input data cell.

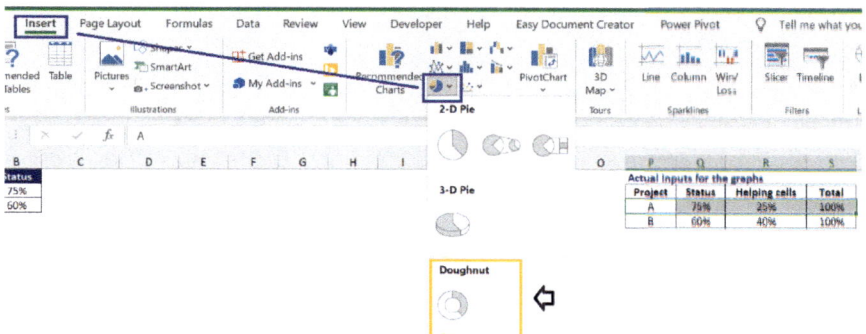

Next, make a **Donut chart**.
- Go to **Insert** tap >>> select **Doughnut**

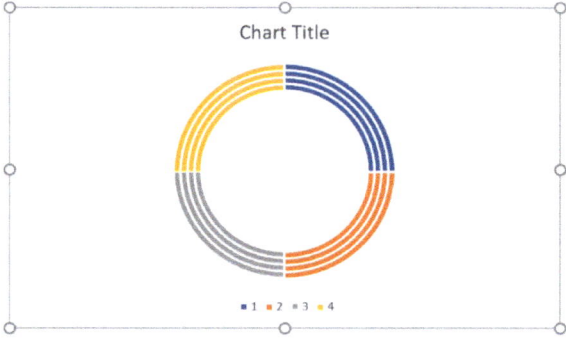

We can see the below chart.

How to remove chart elements:

After clicking a chart, we can see the **plus (+) sign** on right hand side. This is the location where we can control the chart elements.

- Go to chart elements = click **(+)** sign in gray in the chart
- **Remove the chart elements** = Unclick the chart elements which you want to remove

In this case, we unclicked **chart title** from chart elements.

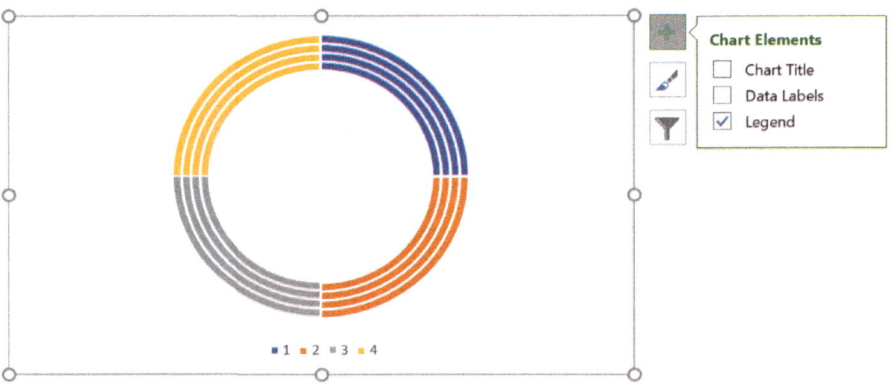

How to adjust size of chart area:

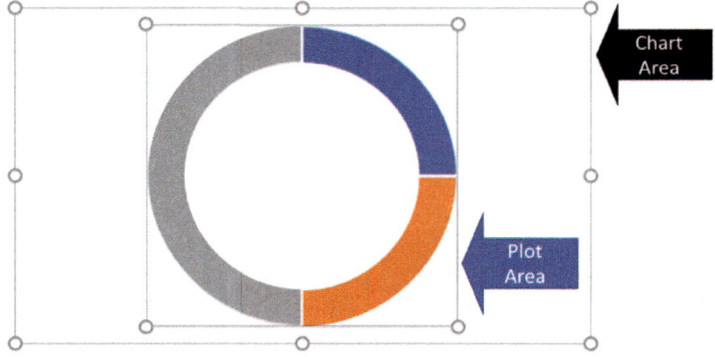

The reason why we need to adjust chart area is to make a right square of the plot.
In order to making it as a right square shape:

- Click chart >>> **Format** tab >>> change size by adjusting values.

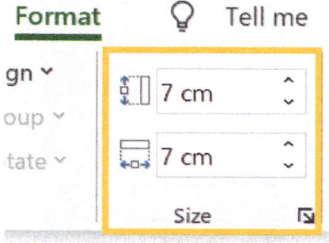

We can see like below.

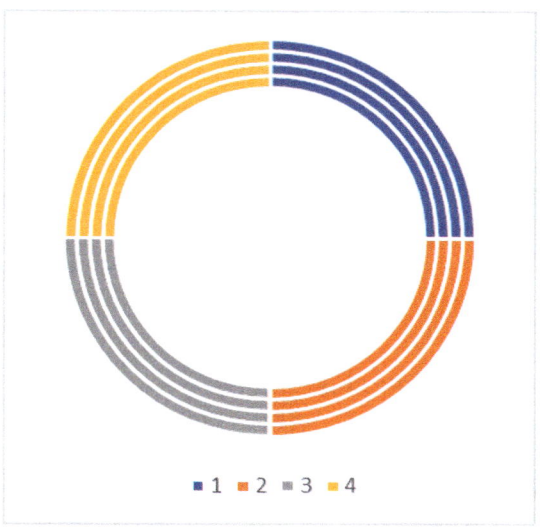

How to remove Gridlines:

- Go to **View** tab and unclick **Gridlines**.

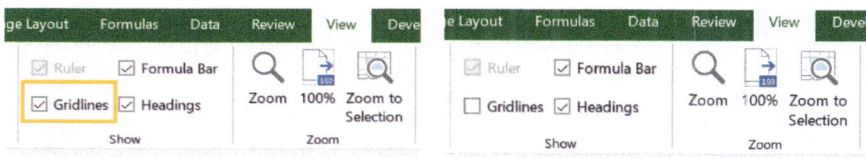

All the grid lines are disappeared in the sheet.
How to remove 'Shape Fill' and 'Shape Outline':

Click a chart >>> Go to **Format** tab. We will change the default settings of **Shape Fill** and **Shape Outline** of the chart.

- **Shape Fill** = No Fill
- **Shape Outline** = No Outline

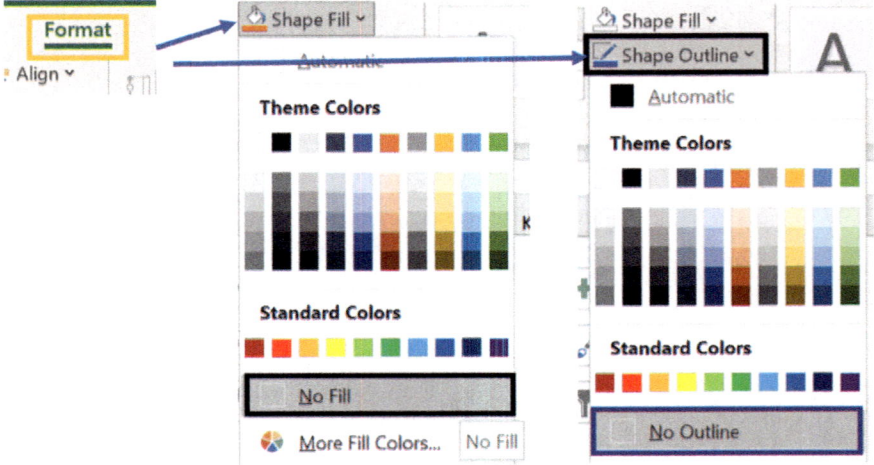

As a result, we can see the following chart.

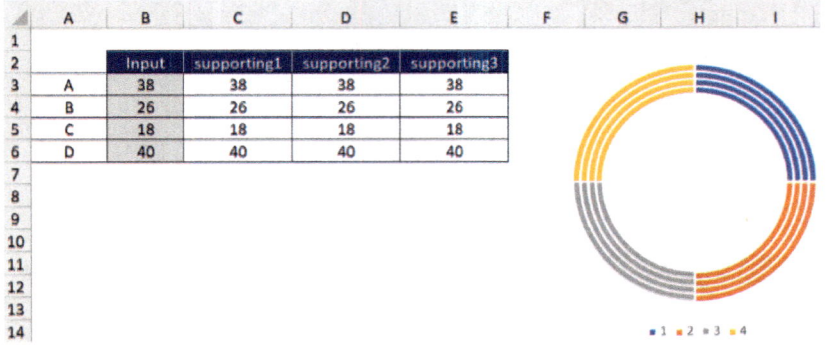

How to change the legend in the chart:

Now, we are going to change 1,2,3,4 to Group A, B, C, D.

- **Select the chart** by using mouse
- Click a **right-hand button** in the mouse
- Select '**Select Data**'

We can see a new pop-up window.
- Select the **Edit** on the Horizontal Axis Labels
- Select the range for A, B, C, D (see below) >>> **OK**

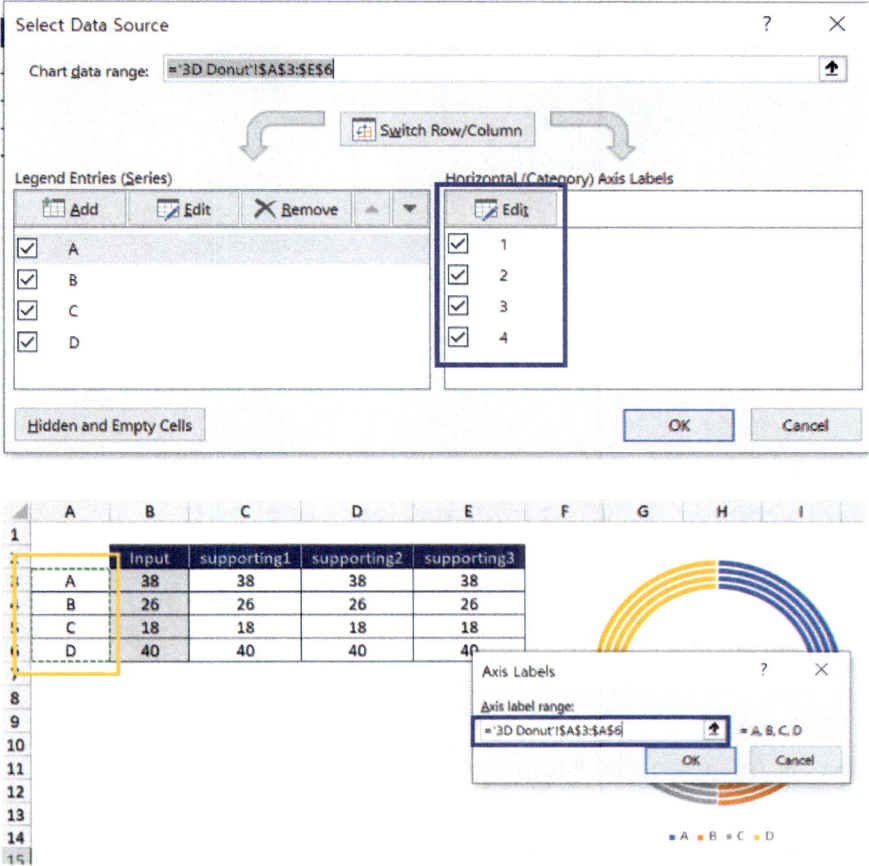

How to change the size of donut:

After changing the label, we need to have the following:

- **Select the chart** by using mouse >>> **Ctrl + 1**
- Click a **right-hand button** in the mouse
- Set 22% for **Doughnut Hole Size**
- (option) you can change a degree of **Angle of first slice**
  The split line degree is changed.

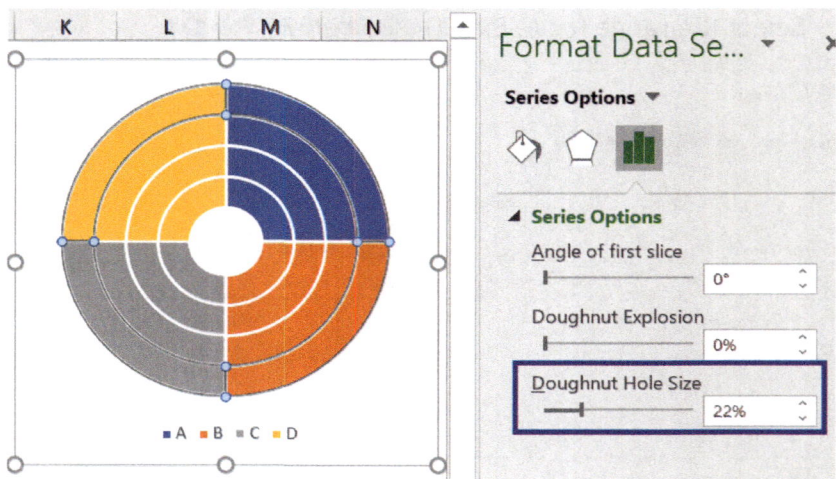

How to change the color of donut layer:

After changing the label, we need to have the following:

- **Select the chart** by using mouse
- Go to **Chart Design** >>> **Change Color**
- Select the color which you wish to change
- In this example, **Monochromatic color** is selected

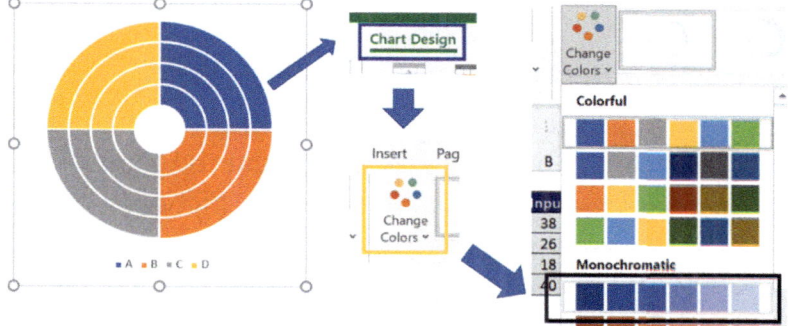

After changing color, we can hide the layer of donut step by step. This step is a bit tedious.

- **Double click a layer of donut >>> Ctrl + 1**
- Select **No fill** for the one specific layer
- In each layer, the number of no filled is increased.

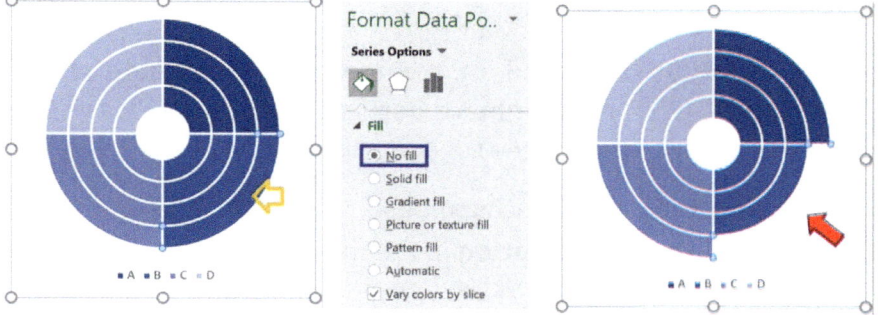

After numerous of **No fills** processes, we can have the following result.

Problem!!!

How to correctly reflect the input values in the chart:

The donut is unchanged even if the actual input value is changed. This because each layer (series) using the same values (please see the orange box in the below picture).

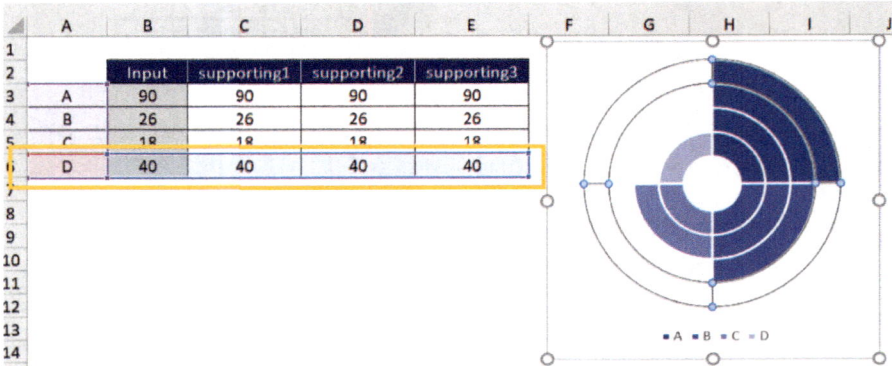

In order to solve this problem, we need to adjust range of layer (series) from horizontal to vertical direction. (Please see the right-side picture below).

- **Select the chart** by using mouse
- Click a **right-hand button** in the mouse
- Select **'Select Data'**

We can see a new pop-up window.
- Select the **one series** (i.e., A) and click **Edit** on the left side
- Select the range for A, B, C, D (see right-hand side) >>> **OK**
- **Repeat** from series A to D

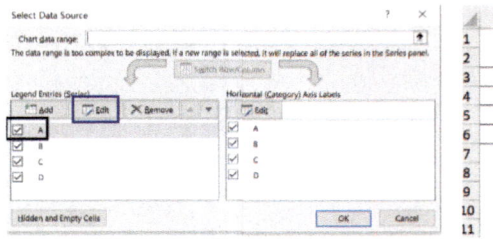 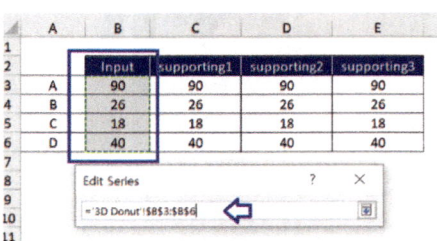

You can see the change after adjusting Serie A (left-side)
It is possible to see the complete-changes (right-side)

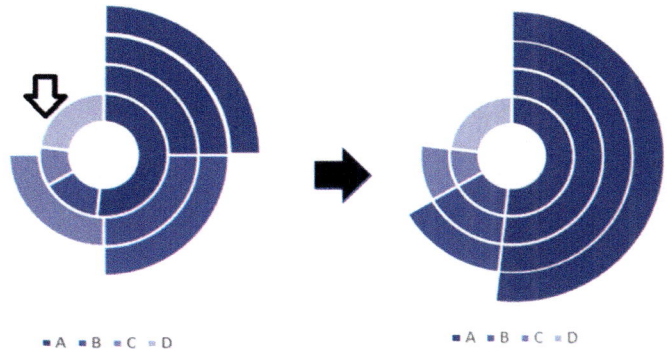

How to remove lines between layers (No lines for each layer):

- **Select the one entire layer** by using mouse >>> **Ctrl + 1**
- Go to **Border** >>> **No line**
- **Repeat** for **all 4 layers** in the case

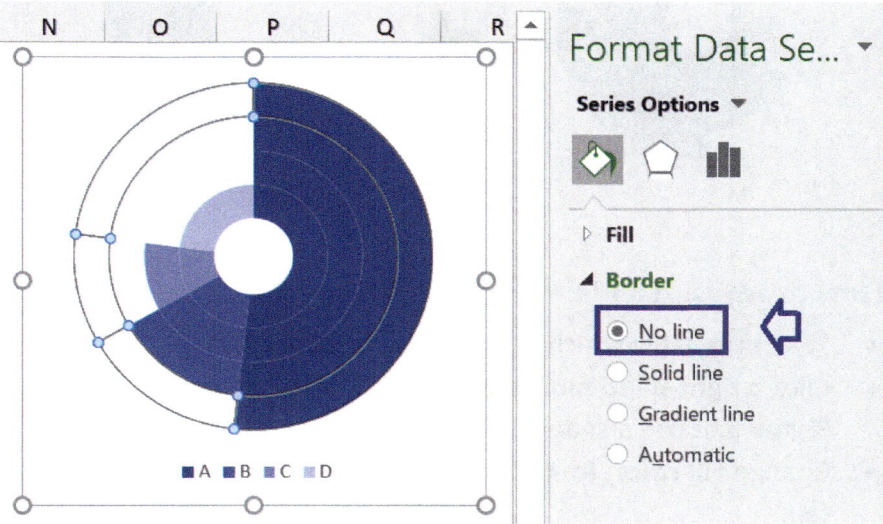

As a result, we can see the below chart.

How to add labels on the donut chart:

- Select the **most outside layer** in each donut by **double clicking**.
- Click a **right-hand mouse button** >>> click **Add Data Labels**
- **Repeat** it 4 times. (i.e., the last label color is black, the rest is white)

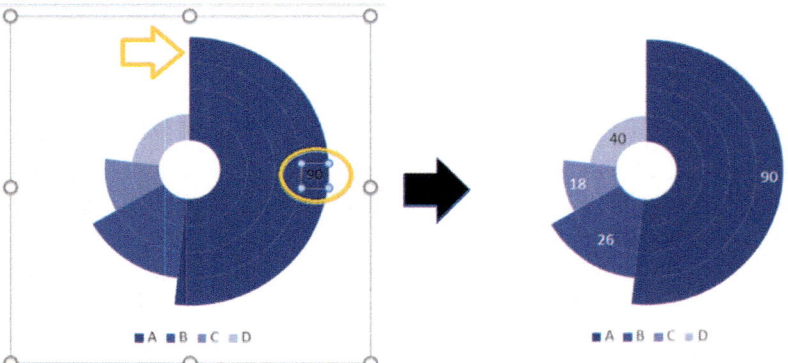

How to adjust data labels on the donut chart:

- Select the label which we made by **double clicking**.
- Click a **right-hand mouse button** >>> click **Chang Data Label Shape** (choose a shape which you like)
- Change **Fill color, font size, font color** for the label using **home** tab
- **Repeat** it 4 times for each label.

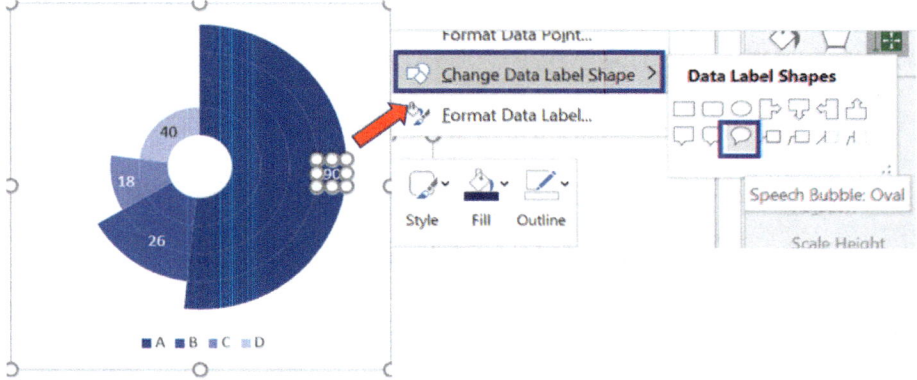

We can complete 2D donut chart.

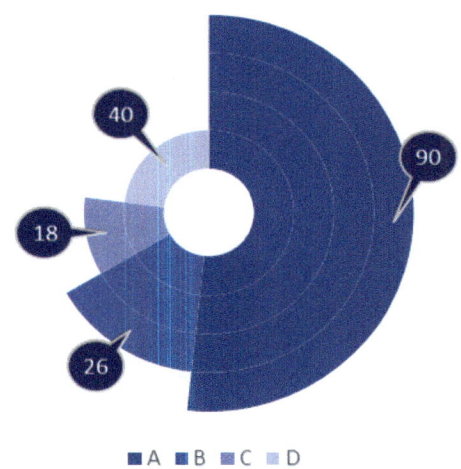

(Optional) Clean-up input table:
- **Copy & paste** the entire input table and relocate it somewhere in the worksheet.
- **Create a new input table** with only the actual input values (without supporting columns)
- **Link** between the new input values with the old actual input values.

The reason why we do this step is to avoid and mistake while we are adjusting the input values (apart from clean-up).

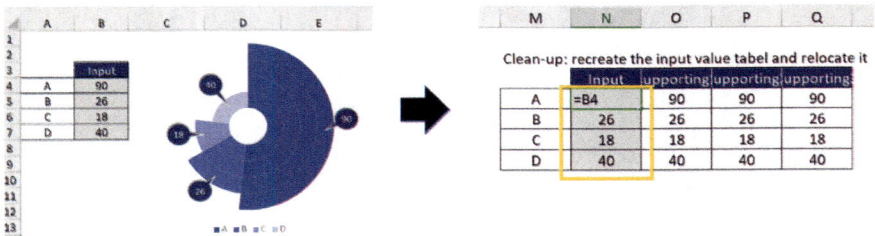

Applied version: 3D unique donut chart:

Depends on the personal preference, we can also add 3D effect into the given chart.

Please note that adding 3 effect is a bit tedious.

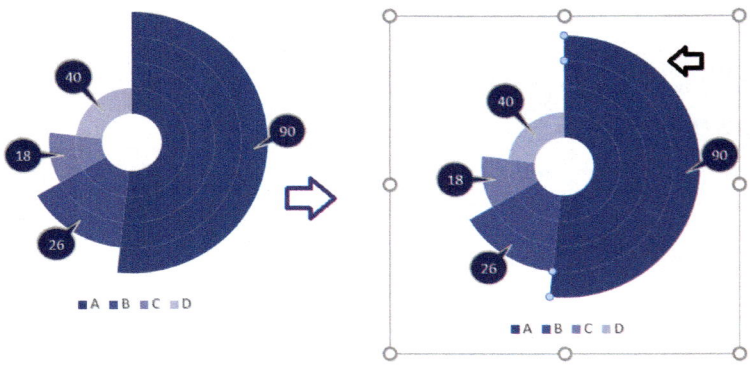

- Copy and paste it and make it 2 charts.
- For a new one, we are going to make a 3D chart.
- **Double click only 1 layer of donut >>> Ctrl + 1**
- In the above (black arrow), we select the one layer.
- We are going to **change Gradient stops settings**.

For the first part of donut, we have 4 layers.

The following setting is for the first layer of first part of donut under **Gradient fill**. (1st and 2nd, 3rd and 4th in the below pictures)

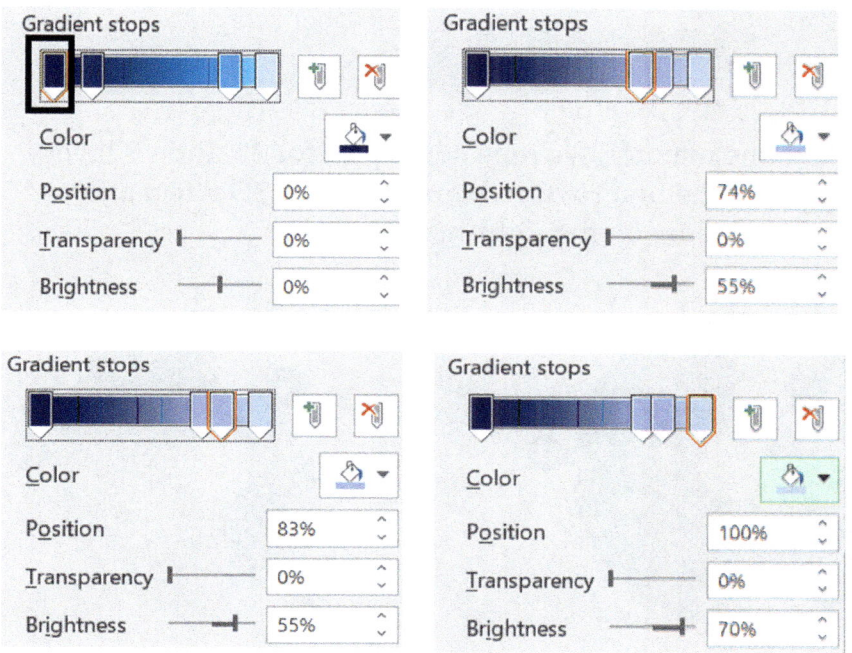

For **the second layer** of first part of donut under Gradient fill: First select only the second layer of the first part by mouse. The settings are same as the first layer.

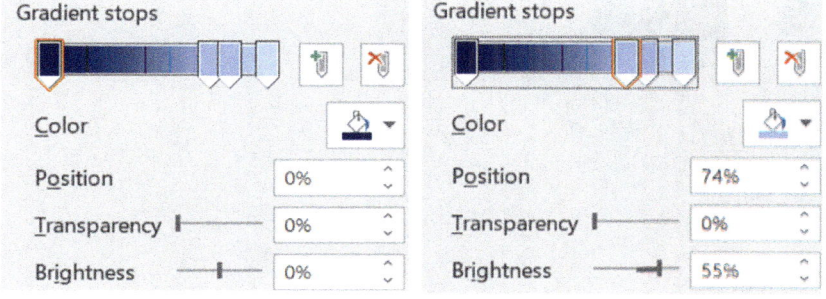

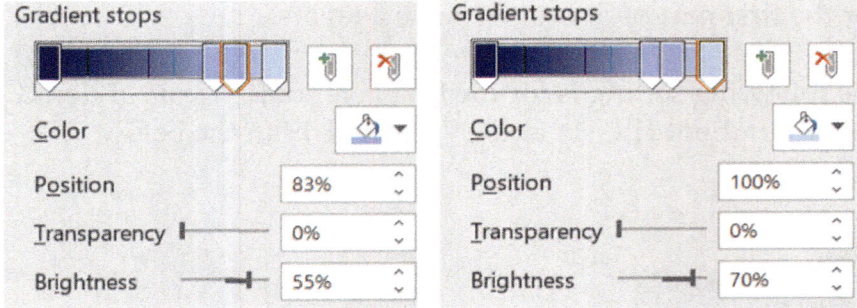

In the same manner, we repeat this part for 3rd and 4th layer. As a result, the first part of donut chart has 3D effect and please see below on the right-hand side.

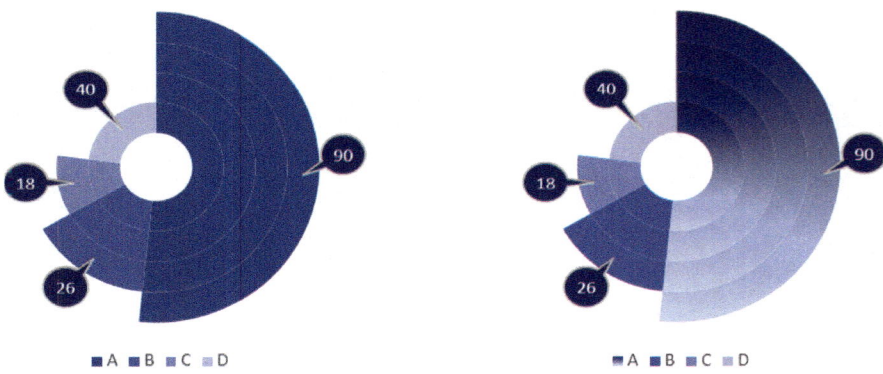

For the second part of donut: repeat it again **3 times**.

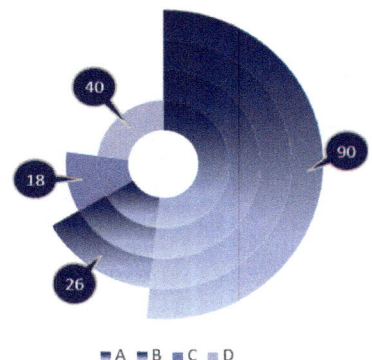

For the third part of donut: repeat it again **2 times**.

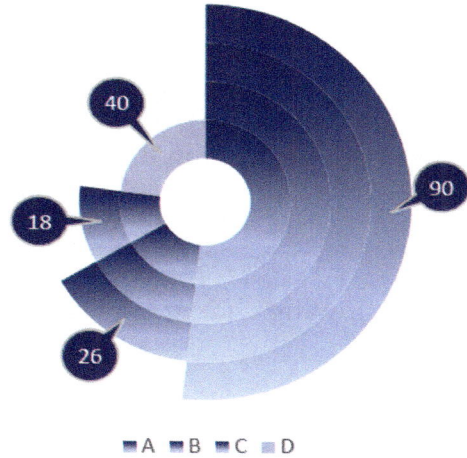

For the fourth part of donut: we do not give 3D effect. This is because it looks less visible for the 4th part of donut. The below picture is with 3D effect for your reference.

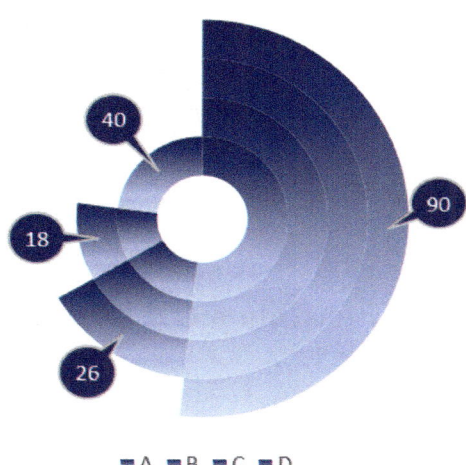

19. Highlighting Bar chart

We are going to make a highlight bar chart which is not really straightforward to make it without knowing the trick. If you are busy, you can just use the graph after updating both input values and chart title.

Target picture:
What we are going to make is the following charts:

The beauty of this graph gives a highlight of a selected quarter by clicking a button.

How to set up input values:

First, create **input cells** and 2 **supporting columns & Quarter index cell (=B15)** in an empty worksheet.

- Supporting column **=IF($B$15=D2, B2, NA())**
  If Quarter index cell is equal to Quarter column, Bring actual input value. If not, bring NA.

- **Quarter column** means 1 = Quarter 1, 2 = Quarter 2, 3 = Quarter 3, 4 = Quarter 4, 5 = Full Year.

C2				fx	=IF($B$15=D2,B2,NA())	
	A	B		C	D	E
1	Month	Sale (2020)		Supporting	Quarter	
2	Jan	3,000		3,000	1	
3	Feb	2,800		2,800	1	
4	Mar	5,000		5,000	1	
5	Apr	5,000		#N/A	2	
6	May	3,000		#N/A	2	
7	Jun	5,000		#N/A	2	
8	Jul	6,600		#N/A	3	
9	Aug	6,000		#N/A	3	
10	Sep	8,000		#N/A	3	
11	Oct	6,500		#N/A	4	
12	Nov	6,000		#N/A	4	
13	Dec	5,000		#N/A	4	
14						
15	Quarter	1		⇐		

How to see 'Developer' tab:

In a default setting, it is not possible to see Developer tab.

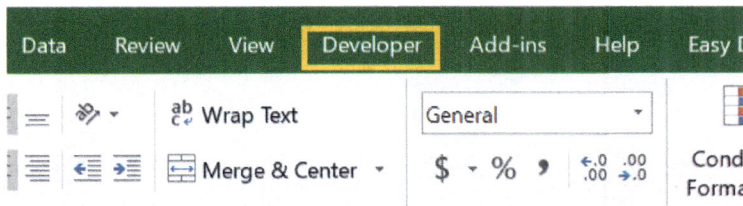

In order to see this tab, please follow the below steps.
- **File** >>> **Options** >>> **Customize Ribbon** >>> **Main Tabs** (right-hand side) >>> **Developer** >>> **OK**

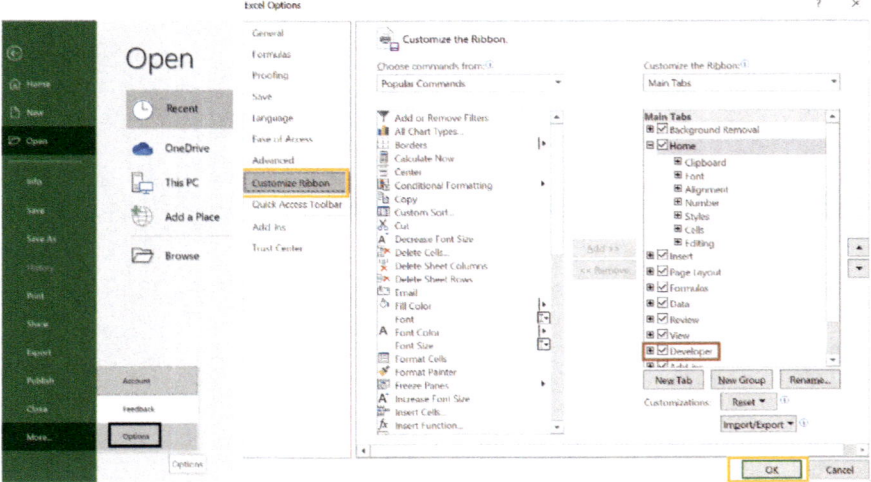

How to make option button:

- Go to **Developer** tab & Click '**Insert**' button
- Select '**Option Button (Form Control)**' & click any location in worksheet
- Drag the check box until the size you would like to have.
- <u>Put the cursor inside of the box</u> (click the box with a right mouse button and click a left mouse button) & change the name

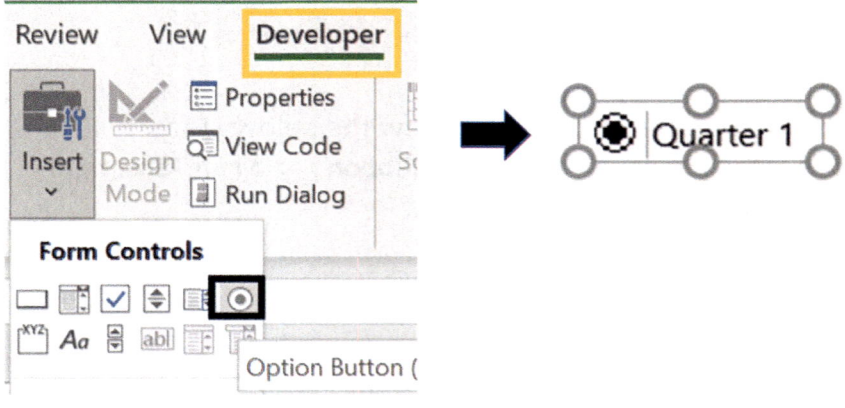

- After selecting the box, click a right-hand mouse button & go to **Format Control** (see below)
- Go to **Control** & Put the cursor inside of '**Cell link:**'
- **Select 'Quarter index cell (=B15)'** for the '**Cell link**' which you will control the check box either checked or unchecked.

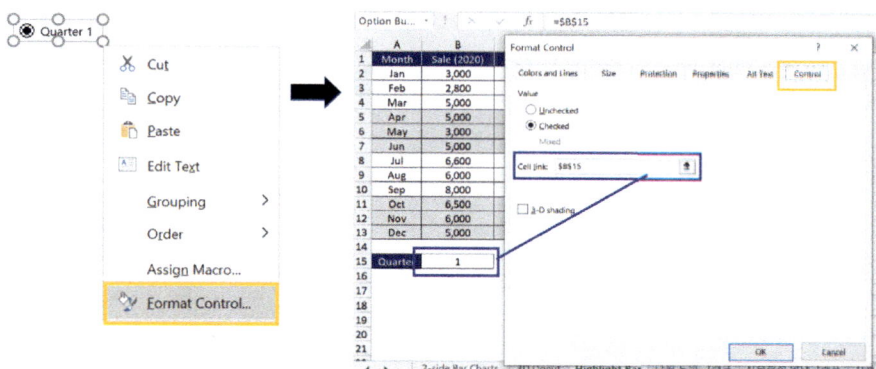

Once one option button is completed, copy and paste it to the worksheet 4 times more.

Changed the name of the box to Quarter 2, 3, 4, and Full Year.

- The Quarter 2 option box shows 2 in 'Quarter index cell (=B15)'
- The Quarter 3 option box shows 3 in 'Quarter index cell (=B15)'
- The Quarter 4 option box shows 4 in 'Quarter index cell (=B15)'
- The Full Year option box shows 5 in 'Quarter index cell (=B15)'.

How to align & group the option button:

- Click one of option buttons & **Alt + A**
- **Shape Format** >>> **Align** >>> **Align Middle**
- **Shape Format** >>> **Align** >>> **Distribute Horizontally**

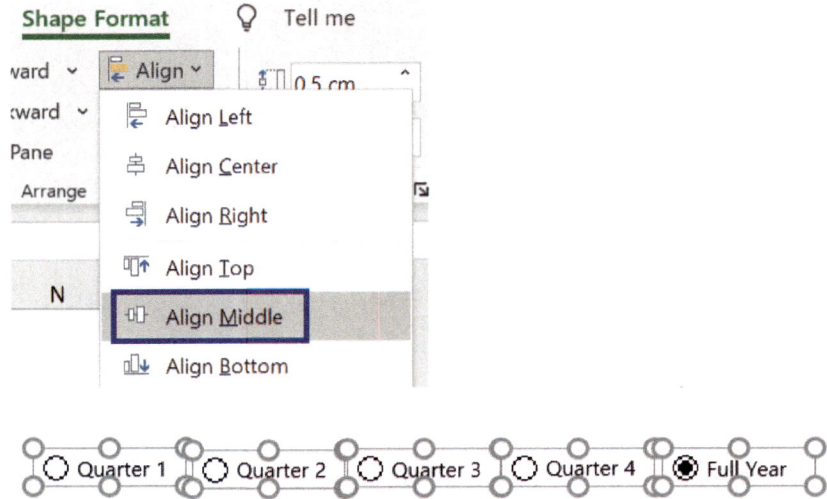

- **Shape Format** >>> **Group** >>> **Group**

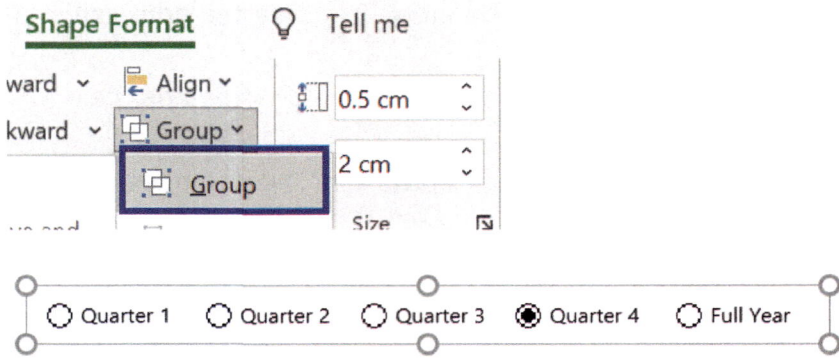

Up to now, we complete both input table and option box.

How to remove Gridlines:

- Go to **View** tab and unclick **Gridlines**.

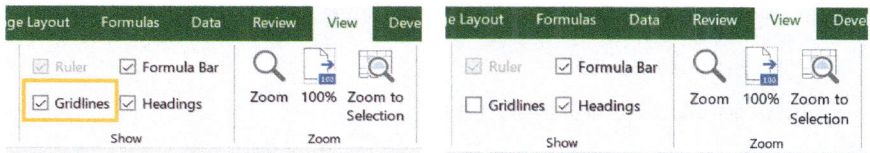

All the grid lines are disappeared in the sheet.

How to create 2-D Stacked bar chart:

- After selecting inputs values (from **Column A to C** & by using mouse dragging), go to **Insert** tab.
- Select **2-D Column** >>> **Clustered Column**.

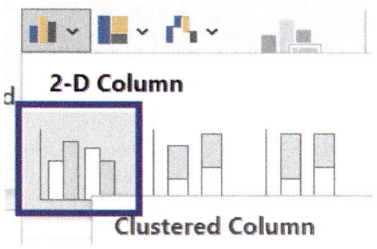

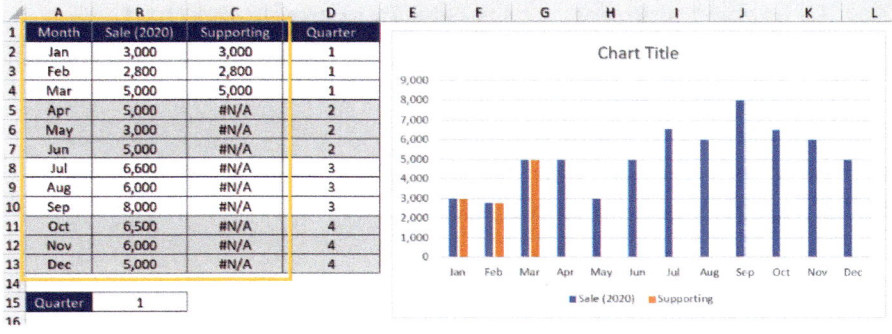

How to remove 'Shape Fill' and 'Shape Outline':

Click a chart >>> Go to **Format** tab. We will change the default settings of **Shape Fill** and **Shape Outline** of the chart.

- **Shape Fill** = No Fill
- **Shape Outline** = No Outline

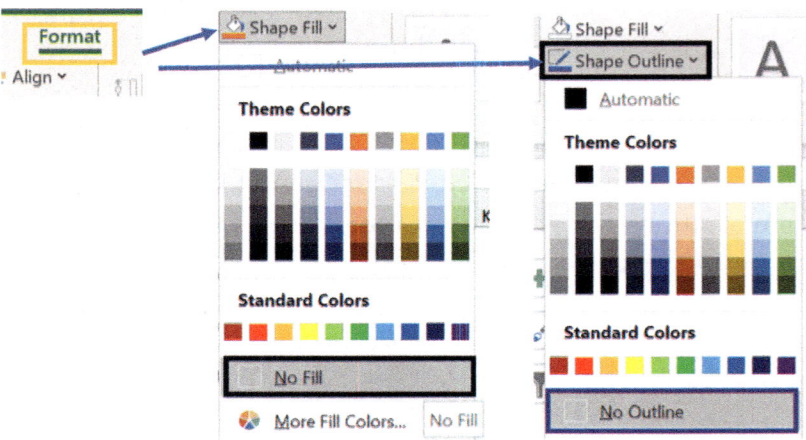

How to remove chart elements:

After clicking a chart, we can see the plus **(+) sign** on right hand side. This is the location where we can control the chart elements.

- Go to chart elements = click **(+)** sign in gray in the chart
- **Remove the chart elements** = Unclick the chart elements which you want to remove

In this case, we unclicked both **Primary Vertical Axes** and **Gridlines** from chart elements.

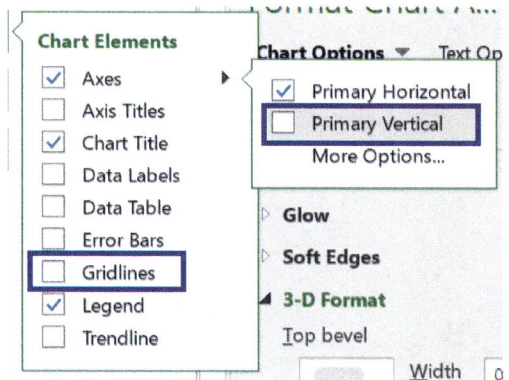

How to combine 2 bars in bar chart:

- After selecting a bar by using mouse >>> **Ctrl + 1**
- Go to **Series Options**
    - **Series Overlap = 100%**
    - **Gab width = 100%**

It is possible to combine 2 bars into one bar.
Actually, the remaining parts is how to make the chart nicely.

How to add labels on the bars:

- Select **actual input vertical bars** (Jan, Feb, …) by a mouse clicking
- Click a **right-hand mouse button** >>> click **Add Data Labels**

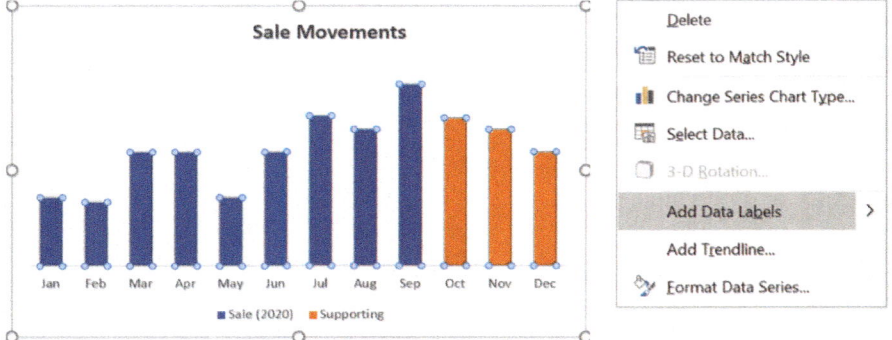

- Select the **labels on bar** by using a mouse
- Adjust color of letter, size, etc. (as you wish)

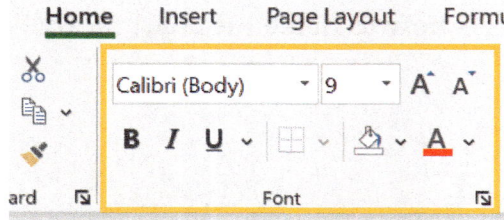

In the same manner, we can adjust a chart title as well. Now, go back to the option button.

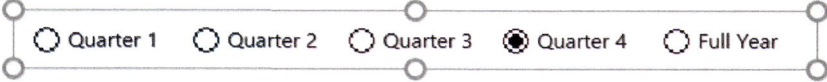

(Optional) How to decorate the option buttons:

- **Insert** tab >>> **Shape** >>> select **Rectangle**
- By using a mouse dragging, put the rectangle in the sheet
- Adjusting the size by mouse button.
- The size should cover up the option buttons.

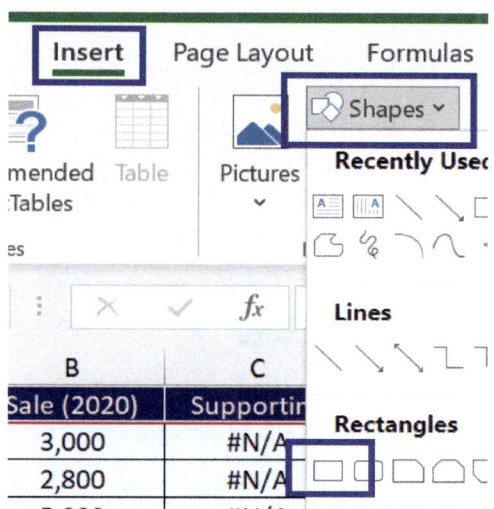

- Overlapping both option buttons and the rectangle.

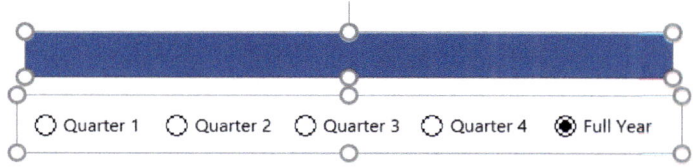

- After clicking both of them, **Shape Format** >>>
- **Align Center** >>> **Align Middle**.

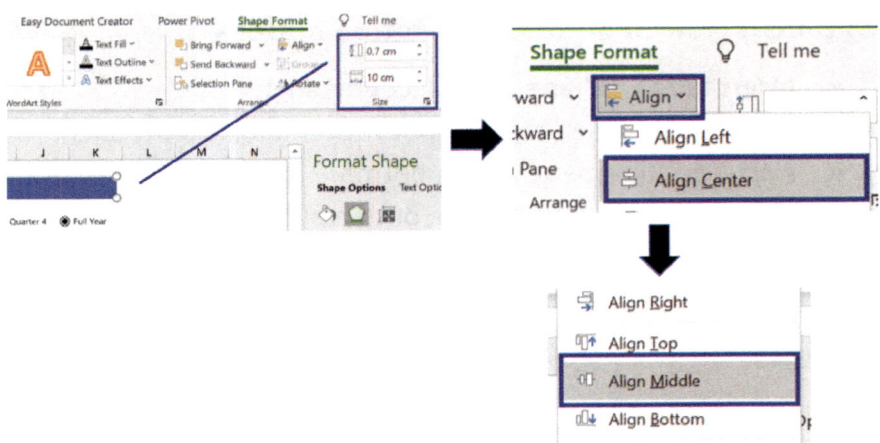

As a result, you can find the below result.

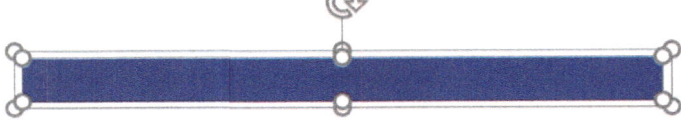

- After clicking the rectangle bar, adjust fill color and line color which you wish to change.
- **Ctrl + 1 >>> Effect >>> Presets >>> Inside >>> Bottom Right**
- Go to **Fill & Lines** >>> **Fill** >>> choose a color which you like.

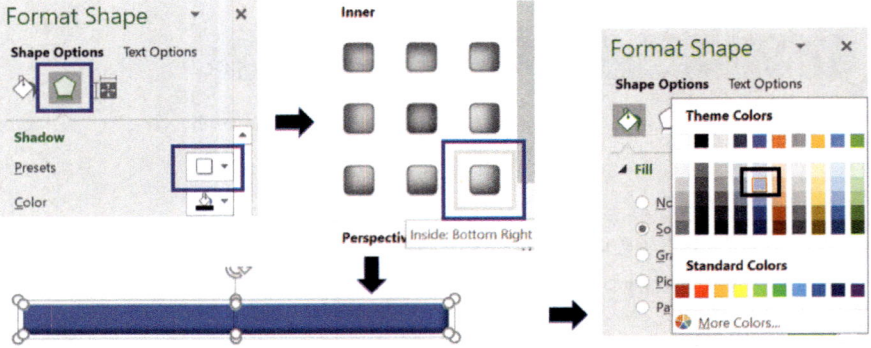

- After clicking the rectangle bar, click a right-hand side mouse button. Click **Send to Back**.

- It is possible to see the option buttons which we made it before.

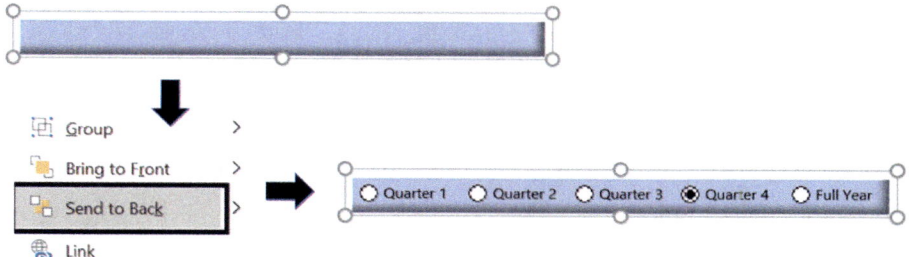

- After clicking the rectangle bar, **Alt + A** (select all)
  (Just explanation (no need to read): We want to select both the rectangle and the option buttons to be Grouping. However, after pressing **Alt + A**, we can also select the bar chart.)

- At this status, press and **hold Ctrl** and **unclick the bar chart** which we do not want to select.

- Click a right-hand side mouse button >>> **Group** >>> **Group**.

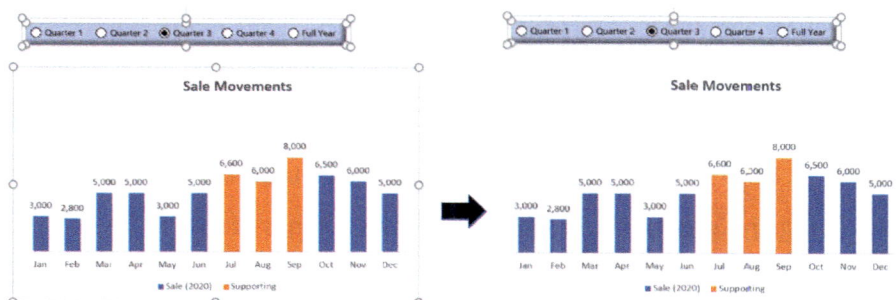

How to adjust plot area:

- Click the graph >>> **Ctrl + 1** (Format Chart Area) >>> click reverse **small triangle** next to 'Chart Options' >>> select **Plot Area** (I just used an old picture below)

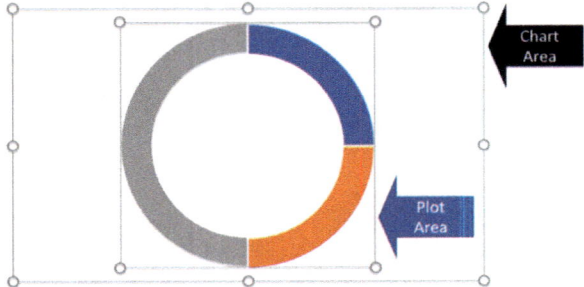

- After **selecting Plot Area** >>> Drag it upwards
- After clicking **legend** >>> press **delete** button

How to combine bar chart and option buttons:

- Drag the grouped option button into the bar chart
- After clicking both of them, **Shape Format** >>> **Align Center**
- Group them

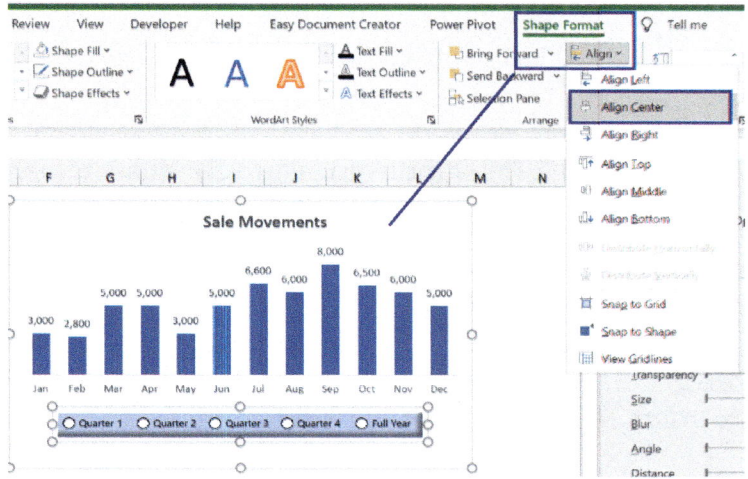

Finally, we can complete the chart.

20. 2D & 3D Index-measure Bar Chart

We are going to make a 2 & 3D index measure bar chart which is not straightforward to make it without knowing the trick.

Depends on your personal preference, you can choose either 2D or 3D graph.

Target picture:
What we are going to make is the following charts:

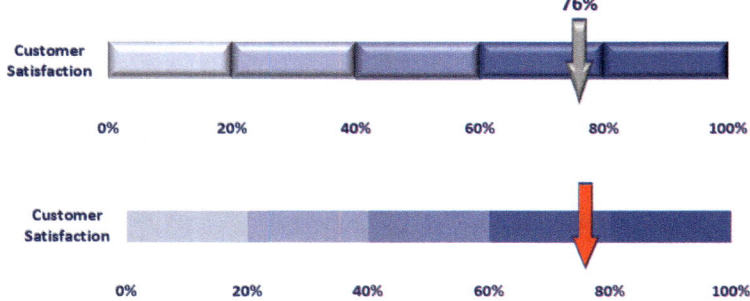

How to set up input values:

First, create **input cell (=A3)** and 2 **supporting columns & Arrow width (=E3)** in an empty worksheet.

- Spilt column = 20% & make 5 of them (if you want to make 5 different indicators, choose 5)
- **Arrow location = Input value – arrow width/2**

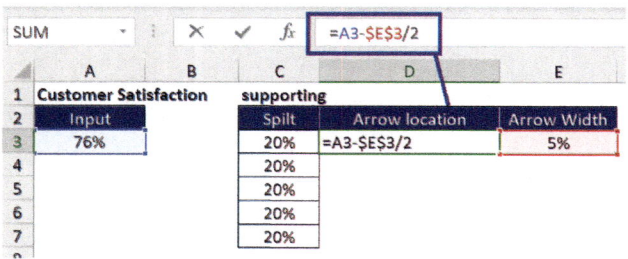

How to remove Gridlines:

- Go to **View** tab and unclick **Gridlines**.

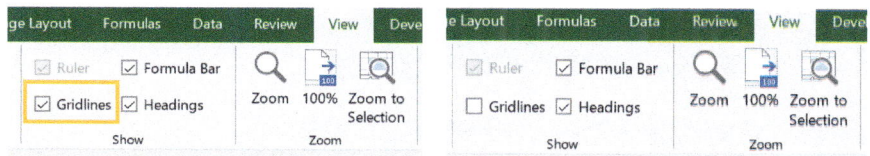

All the grid lines are disappeared in the sheet.

How to create 2-D Stacked bar chart:

- After selecting inputs values (from **Column C** & by using mouse dragging), go to **Insert** tab.
- Select **2-D Bar** >>> **Stacked Bar**.

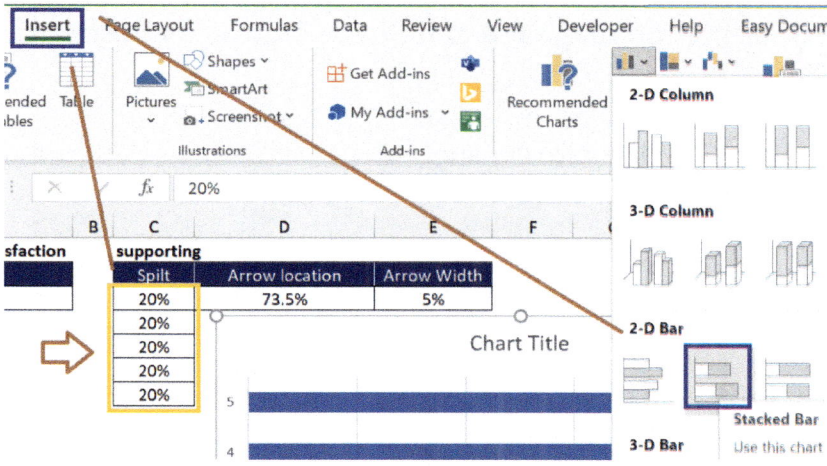

As a result, we can find the following result below.

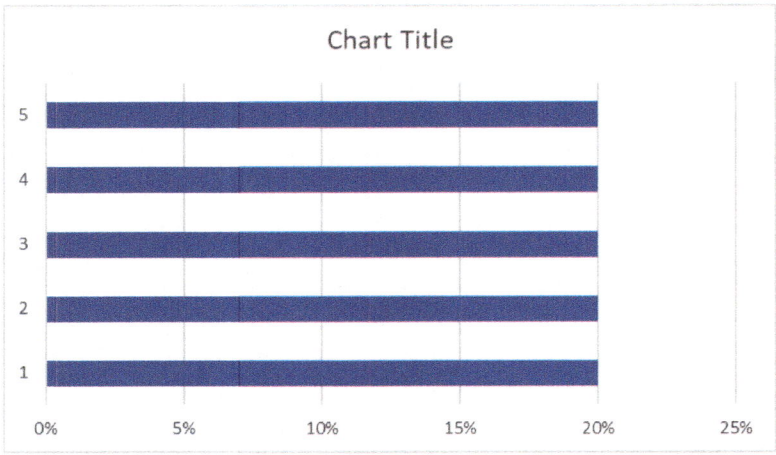

How to remove 'Shape Fill' and 'Shape Outline':

Click a chart >>> Go to **Format** tab. We will change the default settings of **Shape Fill** and **Shape Outline** of the chart.

- **Shape Fill** = No Fill
- **Shape Outline** = No Outline

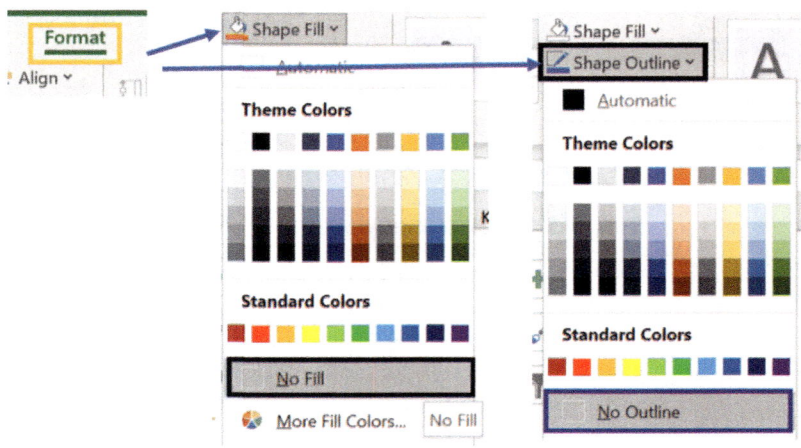

How to switch Row and Column in the chart:

- After selecting chart, click a right-hand side mouse button
- Go to **Select Data** >>> **Switch Row/Column**

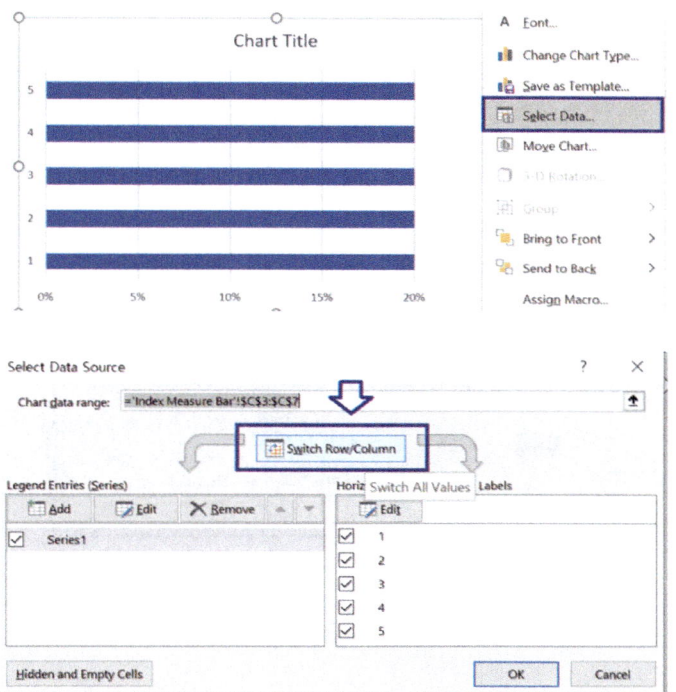

We can find the following:

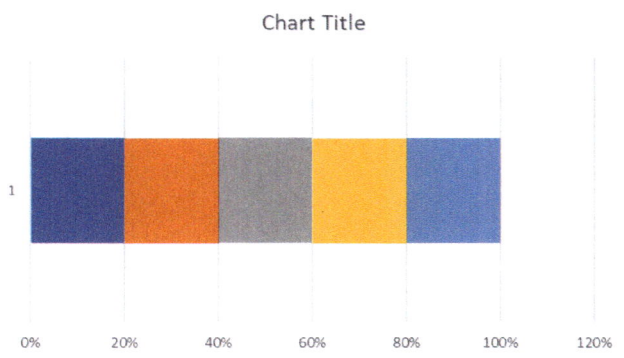

How to change colors in the bar chart:

- After selecting chart, go to **Chart Design**
- Go to **Change Colors** >>> Select the color which you like
- i.e., select **Monochromatic Palette 12**

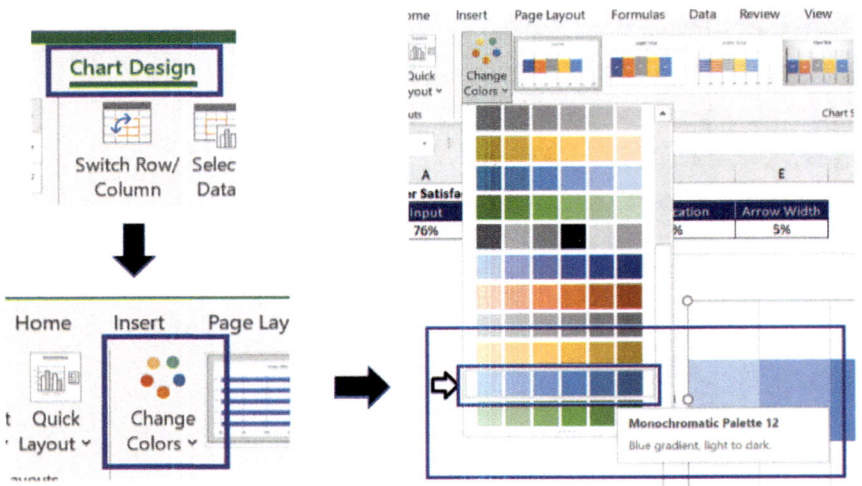

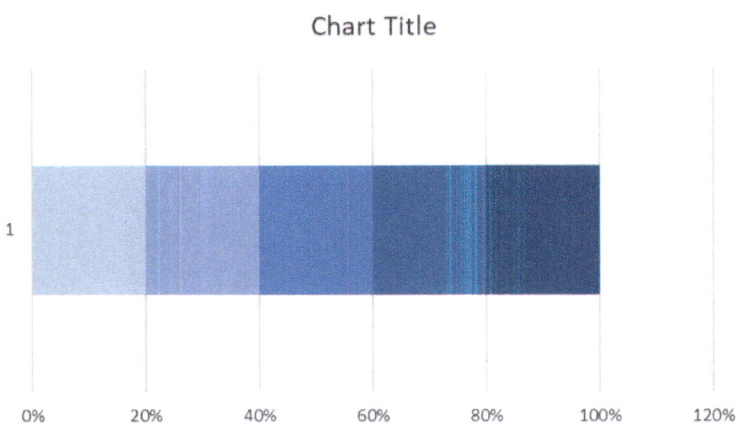

How to add a new value into the bar chart:

- Copy the cell Arrow location (**Ctrl + C**) >>> click the **chart** >>> **Ctrl + V**

If we compare these charts, it looks like below.
On the right-hand side chart, we can see that there is one more value added. So, the total bar is over 150%.

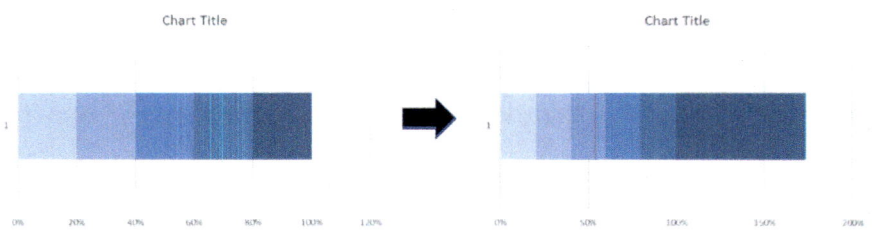

How to adjust the additional Arrow location value (1):

- Click the chart >>> **Ctrl + 1** >>> **Series Options**
- Click the **new Arrow location cell** by mouse

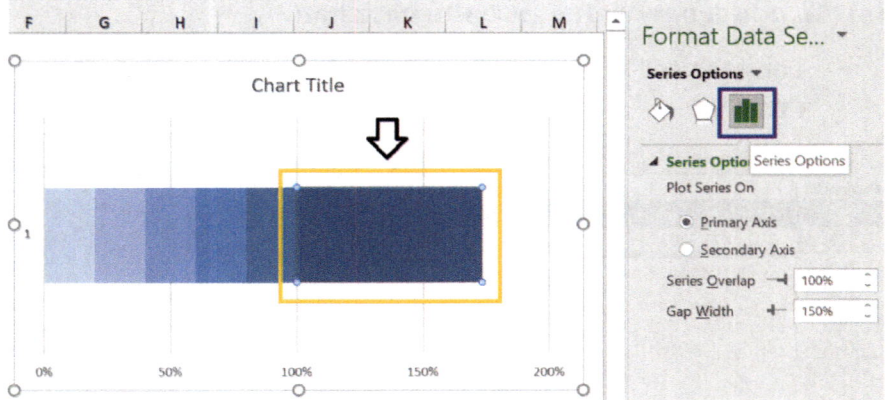

- Select **Secondary Axis** and **Gap Width = 0%**

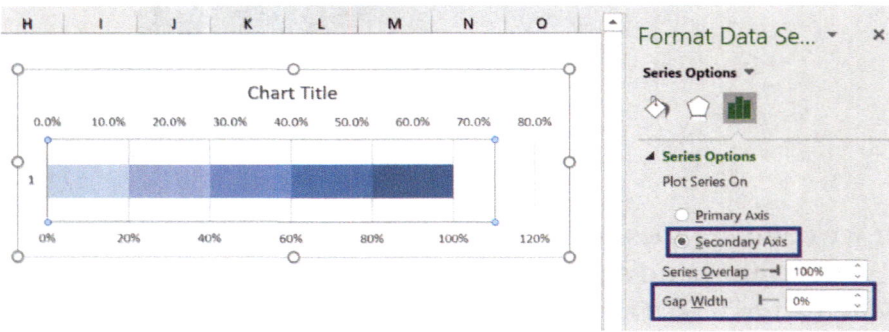

How to remove chart elements:

After clicking a chart, we can see the plus **(+) sign** on right hand side. This is the location where we can control the chart elements.

- Go to chart elements = click **(+)** sign in gray in the chart
- **Remove the chart elements** = Unclick the chart elements which you want to remove

In this case, we unclicked both **Chart title** and **Gridlines** from chart elements.

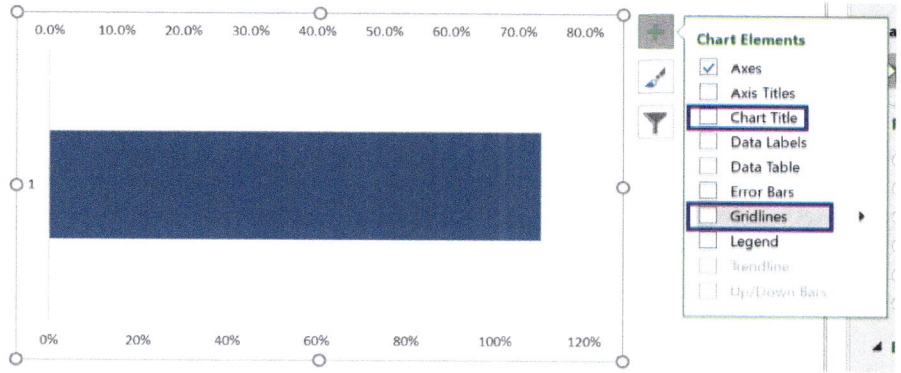

How to adjust the additional Arrow location value (2):

- Click the chart >>> Adjust the height of chart by using mouse
- Click the chart >>> **Ctrl + 1** >>> **Series Options** >>> **No fill**

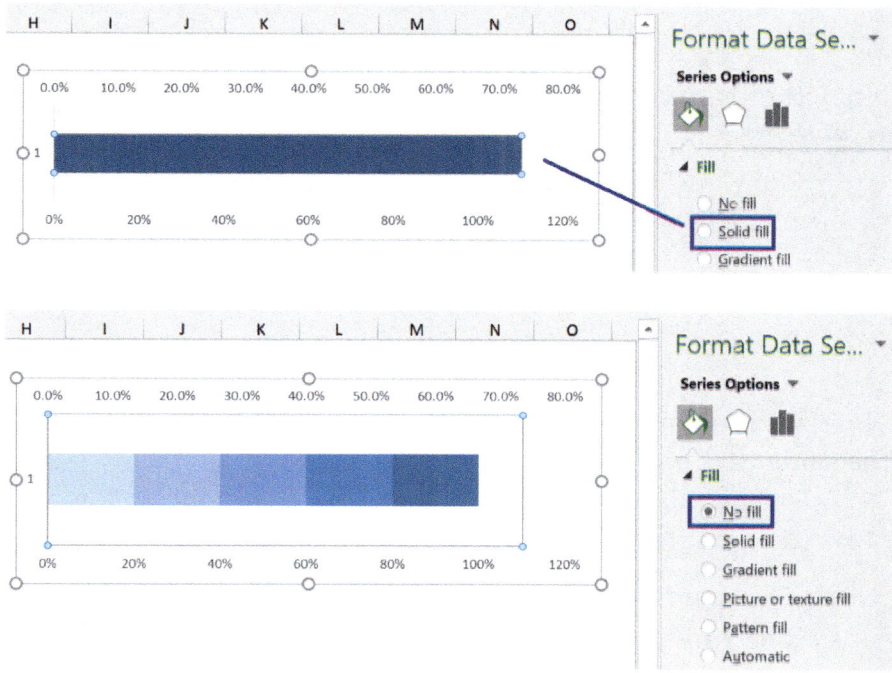

How to add a new value (Arrow width) into the bar chart:

- Copy the cell **Arrow width** (**Ctrl + C**) >>>
- Click the bar in the secondary axis by mouse >>> **Ctrl + V**

In the previous steps, we create a new bar which follows the secondary axis. Now, we are adding a new value into the bar in the secondary axis in the same manner as 'Arrow location' cell.

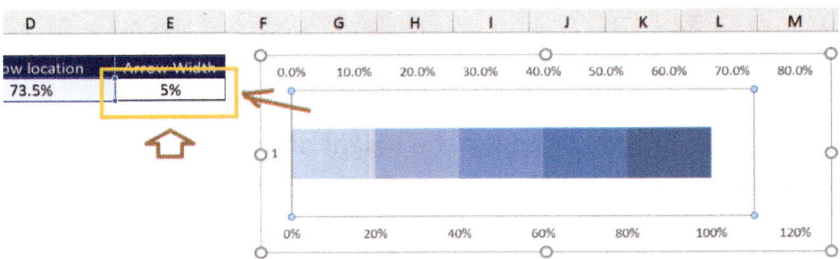

Now, there are 2 values in the secondary axis.

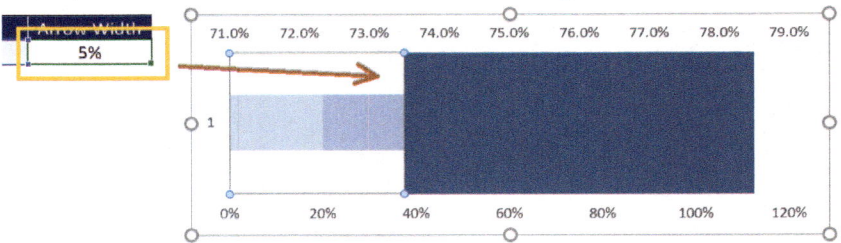

Next, we are going to adjust the range of both vertical axis in the same range.

How to adjust the range of both axes:

- Click the range of primary axis by mouse in the chart.
- **Ctrl + 1** >>> Go to **Axis Options** >>> **Bounds**
- **Minimum: 0** >>> **Maximum: 1**
- Setting is changed from **Auto** to **Reset.**
  It means that the auto-adjusting range is off.

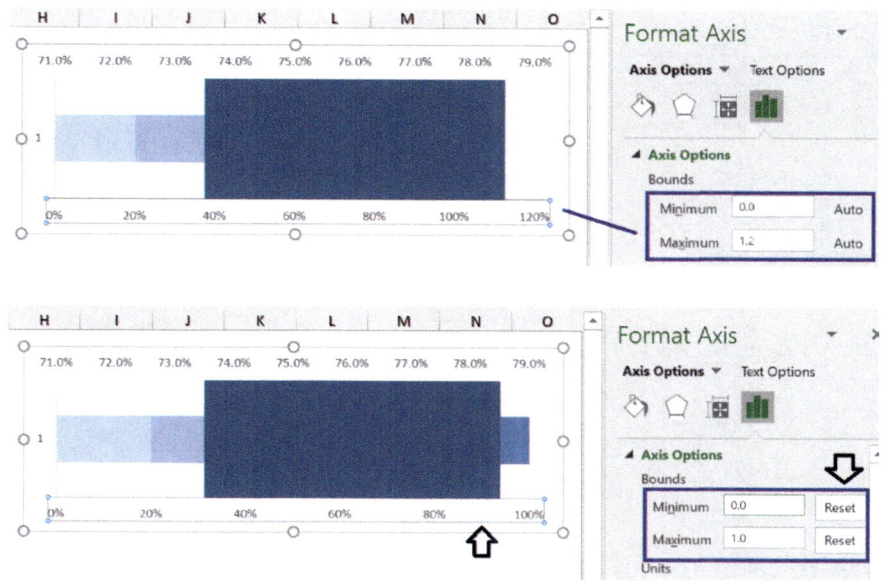

For the secondary axis, we do as same as the primary axis.

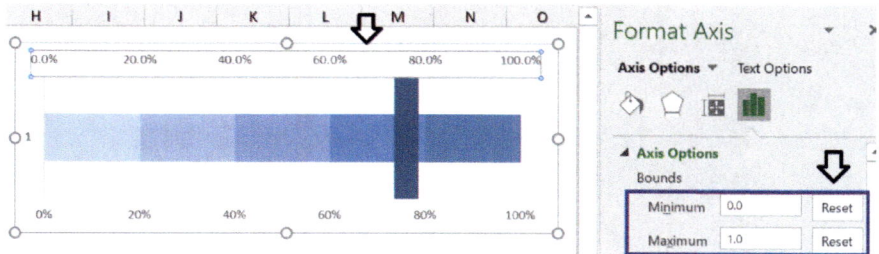

How to create an arrow:

- Go to **Insert** tab >>> **Shape** >>> select **Arrow down**
- **Drag the mouse** somewhere in an empty sheet
- Arrow is ready >>> **Ctrl + 1** >>> **Format Shape**
- Change **Fill** color (i.e., red) & **Line** color, etc.

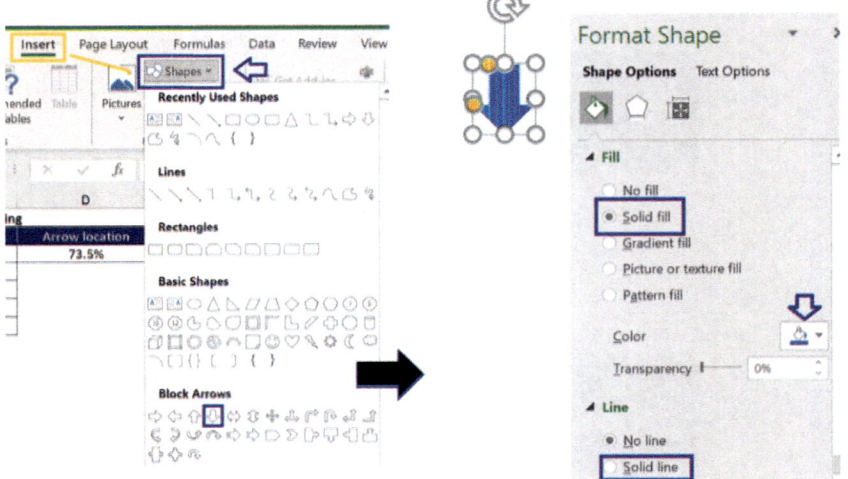

How to combine an arrow icon with the bar chart:

- Click the arrow icon >>> **Ctrl + C**
- Click the horizontal small bar in the chart >>> **Ctrl + V**

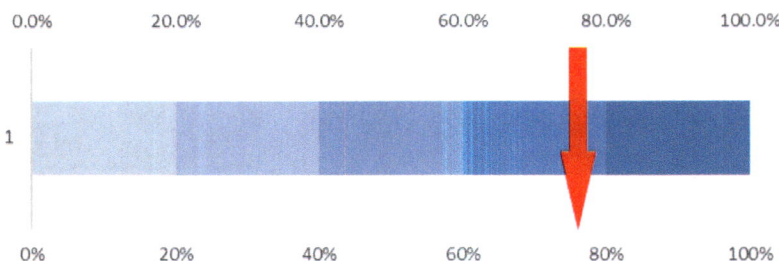

In order to make it nice, you can adjust the size of bar chart by mouse dragging (reducing the height of chart).

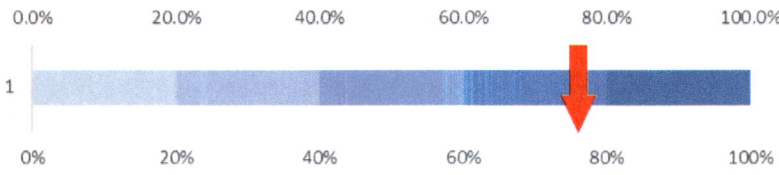

How to adjust vertical axis:

- Click the cart >>> click a **right-hand mouse button**
- Click **Select Data** >>> Click **Edit** on the right-hand side
- Select **Axis Labels** by choosing the cell which you want to appear in the vertical axis >>> **OK**

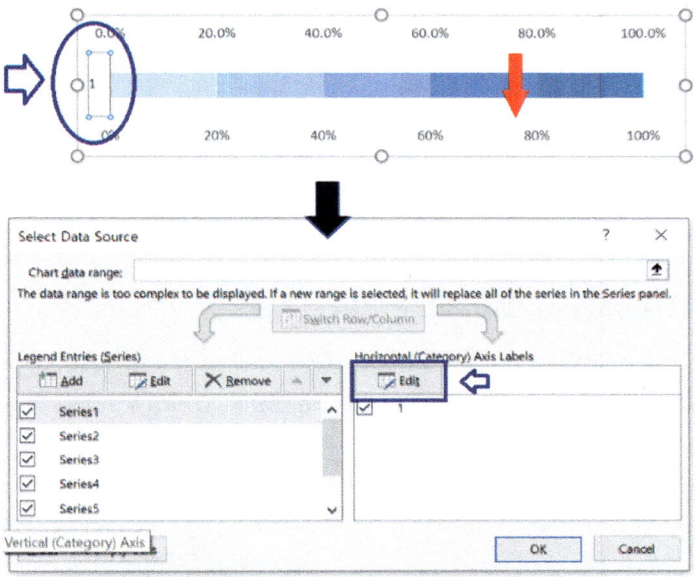

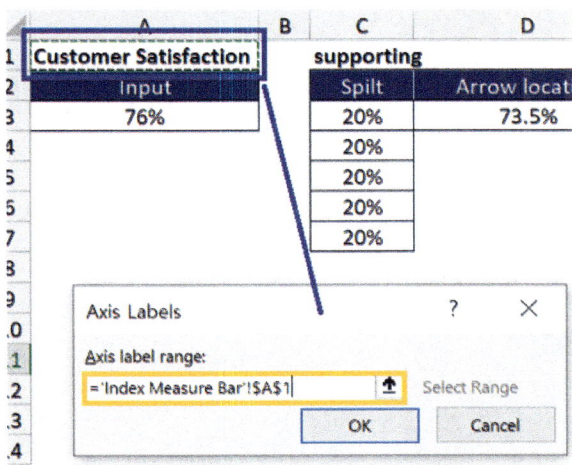

How to adjust vertical axis Label:

- Click the vertical axis label >>> **Ctrl + 1** >>> Click **No line**
- In **Home** tab, you can change font color or style, etc.
- >>> **Ctrl + B** (Bold)

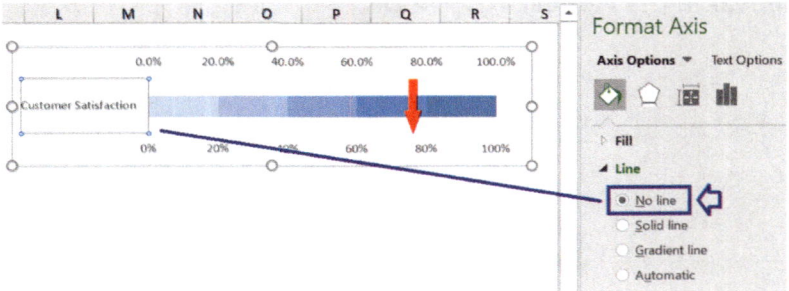

How to remove the secondary axis label:

- Click the horizontal axis label by mouse >>> press Delete button. Also, you can also resize of the chart to look nice.

As a result, we can find the following result.

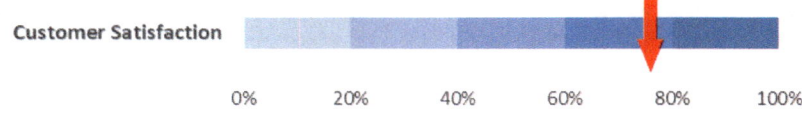

- **Go to Cell A1** where the vertical axis label is located
- Put a curser in the middle of 2 words >>> **Alt + Enter**
- We can make 2 lines in one cell.

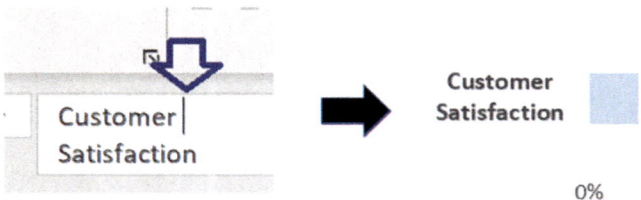

As a result, we can find the following result.

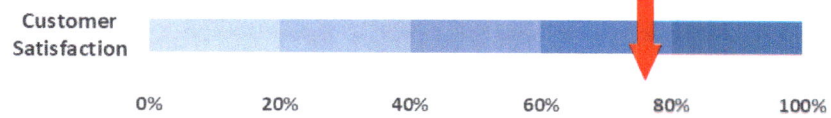

(Optional) How to add the label for arrow:

- Click the arrow >>> Click a **right-hand mouse button**
- Select **Add Data Labels** >>> Click the new label (by mouse) which is overlapped with the arrow >>> **Drag it on the top**.

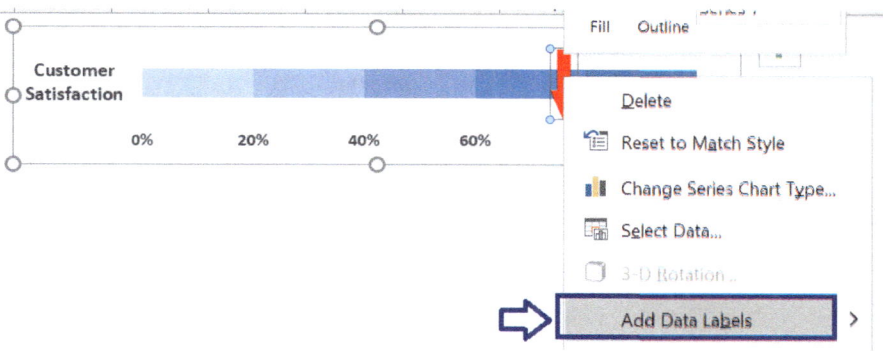

Problem!!!

You might face the problem to put the label on top of the arrow. This is because there is not enough space.

In order to solve this,

- click **Plot Area** >>> **resize the plot area** with making more space on the upper part of bar to put the label.

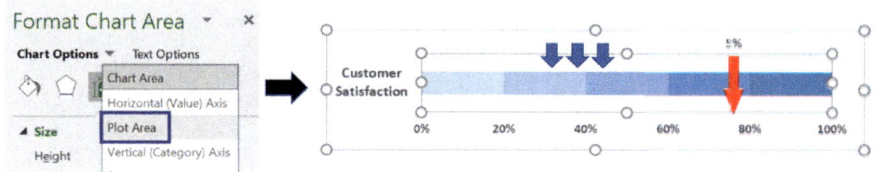

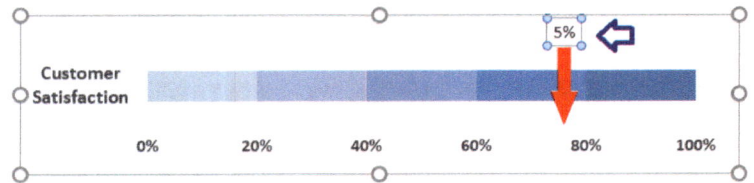

How to re-arrange label for arrow:

- Click the label on the arrow >>> **Ctrl + 1**
- Go to **Label Options** >>> Select **Value form Cells**
- Select the actual input value from the sheet
- **Deselect 'Value'** in the **Label Options**

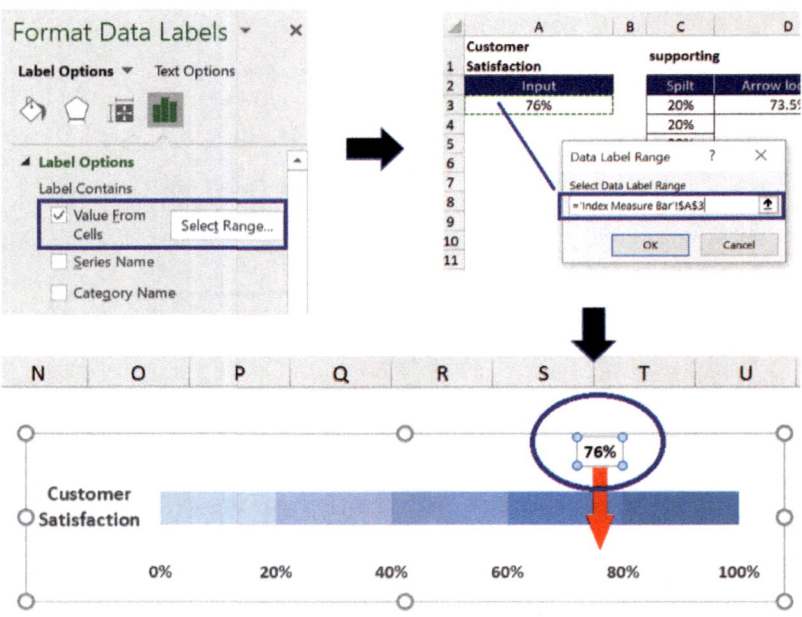

Finally, we can complete 2D index measure bar chart.

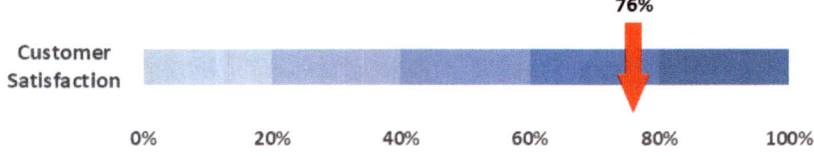

How to add 3D effect into the chart:

First, copy and paste the 2D chart in order to make 3D chart. We are going to change the main horizontal bar part (5 spliced bar).

In order choose the first piece,
- put 1% for the actual input value >>> Click the first piece

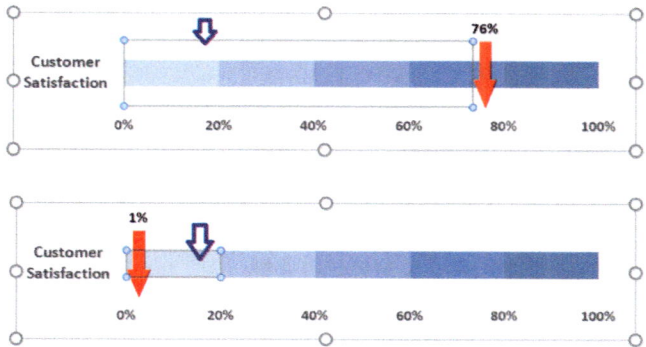

- **Ctrl + 1** >>> **3-D Format** >>> **Top bevel** >>> choose the first one (or which you would like to have) >>> **Repeat 4 times more**

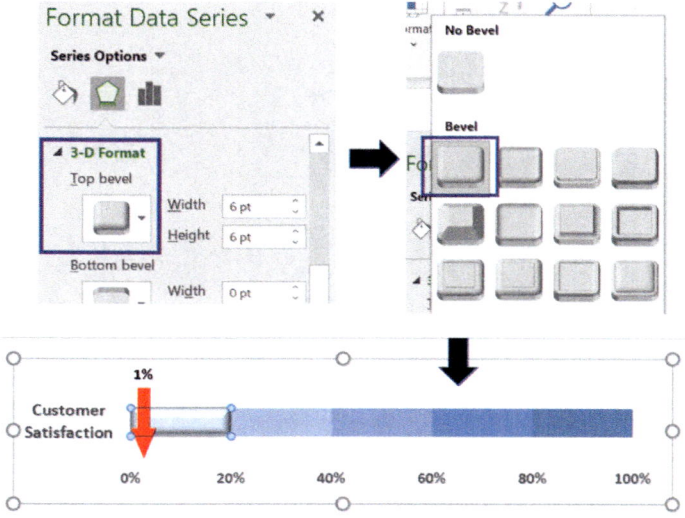

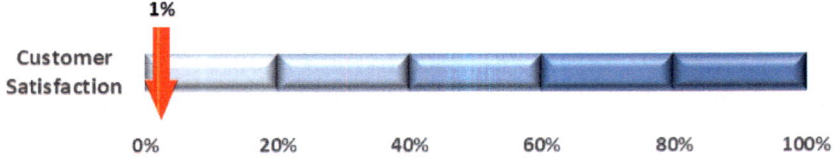

Next, copy and paste the 2D arrow in order to make 3D one. Change the color of the arrow and apply 3D settings in the same manner as before. (You can change the color of the arrow as you wish)

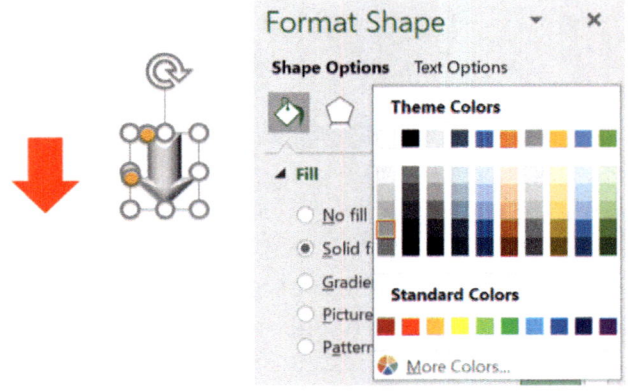

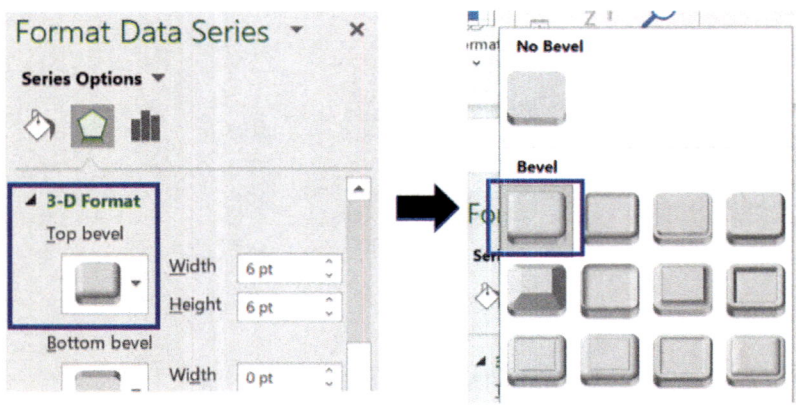

You can add more 3D efforts if you want.

How to combine an arrow icon with the bar chart:

- Click the new 3D arrow icon >>> **Ctrl + C**
- Click the red arrow bar in the chart >>> **Ctrl + V**

Finally, we can complete 3D index measure bar chart.

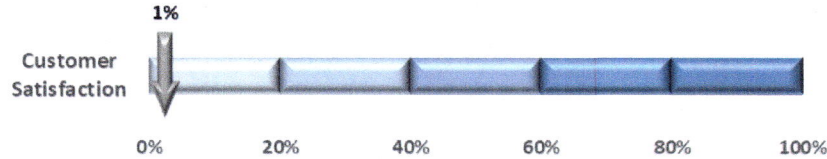

In summary, we can make 2D & 3D index measure bar chars like below. This chart is handy to use your presentation, report or dashboard and so on.

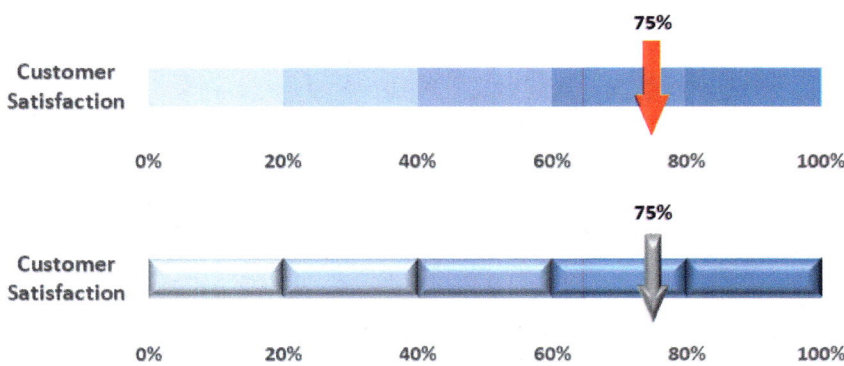

21. Infographic Chart without Chart Functionality

We are going to make an infographic chart and we will not use chart functions to make this chart. However, this cart will dynamically change by input value changes.

Please be aware that the process of making this chart is **a bit complicated**.

Target picture:
What we are going to make is the following charts:

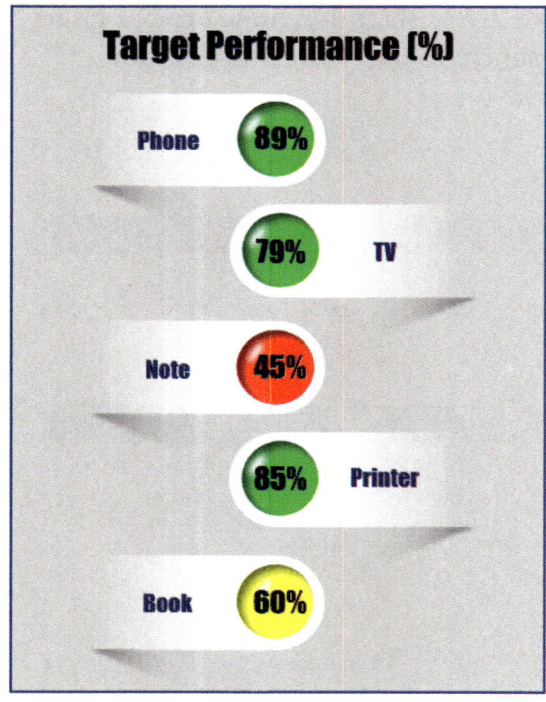

How to set up input values:

First, create **input cells** (=column A & B) and 2 **supporting columns** (=column C & E) in an empty worksheet.

All other inputs are just values except color-index values.

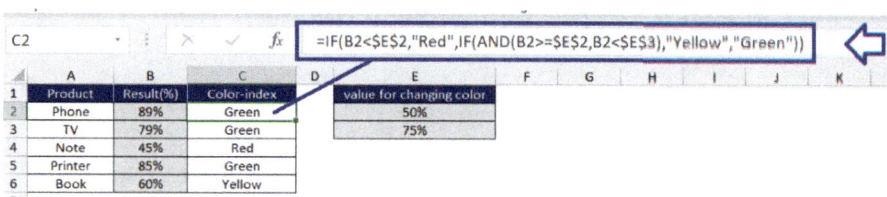

Color-index (column C):

=IF(B2<$E$2,"Red",IF(AND(B2>=$E$2,B2<$E$3),"Yellow","Green"))

Interpretation of IF formula is below:

If **'Result'** value is lower than the first **'value for change color'**, then the **output** is letter **"Red"** >>> **'IF(B2<$E$2,"Red"'**.

If **'Result'** value is Not lower than the first **'value for change color'**, we enter a new condition. >>> **the second IF statement**

If **'Result'** value is greater or equal to the first **'value for change color'** and also then **'Result'** value is lower than the **second** 'value for change color' the **output** is letter **"Yellow"**. If not, "Green" >>>
IF(AND(B2>=$E$2,B2<$E$3),"Yellow","Green")

Example:
Based on the above result, if the result value (column B) is higher than 75%, the color is Green (column C).

- Click the cell C2 >>> **Ctrl + C**
- In this status (**Ctrl + C**), re-select the range until the end of row (i.e., Cell C6) by mouse dragging.

Alternatively,
- In this status (**Ctrl + C**), Click Cell C2 (starting point). Holding **Ctrl + Shift** >>> press an arrow button (↓)

Next step:
- Click **Alt + E + S** (Paste special) >>> a new window will pop up.
- Select **Formula** >>> **OK** >>> table will be filled up with the same formula as the first row of cells.

	A	B	C
1	Product	Result(%)	Color-index
2	Phone	80%	Green
3	TV	79%	Green
4	Note	90%	Green
5	Printer	85%	Green
6	Book	60%	Yellow
7			

If you use the above date selection technique and paste special technique, you can avoid a lot of repetitive tasks.

I strongly recommend to use the above techniques.

How to remove Gridlines:

- Go to **View** tab and unclick **Gridlines**.

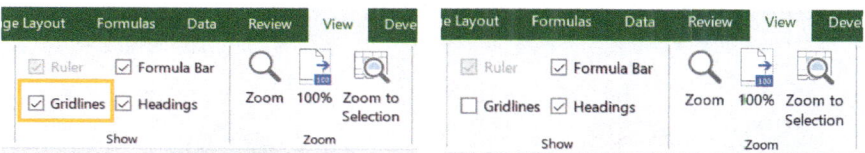

All the grid lines are disappeared in the sheet.

How to make a colored ball icon for the chart:

- **Create a new sheet** & Remove Gridlines again
- **Insert** tab >>> **Presets** >>> the first one in **Inner** section
- After clicking the circle, set **1.4cm** in **Shape Format**
- **Repeat 3 times** with a different color

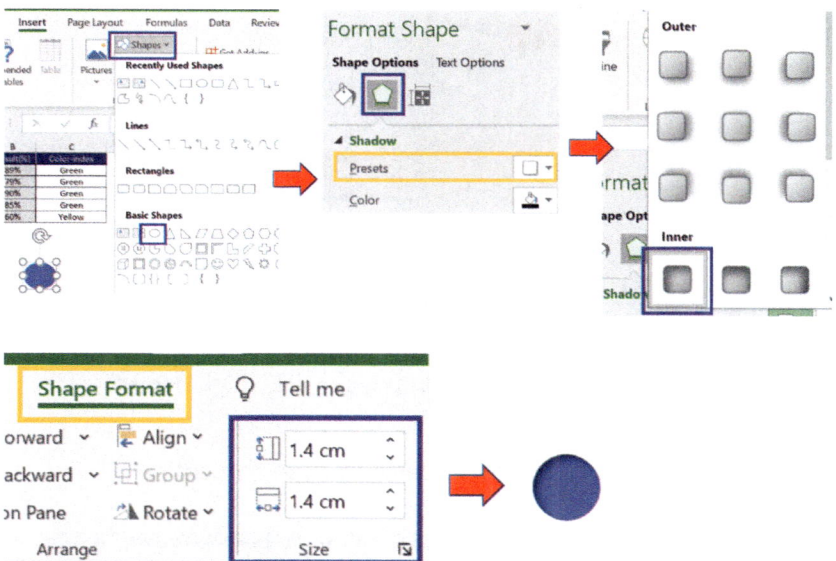

You will see more details in the later section.
The reason why we create a new sheet is to avoid any error by change cell size.

How to allocate the circle icons:

- Go to a new sheet and copy & paste the icons
- (Note) Must locate one circle icon in one cell

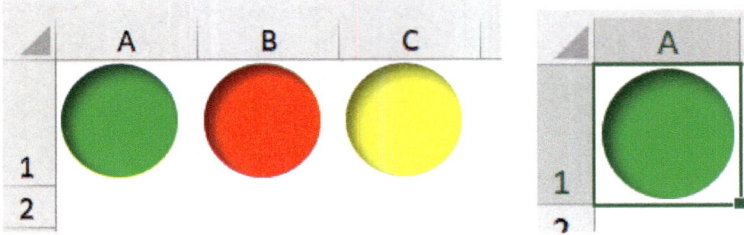

- Select all circle icons in one cell >>> **Align** >>> **Align Middle**

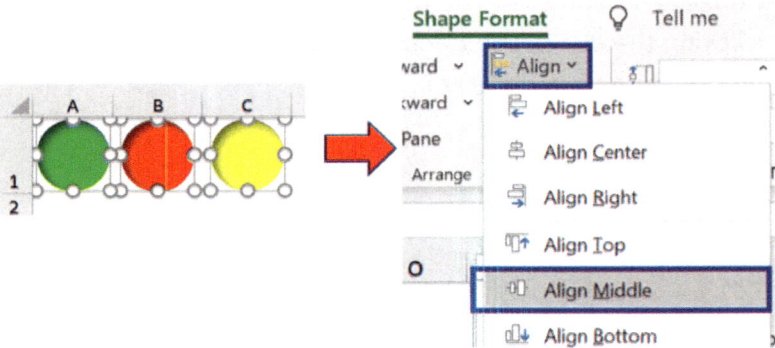

How to align a cell with the circle icon with a new name:

- Select a cell with the circle icon with mouse
- Go to **Formulas** tab >>> **Name Manager** >>> click '**New**'
- **Name** = name of color >>> **OK**
- **Repeat 2 times more** (total 3 new names in the cells)

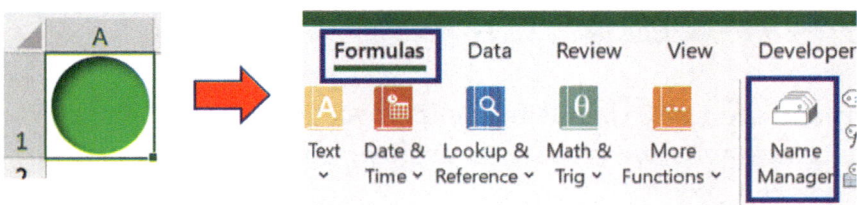

There are 4 circle icons created. Actually, the last one is a dummy one.

Please note that the name of color must be in line with the colors in the 'if formula'.

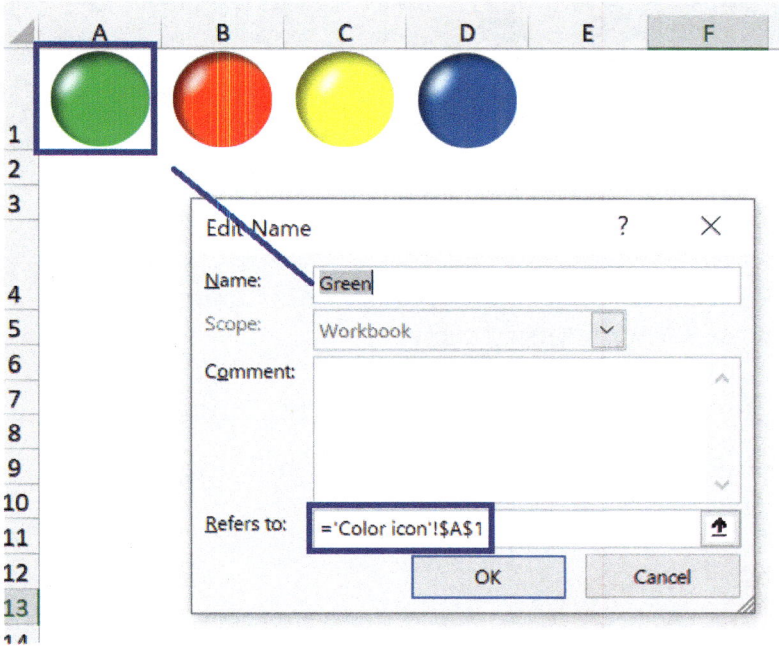

How to make a linked picture:
- Select a cell with the circle icon with mouse >>> **Ctrl + C**
- Go to the sheet where input table is located
- Go to **Home** tab >>> click **Paste** >>> click **Linked picture**
- The linked picture circle icon will be appeared in this sheet
- **Repeat until the total number of products** (i.e., 5 (Column A) in this case)

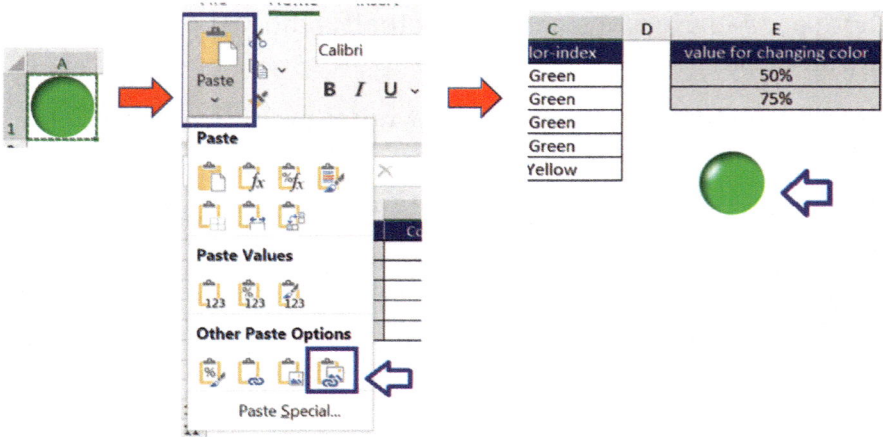

Up to now, we create 3 icons and align 3 new names in the cell. Copy over it with linked picture.

(Optional) How to add the reflection on the circle:

We are going to add the reflection on the circle (See below):

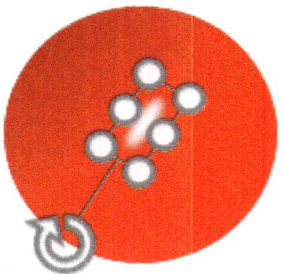

- Select a **circle** in **Insert** tab
- Squeeze the circle like overall shape.
- Select **solid fill** with **white** color
- Go to **Effect** & Select **Soft Edges**. Choose the **third one**.

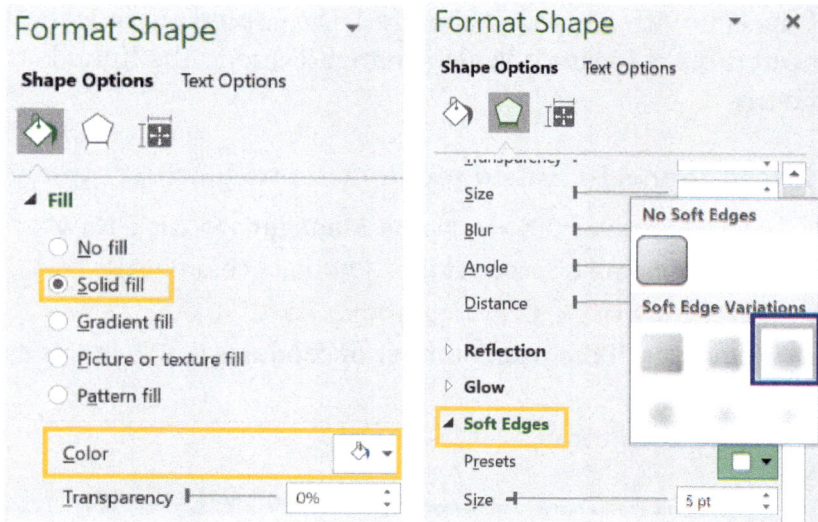

- Put this into the inner circle somewhere at **225 degrees area**.
- **Group** them as one piece.
- **Repeat 2 more times**

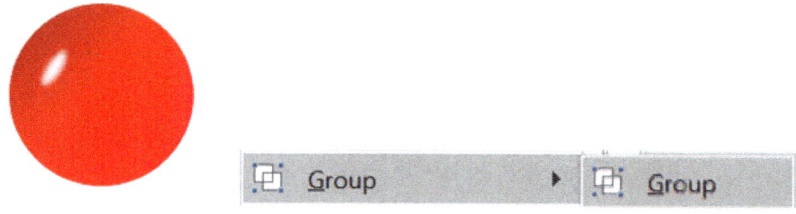

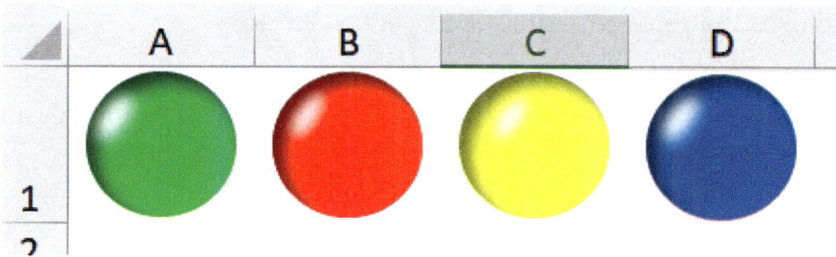

If the cell with an icon is changed, the copied circle icon (in input table is located) is also changed due to the linked picture.

How to connect a linked picture icon with actual inputs:

- Go to **Formulas** tab >>> **Name Manager** >>> click '**New**'
- **Name** = name of product (i.e., Phone in column A)
- **Refer to:** =INDIRECT('Infographic Chart'!$C$2)
- **Repeat until the total number of products** (i.e., 5 in this case) >>> **OK**
- Click **Close** button

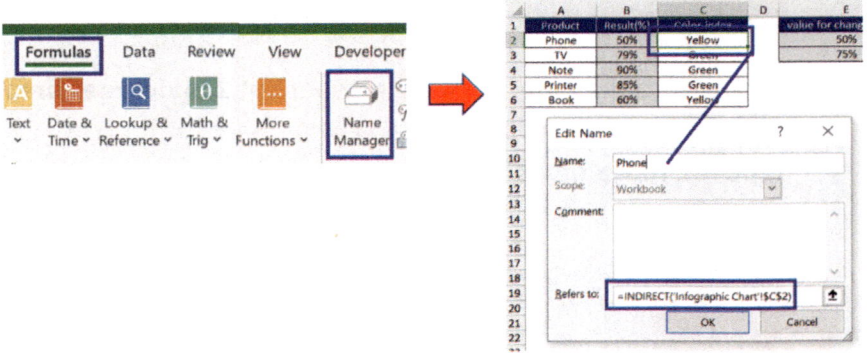

Function: INDIRECT

INDIRECT(ref_text,a1)

Returns the reference specified by a text string.

After repeating 4 more times, we can find the following **Name Manager** (see below).

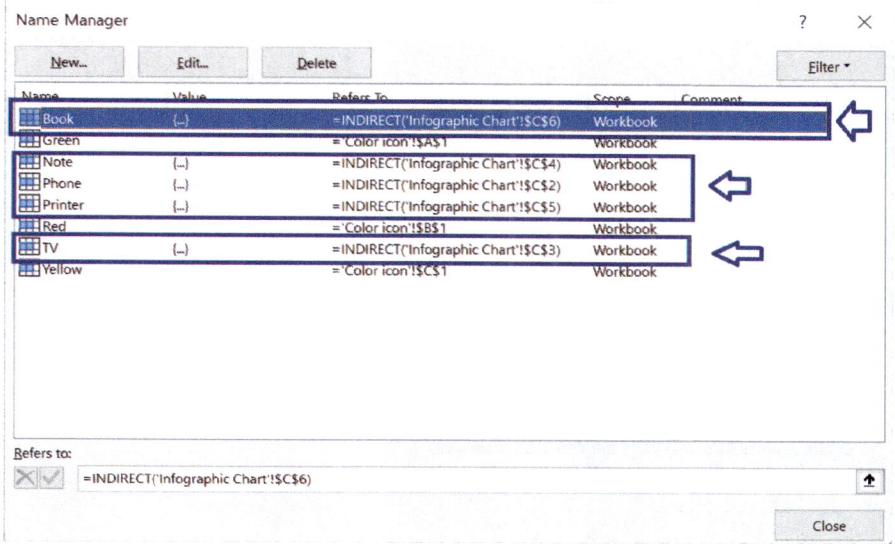

- Starting point: we have 5 circle icons with linked picture.
- Select one of circle icon by using a mouse
- Go to function bar (=fx) >>> type =Phone >>> hit **Enter** button
- **Repeat until the total number of products** (i.e., 5 in this case)

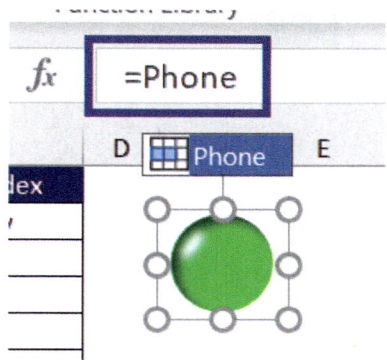

Now, we can complete the connection between a linked picture icon with actual inputs.

Testing: Look at the **Cell B2 & color of circle icon**

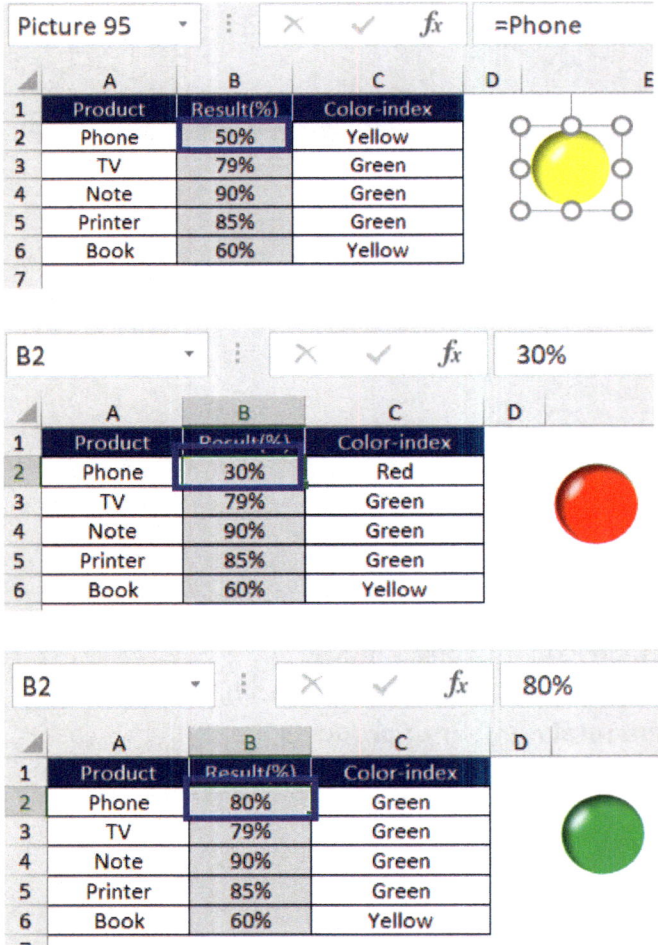

I must say that this connection between icon and input value is a bit difficult to understand at first time.

Happily, the most complicated part is over.

Beauty of this setting:

Simply speaking, **you can create any kind of icons and link it with actual input values.**

How to create a background of infographic cart:

- **Insert** tab >>> **Shape** >>> select **Rectangle**
- By mouse dragging, put the rectangle in the sheet
- Adjusting the size by mouse button.
- The size should cover up the all buttons.
  We can change the size of rectangle later on.
- **Ctrl + 1** >>> **Fill** >>> select the color which you like (i.e., gray)

In the same manner, we can create the following:

- **Insert** tab >>> **Shape** >>> select **Rectangle: Top corners snipped**
- By mouse dragging, put the rectangle in the rectangle which we made it before.
- By controlling the dot (see below), you can control the angle of top-corners snipped rectangle >>> change the direction

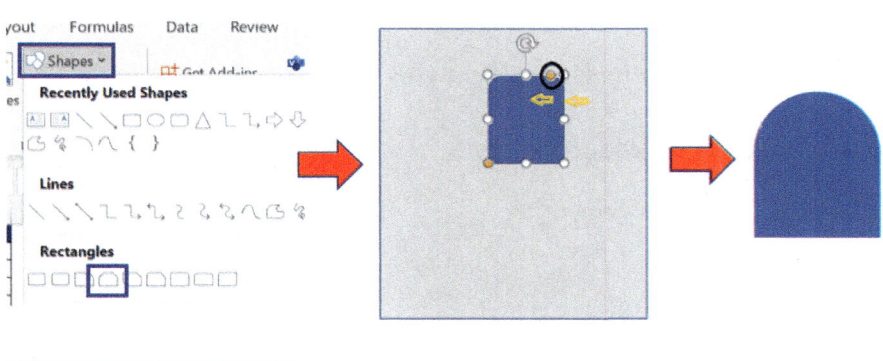

How to set up 3D effect into the inner rectangle:

- Select the horizontal bar by using mouse & **CTRL + 1**.
- Select **Gradient fill**.

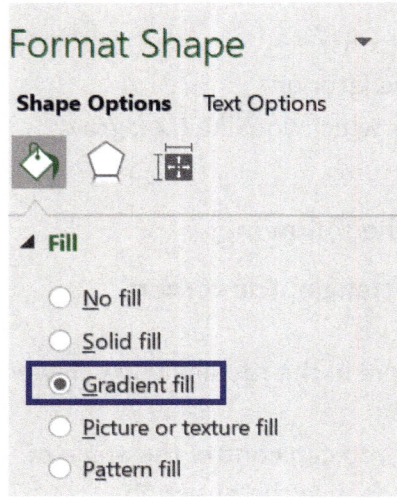

Settings for Gradient stops:

- Color is **white** (first one), **light grey** (middle 2 stops) & **light grey** (last one)
- Positions are **40%, 80%, 100%**.

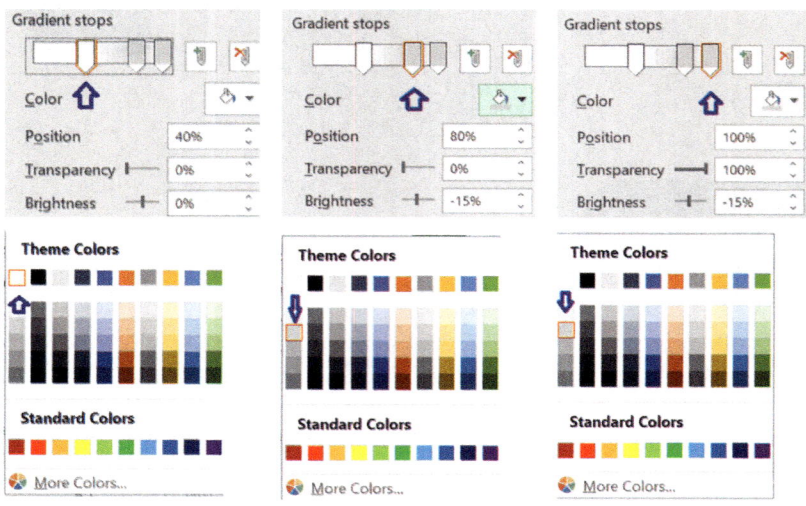

- **Angle = 90 degree** in **Preset gradients**.

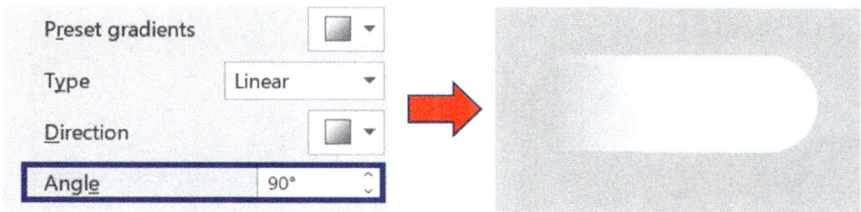

In the above picture (right-hand side), I added a grey background to see the picture clearly. Without the background, it looks like below.

How to make a 3D shadow effect into the inner rectangle:

- **Insert** tab >>> **Shape** >>> select **triangle**
- By mouse dragging, put the triangle in the sheet
- Adjusting the size by mouse button.
  In case of below pictures, the black color for the icons is used to show you clearly.

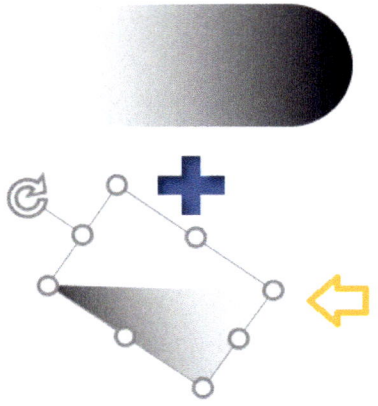

In case of vertical version, you can also use the following way. This part is related to the additional example in the right-hand side of sheet.

Different examples

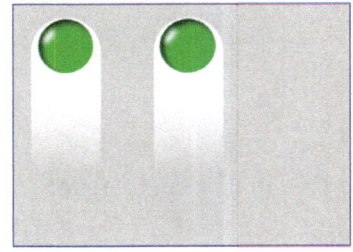
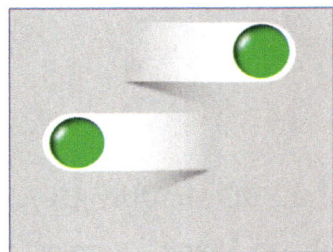

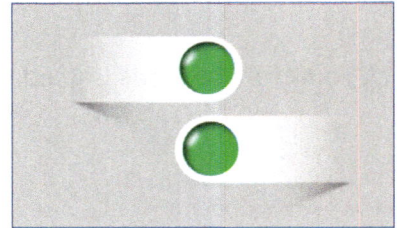

Settings for Gradient stops for the triangle (for shadow):

- Color is **light gray** (first one), **black** (last one)
- Positions are **0%, 100%**.
- Brightness's are **-15%, 0%**.

Please note that you can change the setting of gradient depends on your preference. The above setting is for only examples.

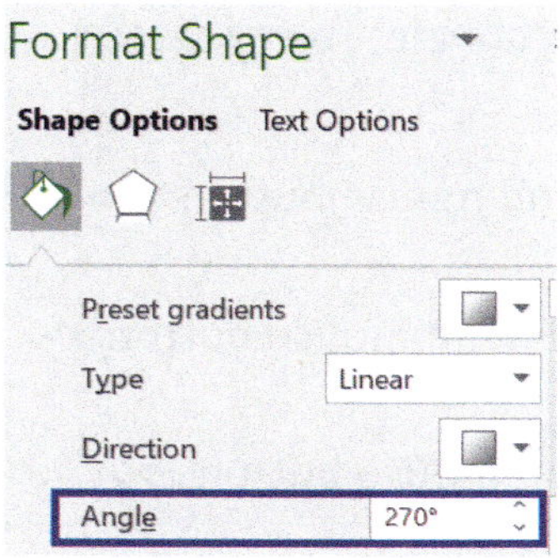

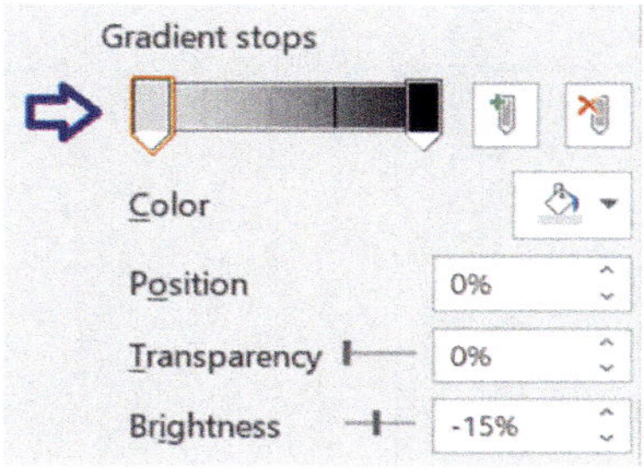

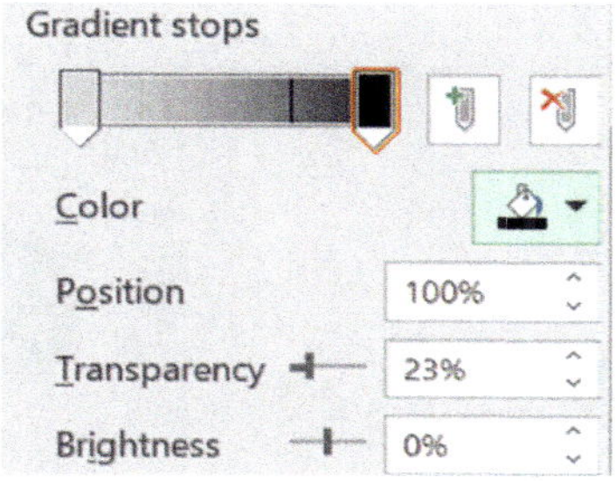

Combine the rectangle and the triangle like the below picture.

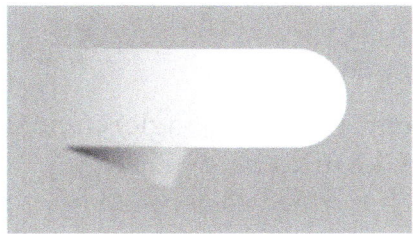

How to combine background, inner rectangle, inner circle and the triangle:

- Click the **background** >>> a right-hand mouse button >>> **Send to back**
- Click the **inner rectangle** >>> a right-hand mouse button >>> **Bring to Front**
- Click the **inner circle** >>> a right-hand mouse button >>> **Bring to Front**
- Combine them all like the below picture.

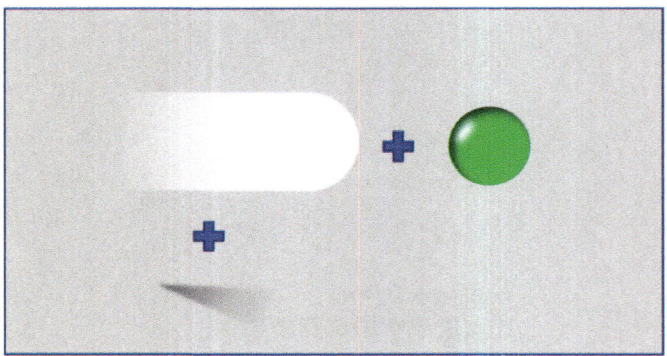

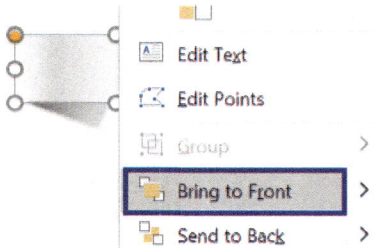

How to align multiple text boxes or charts:

Now, we have 3 pieces of components (inner rectangle, circle, the shadow triangle). In order to make them align nicely, please use the following steps which is much easier than by using mouse.

- **Holding Ctrl** button >>> **select** chart and text boxes **by clicking left-hand mouse button**.
- (Optional) Grouping them >>> after multiple selections, click **Shape Format** >>> **Group** >>> **Group**

It is possible to select multiple items in the sheet.
For example,

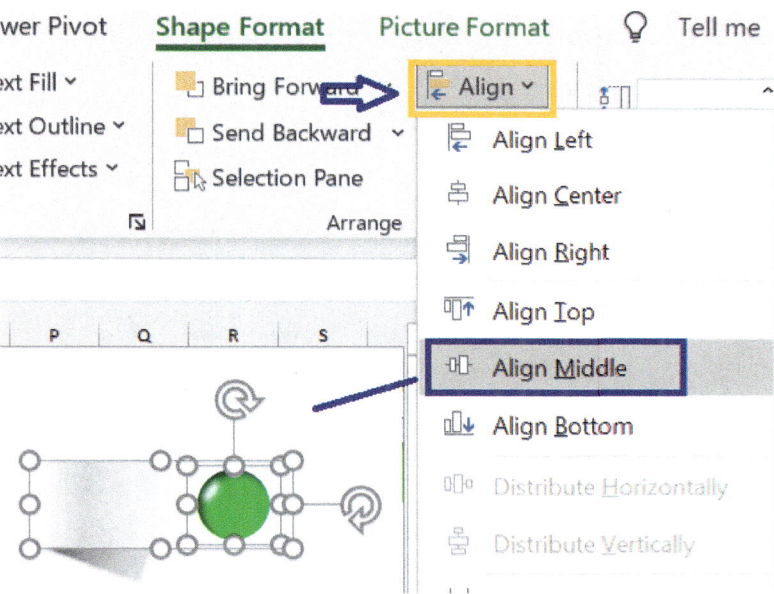

How to make a text box which shows input values:
- Make a text box: **Insert** tab >>> **Shapes** >>>select **Text box**.
- Put a cursor inside of text box & click a function box ( )
- Write '= a cell location (i.e., =B5)' and then hit 'Enter' button. Please see the below picture for the detail. <u>The following picture is not directly from this example</u>. However, the method is more or less identical.

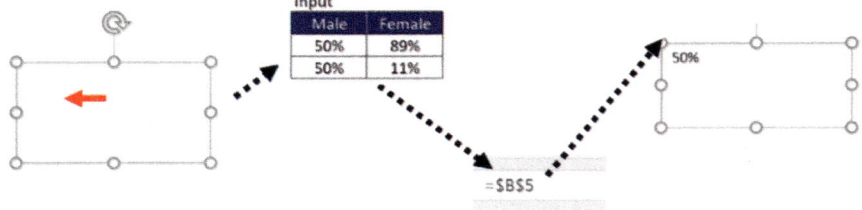

How to make the text box looking good:

Clicking a text box, removing Shape Fill & Shape Outline.

- **Shape Fill** = No Fill
- **Shape Outline** = No Outline

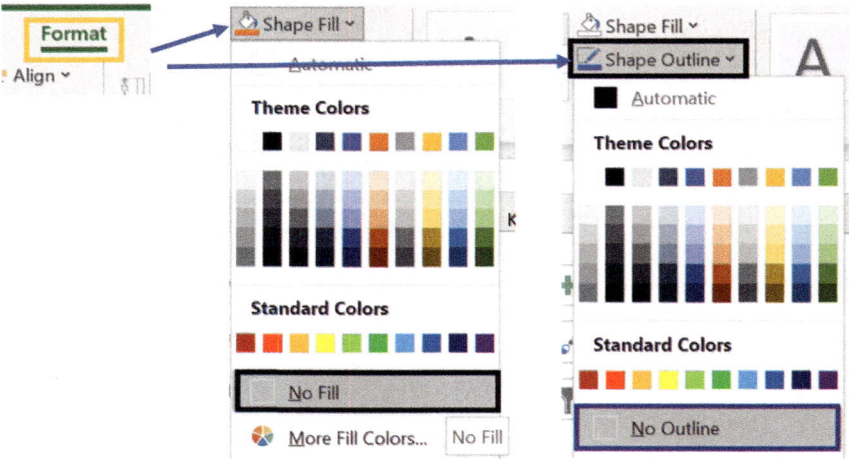

The rest elements (font size, font color, font type, etc.) can be changed by Font tab in **Home** tab (see below)

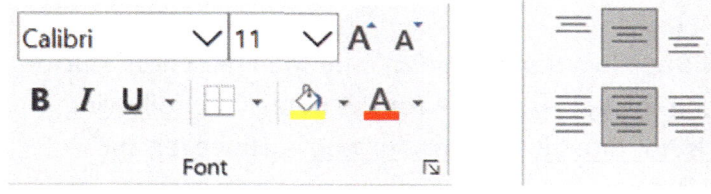

By using alignment & grouping technique, you can combine the previously made shape and the textbox.

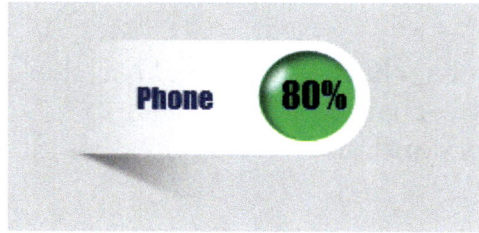

Next, repeat until the maximum number of product (i.e., 5 = Phone, TV, etc.) what we have done to create the above picture.

Please note that the remaining repeating processes are identical as before. Therefore, there will be no explanation on this part in this book.

Finally, we can complete the chart like below.

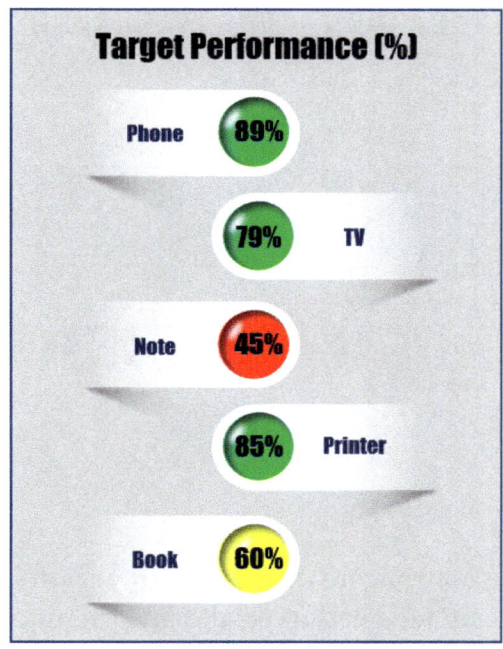

22. Bar of Bar Chart

We are going to make a bar of bar chart. In a normal bar, there is another bar chart inside of bar chart. It is not so easy to show both sum of each category and the individual values at the same time.

Benefit of this chart is to visualize the complicate date simply.

Target picture:
What we are going to make is the following charts:

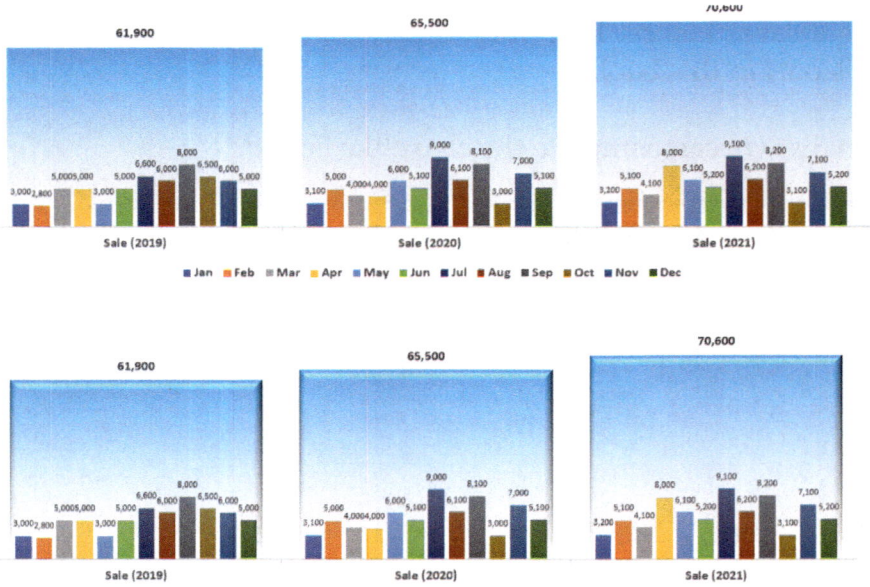

How to set up input values:

Let's assume that we have a complicate data set with various tables. (See below) In this case, we need to re-allocate them to make a chart easily later on.

	A	B	C	D	E	F	G	H
1	Origial Data			Origial Data			Origial Data	
2	Month	Sale (2019)		Month	Sale (2020)		Month	Sale (2021)
3	Jan	3,000		Jan	3,100		Jan	3,200
4	Feb	2,800		Feb	5,000		Feb	5,100
5	Mar	5,000		Mar	4,000		Mar	4,100
6	Apr	5,000		Apr	4,000		Apr	8,000
7	May	3,000		May	6,000		May	6,100
8	Jun	5,000		Jun	5,100		Jun	5,200
9	Jul	6,600		Jul	9,000		Jul	9,100
10	Aug	6,000		Aug	6,100		Aug	6,200
11	Sep	8,000		Sep	8,100		Sep	8,200
12	Oct	6,500		Oct	3,000		Oct	3,100
13	Nov	6,000		Nov	7,000		Nov	7,100
14	Dec	5,000		Dec	5,100		Dec	5,200

As a next step, it is required to make them into one table.

How to sort various tables into one table:

- Create a new table >>> Link between an original data and a sorted data
- Put '=' in the cell >>> Click the location of cell which you would like to link >>> '= cell location' (i.e., =B3)
- In the same manner, you can apply this method from one column to another column (from 2019 to 2021)

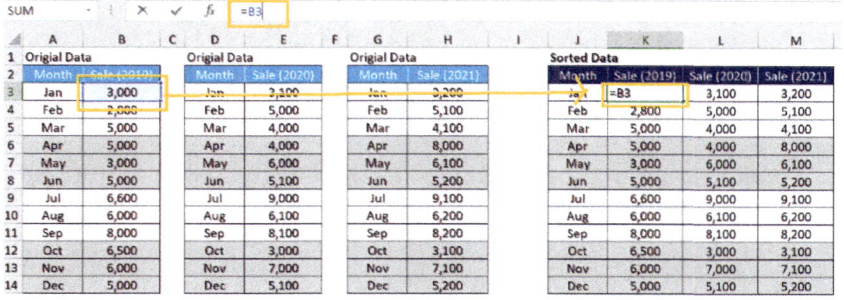

- Now, 3 cells are linked with the original values.
- Select the range by mouse >>> **Ctrl + C**

- In this status (**Ctrl + C**), re-select the range until the end of row (i.e., Dec) by mouse dragging.

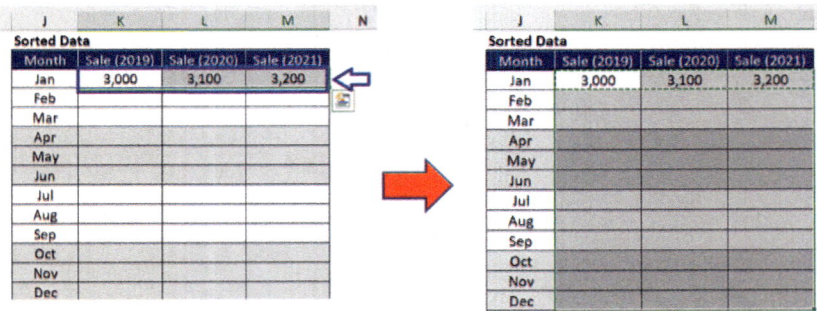

- Click **Alt + E + S** (Paste special) >>> a new window will pop up.
- Select **Formula** >>> **OK** >>> table will be filled up with the same formula as the first row of cells.

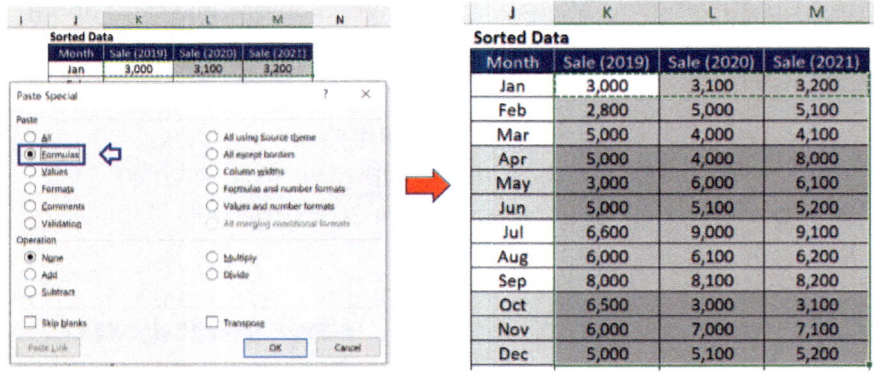

- Select range of 12 months for each year (by using a mouse) >>> put '**= sum (12months cells range)**' >>> hit enter button

- Click the sum calculated cell >>> **Ctrl + C** >>> select the other 2 cells >>> **Ctrl + V**

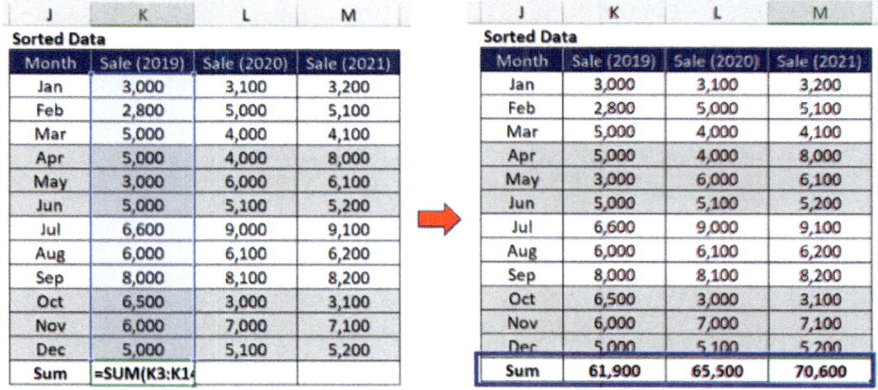

We can complete the sorting of original data and put them into a table.

How to remove Gridlines:

- Go to **View** tab and unclick **Gridlines**.

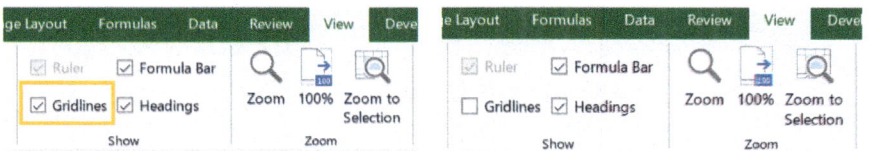

All the grid lines are disappeared in the sheet.

How to create 2-D Stacked bar chart:

- After selecting inputs values (from **Column C** & by using mouse dragging), go to **Insert** tab.
- Select **2-D Column** >>> **Clustered Column**.

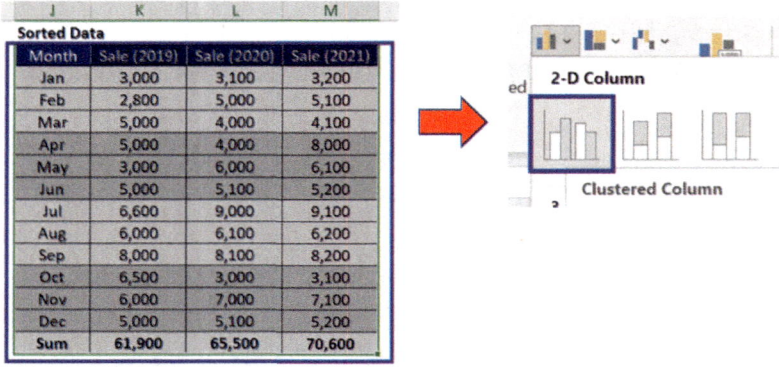

As a result, we can find the following result below.

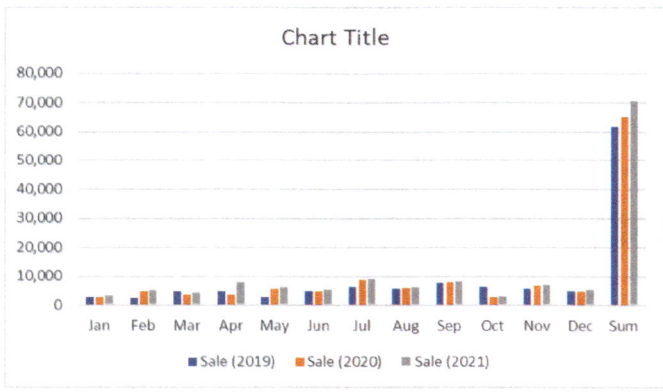

How to remove 'Shape Fill' and 'Shape Outline':

Click a chart >>> Go to **Format** tab. We will change the default settings of Shape Fill and Shape Outline of the chart.

- **Shape Fill** = No Fill
- **Shape Outline** = No Outline

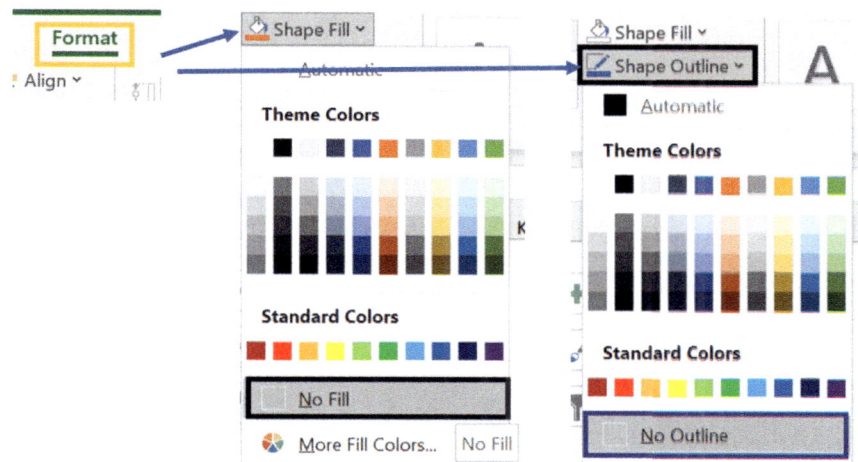

How to switch 'Row and Column' in the chart:

- After selecting chart, click a right-hand side mouse button
- Go to **Select Data** >>> **Switch Row/Column**

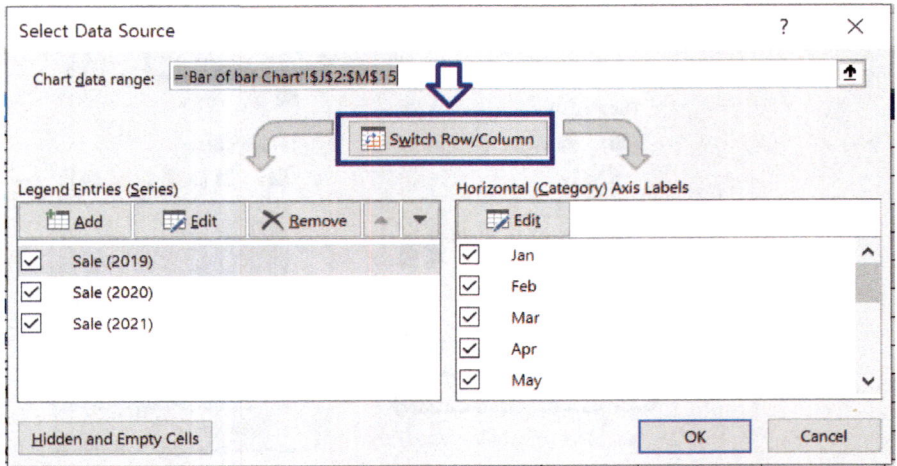

We can find the following:

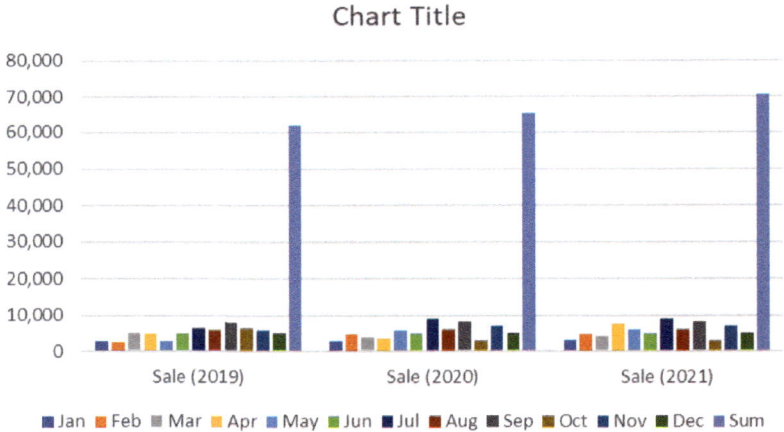

How to remove chart elements:

After clicking a chart, we can see the plus **(+) sign** on right hand side. This is the location where we can control the chart elements.

- Go to chart elements = click **(+)** sign in gray in the chart

- **Remove the chart elements** = Unclick the chart elements which you want to remove

In this case, we unclicked both **Chart Title** and **Gridlines** from chart elements.

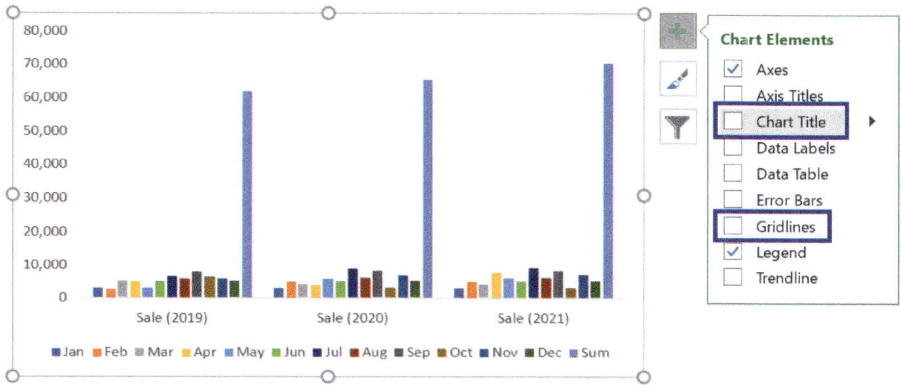

How to adjust the legend in the chart:

- **Select the legend** by using a mouse (all selection)
- **Click one more time with one specific legend** (i.e., 'Sum') which you want to remove (you see select like below)
- Press **Delete** button

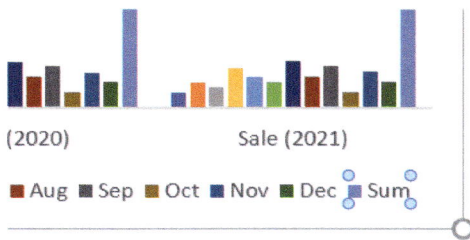

How to add data labels:

- After selecting a vertical bar by using mouse
- Click a **right-hand mouse button** >>> go to **'Add Data Labels'**

- Unfortunately, **repeat until the end of bar** in the chart
- Extend the size of chart by mouse dragging, but only horizontally (to see the labels clearly)

- Reduce the size of label from **9** to **6** (font size)
  The font size 6 is only fitted for this example. You can change the size by your example cases.

- Click each label (i.e., 3 Jan bars) >>> reduce the size
- **Repeat** until the end of bar (**except the sum bar**)

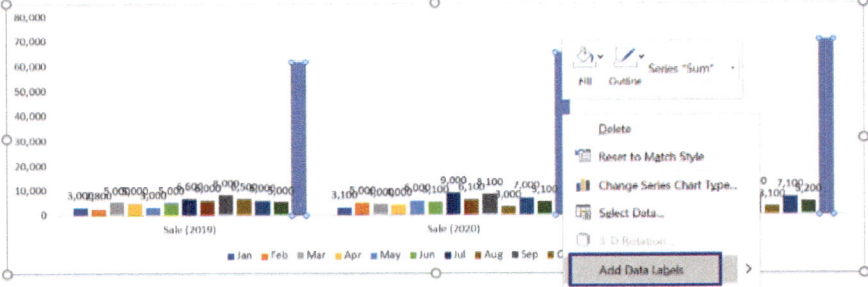

After these steps, we can create the following bar.

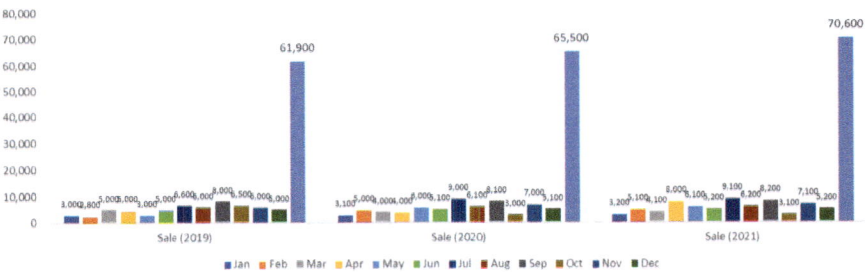

How to select the secondary axis:

We are going to overlap the sum bars with the monthly bars. In order to so, we need to define the sum bars as the secondary axis.

- After selecting vertical sum bars by using mouse
- **Ctrl + 1 >>> Series Options >>> Secondary Axis**

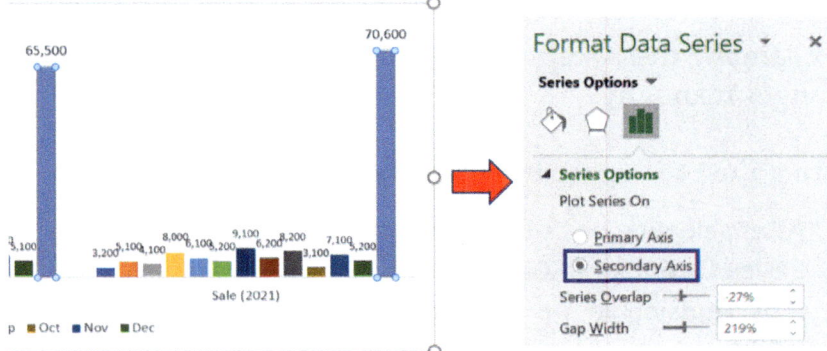

The below chart looks strange because both monthly and sum bars from primary and secondary axis overlapped.

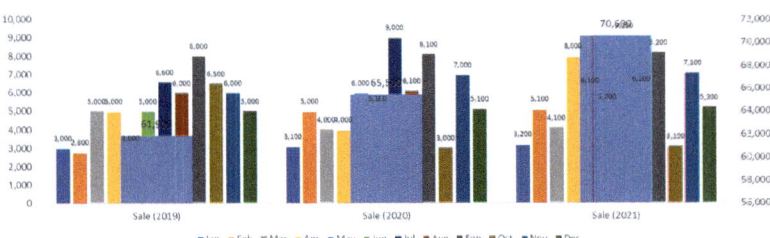

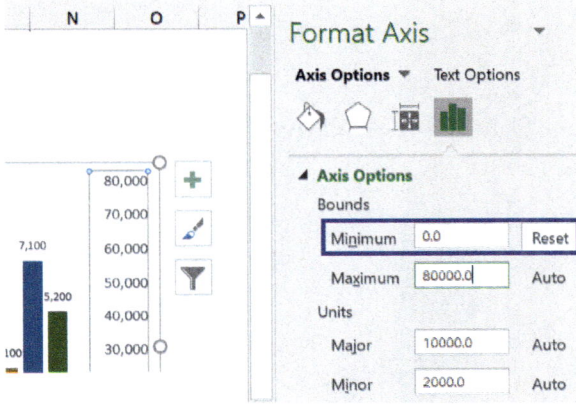

- After selecting the **secondary axis** >>> **Ctrl + 1** >>> **Axis Options**
- **Bounds** >>> **Minimum = 0** (change from **Auto** >>> **Reset**)

After changing these steps, please note that you need to adjust axis ranges manually.

How to adjust the space between bars:

- After selecting one of the **monthly** bars >>> **Ctrl + 1** >>> **Series Options** >>> **Gap Width = 300%**
- It depends on your preference you can change the **Gap Width** as you wish.

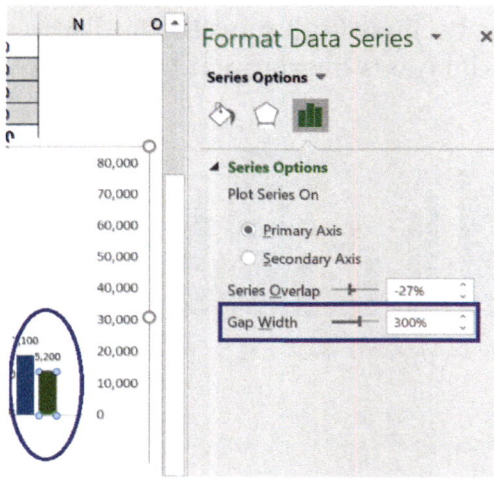

After the setting changes, it looks like below (black bracket).

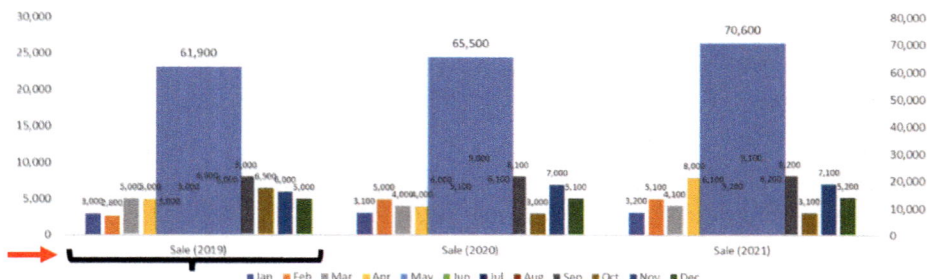

How to adjust the space between bars:

- After selecting one of the **sum** bars (Yearly) >>> **Ctrl + 1** >>> **Series Options** >>> **Gap Width = 15%**
- It depends on your preference you can change the **Gap Width** as you wish.

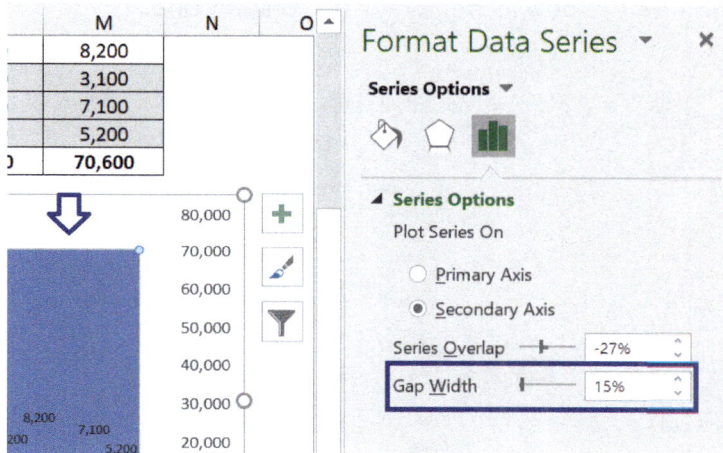

After the setting changes, it looks like below.
Basically, by changing Gap width, it is possible to overlap both monthly and yearly sum bars.

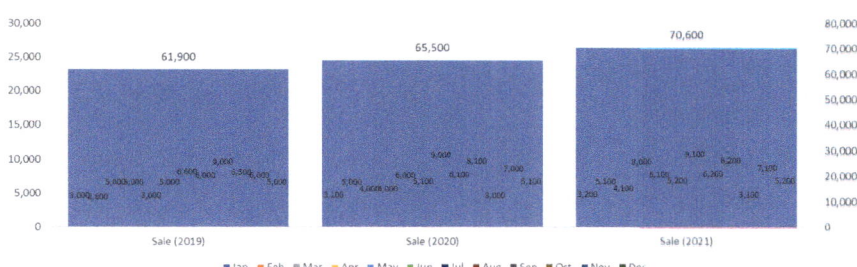

The following steps are how to decorate the bar of bar nicely. Depends on your preference, it can be changeable.

(Optional) Settings for Gradient stops:

- Select the sum bars >>> **Ctrl + 1** >>> **Fill** >>> **Gradients fill** >>> no need to change the first gradient stops (leave it as a default setting) >>> Select the second one (choose the color which you like)
- You can find the details below for the second one.

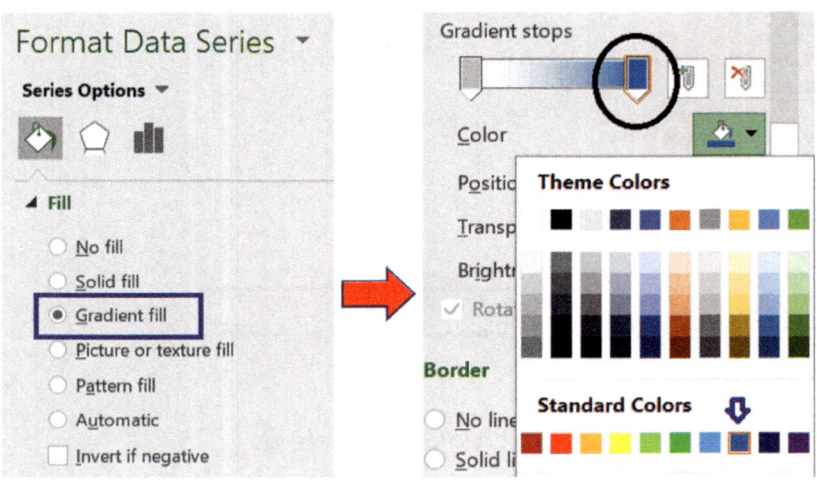

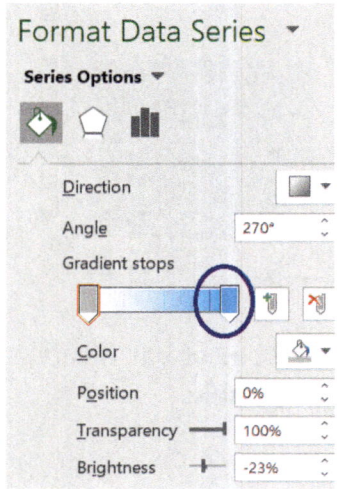

We can create the following picture. It is almost completed.

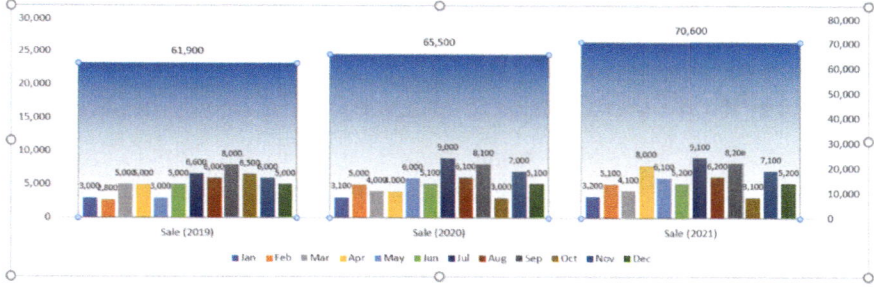

Minor adjustment:
We make both the labels for 3 sum value and year values.

Make it bold:
- Select an item which you want to make it bold >>> **Ctrl + B**

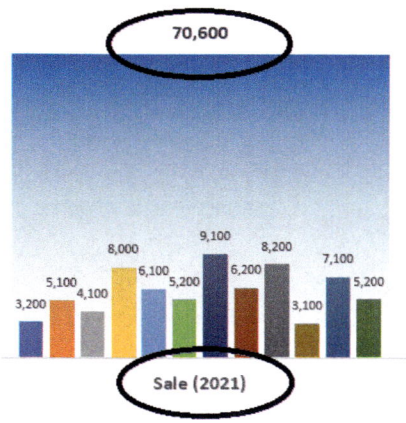

Short summary (up to now):
- Sorting the initial data >>> Adjust into one table.
- Create a bar chart >>> overlapped sum bar with monthly bar
- For the sum bar, give Gradient effect in order to see the overlapped bars.

How to adjust the vertical axis:

At the moment, we have the following 2 vertical axis. Depends on the personal preference, we can leave it like that. However, if you would like to change it, please see below.

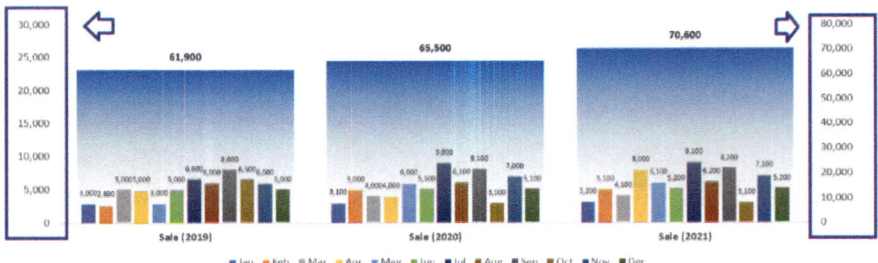

At this point, there are 2 possible options.

Option1:
Removing the primary vertical axis by selecting & **pressing the delete button**.

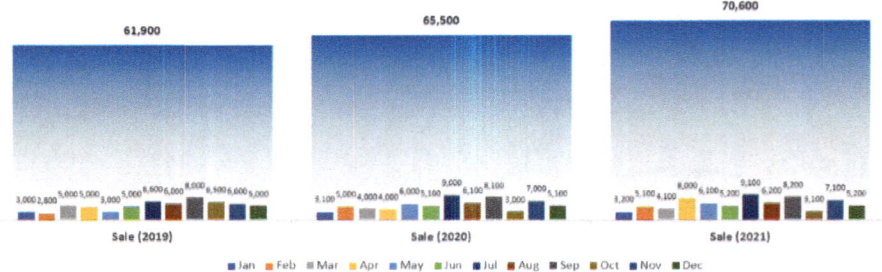

Option2:
Hide the primary vertical axis by selecting & **changing color of axis font color to white**.

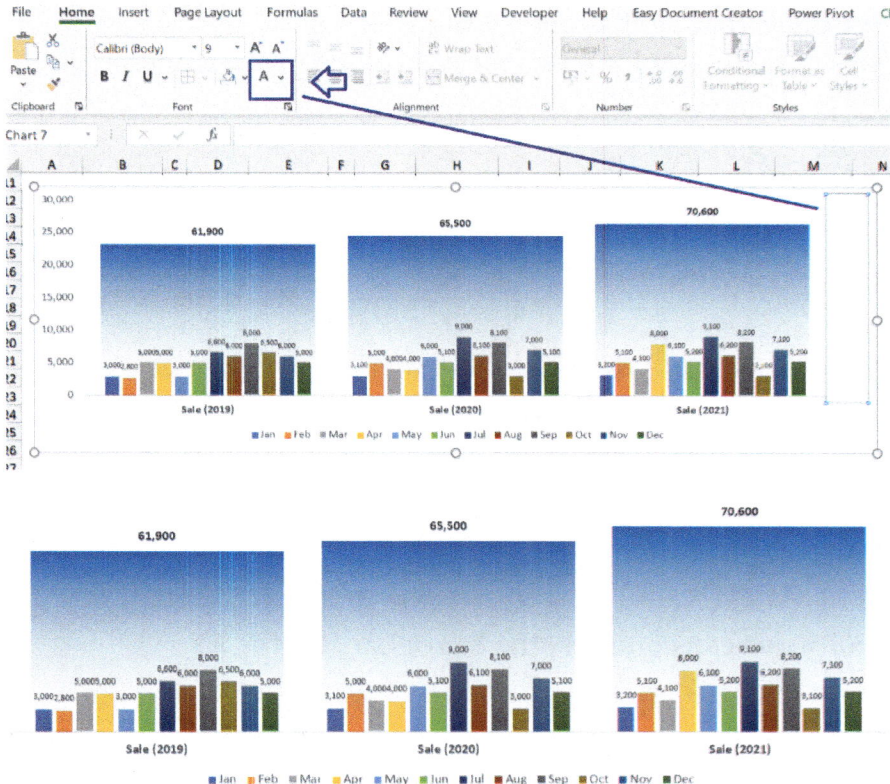

Differences:

The main difference is as follows:
<u>Option1 shows the overall figure more correctly</u>. However, it is a bit difficult to read the monthly bars. Too small.

<u>For Option2 case, it shows the monthly bars clearly</u>. However, the total sum values are proportionally correct.

In the example excel file, both versions are available.
Depends on your preference, it can use either of them.

Optional: change the color of the sum bar
I think that this color looks nicer. I just changed it again.

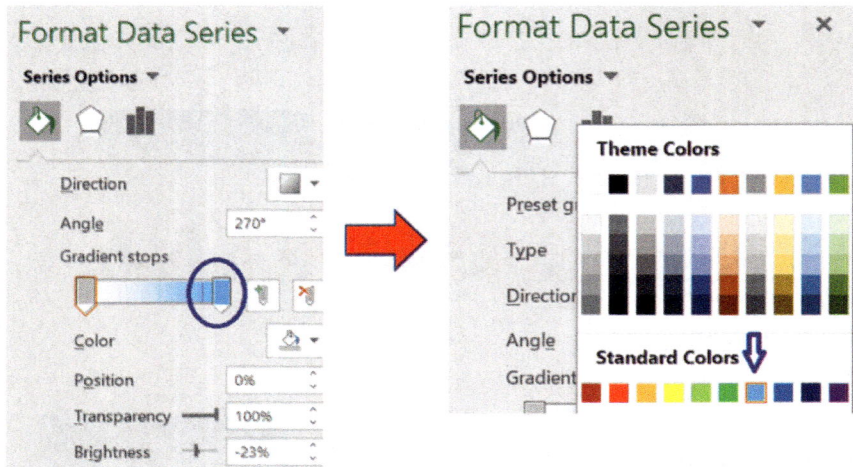

Finally, we can complete the bar of bar chart.

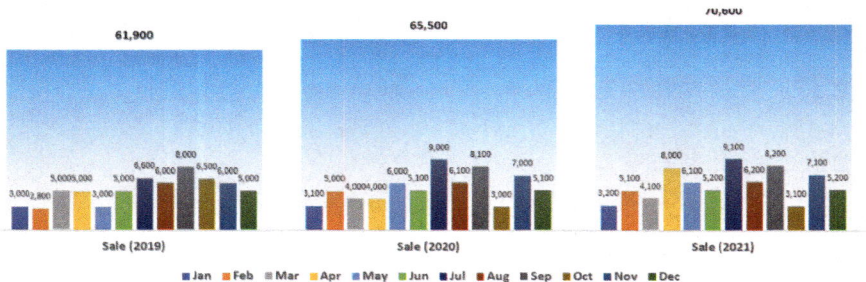

Optional: adding 3D effect to the sum bar

- Selecting sum bar by clicking mouse
- **Ctrl + 1 >>> 3-D Format >>> Top bevel**

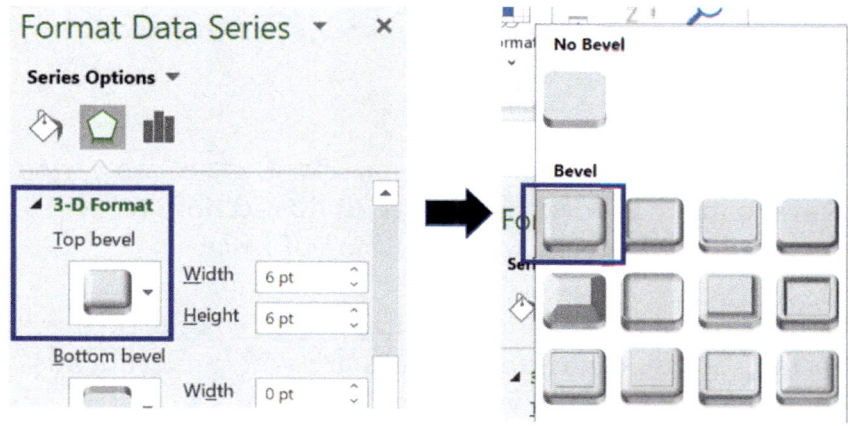

Finally, we can complete the bar of bar chart with 3D effect.

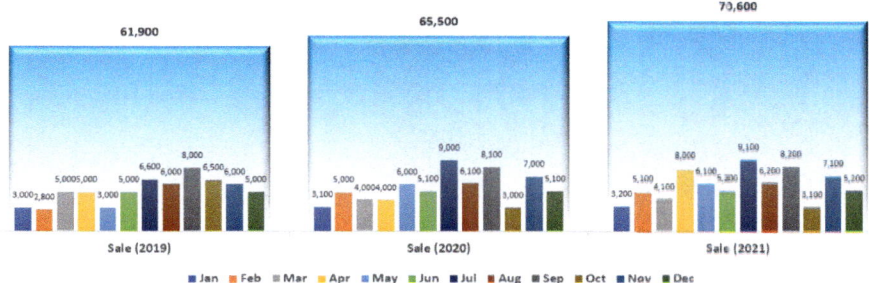

23. World Map Chart

We are going to make a world map chart. There are various ways to make a world map chart. In this section, we will touch the method which can use all version of Excel.

Benefit of this chart is to visualize the given date on the map. As long as you can use a bubble chart, you can create this chart regardless of the version of Excel.

Target picture:
What we are going to make is the following charts:

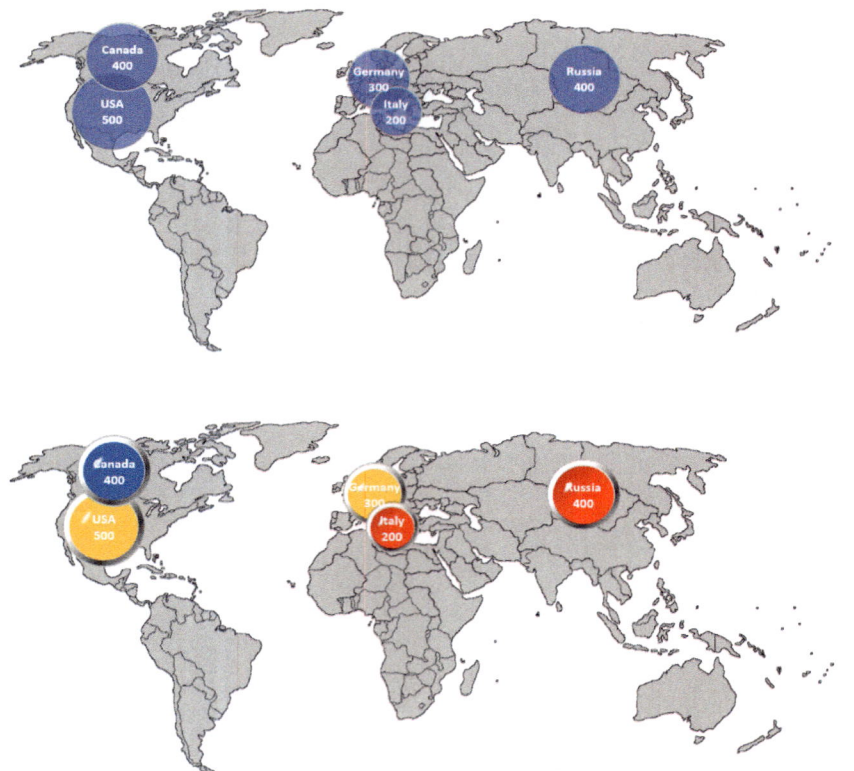

How to adjust the empty sheet:

- Select **25 columns** by using mouse dragging. Select the 'A' column by using mouse and drag it until the Z column.
- After the selection, shrink it until the shape of cells to make right square shapes. (See below)
- We can have **16 x 25 metric** with right square cells.
- Numbering from Cell A16 to upward up to 16 (=Cell A1)
- Numbering from Cell A15 to the right direction up to 14 (=Cell Z25)
- Must start from **0** value.

Please see the detail in the below picture.

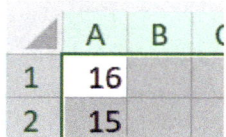

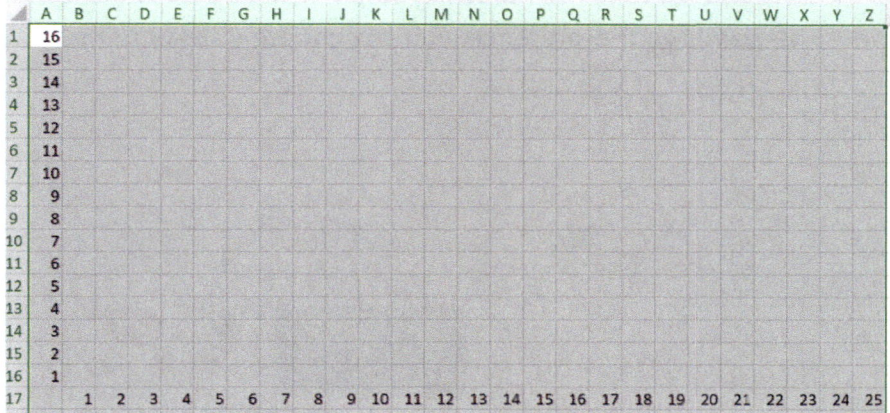

The reason why we make this shape is that we are going to put a world map on the top of this right square metric.

The allocated numbers (x, y) will be the control parameters for the location of countries in the world map chart.

How to find a world map for the chart:

- Go to **Insert** tab >>> **Picture** >>> **Online Pictures**
- **Insert Pictures** window will pop up.
- Go to **Bing Image Search**
- Type '**World map**' >>> press **Enter** button

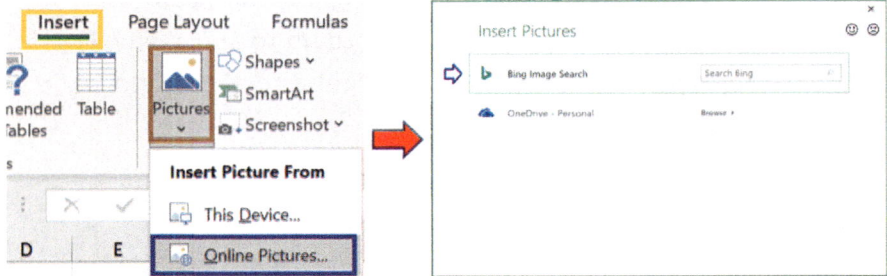

- Online Pictures window will pop up.
- Select **Creative Commons only** >>> which has no copyright normally.
- In this example, the following map is selected for the chart. Depends your preference, you can choose different one.

As a result, we can download the following picture on the sheet.
- Click the below part (= 'This Photo by....')
- Delete the box.

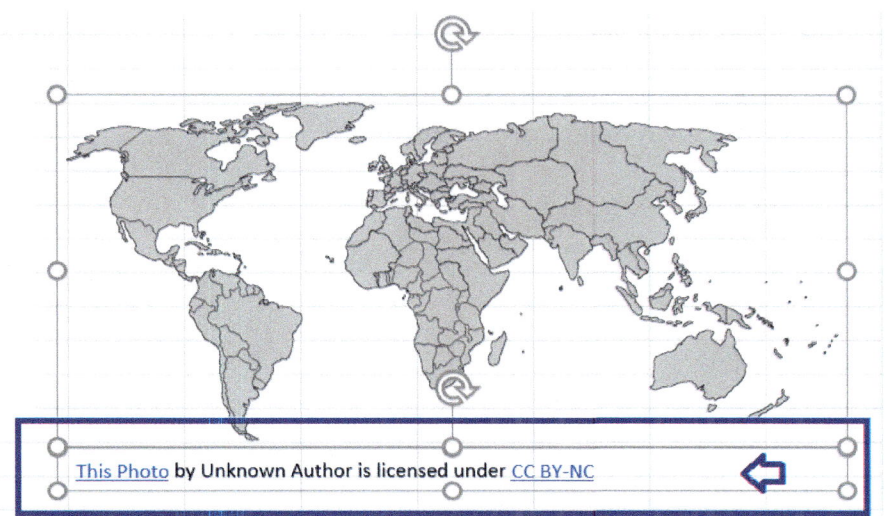

How to combine a world map image with sheet:

- Select the image >>> Put it from cell B2 (starting point) >>>
- **Extend** the image up to Cell Y16 by using a mouse

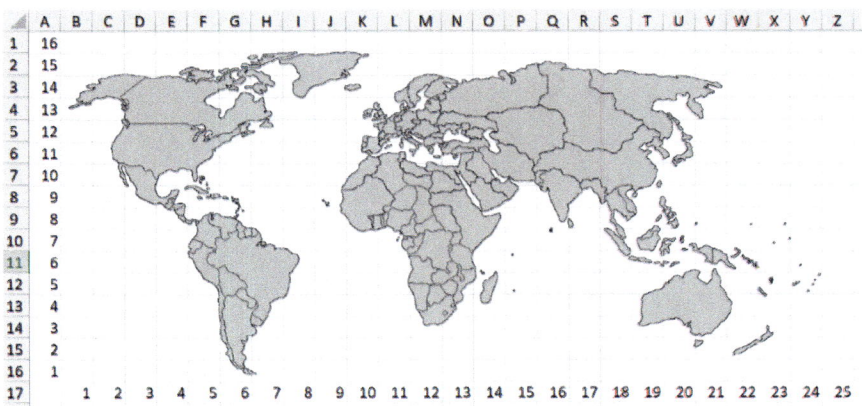

Based on the above picture, we can overlap both image and the right square shape cells.

How to check the size of a world map image:

- Click the image >>> **Picture Format** >>>
- Write down **height** and **width**

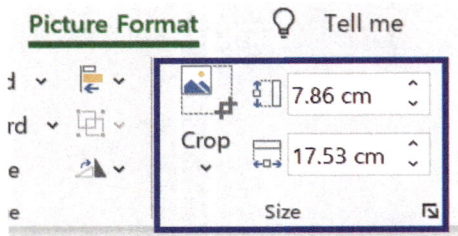

How to create 2-D Bubble chart:

- **Insert** tab >>> **Charts** >>> **Scatter** >>> **Bubble**.

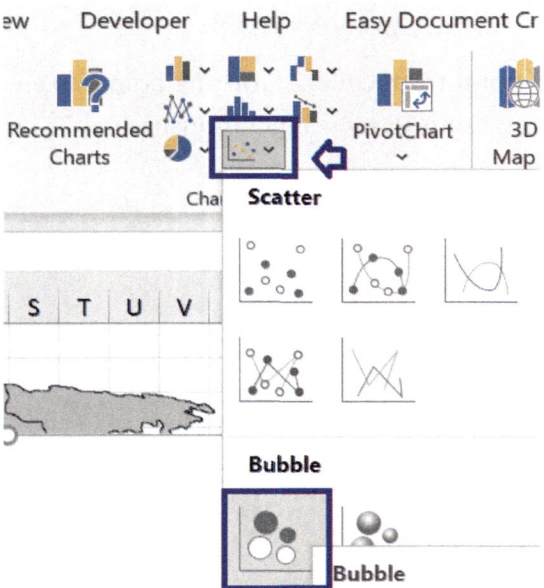

After clicking the bubble chart above, you can find the following empty chart below.

How to resize the size of a bubble chart:

- Click the chart >>> **Format** >>>
- **Change** the **height** and **width size** according to the world map image

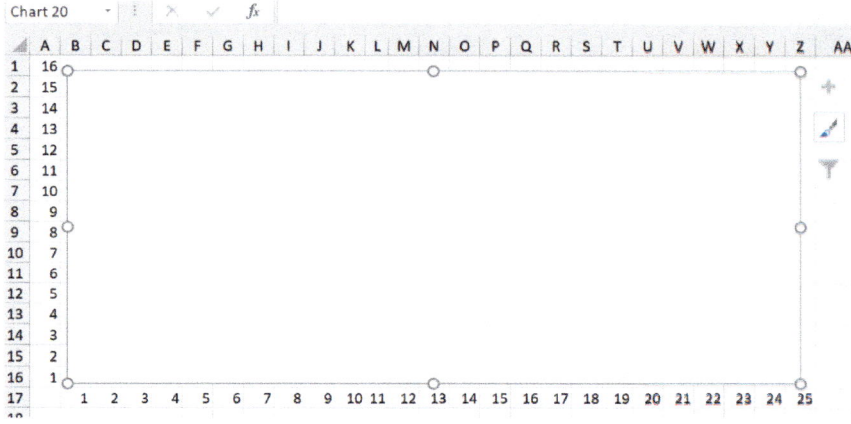

- Click the chart >>> click a **right-hand mouse button** >>>
- Click **Select Data** >>> Click **Add** button (on the left side)

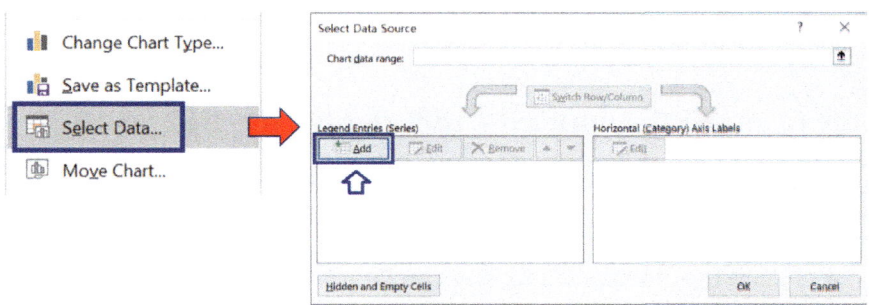

It is possible to see the below **Edit Series** window.
We can update the X, Y, Bubble size from the input values.

At this point, you should not worry about the exact point to show the location of countries. We can change these settings anytime.

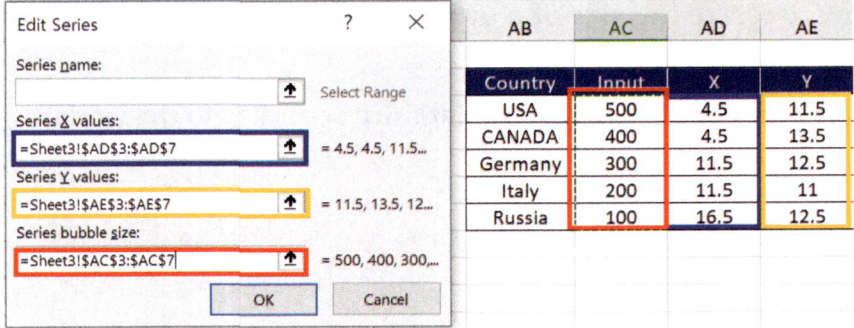

As a result, we can find the following results.

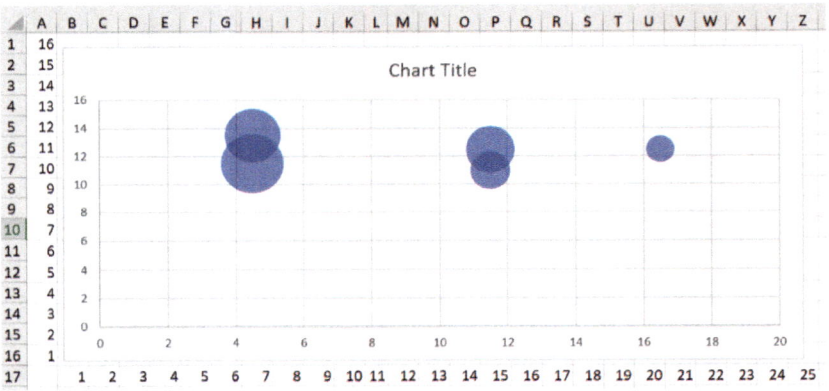

How to adjust the both axis from chart and cells:

As you can see below, it is a bit confused with both the measure from axis in the chart and the measure in cells.

- Click the horizontal axis in the chart >>> **Ctrl + 1** >>> **Axis Options** (i.e., horizontal axis)
- **Bounds** >>> **Minimum = 0** (change from **Auto** >>> **Reset**)
- **Maximum = 24** (change from **Auto** >>> **Reset**)

  The min & max value has to be in line with the min and max values in the cells.

Before:

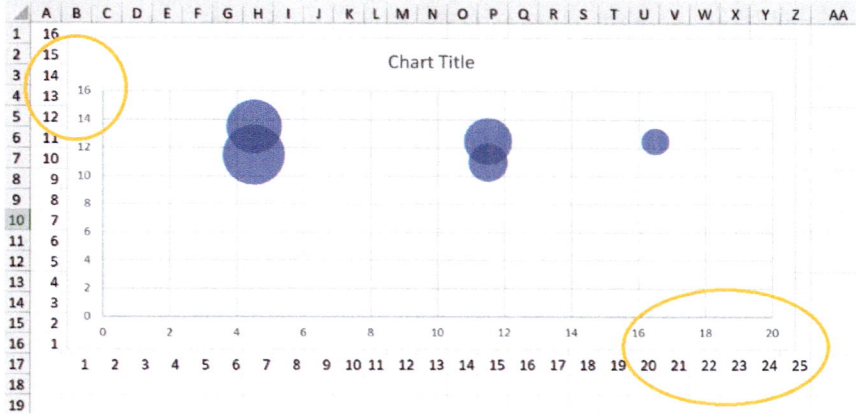

After:

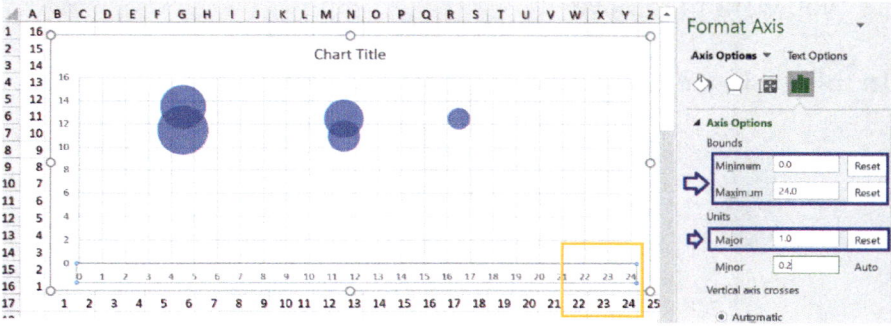

- In the same manner, we can adjust the min and max values for the vertical axis as well.

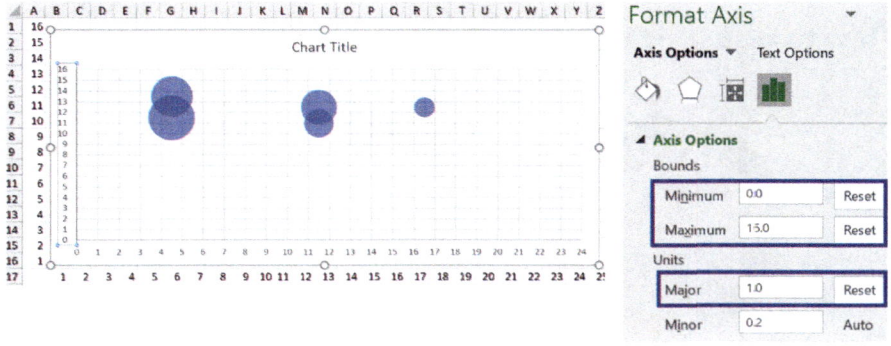

- **Bounds >>> Minimum = 0** (change from **Auto** >>> **Reset**)
- **Maximum = 16** (change from **Auto** >>> **Reset**)

The min & max value has to be in line with the min and max values in the cells.

How to remove chart elements:

After clicking a chart, we can see the plus **(+) sign** on right hand side. This is the location where we can control the chart elements.

- Go to chart elements = click **(+)** sign in gray in the chart
- **Remove the chart elements** = Unclick the chart elements which you want to remove

In this case, we **unclicked all chart elements**.

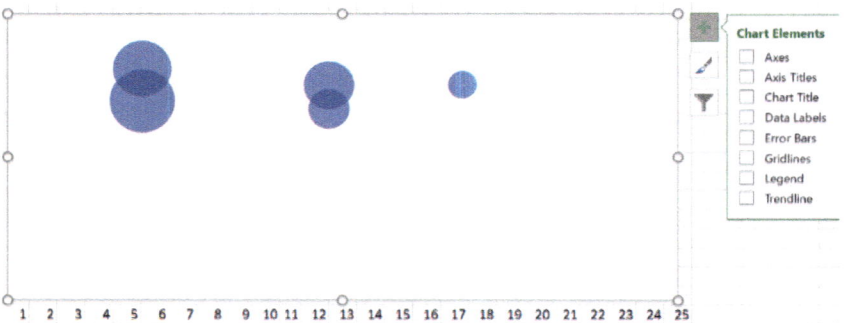

How to adjust size of chart area:

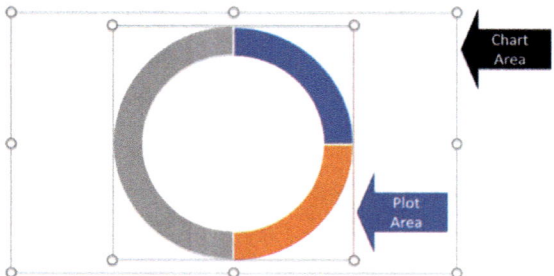

The reason why we need to adjust chart area is to overlap between plot area and chart area.

In order to make them as an overlapped chart:

- Click the plot area >>> **drag it to the corner of chart area** as much as you can.

We can see like below.

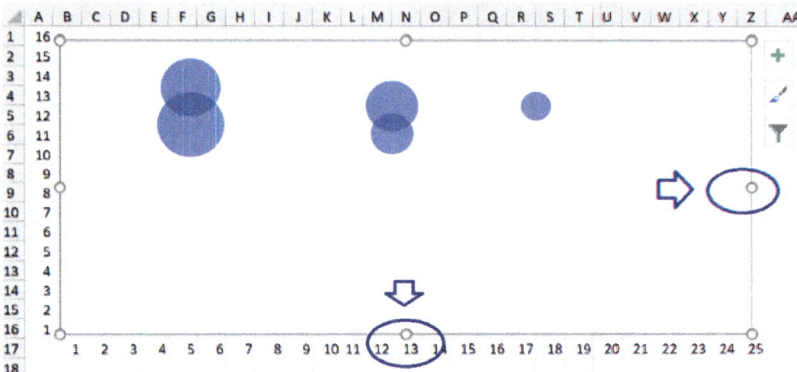

How to select the chart area:

After the above adjustment, it is difficult to select the chart area. If you click the chart, you will select only the plot area. Therefore, you need the following steps.

- Click the chart >>> **Ctrl + 1** >>> select **Chart Area**

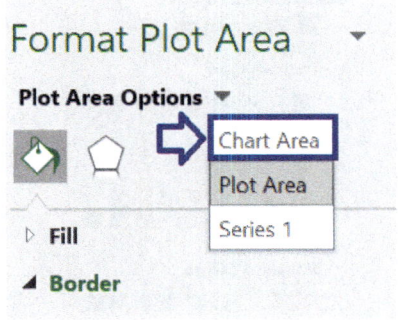

How to group both image and the chart area:

- Select the chart area first (see above) >>> **Alt + A** (assume that there are no other charts apart from image file and the world map chart. If not, please manually deselect the grouping-unwanted chart)
- **Shape Format** >>> **Group** >>> **Group**

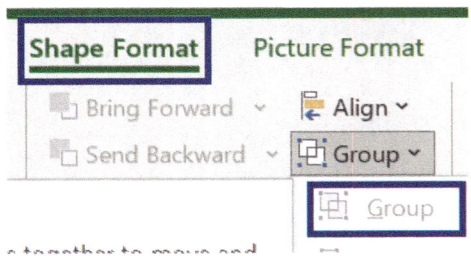

How to remove 'Shape Fill' and 'Shape Outline':

Click a chart >>> Go to **Format** tab. We will change the default settings of **Shape Fill** and **Shape Outline** of the chart.

- **Shape Fill** = No Fill
- **Shape Outline** = No Outline

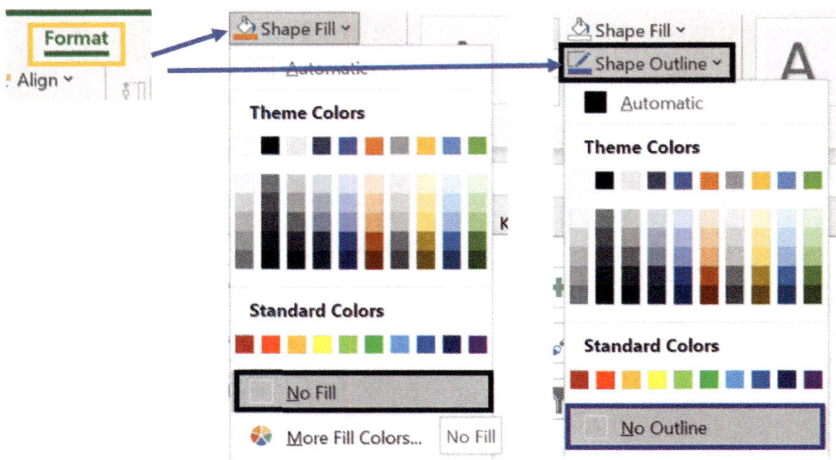

As a result, we can find the following result.

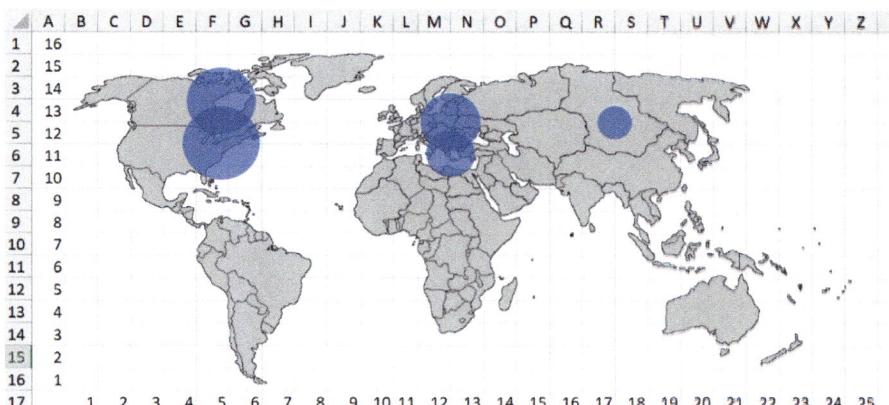

How to remove Gridlines:

- Go to **View** tab and unclick **Gridlines**.

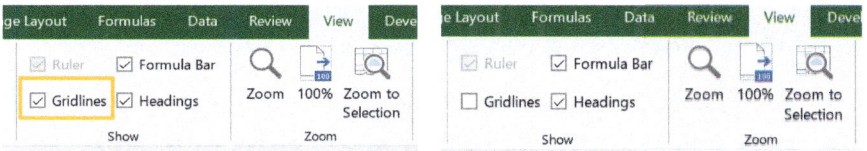

All the grid lines are disappeared in the sheet.

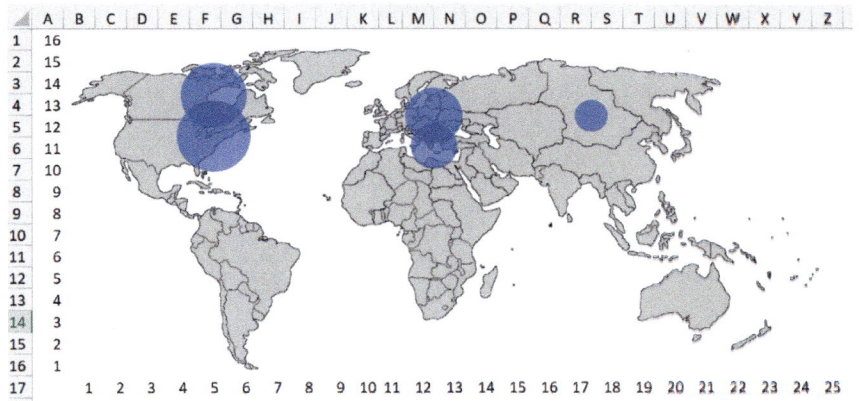

After making the world map chart, we can re-adjust the X, Y values for the location of countries in the chart. After re-adjusting, we can delete the X, Y values on the sheet.

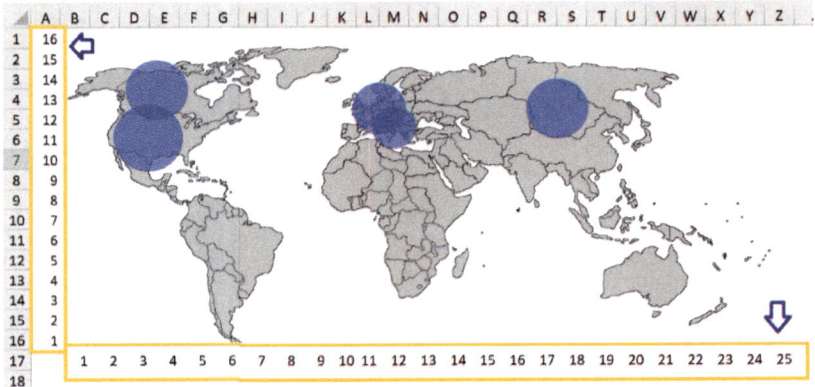

(Optional) How to add data labels:

Depends on your preference, you can change the selection of labels. This is just one of possible cases.

- After selecting a bubble by using mouse
- Click a **right-hand mouse button** >>> go to **'Add Data Labels'**.
- Select **'Bubble Size'** >>> Select **'Value From Cells'** >>> **Select Range** >>> Choose name of country >>> **OK**
- Go to **Separator** >>> select **(New Line)**

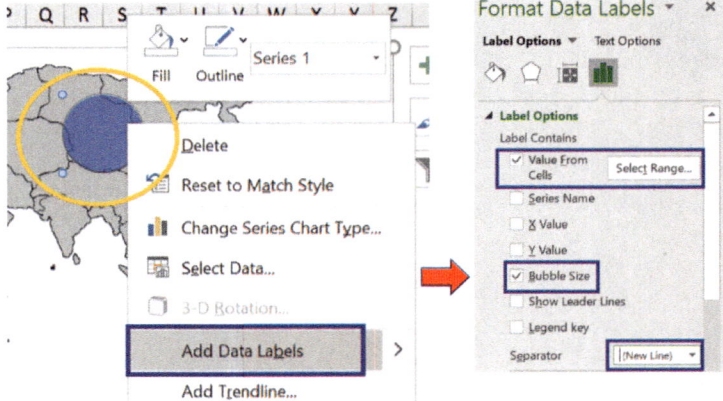

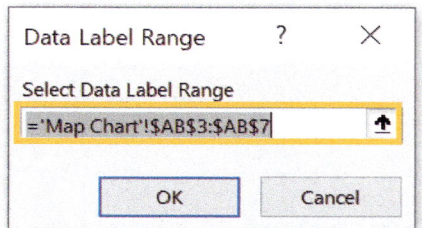

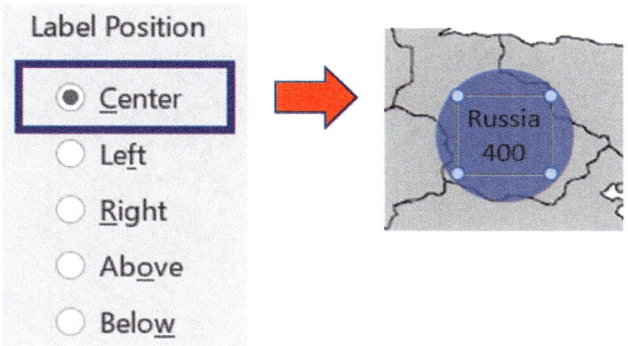

- Go to **Label Position** >>> select **Center**

How to decorate the color, size of fonts will be skipped. This is because these steps are quite straightforward.

Erase the X, Y numbers in cells because we do not need them.

(Optional) How to hide columns or row on the sheet:

You can hide the X, Y values for the location of countries.

By mouse dragging, select 2 columns and a right-hand mouse button. Click **Hide**.

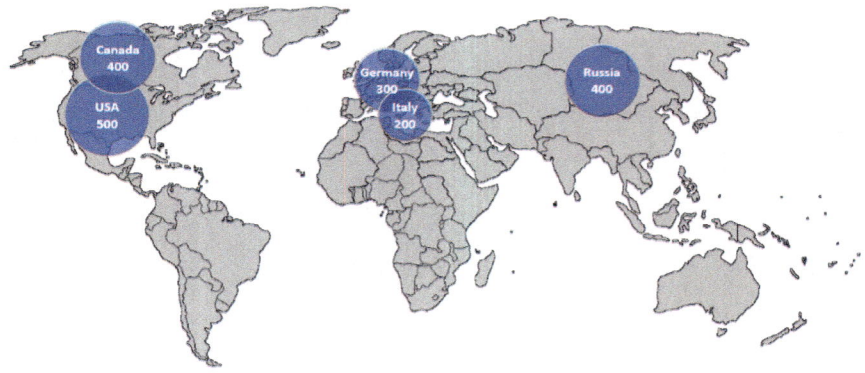

Finally, we can complete the world map chart.

Testing:

Even after changing the shape of map image, the chart is stilll showing values correcltly.

However, if the chart size is reducted too dramatically, the chart looks not good because the size of font is not automtically adjusting (Excel default setting).

- Horizontal: **shirinked** up to N column
- Vertical: **extended** up to Row 23

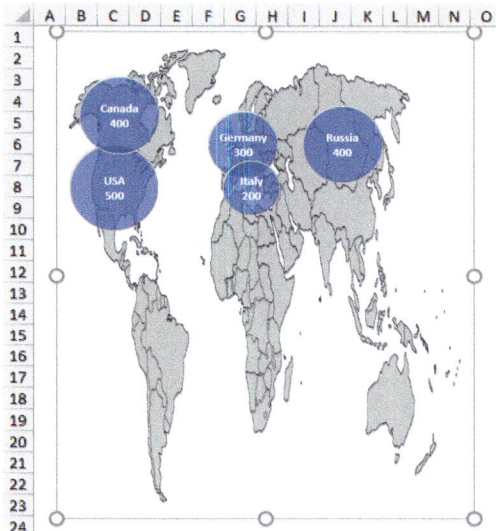

Applied verion: 3D Icon World Map Chart

We are going to make an infographic icon for the world map. This part is totally an optional part.

What we are going to make is the following:

How to make an outer circle:

Please note that all the following settings are based on the given example above.

Insert a circle. The size of outer circle = **6cm**. Line color = **Black** & Width = **0.5**pt. (you can resize it later on)

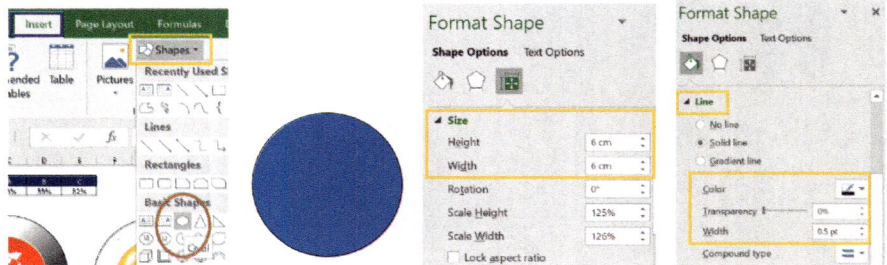

Select **Gradient fill** & Select degree for **225** degrees (see below).

The feeling we want to create is the light is coming from 225 degree to downside.

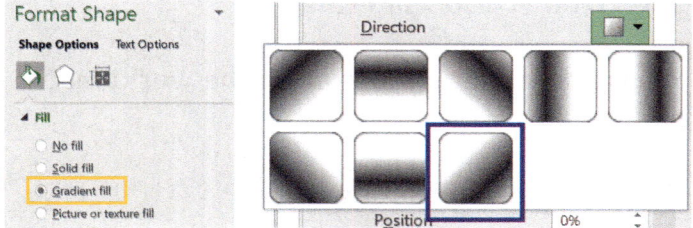

Settings for Gradient stops:

- Color is white except the second stop (Black)
- Positions are 0%, 30%, 66% and 100%.

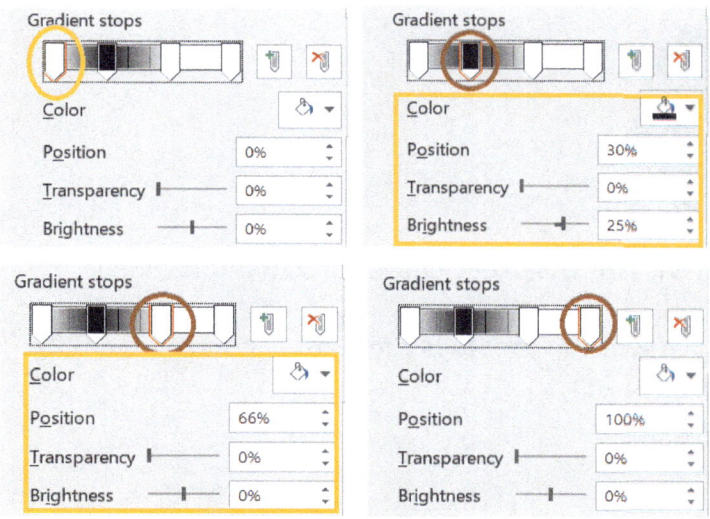

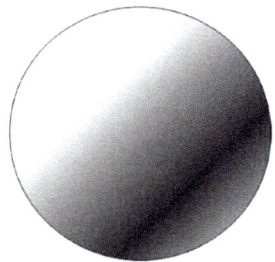

The outer circle is completed.

How to make an inner circle:

The method is pretty much same as the outer circle. Please note that all the following settings are based on the given example above.

Insert a **circle**. The size of outer circle = **4cm**. Line color = **Black** & Width = **1**.

Select **Gradient fill** & Select degree for **225** degrees (see below).

The feeling we want to create is the light is coming from **225** degree to downside.

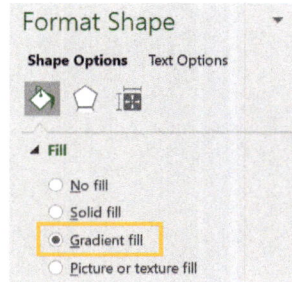 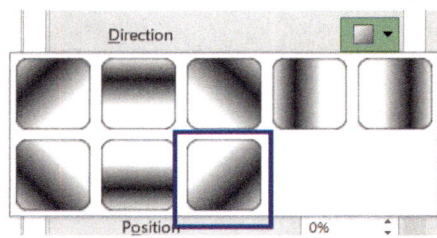

Settings for Gradient stops:

- Color is all **Red** & specify the red color (click '**More Colors …**' >>> select the color you like)
  Why '**More Colors …**'? in order to show you more possibility to choose colors.
- Positions are 0%, 56% and 100%.

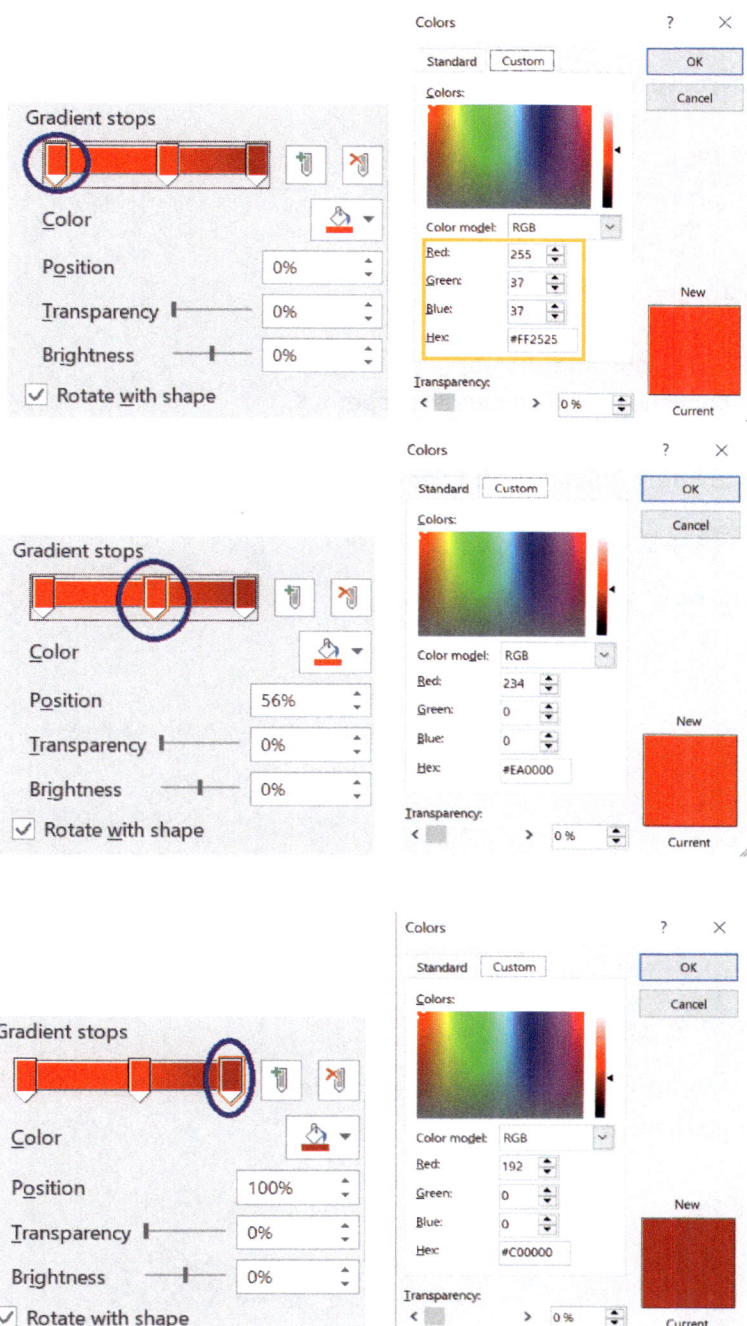

The inner circle is completed.

How to add the reflection on the circle:

The target picture looks like the inside white part (See below):

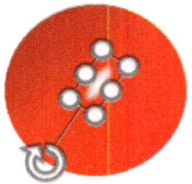

- Select a **circle** in **Insert** tab
- Squeeze the circle like overall shape.
- Select **solid fill** with **white** color
- Go to **Effect** & Select **Soft Edges**. Choose the **third one**.

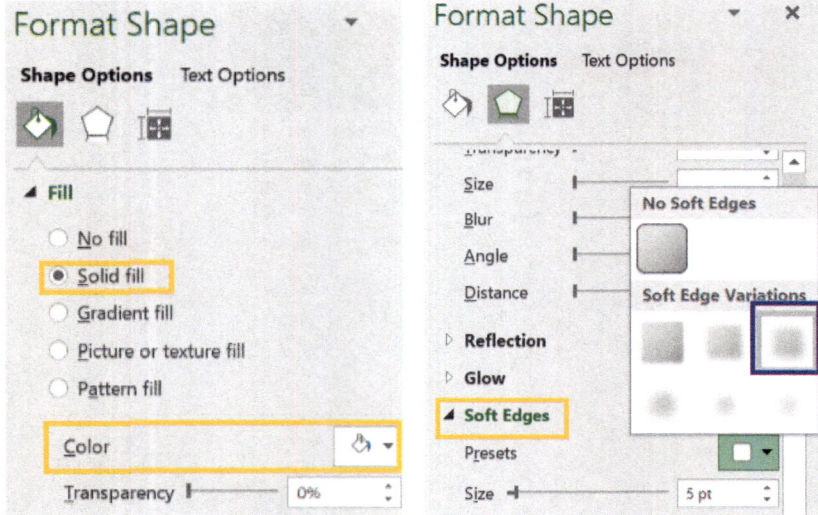

- Put this into the inner circle somewhere at 225 degrees area. Group them.

How to align 2 circles:

Put the inner circle somewhere inside of outer circle. Go to **Format** & select **Align Center** & **Align Middle**.

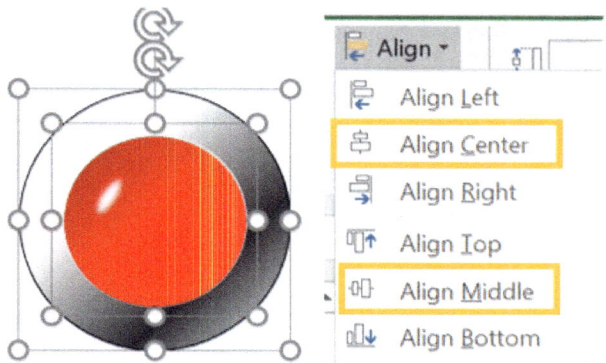

The size of the outer-circle is reduced. After completing one circle completely, copy and paste it. Just change the color of inner circle.

How to combine an icon and the bubble in the chart:

- Click the circle icon >>> **Ctrl + C**
- Double clicks one of the bubbles in the chart >>> **Ctrl + V**

If you selected the single bubble, it looks like below (i.e., Russia).

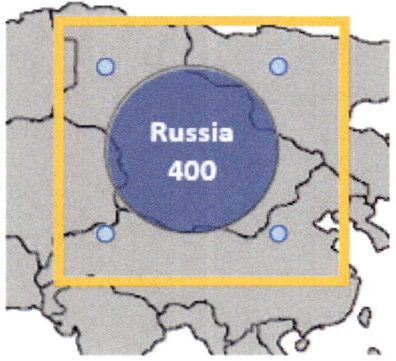

As a result, we can finally complete 3D icon-combined world map chart below.

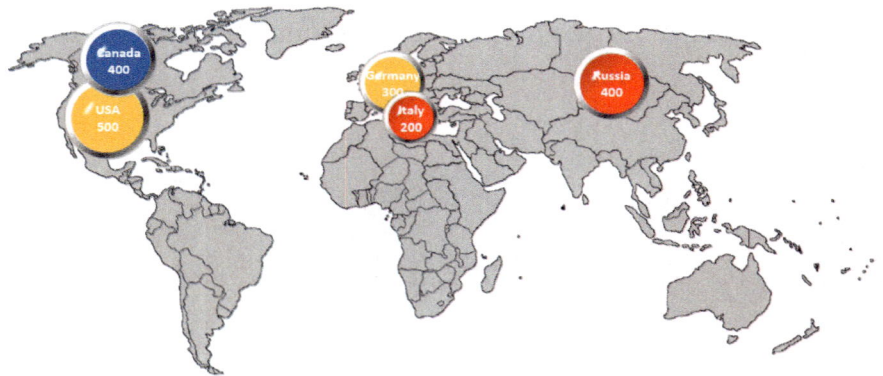

24. Special Range Bar Chart

We are going to make a bar chart with a special range. When you want to emphasize some data in the specific ranges, this chart will be fit for the purpose. The technique in this section will save you some time when you make this type of chart.

Benefit of this chart is to visualize the given data under the specific range in the chart. In addition, you can control the specific range as well.

Target picture:
What we are going to make is the following charts:

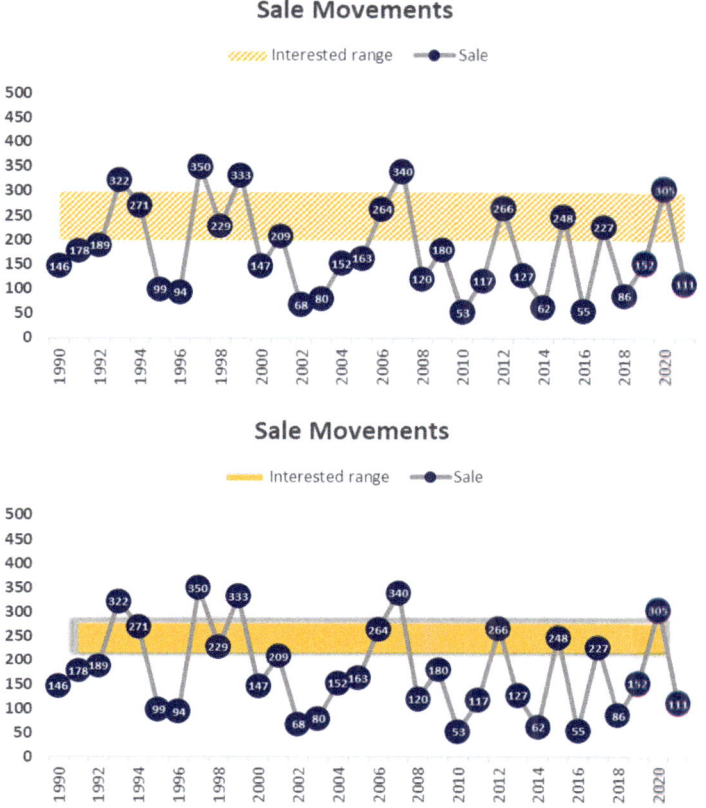

How to set up input values:

Let's assume that we have 32 years of sale data (from 1990 to 2021) in Column B. (See below)

Both lower and upper limit represent the parameters of the special range in the chart.

- Lower limit (Cell C2): 200 (just an example, changeable)
- Upper limit (Cell D2): 300 (just an example, changeable)

	A	B	C	D
1			Lower limit	Upper limit
2			200	300
3				
4	Year	Sale	Lower limit	Upper - Lower limit
5	1990	146	200	100
6	1991	178	200	100
7	1992	189	200	100
8	1993	322	200	100
9	1994	271	200	100
10	1995	99	200	100

For **lower limit column** (column C),
The values are identical as the lower limit value (Cell C2).

SUM			✗ ✓ fx	=$C$2	
	A	B		C	D
1				Lower limit	Upper limit
2				200	300
3					
4	Month	Sale		Lower limit	Upper - Lower limit
5	1990	221		=$C$2	100
6	1991	121		200	100

For **upper limit column** (column D),
The values are Upper limit - Lower limit value (Cell D2- C2).

	A	B	C	D
1			Lower limit	Upper limit
2			200	300
3				
4	Month	Sale	Lower limit	Upper - Lower limit
5	1990	146	200	=$D$2-$C$2
6	1991	178	200	100
7	1992	189	200	100

Formula bar: =$D$2-$C$2

Both 2 columns are showing same values in each cell in each column.

How to remove Gridlines:

- Go to **View** tab and unclick **Gridlines**.

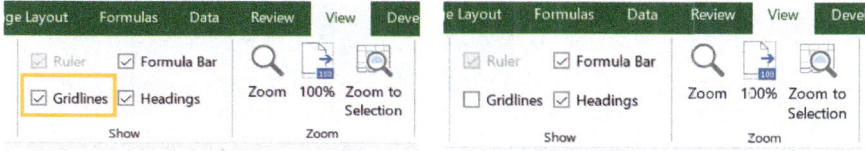

All the grid lines are disappeared in the sheet.

How to create 2-D Stacked area chart:

- Select 'Lower limit' and 'Upper – Lower limit' values (from **Column C & D**). Click Cell C5. Holding Ctrl + Shift >>> press an arrow button (→) >>> press an arrow button (↓)
- go to **Insert** tab >>> **Line and Area chart**.
- Select **2-D Area** >>> **Stacked Area**.

	A	B	C	D	E
1		Parameters	Lower limit	Upper limit	
2			200	300	
3					
4	Year	Sale	Lower limit	Upper - Lower limit	
5	1990	146	200	100	
6	1991	178	200	100	
7	1992	189	200	100	
8	1993	322	200	100	
9	1994	271	200	100	
10	1995	99	200	100	
11	1996	94	200	100	
12	1997	350	200	100	
13	1998	229	200	100	
14	1999	333	200	100	
15	2000	147	200	100	
16	2001	209	200	100	
17	2002	68	200	100	
18	2003	80	200	100	

How to create special area in the chart:

- Select the lower part of area in the chart by using a mouse.
- **Ctrl + 1** >>> go to **Series Options**
- **No fill** >>> **No line**

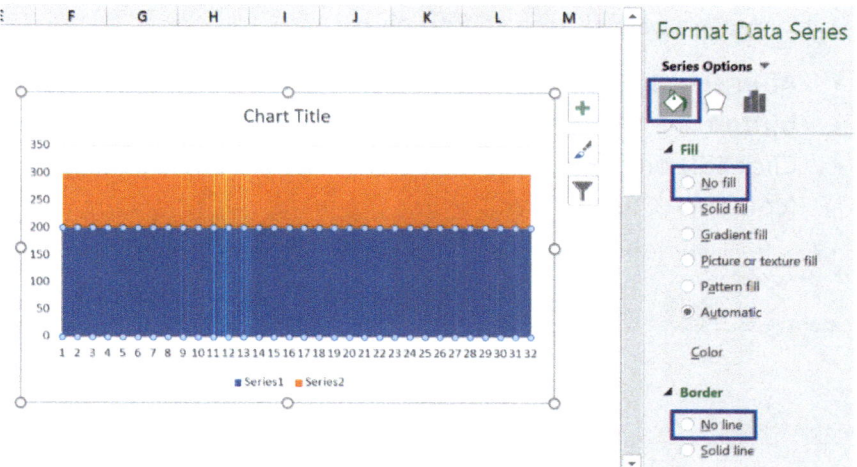

Basically, we already make the special range in the chart. As you can see, the range is from 200 to 300 which is in line with **lower limit column** (column C) and **upper limit column** (column D).

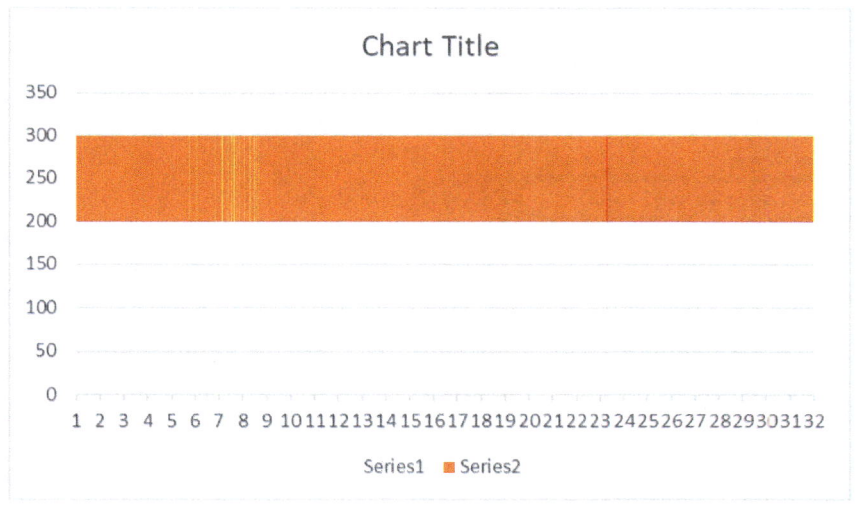

Next, we are going to update the horizontal axis and add the actual values in the chart.

How to create special area in the chart:

- After selecting the chart >>> click a **right-hand mouse button** >>> click **Select Data** >>> a Pop-up window.
- Click **Edit** on the horizontal axis >>> Select the **Year range** (column A). See below.

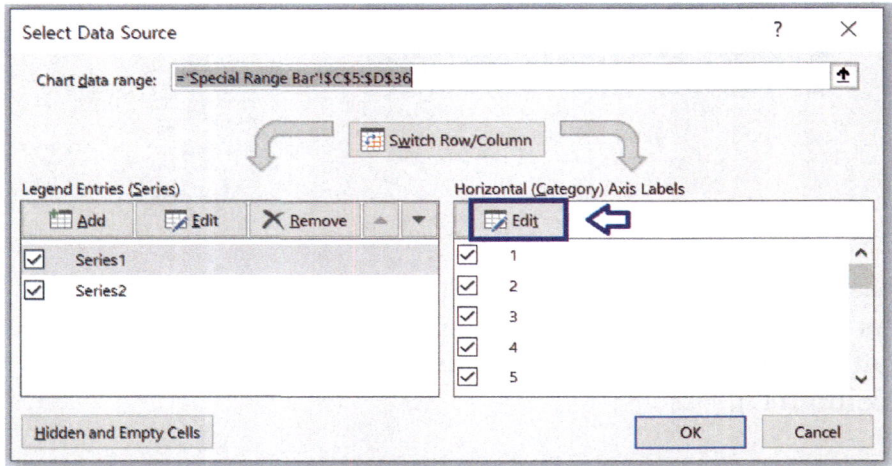

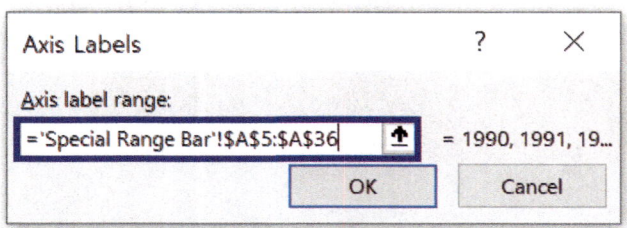

- Select **Series 1** >>> Click **Edit** on the legend entries (left side) >>> Select **Cell C1** to change the series name. See below.

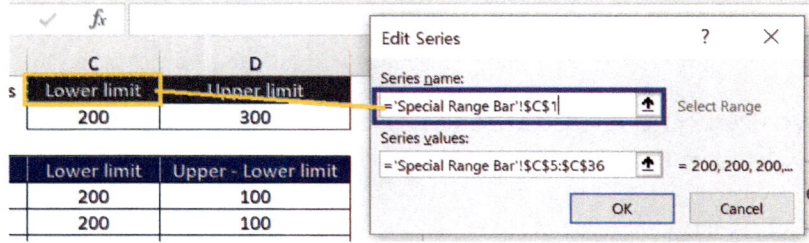

In the same manner for the Series 2, we do the same thing.

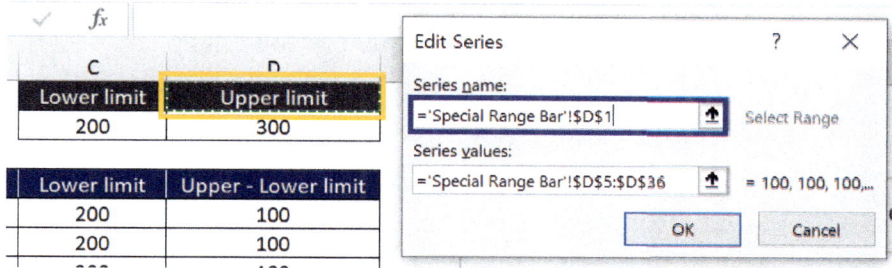

- Click **Add** on the '**Legend Entries**' (left side) >>> Select **Cell B4** to give the series name >>> Select range of '**Sale**' series.

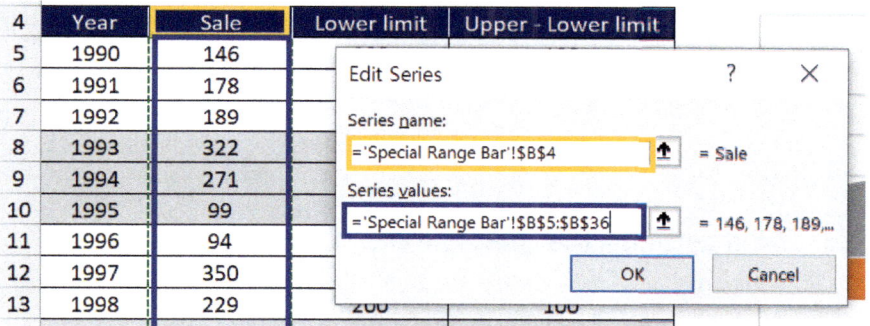

After adding & editing the data, it looks like below. Click **OK**.

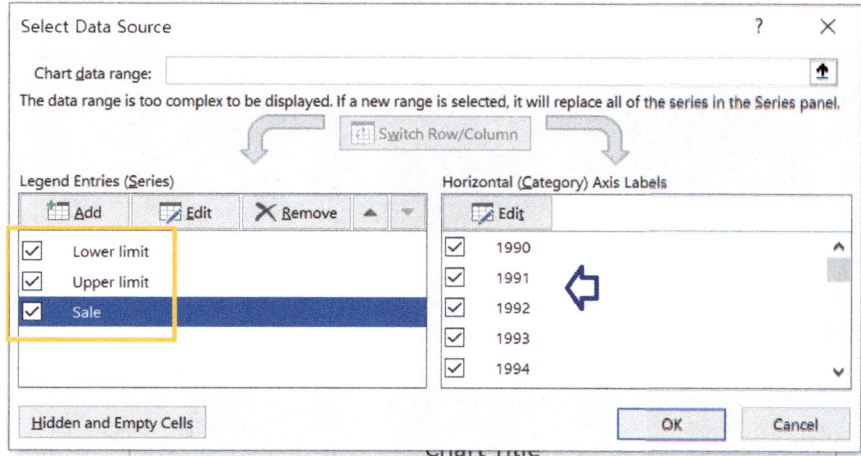

How to change chart type:

After adding the sale series, the chart looks strange. Therefore, we need some adjustments for the chart.

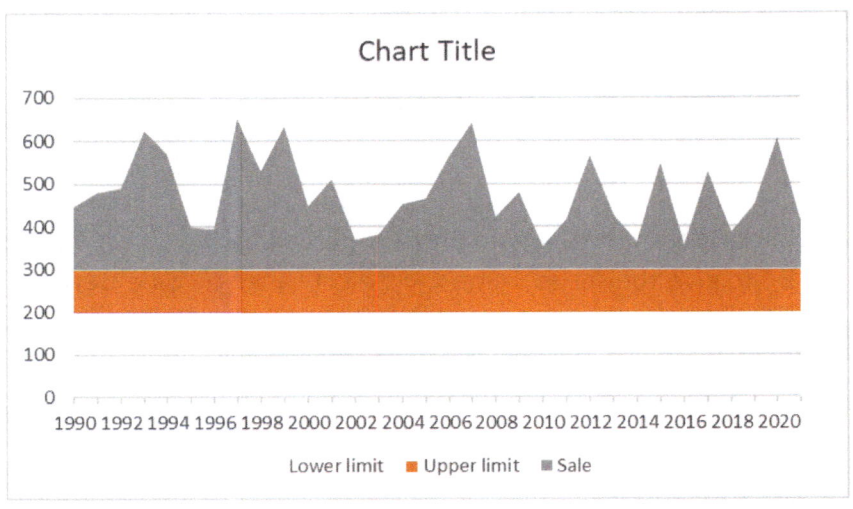

- After selecting the chart >>> click **a right-hand mouse button**
- Click **Change Chart Type** >>> a Pop-up window

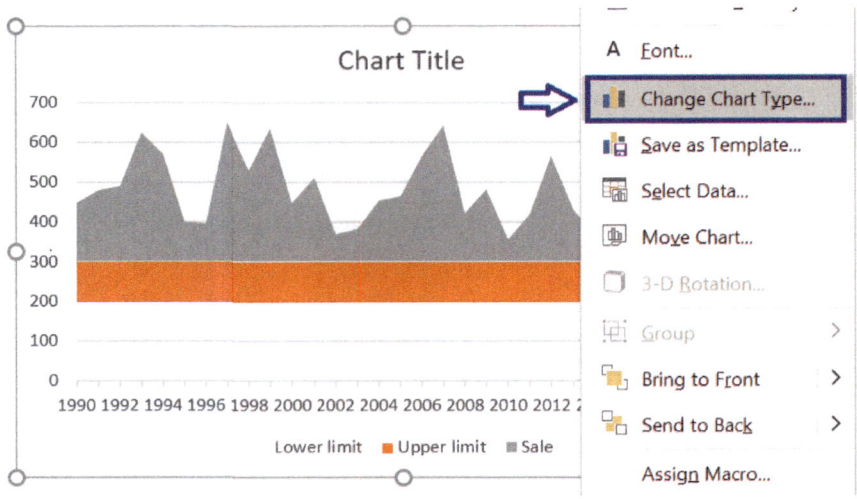

- Click **Combo** >>> Select the chart type like below.
- Lower & Upper limit = **Stacked Area**
- Sale = **Line with Markers** & click **Secondary Axis** >>> **OK**

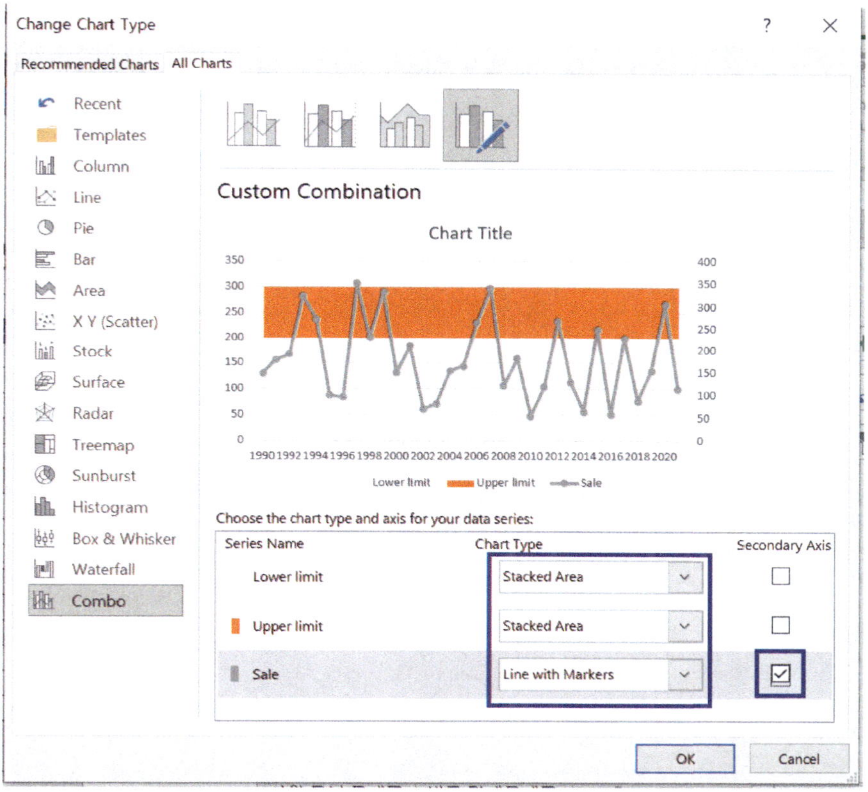

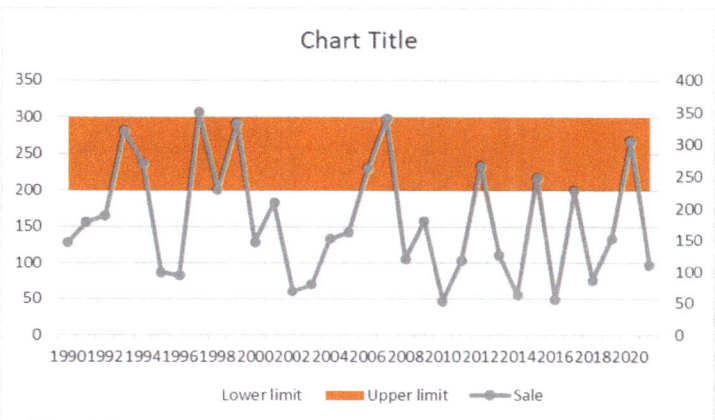

How to adjust the both axis in the chart:

Order of adjusting axis is not important.

- Click the secondary axis in the chart >>> **Ctrl + 1** >>> **Axis Options**
- Bounds >>> **Minimum = 0** (change from **Auto** >>> **Reset**)
- **Maximum = 500** (change from **Auto** >>> **Reset**)
  The <u>min & max value can be changeable</u> depends on your actual data set.
- Do the same thing for primary axis as well.

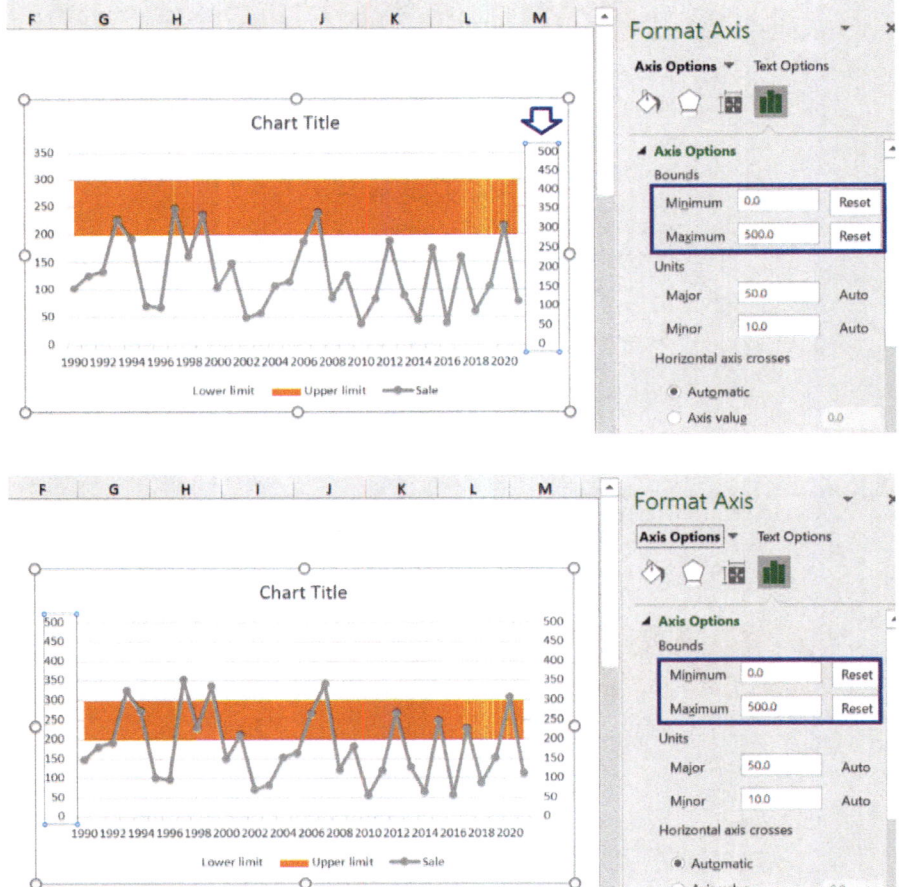

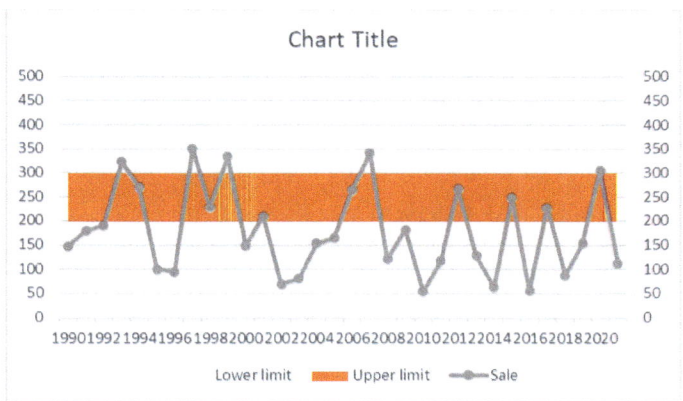

It looks like above now. The general shape of chart is already completed. The following steps are just how to decorate the chart nicely. Depends on your preference, it can be changeable.

How to adjust the legend in the chart:

After checking the legend, it looks a bit misleading. Therefore, we decide to adjust them.

- Double click the **Lower limit** >>> press **Delete** button
- After selecting the chart >>> click a **right-hand mouse button** >>> click **Select Data**
- Select 'Upper limit' series >>> Click **Edit** on the **legend entries** (left side) >>> Change the series name (i.e., Interested range) >>> **OK**

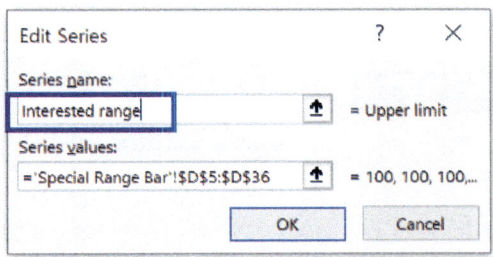

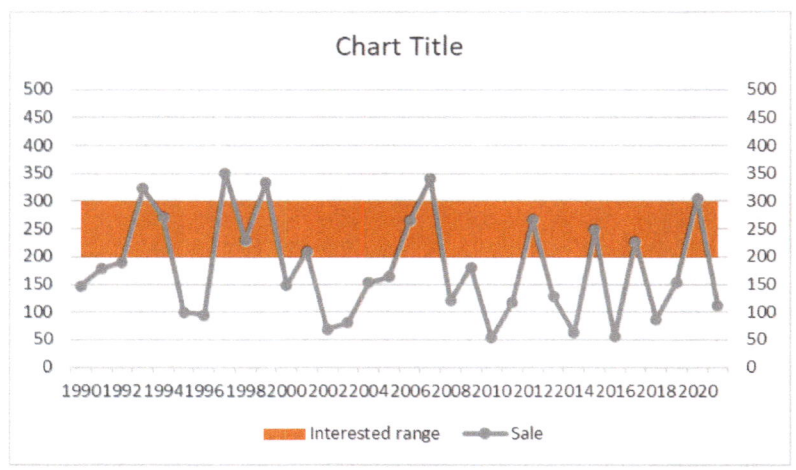

How to remove 'Shape Fill' and 'Shape Outline':

Click a chart >>> Go to **Format** tab. We will change the default settings of **Shape Fill** and **Shape Outline** of the chart.

- **Shape Fill** = No Fill
- **Shape Outline** = No Outline

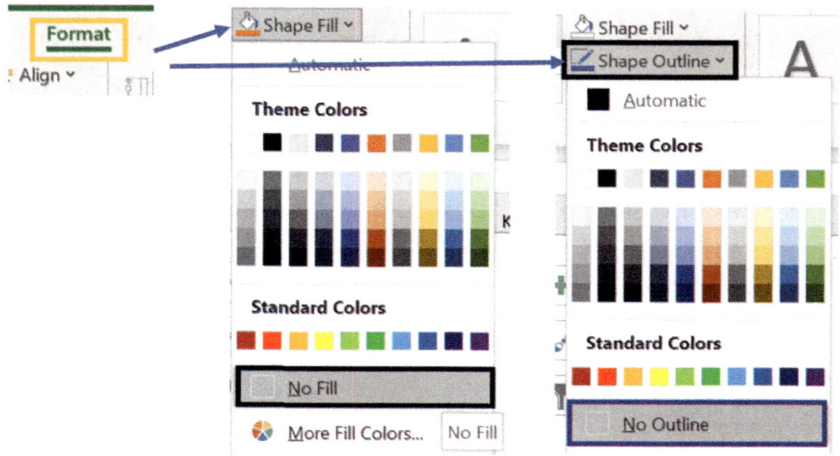

How to remove chart elements:

After clicking a chart, we can see the plus **(+) sign** on right hand side. This is the location where we can control the chart elements.

- Go to chart elements = click **(+)** sign in gray in the chart
- **Remove the chart elements** = Unclick the chart elements which you want to remove

In this case, we clicked both **Chart Title, Axes** and **Legend** from chart elements.

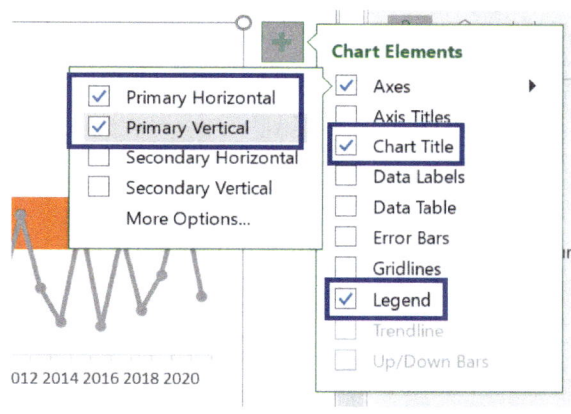

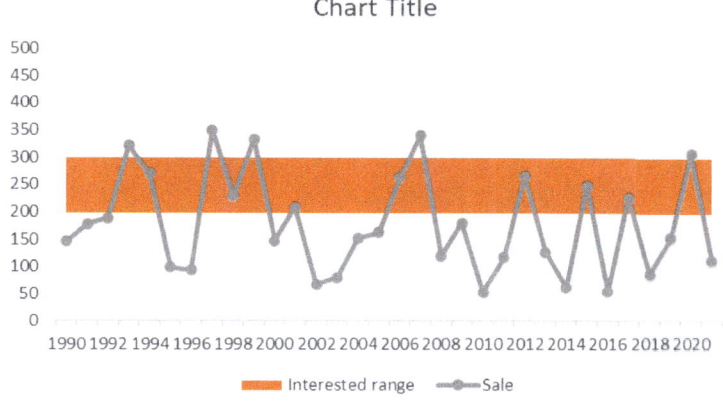

(Optional) How to adjust the horizontal axis in the chart:

- Click the horizontal axis in the chart >>> **Ctrl + 1** >>> **Text Options** >>> go to **Text direction** >>> Select **Rotate all text 270 degree.**

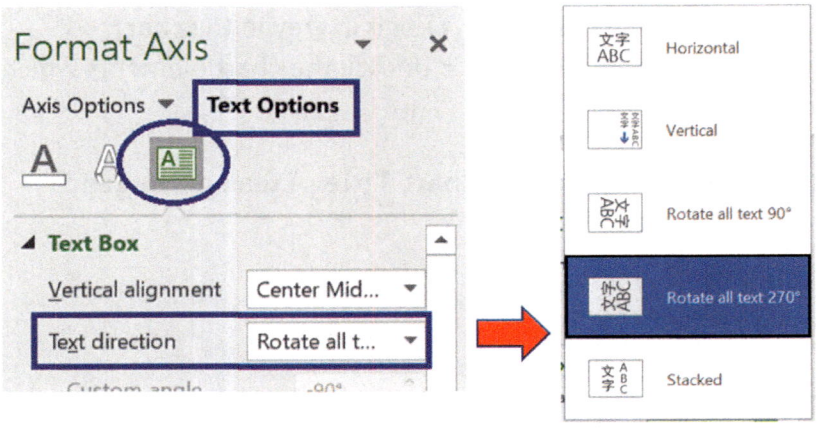

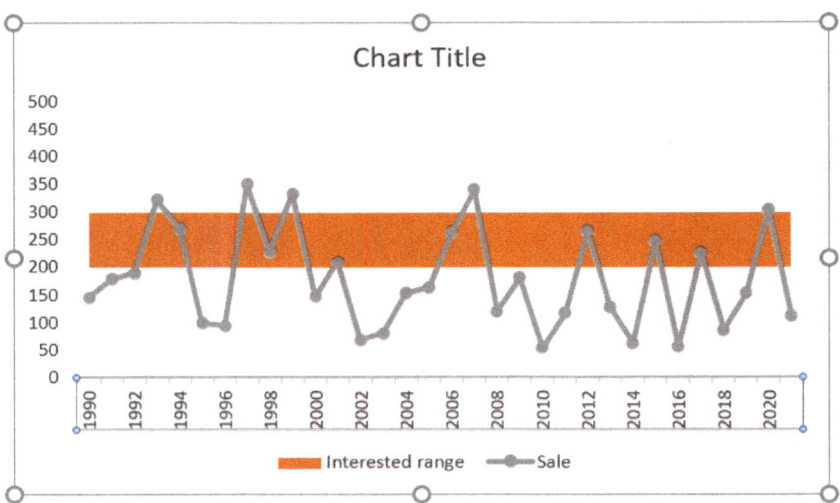

In addition, click the chart title. Update the title as you wish.

(Optional) How to adjust the legend:

- Click the legend in the chart >>> **Ctrl + 1** >>> Go to **Legend Options** >>> click **Top**

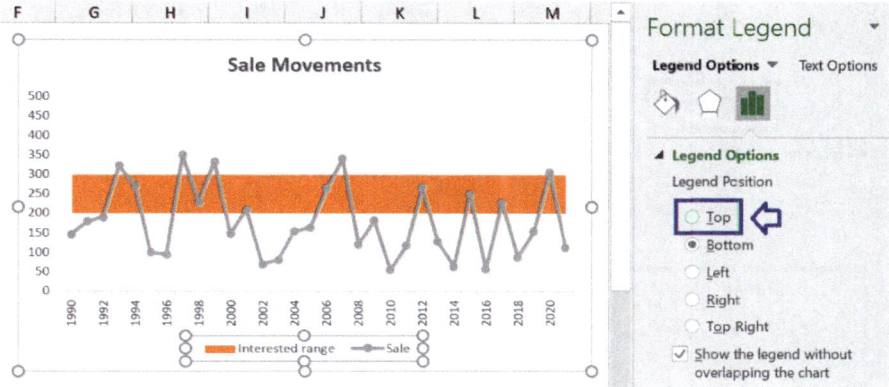

Depends on the personal preference, it is possible to add Axis Title. Click '+' sign >>> **Axis Title**.

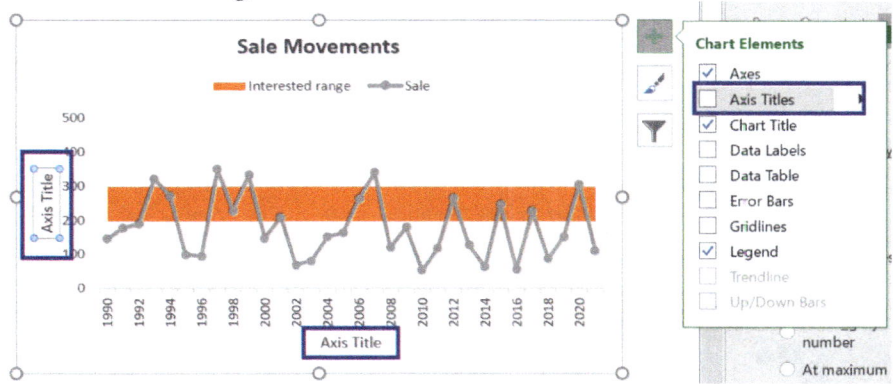

How to adjust Marker in series:

- Click the line in the chart >>> **Ctrl + 1** >>> Go to **Marker** >>>
- Go to **Marker Options** >>> Click **Built-in** >>> Change **color & size** if you want to change. (i.e., dark blue)

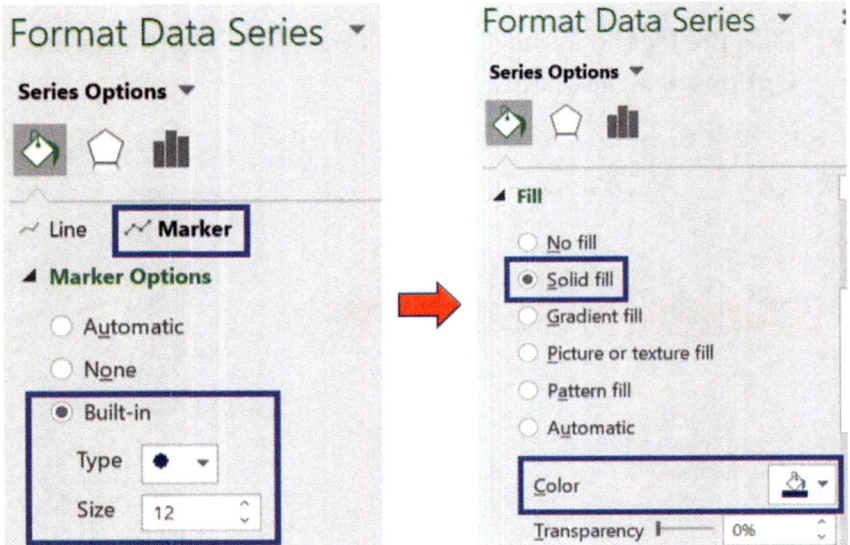

As a result, we can have the following.

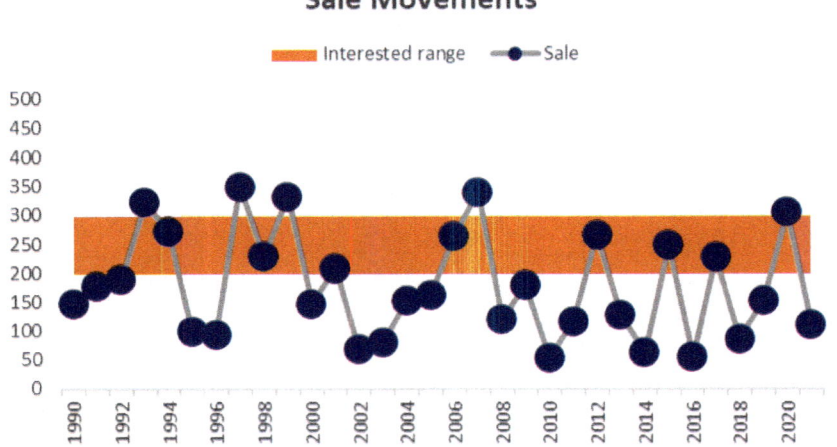

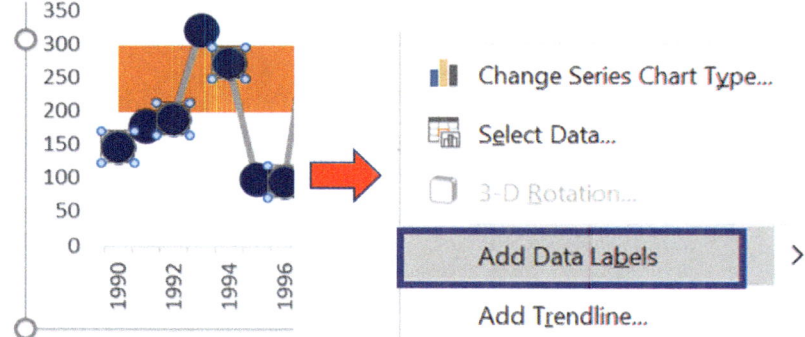

We can have the following result. The labels' locations are not really good at the moment. Therefore, we need to adjust them.

- **Click the label** by mouse >>> **Ctrl + 1** >>> **Label Position** >>> **Center**

- Click the label again >>> **Home** tab >>> change font size, color, and add **Bold**

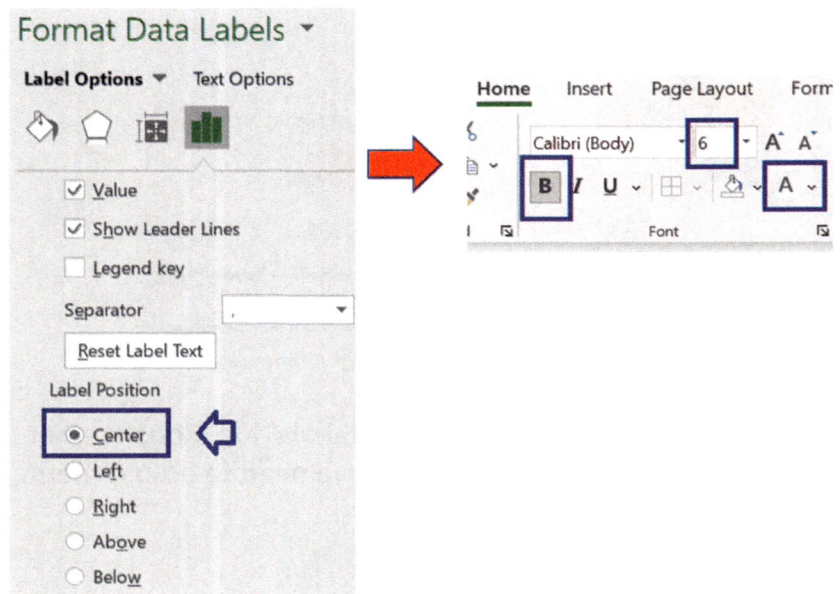

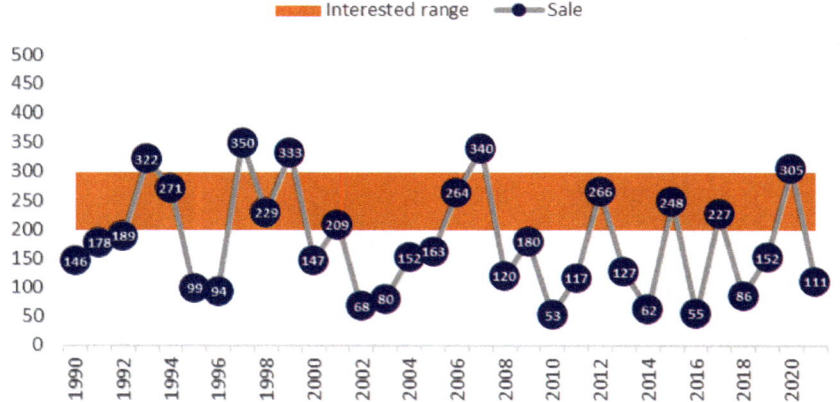

How to adjust special range area in chart:

- Click the range in the chart >>> **Ctrl + 1** >>> Go to **Fill** >>>
- Click **Pattern fill** >>> Select the pattern & color (below of example patterns)

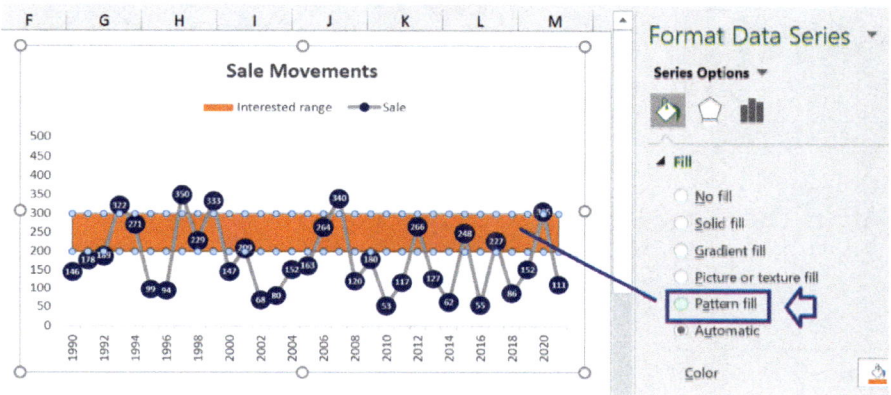

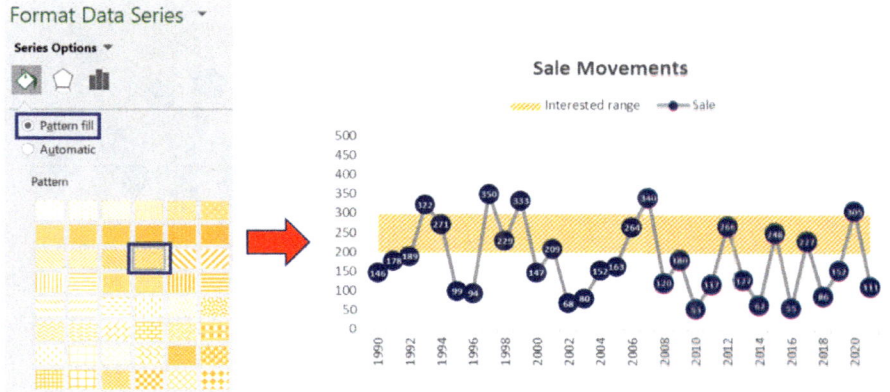

Testing of special range:

- Current setting: Lower limit = 200, Upper limit = 300
- New setting: Lower limit = 150, Upper limit = 400

Before >>> After:

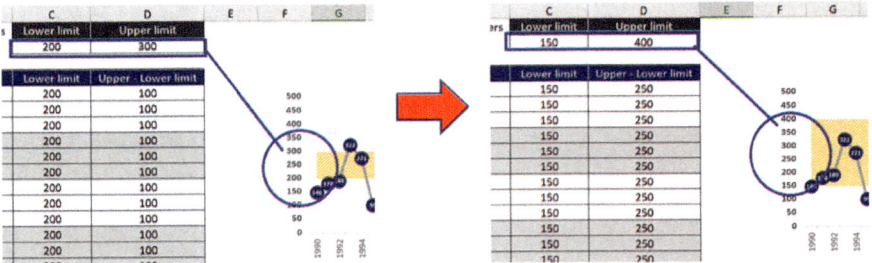

After: The range is changed in the chart.

Finally, we can complete the special range bar chart.

Optional: there is another possible technique to change the special range. First, create an icon and apply the below method. Please note that the creating icon part will be skipped because we had touched it a lot before.

How to combine an icon and the bubble in the chart:
- Click the created icon >>> **Ctrl + C**
- Double clicks the special range area in the chart >>> **Ctrl + V**

(Optional) How to use 'Picture or texture fill' with in chart:

By using this method, we will stack the right square boxes in the chart. (In order to show a new technique)
- Click the **icon-combined bar** >>> **Ctrl + 1**
- Go to **Format Data Series** & Select **Picture or texture fill**
  - Click **'Tile picture as texture'**

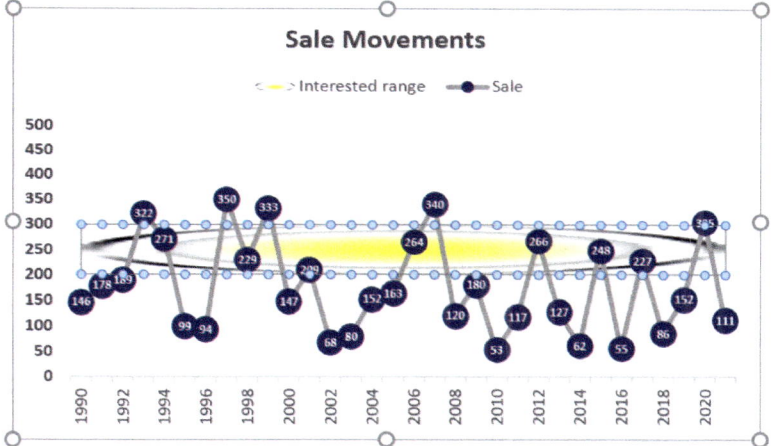

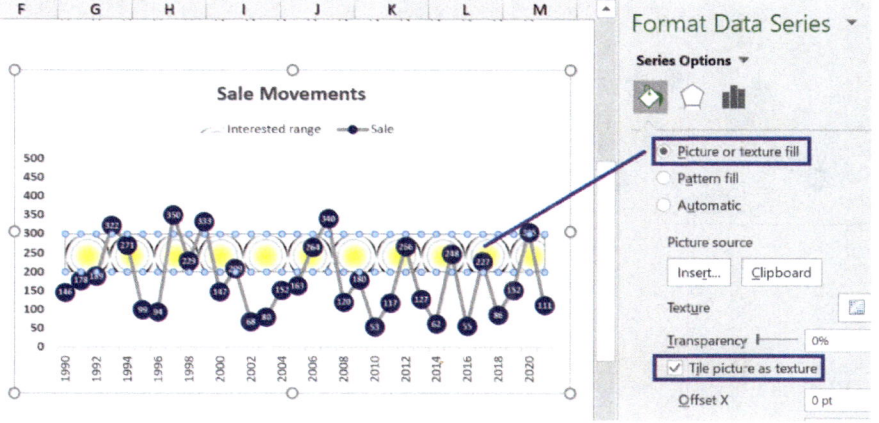

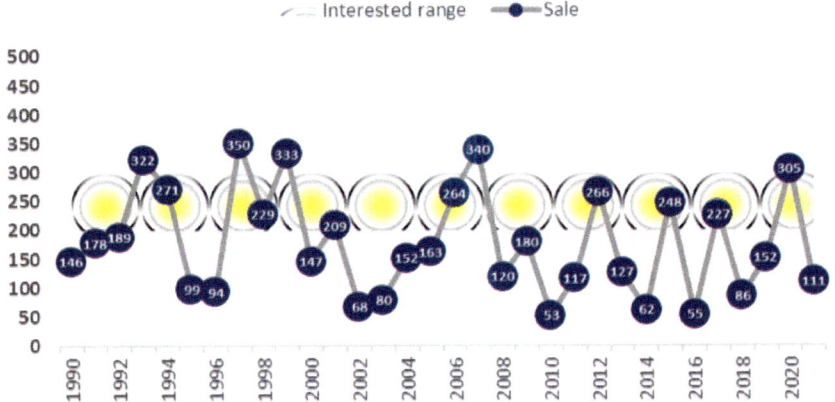

In the above case, it works fine.

However, **please be aware that the combining & 'Picture or texture fill' are not always working**. In spite of this fact, the reason why I show here is to introduce a different type of technique to apply to the chart.

Another example below with a bar icon:

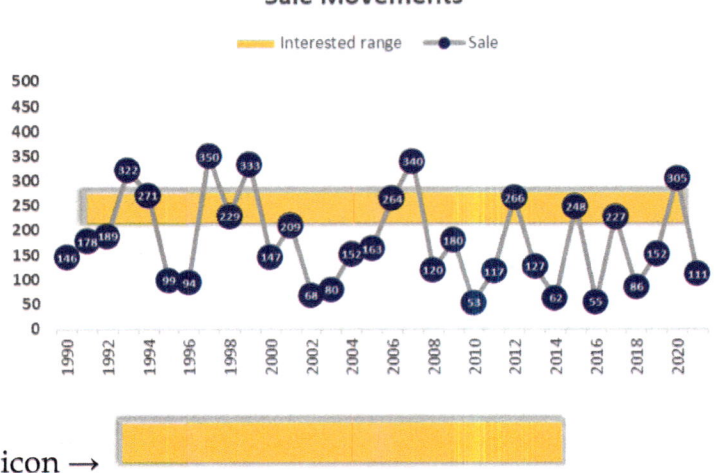

icon →

25. Stylish Donut Chart

We are going to make stylish donut charts which looks nice and relatively easy to make it. However, it is not easy to make them without knowing the techniques of how to make it.

Target picture:
What we are going to make is the following charts:

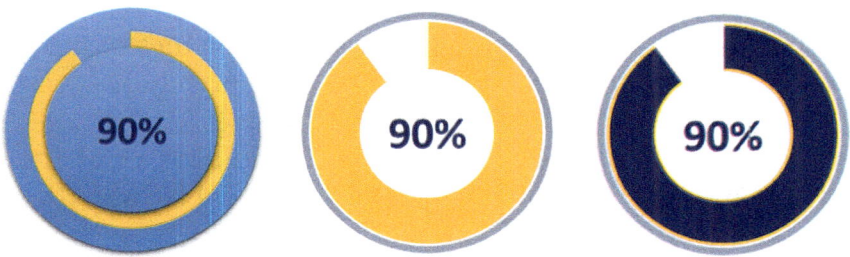

How to set up input values:

First, create **input cells** and **helping cells** in an empty worksheet.
The input values are presented by percentage (%). This is because, normally, reports are used % a lot and % is easy to communicate.

The help cell (=cell O3) has a simple formula which is '**1-input value**'.

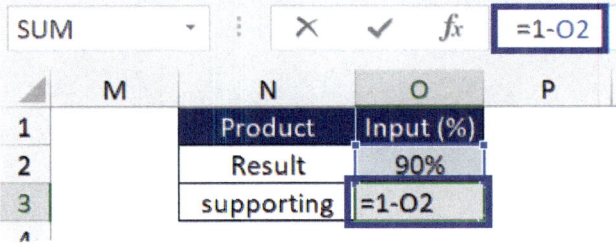

In order not destroy the chart easily, we can re-create the input like below. In this set-up, the user cannot destroy the chart. The actual input for the chart is range O2 to O3 cells.

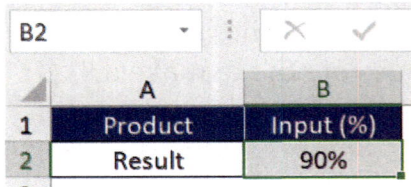

How to create donut chart:
As a starting point, we can simply think that 2 values of input (in the below table in column O) mean one donut chart.

Select input range by dragging mouse with holding a right-hand side button from the starting cell to the end of input data cell.

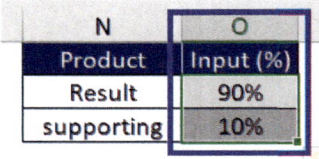

Next, make a **Donut chart**.
- Go to **Insert** tap >>> select **Doughnut** chart

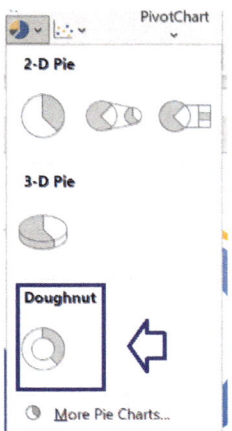

As a result, we can create the below chart.

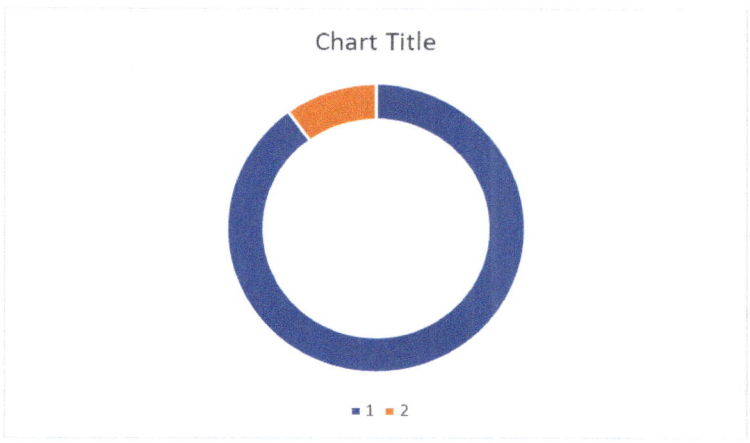

How to remove chart elements:

After clicking a chart, we can see the plus **(+) sign on right hand side**. This is the location where we can control the chart elements.

- Go to chart elements = click **(+)** sign in gray in the chart
- **Remove the chart elements** = Unclick the chart elements which you want to remove

In this case, we unclicked both chart title and legend from chart elements.

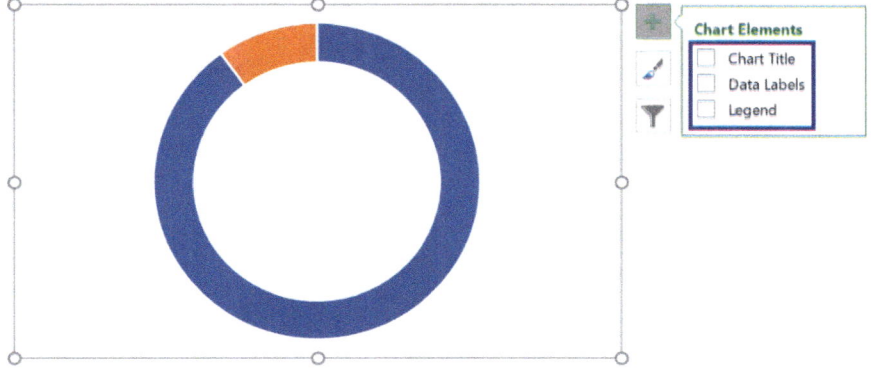

Difference between 'Chart area' and 'Plot area':

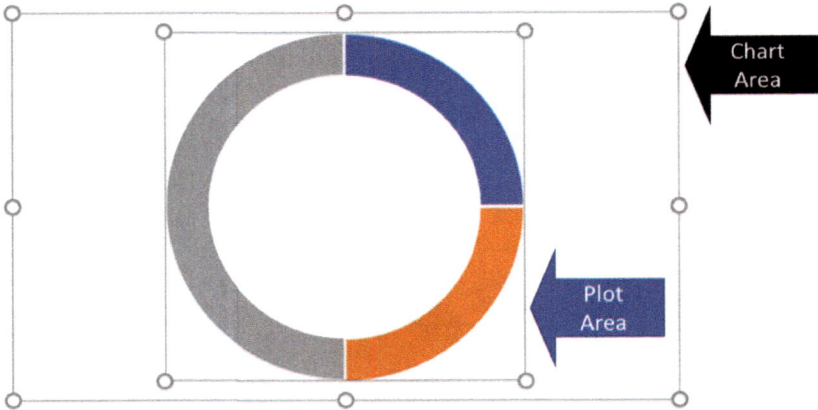

How to select Chart Area:

Simply, you can click the area by using mouse.

Alternatively, you can use the following way:

- Click the graph >>> **Ctrl + 1** (Format Chart Area) >>> click reverse **small triangle** next to 'Chart Options' >>> select **Chart Area**

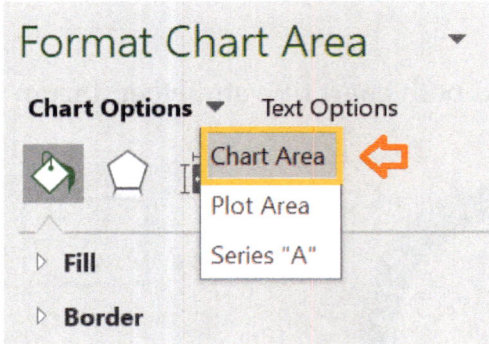

After selecting the chart area, let's make the chart as a right square shape. In order to do:

- Click chart >>> **Format** tab >>> change size by adjusting values.

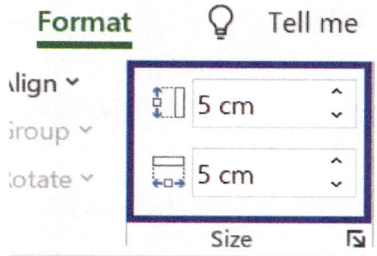

We can see like below.

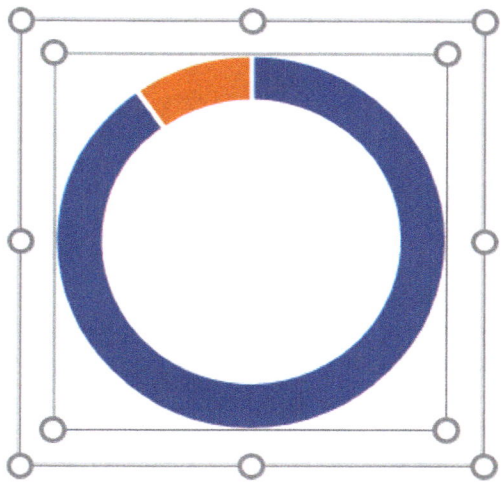

How to remove Gridlines:

- Go to **View** tab and unclick **Gridlines**.

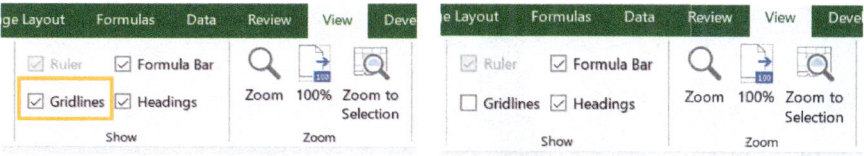

All the grid lines are disappeared in the sheet.

How to remove 'Shape Fill' and 'Shape Outline':

Click a chart >>> Go to **Format** tab. We will change the default settings of **Shape Fill** and **Shape Outline** of the chart.

- **Shape Fill** = No Fill
- **Shape Outline** = No Outline

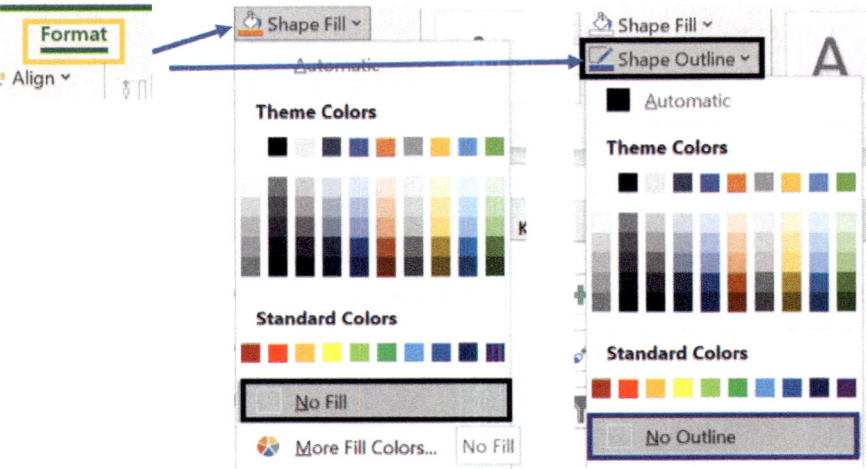

As a result, we can see the following chart.

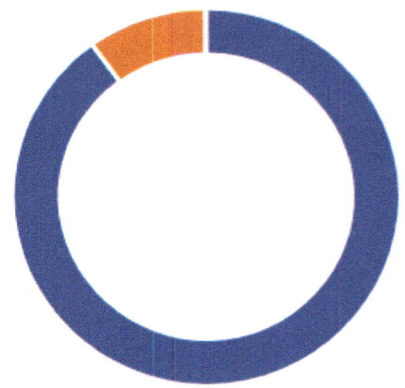

How to remove colors in a piece of donut chart:

Please note that we always need to **change the color one by one in donut charts**.

- Double click the supporting part in the donut chart.
- **Ctrl + 1 >>> No fill**

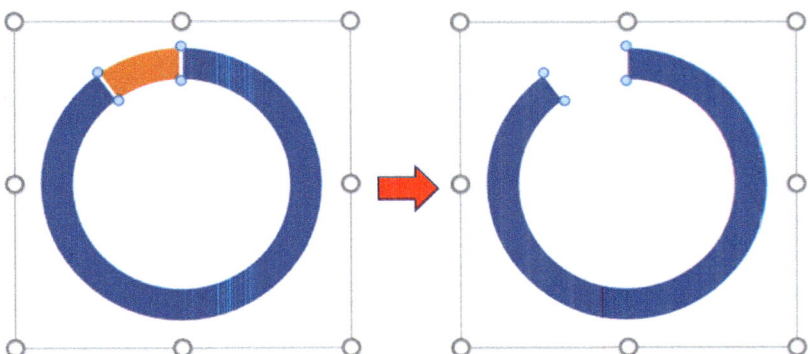

How to change colors in a piece of the chart:

Please note that we need to double clicks for selecting <u>one specific part</u> in the chart.

For the main donut part (=input values):

- Click one of series in the chart (**select main part**) >>>
- **Ctrl + 1** >>> **Format Data Series** >>> **Fill** >>>
- Select **Solid fill** >>> **Select a color** (i.e., dark blue) which you wish to choose.

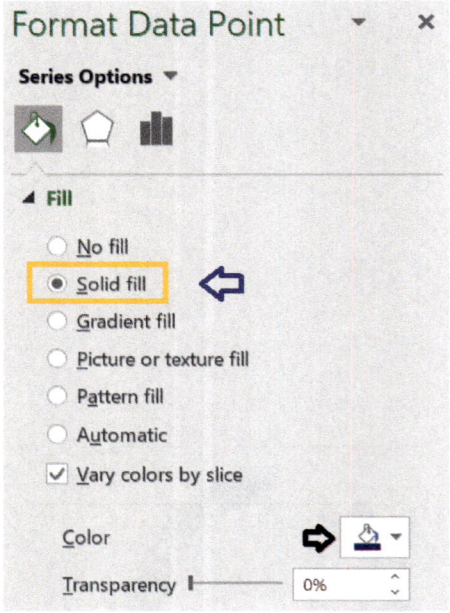

How to change donut hole size:

- Click one of series in the chart (**select main part**) >>>
- **Ctrl + 1** >>> **Format Data Point** >>> **Series Options** >>>
- **Doughnut Hole Size = 60%**. (Control the width of donut)

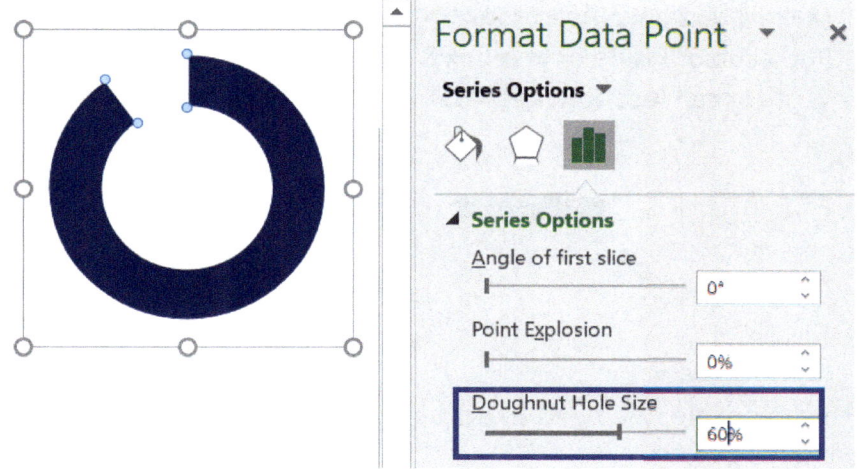

Change the color of border like below.

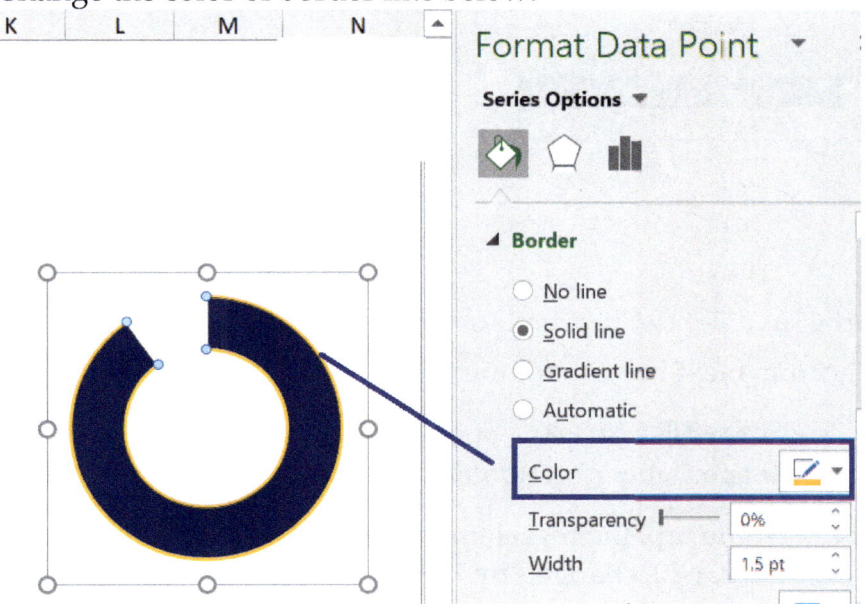

How to make a text box which shows an input value:

Please note that <u>the below pictures are Not directly from this example</u>. However, the methods are identical. Therefore, there is no issue to create a text box.

- Make a text box: **Insert** tab >>> **Shapes** >>>select **Text box**.
- Put a cursor inside of text box & click function box (*fx*)
- Write '**= cell location** (i.e., =B5)' and then hit '**Enter**' button.

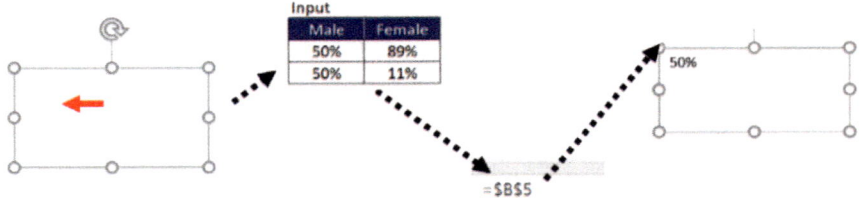

In this example, we need to add =$B$2
Please see below.

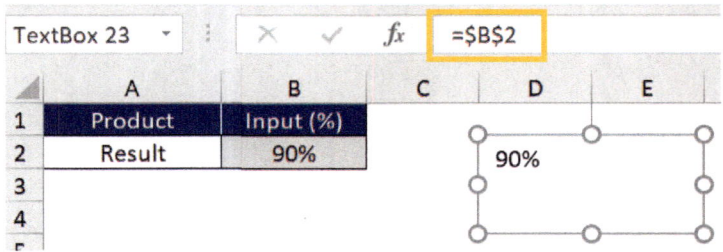

How to make the text box looking good:

Clicking a text box, removing Shape Fill & Shape Outline.

- **Shape Fill** = No Fill
- **Shape Outline** = No Outline

In the **Home** tap, the rest elements (font size, font color, font type, etc.) can be changed by Font tab elements (see below)

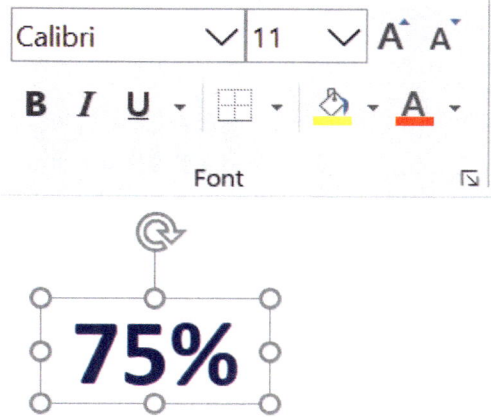

How to make an outer circle:

Insert a **circle**. The size of circle = **4.5cm**.

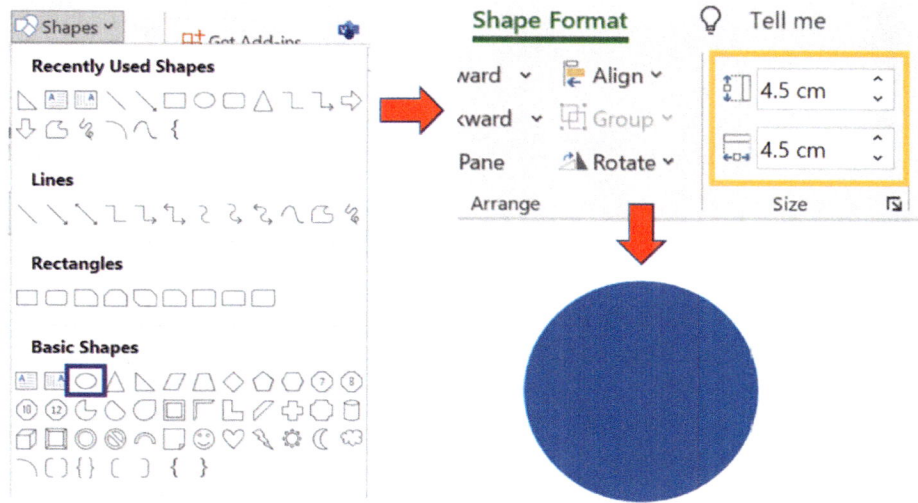

- **Ctrl + 1** >>> **No fill** >>> **Solid line** >>> **Transparency = 60%**
- **Color** = Dark Blue >>> **Width = 4pt** (for this example)

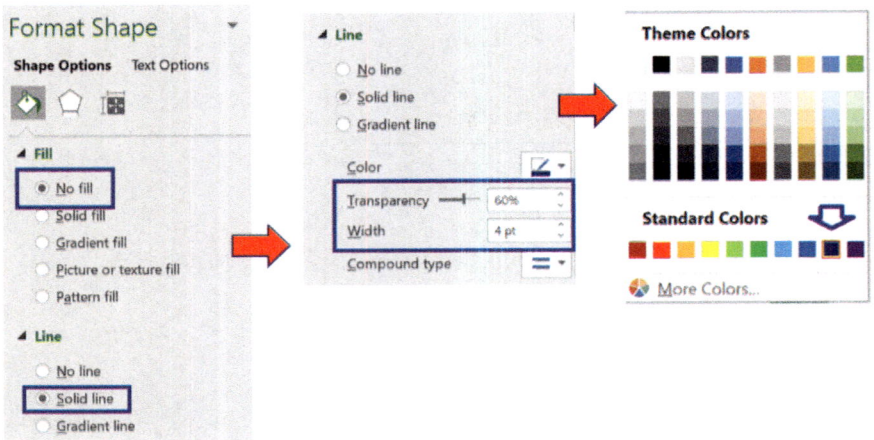

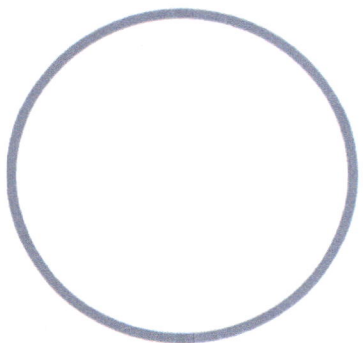

Or, you can create different style of circle as well.
However, you might also need to change the color or donut as well

How to align multiple text boxes or charts:

Now, we have 3 pieces of components (donut chart, 1 text box and 1 outer circle). In order to make them align nicely, please use the following steps which is much easier than by using mouse-dragging.

- **Holding Ctrl** button >>> select chart and the circle by clicking a left-hand mouse button.

It is possible to select multiple items in the sheet.

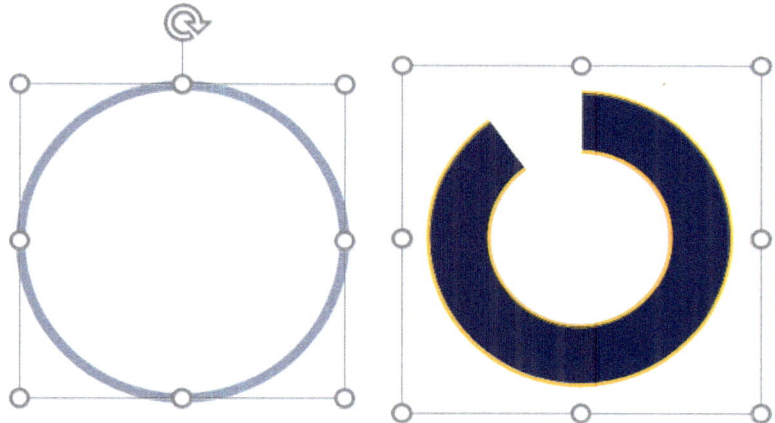

- Go to **Shape Format** >>> **Align** >>> **Align Center**

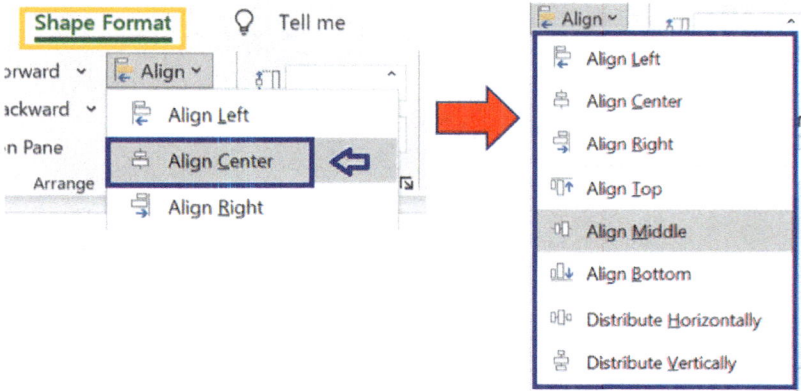

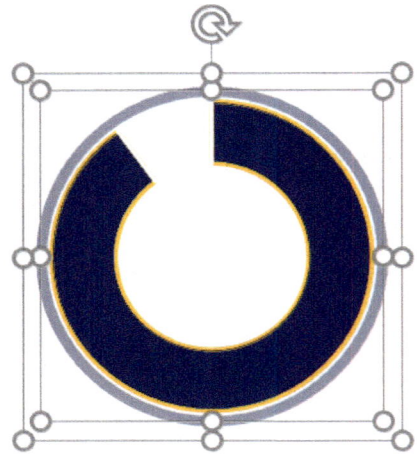

After this step, group them. (In the below section, you can see some more detail of how to group items)

In the same manner, we can align them again and Group them again.

- Go to **Shape Format** >>> **Align** >>> **Align Center**

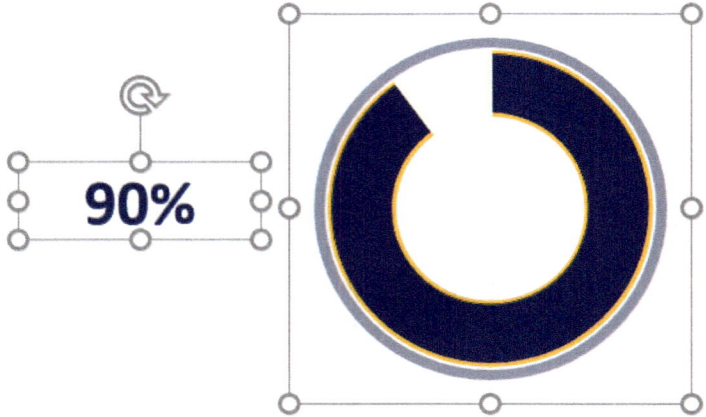

(Optional) How to group objects (or items):

Select more than 2 objects, then click right-hand button on the mouse, you can see '**Group**' in **Shape Format**. Select Group.

More than 2 objects become one object which is handy.
If you don't like it, you can also ungroup it or regroup them.

Select multiple items >>> Go to **Shape Format** >>> **Group**

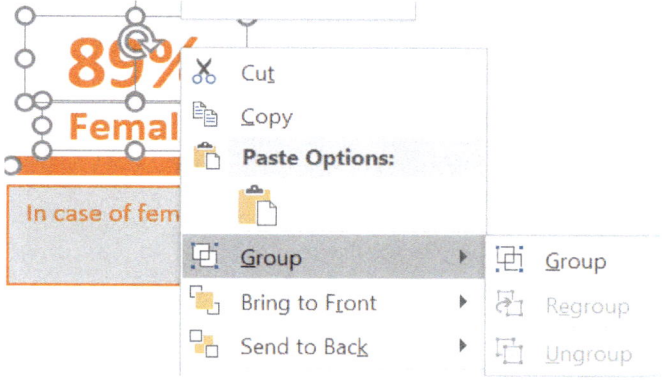

Believe it or not, we already complete a stylish donut chart. This chart is ready to use for your report, blog (as a picture), teaching materials.

Now, we can challenge ourselves to generate more applied version from the basic half-circle donut chart by changing colors.

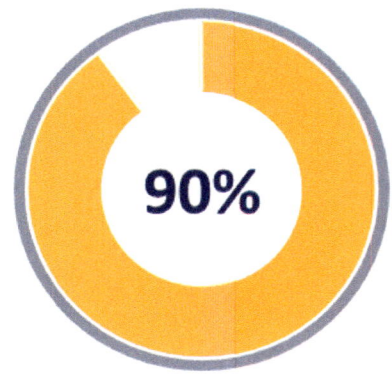

Applied version:

Now, we are going to make 2 circles with 3.6cm and 5.3cm.

Insert a **circle**. The size of circle = 3.6 cm and 5.3 cm.

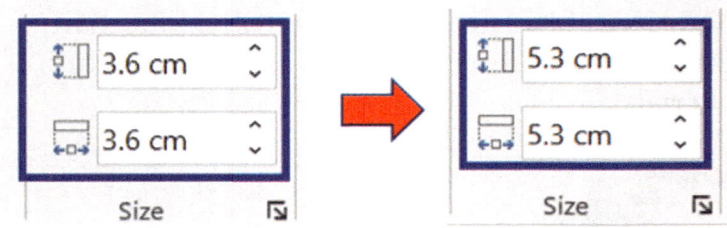

After selecting both circles, go to **Shape Format**.
Click the **Theme Styles** which you like.

Before doing alignments, it is necessary to make a proper order among 2 outer circles and the donut chart.

When we just merged 3 items, the donut chart is automatically the most front. However, we need to put the smaller inner circle must be the most front among 3 items.

Below shows: the donut chart is the most front.

Therefore, we need to the following.

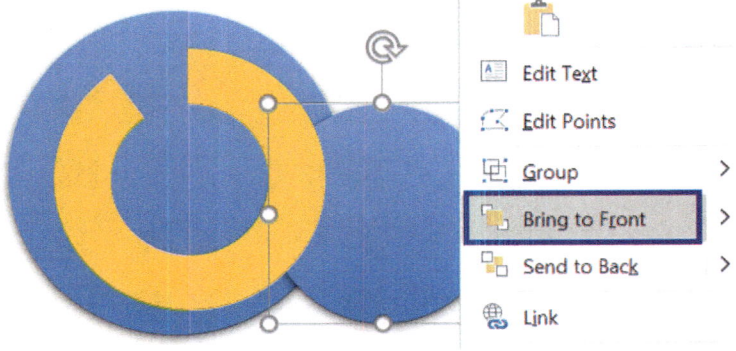

Now, the text box also needs to bring to Front.

How to align multiple text boxes or charts:

Now, we have 4 pieces of components (donut chart, 1 text box and 2 circles). In order to make them align nicely, please use the following steps which is much easier than the mouse dragging.

- **Holding Ctrl** button >>> select chart and the circle by clicking a left-hand mouse button.

It is possible to select multiple items in the sheet.

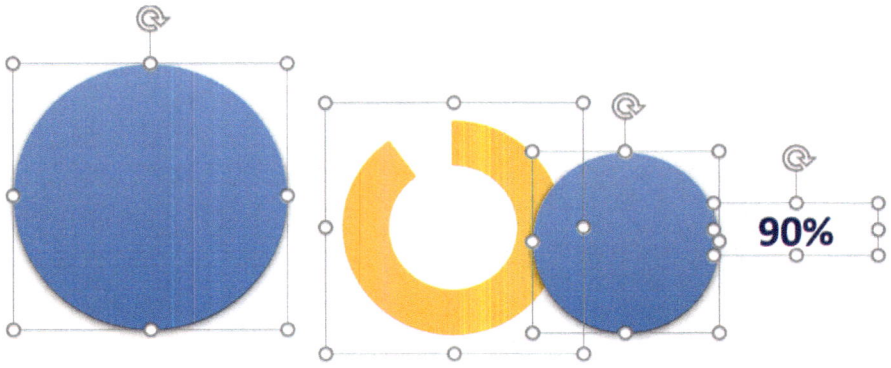

- Go to **Shape Format** >>> **Align** >>> **Align Center** >>> **Align Middle**

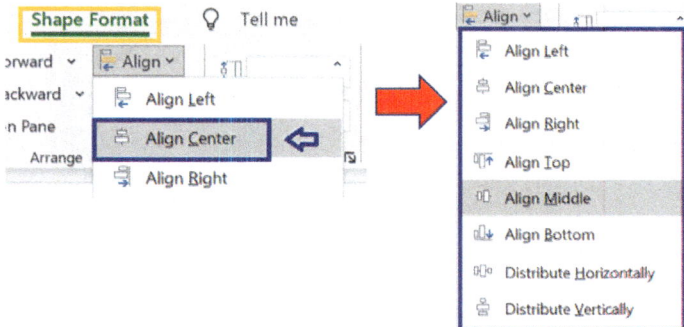

At this status, we can also **group** them.

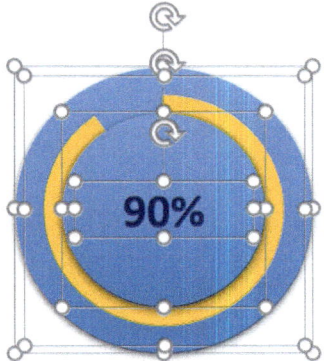

As a result, we can complete the applied version of stylish donut chart.

In summary, we can complete the following charts.

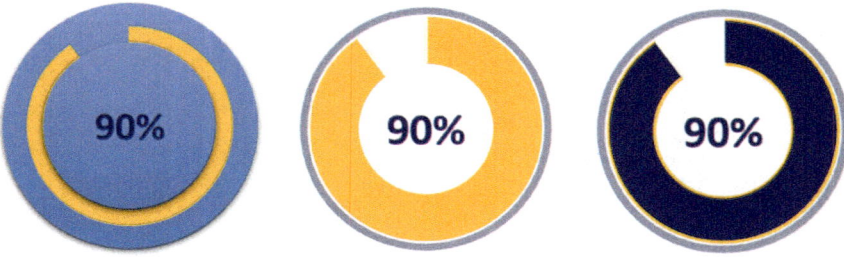

26. Stylish Bar Chart with Error Bars

We are going to make a bar chart which is relatively easy to make it compared to other charts. However, the chart looks nice. And also, it is not easy to make it without knowing the techniques of how to make it.

Target picture:
What we are going to make is the following chart:

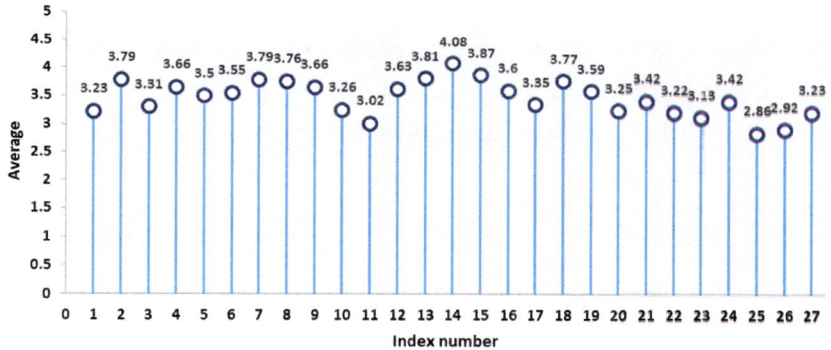

How to set up input values:

Let say, we have around 30 input values. If you put them into a normal bar chart. It looks like below. Which is a bit difficult to read it. Therefore, we are going to create a new bar chart in order to overcome this drawback.

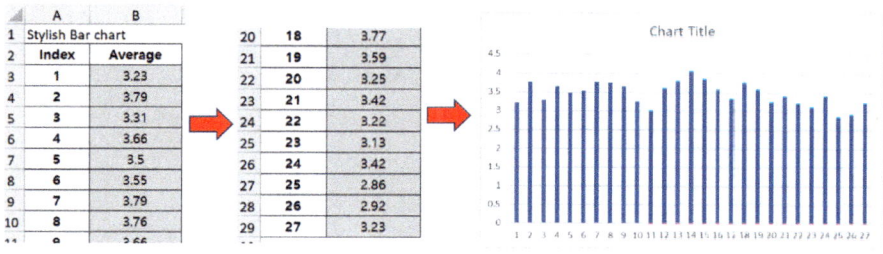

How to remove Gridlines:

- Go to **View** tab and unclick **Gridlines**.

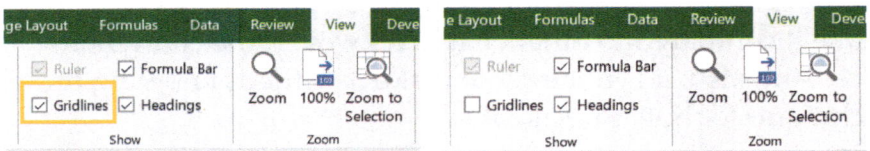

All the grid lines are disappeared in the sheet.

How to create 2 Scatter chart:

- Select 'Average' values (in **Column B**). Click **Cell B3**. Holding **Ctrl + Shift** >>> press an arrow button (↓).
- go to **Insert** tab >>> select **Scatter chart**.

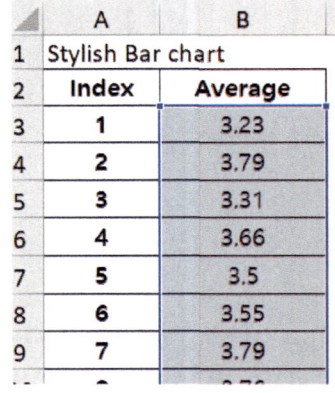

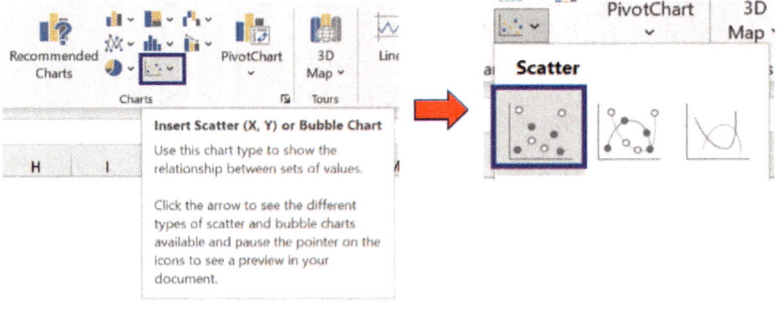

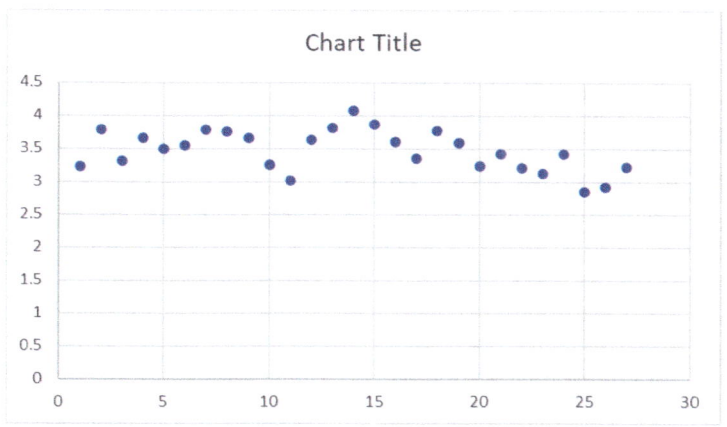

How to remove chart elements:

After clicking a chart, we can see the plus **(+) sign** on right hand side. This is the location where we can control the chart elements.

- Go to chart elements = click **(+)** sign in gray in the chart
- **Remove the chart elements** = Unclick the chart elements which you want to remove

In this case, we unclicked both **Chart Title** and **Gridlines** from chart elements.

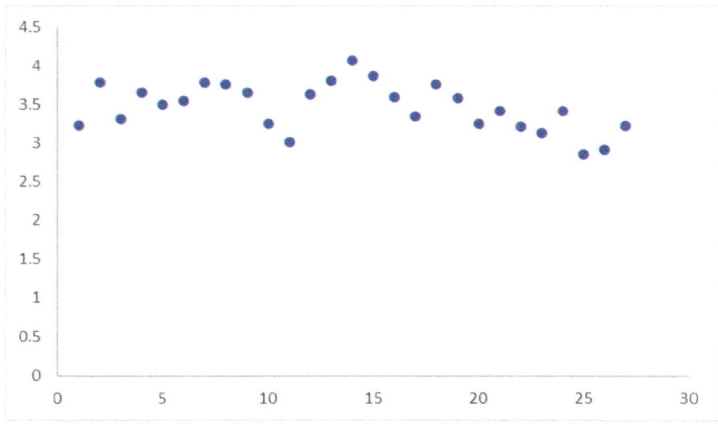

How to make a bubble in scatter plot:

- Click plots (select all points) & **CTRL+1**
- Click **Marker** & Built-in, circle and Size = **7**
- Click **Fill** & Solid fill & Color = **white**
- Click **Border** & **Solid fill** & Color = **dark blue**, Width = **1.75**

You can change the settings depends on your preference.

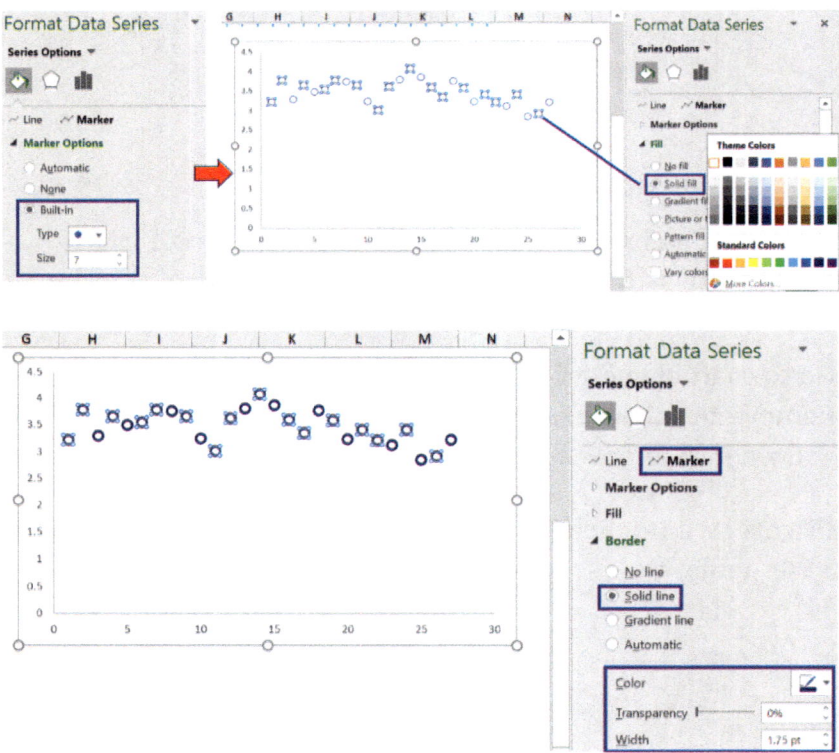

As a result, we can have the following chart.

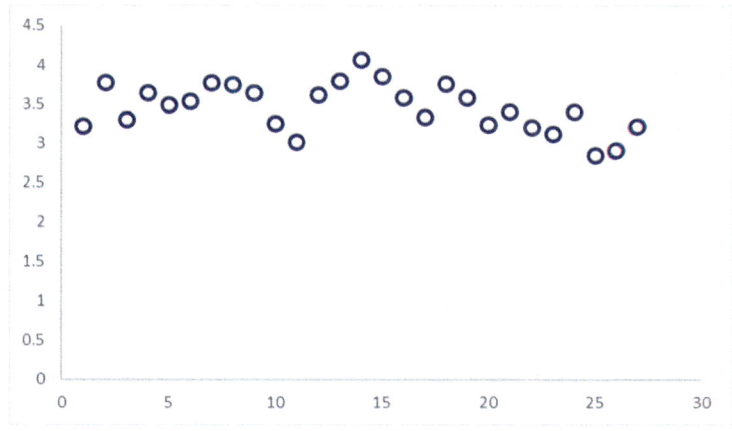

How to use Error Bar functionality:

- Click chart element (+ plus sign) in the chart.
- Select '**Error Bars**' & go to '**More Options...**'

- Go to **Error Bar Options**
- Select a small triangle & Select '**Y Error Bars**'
- **Vertical Error Bar** >> Select **Minus** & **No Cap**
- **Error Amount = 100%**

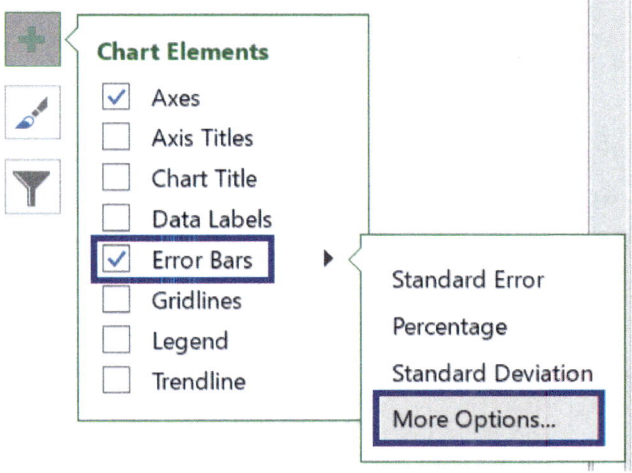

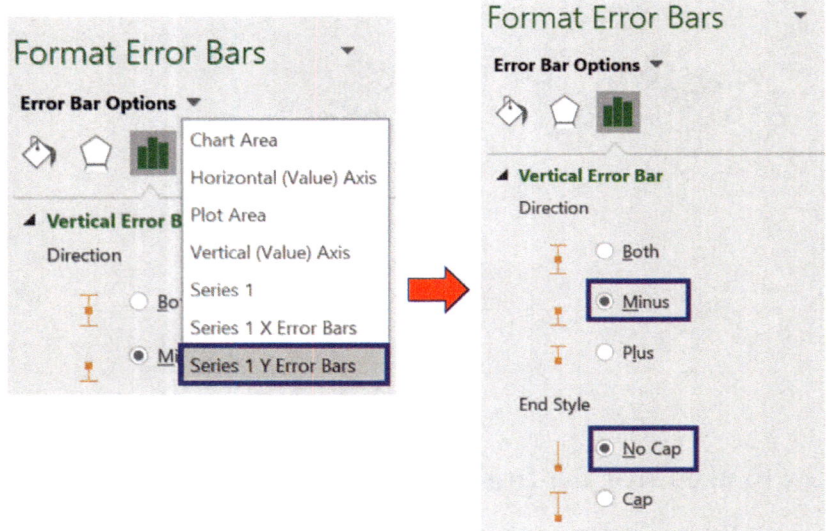

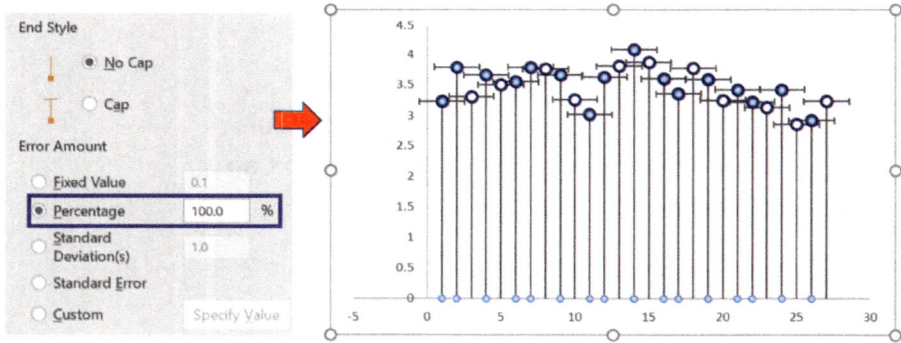

- Click a **horizontal Error Bars** and **remove** them (by pressing delete button). We can have a left-hand side chart below.

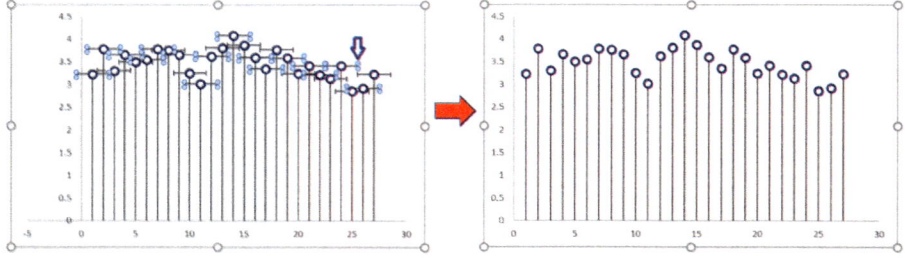

The main part is over and the rest part is how to decorate the cart.

How to adjust the range of axis:

- Click **axis** >>> **Ctrl + 1** >>> Go to **Axis Option** >>>
- Change the Max and Min value according to the data set.
- In the same manner, change the Units as well.
  Due to this setting, the automatic update part is gone.
  Therefore, you need to update it manually.

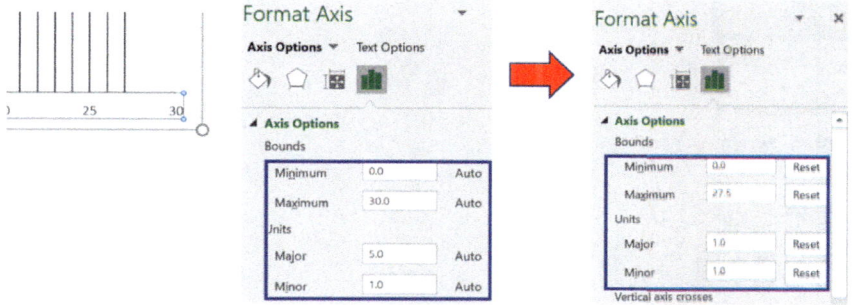

As a result, we can find the following chat (see at the end of the horizontal axis). The empty space is gone now.

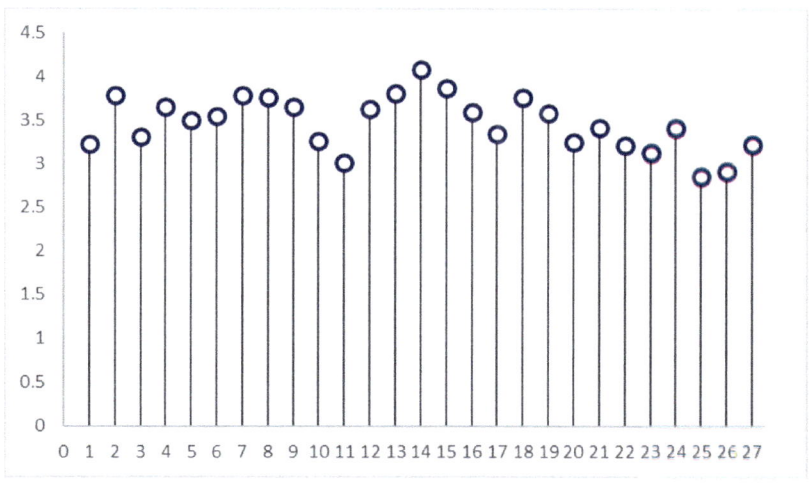

How to remove 'Shape Fill' and 'Shape Outline':

Click the chart >>> Go to **Format** tab (you can see on top of Excel). We will change the default setting of **Shape Fill** and **Shape Outline** of the chart.

- **Shape Fill** = **Select the color** which you like
- **Shape Outline** = No Outline

In this case,

How to adjust Error bar lines:

- Click the vertical line >>> **Ctrl + 1**
- **Change color, width**, etc. (in Line section)

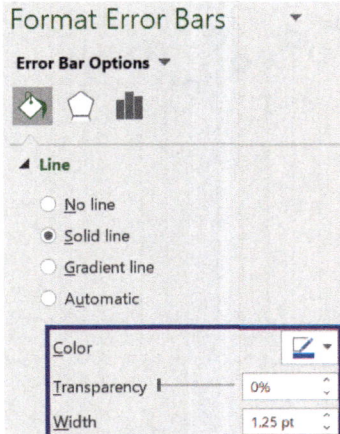

How to add Label in Error Bars:

- Click the scatter plot which you want to add labels
- Click **CTRL +1** >>> Click **'Add Data Labels'**.
- Go to **Format Data Labels** >>> Select **Value from Cells**
- Select **the actual values** from the input table. Click **OK**.

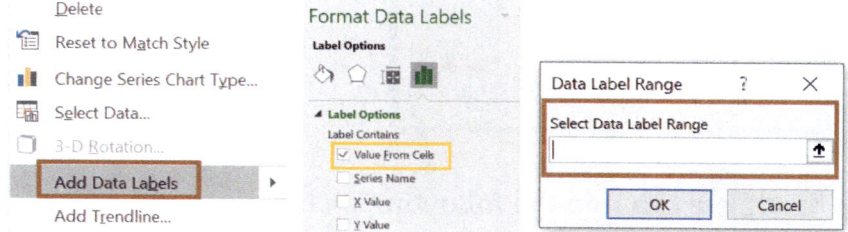

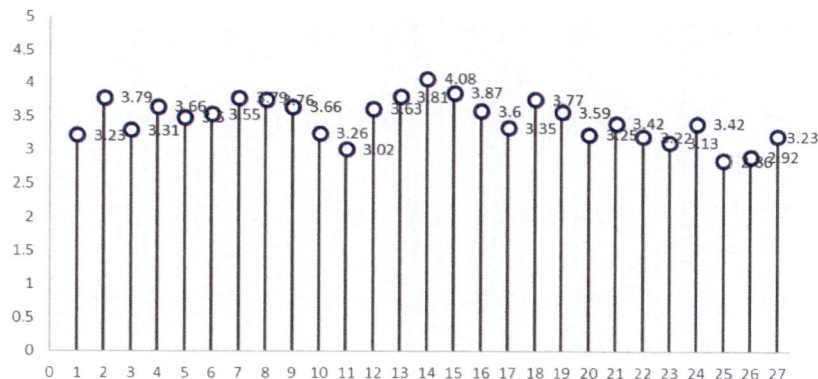

- Label Position = **Above**

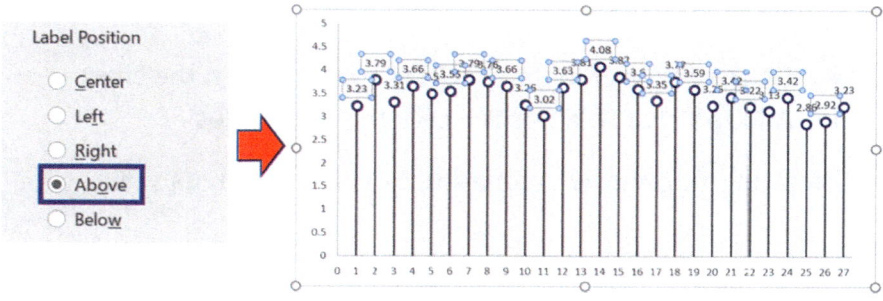

How to adjust Labels:

- Go to **Home** tab >>> change font color, width, etc.
- In the same manner, we can adjust axis font as well.

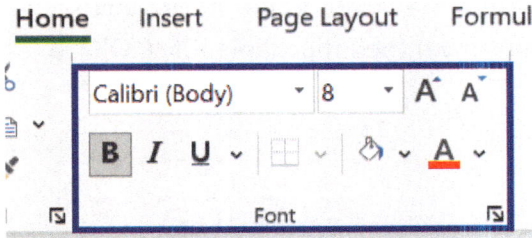

As a result, we can find the following picture.

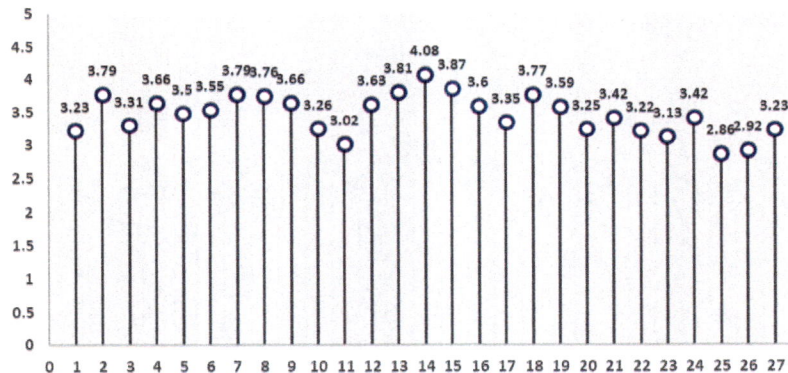

How to add Axis title:

After clicking a chart, we can see the plus **(+) sign** on right hand side. This is the location where we can control the chart elements.

- Go to chart elements = click **(+)** sign in gray in the chart
- **Add the chart elements** = click the '**Axis Titles**'.

In the same manner, we can adjust axis title font as well.

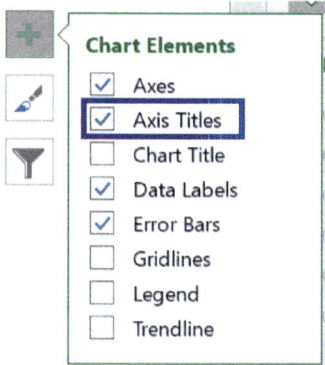

Finally, we can complete the bar chart.

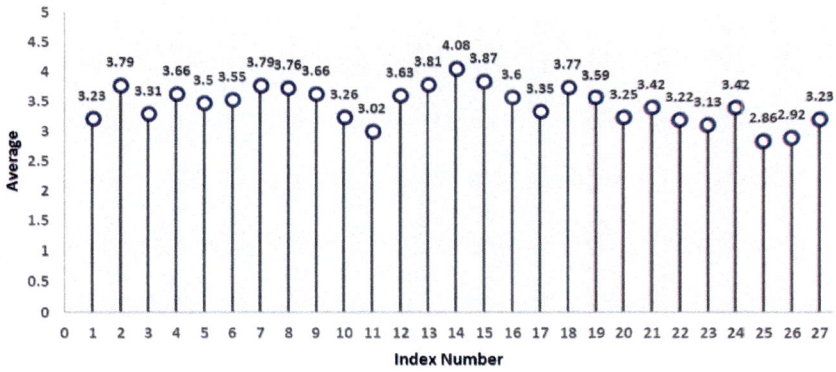

Printed in Great Britain
by Amazon

What they never tau
okay with no

13 Lessons from Therapy Rooms

Real stories. Brutal truths. Gentle wisdom

A Project of

INSTITUTE OF PROFESSIONAL PSYCHOLOGY

*13 Lessons from Therapy Rooms
Copyright © 2025 by Institute of Professional Psychology
All rights reserved.*

No part of this book may be reproduced, distributed, or transmitted in any form or by any means, including photocopying, recording, or other electronic or mechanical methods, without the prior written permission of the author, except in the case of brief quotations embodied in critical reviews and certain other noncommercial uses permitted by copyright law.

This book is a work of nonfiction. Names, characters, organizations, and events described herein are either the product of the author's research and analysis or used in a fictional manner for illustrative purposes. Any resemblance to actual persons, living or dead, or actual events is purely coincidental.

Table of Contents

Introduction – Page # 06

Lesson 1: You Are Not Your Thoughts – Page # 11

Lesson 2: Feelings Are Not Facts – Page # 16

Lesson 3: Boundaries Are Love, Not Rejection – Page # 21

Lesson 4: Healing Doesn't Mean Forgetting – Page # 27

Lesson 5: The Inner Child Always Speaks – Page # 32

Lesson 6: You Don't Have to Fix Everything (or Everyone) – Page # 38

Lesson 7: Shame Dies in Safe Spaces – Page # 44

Lesson 8: Perfectionism Is Fear in Disguise – Page # 49

Lesson 9: Forgiveness Is for You, Not Them – Page # 54

Lesson 10: Self-Sabotage Is a Sign, Not a Sentence – Page # 59

Lesson 11: Anxiety Lies to You – Page # 64

Lesson 12: Love Is a Skill, Not Just a Feeling – Page # 70

Lesson 13: Healing Is Not Linear – Page # 76

Conclusion: Carrying These Lessons Forward – Page # 81

References – Page # 86

About Us – – Page # 91

Dedication

*To the broken,
who kept waking up.*

*To the silent ones,
whose hearts screamed louder than their words.*

*To the seekers,
who searched for peace in pain and found
themselves instead.*

*To the brave souls in therapy rooms,
laying down their masks,
and picking up their truth—
one trembling breath at a time.*

*To the inner child still waiting to be seen,
the adult learning to hold them,
and every version of you in between.*

*This is for you—
not to fix,
but to remind you:
you were never truly broken.*

*You were just waiting
to come home to yourself.*

Why These Lessons Matter

In 1973, a young woman named "Anna" walked into the office of Dr. Irvin Yalom, a renowned existential psychiatrist. She was in her late twenties, yet she carried the exhaustion of someone who had lived a thousand years. As she settled into the chair across from him, she didn't cry. She didn't plead for help. She just sat there, silent. When she finally spoke, her words came out like a whisper. "I don't think I know how to be a person."

Dr. Yalom had heard versions of this before. People often walked into therapy burdened with invisible weights—depression, anxiety, trauma, shame. But Anna's struggle wasn't just sadness. It was something deeper: a quiet, suffocating detachment from life itself.

Over the next several months, they uncovered the layers of her suffering. Anna had spent most of her childhood being what others needed her to be. A perfect daughter. A high-achieving student. A people-pleaser. She had mastered the art of disappearing into roles others created for her. But now, in her late twenties, when life demanded that she show up as herself, she realized something terrifying: she had no idea who that was.

As Dr. Yalom guided her through therapy, Anna slowly started reclaiming her own voice. She learned that healing wasn't about fixing herself—because she was never broken. It was about uncovering the self she had buried beneath years of expectations, fears, and survival mechanisms. It was about unlearning the false stories she had told herself. It was about embracing her imperfections, her pain, her humanness.

This book is about those very lessons—the ones that therapy quietly teaches, the ones that change everything.

Every day, thousands of people walk into therapy rooms, carrying wounds that aren't always visible. Some are reeling from heartbreak, some are drowning in anxiety, others are grappling with childhood scars that refuse to fade. But beneath all of these struggles, there is one fundamental truth: humans are wired for healing. The mind, much like the body, has a natural ability to mend itself—if given the right tools, the right understanding, and the right space to do so.

Yet, the world doesn't exactly teach us how to heal. We're taught how to succeed, how to earn, how to conform. But no one sits us down and says: Here's how to deal with rejection. Here's what to do when your mind turns against you. Here's how to forgive yourself. Therapy, for many, becomes the classroom where these life lessons are finally learned.

But let's be honest, therapy has long been misunderstood. For decades, people saw it as something only meant for those who were "broken" or "mentally ill." This couldn't be further from the truth. The reality is that therapy is not about fixing you. It's about teaching you how to live fully, even with the inevitable messiness of life.

The power of therapy lies in the fact that it does not offer easy answers. There are no quick fixes, no magic formulas. Instead, it offers something far more valuable: insight. Therapy teaches us how to think differently, how to see our pain in a new light, how to rewrite the stories we tell ourselves. And in doing so, it gives us the power to change our lives—not by removing struggle, but by changing the way we respond to it.

A groundbreaking study conducted by Dr. Bruce Wampold at the University of Wisconsin found that the most important factor in successful therapy isn't the type of therapy—it's the relationship between the client and the therapist. What does this mean? It means that healing is not about having the "perfect strategy"; it's about having a safe space where you feel heard, understood, and challenged in the right ways. Consider the work of Carl Rogers, one of the most influential psychologists of the 20th century. Rogers believed that the key to personal transformation wasn't advice or technique—it was "unconditional positive regard." In other words, when people are given a space where they feel unconditionally accepted, they begin to heal. Not because someone tells them how to, but because they finally feel safe enough to be themselves.

But let's go a step further. Why do some people thrive after therapy while others don't? Why do some learn these life-changing lessons, while others seem to remain stuck in the same cycles of pain? The answer lies in one word: integration. Therapy is not just about having deep conversations—it's about what you do with them afterward. It's about the willingness to take what you learn and apply it in real life. Because insight without action is useless.

A study published in Psychotherapy Research found that people who actively practice what they learn in therapy—whether it's self-compassion, boundary-setting, or challenging negative thoughts—show significantly greater long-term improvement compared to those who only engage in therapy passively. This means that the true power of therapy doesn't lie in what happens inside the room—it lies in what you take with you when you leave.

Think about some of the most important lessons you've learned in life. Did they come from books? From lectures? Or did they come from experience—from moments of struggle, pain, and deep reflection? Therapy is one of the few places in life where you are invited to pause, to reflect, to truly understand yourself. And the lessons that emerge from that process? They change everything.

In this book, we will explore 13 of the most profound lessons therapy teaches—lessons that have transformed the lives of countless individuals. Some of them will challenge the way you see yourself. Some will force you to question long-held beliefs. Some will offer you relief in ways you never thought possible. But every single one of them has the potential to reshape your understanding of yourself, your relationships, and your life.

These lessons are drawn from real therapy rooms, from the work of some of the greatest psychologists in history, from research studies, and from the deeply personal journeys of those who have walked the path of healing. They are not abstract theories. They are truths that have been tested in the fire of real human struggle.

And here's the most important thing you need to know: You don't have to be in therapy to benefit from these lessons. You don't have to be at rock bottom. You don't have to wait until things fall apart. Because the best time to learn how to heal is before you desperately need it.

So, as you move through this book, I invite you to read with an open heart. Not just as a passive observer, but as someone who is willing to reflect, to question, and to engage with these lessons in your own life. You may find echoes of your own struggles in these pages. You may see reflections of your own patterns, your own fears, your own hopes.

And if you do, know this: You are not alone. You are not broken. You are simply in the process of becoming.

Therapy, at its core, is not about "fixing" people. It is about giving them permission to be human. And if there is one thing that I hope you take away from this book, it is this:
Your struggles do not define you. Your ability to heal does.
Now, let's begin.

Chapter 1: You Are Not Your Thoughts

In 2011, a man named Omar sat in my therapy office for the first time. He was in his early forties, a well-respected professor, father of two, and by all accounts, someone who had "figured it out." Yet, as he sat across from me, his hands clenched into tight fists, his voice barely above a whisper, he confessed something that he had never said out loud.

"I think I'm a fraud," he said. "Every day, I wake up expecting people to realize that I don't actually know what I'm doing. I feel like… I don't deserve my job, my family, my life. I don't know why, but I can't shake this thought. It's always there."

I had heard versions of this before—dozens, maybe hundreds of times. Different words, different faces, same fundamental fear. A relentless, unshakable voice inside their heads telling them that they were not enough, that they were somehow defective, that they were defined by their worst thoughts.

I leaned forward and asked him, "Do you know what the difference is between someone who feels like a fraud and someone who doesn't?"

He shook his head.

"Nothing," I said. "The only difference is that one believes their thoughts, and the other doesn't."
For the next few months, Omar and I worked through what psychology calls cognitive distortions—faulty ways of thinking that warp our

11

perception of reality. And Omar, like most of us, had fallen into the trap of believing that every thought in his head was a fact. That if his mind told him he was unworthy, it must be true. That if he had a passing thought about being a failure, it meant he was one. But here's the brutal truth: your mind is a liar.

Research from the National Science Foundation suggests that the average person has around 60,000 thoughts per day, and 80% of those thoughts are negative. Even more shocking? 95% of our thoughts are repetitive—which means that most of what we think today, we already thought yesterday. And the day before. And the day before that.

If your mind is a broken record of negativity, self-doubt, and fear, how can you ever expect to feel free? The 20th-century sociologist Charles Horton Cooley once said, "I am not what I think I am. I am not what you think I am. I am what I think you think I am." Let that sink in. So much of our identity is constructed from the imagined judgments of others. We don't even see ourselves clearly—we see a distorted, secondhand reflection built on our assumptions of how others perceive us.

Buddhist philosophy has been teaching this for thousands of years. The core of Buddhist thought on identity is simple: the self is an illusion. Not in a mystical, abstract way, but in a deeply practical one. The self—the version of you that you believe exists—is nothing more than a collection of constantly shifting thoughts, emotions, and experiences. You are not a static entity. You are not your failures, your doubts, or the cruel words you say to yourself in moments of weakness.

The problem is that most people never question the thoughts that arise in their minds. A thought appears, and they take it at face value. But just because a thought exists doesn't mean it's true.

The psychologist Aaron Beck, often called the father of cognitive therapy, spent decades researching how distorted thinking fuels mental illness. He found that people with anxiety and depression aren't experiencing more "bad" things in life than others—they're just processing them differently. Their brains latch onto negative thoughts, amplify them, and repeat them so often that they become automatic.

So how do we escape this trap? How do we stop being held hostage by our own thoughts?

The first step is brutal: you have to prove your mind wrong.
Most therapy models teach basic mindfulness exercises—notice the thought, acknowledge it, let it pass. But in my experience, that's not enough. If your thoughts are aggressive, self-critical, and deeply ingrained, you can't just observe them. You have to challenge them.

Here's a brutal, practical strategy that I've given countless clients, one that forces them to confront the lies their mind tells them.

Step 1: Write down your most persistent negative thoughts. Not just vague concepts—specific sentences. Instead of "I'm not good enough," write "I will fail at this project, and people will think I'm incompetent."

Step 2: List the evidence. Imagine you are a lawyer, forced to prove your thought in court. Where's the proof? Where's the hard, undeniable evidence that this thought is true? And be honest—"I just feel like it's true" doesn't count as proof.

Step 3: List the counter-evidence. Has there ever been a time when this thought was wrong? When you succeeded despite self-doubt? When you received praise or accomplished something that contradicted your fears?

Step 4: Rewrite the thought into something truer. This isn't toxic positivity—it's about accuracy. Instead of "I will fail at this project, and people will think I'm incompetent," you might end up with "I have completed difficult projects before, and even if I struggle, I am capable of learning and improving."
Step 5: Speak the new thought out loud. This sounds ridiculous, but it works. Our thoughts shape our reality, and when we speak them out loud, we reinforce them in a powerful way.

In cognitive behavioral therapy, this process is called cognitive restructuring, and research shows that it is one of the most effective methods for combating anxiety, depression, and self-doubt. A meta-analysis of 269 studies found that CBT is as effective as medication for most anxiety disorders and depression—and in many cases, it has longer-lasting effects.

But here's the part no one wants to hear: this isn't easy. Changing the way you think is like breaking an addiction. Your brain is wired for familiarity, and if you've spent years, maybe decades, believing certain things about yourself, your mind is going to resist change.

Which brings me to the final, hardest truth of all: you will never fully control your thoughts. They will always come. But what you can control is your response.

Think of your thoughts like a radio station. If a channel is playing music you don't like, do you sit there and listen, absorbing every word, letting it ruin your mood? Or do you change the station?

You will never stop negative thoughts from arising. But you can stop believing them. You can stop feeding them. You can stop letting them dictate who you are.

At the end of his therapy, Omar told me something that has stuck with me for years.

"For the first time in my life," he said, "I realize that I don't have to believe everything my mind tells me. I can choose what I accept. And that... that changes everything."

It does. And if there is one thing I want you to take from this chapter, it is this:

You are not your thoughts. You never were. And the moment you stop letting them define you, you are free.

Chapter 2: Feelings Are Not Facts

In the winter of 2017, I met a woman named Ayesha who had spent the last five years convinced that her husband was going to leave her. She had no concrete reason to believe this—he was kind, supportive, and had never given her any indication that he was unhappy in their marriage. And yet, every time he came home late, every time he seemed distracted, every time he didn't respond to a text right away, she felt a familiar wave of panic rise in her chest.

"I just know something is wrong," she told me in one of our sessions. "I can feel it. And if I feel it this strongly, doesn't that mean it's true?"

I asked her a question that I've asked many clients over the years: "If you wake up in the middle of the night and feel like there's someone in the house, does that mean there is?"

She blinked. "No, but that's different."
"Is it?" I asked. "Or is it just that fear, when strong enough, can feel exactly like truth?"

Ayesha wasn't alone in this. We all do it—mistaking our emotions for objective reality. The stronger the feeling, the more convincing it becomes. If we feel unloved, we assume we must be unlovable. If we feel anxious about an event, we take it as a sign that something bad will happen. If we feel disrespected, we assume the other person intended to disrespect us.

But here's the problem: Feelings are real, but they are not always true.

Neuroscience backs this up. Studies show that emotions arise from the limbic system, a primitive part of the brain responsible for survival responses. When we experience strong emotions—fear, anger, sadness—the amygdala, often called the brain's "alarm system," lights up. Its job is to detect threats, but it doesn't distinguish between real dangers and perceived ones. This is why you can feel genuine terror watching a horror movie even though you know it isn't real.

The trouble starts when we use emotions as proof. Psychologists call this emotional reasoning—the belief that if something feels true, it must be true.

In a 1983 study, psychologist Aaron Beck found that emotional reasoning is one of the core distortions in depression and anxiety. Depressed patients often report thoughts like, "I feel worthless, so I must be worthless." Anxious individuals frequently say, "I feel like something bad is going to happen, so it will." And yet, when researchers compare these predictions to reality, they rarely hold up.

A famous study published in the journal Cognitive Therapy and Research found that people with generalized anxiety disorder predicted negative outcomes far more often than they actually occurred. In 91.4% of cases, the feared event never happened. Let that sink in—more than 90% of the time, the feeling of impending disaster was completely false. So why do we trust our feelings so much?

Part of the answer lies in evolution. Thousands of years ago, our ancestors didn't have time to analyze whether their fear of a rustling bush was rational—they ran, because assuming danger increased their survival chances. But in modern life, this instinct can backfire. A critical email from a boss feels like a direct threat. A partner's quiet mood feels like abandonment. Our brain reacts first and asks questions later.

But just because our emotions evolved to keep us safe doesn't mean they're always useful. In fact, they often make things worse.

Take anger, for example. When we feel angry, we instinctively believe that someone else is in the wrong. But a study in Emotion found that anger makes people overestimate their own competence and underestimate the perspectives of others. Essentially, when we're mad, we become convinced that we're right—even when we're not.

Sadness is no different. Research from the University of New South Wales found that people in sad moods are more likely to perceive neutral faces as hostile. In other words, when we feel bad, the whole world starts to look like a threat—even when it isn't.

So if emotions are unreliable narrators, does that mean we should ignore them?
Not at all. Feelings are data, not instructions. They provide important information, but they shouldn't automatically dictate our actions. The key is learning how to validate emotions without being ruled by them.

One of the most powerful tools for doing this is the FACT test. I teach this to many of my clients who struggle with overwhelming emotions:

- **F – Feel the emotion fully.** Don't suppress it, don't ignore it. Let it be there. But don't act on it yet.
- **A – Ask:** What is this emotion telling me? If you feel anxious before a meeting, your brain might be warning you that you care about this. If you feel sad after a conversation, it might signal a deeper unresolved issue.
- **C – Challenge the thought.** Just because you feel something doesn't make it fact. Ask yourself, "What objective evidence supports this feeling?" and "What might I be missing?"
- **T – Take action based on facts, not just feelings.** Sometimes your emotions will align with reality, and sometimes they won't. The goal is to respond with both logic and emotion, not just one or the other.

This is the part where people struggle the most. It's hard to separate what we feel from what is true. But therapy is about learning to do just that.

I once had a client, Rehan, who was convinced that his colleagues hated him. Every time he walked into the office, he felt a wave of self-consciousness. "I can just tell," he said. "The way they look at me, the way they don't invite me to lunch. I know I'm not liked." So we tested his belief. Over the next two weeks, he was instructed to track every interaction where he felt excluded and write down hard evidence. And an interesting thing happened.

He noticed that most of the time, his coworkers were friendly. That the times he wasn't invited to lunch, it was often because people already had plans—not because they were rejecting him. And the biggest revelation? He realized that he was the one who avoided eye contact first, assuming they disliked him before they had a chance to engage.

In short: his feelings were lying to him. And once he recognized this, his entire experience at work changed.

This doesn't mean emotions are useless. Quite the opposite—they are vital for decision-making, relationships, and self-awareness. But they are not facts.

You can feel unworthy and still be deeply valuable. You can feel afraid and still be completely safe. You can feel rejected and still be deeply loved.

And the moment you start questioning your feelings instead of blindly believing them, you take back control of your life.

Chapter 3: Boundaries Are Love, Not Rejection

I still remember the night I learned the real meaning of a boundary—not in a therapy room, but sitting across from my mother at our kitchen table. I was 28, freshly burnt out, emotionally drained, and stretched far too thin between clients, friends, family, and every possible obligation I thought I "owed" the world. My mother looked at me with a kind of soft exhaustion, the way only a parent can when they've seen their child fall into the same pit for the tenth time.

"You think saying yes is love," she said quietly. "But all I see is you disappearing."

That sentence broke me open.
You see, in therapy, we talk a lot about boundaries—how to define them, how to enforce them, how to not feel guilty about them. But what we don't talk about enough is the emotional confusion that surrounds them. People don't just struggle with boundaries because they don't know how. They struggle because setting them feels like rejection. Especially if, like me—and many of my clients—you were raised to equate love with sacrifice.

In therapy sessions, I meet people who are exhausted by their own generosity. They say yes to every friend in crisis, take every late-night call from coworkers, and drop everything for family at the expense of their own peace. And they're not doing this because they don't know how to say no—they're doing it because they believe saying no is cruel.

But here's the truth that changed my life, and the lives of so many clients: boundaries are not walls—they're doors with doorknobs on your side.

When we talk about healthy relationships, we often imagine closeness as being "always available," but in reality, true intimacy can't exist without the ability to say, "This is where I end and you begin." That line is not rejection. It's love in its clearest form—love that honors both people involved.

Psychologist and researcher Brené Brown puts it best: "Daring to set boundaries is about having the courage to love ourselves even when we risk disappointing others." And that's where most people flinch—right at that word: disappoint.

Because to set a boundary often means risking being misunderstood. It means standing firm while someone accuses you of being distant, selfish, uncaring, or cold. But the alternative is worse: it means silently swallowing your needs, eroding your self-respect, and pretending everything is fine while resentment grows like mold beneath the surface.

Therapists often distinguish between three types of boundaries: rigid, porous, and healthy. Rigid boundaries are like barbed wire fences—nothing gets in, and nothing gets out. Porous boundaries are like broken windows—everyone can walk in, rearrange your furniture, and leave without knocking. But healthy boundaries? They're like a well-tended garden: beautiful, defined, with gates that open and close when it feels right.

Statistically, the absence of healthy boundaries is linked to numerous mental health issues. A study published in the Journal of Mental Health Counseling found that people with poor boundary-setting skills are significantly more likely to experience anxiety, burnout, depression, and interpersonal conflict. And among those who identify as people-pleasers or struggle with codependency, boundary issues are almost always central.

One of my clients, Zoya, was a textbook empath. She poured herself into everyone around her, often to the point of emotional depletion. By the time she came to therapy, she was having daily panic attacks and had no idea why. When we traced the triggers, we found they were all related to guilt. Guilt for saying no. Guilt for not picking up the phone. Guilt for not being "there" for everyone. But when I asked her who had ever shown up for her the way she showed up for others, she went silent.

This is where the real work of therapy began. Not in learning new scripts, but in unlearning the ones she was raised with. The belief that her worth was tied to being needed. The fear that a boundary was a betrayal. The unconscious rule that being a "good person" meant being endlessly available.

We didn't start with big steps. That would've been too much. Instead, I asked her to do one thing: pause before every yes. Not say no. Just pause. Breathe. Give herself five seconds to ask, "Do I want to do this, or do I feel I have to?"

That one practice shifted her entire world.

Setting boundaries isn't about building a fortress. It's about drawing a map. It's saying to the people in your life: Here's how to love me. Here's what helps me feel safe. Here's what I can and cannot offer right now. And yes, sometimes people will not like your map. But the ones who respect it? Those are your people. Culturally, this isn't always easy. In collectivist societies, boundaries are often seen as disrespectful. The idea of saying no to a parent, declining an invitation, or refusing to share personal information is sometimes met with shock. But loving others does not mean abandoning yourself.

In fact, clinical psychologist Dr. Henry Cloud explains in his work that boundaries are essential for preserving love. Without them, relationships become resentful, manipulative, and enmeshed. "We can't genuinely love someone if we feel we have no choice," he writes. And he's right. Love requires freedom, not obligation.

From a practical standpoint, setting and maintaining boundaries isn't just about having a hard conversation. It's about consistency. It's about noticing the small moments—like when your phone rings at 11 p.m. and you always pick up, even though you're exhausted. Or when your coworker drops extra work on your desk and you smile and say, "No problem," even though you want to scream.

It starts there. In the pause. In the moment where you ask yourself, "If I say yes to this, what am I saying no to?" Because every yes costs something. And you deserve to count the cost.

Here are a few brutally honest practices I often share with clients working on boundaries:

- **Stop over-explaining.** You don't owe people a detailed report on why you're declining. A simple, "I can't this time" is enough. The right people won't demand a thesis.
- **Anticipate pushback.** Expect discomfort. Boundaries are often hardest on the people who benefited from your lack of them.
- **Script it out.** In early stages, having a go-to phrase can help. Try: "I want to help, but I can't right now." Or "I need some time to think about this—I'll get back to you."
- Don't rescue your guilt. Feeling guilty doesn't mean you're doing something wrong. Sometimes it just means you're doing something new.
- Reward the boundary. Every time you hold a line, celebrate it. Treat it like the radical act of self-love it is.

Over time, boundary-setting becomes less of a terrifying act and more of a quiet rhythm. It's not about pushing people away; it's about inviting the right people closer, without losing yourself in the process.

And here's what's beautiful: boundaries don't just protect your mental health—they also deepen your relationships. When people know your limits, they can trust your yes. When you honor your time, your energy, and your needs, you model what respect really looks like.

So the next time you feel that pang of guilt after drawing a line, remember this: Boundaries aren't a rejection of others. They are a commitment to yourself. And self-respect? That's the foundation of every kind of love worth building.

Chapter 4: Healing Doesn't Mean Forgetting

Dr. Thema is one of the most influential minds when it comes to research on trauma. He said, "Just because the wound no longer bleeds doesn't mean it has vanished." That line stayed with me for months—echoing in the silence after sessions, rising in the stories of my clients, and whispering in the corners of my own history. It struck something deeper than just a clinical truth; it uncovered a lie so many of us unconsciously live by—the myth that healing means moving on, wiping the slate clean, pretending it never happened.

But what if healing doesn't look like forgetting? What if it looks like remembering differently?

There was a client—I'll call him Adil—who walked into my therapy room one rainy evening with a line I've heard in countless variations: "I just want to be over it." He had lost his father in a sudden accident five years earlier. He had done "everything right," he told me. Therapy, journaling, volunteering, self-help books. But he still flinched when he heard certain songs. Still avoided roads that reminded him of that day. Still felt the weight of guilt every time he laughed a little too hard. "I thought I was supposed to move on by now," he said.

That belief—that we are meant to move on from pain like changing lanes on a highway—is one of the most persistent and damaging cultural messages about healing. And it's flat-out wrong.

What I told Adil, and what I want to tell you, is this: healing doesn't erase the scar. It teaches you how to live with it. You don't forget. You grow around the memory.

Neuroscience backs this up in powerful ways. Studies from the University of Wisconsin show that traumatic memories are not stored like normal memories. They lodge deeper in the brain's amygdala, tied to sensory and emotional centers. That's why the smell of smoke or the sound of breaking glass can bring back a panic attack years later. The trauma isn't just remembered—it's relived.

And yet, over time, with therapeutic support, those neural connections can soften. They don't vanish. But they lose their chokehold. This is known as neuroplasticity, the brain's ability to rewire itself based on new emotional experiences. It's not forgetting—it's reprocessing.

One of the most groundbreaking approaches to this kind of healing is EMDR—Eye Movement Desensitization and Reprocessing. Developed by Dr. Francine Shapiro, this therapy helps people access and reframe traumatic memories, not to delete them, but to detach the terror. Patients often describe it not as forgetting the event, but finally seeing it as something that happened, instead of something that's still happening.

The distinction is critical.
Another powerful therapeutic lens comes from narrative therapy, which invites people to become the authors of their own stories, instead of passive

characters. The trauma remains in the story—but the person is no longer defined by it. They're the one turning the pages.

Think of how trees grow. If a branch breaks, the tree doesn't discard the wound—it grows around it. Forms new bark. Continues upward. The wound becomes part of its shape, part of its strength. That's what we're aiming for in healing.

But our culture doesn't like this idea. We prefer clean endings. Closure. The "before and after." It's why people ask, "Aren't you over that yet?" or "Shouldn't you be happy by now?" It's why so many trauma survivors carry a second wound: shame for not being "better" yet.

This shame silences people. It stops them from reaching out. From telling the truth. From grieving honestly.

Yet in every therapy room I've ever worked in, the opposite is true: the most courageous clients are not the ones who've "moved on"—they're the ones who've learned how to stay present with pain without letting it define their worth.

This is especially true for survivors of complex trauma—childhood abuse, domestic violence, systemic racism, or long-term neglect. Healing here is not linear. It's cyclical. It comes in waves. Sometimes you'll feel like you've conquered the mountain, only to be triggered and feel like you're back at the base. That's not failure. That's human.

In Buddhist philosophy, suffering is not an error to be fixed—it's part of the contract of living. But the Buddha also taught that clinging to pain or trying to push it away only creates more suffering. The path to freedom lies in acceptance—not resignation, but the quiet strength of sitting with reality as it is. Of saying, yes, this happened. Yes, it hurt. Yes, I'm still standing. Holocaust survivor and psychiatrist Viktor Frankl, in his extraordinary book Man's Search for Meaning, wrote: "When we are no longer able to change a situation, we are challenged to change ourselves." Frankl didn't mean erasing the past. He meant choosing how we relate to it.

So what does that look like in real life?

Let's get brutally practical.

First, stop waiting for the day when the memory stops hurting completely. It may come. It may not. Instead, track your relationship to the pain. Are you less reactive? Do you recover faster? Are you able to comfort yourself now, instead of collapsing? That's growth.

Second, learn to name the pain without drowning in it. Use grounding techniques—describe what you see, hear, feel. Anchor yourself in the now. When the past shows up, remind yourself: this is a memory, not a prophecy.

Third, reject the myth of closure. Closure isn't a door that shuts. It's a window that opens—where the view includes both joy and loss. And that's okay.

Fourth, tell your story—but on your own terms. Not for others' comfort. Not to prove anything. But because in speaking your truth, you take back authorship.

Finally, turn your wounds into wisdom. Not in a toxic positivity way—not all pain needs to be "productive." But some of your greatest insights, strengths, and empathies will come from what you've survived. Let that shape how you move through the world.

Adil never "moved on" from his father's death. But a year later, he spoke at a local grief support group, sharing the things no one had told him about loss. He still had hard days. But the weight wasn't crushing anymore—it was just a part of his story.

And you? You don't need to erase your past to heal. You just need to stop believing that it defines your future.

Just because the wound no longer bleeds doesn't mean it has vanished. But maybe, just maybe, it can become the place where something beautiful grows.

Chapter 5: The Inner Child Always Speaks

It took me years as a therapist to understand that some of the most adult-looking problems—burnout, perfectionism, emotional shutdown, fear of abandonment—were often echoes of a much smaller voice. Not the one that negotiates salaries or juggles calendars. But the one that once cried silently in a dark room. The one that learned, way too early, that love might be conditional. That being "too much" was dangerous. That asking for your needs might lead to rejection. That voice? It never disappears. The inner child doesn't age. It waits.

I remember a client, Zara, who came to therapy in her late thirties. Successful, composed, and, in her words, "emotionally dead inside." She wasn't depressed in the clinical sense. She functioned well. But joy felt like a distant memory. So did tears. Her relationships were shallow; her laughter, rehearsed. We worked together for months, peeling back layers of her adult narrative until one day, in a quiet session, she whispered something that cracked the room open: "I used to sit outside my parents' door at night just to hear them talk. Just to know they were still there."

That was the moment I met her inner child.
The idea of the "inner child" might sound like pop psychology fluff, but it's deeply grounded in clinical theory and human experience. Psychologist John Bradshaw was one of the early pioneers of inner child work. His books in the '80s and '90s, especially

Homecoming, explored how unresolved childhood pain silently scripts adult behavior. And research backs him up. Studies in developmental psychology show that early attachment patterns—especially those formed before age seven—become internal templates that shape how we relate to ourselves and others. These are called internal working models, and they don't vanish with age. They evolve unless we consciously rewrite them.

So what exactly is the inner child?

Think of it as the emotional blueprint you formed before you had words to process the world. It holds your earliest fears, joys, confusions, and unmet needs. It's where your rawest instincts live. The part of you that still hopes to be chosen. Still fears being abandoned. Still wants to be held.

You might not hear this part clearly, but you feel it—when you get irrationally panicked in a relationship fight, when you shut down after making a mistake, when you ache for validation after a tiny success, when you lash out and don't know why. That's not your adult logic reacting. That's your inner child flinching.

And here's the kicker: your inner child always speaks. The question is—are you listening?

Sometimes the inner child shows up as anxiety that won't shut off. Other times, it's the chronic overachiever, the peacemaker, the one who can't say no. Each of these is a survival strategy that made sense when you were small and powerless—but may be harming you now that you're grown and capable. The good news is: the past isn't fixed. You can't change what happened, but you can change how it lives inside you.

This is where reparenting comes in.

Reparenting is exactly what it sounds like: becoming the caregiver you needed. It's not about blaming your actual parents endlessly, though let's be honest—some of us were raised in emotional deserts. But it is about acknowledging that gaps were left behind. And if you don't fill them, those gaps become triggers, addictions, self-sabotage.

To reparent, you start small.

You tune in. You ask yourself questions your parents may have never asked you: What do I need right now? What hurts? What am I afraid of?

And then, most importantly—you respond. With compassion. Not shame. You stop abandoning yourself when you're in pain. You stop calling yourself lazy when you're overwhelmed. You stop silencing your joy because someone once told you not to make a scene.

One of the most powerful moments in reparenting work is giving your inner child a voice. I often ask clients to write a letter from their younger self. What do they wish someone had said to them? What were they scared of? What did they believe about love, safety, and worth?

Then we flip it—write a letter to that child. Not to fix them. But to witness them.

Zara once wrote: "I'm so sorry you thought you had to earn love by being quiet. You don't. You never did." She sobbed when she read it aloud. It wasn't theatrical. It was decades of silence breaking open.

Now, none of this is magic. Reparenting isn't about hugging a pillow and being healed. It's work. Messy, repetitive work. It means changing how you speak to yourself. Setting boundaries that your childhood never allowed. Soothing your fears instead of yelling at them to shut up. Celebrating yourself even when no one claps.

It means becoming, finally, the adult your younger self dreamed of.

Psychologist Carl Jung said, "In every adult, there lurks a child—an eternal child, something that is always becoming, is never completed, and calls for unceasing care, attention, and education."

Ignoring your inner child doesn't make you stronger. It makes you disconnected. And disconnected adults disconnect others.

Let's talk science for a second. Trauma research shows that emotionally neglected children often develop hyper-independence as adults. They don't trust others to show up. But this "strength" often hides deep loneliness and a lack of self-worth. According to a 2019 study in the Journal of Personality, unresolved childhood emotional neglect was a strong predictor of adult depressive symptoms—even decades later.

That's how far the child reaches. Across time. Across choices. Across relationships.

But the most incredible thing? That same study also found that self-compassion practices and secure adult relationships could actually mediate these effects. In other words, you can heal backwards through how you live forward.

Isn't that beautiful? So how do you start? Here are some real, no-fluff practices:

- **Create a visual of your inner child.** Find a photo. Draw them. Keep it where you can see. This makes the connection real. When you're hard on yourself, look at it. Would you speak that way to them?
- **Track your triggers.** When you overreact, pause. Ask: what age part of me is reacting right now? Is this a 30-year-old response or a 6-year-old fear?
- **Create rituals of care.** Not bubble baths. I mean accountability. Go to bed when you say you will. Eat nourishing food. Speak kindly. Keep promises to yourself. These are the things your child self longed for: consistency and love.
- **Seek corrective emotional experiences.** This might mean therapy. Or being vulnerable with a safe person. Or practicing boundaries that your family never modeled.

> Each of these experiences tells your nervous system: it's different now. We're safe.

Because ultimately, that's what healing the inner child means—it's not about reliving the past. It's about reloving yourself now.

Zara's work didn't end with that letter. She slowly began showing up differently—with herself, with friends, with her own children. She told me once, "I thought I had to forget who I was to survive. But now I realize, I just had to come back for her."

And maybe that's what we all need: to come back for the younger versions of ourselves who waited. Who watched. Who hoped someone would choose them. That someone is you.

Chapter 6: You Don't Have to Fix Everything (or Everyone)

There was a time early in my career when I thought I was doing therapy "right" if every client left feeling better, lighter, clearer. If someone cried in a session, I felt responsible to soothe them. If someone sat in silence, I filled the space. If they didn't make progress fast enough, I stayed up reviewing my notes, wondering what I'd missed. I was trying to be the "good therapist." The one who healed. The one who saved. It took me burning out—and sitting across from a client who mirrored my very behavior—for me to realize: trying to fix everyone isn't help. It's control in disguise.

Her name was Saba. A kind, generous soul in her forties, always doing something for someone—her parents, her husband, her kids, her boss. She was tired, emotionally wrung out, yet deeply afraid to stop giving. "If I don't do it," she said once, eyes rimmed red, "everything falls apart." She came to therapy because she was angry—not at others, but at herself. For being exhausted. For being resentful. For not being "strong enough."

I looked at her, and in a strange, surreal moment, it felt like I was looking in a mirror. Not just as a therapist—but as a person who'd learned, long ago, that being needed was the safest way to be loved.

This chapter is for anyone who carries the rescuer's burden. The fixer. The peacemaker. The one who takes on others' pain like it's a project. It might feel noble. It might even feel like love. But more often than not, it's a trauma response dressed up as kindness.

Let's talk psychology for a minute. The rescuer complex, often rooted in childhood experiences, refers to the compulsive need to help or save others—sometimes at the expense of one's own wellbeing. It's a common dynamic in codependent relationships, where one person over-functions and the other under-functions. Stephen Karpman's Drama Triangle, a well-known psychological model, breaks this down into three roles: the Victim, the Persecutor, and the Rescuer. The Rescuer believes they must solve others' problems, but often ends up enabling dependency, avoiding their own issues, and becoming emotionally depleted.

I've met hundreds of clients who unknowingly live their lives in this triangle. They come into therapy thinking they're being "too caring," but underneath that is usually something deeper—an old wound. Maybe they grew up in chaotic homes where they had to manage emotions way beyond their age. Maybe love was tied to usefulness. Maybe they were told, directly or subtly, that their needs came second—or didn't matter at all.

Fixing became survival. Helping others became a way to feel enough.

But here's the truth no one teaches us growing up: not everything broken is yours to repair. And often, the greatest act of love is not rescuing—but respecting someone else's capacity to navigate their own pain.

This is where compassionate detachment comes in. It's a concept rooted in both psychology and spirituality. Buddhist teachings call it upekkha—equanimity. A loving awareness that holds space without clinging, controlling, or rescuing. It's the difference between standing beside someone in the storm and trying to shield them from the rain. The first honors their strength. The second assumes they have none.

Of course, this is easier said than done. The desire to fix can feel instinctive. You see someone struggling, and your brain floods with ideas, solutions, urges. But we often forget that unsolicited fixing sends a message: I don't believe you can handle this. That's not empowerment. That's erasure.

Let's talk neuroscience for a second. Studies on mirror neurons—the brain cells that allow us to empathize with others—show that when we see someone in pain, our own brains light up as if we're experiencing it ourselves. This is powerful. It fuels human connection. But if we don't regulate it, it can also lead to empathetic distress, where we absorb the other person's suffering to the point of dysfunction. Therapists, caregivers, and highly sensitive people are especially prone to this.

So what do we do with this empathy?

We practice boundaries—not as walls, but as clarity. We ask ourselves, What's mine, and what's theirs? We remind ourselves: I can care deeply without carrying completely.

This doesn't mean becoming cold or indifferent. It means cultivating something called emotional sovereignty—the ability to stay grounded in your own emotional world, even as you support someone else's.

One of the most liberating shifts I've seen clients make is learning to say, "That sounds really hard. I'm here for you. What do you need from me?" Instead of jumping in with advice, fixing, or unasked-for pep talks, they learn to pause. To listen. To trust that others can ask for what they need—and that silence is not failure, it's space.

And let me be honest: this is hard for many of us. Especially if we've built our self-worth around being "the strong one." Letting go of fixing means confronting the fear that if we're not needed, we're not wanted. But that's a lie. You are lovable for who you are—not for how useful you are.

I often return to this quote by Ram Dass: "We're all just walking each other home." Not dragging, not carrying, not rescuing. Walking. Side by side. That's what true connection looks like.

I also want to name the gendered piece here. Women, in particular, are often socialized to be caretakers, nurturers, emotional laborers. From a young age, many are taught to prioritize others' needs above their own. The result? A lifetime of burnout, resentment, and internalized guilt for even thinking of saying no.

A 2021 study in the Journal of Clinical Psychology found that women who over-function in emotional labor roles are significantly more likely to experience anxiety, depression, and somatic symptoms. And yet, many continue because it feels normal. Even good. Even feminine.

But caregiving that costs you your mental health is not kindness. It's self-erasure.

So how do we start letting go?

Here are some brutally honest practices that go beyond surface-level advice:

- Stop answering immediately. Give yourself permission to pause when someone vents or asks for help. Ask yourself: Am I about to respond from guilt, habit, or choice?
- Check your motive. Before you help, ask: Am I doing this because they need me, or because I need to feel needed?
- Sit in the discomfort of powerlessness. Practice witnessing someone struggle without jumping in. Name your urge. Breathe through it. Stay present without fixing.
- Have "non-rescue" mantras. Try: "I can't heal this for them." Or, "They're allowed to be in pain without me saving them." Or, "Support is not the same as sacrifice."
- Go to therapy yourself. If helping others feels compulsive, there's a story behind it. Explore

it. Untangle it. You deserve your own healing too.

I remember the day Saba said, "I'm learning to let people fall—not because I don't care, but because I trust they can rise." That was her turning point. Not when she stopped loving people, but when she stopped abandoning herself in the name of love.

And maybe that's the lesson we all need: that real love has limits. That fixing isn't always helpful. That you can be compassionate and still say, "This is not mine to carry."

You're not a machine. You're not a savior. You're a person—with needs, limits, and a right to your own peace. Letting go doesn't mean giving up on others. It means showing up differently—wiser, lighter, and more whole.

And if no one's told you yet: that's enough. You're enough. Even when you're not fixing a single thing.

Chapter 7: Shame Dies in Safe Spaces

I will never forget the silence in the room when Sarah whispered, "I hate who I've become." She was sitting across from me, gripping the sleeves of her sweater like they were the only things keeping her from falling apart. Her voice trembled, not from fear of judgment—though that was certainly there—but from the unbearable weight of shame she had carried alone for years. What broke me was not what she shared—it was the look in her eyes, this raw desperation for someone to tell her, you're still worthy, even with this. That moment stayed with me because it reminded me of something fundamental: shame thrives in secrecy, and it dies in safe spaces.

Sarah was not a criminal. She wasn't dangerous. She wasn't unkind. She was human—hurting, flawed, deeply self-aware, and desperate for redemption. And yet, the story she had come to believe about herself was that she was fundamentally broken. That if people knew who she really was, they'd walk away.
Therapy has shown me, time and time again, that shame is not about what we do—it's about who we believe we are. It's the voice that says, "I'm not just wrong—I am wrong." And unlike guilt, which says, "I did something bad," shame whispers, "I am bad." That distinction is everything.

The first person to really untangle this difference was Dr. Brené Brown whose groundbreaking research on shame and vulnerability transformed how we understand emotional pain. She explains it like this: guilt is adaptive—it pushes us to repair. Shame is corrosive—it convinces us we are unworthy of repair.

And that's why it's so dangerous. Because once you believe you're unworthy, you stop trying to heal. You stop asking for help. You stay silent.

There's a reason shame is called "the master emotion." It hides beneath anger, anxiety, addiction, perfectionism, even depression. According to studies published in Psychological Science, people who experience chronic shame have higher rates of social withdrawal, suicidal ideation, and chronic health problems. Shame literally changes the body—it increases inflammation, raises cortisol levels, and compromises immunity. It's not just an emotional burden; it's a biological one.

And here's the kicker: shame isn't just a personal feeling. It's cultural. We're raised in societies that weaponize shame to control behavior—don't cry like a girl, man up, good girls don't do that, you should be ashamed of yourself. We internalize these messages, and they become the lens through which we see ourselves. It doesn't matter if the voice is gone—the echo stays.

I once had a client who couldn't speak in full sentences about her childhood without flinching. She had grown up in a home where mistakes were punished with silence, sarcasm, or shame. As a child, she learned that being herself was dangerous. So she became a master at hiding. Performing. Numbing. And by the time she reached adulthood, she didn't even know who she was beneath the mask.

That's what shame does. It disconnects us from ourselves. And the only thing that reconnects us is safety—not in the sense of comfort, but in the sense of emotional permission. Permission to be real. Messy. Incomplete. Permission to be seen and not shamed.

Which brings us to the most powerful antidote we have: vulnerability.

Now, I know vulnerability has been tossed around so much lately it's starting to sound like a cliché. But here's what it really means in the therapy room—it means telling the truth when you're terrified of being judged. It means letting someone see the parts of you you've been taught to hide. It means saying, "I'm not okay," and allowing yourself to be held.

But vulnerability only works when there's psychological safety. You can't be vulnerable with someone who shames you. You can't heal in an environment where honesty is punished. And that's why so many people never talk about their pain—they've never been given a safe space to do it.

So, what makes a space safe?

It's not just silence. Or presence. It's compassion without condition. It's the ability to hold someone's pain without trying to fix, minimize, or judge it. It's saying, "I see your mess, and I still choose to stay."
Creating this kind of space—for yourself and for others—takes intention. It starts with language. The words we use matter. Shame flourishes in phrases like "What's wrong with you?" "You always do this," or "You're so dramatic." But it weakens when we say

things like, "That must have been really hard," "I'm glad you shared this," or "You're not alone."

Sometimes, the most powerful thing we can do is simply sit with someone in their truth without flinching.

But what if you've never had that kind of space before? What if no one has ever responded to your pain with gentleness?

Then your healing might begin with creating that space within yourself.

This is where self-compassion becomes more than a buzzword—it becomes survival. And it's not about letting yourself off the hook or avoiding accountability. It's about refusing to abandon yourself when you're at your most human. Dr. Kristin Neff, a pioneer in the study of self-compassion, found that people who practice it are less anxious, less depressed, and more resilient in the face of failure. Not because they avoid discomfort—but because they stop weaponizing it.

Here's one brutally honest truth about shame: it loses its power the moment it's spoken in the presence of empathy. That's why support groups work. That's why trauma-informed therapy is so transformative. That's why even one safe relationship can rewire your entire belief system.

But don't mistake safety for softness. Sometimes the safest thing you can do is tell the hard truth—to yourself or someone else. Sometimes it means walking away from people who consistently make you feel like you're too much or not enough. Sometimes it means saying, "I will no longer participate in my own shaming."

And if you're someone who's still carrying a story of shame—about your past, your choices, your body, your mental health—please know this: your worth has never been up for debate. You don't have to prove yourself pure. You don't have to earn love through perfection. You are allowed to be a full, flawed human being. You are allowed to exist in your truth, even if that truth is messy.

As I write this, I think back to Sarah. It took her months of weekly sessions to look me in the eye and say, "I'm starting to believe I'm not a bad person." That was her win—not because she had fixed everything in her life, but because she stopped abandoning herself. She built a space inside where shame didn't get to make the rules anymore.

That's the kind of healing we all deserve.

Because shame cannot survive the light. And sometimes, all we need is for someone to sit beside us, turn on a lamp, and say, "You're not alone in this."

Chapter 8: Perfectionism Is Fear in Disguise

I remember the day one of my most seemingly "high-functioning" clients finally broke. Her name was Amina. She was a young architect, the kind of person you'd think had it all together—sharp, articulate, dressed immaculately, always prepared with a notebook full of bullet points and backup plans. She walked into the therapy room every week with a polished smile. But that day, she didn't sit the way she usually did. She collapsed into the couch like the weight of her own mind had finally pulled her down. "I'm exhausted," she said. "I'm tired of never being enough. No matter what I do, it never feels like it's safe to stop."

That sentence hit me like a punch in the chest. Because I've heard it before—over and over—from students, artists, doctors, teachers, mothers, sons. People who appear driven, disciplined, successful. And underneath all that gold-star living? Terror.

The truth is, perfectionism is not about high standards—that's what people get wrong. It's about fear. It's the voice that says, If I don't do it perfectly, I will be judged, abandoned, or worthless. It's not ambition—it's anxiety in a tailored suit.

Psychologist Dr. Gordon Flett, a leading researcher in the field, defines perfectionism as "the need to be or appear to be perfect, and to believe that anything less than perfect is unacceptable." But here's the kicker: perfectionism is strongly linked to depression, anxiety, OCD, and eating disorders. In fact, in a longitudinal study published in Psychological

Bulletin, perfectionism has been rising significantly in young people over the last 30 years—especially what's called socially prescribed perfectionism, which is the belief that others expect me to be perfect.

It's a cultural epidemic, not a personal flaw.

And it starts early. Think about it—how many of us were praised not just for trying, but for being the best? For getting straight A's? For not making waves? For doing things "right" the first time? Slowly, we learned that love, approval, and belonging were conditional. We internalized this idea: My worth depends on my performance.

So we hustled. We cleaned up. We stopped showing people the mess. And we grew into adults who felt like failures if our living rooms weren't spotless, if our emails weren't perfectly worded, if our parenting didn't look Instagram-worthy, if our mental health slipped out of sight.

But here's the uncomfortable truth: perfectionism is a defense mechanism. It's a strategy the nervous system uses to avoid rejection, humiliation, or even shame. It says, If I do everything right, no one can criticize me. And when we live like that long enough, it becomes automatic. You stop being aware of how much you're chasing, and start believing that this constant pressure is just who you are.

It's not.

Let's talk neuroscience for a second. Our brains are wired for survival, not excellence. The amygdala, the part of the brain responsible for threat detection, doesn't distinguish between a tiger and a typo on a presentation. If you grew up in a home or society where mistakes were punished, your brain may register imperfection as danger. Over time, the "perfection equals safety" loop gets hardwired. That's why it's not enough to say, "Just let it go." It's like telling someone with a fear of flying to just relax. It takes rewiring, not willpower.

The Buddhists have a beautiful concept called "wabi-sabi"—it's the acceptance of transience and imperfection. It's the idea that beauty exists in what is flawed, broken, or incomplete. Imagine what would happen if we embraced our lives the same way. If instead of polishing every rough edge, we held it like a sacred reminder: this is real. This is human.

But how do we start to shift out of perfectionism?

Well, first, we need to recognize the fear behind the behavior. Ask yourself: What am I afraid will happen if I don't do this perfectly? The answer will tell you everything. Often, it's not about the task itself. It's about what the task represents—being loved, being accepted, being safe.

Then, there's the next step: start practicing "good enough." This is not the same as giving up or doing things carelessly. It's a conscious decision to stop sacrificing your mental health at the altar of someone else's expectations.

Start small. Send an email without rereading it five times. Wear the outfit that's comfortable, not the one that looks curated. Let the project go out at 90% instead of 110%. The world won't collapse. In fact, most of the time, no one even notices.

One of the most brutally honest practices I offer clients is this: set a "B minus" goal for the week. Not an A+. Not perfect. Just good enough. And then actually follow through with it. If your instinct is to scream at the idea, that's your nervous system learning to tolerate discomfort. That's where the healing is.

Another tool is exposure. Expose yourself—gently and intentionally—to imperfection. Skip the makeup for a day. Tell someone you're struggling. Ask for help without having all the answers. Every time you survive that moment without losing love or respect, your brain rewires. It learns: I can be imperfect and still belong.

And if you're raising kids—or mentoring anyone—please model this for them. Let them see you mess up. Let them see you recover. Let them hear you say, "I made a mistake, and I'm still worthy of love." We don't teach resilience by teaching them to be perfect—we teach it by showing them how to be human.

There's also something else we have to say out loud: perfectionism can be a trauma response. If you grew up in chaos, being perfect might have felt like the only way to control anything. If you were neglected or abused, perfectionism might have been your way of earning scraps of attention. Naming this doesn't make you weak. It makes you brave.

In fact, if you're someone who's constantly battling the feeling that nothing you do is enough—I want you to hear this clearly: you are not the problem. The system that taught you perfection was the only path to worth? That's the problem.

Healing perfectionism isn't about becoming lazy. It's about reclaiming your life. Reclaiming your weekends. Your sleep. Your identity. It's about realizing that your value is not in what you produce— it's in who you are when you stop producing.

You might still have standards. You might still have goals. That's okay. But let them come from love, not fear. Let your efforts be an expression of passion, not punishment.

Because perfection is a lie.

And your humanity is not a flaw. It's the best part of you.

Chapter 9: Forgiveness Is for You, Not Them

I wasn't planning to talk about forgiveness that day. It was a group therapy session on grief and loss, and most people in the room were mourning someone they had loved deeply. But then an older man—quiet, with eyes that looked decades heavier than his age—said something that changed the entire energy in the room.

"I don't miss her," he said, "I miss who I thought she was. But I can't seem to let go of the anger."

That moment stayed with me long after the chairs were stacked and the room was empty. Because what he said was so raw, so painfully honest—and it reflected something I see almost daily in therapy: our deepest wounds are often tied not just to what happened, but to what should have happened and didn't. And forgiveness? It's not about saying, "It's okay." It's about saying, "It's not okay—but I'm not going to let this own me anymore."

Most people misunderstand forgiveness. They think it's about the other person—about absolving them, reconciling, or forgetting what they did. But the truth is, forgiveness is not for the person who hurt you—it's for the part of you that's still hurting.

Let's break that down.

Resentment, according to psychiatrist Carl Jung, is like "drinking poison and waiting for the other person to die." When we hold onto anger, betrayal, and unresolved pain, we create a feedback loop in the body—an ongoing stress response. Studies have shown that chronic anger and rumination are directly linked to increased cortisol levels, higher blood pressure, and weakened immune functioning. One study from Johns Hopkins found that people who practice forgiveness regularly experience lower risks of heart disease and higher quality of sleep. This isn't just emotional—it's biological.

But here's the trick: forgiveness doesn't mean forgetting, and it sure as hell doesn't mean pretending something didn't hurt. Real forgiveness starts with validation. With facing the full weight of what was lost, broken, or betrayed—and choosing, over time, to let the pain stop dictating your inner world.

You might be wondering, But how do I forgive someone who isn't sorry? Or someone who keeps doing the same thing?

Let me say something that I often have to remind my clients: forgiveness doesn't require reconciliation. In fact, sometimes it's safest to forgive from a distance. You can let go of the grip they have on your thoughts while still protecting yourself with healthy boundaries. You can release the venom without shaking hands with the snake.

The Buddhist teacher Jack Kornfield writes, "Forgiveness is giving up all hope for a better past." That hits. Because most of the time, what we're wrestling with isn't just what happened—it's that loop in our heads that keeps asking, Why did this happen to me? What if I had done something differently? What if they never change?

These questions don't heal—they bind.

But when we start to understand forgiveness as a process of liberation, things shift. In fact, MRI research from the University of Pisa in Italy showed that when people actively engage in forgiveness practices, the neural networks associated with empathy and emotional regulation light up. Forgiveness, in the brain, looks like freedom.

That doesn't mean it's easy. Forgiveness is rarely one moment. It's a thousand micro-decisions. It's waking up and choosing, again and again, to not let bitterness build a home inside you.

Now let's be brutally honest—some wounds are deep. There are people who have done unthinkable things. Childhood abuse. Betrayal by a spouse. Abandonment by a parent. These aren't petty grievances. These are core injuries. And in those cases, forgiveness might not feel possible yet. That's okay. You're not broken for needing time. In fact, trauma therapist Janina Fisher notes that "forcing forgiveness before someone is ready can be a form of retraumatization." Healing comes first. Forgiveness can come later.

What I often explore with clients is the idea of grief before forgiveness. Grieving the loss of what should have been—the parent who never protected you, the friend who wasn't loyal, the partner who disappeared when you needed them most. That grief is sacred. It's necessary. Because only when we've felt the weight of the loss can we begin to release the chain it holds on our present.

Sometimes people say, "But if I forgive them, doesn't that mean what they did was okay?" Absolutely not. Forgiveness is not approval. It's not denial. It's the opposite—it's truth-telling. It says: This was real. This hurt. And I am no longer letting it rule my life.

In fact, forgiveness is the ultimate act of reclaiming power. Because as long as you're consumed by the pain, the person who hurt you still holds the pen in your story. Forgiveness is taking the pen back.

But here's something even more tender. Sometimes, the person we need to forgive is ourselves. For not leaving sooner. For not seeing the signs. For the mistakes we made in survival mode. And that kind of forgiveness? It's often the hardest of all.

Self-forgiveness requires a deep confrontation with shame. Shame says, I am bad. But forgiveness says, I made a mistake—and I am still worthy. And that shift? That's where the healing really begins.

So how do we start to forgive?

First, name the harm. Be honest. Write it down. Say it out loud. Give yourself permission to feel the anger, the sadness, the betrayal.

Second, connect to the impact the resentment is having on your life. Not the event—what it's doing to you now. Your energy. Your health. Your relationships.

Third, decide what forgiveness would look like for you. Maybe it's writing a letter you never send. Maybe it's finally saying what you never got to say. Maybe it's something symbolic—like burying a note, burning a memory, or creating something in honor of your healing.

And finally, start the practice. You don't have to believe it fully at first. You just have to begin.

Say it gently, like a whisper:
I am ready to let this go.
I am ready to be free.
I am ready to stop carrying what isn't mine.

Because forgiveness isn't about them.
It never was. It's about you—your peace, your future, your healing. And you deserve every inch of that freedom.

Chapter 10: Self-Sabotage Is a Sign, Not a Sentence

I once had a client named Rachel who was, in every external sense, doing incredibly well. She was in her early thirties, held a senior position at a marketing firm in Chicago, made six figures, and had a close-knit circle of friends. But every time she got close to something she really wanted—whether it was a promotion, a relationship that seemed solid, or even sticking to a personal health goal—she would quietly, almost invisibly, pull the plug. She'd skip important meetings without explanation, ghost someone she really liked, or break her routines just as they were beginning to help.

"I don't know what's wrong with me," she confessed one day in session, eyes wide with shame. "It's like I have this part of me that's allergic to good things."

I've heard variations of that line hundreds of times over the years. And I'll tell you something I wish more people knew: self-sabotage isn't proof that you're broken—it's proof that something inside you is trying to protect itself. Not in a healthy way, maybe. But with good reason.

The term self-sabotage sounds harsh, doesn't it? It conjures images of someone actively destroying their own future, like setting fire to a house they just finished building. But more often than not, self-sabotage is subtle. It hides in the excuses we make, the tasks we procrastinate, the texts we don't send, and the opportunities we quietly turn away from.

What if I told you that self-sabotage is not a flaw—it's a message?

According to Dr. Judy Ho, a clinical neuropsychologist and author of Stop Self-Sabotage, the root of self-defeating behavior usually lies in one of four things: low self-esteem, fear of change, fear of failure, or fear of success. Each one of those fears carries its own complex history. Take fear of success, for instance. It might sound strange at first—why would anyone fear getting what they want? But if success in the past came with isolation, jealousy from others, or burnout, your brain might link "achievement" with "danger."

Rachel's story, as it turned out, wasn't just about being "bad at follow-through." When we explored her past, we uncovered a childhood where attention and affection were doled out only when she was struggling. She learned, at a young age, that suffering earned her love. So thriving? That felt unfamiliar. Unsafe. Her nervous system had coded dysfunction as normal—and stability as suspicious.

This is something we now understand more clearly through neuroscience. The brain, especially in trauma survivors, prioritizes what's familiar over what's healthy. Even if you consciously want change, your subconscious will resist what it hasn't learned to trust. This is where self-sabotage lives—in the tension between conscious desire and unconscious defense. And here's the kicker: self-sabotage often looks like self-protection in disguise.

Take another client, Mark, a 26-year-old software developer from Seattle. He'd been passed over for a leadership role and was spiraling. But as we unpacked his performance, it wasn't that he lacked the skills—

he had actually withdrawn from participating in projects just as his boss was evaluating him. "I didn't want to look too eager," he said. But underneath that? A deep fear of being seen as arrogant. He'd grown up with a narcissistic parent, and any hint of ambition felt like he was becoming them. His self-sabotage was, in essence, an act of self-reassurance: I'm not like them.

Psychologist Gay Hendricks calls this "The Upper Limit Problem"—the idea that each of us has an internal thermostat for how much success, joy, or intimacy we believe we're allowed. When we exceed it, we unconsciously bring ourselves back down. We self-regulate... by self-sabotaging.

So the question becomes: How do we transform this pattern into something helpful? How do we turn self-sabotage into self-support?

First, we have to name the pattern. Not judge it. Not shame it. Just name it.

Ask yourself: Where in my life do I keep hitting the same wall? What do I do right before things start going well?

This is uncomfortable work, but it's powerful. Because once you recognize the pattern, you begin to reclaim agency. It's like turning the lights on in a room you've always navigated in the dark.

Second, get curious about the function of the behavior. What is this self-sabotage doing for you? What feeling is it helping you avoid? For some, it's anxiety. For others, it's exposure. You might find that it's protecting a younger part of you that didn't feel safe being seen or praised or depended on. That part deserves your attention—not your punishment.

This is where the work of Internal Family Systems (IFS) can be incredibly useful. IFS teaches us that we all have different "parts" within us—protectors, exiles, managers—and self-sabotaging parts are often protectors that have been working overtime. They just need a new job description.

And here's something important: you don't overcome self-sabotage by pushing harder. You overcome it by listening deeper. You can't discipline your way out of emotional resistance. But you can build trust with the part of you that's scared.

Try this: the next time you catch yourself procrastinating, underperforming, or disengaging, ask that part of you, "What are you afraid might happen if I succeed here?" Then listen. Really listen. Write it down. Talk to someone about it. The answer might surprise you.

Of course, self-awareness isn't enough without action. But your actions have to be aligned with your nervous system's capacity. If your body is used to chaos, stability will feel boring. If your identity has been shaped around struggle, ease might feel like you're doing something wrong.

That's why one of the most radical things you can do is practice tolerating success. Stay in the moments that go well. Let yourself be celebrated. Don't rush to the next problem. Take up space in the good.

And finally, create environments that support your higher self. Your habits, your calendar, your relationships—they should all reflect the version of you you're becoming, not the one you're trying to outgrow. That might mean saying no more often. Turning your phone off after 9pm. Not dating people who activate your insecurity. These are not just lifestyle tweaks. They're declarations of self-worth.

Self-sabotage loses power when we stop treating it like a curse and start treating it like a signal. It tells us where the fear lives. It tells us where the healing needs to happen. And when we listen, not with criticism but with compassion, we start to see the truth:

You were never trying to fail. You were trying to feel safe.

But now? It's safe to thrive.

Lesson 11: Anxiety Lies to You

I remember a client named Laura, a 34-year-old lawyer in New York City, who came into therapy one afternoon visibly exhausted. She was a high achiever, meticulous about her career, but she had been battling anxiety for as long as she could remember. Her anxiety, though, wasn't about the usual "what ifs" that we often associate with anxiety—it was much more subtle, much more convincing.

Laura had a recurring thought that kept her awake at night: "If I mess up, everything will fall apart." This thought wasn't just about a small mistake—if she made even a minor error in a brief, she would catastrophize it into an irreversible disaster. She imagined the worst-case scenarios: losing her job, her colleagues thinking less of her, and ultimately, failing in life. But when we examined the situation more closely, it became clear that her fears were not grounded in reality. The mistakes she feared were often not even noticeable to others, and the consequences were far less dire than she had convinced herself.

What Laura was experiencing is not unusual. In fact, it's one of the most common symptoms of anxiety— the tendency to distort reality by focusing on worst-case scenarios. This is what cognitive psychologists often refer to as catastrophic thinking. When we're anxious, our minds often overestimate danger and underestimate our ability to cope with it. Anxiety, in its essence, creates an alternate reality that feels more real than the one around us.

What Laura's case illustrates is how anxiety lies to us. Anxiety distorts our perception of reality, convincing us that something bad is going to happen, even when there is little or no evidence to support it. When you're anxious, your brain doesn't just predict bad things; it amplifies them, making them feel inevitable and all-consuming.

Anxiety also triggers what's known as the fight-or-flight response. This is a natural physiological reaction to perceived danger, designed to protect us. But when it's activated in response to imagined threats, it's no longer helpful—it's just harmful. The physical symptoms—rapid heartbeat, shallow breathing, dizziness—are often disproportionate to the actual threat, but they feel very real. And because the body responds so strongly, anxiety often convinces us that we must be in danger.

In fact, according to research from the National Institute of Mental Health, anxiety disorders affect over 40 million adults in the United States alone, making them the most common mental health conditions in the country. That's roughly 18% of the adult population. These statistics paint a clear picture of just how widespread the experience of anxiety is, and how many people—like Laura—are living in a distorted reality of fear and doubt.

When you begin to challenge anxiety, you realize something important: your anxious thoughts are not necessarily facts. They're projections, predictions, or even assumptions that have no real evidence. They're an echo of your fear, rather than a reflection of reality.

So, how do we begin to challenge these lies that anxiety tells us? The first step is recognizing that your thoughts are not inherently true, no matter how strong they feel in the moment. This is where cognitive-behavioral therapy (CBT) plays a pivotal role. CBT helps individuals like Laura identify negative thought patterns and replace them with more balanced, realistic perspectives. Instead of automatically assuming that a minor mistake will lead to catastrophic consequences, CBT teaches you to examine the evidence and assess the probability of that outcome.

One powerful technique in CBT is cognitive restructuring, where you systematically challenge irrational thoughts and replace them with more rational ones. For example, if you're thinking, "If I fail this test, my whole life will fall apart," you can ask yourself: "What evidence do I have that this will happen?" You'll quickly find that there's no solid proof to support such an extreme thought. Yes, failing a test may be disappointing, but it doesn't mean that your life is over. By consistently challenging these irrational thoughts, you begin to weaken the grip anxiety has over your life.

Research supports the effectiveness of this method. A study published in the Journal of Consulting and Clinical Psychology found that individuals with anxiety disorders who underwent CBT experienced significant reductions in anxiety and improvements in functioning. This is because CBT doesn't just focus on reducing symptoms; it aims to change the thought patterns that fuel anxiety in the first place.

But challenging thoughts alone isn't enough. You also need tools to ground yourself in the present moment, especially when anxiety hijacks your thoughts and emotions. Grounding techniques are one of the most effective ways to do this. Grounding is all about reconnecting with your body and the present moment, rather than getting lost in anxious thoughts.

Take, for example, the 5-4-3-2-1 grounding technique. This simple exercise involves identifying five things you can see, four things you can touch, three things you can hear, two things you can smell, and one thing you can taste. This exercise works by engaging your senses, which pulls you out of your anxious thoughts and back into the present moment. It reminds you that you're safe right now, that there's no immediate danger, and that the catastrophic scenario your mind is presenting isn't real.

Another grounding technique is deep breathing. Deep breathing activates the body's parasympathetic nervous system, which helps calm the fight-or-flight response. One technique I often recommend is box breathing: inhale for four counts, hold for four counts, exhale for four counts, and hold again for four counts. Repeat this for a few minutes, and you'll notice a significant reduction in anxiety. This technique not only calms your body but also shifts your focus away from anxious thoughts and back to your breath.

I always tell my clients that while these grounding techniques are incredibly helpful, they're not a cure-all. Anxiety is deeply ingrained in our biology, and it takes time and practice to rewire our brains. But grounding exercises, when practiced regularly, can serve as a lifeline in moments of heightened anxiety. They give you back control when it feels like anxiety is taking over.

At the same time, challenging catastrophic thinking isn't just about fighting against your anxiety—it's about making room for more realistic, balanced thinking. For instance, instead of catastrophizing, you can begin to ask yourself questions like: "What is the most likely outcome here?" or "What's the worst thing that could happen, and how would I handle it?" This kind of inquiry creates space between you and your anxious thoughts. It doesn't mean the anxiety disappears, but it means you no longer have to take it as gospel. You can live with the uncertainty, rather than being consumed by it. You can acknowledge the anxiety and its presence, but you can also recognize that it doesn't get to define your reality.

Anxiety will always be part of the human experience to some extent. It's a natural response to stress, uncertainty, and change. But it doesn't have to dictate your life. With the right tools and perspective, you can begin to see anxiety for what it truly is: a series of distorted thoughts, a series of lies that your mind tells you to keep you in a state of fear.

Laura learned to challenge her anxiety over time, and while it never disappeared entirely, it no longer controlled her. Instead of imagining disaster at every turn, she learned to ask herself, "What's the evidence?" She also practiced grounding techniques like deep breathing and mindfulness, which helped her reconnect to the present moment. And most importantly, she began to understand that anxiety doesn't define who she is. It's simply a feeling that comes and goes, just like any other.

So, next time anxiety strikes, remember: it's not telling you the truth. It's trying to protect you, but it's doing so in a way that distorts your perception. Challenge it, ground yourself in reality, and you'll be able to regain control.

Lesson 12: Love Is a Skill, Not Just a Feeling

I remember working with a client named Emily, a 28-year-old marketing professional from Boston, who had always believed that love should come effortlessly. She'd grown up reading fairy tales and watching romantic movies where love was portrayed as this magical, almost serendipitous feeling that swept you off your feet. Emily had always hoped that when she met "the one," everything would fall into place with ease. But when her relationships didn't live up to this ideal, she felt defeated, as if love was somehow slipping through her fingers.

After a series of failed relationships, she found herself sitting across from me, frustrated and confused. "Why is it so hard for me?" she asked. "Why can't I just find someone who loves me the way I want to be loved?"

What Emily didn't realize at the time was that love is not simply a feeling that arrives when we least expect it. Love, in its deepest form, is a skill—a skill that requires effort, self-awareness, and active growth. It's easy to assume that love should come naturally, but the truth is that building and maintaining meaningful relationships takes work.

This misconception about love is deeply ingrained in our culture. We've been sold the idea that love is a magical spark that either exists or it doesn't. But the reality is far more complex. Love is a dynamic process—one that requires intentionality, effort, and an understanding of ourselves and our partners. Relationships are not static; they're constantly evolving, and the work that goes into them is what allows them to grow and deepen.

One of the key aspects of building love as a skill is understanding attachment styles—the patterns of behavior we develop in our early relationships with caregivers. These patterns influence how we approach intimacy and connection in adulthood. There are four primary attachment styles: secure, anxious, avoidant, and disorganized.

People with a secure attachment style tend to have healthy, balanced relationships. They are comfortable with intimacy, are able to express their emotions, and are generally able to rely on others while also maintaining their independence. For Emily, it was clear that her struggle in relationships stemmed from her anxious attachment style, which made her crave constant reassurance and fear abandonment. Her inability to trust that love could be stable and consistent often led to her sabotaging relationships.

People with an anxious attachment style tend to be preoccupied with their relationships and are often overly dependent on their partner for validation. They may become emotionally overwhelmed when they perceive any hint of rejection or distance from their partner, even if it's not intentional. This style often leads to a cycle of seeking reassurance, feeling insecure, and sometimes creating conflicts where none need to exist. Emily's past relationships had often followed this pattern, and she would often find herself feeling anxious or insecure, which would push her partner away.

On the other hand, individuals with an avoidant attachment style are uncomfortable with intimacy and tend to withdraw emotionally when relationships get too close. They often value their independence and may struggle to express their emotions or meet the emotional needs of their partner. Avoidants often push their partners away when they sense the relationship becoming too emotionally demanding. This style can create a sense of distance in relationships, and individuals with this attachment style may often feel overwhelmed by emotional closeness.

Finally, the disorganized attachment style is characterized by a combination of anxious and avoidant behaviors. People with this style often have a history of trauma or inconsistent caregiving, and they may struggle with both emotional closeness and emotional distance. Their relationships can feel chaotic and unstable, and they may have difficulty trusting others or allowing themselves to be vulnerable.

Understanding these attachment styles is critical for developing healthier relationships because they shape how we interact with our partners and respond to intimacy. By recognizing our attachment style, we can begin to identify the patterns that are holding us back and work to change them. Emily, for example, had to learn to recognize her anxious tendencies and find ways to feel secure within herself, rather than relying solely on her partner for reassurance.

But attachment styles aren't the only thing that influence love. Relationship patterns—the ways in which we behave and communicate in relationships—are also key to cultivating deep and meaningful connections. For example, many of us fall into patterns of negative communication, such as stonewalling, criticism, or defensiveness, which can lead to escalating conflicts. These behaviors can be learned in childhood or develop over time as a way of protecting ourselves from emotional pain.

One of the most influential psychologists in the field of relationships, John Gottman, has spent decades studying couples and what makes relationships successful. Through his research, he identified four horsemen—patterns of behavior that are highly predictive of relationship breakdowns. These four horsemen are criticism, contempt, defensiveness, and stonewalling.

Criticism involves attacking your partner's character rather than addressing specific behaviors. Contempt is the most damaging of the four horsemen, as it involves treating your partner with disrespect, such as mocking them or using sarcasm. Defensiveness occurs when we respond to criticism by denying responsibility or blaming our partner, while stonewalling happens when one partner withdraws emotionally from the conversation and shuts down communication.

Gottman's research shows that couples who engage in these behaviors are more likely to experience relationship breakdowns, as they prevent constructive communication and create emotional distance between partners. To build love as a skill, it's essential to replace these negative patterns with healthier communication strategies, such as active listening, expressing appreciation, and problem-solving together.

For Emily, learning to communicate openly and honestly about her needs was a crucial step toward improving her relationships. She had spent so much time trying to avoid conflict that she never truly expressed her feelings or needs. Through therapy, Emily learned to articulate her emotions in a way that was vulnerable but not accusatory. She also worked on recognizing when her anxiety was influencing her communication and tried to counteract those impulses with self-soothing techniques.

Cultivating love as a skill also involves self-awareness—understanding our own emotional needs and triggers. Self-awareness allows us to set healthy boundaries and communicate those boundaries clearly to our partner. It also helps us recognize when we need to give our partner space, when we need to ask for support, and when we need to practice self-care.

As we continue to build our emotional toolkit, it's important to remember that love is a dynamic process. It's not something that stays the same over time. The work we put into our relationships—whether it's learning better communication skills, addressing our attachment wounds, or building trust—is what allows love to deepen and grow. Emily, over time, learned to see love as something she could actively create, not just something that happened to her.

Building love as a skill also means being willing to invest in the relationship, especially when challenges arise. There will always be ups and downs in any relationship, but by choosing to grow together, partners can develop a deeper, more resilient love that withstands life's difficulties.

If you want to build a meaningful connection with another person, you have to be willing to put in the work. Love isn't just about feeling good—it's about making conscious decisions to create a relationship that is rooted in trust, respect, and mutual growth. The beauty of love, when approached as a skill, is that it's never too late to learn.

Lesson 13: Healing Is Not Linear

I remember a moment in my early years of therapy when I sat with a client named Andrew, a 35-year-old teacher from New York, who was struggling with severe depression and anxiety after a difficult divorce. He came into my office feeling defeated, convinced that he wasn't making any real progress. "I've been doing all the right things," he said. "I've been going to therapy, I've been working on myself, but I still feel like I'm back at square one."

Andrew was frustrated. He'd hoped for quick, sweeping changes in his mental health, but the reality of his healing journey was much messier than he anticipated. Some days, he felt empowered, like he was finally taking control of his life again. But other days, the weight of his emotions seemed unbearable, and he found himself spiraling back into dark thoughts.

This is where many people get caught up in their healing journey—the misconception that it should be a smooth, linear process. When progress doesn't happen in a straight line, it can feel disheartening, almost as if we're not getting anywhere at all. But this is one of the biggest truths about healing that I've come to understand: healing is not linear.

In fact, the ups and downs of the healing journey are not only normal but expected. Progress in therapy and personal growth doesn't look like a steady upward trajectory. Instead, it often feels more like a series of highs and lows—like climbing a mountain where, at times, you take a step back before you can move forward again.

If we look at Andrew's story, the key to understanding his struggle was recognizing that he was holding onto an ideal of healing that wasn't realistic. Healing doesn't happen in a tidy package. It's messy, it's emotional, and it's filled with setbacks. But those setbacks don't mean you're failing. In fact, they're often part of the process.

Research into the nature of trauma and recovery, particularly neuroscience, has shown that healing from emotional wounds doesn't follow a straight line. In fact, it's often much more complicated. Studies on trauma have revealed that the brain has an incredible capacity for neuroplasticity, meaning that it can rewire itself based on new experiences and behaviors. But this process of rewiring isn't immediate. It takes time. And during that time, you'll experience moments of growth alongside periods of challenge.

One of the core reasons for the non-linear nature of healing is that our emotions and our psyche don't work in the same way that other aspects of our body do. For example, if you break your arm, you can usually expect that with enough rest and physical therapy, it will heal. Emotional wounds, on the other hand, are more complicated. They don't have a clear, predictable timeline. They can resurface unexpectedly, and the pain can sometimes feel just as intense as it did when the trauma first occurred.

Consider the concept of emotional triggers. These triggers can be something as simple as a song on the radio or a smell that reminds us of a difficult experience. When a trigger appears, it may seem like you've taken a step back in your healing journey. But in reality, it's just a sign that your brain and body are trying to process and integrate the experience. These triggers often arise as part of your brain's effort to "revisit" the pain in order to heal it. And while it can feel like regression, it's really a sign that your body is trying to reconcile the trauma.

And this brings us to an important point: healing is cyclical, not linear. It's natural for healing to take the form of a spiral rather than a straight line. This means that there will be periods where you feel like you're making huge strides forward, followed by moments when you feel as though you're back in the same place. But the key to remember is that each time you circle back to a previous point, you're not exactly where you were before. You're a little further along, a little stronger, and a little more aware of your triggers and how to manage them.

This idea is beautifully captured by Brene Brown, who says, "The process of healing is not about 'getting over it.' It's about making sense of it, transforming it, and learning how to live with it." Healing is not about erasing the past but about learning how to carry it in a way that doesn't prevent you from moving forward. It's about integrating your experiences into your sense of self so that they no longer have the power to define you.

One of the most difficult parts of the healing journey is measuring progress. We live in a world that values instant results, and when progress isn't immediately visible, it's easy to feel discouraged. But measuring progress in therapy and personal growth requires a different mindset. It's not about comparing where you are today to where you were yesterday; it's about recognizing the small, meaningful shifts that happen over time.

For Andrew, his progress wasn't measured in big, dramatic changes but in the small steps he took to understand himself better. He began recognizing when his anxious thoughts about his past relationship were starting to control him. He learned how to interrupt those thoughts and reframe them in a more compassionate way. The true measure of his progress wasn't the absence of pain—it was his ability to cope with pain in a healthier way.

Another important aspect of healing is self-compassion. It's easy to fall into the trap of self-criticism when we feel like we're not progressing as quickly as we'd like. We may start thinking that we're not "doing it right," or that we should be further along than we are. But this kind of thinking is counterproductive and can lead to feelings of shame or frustration. Instead, it's important to practice self-compassion—to treat yourself with the same kindness and understanding that you would offer a friend who was struggling.

In fact, self-compassion has been shown to play a crucial role in healing. Research by psychologist Kristin Neff found that individuals who practiced self-compassion were better able to cope with difficult emotions and recover from trauma. Self-compassion involves acknowledging that healing is a process and that setbacks are a natural part of that process. Instead of berating yourself for not "getting over it," self-compassion allows you to gently guide yourself through the ups and downs of the journey.

As we come to the end of this journey together, I want you to remember one final thing: healing is not a race. It's not something that can be rushed, and it's not something that can be measured in conventional terms. Your healing journey is uniquely yours, and it will unfold in its own time. There will be moments when you feel like you've made tremendous progress, and other times when you feel like you've taken a step backward. And that's okay.

The important thing is to stay engaged in the process—to keep showing up for yourself, even on the days when it feels like nothing is changing. Progress is often slow, but every small step forward is a step toward healing. And most importantly, remember that you are worthy of that healing, no matter how long it takes.

Carrying These Lessons Forward

Throughout this book, we've explored some of the most powerful lessons that can emerge from therapy—the lessons that have not only shaped my understanding as a therapist but also the way I approach life itself. These lessons, while deeply rooted in therapy and the healing process, extend far beyond the confines of the therapy room. They are life lessons—practical, profound, and transformative—meant to be applied to everyday living.

I've shared stories, research, and tools that you can use to challenge your thoughts, validate your emotions, set healthy boundaries, forgive, and ultimately heal. But now, as we come to the close of this journey, I want to talk about something equally important: carrying these lessons forward. How do you take what you've learned here and apply it to your daily life in a way that makes a meaningful difference? First and foremost, therapy insights are not just something to be learned; they are something to be lived. The insights we gain from therapy, whether it's about managing anxiety, healing past wounds, or developing deeper connections, are not meant to sit on a shelf in our minds like a book gathering dust. They are meant to be woven into the fabric of our daily experiences. Therapy is not a quick fix; it's a lifelong process, and so is applying these lessons.

Take the lesson about boundaries, for instance. Setting boundaries isn't a one-time event. It's something that needs to be practiced consistently. You can't just decide one day to set a boundary and expect it to hold forever. Life, people, and circumstances will challenge that boundary time and time again. But each time you practice setting a healthy boundary—whether it's saying "no" to an overbearing colleague or taking time for yourself when you need it—you're reinforcing that lesson in real time. It's not always easy, and it's not always comfortable, but it's always worth it. These lessons, when applied consistently, will gradually transform the way you interact with the world and with yourself.

The same applies to the lesson of self-sabotage. It's not enough to simply recognize when you're blocking your own success. You have to actively engage with those patterns, day in and day out. We all have moments when we default to old, familiar ways of thinking and behaving. But by recognizing those moments and choosing a different path, we slowly rewire the way we respond to challenges. Healing from self-sabotage requires vigilance, self-awareness, and a commitment to self-support. This isn't a lesson you learn once and forget; it's one that requires ongoing effort and practice.

Self-reflection is another key aspect of carrying these lessons forward. Throughout this book, I've encouraged you to reflect on your thoughts, your emotions, your behaviors, and your relationships. But self-reflection doesn't stop here. In fact, continuous learning is essential for growth. As you move forward, I encourage you to keep asking yourself important questions: How am I showing up for myself today? What boundaries do I need to set? How am I practicing compassion for myself and others? This is a process that never really ends. It's not about reaching a destination, but rather about embracing the journey of becoming the person you're meant to be.

One of the most empowering things about therapy—and life in general—is that you are always in a position to grow. Even on the days when it feels like you're not making progress, even on the tough days when the setbacks feel overwhelming, know that each moment is an opportunity to reflect, learn, and grow. Sometimes growth comes in small, quiet ways that are easy to overlook. But over time, those small changes compound into something meaningful.

It's also essential to recognize that help is always available when you need it. As much as we can learn from books, self-reflection, and the insights we gain from others, there will always be times when we need the support of someone who can offer a fresh perspective—a therapist, a mentor, a close friend. Seeking help is not a sign of weakness, but rather a powerful step toward healing. Therapy isn't a one-time fix—it's a partnership that can support you throughout your journey. And if you're reading this and feeling overwhelmed by the prospect of applying these lessons, remember that seeking help is the first step toward understanding and integration.

In my own experience as a therapist, one of the most profound realizations has been that healing doesn't happen in isolation. We are all interconnected. We all need support, validation, and love in order to heal and grow. Whether that support comes from friends, family, or professional guidance, it is crucial to recognize that you don't have to do this alone. You are not alone in your struggles. There are people and resources available to help you on your journey.

This book is just one step on the path of your personal growth, but it's a step worth taking. The lessons shared here are only valuable if they are put into practice. The stories of transformation I've witnessed, the research findings that back these lessons, and the tools I've shared—all of this is meaningless unless you take it forward into your daily life and use it to better understand yourself, heal your wounds, and build the life you desire.

Remember, healing is not a race. It's not a competition. And it's certainly not about perfection. It's about making progress, one day at a time. It's about learning to embrace your flaws, forgive your mistakes, and show up for yourself, even when it's difficult. It's about accepting that you're worthy of love, care, and growth, even on your hardest days. Be kind to yourself as you continue this journey. Every step you take is a victory.

I hope this book has served as a guide—one that you can return to whenever you need a reminder of how far you've come and how much further you can go. Healing is possible. Growth is possible. You are worthy of both.

Carry these lessons forward with you, and remember that the journey of becoming whole is never truly complete. It's a beautiful, messy, and deeply rewarding process. And above all, never forget that you are not alone on this journey. There is always support available, and the world is full of people ready to walk alongside you as you heal, grow, and flourish.

References

- Brown, B. (2012). *The Gifts of Imperfection: Let Go of Who You Think You're Supposed to Be and Embrace Who You Are.* Hazelden Publishing.
- Gilbert, P. (2009). *The Compassionate Mind: A New Approach to Life's Challenges.* New Harbinger Publications.
- Gendlin, E. T. (1997). *Focusing.* Bantam Books.
- Hayes, S. C., Strosahl, K. D., & Wilson, K. G. (2011). *Acceptance and Commitment Therapy: The Process and Practice of Mindful Change.* Guilford Press.
- Yalom, I. D. (2002). *The Gift of Therapy: An Open Letter to a New Generation of Therapists and Their Patients.* HarperCollins.
- Neff, K. D. (2011). *Self-Compassion: The Proven Power of Being Kind to Yourself.* William Morrow.
- Linehan, M. M. (1993). *Cognitive-Behavioral Treatment of Borderline Personality Disorder.* Guilford Press.
- Siegel, D. J. (2010). *The Mindful Therapist: A Clinician's Guide to Mindsight and Neural Integration.* W. W. Norton & Company.
- Van Der Kolk, B. (2014). *The Body Keeps the Score: Brain, Mind, and Body in the Healing of Trauma.* Viking.
- Brene Brown. (2010). *The Power of Vulnerability: Teachings of Authenticity, Connection, and Courage.* Sounds True.
- Freud, S. (1917). *Introductory Lectures on Psychoanalysis.* Liveright.

- Jung, C. G. (1961). *Memories, Dreams, Reflections.* Pantheon Books.
- Beck, A. T. (1976). *Cognitive Therapy and the Emotional Disorders.* Meridian.
- Ellis, A. (2001). *Reason and Emotion in Psychotherapy.* Citadel Press.
- Kohut, H. (1971). *The Analysis of the Self.* International Universities Press.
- Linehan, M. M. (1997). *Dialectical Behavior Therapy for Borderline Personality Disorder.* The Guilford Press.
- McLaren, R. (2002). *Boundaries in Therapy: A Guide to Practitioners.* Routledge.
- Meyer, B. (2014). *Overcoming Perfectionism: A Self-Help Guide to Coping with Anxiety and Perfectionistic Tendencies.* CreateSpace Independent Publishing.
- Whitfield, C. L. (1995). *The Truth About Denial: Drugs, Alcohol, and Behavior in Society.* The Hazelden Foundation.
- Russell, B. (1959). *The Conquest of Happiness.* George Allen & Unwin.
- Seligman, M. E. P. (2002). *Learned Optimism: How to Change Your Mind and Your Life.* Vintage Books.
- Siegel, D. J. (2015). *The Developing Mind: How Relationships and the Brain Interact to Shape Who We Are.* Guilford Press.
- Van Der Kolk, B. (2005). *Trauma and Memory: Brain and Body in a Search for the Living Past.* The New England Journal of Medicine.
- American Psychiatric Association. (2013). *Diagnostic and Statistical Manual of Mental Disorders, 5th Edition (DSM-5).* American Psychiatric Association.

- Finkelhor, D. (1995). *The Victimization of Children: Developing a Research Agenda.* American Journal of Orthopsychiatry.
- Leary, M. R. (2007). *The Curse of the Self: Self-Awareness, Egotism, and the Quality of Human Life.* Oxford University Press.
- Miller, W. R., & Rollnick, S. (2002). *Motivational Interviewing: Preparing People for Change.* The Guilford Press.
- Prouty, D. (2012). *The Power of Change: The Power of Uncertainty in Personal Development.* New World Library.
- Beck, A. T. (2005). *Cognitive Therapy: Basics and Beyond.* The Guilford Press.
- Hart, T. (2010). *The Art of Self-Reflection.* J. Wiley & Sons.
- Harlow, H. F. (1958). *The Nature of Love.* American Psychologist.
- Masten, A. S. (2014). *Ordinary Magic: Resilience in Development.* Guilford Press.
- Rogers, C. R. (1961). *On Becoming a Person: A Therapist's View of Psychotherapy.* Houghton Mifflin Harcourt.
- Mahoney, M. J. (1991). *Human Change Processes: The Scientific Foundations of Psychotherapy.* Basic Books.
- Goleman, D. (1995). *Emotional Intelligence: Why It Can Matter More Than IQ.* Bantam.
- Kuhl, J. (2000). *A Theory of Action Control and Self-Regulation.* International Journal of Psychology.
- Linehan, M. M. (2008). *DBT Skills Training Manual.* The Guilford Press.
- Murphy, J. (2017). *Healing Emotional Pain: How to Move Beyond Your Past Wounds and Start Living Again.* HarperOne.

- Williams, M., & Penman, D. (2011). *Mindfulness: A Practical Guide to Finding Peace in a Frantic World.* Piatkus.
- Kabat-Zinn, J. (1990). *Full Catastrophe Living: Using the Wisdom of Your Body and Mind to Face Stress, Pain, and Illness.* Delta Trade Paperbacks.
- Sutherland, S. (1992). *The Psychology of Self-Esteem: A Cognitive Perspective.* HarperCollins.
- Tolan, P. H. (2008). *The Development of the Child's Social and Emotional Competence.* Lawrence Erlbaum Associates.
- Yip, L., & Cumming, J. (2003). *Exploring Trauma and its Effects on Personal Development.* Journal of Psychotherapy Integration.
- MacIntyre, D. (2012). *The Role of Compassion in Mental Health Recovery.* Mental Health Journal.
- National Institute of Mental Health. (2015). *Understanding Anxiety Disorders: What You Need to Know.* U.S. Department of Health and Human Services.
- Holmes, E. A., & Mathews, A. (2005). *Mental Imagery and Emotion: A Review of the Literature.* Cognitive Therapy and Research.
- McGonigal, K. (2015). *The Upside of Stress: Why Stress Is Good for You, and How to Get Good at It.* Avery.
- Emmons, R. A., & McCullough, M. E. (2003). *Counting Blessings versus Burdens: An Experimental Investigation of Gratitude and Subjective Well-Being in Daily Life.* Journal of Personality and Social Psychology.

- Walden, T. A., & Peters, D. (2012). *The Development of Emotion Regulation and Coping Strategies in Childhood.* Early Childhood Development.
- Gilbert, P., & Irons, C. (2004). *The Compassionate Mind: A New Approach to Life's Challenges.* New Harbinger Publications.

About the Author

This book is a project of "The Institute of Professional Psychology" which isn't just a platform for learning—it's a movement dedicated to unlocking human potential through the power of psychology. With a global community of over 20,000 students across 180+ countries and a strong presence on both Udemy and Amazon, we have made it our mission to bridge the gap between academic psychology and real-world application.

Beyond online education, we are proud to have over a dozen published books on Amazon, covering a wide range of psychological topics—from emotional intelligence and cognitive behavioral therapy (CBT) to resilience, motivation, and personal transformation. Our books are not just collections of theories; they are practical guides designed to help readers navigate life's challenges with clarity, resilience, and purpose.

Our journey began with a simple yet powerful belief: psychology isn't just for therapists or researchers—it's a tool for everyone. Whether you're a student, professional, or simply someone seeking personal growth, understanding the human mind can transform how you think, feel, and interact with the world. Through our courses and books, we make even the most complex psychological concepts accessible, engaging, and actionable.

With thousands of five-star reviews and a dedicated following, our work has helped readers and learners alike overcome obstacles, develop stronger mindsets, and create meaningful change in their personal and professional lives. Our approach is rooted in scientific research, real-world case studies, and practical strategies, ensuring that everything we teach is not just insightful—but truly transformative.

At the heart of our mission is a commitment to empower individuals to thrive. Whether it's through an online course or the pages of a book, we are here to guide you on your journey toward self-discovery, emotional mastery, and lasting success.

Join us in exploring the fascinating world of psychology—where knowledge isn't just power, but the key to unlocking your fullest potential.

Printed in Great Britain
by Amazon